THE UNITED NATIONS IN GLOBAL TAX COORDINATION

The United Nations in Global Tax Coordination fills the decade-long knowledge gap in international tax history concerning the UN Fiscal Commission, which functioned as the overarching fiscal authority during the early post–World War II economic order. With insights from political economy and international relations scholarship, this critical archival examination chronicles the tenacious activism by postcolonial developing countries to preserve source taxation rights, and by the UN Secretariat in championing the development of equitable tax rules. Such activism would ultimately lead developed countries to oust the UN as a forum for international tax norm setting. The book includes a revealing prehistory of the wartime work of the League of Nations that questions the legitimacy of the Mexico Model, the first model tax convention between developed and developing countries. This expertly researched work is essential reading for understanding the roles of politics, states, secretariats and private actors in directing global tax coordination.

NIKKI J TEO is a postdoctoral research affiliate at the University of Sydney.

CAMBRIDGE TAX LAW

Tax law is a growing area of interest. It is included as a subdivision in many areas of study and is a key consideration in business needs throughout the world. Books in this series expose the theoretical underpinning behind the law to shed light on taxation systems, so that the questions to be asked when addressing an issue become clear. These academic books, written by leading scholars, are a central port of call for information on tax law, with content illustrated by case law and legislation. The books will be of interest to those studying law, business, economics, accounting and finance courses.

Series Editor

Professor Peter Harris, Law Faculty, University of Cambridge, Director of the Centre for Tax Law.

Professor Harris brings a wealth of experience to the series. He has taught and presented tax courses at more than a dozen different universities in as many countries and has acted as an external tax consultant for the International Monetary Fund for over twenty years.

THE UNITED NATIONS IN GLOBAL TAX COORDINATION

Hidden History and Politics

NIKKI J TEO

University of Sydney

CAMBRIDGE
UNIVERSITY PRESS

CAMBRIDGE
UNIVERSITY PRESS

Shaftesbury Road, Cambridge CB2 8EA, United Kingdom

One Liberty Plaza, 20th Floor, New York, NY 10006, USA

477 Williamstown Road, Port Melbourne, VIC 3207, Australia

314–321, 3rd Floor, Plot 3, Splendor Forum, Jasola District Centre, New Delhi – 110025, India

103 Penang Road, #05–06/07, Visioncrest Commercial, Singapore 238467

Cambridge University Press is part of Cambridge University Press & Assessment, a department of the University of Cambridge.

We share the University's mission to contribute to society through the pursuit of education, learning and research at the highest international levels of excellence.

www.cambridge.org
Information on this title: www.cambridge.org/9781009180467
DOI: 10.1017/9781009180450

First published 2023

A catalogue record for this publication is available from the British Library.

Library of Congress Cataloging-in-Publication Data
Names: Teo, Nikki Jern-li, author.
Title: The United Nations in global tax coordination : hidden history and politics / Nikki J Teo, University of Sydney.
Description: Cambridge, United Kingdom ; New York, NY : Cambridge University Press, 2023. | Series: Cambridge tax law | Based on author's thesis (doctoral - Sydney Law School, 2021) issued under title: Developing Countries at the Double Taxation Negotiating Table and the United Nations' False Start at Global Tax Coordination : The Fiscal Commission Years (1946–1954). | Includes bibliographical references and index.
Identifiers: LCCN 2022029375 (print) | LCCN 2022029376 (ebook) | ISBN 9781009180467 (hardback) | ISBN 9781009180450 (ebook)
Subjects: LCSH: Taxation – Law and legislation – International unification – History – 20th century. | International business enterprises – Law and legislation – International unification – History – 20th century. | United Nations. Fiscal Commission – History.
Classification: LCC K4475 .T463 2023 (print) | LCC K4475 (ebook) | DDC 341–dc23/eng/20221101
LC record available at https://lccn.loc.gov/2022029375
LC ebook record available at https://lccn.loc.gov/2022029376

ISBN 978-1-009-18046-7 Hardback

CONTENTS

FOREWORD

It is a great pleasure to provide a foreword to Nikki Teo's book, *The United Nations in Global Tax Coordination: Hidden History and Politics*.

During the public fuss over multinational enterprises not paying their fair share of tax, the OECD Base Erosion and Profit Shifting project, which is leading to major rewrites of the international tax rules, has been the international response. As part of this process, appeals are often made to history to justify changes. The appeals mainly relate to technical issues, such as the permanent establishment threshold for the taxation of business profits and transfer pricing rules, but the political dimension of the project – giving a voice in international taxation to developing countries – arguably is more important. We are seeing a return in tax policy discourse to the pursuit of fairness, and inter-nation equity is one dimension of that shift.

Tax history has also seen a resurgence with scholars obtaining access to archival material of international organisations and national governments as a way of finding what went on behind the scenes. Up to now this history has mainly consisted of telling the technical story rather than providing the political and international context which allows linking of the technical debate to the inevitably political global context.

Nikki's book is a timely exploration of a generally forgotten part of international tax history – the early years of the United Nations – and breaks new ground by linking international, national and personal archives to a detailed analysis of the international relations context. In a fairness sense she shows that it was a shameful period with an unlikely alliance of the Soviet bloc combining with the United Kingdom and the United States to thwart the undeniably strong claims for fairer international tax policies by the developing world.

The period is generally forgotten because in an external sense very little happened: no new model treaties or international tax policies were developed. But in a geopolitical sense, it was a rebuff of the newly emerging developing world and bound to contribute to lasting resentments that have never gone away.

The OECD is now racing to implement its Two Pillars solution to international tax problems which is intended to produce a grand settlement of both the technical and the political issues in international taxation, avowedly with the full involvement of developing countries. It is salutary for those interested in taxation, economic history and international relations more broadly to take time to read this book and ask themselves: is the world really changing for the better, or is it just more of the same? Nikki's book is a great read with enough political intrigue, Machiavellian tactics and obscure technicalities to make it a tax thriller.

Richard Vann

PREFACE

This book had its beginnings in a quest to discover how and why developing countries, having long resisted joining the bilateral tax treaty network since the time of the League of Nations, came together in 1968 under auspices of the UN to formulate a model double tax convention with developed countries which, from most points of view, signed away many of their source taxing rights. Such cooperation today would appear singular in history in view of the multitude and protracted multilateral tax coordination efforts that have arisen over the past two decades to find middle ground in the contention for a satisfactory division of global revenue, within which developing countries continue to struggle for voice and influence in international tax policymaking.

In combing through several archives, however, I came upon a surprising trove of material from an earlier UN period that seemingly contradicted prevalent historical narratives that indicate that little international tax coordination of significance took place during the first post–World War II decade. Comprehending and making coherent sense of this material itself might have been a futile endeavour were it not for the profoundly rich works of many historians and scholars of international tax, international economics, international institutions and international relations that enabled me to synthesise the surrounding and supporting framework and context. The result is a chronicle that is far from insignificant in the annals of international tax history. It is, in fact, the connecting piece that not only explains the unbroken continuity Western powers have had in dictating the international tax regime but also demonstrates the inseparability of international tax relations between developed and developing countries from wider considerations of international political economy, global governance and development.

The narrative of the UN Fiscal Commission years presented here is not an exhaustive account of all that this body did regarding fiscal matters. Rather, the focus is on double taxation, the subject of greatest international concern at the time and which provoked the most controversial debates. The story itself is complex, having a genesis in the wartime activities of the League in the Americas and extending to involve various UN bodies and specialised agencies, regional intergovernmental organisations, industry interests and private foundations. As no thorough or chronological exposition exists on the Commission, including its set-up and workings, or its public finance and technical assistance efforts, it has furthermore been necessary to sacrifice detail for concision in order to present history in its proper and relevant context.

The primary source material for this book has mainly been drawn from the UN Archives and Records Management Section (New York); the UN Office at Geneva Library and Archives, which also houses the League of Nations Archives; the British National Archives (Kew); and the United States National Archives (College Park, Maryland). Online archival databases, such as those of the UN, the International Civil Aviation Organization and the US Department of State's Office of the Historian, have also been availed. The integration of the American and British private positions and considerations as found among their records bring crucial insight to the narrative as both countries were the main decision-makers, the largest funders and the biggest capitalist powers of the UN system. Collectively, they functioned as major gatekeepers to the international tax rules that could be shaped and the direction of fiscal work that could be undertaken in the UN. Regrettably, this work does not have the benefit of archival material from informational sources of developing countries (or of other countries) which were active in double taxation matters during this period, although their positions, expressed in terms of broad policy arguments, are made known from the UN records. It is hoped that researchers in the field might unearth and furnish such narratives where they exist. This work has also been predominantly based on English language source material, the remainder comprising French and Spanish texts. In relation to the collection of archival documents, this limitation was greatly circumvented by English being, firstly, the primary working language of the UN and of the League's Princeton Mission due to their headquartering in the United States, and, secondly, the language of the two above-mentioned powers. As English is, moreover, the dominant common language of international taxation, authoritative English academic sources have generally been considered to provide a reliable survey of information generally known about the Commission and the double taxation work of this period.

In an age where international tax appears to have become intensely politicised due to power shifts, financial crises, interinstitutional jurisdictional conflict, impact of non-governmental actors and the rise of the South, this book illuminates that such developments are not unique to the twenty-first century but were already played out at the earliest attempt at inclusive tax cooperation, with detrimental outcomes for developing countries and the UN. It is most fortuitous and fascinating that this work was undertaken at a time when scholarship has begun to scrutinise the political, diplomatic and behavioural determinants of global tax governance with the aim of reforming international taxation, particularly in view of developing countries' propensity to fare poorly in the international tax system. This book, as the first archival research analysing international tax coordination at the institutional level through an international relations lens, provides the historical empirical analysis to such endeavours as well as an extended case study to the international relations scholarship on international institutions. It is hoped that this interpretation of international tax history will encourage international tax scholarship towards interdisciplinary approaches that increase our understanding of how international tax law is truly shaped in order to bring us closer to achieving tax justice in the globalised world.

ACKNOWLEDGEMENTS

First and foremost, a depth of gratitude to Professor Richard Vann for his vast knowledge, wisdom and networks of tax history ages, and for mentoring me in writing tax history. This book is the product of a long PhD journey, and I am indebted to Professor Lee Burns for funding much of my archival field research and to the tax cluster of the University of Sydney Law School for providing the facilities to carry out my work and the opportunities to develop as a scholar. To my Sydney Law School colleagues Nancy Carrasco, Dr Penelope Crossley, Dr Celeste Black, Melissa Ogier and Dr Fady Aoun, your moral support sustained me over the years. A sincere thanks to Professor Sunita Jogarajan at the University of Melbourne whose work and warm and insightful conversations have been an inspiration. I am grateful to Dr Elaine Lindsay for her incisive editorial assistance on my thesis which improved its readability. I also extend my deepest appreciation to Professor Peter Harris, Dr John Avery Jones and Dr Mark Brabazon for their invaluable encouragement in supporting the publication of this research.

I received vital assistance from various archivists and librarians in conducting my research at several archival institutions and libraries. I particularly want to thank Jacques Oberson and Carla Bellota at the United Nations Archives and Library at Geneva for their incredible help with my searches, which included digitising documents to send to me. Amanda Leinberger similarly deserves special mention for facilitating my archival hunting at the United Nations Archives and Records Centre in New York.

Finally, my heartfelt gratitude to my husband, Benjamin, and my toddler, Eliana, for their overwhelming love, support, sacrifice and motivation. A special thanks also to Eliana's grandparents, Albert and Catherine, and Aunt Shana, who were her weekend escapes during COVID-19 times: you enabled me to complete my thesis knowing that my precious one was in the best of hands and hearts. And little Ezra, you have been a most agreeable baby, enduring a distracted and absent mother while she turned her thesis into a book!

CHRONOLOGY OF KEY EVENTS

September 1939	Outbreak of World War II
June 1940	First 'Regional Meeting' of the League's Fiscal Committee, Mexico
September 1940	First group of staff members from the League's Economic, Financial and Transit Department arrive at Princeton; establishment of the Princeton Mission
August 1941	Atlantic Charter released
December 1941	Bombing of Pearl Harbour
January 1942	Third Meeting of Ministers of Foreign Affairs of the American Republics, Rio de Janeiro
July 1943	Second 'Regional Meeting' of the League's Fiscal Committee, Mexico
July 1944	United Nations Monetary and Financial Conference, Bretton Woods; establishment of International Monetary Fund and World Bank
November 1944	International Civil Aviation Conference, Chicago
February–March 1945	Inter-American Conference on Problems of War and Peace, Chapultepec
April 1945	Death of President Roosevelt; President Truman sworn in
May 1945	Surrender of Nazi Germany
April–June 1945	United Nations Conference on International Organization, San Francisco; UN Charter signed
July 1945	Churchill's defeat in British general elections
August 1945	Atomic bombings of Hiroshima and Nagasaki
September 1945	Surrender of Imperial Japan
October 1945	UN Charter enters into force; establishment of the UN Organization
August–November 1945	Meeting of the Executive Committee of the UN Preparatory Commission, London
November–December 1945	Meeting of the UN Preparatory Commission, London

January–February 1946	First Session of ECOSOC, London
March 1946	Tenth Session of the League's Fiscal Committee, London
	UN moves from London to New York
April 1946	League of Nations dissolved
May–June 1946	Second Session of ECOSOC, New York
September–October 1946	Third Session of ECOSOC; establishment of the UN Fiscal Commission
March 1947	Truman Doctrine announced to Congress
April 1947	Permanent ICAO comes into being
May 1947	First Session of the UN Fiscal Commission
June 1947	Marshall Plan announced
August 1947	Independence and partition of India
February 1948	Establishment of ECLA
November 1947–March 1948	United Nations Conference on Trade and Employment, Havana
April 1948	Establishment of the OEEC
March–May 1948	PAU/OAS Ninth International Conference of American States, Bogotá
January 1949	Second Session of the UN Fiscal Commission
	Truman's Point Four Program announced
August 1949	Launch of the UN Expanded Programme of Technical Assistance
	USSR detonates its first atomic bomb
October 1949	Chinese Communist Party victory; establishment of the PRC
February 1950	Speech by Senator McCarthy that launches Red Scare
June 1950	Outbreak of the Korean War
May 1951	Third Session of the UN Fiscal Commission
October 1951	Egypt declares void Anglo-Egyptian Treaty of 1936
October 1952	Permanent UN headquarters in Manhattan completed
November 1952	UN Secretary-General Lie resigns
January 1953	President Eisenhower inaugurated
	FBI begins operations in UN headquarters as part of McCarthy investigations
March 1953	Death of Stalin
April 1953	Hammarskjöld elected as new UN Secretary-General
April–May 1953	Fourth Session of the UN Fiscal Commission
August 1953	USSR detonates its first thermonuclear bomb

May 1954	Viet Minh victory at Dien Bien Phu, Vietnam; France withdraws from Indochina
June 1954	US-supported coup in Guatemala to overthrow President Arbenz
July 1954	ICC calls upon the OEEC to take up double taxation matters
August 1954	Dissolution of the UN Fiscal Commission
March 1956	Establishment of the OEEC Fiscal Committee

ARCHIVAL SOURCES

United Nations Archives and Records Management Section, New York (UNARMS)

AG-009	Preparatory Commission of the United Nations (1945–1946) Fonds
AG-025-002	United Nations Registry Section (1946–1979) Fonds
S-0441	Branch Registries, vol I–IV
AG-004-001	Department of Economic and Social Affairs (DESA) Fonds
S-0991	Economic and Social Council Secretariat Records
S-0979	Fiscal Division Records

United Nations Office at Geneva Registry, Records and Archives (UNOG)

PO	Princeton Office Files (contained in League of Nations External Fonds)
OSG	Office of the Secretary-General Files (contained in League of Nations Secretariat Fonds)
UNOGRFP	UNOG Registry First Period Fonds

United States National Archives and Records Administration, College Park, Maryland (NARAII)

RG59	Department of State Record Group
RG56	Department of Treasury Record Group

British National Archives, Kew (TNA)

IR40 Board of Inland Revenue Files: Stamps and Taxes Division Registered Files

FO371 Foreign Office Files: Political Departments: General Correspondence from 1906–1966

Department of State's *Foreign Relations of the United States* (FRUS) Records

As archived at the Office of the Historian website <https://history.state.gov/>

ABBREVIATIONS

ABA	American Bar Association
ATC	Air Transport Committee (ICAO)
BEPS	Base Erosion and Profit Shifting
CAB	Civil Aeronautics Board (US)
CEIP	Carnegie Endowment for International Peace
CSCIO	Cabinet Steering Committee on International Organisations (UK)
DEA	Department of Economic Affairs (UN Secretariat)
DESA	Department of Economic and Social Affairs (UN Secretariat)
DIESA	Department of International Economic and Social Affairs (UN Secretariat)
DTA	Double Taxation Agreement
ECAFE	Economic Commission for Asia and the Far East
ECE	Economic Commission for Europe
ECLA	Economic Commission for Latin America
ECOSOC	Economic and Social Council
EFTD	Economic, Financial and Transit Department (League Secretariat)
FAO	Food and Agriculture Organization
FDI	Foreign Direct Investment
FPILA Taxation	Taxation in capital-exporting and capital-importing countries of foreign private investment in Latin America (UN Secretariat study)
FTC	Foreign Tax Credit (US)
G20	Group of Twenty
GA	General Assembly
GATT	General Agreement on Tariffs and Trade
GDP	Gross Domestic Product

HLS	Harvard Law School
IABA	Inter-American Bar Association
IACCP	Inter-American Council of Commerce and Production
IAS	Institute for Advanced Study, Princeton
IATA	International Air Transport Association
IBFD	International Bureau for Fiscal Documentation
ICAN	International Commission for Air Navigation
ICAO	International Civil Aviation Organization
ICC	International Chamber of Commerce
IDAB	International Development Advisory Board (US)
IFA	International Fiscal Association
IFC	International Finance Corporation
ILO	International Labour Organization
IMF	International Monetary Fund
ITA	International Tax Agreements (UN publication series)
ITD	International Tax Dialogue
ITO	International Trade Organization
League	League of Nations
NAM	National Association for Manufacturers (US)
NFTC	National Foreign Trade Council (US)
NGO	Non-Governmental Organisation
OAS	Organization of American States
OCIAA	Office of the Coordinator of Inter-American Affairs (US)
OECD	Organisation for Economic Co-operation and Development
OECD Model	OECD Model Tax Convention on Income and on Capital
OEEC	Organisation for European Economic Co-operation
Pan Am	Pan American Airways
PAU	Pan-American Union
PCT	Platform for Collaboration on Tax
PE	Permanent Establishment
PFI Conditions	Conditions of Private Foreign Investment (League study)
PRC	People's Republic of China

SoCtyTax/ResCtyExempt(FoInvInc)	Exclusive source-country taxation of income from foreign investments in under-developed countries, with corresponding residence-country exemption of foreign-source income by capital-exporting countries (Proposed double taxation solution)
SUNFED	Special United Nations Fund for Economic Development
TAA	Technical Assistance Administration (UN Secretariat)
UN	United Nations
UNEC	United Nations Economic Subcommittee of the Executive Committee on Economic Foreign Policy (US, chaired by the State Department)
UN Model	UN Model Double Taxation Convention between Developed and Developing Countries
USGPO	United States Government Printing Office
USSR	Union of Soviet Socialist Republics
World Bank	International Bank for Reconstruction and Development

1

Introduction

1.1 Introduction

In the 100 years of international tax coordination since the League of Nations (League) took up the study of double taxation in 1921,[1] there is generally a hiatus in tax history between 1946 and 1954 after the League's Fiscal Committee was dissolved[2] and before the Organisation for European Economic Co-operation (OEEC) adopted double taxation as its first international tax concern in 1955.[3] This was the postwar decade in which the Fiscal Commission of the United Nations (UN) functioned as the successor to the League's Fiscal Committee, which had concluded its double taxation work with two conflicting and incomplete model conventions (the pro-source country 1943 Mexico Model and the pro-residence country 1946 London Model),[4] urging the UN to review and further develop the two models in a forum of 'a balanced group of tax administrators and experts from both capital-importing and capital-exporting countries and from economically advanced and less-advanced countries'.[5]

[1] GWJ Bruins et al, *Report on Double Taxation Submitted to the Financial Committee*, League Doc E.F.S.73.F.19 (5 April 1923) 3 ('*Economists' Report*').

[2] *Resolution for the Dissolution of the League of Nations*, League Assembly, League Doc A.32(1).1946.X (18 April 1946) 12–16.

[3] OEEC Council, Recommendation of 25 February 1955: see Organisation for Economic Co-operation and Development (OECD), *Model Tax Convention on Income and on Capital 2017 (Full Version)* (2019) vol 1, I-1 [4] ('*OECD 2017 Model*').

[4] Fiscal Committee, *Report on the Work of the Tenth Session*, League Doc C.37.M.37.1946.II.A (25 April 1946) 7–8 ('*Tenth Session Report*').

[5] Ibid 8.

The work of the Fiscal Commission has never been investigated in depth, but the reports[6] and scarce accounts[7] of its four sessions indicate that its international tax work became politically engulfed in the East–West, North–South dichotomies and suffered from a lack of financing. Importantly, these texts highlight that keen, even heated, debate arose concerning the allocation rules and preferred method of double taxation relief to apply for certain types of income with respect to relations between developed and developing countries. Moreover, the resolutions adopted by the Commission called not only for the widespread conclusion of double taxation agreements (DTAs) among UN member states, but also for developed countries to consider granting more source taxation rights to developing countries in view of their development needs. Despite these promising developments of the UN as a forum for double taxation matters and the interested participation of non-European, post-colonial developing countries in the subject, the UN did not make an official contribution to international tax law in the form of a model convention by the time of the Commission's dissolution in August 1954.[8] What is more, the reports and resolutions of this period would never be broached again in successive international double taxation efforts.

In March 1956, the OEEC (later succeeded by the Organisation for Economic Co-operation and Development (OECD)) established its Fiscal Committee whose model conventions and related work[9] soon eclipsed the UN's progress in the field, leading to DTAs flourishing in the developed world under international tax rules that favoured residence-based taxation. Efforts by developed countries to conclude DTAs with developing countries would only gain momentum when the UN re-entered the international tax arena through its 1968 Ad Hoc Group of Experts on Tax Treaties between

[6] Fiscal Commission, *Report to the Economic and Social Council on the Work of the First Session of the Commission by ARF Mackay, General Rapporteur*, UN Doc E/440 (29 May 1947); Fiscal Commission, *Report to the Economic and Social Council on the Second Session of the Commission, Held at Lake Success, New York, 10 to 25 January 1949*, UN Docs E/1104/Add.1 and Corr.1 (also E/CN.8/49/Rev.2) (3 February 1949); Fiscal Commission, *Report to the Economic and Social Council on the Third Session of the Commission, Held at Lake Success, New York, 7–17 May 1951*, UN Doc E/1993 (also E/CN.8/62) (31 May 1951); Fiscal Commission, *Report to the Economic and Social Council on the Fourth Session of the Fiscal Commission, Held at Headquarters, New York, from 27 April to 8 May 1953*, UN Doc E/2429 (also E/CN.8/78) (8 May 1953).

[7] See Section 1.2.

[8] *Fiscal Commission*, ESC Res 557C II (XVIII), UN ESCOR, UN Doc E/2654 (15 August 1954, adopted 5 August 1954).

[9] See *OECD 2017 Model*, I-1–I-3 [4]–[9].

Developed and Developing Countries (Group of Experts),[10] which culminated in the 1980 UN Model.[11] Despite the success of the Group of Experts' work in bringing developing countries back to the negotiating table and into the bilateral tax treaty network, the UN Model was largely considered by many experts as too similar to the OECD Model to be considered a true compromise in securing source-based taxing rights for developing countries.[12] In this regard, the UN has been criticised for failing the objective set by the Secretary-General to safeguard the revenue base of developing countries,[13] and for spreading the OECD's tax influence in the developing world[14] through the regularly updated OECD Model and Commentary, which are widely held to be the most influential infrastructure in tax treaty design[15] and the original locus of the OECD's soft law power.[16] To this day,

[10] The Group of Experts was set up pursuant to ESC Res 1273 (XLIII) (entitled *Tax Treaties between Developed Countries*), UN ESCOR, UN Doc E/4429 (1967, adopted 4 August 1967).

[11] Department of International Economic and Social Affairs (DIESA), *United Nations Model Double Taxation Convention between Developed and Developing Countries*, UN Doc ST/ESA/102 (UN, 1980) ('*UN Model 1980*'). Prior to this the UN published the *Manual for the Negotiation of Bilateral Tax Treaties between Developed and Developing Countries* (1979) and *Guidelines for Tax Treaties between Developed and Developing Countries* (1974).

[12] See, for example, Jan de Goede and Fraser Dickinson, 'The UN Model (2001) Special Issue - The Context and Contents' (2012) 66(11) *Bulletin for International Taxation* 587, 587; Leif Mutén, 'Double Taxation Conventions between Industrialised and Developing Countries' in International Fiscal Association (IFA), *Double Taxation Treaties between Industrialised and Developing Countries: OECD and UN Models, a Comparison* (Kluwer, 1990) 3, 3–4; JF Court, 'Some Reflections on the Experience of the UN Model in Tax Treaties between Developed and Developing Countries' in IFA, *Double Taxation Treaties between Industrialised and Developing Countries: OECD and UN Models, a Comparison* (Kluwer, 1990) 15, 18; NM Qureshi, 'Tax Treaty Needs of Developing Countries' in IFA, *UN Draft Model Taxation Convention* (Kluwer, 1979) 31, 33–9.

[13] AH Figueroa, 'Comprehensive Tax Treaties' in IFA, *Double Taxation Treaties between Industrialised and Developing Countries: OECD and UN Models, a Comparison* (Kluwer, 1990) 9, 12–13.

[14] Philip Baker, *Double Taxation Conventions and International Tax Law: A Manual on the OECD Model Tax Convention on Income and on Capital of 1992* (Sweet & Maxwell, 2nd ed, 1994) 5; Victor Thuronyi, *Comparative Tax Law* (Kluwer Law International, 2003) 288; Roy Rohatgi, *Basic International Taxation* (BNA International, 2nd ed, 2005) 3, 74–5.

[15] Diane M Ring, 'Who Is Making International Tax Policy? International Organizations as Power Players in a High Stakes World' (2010) 33(3) *Fordham International Law Journal* 649, 700; Yariv Brauner, 'An International Tax Regime in Crystallization' (2003) 56(2) *Tax Law Review* 259, 310; Joseph Isenbergh, *International Taxation* (Foundation Press, 3rd ed, 2000) 224.

[16] Allison Christians, 'Hard Law, Soft Law, and International Taxation' (2007) 25(2) *Wisconsin International Law Journal* 325, 326 nn 5–6, 331–2; Arthur J Cockfield, 'The

the UN's involvement in international tax coordination remains selective and supplementary to the OECD – a status quo that concerns many, no less the developing country caucus forming the bulk of the UN's 193 members, who consider the inclusive organisation as better poised to ensure that the promotion of foreign direct investment (FDI) in developing countries is done in an equitable manner that preserves sufficient taxing rights for source countries.[17]

For the past two decades, general discontent over these concerns has seen the rise of unprecedented international tax activity, in particular non-conformist responses by emerging economies towards the long-standing tax treaty principles;[18] the revision of the UN Model in 2001, 2011 and 2017;[19] the revisions of the UN Manual for negotiating DTAs between developed and developing countries published in 2003 and 2019;[20] the OECD/Group of Twenty (G20) Base Erosion and Profit Shifting (BEPS) projects launched in 2012 and 2017; the joint initiative of the European Commission, International Monetary Fund (IMF), Inter-American Development Bank, OECD, World Bank Group and Inter-American Center of Tax Administrations on the International Tax Dialogue (ITD) begun in 2002;[21] the joint initiative of the IMF, OECD, UN and World Bank Group on the Platform for Collaboration on Tax (PCT) launched in 2016;[22]

Rise of the OECD as Informal "World Tax Organization" through National Responses to E-commerce Tax Challenges' (2006) 8 *Yale Journal Law and Technology* 136, 167.

17 See Michael Lennard, 'The Purpose and Current Status of the United Nations Tax Work' (2008) 14(1) *Asia-Pacific Tax Bulletin* 23, 30; Eva Andrés Aucejo, 'The Primary Legal Role of the United Nations on International Tax Cooperation and Global Tax Governance: Going on a New International Organization on Global Tax Cooperation and Governance under the UN "Family"' (2020) 21 *Revista de Educación y Derecho*, 31297: 1–34 <https://revistes.ub.edu/index.php/RED/issue/view/2311>.

18 See, for example, Lara Friedlander and Scott Wilkie, 'Policy Forum: The History of Tax Treaty Provisions – and Why It Is Important to Know about It' (2006) 54(4) *Canadian Tax Journal* 907, 908; Richard M Bird, 'Taxing Electronic Commerce: The End of the Beginning?' (2005) 59(4) *Bulletin for International Taxation* 130, 137.

19 Department of Economic and Social Affairs (DESA), *United Nations Model Double Taxation Convention between Developed and Developing Countries* (UN, 2001) ('*UN Model 2001*'); DESA, *United Nations Model Double Taxation Convention between Developed and Developing Countries* (UN, 2011) ('*UN Model 2011*'); DESA, *United Nations Model Double Taxation Convention between Developed and Developing Countries: 2017 Update* (UN, 2017) ('*UN Model 2017*').

20 DESA, *Manual for the Negotiation of Bilateral Tax Treaties between Developed and Developing Countries* (UN, 2003); DESA, *Manual for the Negotiation of Bilateral Tax Treaties between Developed and Developing Countries 2019* (UN, 2019).

21 See *International Tax Dialogue* (Web Page) <www.itdweb.org/>. The last activity of the ITD was in 2015.

22 See *Platform for Collaboration on Tax* (Web Page) <www.tax-platform.org/>.

and the PCT's 2021 Toolkit on Tax Treaty Negotiations.[23] These manifold efforts have underscored core and persistent themes troubling international tax relations between the two groups of countries, which may be narrowed down to questions concerning the appropriate forum for dealing with international tax issues between developed and developing countries; the division of taxing rights between source and residence countries; the role of tax jurisdiction in influencing FDI in developing countries; and the suitability of tax treaties for application between developed and developing countries.

In the search for answers to guide future discourse, it is necessary to confront the neglected history of the UN's first attempt at global tax coordination to understand how and why the only genuine universal forum vacated its original mandate, leaving an organisation mainly formed of developed countries to assume its role in steering international tax policy development. The Commission story presented in this book will surprise many. It is rife not only with the tenacious endeavours of developing countries and the UN Secretariat to forge new international tax principles and practices, but also the Secretariat's efforts to secure the UN's position as the overarching world fiscal authority. It even has a genesis in the League's work in the Americas when the organisation sought refuge at Princeton during World War II. This narrative altogether will, firstly, reveal how the double taxation work of the 1940s, the initiation of developing countries into international tax coordination and the creation of the Commission were achieved under questionable circumstances, motivations and theories of economic development. Secondly, it will explain why the UN never reconciled the Mexico and London Models, how double taxation came to be imbued with a development purpose and why most developing countries were not motivated to conclude DTAs with developed countries despite official encouragement. Thirdly, it will show how the activism of the Secretariat led to its loss of broad fiscal jurisdiction, and how the activism of developing countries resulted in the abrupt abolition of the Commission and the loss of their place at the double taxation negotiating table. Finally, and above all, it will show how American[24] and, to a lesser

[23] PCT, 'Toolkit on Tax Treaty Negotiations' (May 2022) <www.tax-platform.org/publications>.

[24] With apologies to the broad Americas, the terms 'America' and 'American' in this book are synonyms for the United States and its citizens, except in the context of the American continent.

extent, British hegemony of this period controlled the double taxation policies and principles that could be developed.

In short, this book provides the historical foundation needed to better understand how the present international tax system came to be, demonstrating that past international tax coordination was more nuanced than a straightforward negotiation of technical rules but rather involved considerations of hegemonic influences, power imbalances, information asymmetries, global governance and private business pressures. This background in turn offers new perspectives to evaluating the fairness, inclusivity and comprehensiveness of current developments on global multilateral tax cooperation, especially regarding the UN's role as participant in the complex policy formation process and facilitator in reconciling the developed and developing countries' positions.

1.2 Prevailing Narratives

Modern tax literature regarding the Fiscal Commission is sporadic and sketchy. Many prominent works that outline international tax history overlook the Commission altogether, citing the OECD's Fiscal Committee as the effective successor to the League's Fiscal Committee.[25] Similarly, several texts (including the later UN Models) imply that the UN only made its debut in double taxation in 1968 with the creation of the Group of Experts.[26] Publications, including those by the UN, that do mention the Commission's existence indicate that it did not progress double taxation.[27] Very few have flagged this gap in history

[25] *OECD 2017 Model*, I-1–I-2 [4]–[6]; Ekkehart Reimer and Alexander Rust (eds), *Klaus Vogel on Double Taxation Conventions* (Kluwer Law International, 4th ed, 2015) vol 1, 1; Mitchell B Carroll, 'The Historical Development of Tax Treaties' in Jon E Bischel (ed), *Income Tax Treaties* (Practising Law Institute, 1978) 51, 58–9; Baker, *Double Taxation Conventions*, 1; David R Davies, *Principles of International Double Taxation Relief* (Sweet & Maxwell, 1985) 36.

[26] See, for example, Ring, 'Who Is Making', 698 n 232; *UN Model 2011*, vi–vii; *UN Model 2017*, iii–iv; Court, 'Some Reflections', 15.

[27] International Chamber of Commerce (ICC), *Settlement of Difficulties and Disputes Arising Out of Double Taxation Agreements: Statement Adopted by the Executive Committee of the ICC (February 1959) and Report of Its Commission on Taxation* (1959) 18–19; AJ Van den Tempel, *Relief from Double Taxation* (International Bureau for Fiscal Documentation (IBFD), 1967) 7–9; Richard J Vann, 'A Model Tax Treaty for the Asian-Pacific Region?' (1991) 45(3) *Bulletin for International Fiscal Documentation* 99, 103 n 15; Ken Messere, 'The 1992 OECD Model Treaty: The Precursors and Successors of the New OECD Model Taxation Convention on Income and Capital' (1993) 33(8) *European Taxation* 246, 246; Baker, *Double Taxation Conventions*, 1; Rohatgi, *Basic International Taxation*, 3, 65; Peter Andrew Harris, *Corporate/*

as peculiar.[28] The following provides a brief overview of contemporaneous and subsequent works containing more than cursory insights into the Commission that have largely shaped prevailing narratives of that body.

1.2.1 *Contemporaneous Narratives*

During the Commission's lifespan, it was the subject of only one scholarly work,[29] which stemmed from lectures delivered by tax law professor Chrétien under the auspices of The Hague Academy of International Law (*Académie de Droit International de La Haye*).[30] Chrétien was a consultant expert to the Fiscal Division (the UN Secretariat staff serving the Commission) but did not attend the Commission's sessions so his knowledge of the deliberations was based on the content of the Commission's reports. Chrétien's account was part of a broader study directed at explaining the role of international organisations in developing the relatively new field of international tax law. This work covered the League's and UN's fiscal work

Shareholder Income Taxation and Allocating Taxing Rights between Countries: A Comparison of Imputation Systems (IBFD, 1996) 307–8; Peter Harris and David Oliver, *International Commercial Tax* (Cambridge University Press, 2010) 17. For UN sources, including works by its officials, see, for example, *UN Model 1980*, 8; *UN Model 2001*, xvii [26]; Lennard, 'United Nations Tax Work', 23.

28 Vann, 'Model Tax Treaty', 103 n 15.

29 Four other articles concerning the Commission's sessions were written by those privy to the Commission's meetings: Nathan N Gordon, 'The Second Session of the United Nations Fiscal Commission' (1949) 2(2) *National Tax Journal* 166; José Perez Cubillas, 'New Decisions of Fiscal Commission: Review of Third Session' (1951) 10(12) *United Nations Bulletin* 598; Mitchell B Carroll, 'Report on the Meeting of the United Nations Fiscal Commission, Lake Success, May 7–17, 1951' (1951) 5(5) *Bulletin for International Fiscal Documentation* 309; Mitchell B Carroll, 'Action on Tax Treatment of Foreign Income at Session of United Nations Fiscal Commission, April 27 to May 8, 1953' (1953) 7(5) *Bulletin for International Fiscal Documentation* 183. These narratives are of less assistance to academic study as they are a mix of historical narrative and advocacy for the bodies that the authors represented. The accounts of Gordon, as a member of the US delegation to the Second Session, and Perez, as the Cuban representative and Chairman of the Third Session, were generally descriptive overviews. Carroll's accounts were as an observer representing industry interests and focused on the deliberations of relevance to Western business concerns.

30 The lectures were published in the Academy's Collected Courses (*Recueil des Cours*): Maxime Chrétien, 'Contribution a l'Étude du Droit International Fiscal Actuel: Le Rôle des Organizations International dans le Règlement des Questions d'Impôts entre les Divers États' (1954 II) 86 *Recueil des Cours* 5 (*Translation:* Contribution to the Study of Current International Tax Law: The Role of International Organisations in the Settlement of Tax Matters among Various States).

between 1921 and 1954[31] and to date represents the most thorough academic exposition of the Commission. In it, Chrétien evaluated the Commission through a comparative lens with the League's Fiscal Committee, which included an examination of the institutional structures within which they operated, their functions and practices, and their scope and influence.[32]

In summary, Chrétien considered that the League and UN counterparts were alike in most respects, including in their (1) advisory functions;[33] (2) role in settling tax issues to achieve a level of uniformity through DTAs and domestic laws;[34] (3) tasks in developing model conventions, publishing compendiums of DTAs and running a fiscal information service;[35] (4) priority responsibility over fiscal matters with little interference from the principal organs (i.e. the respective Assemblies and Councils), which largely adopted their recommendations;[36] (5) close collaboration with their respective Secretariats, the latter bearing a considerable burden of the preparatory and implementation work;[37] (6) use of temporary committees of experts to deal with specific issues, occasionally assigning projects to groups of experts or a single expert;[38] and (7) active work with the International Chamber of Commerce (ICC), which attended all their meetings.[39] He also noted the continuity between the League and UN Secretariats with Paul Deperon, the last Secretary of the League Committee, becoming the first Secretary of the UN Commission.[40]

Nevertheless, Chrétien emphasised that the UN Commission's departure from the League Committee in composition and mandate ultimately hampered progress of the former's tax work. Regarding composition, the League Committee had comprised of both 'full' and corresponding members,

[31] The study was completed before the Commission's abolition and Chrétien wrote of the Commission in the present tense, expecting it to continue in its activities: Ibid 7 [3], 22 [18], 33–4 [30].

[32] Ibid 7 [3].

[33] Ibid 7–8 [3]–[4], 18–20 [13]–[14], 37 [37].

[34] Ibid 37 [37].

[35] Ibid.

[36] Ibid 21–5 [16]–[20].

[37] Ibid 21–2 [17], 29 [25], 34 [31].

[38] Ibid 22 [18], 35–6 [33]–[36].

[39] Ibid 28 [24], 28 [30]. Chrétien nevertheless pointed out that in the UN, the ICC was criticised by some members for using the Commission for capitalist purposes. He also highlighted that the Commission collaborated with IFA (at 29 [25]) and with universities, specifically Harvard, the latter cooperation being more promising and disinterested (at 28 [30]).

[40] Ibid 29 [25].

drawn from both League member and non-member states, who were technical experts appointed in their personal capacities primarily to represent a variety of tax systems, especially the major systems.[41] Conversely, the members of UN Commission were only drawn from UN member states, acted in the capacity of government representatives, and were mostly from their state's Treasury or Finance departments.[42] Chrétien criticised the latter composition for resulting in (1) a narrower range of expert skills and variety of world tax systems represented on the Commission (and accordingly its temporary committees);[43] (2) inequitable representation across large, medium and small states, because of the de facto permanent places given to the 'Big Five' UN powers (the United States, the Union of Soviet Socialist Republics, the United Kingdom, France and China); and (3) East–West ideological differences being played out at the Commission level with regard to China's representation despite the Commission having no jurisdiction to resolve the matter.[44] Regarding its mandate, the UN Commission had replaced both the League's Fiscal Committee and its Financial Committee,[45] which revived the status quo in the League as it was prior to 1928 when the taxation issues were dealt with by the Financial Committee.[46] Chrétien criticised this merger, indicating that it caused a duality in the Commission from the start as the Commission would divide into two working groups to deal, respectively, with tax and finance issues, sitting in plenary only at the beginning and at the end of each session. Nevertheless, the merger appeared only partial as the Commission's work programme showed it was more interested in taxation than finance and because the existence of the IMF and the International Bank for Reconstruction and Development (World Bank) reduced some of the public finance functions of the Commission.[47] The Commission's tax work, however, was deprioritised with the emergence of its function of providing technical assistance to underdeveloped countries, which it executed in cooperation with the Secretariat, other UN bodies and specialised agencies.[48] Eventually, this too was downsized by the creation of other ad hoc bodies.[49]

41 Ibid 26–8 [23].
42 Ibid 29–31 [27]–[28].
43 Ibid 26–8 [23], 35–6 [34].
44 Ibid 30–1 [28].
45 Ibid 29 [26].
46 Ibid 32–3 [29].
47 Ibid 34–5 [32].
48 Ibid 37–8 [37]–[38], 86–9 [101]–[104].
49 Ibid 34–5 [32].

In relation to the scope of double taxation work continued by the UN, Chrétien observed that the Commission's work on reconciling the Mexico and London Models had ceased by 1951 as the Secretariat did not receive sufficient or adequate government responses to enable it to establish new texts.[50] Instead, the Commission formulated principles on two difficult issues that were indirectly related to revising the model conventions, namely the general allocation principles to apply in relations between developed and undeveloped countries, and the taxation of international air transport. The first issue was examined in cooperation with the ICC and led to heated debates and nearly identical resolutions in 1951 and 1953 that, inter alia, recognised the primary taxation right of source countries.[51] In addition, in 1953, faced with an impasse concerning the principle of exclusive source-country taxation of income from FDI advocated by the capital-importing countries but opposed by the capital-exporting countries, the Commission adopted a compromise that urged capital-exporting countries to sympathetically consider taxing such income only or mainly in underdeveloped countries. The second issue was considered in collaboration with the International Civil Aviation Organization (ICAO) and led to acrimonious debate and an inconclusive resolution in 1951.[52] Chrétien concluded that the Commission and its Secretariat were still at the stage of preliminary studies for the revision of the Mexico and London drafts, and that the slow pace was justified by the need to proceed cautiously. Furthermore, the UN's fiscal information service, which was more extensive than that achieved by the League, was supplementing the international tax work by providing the background on tax systems to facilitate DTA negotiations.[53] He nevertheless doubted the Commission's ability to establish a model treaty providing a common solution for relations between developed and developing countries since the two groups could not reach consensus on what amounted to equality of sacrifice.[54]

Chrétien generally found the influence of the UN's work on states' tax systems difficult to assess.[55] While there was high demand for its technical assistance activities, such work rarely resulted in publications in contrast to the League's more prolific taxation output, particularly the

[50] Ibid 62 [71].
[51] Ibid 62–3 [72].
[52] Ibid 64 [73].
[53] Ibid 83–4 [98].
[54] Ibid 65 [74].
[55] Ibid 90 [105].

model conventions.[56] There was evidence that the income tax systems of less developed countries were influenced by the modern ones of more developed countries, but it was less clear whether this was due to technical assistance activities or the progressive democratisation of states.[57] Even if it were attributable to technical assistance, it was unclear whether the influence was beneficial or not.[58]

1.2.2 *Subsequent Narratives*

Up until the early 1970s, anecdotal reasons for the Commission's termination were provided by those who had attended the Commission's sessions. These reasons included that it had been 'suppressed . . . on the grounds of economy' and that its composition had made 'achieving unanimity' impossible;[59] that it had 'been moribund almost from the start' because of the wide and incongruent 'economic and political spectrum' of its composition, and that its disbandment had left 'few mourners in its wake';[60] and that it had been 'adjourn[ed] *sine die*' due to 'opposition of certain elements in Eastern Europe'[61] or because 'certain antagonistic elements used its technical meetings as a forum for political denunciations'.[62]

Since Chrétien, Pires has provided the only scholarly analysis[63] of the Commission's double taxation work in his 1989 comparative study of

56 Ibid 90 [105], 91 [106].

57 Ibid 91 [106].

58 Ibid 91–4 [106]–[108].

59 ICC, *Settlement of Difficulties*, 18–19.

60 Nathan N Gordon, 'The Role of Tax Treaties' (July 1965) 46(7) *Taxes – The Tax Magazine* 463, 464.

61 Mitchell B Carroll, 'IFA's Growth with International Tax Law' (1971) 5(3) *The International Lawyer* 558, 562 (emphasis in original).

62 Mitchell B Carroll, 'Income Tax Conventions as an Aid to International Trade and Investment' (1962) 6(3) *Section of International & Comparative Law Bulletin* 16, 19.

63 Three other academic/reference works by Dirksen, Farrell and Hearson marginally discuss the Commission with reference to archival material. Dirksen, in authoring IFA's golden jubilee book from IFA's archival records, refers to relations between the UN and IFA (Willem Dirksen, *IFA: International Fiscal Association, 1938–1988* (Kluwer Law and Taxation, 1988) 45). Farrell, writing from an international trade perspective based on the records of the Havana negotiations of the International Trade Organization (ITO), reports on the 'direct dialogue' between representatives for the Fiscal Commission and ITO delegates regarding crossover competencies on double taxation (Jennifer E Farrell, *The Interface of International Trade Law and Taxation* (IBFD, 2013) 15–23). Hearson, writing from a political economy perspective and from his survey of the British National Archives records, draws attention to Soviet denunciations of the Commission's

international juridical double taxation.[64] He sourced his information from the Commission's reports and the Economic and Social Council (ECOSOC) resolution that abolished the Commission. Accordingly, this account was largely a summary of the work programme and decisions related to double taxation. He did, nevertheless, infer from the Commission's 1951 resolution recognising source countries' 'undeniable right' to tax income and the responsibility of residence countries to eliminate double taxation, that '[t]he approach of the London model was therefore abandoned in favour of the Mexico model'.[65] Other notable research has generally relied on the works of Chrétien, Carroll[66] and Pires to chronicle the Commission's double taxation work,[67] leading to fragmented and varying accounts of the Commission in the tax literature.

1.3 The 'Developing Countries' of Early International Tax Coordination

This section explains the meaning of the term 'developing countries' intended by this book, charting how the concept, where used generally in reference to the League's double taxation work, evolved to acquire

double taxation work and ICAO's proposal for reciprocal exemption of airline income to highlight Western industrialised countries' first-mover advantage already established and at work by the time of the UN efforts at global tax coordination: Martin Hearson, *Imposing Standards: The North–South Dimension to Global Tax Politics* (Cornell University Press, 2021) 41. On his website, Hearson also surmised that the Commission's end appeared 'a matter of failure to gather institutional momentum, in part due to the lack of effective secretariat support, and lukewarm support from across the board', in particular that '[t]he UK and US were never strongly in favour of a permanent international committee examining taxation issues': Martin Hearson, '"Futile and Unrewarding": The Wilderness Years of the International Tax Regime', *Martin Hearson* (Web Page, 28 June 2018) <https://martinhearson.net/2018/06/28/futile-and-unrewarding-the-wilderness-years-of-the-international-tax-regime/>.

64 Manuel Pires, *International Juridical Double Taxation of Income* (Kluwer Law and Taxation, 1989) 98–100.

65 Ibid 99.

66 See n 29.

67 For example, Van den Tempel, in his study comparing the international tax work of the League and the OEEC/OECD, referred to Chrétien for the history of the UN's involvement (Van den Tempel, *Relief from Double Taxation*, 7–9); Picciotto, in his coverage of seventy years of the development and operation of international business taxation referred mainly to Carroll's contemporaneous accounts and Chrétien (Sol Picciotto, *International Business Taxation* (Quorum Books, 1992) 48–52); and Rohatgi, in his handbook on international taxation, referred to Pires for his summary of the Commission's progress (Rohatgi, *Basic International Taxation*, 3, 65).

a particular meaning during the Fiscal Commission years that is fundamentally still the connotation the term carries today.

1.3.1 The League Era

For most of the League period, the concept of 'developing countries' was not clearly defined and no consistent terminology was created to recognise the different sub-groups contained within the concept. Politically speaking, the world was traditionally divided into great and small powers based on military and economic strength.[68] The great powers were largely recognised as the 'inner circle' of the League's decision-makers – that is, the intended or actual permanent members of the League Council (Italy, Japan, Germany, the United Kingdom, the United States and the USSR).[69] Economically however, the United Kingdom remained, and the United States emerged, as the only major capital-exporting and creditor countries.[70] The other member states represented the small powers irrespective of factors such as population or area size, form of government, colonial possessions, per capita wealth and so on.[71] They were an eclectic mixture of war-devastated European states, some of which still held large colonial and trade interests; new nation-states from the carved-up Austro-Hungarian, Ottoman, Russian and German empires; New World republics of Latin America; some members of the British Empire (Australia, Canada, India, New Zealand and the Union of South Africa (South Africa)); and miscellaneous African, Arab and Asian states (e.g. Afghanistan, China, Egypt, Ethiopia and Liberia). The categorisation of states into great or small powers did not significantly impact the League's economic work due to the unanimity principle and the lack of meaningful distinction between these powers in the League Covenant; the mostly non-political nature of

[68] David Vital, *The Inequality of States: A Study of the Small Power in International Relations* (Clarendon Press, 1967) 7–8; Alan K Henrikson, 'Great Powers, Superpowers, and Global Powers: Managerial Succession for a New World Order' in Dimitris Bourantonis and Marios Evriviades (eds), *A United Nations for the Twenty-First Century: Peace, Security and Development* (Kluwer Law International, 1996) 65, 65–6.

[69] Zara Steiner, 'Introductory Essay' in UN Library/Graduate Institute of International Studies, *The League of Nations in Retrospect: Proceedings of the Symposium* (Walter de Gruyter, 1983) 1.

[70] Reuven S Avi-Yonah, *Advanced Introduction to International Tax Law* (Edward Elgar, 2015) 4; Inderjeet Parmar, *Foundations of the American Century: The Ford, Carnegie, & Rockefeller Foundations in the Rise of American Power* (Columbia University Press, 2012) 35.

[71] William E Rappard, 'Small States in the League of Nations' (1934) 49(4) *Political Science Quarterly* 544, 544.

the technical activities; and the open participation by non-League members.[72] Accordingly, the double taxation work mostly utilised economic distinctions based on capital-exporting or capital-importing considerations.

With regard to the fiscal work, in the 1923 Economists' Report as well as in the 1925 report of the Technical Experts, the term 'debtor' country (as opposed to 'creditor' country) was used to represent economically weaker nations that were in need of foreign capital injection for the growth of their agriculture or industry.[73] This term was broadly understood to reflect (1) most of continental Europe that had been reduced to debtor countries by World War I;[74] (2) former colonies which were foreign borrowers, such as Argentina, Australia, Brazil and New Zealand;[75] and (3) the newly created European states.[76] Nevertheless, the economists and 1925 Experts did briefly recognise a subset of less-developed capital-importing countries which had good cause to insist upon significant source-based taxing rights. The economists referred to countries in this position as 'semi-developed' or 'economically undeveloped',[77] while the 1925 Experts referred to them as 'developing' or 'new' countries as distinguished from '[m]ost of the other nations in Europe and America' which were slowly adopting the domicile-based concepts of personal tax already in use in the United Kingdom and the United States.[78] Apart from this, those of the 1925 Experts who represented European debtor countries did not consider the situation of debtor countries to be 'the "norm"' or 'a priority'.[79]

In the 1927 and 1928 reports of the Committees of Technical Experts, the range of participants was broadened to include experts from other

[72] See Thomas Hovet Jr, *Bloc Politics in the United Nations* (Harvard University Press, 1960) 1; A Alexander Menzies, 'Technical Assistance and the League of Nations' in UN Library/ Graduate Institute of International Studies, *The League of Nations in Retrospect: Proceedings of the Symposium* (Walter de Gruyter, 1983) 295, 296–8; Arthur Sweetser, 'The Non-Political Achievements of the League' (1940) 19(1) *Foreign Affairs* 179, 182.

[73] Bruins et al, *Economists' Report*, 9, 10, 35, 38, 40, 41, 48, 49, 50, 51; Technical Experts to the Financial Committee of the League of Nations, *Double Taxation and Tax Evasion, Report and Resolutions*, League Doc F.212 (7 February 1925) 14 ('*1925 Report*').

[74] Sunita Jogarajan, *Double Taxation and the League of Nations in the 1920s* (Cambridge University Press, 2018) 251.

[75] Bruins et al, *Economists' Report*, 40, 50.

[76] Technical Experts, *1925 Report*, 14–15.

[77] Bruins et al, *Economists' Report*, 50–1. The economists also recognised the existence of 'an undeveloped primitive country' but this was not the object of their work (at 12).

[78] Technical Experts, *1925 Report*, 14.

[79] Jogarajan, *Double Taxation*, 251.

economically weaker newly created European states, such as Danzig and Estonia, and other non-European countries, such as Argentina, China, Japan, South Africa and Venezuela, for the purposes of reflecting other important economies and a wide variety of fiscal systems, national economic interests and income concepts.[80] At this stage, however, the situation of debtor countries was considered to have been sufficiently catered for in the 1925 report despite conflicting views expressed by Argentina and Venezuela.[81] The deliberations resulted in the adoption of three alternative model conventions to cater for two main considerations, being differing tax systems (i.e. based on personal or impersonal taxation), and the conflict between capital-exporting and capital-importing countries over which should have the right to tax interest and dividends.[82]

No further country distinctions regarding double taxation arose in the Fiscal Committee's reports between 1929 and 1938.[83] Only in 1946 did

[80] Committee of Technical Experts on Double Taxation and Tax Evasion, *Double Taxation and Tax Evasion: Report*, League Doc C.216.M.85.1927.II (April 1927) 6, 9 ('*1927 Report*'); General Meeting of Government Experts on Double Taxation and Tax Evasion, *Double Taxation and Tax Evasion: Report*, League Doc C.562.M.178.1928.II (October 1928) 37–8 ('*1928 Report*'). See also Technical Experts, *1925 Report*, 29. Note that replies were received from some non-European governments (e.g. India, Chile) as well as other European governments in response to requests sent by the League Secretariat for their observations on the 1927 report: see Jogarajan, *Double Taxation*, 183–4.

[81] Jogarajan, *Double Taxation*, 251.

[82] Government Experts, *1928 Report*, 7–21.

[83] Loose distinctions were used in the context of some of the Committee's other tax work, but they indicated no uniform or clear attempt to group countries. For example, the League's 1932–1933 enquiry into the tax laws of thirty-five countries on enterprise income, which was aimed at developing methods of allocating or apportioning income of multinational enterprises, simply divided countries into European and non-European states: League of Nations, *Taxation of Foreign and National Enterprises* (1932–3) vols 1–3 (volume 3 contained the tax systems of British India, Canada, Japan, Mexico, Netherlands East Indies (now Indonesia), South Africa and three US states, collectively categorised as 'non-European States' in contrast to the 'European countries' addressed in volumes 1 and 2). Also, the term 'debtor' country resurfaced in the Committee's reports of its Eighth and Ninth Sessions: in the former, it was used among the terms of agricultural, industrial or creditor countries in relation to the Committee's study concerning the principles of taxation (Fiscal Committee, *Report to the Council on the Work of the Eighth Session of the Committee*, League Doc C.384.M.229.1938.II.A (25 October 1938) 2); in the latter, it was used in relation to customs duties (Fiscal Committee, *Report to the Council on the Work of the Ninth Session of the Committee*, League Doc C.181.M.110.1939.II.A (21 June 1939) 11). The report of the Ninth Session further referred to a type of underdeveloped country not previously considered by the Committee, namely, countries 'where the standard of living is low or where internal taxes and Customs duties on articles of consumption are heavy' (at 19). This distinction had arisen in response to the Assembly's request to the

the terms 'capital-importing' or 'capital-receiving' (in contrast to 'capital-exporting'), and 'economically-less-advanced' (in contrast to 'economically-advanced') countries surface in the Committee's report of its Tenth Session ('*Tenth Session Report*')[84] and Commentary to the Mexico and London Models ('*Mexico/London Models Commentary*').[85] Such distinctions were reported as having arisen because the membership at London had 'differed considerably' from the participants at Mexico.[86] Although the Fiscal Committee did not elaborate on the income item(s) of main concern or the structure of the tax system that the Mexico or London Models catered to (as contrasted with the commentary provided for Draft Conventions 1*b* and 1*c* of the Geneva models[87]), the Mexico Model is implicitly understood to be applicable to 'economically less-advanced' countries, such as Latin America, due to its strong emphasis on source taxation, while the London Model applied to systems that adhered to residence taxation.

In summary, the League's double taxation work showed that the traditional differentiation between capital-importing and capital-exporting countries had always been a key factor determining the solutions for relief. While there had been some brief recognition of a subset of capital-importing countries that were less developed and more needful of source-based taxation principles, no further effort was made to categorise or address the situation of this group.[88] This is understandable as the prevailing notions on economic development at that time were dominated by the opposing views of those who espoused Adam Smith's capitalism and Karl Marx's socialism.[89] Development theories would only begin to emerge in the late 1940s and were not only economic and Eurocentric, but also based on the ruling paradigm that viewed economic progress as an unproblematic, unilinear process with investments as the primary

Economic and Financial Organisation that it study the influence of taxation on standards of living.

84 Fiscal Committee, *Tenth Session Report*, 8.

85 Fiscal Committee, *London and Mexico Model Tax Conventions: Commentary and Text*, League Doc C.88.M.88.1946.II.A (November 1946) 6, 26.

86 Fiscal Committee, *Tenth Session Report*, 7.

87 Government Experts, *1928 Report*, 18, 21.

88 It is worth noting that up to 1938, the League's World Economic Survey that reported 'on "world business activity" paid virtually no attention to what were by the 1940s called the underdeveloped countries': John Toye and Richard Toye, *UN and Global Political Economy: Trade, Finance, and Development* (Indiana University Press, 2004) 89.

89 Giang Dang and Low Sui Pheng, *Infrastructure Investments in Developing Economies: The Case of Vietnam* (Springer, 2015) 15–16.

mover of per capita growth and with every economy assumed to have the necessary conditions allowing them to pass through the same single trajectory of historical stages of growth.[90] In a similar vein, the League's work reflects the approach that less-developed countries were qualitatively different neither from their more developed counterparts nor from each other, and that every economy had the same capacity to transition from underdevelopment to modernisation following the Western model of development.[91] Such optimism is evident in the Economists' Report when the experts predicted that uniformity based on residence-taxation principles would eventually be possible as underdeveloped economies became more industrialised.[92] Also, the 1928 model conventions were based on the existence of personal/general taxes in negotiating states even though participating countries such as Argentina and Venezuela (then the more economically advanced of their region) in the 1927 technical meetings had yet to implement such taxation.[93] The Fiscal Committee's *Tenth Session Report* furthermore indicated that, irrespective of the level of development between states, tax treaties were the recommended

[90] Ibid 16; Björn Hettne, 'The Development of Development Theory' (1983) 26(3/4) *Acta Sociologica* 247, 248–9; Mauro Boianovsky, 'Beyond Capital Fundamentalism: Harrod, Domar and the History of Development Economics' (2017) 42(2) *Cambridge Journal of Economics* 477, 489–93; Richard Jolly, Louis Emmerij and Dharam Ghai, *UN Contributions to Development Thinking and Practice* (Indiana University Press, 2004) 49–50; Adam Szirmai, *The Dynamics of Socio-Economic Development: An Introduction* (Cambridge University Press, 2005) 79–81. The Cold War, moreover, appears to have been instrumental in entrenching such ideas as US policymakers promoted these theories to the global South using America as 'a universal model for development' in the attempt to expand American hegemony and curb Communist influence in post-colonial countries: Mark Philip Bradley, 'Decolonization, the Global South, and the Cold War, 1919–1962' in Melvyn P Leffler and Odd Arne Westad (eds), *The Cambridge History of the Cold War* (Cambridge University Press, 2010) vol 1: Origins, 464, 476. See also WW Rostow, *The Stages of Economic Growth: A Non-Communist Manifesto* (Cambridge University Press, 1960).

[91] This thinking was grounded in the British and European industrialisation experience where big changes in their economic structures arose from great leaps in the technological sophistication of their production mechanisms. The theory appeared confirmed when the later-developing countries of Germany, Japan and Russia were able to not only adopt and adapt such technology but also achieve higher rates of growth than the older-rich countries, allowing them to bypass intermediate stages of development. In short, scientific and technological knowledge was believed to herald development progress: Hans W Singer and Javed A Ansari, *Rich and Poor Countries* (Allen & Unwin, 2nd ed, 1978) 32–3, 43.

[92] Bruins et al, *Economists' Report*, 51. See also Mitchell B Carroll, *Prevention of International Double Taxation and Fiscal Evasion: Two Decades of Progress under the League of Nations* (League of Nations, 1939) 15.

[93] Jogarajan, *Double Taxation*, 107–8.

solution for double taxation relief, and that any divergences, particularly on interest and dividends, were reconcilable through tax treaty negotiations alone, pending study of the various legal, administrative and economic aspects of the problem.[94]

It may be concluded that the 'developing countries' of the League's pre-war double taxation work were a select group comprising European countries, the British Empire dominions and the more advanced Latin American states. In relation to the former two, unilateral and bilateral arrangements to prevent double taxation had already been in existence even prior to World War I[95] and the Geneva models catered for these historical practices. Meanwhile, the involvement of Latin America in the 1920s work failed to lead to any tax treaties with this region. The negotiation success of the Mexico Model, however, ostensibly signalled the adaptability of tax treaties to a continent of developing countries that had virtually no history of such arrangements, no general income taxes, low taxation rates and territorial tax systems. It is important to note, however, that Latin America at this stage 'could not be considered "poor"' with reference to the conventional narrow measure of Gross Domestic Product (GDP) per capita,[96] which placed average incomes in the region during the interwar years 'well above subsistence levels and comparable with those obtained in Southern and Eastern Europe'.[97] In fact, '[i]ndustry in the region was viewed by outside observers as relatively dynamic'[98] with accelerating GDP between 1930 and 1950, while the rest of the world was doing poorly from the collapse of international trade and World War II.[99] Accordingly, the expectation expressed in the

[94] Fiscal Committee, *Tenth Session Report*, 8, 10.

[95] Matthew J Kust, 'Tax Treaties with the Underindustrialized Countries' (1961) 13(3) *Tax Executive* 175, 176.

[96] GDP per capita was introduced in the 1930s and was the principal indicator of economic progress with more modern approaches to preparing composite indices emerging only from the mid-1970s: see Maria Francesca Cracolici, Miranda Cuffaro and Peter Nijkamp, 'The Measurement of Economic, Social and Environmental Performance of Countries: A Novel Approach' (2010) 95(2) *Social Indicators Research* 339, 340–3; Robert Costanza et al, *Beyond GDP: The Need for New Measures of Progress* (The Pardee Papers No 4, The Frederick S Pardee Center for the Study of the Longer-Range Future, Boston University, January 2009) 3.

[97] EVK FitzGerald, 'ECLA and the Formation of Latin American Economic Doctrine' in David Rock (ed), *Latin America in the 1940s: War and Postwar Transitions* (University of California Press, 1994) 89, 90.

[98] Ibid 90.

[99] This was particularly in relation to countries which had large domestic markets and some industrial base predating 1929, for example, Argentina, Brazil, Colombia and

Fiscal Committee's *Tenth Session Report* that the UN Fiscal Commission could reconcile the differences between capital-exporting and capital-importing, and economically advanced and economically less-advanced countries may have seemed possible in view of the perceived narrowing gap of economic development between these countries and the presumed ability of developing nations to replicate the historical experience of developed countries.

1.3.2 *The UN's First Decade*

During the Fiscal Commission years, the concept of developing countries in the fiscal work began to evolve to take on more political and socio-economic characteristics due to a combination of the following factors.[100] Firstly, a closer connection emerged between the fiscal work and the broader economic and social activities of the UN. Secondly, the official start of the Cold War in 1947 distanced the growing Soviet bloc and Western Europe from the international economy, the latter case being due to the Marshall Plan that promoted regional economic integration. Thirdly, the great wave of decolonisation beginning around the end of World War II would introduce over ninety economically poor and unindustrialised former colonies, initially from the Asia-Arab bloc, to UN membership.[101] Fourthly, and most importantly, political alliances began to form among the Latin American, Asian and Middle East countries in their solidarity against imperialism and intent to pursue development aid from richer countries. These events ushered in a rapid evolution of the concept towards the meaning understood by the terms 'Third World' and 'South', although this was not yet clearly defined at the time of the Commission's closure.

Economically, the United States was the only capital-exporter country after World War II. All other member states, aside from the insulated Soviet economies, were capital-importing countries. These countries covered a diverse spectrum and included China (one of the Big Five);

Mexico: André A Hofman, *The Economic Development of Latin America in the Twentieth Century* (Edward Elgar, 2000) 31–2.

100 These developments are further elaborated in Chapter 4, Section 4.1.

101 Heather Streets-Salter and Trevor R Getz, *Empires and Colonies in the Modern World: A Global Perspective* (Oxford University Press, 2016) 440–5; Dane Kennedy, *Decolonization: A Very Short Introduction* (Oxford University Press, 2016) ch 1. Africa's decolonisation would only begin in the late 1950s, whereas the independence of most Latin American and Caribbean countries took place much earlier in the nineteenth century.

the war-impaired Western European countries and colonial powers; the British Commonwealth; Latin America; and the growing number of newly decolonising colonies. As the UN's economic and social activities assumed a development aspect, the expression 'underdeveloped'[102] (and occasionally 'developing', 'undeveloped' and 'less-developed', in contrast to 'developed', 'more industrialized' or 'more economically advanced') was applied to describe the economically weak countries of Latin America, Asia and the Middle East,[103] although other countries, such as Australia, China and New Zealand, also identified with the classification.[104] Very soon two types of divisions on economic questions emerged, reflecting the separation of countries into 'the rich and poor' and 'the less and least developed' categories.[105] By 1950, a theory had developed of the existence of a sharp North–South dichotomy underpinned by the belief 'that developing countries confronted a socially specific reality that was relatively homogenous within the group, but different from that of the industrialised countries'.[106] This

[102] The term, sometimes hyphenated in usage, is noted to have become 'almost universally accepted' after it was used in US President Truman's inaugural address in January 1949 which launched the Point Four Program and 'established the hegemony of the modernization paradigm by dividing the world into developed and underdeveloped countries': Jolly, Emmerij and Ghai, *UN Contributions*, 50. This Point Four speech has been credited for having initiated discussions concerning development (then considered a novel idea) and a vast development program in the UN: Thomas G Weiss, Ramesh Thakur and John Gerard Ruggie, *Global Governance and the UN: An Unfinished Journey* (Indiana University Press, 2010) 158. See Chapter 7, Sections 7.4 n 115 and 7.5, and Chapter 10, Section 10.2 n 12, for further on the Point Four Program.

[103] See, for example, 'Economic and Social Questions' [1947–8] *Yearbook of the United Nations* 512; *Study of Factors Bearing upon the Establishment of an Economic Commission for the Middle East*, GA Res 120 (II), UN Doc A/RES/120(II) (31 October 1947) para 1; *Methods of Financing Economic Development of Under-Developed Countries*, ESC Res 222D (IX), UN ESCOR, UN Doc 1553 (15 August 1949, adopted 14 August 1949). The phrase 'underdeveloped' was soon 'considered rude' and was replaced with 'developing countries': Weiss, Thakur and Ruggie, *Unfinished Journey*, 158. See also DESA, *World Economic and Social Survey 2017: Reflecting on Seventy Years of Development Policy Analysis*, UN Doc E/2017/50/Rev/1 (also ST/ESA/365) (UN, 2017) 24 n 2 (explaining that the UN's recurrent *World Economic Survey* publication only began to employ the term 'developing countries' from 1962).

[104] See UN Yearbook 1947–48, 'Economic and Social Questions', 516; Fiscal Commission, *Summary Record of the 31st Meeting*, 4th sess, 31st mtg, UN Doc E/CN.8/SR.31 (21 May 1953) 5.

[105] Evan Luard, *The United Nations: How It Works and What It Does* (Palgrave Macmillan, 1979) 43.

[106] José Antonio Alonso, Ana Luiza Cortez and Stephan Klasen, 'LDC and Other Country Groupings: How Useful Are Current Approaches to Classify Countries in a More

was considered a 'reasonable assumption'[107] for the period on the basis of per capita income levels, with those of Western Europe, the United States, Canada, Australia and New Zealand being twice that of Latin America,[108] and around eight to ten times higher than those in Africa and Asia.[109]

In the UN's international tax studies, this dichotomy was addressed by the Fiscal Division of the Secretariat from 1949 in its recognition of the 'special situation' of underdeveloped countries in addition to the traditional capital-exporting, capital-importing considerations.[110] The definition formulated, however, was ambiguous and closely related to the UN's technical assistance work,[111] which itself was inseparably connected to the US Point Four Program.[112]

While the aforementioned dichotomy was being laid out in budding development approaches, Western political scientists were challenged to both describe and develop a framework for understanding the emerging nations that were distinct not only from the older European and North American states but also from the Eastern European countries.[113] Another layer of categorisation was soon superimposed by the political currents that divided the world into the ideologically defined blocs of the First World (the advanced, capitalist democracies of Europe, North America, and the White Dominions of Australia, New Zealand, and

Heterogeneous Developing World?', UN Doc ST/ESA/2014/CDP/21 (Committee for Development Policy Background Paper No 21, UN, September 2014) 6.

107 John W McArthur and Eric Werker, 'Developing Countries and International Organizations: Introduction to the Special Issue' (2016) 11(2) *Review of International Organisations* 155, 156.

108 Latin American levels were generally slightly higher than the Iberian levels, and countries such as Argentina, Uruguay and Venezuela had higher levels than those of Western Europe: McArthur and Werker, 'Special Issue', 156; Hofman, *Economic Development*, 99; Court, 'Some Reflections', 18.

109 Alonso, Cortez and Klasen, 'Heterogeneous Developing World?', 6.

110 See Department of Economic Affairs (DEA), *The Effects of Taxation on Foreign Trade and Investment*, UN Doc ST/ECA/1 (UN, 1950) 1.

111 According to the Secretariat, 'developed' and 'underdeveloped' economies were then considered as two heterogeneous, rather than homogenous, groups although generalisations could be made based on the dominant 'significant differences' between the two: Technical Assistance Administration, *Taxes and Fiscal Policy in Under-Developed Countries: A Report Based on Technical Assistance Experience, with Special Reference to Field Missions and to the Technical Assistance Conference on Comparative Fiscal Administration, Geneva, 16–25 July 1951*, UN Doc ST/TAA/M.8 (UN, 1954) 1. Moreover, underdeveloped countries were 'not necessarily restricted to those at the lowest stage of development' but 'could include countries that were in higher stages but still under-developed in a relative sense' (E/CN.8/SR.31, 5).

112 See n 102.

113 Jeff Haynes, *Third World Politics: A Concise Introduction* (Blackwell, 1996) 3.

apartheid South Africa); the Second World (the industrialised socialist countries in Eastern Europe); and the Third World (the post-colonial countries of Africa, Asia, Latin America and the Middle East).[114] The concept of the 'Third World', introduced in 1952, thus had several related meanings in the sense of emerging sovereign countries which were underdeveloped, marginal (politically, economically and culturally) in the international community, neutral in the Cold War and which had great ambitions to become a third pole of influence in the international order.[115]

It is these political, socio-economic dimensions of the Third World that are encompassed in the term 'developing countries' used in this book as they embody the subset of developing countries prominent in the double taxation work of the Commission period[116] and which would later unite under the Non-Aligned Movement.[117] These comprised low development, post-colonial countries that were not only desperate to create nation-states and to build up national income to develop their productive capacities, but which also began to assert pro-source taxation principles under the UN agenda of financing economic development in underdeveloped countries through FDI.

1.4 Structure of the Book

This book has fourteen chapters. Chapter 2 provides a history of developing countries' involvement in the League's fiscal work, focusing on the activities of the Princeton Mission and inter-American relations between

[114] See Jeff Haynes, *Politics in the Developing World: A Concise Introduction* (Blackwell, 2002) 6; Szirmai, *Socio-Economic Development*, 16.

[115] Marcin Wojciech Solarz, '"Third World": The 60th Anniversary of a Concept that Changed History' (2012) 33(9) *Third World Quarterly* 1561, 1561–6. The concept was coined by French scholar Alfred Sauvy, and while the expression was widespread among political scientists, it was never officially used in the UN during the Commission years. See also Leslie Wolf-Phillips, 'Why Third World?' (1979) 1(1) *Third World Quarterly* 105, 105–8; Haynes, *Politics in the Developing World*, 6–7; Haynes, *Third World*, 3.

[116] It is worth noting here that by the time of the OECD's first fiscal report concerning developing countries in 1965, developing countries were generally understood to refer to the Third World, although just based on per capita income levels: OECD, *Fiscal Incentives for Private Investment in Developing Countries: Report of the Fiscal Committee* (1965) 9.

[117] The Non-Aligned Movement's early beginnings are traceable to the 1955 Bandung Conference of Afro-Asian leaders, although it was only later formalised in 1961: Shirley Hune and Jayantha Dhanapala, 'Non-Aligned Movement' in Joel Krieger (ed), *The Oxford Companion to International Relations* (Oxford University Press, 2014) [e-Resource]; Jürgen Dinkel, *The Non-Aligned Movement: Genesis, Organization and Politics (1927–1992)*, tr Alex Skinner (Brill, 2018) 82–3.

1940 and 1946 that led to the successful negotiation of the Mexico Model. The purpose is to reveal the stimuli behind and the conditions facilitating such international tax coordination in order to provide, firstly, a better understanding of the premise on which developing countries were initiated into double taxation, and secondly, a more accurate base for evaluating the UN's own attempt to progress the work achieved by the League.

Chapter 3 sets out how the Fiscal Commission was brought into existence, its intended function and scope within the new postwar international economic order and how the eventual construct created under the ECOSOC structure departed from its blueprint. Chapter 4 outlines the dynamics and shifts in the global political economy and institutional order that affected not only the UN's capacity for international tax coordination but also postwar international financial flows. The aim is to explain how and why the Commission and the Fiscal Division could not function in the manner of their League predecessors; the impetus and facilitators behind the direction of the international tax work of this period; and the major role that FDI flows assumed in the postwar economy that would lead to double taxation questions being imbued with a development purpose where developing countries were concerned.

Chapters 5–13 discuss the progress of double taxation in the UN during the Fiscal Commission years. The narratives are arranged around the four sessions of the Commission and are set within the wider context surrounding these efforts. This context includes, firstly, the broad work the Commission and Division embarked on with the aim of becoming the world fiscal authority; secondly, the progress of double taxation as raised in other intergovernmental and non-governmental forums; thirdly, the contemporaneous political and bureaucratic backdrop that impacted the positions of states in negotiations, the Secretariat's operations and the Commission's fate; and fourthly, American and British influence over the UN's work and their foreign economic policy positions. These dimensions collectively enable a comprehensive assessment of how double taxation was being approached, the policies being pursued and the countries pursuing them, the extent of progress in this field in comparison to other fields, and various other influences impacting the Division's and Commission's work. Chapters 5, 7, 9 and 12, respectively, address the work and events relating to the Commission's four sessions, covering the preparatory documents of the Division; the deliberations in the Commission, ECOSOC and, where such transpired, the General

Assembly; and the subsequent work undertaken by the Division. Chapters 6, 8 and 10 outline the relevant developments that took place in the intervening periods between the Commission sessions, including the double taxation movement in other UN bodies and specialised agencies, as well as among business-related interests; the status of US DTA negotiations with developing countries; and great power foreign economic policies that affected or concerned developing countries. Chapter 11 separately deals with the background and narrative concerning the taxation of international air transport as this was a multifaceted and protracted affair spanning several years and following parallel developments in ICAO. Chapter 13 traces the developments leading to the closure of the Commission and recounts the Division's role in the OEEC's entry into double taxation matters.

Chapter 14 concludes the book by summarising the main threads of the Commission story and prehistory that call for a revision of many of the prevalent but inaccurate assertions in the literature concerning international tax history. It also briefly discusses the impact of the events of the Commission period on the development of international tax law and theorises, with reference to broader shifts in the global balance of power and the UN's general track record for economic activities, what might have eventuated had the Commission not met its demise. The chapter ends by highlighting the parallels and transformations of various themes in the Commission story in the recent developments stemming from the revival of global multilateral cooperation under the BEPS projects.

2

Prelude to Global Tax Coordination

The League's Princeton Mission in the Americas

This chapter examines developing countries' first connections with the League's fiscal work, focusing on the events of 1940–3 and inter-American relations which brought about the successful negotiation of the Mexico Model. Its purpose is to provide a deeper understanding of the early motivations and circumstances for tax relations and DTAs between developed and developing countries by examining the business, economic and political imperatives that facilitated this unprecedented cooperation. This background in turn illuminates the expectations, objectives and issues confronting the UN as it set about taking on the task of global tax coordination.

Section 2.1 chronicles the League's engagement with developing countries in its fiscal work and the aberration that the Mexico Model represented in contrast to the general trend of its double taxation work,[1] highlighting the questionable legitimacy of the League's work in the Americas. Section 2.2 details the impact of wartime inter-American relations in facilitating the League's pioneering activities into Latin America. Section 2.3 concludes with a commentary that proposes a reconsideration of the Mexico Model in the scheme of international tax history.

2.1 Developing Countries in the League's Fiscal Work

2.1.1 Participation until 1940

Developing countries (at this time mostly represented by Latin America) generally had very little connection to the League's economic activities, and those which were League members hardly obtained any economic and social

[1] Existing literature has tended to focus on the rules negotiated. This section's narrative builds on such research with the addition of relevant archival insights to highlight the importance of the context that enabled such tax cooperation to be achieved.

betterment from their membership.[2] Until just prior to World War II, developing countries had negligible involvement with the League's double taxation work or with DTAs, and for the most part showed scarce interest in the Fiscal Committee's work.[3] Although Argentina and Venezuela had been part of the 1926–7 sessions which involved thirteen technical experts and produced the 1927 report on double taxation,[4] they were not involved in the 1928 meeting despite the repeated participation of the other eleven countries.[5] Their involvement moreover did not encourage any DTAs by those governments or by any other Latin American government.[6]

In 1933, the Fiscal Committee included four non-European developing countries – British India, Netherlands East Indies, Mexico and South Africa – as part of its *Taxation of Foreign and National Enterprises* survey of thirty-five countries,[7] which was ultimately used to formulate the 1935 Draft Convention on the Allocation of Business Income ('1935 Allocation Draft').[8] This was a data-gathering exercise rather than a specific action to engage directly with developing countries. The countries were not chosen because of their developing status (three were at this stage colonies/dominions) but because they represented tax systems and economies that were primarily based on mining and agricultural enterprises carried on by foreign companies.[9] From 1935, the League persisted in building up its network of corresponding members in Latin

2 John A Houston, *Latin America in the United Nations* (Carnegie Endowment for International Peace, 1956) 4–5.

3 Paul Deperon, 'Mission in Latin America (October 7, 1941–January 30, 1942)', 30 January 1942, 14, UNOG:PO—C.1643/27/4/1 ('LA Mission').

4 Committee of Technical Experts on Double Taxation and Tax Evasion, *Double Taxation and Tax Evasion: Report*, League Doc C.216.M.85.1927.II (April 1927) 6.

5 General Meeting of Government Experts on Double Taxation and Tax Evasion, *Double Taxation and Tax Evasion: Report*, League Doc C.562.M.178.1928.II (October 1928) 37–8.

6 In a 1942 memorandum of the Fiscal Committee prepared by Deperon, he would attribute the limited Latin American participation in the work of experts at Geneva to income taxation having been in its infancy in their region: Fiscal Committee, *Mexico Draft Model Convention for the Prevention of International Double Taxation of Income and Property, Secretariat Memorandum*, League Doc F/Fiscal/128 (15 September 1942) 9.

7 See League of Nations, *Taxation of Foreign and National Enterprises* (1933) vols 1–3. Carroll was director of this survey: Fiscal Committee, *Report to the Council on the Fourth Session of the Committee*, League Doc C.399.M.209.1933.II.A (26 June 1933) 1.

8 Carroll was the author of volume 4 (*Methods of Allocating Taxable Income* (1933)) of the series. He states that Chapter 12 of this volume formed the basis for the 1935 draft convention: Mitchell B Carroll, 'International Tax Law: Benefits for American Investors and Enterprises Abroad: Part I' (1968) 2(4) *The International Lawyer* 692, 703–4 ('ITL (1968)').

9 Mitchell B Carroll, *Prevention of International Double Taxation and Fiscal Evasion: Two Decades of Progress under the League of Nations* (League of Nations, 1939) 27.

America,[10] and in 1937 included Argentina and Peru in its study on the evolution of tax systems of fourteen countries, the country studies of which were facilitated by the respective revenue authorities.[11]

In September 1938, at Mexico's request, the Assembly tasked the Fiscal Committee with studying the technical principles of taxation for chief categories of taxes (e.g. income, property and turnover taxes) to serve as a guide to various types of economies, especially to 'states which might desire to modify or improve their fiscal legislation'.[12] The Committee was to 'naturally have regard, as far as possible, to ways and means of adapting its conclusions to the various types of national economy'.[13] This request was reportedly the 'first symptom of improvement' in the stirring of Latin American interest in the League's fiscal work.[14] In October 1938, Peru attended the Committee's Eighth Session as a member,[15] and in June 1939, Argentina, Egypt, Mexico and Uruguay attended the Ninth Session as corresponding members.[16] The Committee's work at this time had moved away from double taxation to focus on fiscal evasion and the behaviour of tax systems in relation to economic fluctuations. The Committee nevertheless did express its intention in the context of the technical principles of taxation project to take into consideration principles to be introduced in national laws purposed at eliminating extraterritorial taxation and double taxation.[17]

By the time the war broke out in September 1939, only the work concerning the principles of income taxation had been completed. Carroll arranged through the Mexican corresponding member (Luciano Wiechers) and the Mexican Minister of Finance (Edouardo Suarez) to hold a meeting in Mexico City in June 1940 to consider the report.[18] The

[10] Deperon, 'LA Mission', 14; Stefano Simontacchi, *Taxation of Capital Gains under the OECD Model Convention: With Special Regard to Immovable Property* (Kluwer, 2007) 84–5.

[11] Fiscal Committee, *Report to the Council on the Seventh Session of the Committee*, League Doc C.490.M.331.1937.II.A (16 October 1937) 5.

[12] Fiscal Committee, *Report to the Council on the Work of the Eighth Session of the Committee*, League Doc C.384.M.229.1938.II.A (25 October 1938) 2 ('*Eighth Session Report*') (quoting League Assembly Res (29 September 1938)).

[13] Ibid 2.

[14] Deperon, 'LA Mission', 14. See also Simontacchi, *Taxation of Capital Gains*, 85.

[15] Fiscal Committee, *Eighth Session Report*, 1.

[16] Fiscal Committee, *Report to the Council on the Work of the Ninth Session of the Committee*, League Doc C.181.M.110.1939.II.A (21 June 1939) 1.

[17] Fiscal Committee, *Eighth Session Report*, 2.

[18] Mitchell B Carroll, 'Income Tax Conventions as an Aid to International Trade and Investment' (1962) 6(3) *Section of International & Comparative Law Bulletin* 16, 18. See

League, however, also had a double taxation motive for convening this 'first meeting of the kind to be held on the American Continent' because the continent, unlike Europe, 'had, on the whole, remained aloof from the movement towards the elimination of double taxation'.[19]

2.1.2 *The 1940 Mexico Meeting and the Princeton Mission*

The 1940 meeting (referred to as a 'regional meeting' of the Fiscal Committee) was held in the first half of June and was attended by senior officials from seven countries (Argentina, Brazil, Canada, Mexico, Peru, the United States and Venezuela).[20] In addition to the technical principles of taxation report,[21] the League (represented by Carroll,[22] and members of the Secretariat, Louis Rasminsky and Manuel Perez-Guerrero) introduced a first reading of its proposed revision of the 1928 Geneva model drafts – the 1940 Mexico Draft – which was adopted by the attendees.[23] For most of the Latin republics, this was their first encounter with the presentation of double taxation, and the meeting '[did] little else than adopt [the draft]',[24] which was 'considered very hurriedly'.[25] The draft was itself substantially based on the 1940 Hague draft of the Fiscal Committee's Sub-Committee[26]

also Carroll, 'ITL (1968)', 707; Mitchell B Carroll, 'International Double Taxation' in Harriet Eager Davies (ed), *Pioneers in World Order: An American Appraisal of the League of Nations* (Columbia University Press, 1944) 171, 174 ('IDT (1944)'). In the first-mentioned article, Carroll states that he arranged both Mexico meetings. In the latter two articles, he states that they were arranged by the League.

19 P Deperon, 'Note on the Fiscal Committee and Its Activities', undated (around end 1944), 3, UNOG:PO—C.1643/27/5.

20 Fiscal Committee, *Second Report of the Meeting of Members and Corresponding Members of the Fiscal Committee, Mexico City*, League Doc F/Fiscal/127 (25 June 1940).

21 Fiscal Committee, *First Report of the Meeting of Members and Corresponding Members of the Fiscal Committee, Mexico City*, League Doc F/Fiscal/126 (15 June 1940).

22 The Peruvian expert (Carlos Jimenez) was the only other Committee member but he is not mentioned as having a significant role in the meeting. Carroll was accompanied by two other Americans, Eldon King and Harry Turkel, representing the US Departments of Treasury and State, respectively. Rasminsky reported US interest in concluding tax treaties with countries of the hemisphere: Letter from Rasminsky to Loveday, 30 September 1940, 3, UNOG:PO—C.1643/27/5; Louis Rasminsky, 'Comments on Future Program of Fiscal Committee Work in the Western Hemisphere', 15 July 1940, 3, UNOG:PO—C.1643/27/5.

23 League Doc F/Fiscal/127.

24 Deperon, 'LA Mission', 14.

25 Rasminsky, 'Comments on Future Program', 3 (further noting that the Latin American experts 'should be given an opportunity to reconsider' the draft at a further meeting).

26 Fiscal Committee, *Proposed Revision of the Model Bilateral Convention for the Prevention of Double Taxation in the Field of Direct Taxes*, No I(c) of 1928, Provisional Report of the

and Carroll's own 1940 study[27] produced earlier in April that synthesised the three 1928 draft conventions, the 1935 Allocation Draft and major tax treaty trends.[28] Carroll's presence and influence were regarded as instrumental to the solutions agreed upon at the Mexico discussions.[29] The meeting's participants recommended that another tax conference be convened with a larger representation of the region 'in the near future to pursue the work on double taxation, fiscal evasion, technical principles of taxation and coordination of central and local finance'.[30]

There were clear indications that the Latin Americans then had no genuine interest in double taxation problems. Some, in fact, were suspicious of the introduction of the subject: Rasminsky reported that several 'evidently regarded it as an American ramp to keep them from taxing American enterprises as heavily as they wished';[31] the Argentinian expert (Avelino Lerena) 'refrained from giving an opinion about anything' as he 'was not in agreement with the way the matter was brought up and treated';[32] and Brazil abstained from participating in the discussion because the draft's provisions were inconsistent with Brazilian legislation.[33] Rasminsky himself noted that the income tax structure in these countries, where it existed, was 'still pretty rudimentary in form' and that the meeting 'was so overshadowed by the French collapse'[34] that it was 'difficult to appraise it

Sub-Committee, 12–16 April 1940, League Doc F/Fiscal/124 (4 May 1940). The Sub-Committee had met in April 1940 at The Hague but its work was interrupted when Rotterdam was attacked on 10 May 1940: Carroll, 'ITL (1968)', 707.

27 Fiscal Committee, *Study by Mitchell B Carroll on the Draft Conventions Prepared by the General Meeting of Government Experts on Double Taxation and Tax Evasion of 1928*, League Doc F/Fiscal/123 (3 April 1940).

28 Deperon, 'LA Mission', 14; Simontacchi, *Taxation of Capital Gains*, 65–6, 75–7, 85, 90–1.

29 Rasminsky letter, 30 September 1940, 2, 5. See also Simontacchi, *Taxation of Capital Gains*, 90–2, 112; Mitchell B Carroll, 'Development of International Tax Law in the Americas' (1941) 8(4) *Law and Contemporary Problems* 793, 799 ('ITL in Americas'). Deperon was responsible for all the preparatory work but was not able to attend the conference: Memorandum by Loveday, 25 February 1941, UNOG:PO—C.1626/523/10/1.

30 Deperon, 'LA Mission', 14. See also Rasminsky letter, 30 September 1940, 4–5 (crediting Carroll as being behind the initiative for 'a further meeting of an American group').

31 Rasminsky letter, 30 September 1940, 2.

32 Letter from Lerena to Rasminsky, 27 October 1941, UNOG:PO—C.1644/28/1.

33 Paul Deperon, 'Report on Brazil', December 1941, UNOG:PO—C.1643/27/4/2.

34 By early June, Denmark, Norway, Belgium and the Netherlands had fallen, and German troops had invaded France. As the meeting took place, hostilities were spreading throughout the Mediterranean and into Africa, Italy had entered the war against France and Britain and Spanish troops occupied the International Zone of Tangier: US Department of State (State Department), *Postwar Foreign Policy Preparation 1939–1945* (US Government Printing Office (USGPO), 1949) 31.

objectively at the time'.[35] Nevertheless, following the conference, a number of DTA negotiations were reportedly begun between the United States and several Latin American countries (Argentina, Brazil and Peru) based on the Mexico Draft.[36] The Secretariat would report the meeting to have 'proved outstandingly successful' although it did appear to have some unease that such negotiations had been initiated despite the draft having 'not yet been officially approved by the Fiscal Committee in plenary session'.[37] Meanwhile, Deperon considered this 'rapid change of attitude' in the American continent as 'a striking example of the benefits which countries may derive from a technical collaboration with the Fiscal Committee'.[38] The Mexican officials even offered to print the reports of the meeting in Mexico 'at the expense and under the auspices of the Minister of Finance'.[39]

In the same month as the 1940 meeting, because of the isolation of Geneva in the war, Princeton University, the Institute for Advanced Study (IAS) and the Rockefeller Institute for Medical Research made a joint offer to the League's Secretary-General to continue the League's economic and social services that were financially self-sufficient at the university so as not to lose the results and contacts so far achieved.[40] Although there were political problems associated with this invitation,[41]

[35] Rasminsky letter, 30 September 1940, 3, 2.

[36] Officials from Argentina and Peru also visited the US Internal Revenue Bureau to 'become better acquainted with the American tax system': Rasminsky, 'Comments on Future Program', 5; Rasminsky letter, 30 September 1940, 3.

[37] 'Extract from Draft Report to the Members of the League', 10 October 1940, 1–2, UNOG: PO—C.1643/27/5. In the official report, the statement regarding the new model convention as not yet approved by the Fiscal Committee was eliminated: see League of Nations, *Brief Statement on the Activities of the League of Nations and Its Organs in 1940 and 1941, Submitted by the Acting Secretary-General*, League Doc C.41.M.38.1941 (June 1941) 8–9 (*'Brief Statement on 1940 and 1941 Activities'*).

[38] Deperon, 'Note on the Fiscal Committee', 4.

[39] Letter from Rasminsky to Deperon, 2 October 1940, 2, UNOG:PO—C.1643/27/5. Deperon completed the Spanish manuscript of the reports in November 1940 (Letter from Deperon to Carroll, 22 November 1940, 1, UNOG:PO—C.1643/27/5) but there is no indication that Mexico followed through on its offer.

[40] The Fiscal Committee was then comfortably operating off its most recent Rockefeller grant. See Letter from Dodds, Tenbroeck and Aydelotte to Avenol, 12 June 1940; Memorandum by Livingston, 21 June 1940; Telegram from Norwegian Minister (London) to Avenol, 25 June 1940, UNOG:PO—C.1624/521/8/5.

[41] Secretary-General Joseph Avenol initially rejected the invitation on the grounds that the League's statutory seat was at Geneva and the United States was not a League member: Letter from Avenol to Dodds, undated (around June 1940); Telegram from Hull to American Consul Geneva, 29 June 1940, UNOG:PO—C.1624/521/8/5. The United States also hesitated to issue the invitation without Congress' approval although Britain and Norway supported

it was eventually accepted and part of the Economic, Financial and Transit Department of the Secretariat relocated to Princeton between September 1940 and February 1941, financed by the Rockefeller Foundation.[42] This Princeton Mission, as it was called, was headed by Alexander Loveday[43] and continued the League's work by focusing on developments outside of Europe.[44] The Mission was small[45] and Deperon was effectively the only Secretariat member responsible for the fiscal work.[46] The Mission's activities were not self-sustaining for long: already

the move: Memorandum, 27 June 1940, UNOG:PO—C.1624/521/8/5; Norwegian Minister telegram, 25 June 1940. Tournès notes that Secretary of State Hull indicated 'that an official invitation from the federal government would be out of the question' but 'gave the green light to an invitation of the EFTD [Economic, Financial and Transit Department] by private institutions' as 'the research of the EFTD was of particular interest to the Department of State, which had long been in favour of a thorough overhaul of the rules governing the international economy and, especially, of liberalising international trade': Ludovic Tournès, 'The Rockefeller Foundation and the Transition from the League of Nations to the UN (1939–1946)' (2014) 12(3) *Journal of Modern European History* 323, 327. The League's own concerns appeared to have been settled with the Princeton location intended to be a mere branch of the League operating physically outside Geneva: Letter from Avenol to Loveday, 30 July 1940, 1; Letter from Dodds, 12 July 1940, UNOG:PO—C.1624/521/8/5. This arrangement, however, soon became 'pure fiction' with Geneva 'hardly more than a local branch ... confined to collecting statistics': Memorandum to Loveday, 5 December 1944, UNOG:PO—C.1633/529/17/4-1.

42 Letter to Dobbs, 26 July 1940, UNOG:PO—C.1624/521/8/5; Bob Reinalda, *Routledge History of International Organizations: From 1815 to the Present Day* (Routledge, 2009) 273; Patricia Meria Clavin, 'The League of Nations at IAS', *IAS* (Web Page, 2009) <www.ias.edu/ideas/2009/league-nations-ias>; Patricia Clavin, *Securing the World Economy: The Reinvention of the League of Nations, 1920–1946* (Oxford University Press, 2013) ch 8.

43 Loveday was effectively 'by agreement the Acting Secretary-General of the League in the USA': Clavin, *Reinvention of the League*, 267.

44 The general policy of Sean Lester, the last Secretary-General of the League (31 August 1940–18 April 1946), was 'to support in everyway possible ... [the Mission's] activities and initiatives [which] must in the present circumstances often be non-european': Letter from Lester to Loveday, 8 May 1941, UNOG:PO—C.1774/159/3-2, 1. Lester, however, advised the Mission to 'always' consider the additional 'certain psychological and political implications' faced in its initiatives because of the 'troubles arising from inter-american relations'.

45 In September 1943, the Princeton staff numbered around thirty-five; twelve remained in Geneva, headed by Lester: Letter from Loveday to Jamieson, 21 September 1943, UNOG: PO—C.1756/140/1-1. Lester 'served primarily as caretaker of the League's assets during the Second World War': Thant Myint-U and Amy Scott, *The UN Secretariat: A Brief History (1945–2006)* (International Peace Academy, 2007) 2.

46 Memorandum by Loveday to Lester, 24 February 1941, UNOG:PO—C.1626/523/10/1 (in which Loveday stated: 'If we lost M Deperon, the League work in the field of double taxation would quite simply cease'). Deperon was credited as having single-handedly organised the 1943 Mexico conference, which included all the preparatory

in 1941, the League's income was half of that in 1940, which itself was one-third of that in 1939, and the Mission would be supplemented by grant from the Rockefeller Foundation and IAS,[47] the former benefactor noted to have financed 'all of its work during the Second World War'.[48] The Mission found keen support among American internationalist circles, and with the aid of IAS, Princeton University and the Rockefeller Foundation, soon 'forg[ed] ... productive and sustained connections with the State Department, the US Treasury, the Federal Reserve board, and key advisers'.[49] From February 1941 in fact, the Mission 'was confident it could direct the "whale-like" US administration' in influencing and shaping US policy regarding postwar reconstruction, international governance and economic, financial and political relations, although such efforts had to be conducted with diplomatic tact and by 'dovetail[ing] discreetly' into US planning itself.[50]

2.1.3 The 1940 Mexico Draft Aftermath

In US publications, Carroll promoted the 1940 draft as the outcome of 'a joint effort of experts from many ... [Western Hemisphere states] to formulate a model that ... [could] be followed in negotiating bilateral treaties among themselves'[51] and which had 'taken into account the basic requirements of their existing tax legislation'.[52] He also stated that the

documentation, report coverage, liaison with correspondents, determining the attendees and handling the diplomatic negotiations. He 'ran the Conference singlehanded in a foreign country, in a foreign language, with nothing but the help of quite inexperienced Spanish-speaking Mexican officials': Letter from Loveday to Acting Secretary-General, 2 February 1944, UNOG:PO—C.1626/523/10/1.

47 Clavin, *Reinvention of the League*, 267.

48 Tournès, 'Rockefeller Foundation', 324; see also 327, 328.

49 Clavin, *Reinvention of the League*, 271; see also 269 (where Clavin notes that '[t]he League group regularly visited the State Department, the Federal Reserve and the Treasury, and these departments sent officials to Princeton to review reports being compiled by the League'). See also Tournès, 'Rockefeller Foundation', 328. For a discussion of the corporate community links within this internationalist network via the Council on Foreign Relations policy discussion group, which was also sponsored by the Rockefeller Foundation and was highly influential in the White House and State Department regarding foreign policy and postwar economic planning, see G William Domhoff, 'The Council on Foreign Relations and the Grand Area: Case Studies on the Origins of the IMF and the Vietnam War' (2014) 2(1) *Class, Race and Corporate Power* 1:1–41, 1–9.

50 Clavin, *Reinvention of the League*, 268; see also 269, 272 and ch 8 generally.

51 Carroll, 'ITL in Americas', 800.

52 Mitchell B Carroll, 'Tax Trends and Relief for US Companies Trading Abroad' (6 December 1943) *Export Trade and Shipper* 5, 14. See also Mitchell B Carroll, 'Future

draft and the US–France and US–Sweden treaties were useful models for negotiating DTAs with Latin America 'for the purpose of imposing limits on tax jurisdiction, simplifying and clarifying the bases of taxation, and assuring the prevention of double and discriminatory taxation'.[53] According to Carroll, problematic issues with the Latin American tax laws included the taxation of income earned by short duration foreign business visitors; taxation of foreign companies operating through sales agents; allocation of profits between the foreign company and local branch; and 'dividend' taxation of branches in addition to the tax on net profit.[54] The key concern was not just for double taxation[55] but also for discriminatory and extraterritorial taxation of American enterprises, and Carroll advocated that DTAs could remove these obstacles by providing for, inter alia:[56]

- reciprocal exemption of temporary business visitors; transactions effected through travelling salesmen, brokers, commission agents or custodians; shipping and air navigation profits; and patent and copyright royalties;
- taxation of business income only to the extent attributable to a permanent establishment (PE), with allocation of profits based on the separate accounting principle;
- reduction of source taxation rates on dividends, interest and other recurring items; and
- incorporation of the foreign tax credit (FTC) and the foreign taxes to which it applied.

The above indicate almost complete concern for US foreign enterprise, with no consideration of the essentially one-way investment flows and

Work of the Fiscal Committee of the League of Nations' in Report of the League's Conference, 'World Organization: The League of the Future, the Future of the League' (Preliminary Draft) held in Princeton, 11–12 December 1943, to be published by the Woodrow Wilson Foundation, 1, UNOG:PO—C.1756/140/1-3 (where Carroll stated that the 1940 meeting 'made a first draft of a model convention predicated upon the tax laws and economic needs of the indicated countries of the Western Hemisphere').

53 Mitchell B Carroll, 'Removal of Tax Barriers to American Foreign Trade' (1940) 18(10) *Taxes - The Tax Magazine* 616, 617, 619.

54 Ibid 617–20.

55 Although the United States had provided for foreign tax credit relief since 1918 (*Revenue Act 1918*, sections 222 and 238), the concern was whether various Latin American taxes were creditable taxes.

56 Carroll, 'Removal of Tax Barriers', 619; Carroll, 'ITL in Americas', 800–1. See also, MB Carroll, 'History of Movement to Remove Tax Barriers to International Trade' (Speech prepared for the Tax Institute Meeting, Chicago, 2–3 December 1940, document dated 27 November 1940) 19, UNOG:PO—C.1774/159/3-1.

revenue concerns of the Latin American countries, or the fact that many of their economies were dependent on one or two export commodities.[57] Despite the overall rudimentary state of the latter's income tax systems, Carroll reported that:

> At present, Argentina, Brazil, Bolivia, Chile, Colombia, Cuba, Ecuador, Mexico and Peru have fairly complete systems of income taxes. Costa Rica, El Salvador, Guatemala, Haiti, Panama, and Paraguay have taxes on business profits and certain other classes of income. The Dominican Republic, Honduras, Nicaragua, Uruguay, and Venezuela apparently still find other sources of revenue sufficient, but the introduction of an income tax in Venezuela is expected.[58]

With Europe now enveloped by the war, any fiscal work could only progress in the Western Hemisphere and the Mission was keen to complete the double taxation and technical principles of taxation work, necessarily through further regional meetings 'each time, in a different country' and 'most appropriately . . . in Latin America, as there is a great task of fiscal coordination and education to be accomplished in that part of the world'.[59] These meetings were anticipated to 'stimulate the interest of the various countries in the work of the Committee; enhance the intrinsic value of that work through better acquaintance with national conditions; and create fresh personal contacts between the representatives of the Fiscal Committee and executives in the different countries'.[60] Also, the League anticipated that 'recurring meetings of officials from the various Latin American countries would lead to treaty negotiations in this hemisphere' just as 'the periodical meetings at Geneva of experts from the various European countries during the last twenty years contributed directly to the conclusion of treaties between them'.[61] Although Deperon indicated some concern that the Secretariat's proposals could not be submitted to the Committee, he determined 'that they would have met with an entire approval from the rest of the Committee, as they fell

[57] Darlene Rivas, *Missionary Capitalist: Nelson Rockefeller in Venezuela* (University of North Carolina Press, 2002) 37.

[58] Carroll, 'Removal of Tax Barriers', 617.

[59] Deperon, 'Note on the Fiscal Committee', 8–9. King also indicated keenness for another meeting to take place in 1941 with preference for a Mexican, Lima or Buenos Aires location: P Deperon, 'A Report on Attendance at the Meeting of the Tax Institute Meeting in Chicago, December 2nd and 3rd', 6 December 1940, 4, UNOG:PO—C.1774/159/3-1.

[60] Deperon, 'Note on the Fiscal Committee', 8.

[61] Rasminsky, 'Comments on Future Program', 3.

perfectly into line with the original programme of work' and could mostly 'be carried out on the American continent'.[62]

By the end of 1940, Deperon was uncertain about the priority of work to be carried out and contemplated expanding the technical principles of taxation work to address US domestic concerns.[63] Carroll, however, saw the main task of the upcoming regional meeting as promoting DTAs.[64] He and Deperon were seeing success in their efforts to promote the Fiscal Committee's work in the United States,[65] and such favourable reception had given 'considerable encouragement [to Treasury official King] in fostering a program of tax treaties with Latin American countries'.[66] At this time, six South American countries[67] contemplated creating a customs union and Carroll thought that the arrangements could be helpfully supplemented by 'a tax treaty embodying the same basic principles as those contained in the Mexico City draft', potentially even a multilateral treaty.[68]

Attempts to reconvene another meeting shortly after the 1940 Mexico meeting, however, fell through.[69] Between January and June 1941, at the suggestion of the Rockefeller Foundation, the League planned a programme of tax tours for tax officials from nine Latin American countries to visit the United States and Canada for approximately three months to study their fiscal systems and administrations.[70] The primary aim of the tours was to 'be regarded as being to promote improvements in

[62] Deperon, 'Note on the Fiscal Committee', 9. Deperon considered it 'desirable that these studies ... be carried on with diligence, so that the Fiscal Committee should be able to make up for the time lost when it can meet again'.

[63] King had advised that there was 'little use' in circulating the Mexico double taxation report in the United States, but 'that there would certainly be no harm in giving a rather extended distribution to the report on principles of income tax': Deperon, 'Report on Attendance', 4. Deperon's own preliminary scoping in US tax circles indicated that the predominant interest was on the question of allocation of tax jurisdiction in federal states and he wished to focus on this subject within the technical principles of taxation study (at 5). Only the technical principles of taxation report would be sent to tax academics around the country for expert comment. Both reports of the 1940 meeting were nevertheless sent to the Latin American participants and other contacts: see lists and correspondences in UNOG:PO—C.1644/28/1.

[64] Deperon, 'Report on Attendance', 5.

[65] These efforts are elaborated in Section 2.2.2.

[66] Letter from Carroll to Loveday, 4 December 1940, UNOG:PO—C.1774/159/3-1.

[67] Argentina, Bolivia, Brazil, Chile, Paraguay and Uruguay.

[68] Letter from Carroll to Loveday, 23 December 1940, UNOG:PO—C.1643/27/5.

[69] See correspondence between Carroll, Deperon and Loveday between December 1940 and January 1941 in UNOG:PO—C.1643/27/5; Deperon, 'LA Mission', 15.

[70] See correspondence and related documents in UNOG:PO—C.1744/159/3-2.

the tax administration and legislation of the Latin American countries', and secondarily 'to have personal exchanges of views – possibly leading to durable contacts'.[71] However, they were privately also expected to bring about 'greater uniformity in national tax laws and practices', and to serve as 'an excellent preliminary for leading up to parleys on [schemes or policies for the conclusion of DTAs] . . ., provided no premature haste or insistence . . . [was] shown in this respect'.[72] Although the League obtained the approval of the US and Canadian governments for the tours,[73] they did not eventuate as the Foundation found it could not afford to finance them.[74]

By September, '[t]he Secretary-General . . . [was] anxious that a study tour should be made in Latin America in order to follow up the [1940] Conference', and Deperon was entrusted with this mission.[75] Deperon was to renew contacts with participants of the 1940 meeting and create new desired contacts, ascertain what use had been made of the work of the 1940 meeting and what national administrations desired of the future orientation of the League's fiscal work,[76] and examine the possibility of holding a tax conference in a Latin American state in 1942.[77] But the mission to Latin America also had broader aims beyond the fiscal programme: Deperon was to follow up on other work of the League (e.g. nutrition, statistics, narcotics, customs nomenclature, postwar problems) and to inquire into government contributions to the League budget, Spanish editions of League publications, and the loan of government and central bank officials to the League.[78] Nevertheless, '[s]o as to

[71] 'Tax Tours: Tentative Plan' (Extracts of a Minute of 16 January 1941), 1, UNOG:PO—C.1774/159/3–2.

[72] Ibid.

[73] Draft Letter from Loveday to Lester, undated (around early May 1941), 2, UNOG:PO—C.1774/159/3–2.

[74] Letter from Loveday to Lester, 19 June 1941, UNOG:PO—C.1774/159/3–2.

[75] Letter from Loveday to Deperon, 17 September 1941, UNOG:PO—C.1643/27/2.

[76] Loveday would advise Deperon to discuss 'questions of agriculture and raw materials' (i.e. issues that the Latin Americans were 'particularly interested in') as it was 'useful' to project that the League's postwar work programme, 'while not being formally constructed by an inter-governmental committee', would reflect 'issues with which governments are in fact especially concerned': Letter from Loveday to Deperon, 19 November 1941, UNOG:PO—C.1626/523/10/1.

[77] Loveday letter, 17 September 1941.

[78] Ibid; Deperon, 'LA Mission', 1. League members that were visited and which were in arrears were Argentina, Bolivia, Colombia, Cuba, Ecuador, Mexico, Uruguay, Panama and Peru. Deperon's tours indicated a degree of success in increasing the League's chances of obtaining contributions from both members and non-members: Deperon, 'LA Mission', 4–10; Letter from Waterson to Hambro, 24 October 1941, UNOG:PO—C.1643/27/1.

emphasize the non-political character of the mission it was called a study tour'.[79]

The mission took place between October 1941 and January 1942 to twelve Latin American countries[80] and was successful in that, in nearly all countries, Deperon obtained access to ministers of finance, foreign affairs, labour, health and national economy, even in spite of the lack of official introductions.[81] Deperon reported that the Latin American countries were pleased with the League's broad interest in them[82] and that he had, in his discussions on postwar problems, 'indicated that the necessity was recognized of taking into special account the needs and possibilities of Latin America, in view of the future that would no doubt be open for that part of the world when peace is restored'.[83] Regarding fiscal studies, the tour indicated that the Latin American countries were generally more interested in the technical principles of taxation work as they wished to reform their tax systems to move away from dependence on import duties to internal taxation (including income, sales and land taxation and death duties).[84] The 1940 Mexico Draft on double taxation had only been considered by a handful of countries (including Argentina, Chile and Peru); other countries were less interested due to their unfamiliarity with the subject.[85] However, Deperon appeared to have been influential: he would report that they were 'impressed' by the 'value for American countries' shown by the Fiscal Committee in its work, and that the 'important countries in this hemisphere regarded a conference organized under the auspices of the Fiscal Committee as an especially appropriate means of approaching authorities of other countries with a view to eliminating international double taxation and fiscal evasion'.[86] He also indicated that the governments

[79] Deperon, 'LA Mission', 1.

[80] Argentina, Bolivia, Brazil, Chile, Colombia, Cuba, Ecuador, Mexico, Panama, Peru, Uruguay and Venezuela. The countries were selected based on where the Fiscal Committee had members and corresponding members: Deperon, 'LA Mission', 2. Only Argentina, Brazil, Chile, Mexico, Peru and Venezuela were considered 'essential from the point of view of the Fiscal Committee'; the others were 'in any case, on the way': Memorandum by Deperon to Loveday, 11 September 1941, UNOG:PO—C.1645/29/20.

[81] Deperon, 'LA Mission', 2.

[82] Ibid 2–3.

[83] Ibid 22.

[84] Ibid 15–16; Paul Deperon, 'Report on Mission in Washington (February 24–28, 1942)', undated, 4, UNOG:PO—C.1643/27/4/1 ('Washington Mission').

[85] Deperon, 'LA Mission', 16.

[86] Ibid 14–15. In Mexico, Deperon was able to influence the setting up of an unofficial interdepartmental committee to study the 1940 Draft: Letter from Deperon to Loveday, 18 October 1941, UNOG:PO—C.1683/67/1.

were 'most favorable' to his enquires whether they would pay the expenses of their representatives to the conference.[87]

Deperon subsequently visited Washington where he reported to Treasury and State Department officials that 'the Latin American countries now understand that double taxation and fiscal evasion are problems that should be dealt with on account of reasons relating both to revenue and general economic policy', that 'they realise in this connection the utility of the work of the Fiscal Committee', and that they were 'favourably disposed in principle to negotiations' and an upcoming tax conference.[88] Carroll later reported to Princeton that the US officials were much impressed with Deperon and his account of his mission, and that '[h]is views on the possibility of concluding tax treaties with various countries to the South ... [had] given considerable stimulus to the movement for such treaties'.[89]

Deperon's inroads in Latin America made him determined to confine the agenda of the planned conference in principle to double taxation and fiscal evasion but not to neglect the other fiscal work.[90] He encouraged Mexico to initiate DTA treaty negotiations with the United States even though the latter at that time was prioritising commercial treaties.[91] At this time, the US–Canada DTA, which was based on the 1940 draft and mainly purposed at restricting withholding taxes on American corporations,[92] was shortly to be concluded. The United States was now keen to approach Mexico, Brazil, Argentina and Colombia about international tax problems; all countries in which the League had 'very good connections'.[93] It would later amend its

[87] Deperon, 'LA Mission', 8–9.

[88] Deperon, 'Washington Mission', 3–4. Deperon also reported that 'one Government had offered a special grant for the work on taxation, and that other Governments had expressed their willingness to pay the expenses of their representatives at the meeting' (at 4).

[89] Letter from Carroll to Loveday, 11 March 1942, UNOG:PO—C.1645/29/20.

[90] Deperon, 'LA Mission', 19.

[91] Letter from Deperon to Loveday, 23 March 1942, UNOG:PO—C.1643/27/4/1.

[92] Roy D Hogg, 'Canada–US Tax Relations' (1995) 43(5) *Canadian Tax Journal* 1547.

[93] Deperon, 'Washington Mission', 3. US interest in these states was likely attributable to geopolitical and economic considerations. Both Brazil and Mexico were sending combat troops overseas to join American armed forces, and the United States was supplying substantial financial assistance for the Brazilian Volta Redonda steel mill (the first in South America) and Mexican railway improvements. Brazil was strategically significant to the United States due to the former's raw materials, fascist sympathies, geographic vulnerability to external aggression and vital position in the Lend-Lease supply route to the Mediterranean front. It had also allowed the United States to build naval and air bases on Brazilian soil (thereby incurring German retaliation) and had influenced other Latin American countries to break relations with the Axis. Colombia and Argentina were significant suppliers of raw materials for the Allies and the United States was attempting to heavily pressure Argentina, which had pro-Nazi leanings and close ties with Germany, into aligning itself with the Allies: Darlene Rivas, 'United

Revenue Act of 1941 (Section 109) to provide, via treaties, Western Hemisphere Trade Corporations with reduced withholding taxes at source.[94] State Department officials also saw a connection between the technical principles of taxation work and inter-American trade relations, stating that 'if Latin American countries had a more developed system of internal taxes, commercial negotiations would become easier, as tariffs concessions on the part of those countries would represent a smaller proportional sacrifice of revenue'.[95]

Following Deperon's mission to Latin America, Argentina led the Latin American countries in expressing firm positions[96] which, while generally in favour of the draft, contained reservations relating 'to the taxation of income from capital, royalties, purchasing profits, profits of enterprises doing business in a country without possessing an establishment therein'.[97] Simontacchi summed up the Latin Americans' main concerns as follows:[98]

(1) They could not afford a limitation to their taxing rights in relation to income from imported capital (dividends, interest, service of loans)

States-Latin American Relations, 1942–1960' in Robert D Schulzinger (ed), *A Companion to American Foreign Relations* (Blackwell, 2006) 230, 232–4 ('US–LA Relations'); Joseph Smith, *The United States and Latin America: A History of American Diplomacy, 1776–2000* (Routledge, 2005) 103–7. See also Erik Benson, 'Flying Down to Rio: American Commercial Aviation, the Good Neighbor Policy, and World War Two, 1939–45' (2001) 19(1) *Essays in Economic and Business History* 61, 70.

94 *Revenue Act of 1942*: Public Law 753, 77th Congress, ch 619, 2d Session (HR 7378), approved 21 October 1942, 838. See also Carroll, 'ITL in Americas', 793.

95 Deperon, 'Washington Mission', 4.

96 'Translation of a Letter and Memorandum [Dated February 1942] Sent by Dr Ernesto Malaccorto, Director General of Income Tax, Argentina, to the South American Members and Corresponding Members of the Fiscal Committee of the League of Nations', UNOG:PO—C.1646/30/6-1.

97 Letter from Deperon to Carroll, 20 April 1942, 1, UNOG:PO—C.1646/30/6-1. Deperon considered Malaccorto's memorandum not only 'the first clear and reasoned statement of a Latin American country's attitude concerning double taxation' but also useful for delimiting the problems, thus facilitating preliminary discussions for the tax conference. Deperon felt that Malaccorto's exceptions to the draft were possibly 'less divergent' than they prima facie appeared, hence requiring only 'changes in drafting or explanations as to the factual situation he has in view' (at 1–2). Carroll saw Malaccorto's views as protecting the position of the 'pays pénétrés' (penetrated countries) in taking a 'directly opposite position to anything' the United States proposed, and hence stirring 'stimulating' discussion: Letter from Carroll to Deperon, 22 April 1942, UNOG:PO—C.1643/27/5. King appeared unfazed by the variance between Malaccorto's views and the draft, stating to Deperon that 'by swinging somewhat to the extreme on several key points, this may tend to better define the issues and stimulate interest and there is always hope of dropping back to a middle ground from the extremes': Letter from King to Deperon, 29 April 1942, UNOG:PO—C.1643/27/5.

98 Simontacchi, *Taxation of Capital Gains*, 95.

as source countries (i.e. country of the fiscal domicile of the debtor). For Argentina, such receipts comprised a third of the revenue collection and it was estimated that a similar figure was true for the other Latin American countries.

(2) They preferred a lower threshold for the attribution of source-country taxing rights for business income, that is an entitlement to tax even in the absence of a PE.

(3) They envisaged the United States as their capital-exporting treaty partner and expected that double taxation could be solved by the United States forgoing its right to tax the income derived by its nationals from foreign capital investments.

In particular, the Latin Americans believed, encouraged by Deperon, that the principle contained in the third point could be accepted by the United States if they 'should present in an international conference a unanimous opinion in this connection'.[99] This to them represented an extension of the principle applying to business income from movable capital, and that the source country should be regarded as the country in which the capital was invested.[100]

In the ensuing months, the League doggedly persevered to convene the tax conference despite several setbacks, including Colombia's withdrawal of its acceptance to host the conference in the League's preferred city of Bogotá,[101] and the League having to bear the costs of the meeting, including the travel and subsistence expenses of the experts.[102] By March 1943, the new host county, Mexico, 'had done nothing about arranging the meeting', and during his trip in Latin America, Carroll worked to 'assure them [Mexican officials] of the interest of our Treasury Department in it'.[103]

99 Malaccorto memo (as translated), 2.

100 Ibid.

101 Letter from Urrutia to Deperon (Translation), 24 November 1942, UNOG:PO—C.1645/29/2. This withdrawal was attributed to Colombian President Alfonso López's long-held criticism of the League for having 'neglected to execute the purposes it for which it was created' and his determination 'not to include in the budget of the State . . . the payment of . . . the old fees owed by Colombia to the League'.

102 Fiscal Committee, 'Invitation from the Mexican Government to Hold a Regional Tax Conference in Mexico City from July 19th to July 24th, 1943', 5 May 1943, 3, UNOG: PO—C.1645/29/2. The meeting cost was estimated at $14,000 ($216,000 in today's equivalent) with the greater proportion to be borne by the Rockefeller grant and the remainder to be funded by the Geneva League: Cablegram by Loveday to Lester, 18 March 1943, UNOG:PO—C.1645/29/2.

103 Letter from Carroll to Loveday, 4 March 1943, 2, UNOG:PO—C.1645/29/2. Carroll also made the same representations in Guatemala.

Carl Hambro, the League's Norwegian president based at Princeton, encouraged the Mission's efforts, considering it 'essential that the Conference should take place, in view of the interest ... found to exist among leading business and financial circles for problems of double taxation and fiscal evasion'.[104] There were matters of contention relating to the lack of procedural formalities and political influences: the Secretary-General felt that any meeting held, especially one organised 'from US soil', needed to 'be kept well within the frame-work of the League Organization' by inviting some European members of the Fiscal Committee to attend the conference or nominate representative substitutes.[105] Such 'non-American elements, or at least emphasis on the League auspices', were envisaged to enable the meeting's success 'in view of the sometimes delicate inter-American relationship and balance of interests'.[106] The concern regarding the uneven powers at stake was perhaps merited considering the degree of US influence on the conference's attendance. States were invited based on a combination of factors: League membership and relative importance in the region, interest shown in the League's work, and states in which the United States was interested.[107] Accordingly, while the League was opposed to inviting Paraguay on the basis that it was 'a country of quite minor importance' and

[104] Memorandum by Deperon for Loveday, 19 March 1943, 1, UNOG:PO—C.1645/29/2. Hambro also indicated that '[t]here should be no difficulty about the cost of the meeting' and that he would contact the Treasurer and other members of the Supervisory Committee about it.

[105] Telegram from Lester to Loveday, 7 March 1941, UNOG:PO—C.1645/29/2. Hambro was similarly keen that the conference 'not be purely regional', advising that in the case of European members who had died or who were in occupied countries that their governments be asked to designate substitutes available in America. Deperon, however, privately 'doubted ... [European participation] necessary': Deperon memo, 19 March 1943, 1.

Note that similar concerns arose regarding other League Committees. For example, plans to convene a meeting of the Economic Committee were set aside due to a composition of six available members being considered insufficient 'to constitute an adequate "rump" of the Committee' and to be 'rather over-weighted with Americans and British': Letter from Loveday to Grady, 27 November 1941, 1–2, UNOG:PO—C.1630/526/14/2–1. To overcome these issues, the League decided instead to convene a combined meeting of the Economic and Financial Committees.

[106] Lester telegram, 7 March 1941.

[107] Memorandum by Deperon to Loveday, 15 March 1943, UNOG:PO—C.1645/29/2. Canada's own group of states which it was interested in was also given weight from an early stage in the planning, with the Mission having to draw up the invitation list so as not to 'have an unfavourable effect on the sensibility of our Latin-American friends' as '[y]ou know how careful one has always to be on this score': Letter from Loveday to Carroll, 9 January 1941, UNOG:PO—C.1643/27/5.

in large arrears to the League,[108] the US authorities were 'most anxious' for its participation as US–Paraguay DTA negotiations were at an advanced stage.[109] The conference was clearly significant to the United States: in addition to Eldon King (Special Deputy Commissioner of Treasury's Bureau of Internal Revenue), Frederick Livesey (Chief of the Financial Division of the State Department) would attend, unlike the 'only a junior official [sent] ... to the 1940 conference'.[110]

2.1.4 *The 1943 Mexico Meeting*

In July 1943, the second Mexico regional tax conference was convened, reportedly attended by thirteen countries.[111] The meeting not only formulated three draft conventions for double taxation of income, double taxation of death duties and administrative and judicial assistance in the application of DTAs, but also prepared a preliminary report on postwar fiscal policy.[112] The model convention on the double taxation of income (the Mexico Model)[113] has been described as being 'predicated almost entirely on the principle of taxation at

108 Experts from other countries with consolidated arrears (e.g. Cuba, Costa Rica, Nicaragua) were also vetoed by the League on the grounds of an earlier Assembly resolution which 'denie[d] the benefits of the technical activities of the League to countries ... in default': Deperon memo, 19 March 1943, 1.

109 Memoranda by Deperon to Loveday, 4 May and 6 April 1943; Minute from Loveday to Deperon, 16 March 1943, UNOG:PO—C.1645/29/2. Countries that were geographically near to states of US interest (e.g. Cuba) were also invited.

110 Deperon memo, 6 April 1943, 1. See, however, n 111.

111 Argentina, Bolivia, Canada, Chile, Colombia, Cuba, Ecuador, Guatemala, Mexico, Peru, Uruguay, Venezuela and the United States: 'Account of the Proceedings by the Secretary', Fiscal Committee, *Second Regional Conference in Mexico, Account of the Proceedings by the Secretary* (4 December 1943), 2, UNOG:PO—C.1645/29/2. Note, however, that Cuba and Guatemala were not stated as being among the countries represented in the formal report on the work of the conference: Fiscal Committee, *Second Regional Conference in Mexico, Report on the Work of the Conference* (29 July 1943), 1–2, UNOG:PO—C.1674/58/1. WV Whittington (Assistant Chief of the State Department's Treaty Division) substituted for Livesey at the conference, the latter held up by 'negotiations with the United Nations on monetary matters' (see Deperon memo, 6 April 1943, 1).

112 This report comprised a descriptive general survey of the role of fiscal policy in the solution of anticipated postwar commercial, monetary and economic problems: *Post War Fiscal Policies, Paper Submitted by the IV Subcommittee to the Plenary Session of the Second Regional Conference on Taxation, Mexico* (28 July 1943), UNOG:PO—C.1684/68/5–14.

113 Fiscal Committee, *Model Bilateral Conventions for the Prevention of International Double Taxation, Second Regional Tax Conference, Mexico 1943*, League Doc C.2.M.2.1945.II.A (1945).

source',[114] and accordingly 'the first assertion in the League's work of the needs of developing countries'[115] and 'a complete reversal' of the Fiscal Committee's approach up to that point.[116]

In particular, the Model gave the source country primary right of taxation over business income and income from invested capital (e.g. interest, dividends, royalties, annuities, and pensions),[117] and also clarified that all business income derived by a non-resident enterprise in a source country that was not attributable to a PE and was more than 'isolated or occasional' would be taxable in that country.[118] In other words, source-country taxation of foreign industrial, commercial or agricultural enterprise was not limited to the presence of a PE but to any economic activity which gave rise to income as this was deemed as amounting to production in the source jurisdiction.[119] A protocol to the model provided rules for attributing income to a PE using the standard PE definition found in the 1935 Allocation Draft, but as the Model had expanded the scope of source-country taxation rights over business income, the application of these PE attribution rules would appear to limit rather than enable source-country taxation.[120] On other provisions, the Mexico Model followed the 1940 Draft, including concerning exclusive residence-country taxation of ships and aircraft.[121] The Mexico tax conference volume was completed around May 1944.[122] While Mexico

114 Carroll, 'ITL (1968)', 708.

115 David R Davies, *Principles of International Double Taxation Relief* (Sweet & Maxwell, 1985) 35.

116 Bret Wells and Cym Lowell, 'Tax Base Erosion and Homeless Income: Collection at Source Is the Linchpin' (2012) 65(3) *Tax Law Review* 535, 564.

117 Articles IV, IX, X and XI. The source country for investment income was here defined as the state of the payer. While the state of domicile could tax worldwide income, it was required to grant a credit for all source taxes levied.

118 Sol Picciotto, *International Business Taxation* (Quorum Books, 1992) 49–50; Michael J McIntyre, 'Developing Countries and International Cooperation on Income Tax Matters: An Historical Review' (Unpublished manuscript, 2005) 4; Wells and Lowell, 'Tax Base Erosion', 564.

119 Carroll, 'ITL (1968)', 712; Mitchell B Carroll, 'Germany, Japan and Sweden Show the United States How to Reach Tax Treaties with South American Countries' (1969) 38(2) *George Washington Law Review* 199, 201. Article IV also contained, clearly at the insistence of the Latin Americans, a provision allowing the country that produced agricultural or mineral products to measure the income attributable to sources in its territory by world market prices or arm's length prices.

120 McIntyre, 'Developing Countries', 4; Wells and Lowell, 'Tax Base Erosion', 564; Carroll, 'ITL (1968)', 709.

121 Article V.

122 'Note on Section Meeting', 6 April 1945, 3, UNOG:PO—C.1624/521/8/3.

had initially promised to publish the report in Spanish,[123] by April 1945, this task appeared to have fallen to the League.[124]

Although the Mexico Model incorporated many pro-source country provisions from an Anglo-American/European perspective, the Latin Americans at Mexico were suspicious of the negotiations: they expressed fears to Deperon that 'the import of capital might result in their countries being despoiled of their national resources or in foreign control over their economic and financial destiny'.[125] Fraser Elliott (the Canadian representative) also reported to Deperon that the Latin Americans repeatedly turned to him for leadership regarding Canada's 'interpretation', 'attitude' or 'reaction' as a 'debtor nation', despite Canada being 'most closely associated with the US', and that they

> evinced an apprehension of the power of the United States being imposed upon them in such a way that the development of their natural resources and indeed their industrial development would take place to the advantage of the United States . . . they were always fearful that the United States was getting the best, by virtue of their strong position, on all Agreements, Conventions or proposed joint activities.[126]

Elliott suggested to Deperon that Canada's unique position gave it a 'mission' in future conferences of 'properly interpreting' the United States as 'not the grasping nation' as might have been their 'factual experience in the last fifty years' but as 'the wealthy creditor nation' that 'stood ready to approach the joining of efforts' directed towards 'assisting these countries'.[127] Such statements appear to indicate that DTAs were considered, at least by Canada, the United States and the Mission, as a method of development assistance for Latin America.

[123] 'Notes on Department Meeting Held on January 10, 1944', undated, 6, UNOG:PO—C.1624/521/8/3.

[124] At this time Geneva had approved only 500 copies and Deperon was seeking authorisation for another 500 (Section meeting note, 6 April 1945, 3).

[125] Economic and Financial Committees, *Status of Foreign Investment in Undeveloped Countries*, League Doc PEF/12 (December 1943), 1–2, UNOG:PO—C.1630/526/14/2–3.

[126] Letter from Elliott to Deperon, 22 September 1943, 2–3, UNOG:PO—C.1645/29/6. Carroll states that Canada had 'wished to be classified with the countries to the south, i.e., as an "underdeveloped" country' at the conference because it sought US investment, despite it having adopted income classifications, the PE definition and basic allocation principles based on the League's 1928 and 1935 models in its DTA concluded with the United States the year prior (Carroll, 'Germany', 199, 202).

[127] Elliott letter, 22 September 1943, 4, 2.

From January 1944, Carroll attempted to arrange another 'meeting of the Fiscal Committee' in Caracas but nothing eventuated and no further tax meeting was held again by the League in Latin America.[128]

2.1.5 The 1946 London Meeting

In September 1944, anticipating the end of the war, the Mission planned to hold 'a meeting of the Fiscal Committee on European questions'.[129] For its preparation, Deperon was to 'go to London and inform the Allied Governments there of the work done with the American countries on [double taxation]' and it was thought that a meeting could be held in June 'after a good deal of travelling to make preliminary contacts'.[130] By July 1945, this had yet to transpire and the UN Charter had been signed.[131] The League sought to reconvene a final meeting of the Committee in Europe later that year or in early 1946 on the basis that it was 'desirable ... to review the work which has been done on the question of double taxation' at the Mexico meetings before the work was transferred to the new UN.[132] It was thought that the meeting could be formed with four of the Committee's members who were still active in fiscal matters, together with replacements for two of its deceased members.[133] Carroll proposed that the meeting examine the regional

[128] Letter from Carroll to Deperon, 26 January 1944, UNOG:PO—C.1645/29/16; Letter from Carroll to Loveday, 7 March 1944; Letter from Loveday to Carroll, 8 March 1944, UNOG:PO—C.1643/27/5.

[129] 'Note on Department Meeting Held on September 1, 1944', undated, 3, UNOG:PO—C.1624/521/8/3.

[130] Ibid.

[131] *Charter of the United Nations*, opened for signature 26 June 1945, 1 UNTS XVI (entered into force 24 October 1945).

[132] Economic, Financial and Transit Department, 'Recent Work and Work in Hand', 1 August 1945, 4, UNOG:PO—C.1757/141/13-2. See, for example, Letter from Loveday to Lester, 12 July 1945, 5, UNOG:PO—C.1623/520/7/2.

[133] Loveday letter, 12 July 1945, 4–5. These four were Carroll, Rodolphe Putnam (Belgium), Clifford Wakely (Britain) and Carl de Kuylenstierna (Sweden). The League had lost contact with its French (Marcel Borduge) and Dutch (Sinninghe Damste) members, the Greek member (Georges Mantzavinos) was no longer interested in fiscal questions and the Swiss (Hans Blau) and Peruvian (Jimenez) members had passed away. Initial plans were to replace the deceased members with Elliott, who by then was 'Deputy Minister of Internal Revenue and ... ha[d] attended all recent meetings on this side of the Atlantic', and Carlos Lleras Restrepo (Colombia), who had 'been a useful member at some of the recent tax conferences' (at 4). By early March, Damste had been found: see 'Fiscal Committee, London, March 20–25, 1946, Estimate of Cost', attached to Memorandum by Deperon to Watterson, 6 March 1946; cf Memorandum by Deperon to Loveday, 13 February 1946, UNOG:PO—C.1647/31/2.

Mexico models 'from the viewpoint of their usefulness in connection with the negotiation of treaties between countries in Europe and in the Western Hemisphere to facilitate the resumption of trade and investments', and also for '[t]heir applicability as a basis for treaties with countries in the Near and Far East and Africa'.[134] By December 1945, the UN was not proposing, at least immediately, to set up a Fiscal Commission and the League considered it 'all the more important' to convene the meeting before the League transfer to the UN was effected, particularly so that the 'set of draft conventions, revised at the two Mexican Conferences, ... be submitted to the Committee as a whole, and more especially to the European members of it, in order to give them the status they require to be fully effective'.[135]Although Deperon had intended the meeting's programme to consist of (1) enlarging and making more comprehensive the Mexico models, (2) making a study of the recent US DTAs, and (3) discussing possible future international tax work, he had to forgo the second agenda item as a result of rushed plans for the meeting to coincide with the planned League Assembly in Europe in January, for which Deperon would be sent to assist the Secretariat.[136]

By this time, the Mission appeared to have retreated from some of the key concessions offered to source countries in the Mexico Model, even indicating a degree of US influence in its preferred method of double taxation relief. This was made evident in its Special Joint Committee's *Conditions of Private Foreign Investment* ('*PFI Conditions*') report, which contained a section on international taxation that, inter alia, recommended that the business income of foreign enterprises was to be taxable only in countries where PEs were maintained, and that the profits of PEs should be computed according to the separate-entity arm's length principle.[137] The credit mechanism was also recommended over

[134] Letter from Carroll to Deperon, 11 September 1945, UNOG:PO—C.1643/27/5.

[135] Letter from Loveday to Lester, 17 December 1945, UNOG:PO—C.1626/523/10/1.

[136] 'Note II on Department Meeting Held on 7 December 1945', 3; Letter from Loveday to Rosenborg, 2 October 1945; Loveday letter, 17 December 1945; Letter from Lester to Loveday, 22 January 1946, UNOG:PO—C.1647/31/2.

[137] Economic and Financial Organization, *Conditions of Private Foreign Investment: Report by the Special Joint Committee*, League Doc C.14.M.14.1946.II.A (League of Nations, 1946) 38. Carroll played a lead role in the preliminary meetings of this Committee and in the report's drafting (at 7). The Special Joint Committee comprised a mixture of eighteen financial, economic and fiscal experts with backgrounds in government, banking and business, with two-thirds from industrialised nations (including colonial administrations) (at 6–8). Of the eighteen, five were fiscal experts, namely Carroll, Elliott, H Heward

'[u]nqualified exemption' by residence countries of foreign derived income.[138]

The Fiscal Committee reconvened for its Tenth Session in London in March 1946 for a meeting which was almost entirely preoccupied with work on the model conventions and which was overwhelmingly represented by developed countries (Belgium, Canada, the Netherlands, Norway, Sweden, Switzerland, the United Kingdom and the United States), with only one Latin American representation (Mexico) present.[139] There were altogether twelve participants representing these nine states,[140] which mirrored the size of some of the earliest sessions held in 1930–1.[141] Although modern literature describes the London meeting as composed of 'a full complement of members',[142] in reality, only four fully fledged members were present.[143] The other 'attendants' (the term used in the Committee's *Tenth Session Report*) comprised four replacements (for one current member and two deceased members),[144] one corresponding member (Elliott) and three other persons.[145] Four of these attendants were local embassy representatives substituting for three European experts

Stikeman (Elliot's assistant in the Canadian Inland Revenue), Wiechers and Medardo Goytia (Chile). This would have made for three developed country representatives and one Fiscal Committee corresponding member (Wiechers), which perhaps explains, along with the fading US interest in Latin America (see Section 2.2.1.4), why the report's recommendations that were related to double taxation overlooked the special pro-source taxation provisions of the Mexico Model.

138 Ibid 39.

139 See Fiscal Committee, *Report on the Work of the Tenth Session*, League Doc C.37. M.37.1946.II.A (25 April 1946) 5 ('*Tenth Session Report*'). The invitation list was only established at end January (Deperon memo, 13 February 1946). Less than three weeks before the start of the Tenth Session on 20 March, the meeting's location was changed from Geneva to London (Telegram from Rosenborg to Smith, 28 February 1946, UNOG: PO—C.1647/31/2), prompting a late substitution of experts from certain invited countries (see, e.g., Letter from Deperon to Valensi, 6 March 1946; Letter from Deperon to Grässli, 6 March 1946, UNOG:PO—C.1647/31/2). This may have caused the lack of French representation given that the French embassy in Washington, D.C., had earlier indicated that Borduge would likely represent France at Geneva: Letter from Valensi to Deperon, 13 February 1946, UNOG:PO—C.1647/31/2.

140 Another two participants represented the ICC.

141 Between 1933 and 1939, the average attendance fell to seven persons.

142 McIntyre, 'Developing Countries', 4. See also Carroll, 'ITL (1968)', 708 (using the description 'the full Fiscal Committee').

143 Carroll, Putnam, Wakely and Damste.

144 Björn Prytz (Sweden) replaced Kuylenstierna; Armando Servin (Mexico) replaced Jimenez; and AM Escher and Eric Barbey (Switzerland) replaced Blau.

145 Jacob Stein Bergh-Jacobsen (Norway), representing M Christen Urbye (Norway); Robert Willis (the United Kingdom), participating as assistant secretary to Wakely; and Herbert Fales (the United States), Secondary Secretary of the US embassy in London.

(Norway, Sweden and Switzerland) while the fifth embassy representative (the United States) substituted for King (although this is not stated in the report, presumably because the United States was not a League member).[146] The invitation to attendees who were not Committee members was heavily influenced by political factors, namely: noteworthy contributors to the League's double taxation work,[147] countries that could influence the continuance of the Committee in the UN,[148] funding,[149] and perhaps even

[146] The Mission had invited King and Livesey, the latter declining on the basis that 'my presence would be much less useful and I am afraid I cannot accept' (referring to his new position as Adviser of the State Department's Office of Financial and Development Policy): Letter from Livesey to Deperon, 27 February 1946, UNOG:PO—C.1647/31/2. King suggested to Deperon, after consultation with State Department officials, to invite Fales in his place: Letter from Deperon to Fales, 8 March 1946, UNOG:PO—C.1647/31/2. Apart from Fales, all the other attendees who were not fully fledged Committee members were from League member states, highlighting the Mission's efforts to secure as close a connection with the League as possible. Such concern for formalities appeared to have become critical once the war was over: the inclusion of a Brazilian expert in the Special Joint Committee on the *PFI Conditions* study was vetoed by the Geneva League's Supervisory Committee on the grounds that Brazil was not a League member (Letter from Deperon to Loveday, 25 June 1945, UNOG:PO—C.1625/522/9/1). Fales' attendance at the Fiscal Committee's Tenth Session as the only embassy representative who was neither an expert (or a replacement for one) nor from a League member state would thus appear to have been politically motivated: the United States was host country to the Mission and future UN; the superpower steering the postwar world order; and a key supporter for the Fiscal Commission's establishment (see Chapter 3, Section 3.3.1).

[147] Elliott was singled out for being 'one of the most active persons associated with the Fiscal Committee' and because he was then 'engaged ... in negotiating tax treaties' in his official capacity. The Mission had also invited Wiechers based on having 'for a long period of time been the most active of the South American members or participants at the conferences organized by the Committee', and Goytia for playing 'a leading part' in the 1943 conference and on the Special Joint Committee: Letter from Loveday to Lester, 5 February 1946, UNOG:PO—C.1647/31/2.

[148] Canada and Chile were earmarked as the Mission considered it was 'obviously sound tactics' to use experts from governments which held seats in the new ECOSOC: Ibid. A Colombian representative (Jorge Soto del Corral) was also supposed to attend and flight reservations had been purchased (see Letter from Deperon to Belanus, 5 March 1946, UNOG:PO—C.1647/31/2; Estimate of Cost attached to Deperon memo, 6 March 1946), likely because Colombia was an ECOSOC member and its representative at ECOSOC's First Session in February had strongly urged the creation of the Fiscal Commission (see Chapter 3, Section 3.3.1).

[149] Lester had hoped for the meeting to be chargeable to the Rockefeller grant. Formalities, however, required the costs of the meeting to be borne by the League, but the Mission arranged to charge the expenses of non-European, non-full-fledged members (then proposed as Elliott, Wiechers and Goytia) to the grant: Loveday letter, 5 February 1946.

Hambro's preferred countries[150] and countries which had hosted the League's wartime work.[151]

At the London meeting, the Committee agreed on the basic structure of the Mexico Model but not on its strong source taxation principles, choosing instead to adopt a new version, the London Model, which reasserted the principle of primacy of residence-country taxation by restoring to the residence country the primary right of taxation over business income, dividends, interest and royalties.[152] Source countries were only entitled to tax business income if a PE existed, and then only that portion that was attributable to the PE.[153] On other points, new articles were inserted to reflect innovations of the 1945 US–UK DTA.[154]

In his draft suggesting studies for the future UN Fiscal Commission which were to be included in the *Tenth Session Report*, Deperon wrote that the Mexico and London outcomes were inadvertent products of the circumstances (rather than of any planning or encouragement by the League). Specifically, the Mexico Model 'perhaps [placed] greater emphasis ... upon taxation at source than would otherwise have occurred, due to the circumstances in which the meeting was held', that is, 'formulated ... while the war was still in progress ... without the co-operation of

150 In his desire for European presence at the 1943 Mexico conference, Hambro had particularly favoured Norway and Sweden (perhaps attributable to Hambro's Norwegian nationality) and had been 'very anxious' for Switzerland (likely because of the League's nominal Geneva seat): Deperon memo, 19 March 1943, 1.

151 The Mission's early plans indicated that a Mexican representative (Loyo, rather than Wiechers) had been intended, along with Goytia, to be the two Latin American participants at the meeting, then contemplated to be formed of nine persons (the other seven comprising the five fully fledged members, Elliott and Deperon): 'Fiscal Committee, Meeting, Geneva, March 1946, One Week, Tentative Estimate of Expense: in US $', undated (around January 1946), UNOG:PO—C.1647/31/2. As Loyo was not recorded among the 1943 conference participants nor was part of the Special Joint Committee, his inclusion was perhaps attributable to Mexico's hosting of the regional tax conferences, not to mention being the Mexico Model's namesake. Mexico's presence would have also served to affirm the work of the Mexico conferences. See n 146 regarding the recognition of host country the United States.

152 Davies, *Principles*, 36; Picciotto, *International Business Taxation*, 50. Dividends were taxable by the state of the payer but were to be exempt if paid by a subsidiary to a parent company. Meanwhile, patent royalties could only be taxed by the state of the paying company (i.e. country of exploitation of the patent) if paid to a related company.

153 McIntyre, 'Developing Countries', 4; Wells and Lowell, 'Tax Base Erosion', 564. A PE was defined basically as an installation or fixed place of business of productive character. Ancillary activities (e.g. warehousing, research laboratories and independent agents/brokers) were excluded.

154 Fiscal Committee, *Tenth Session Report*, 8.

representatives of European countries'.[155] On the other hand, the London meeting 'was attended by only one representative of Latin American countries, inasmuch as the circumstances of the moment precluded the attendance of others who had been invited'.[156] Due to the 'evident conflict of viewpoint between certain of the provisions, particularly those relating to taxation of income from capital' that had arisen, Deperon proposed it would be 'desirable to have the tentative London draft examined by a better balanced group of European and Western Hemisphere experts'.[157] In the *Tenth Session Report*, this phrase was replaced by a more generic reference to both models being examined by capital-exporting/importing and economically advanced/less-advanced countries.[158] This change was perhaps made in view of the broad UN membership, where middle and small powers were keen participants in securing a greater role for themselves in the new organisation,[159] as well as Deperon's efforts to gain international support for the establishment of the Fiscal Commission.[160]

2.1.6 *Reframing the Prevailing History of International Tax Coordination in the Americas*

The aforementioned narrative challenges many portrayals in League publications and the prolific writings of Carroll concerning the Mexico Model and the nature of the League's double taxation work in the Western Hemisphere. Such works have generally depicted Latin America as having been attracted to, and greatly interested in, the League's double taxation work, and the Committee as continuing to function during the war. For example, despite Latin America having had little exposure to the subject up to 1940, Carroll reported the 1940 meeting as having provided 'the less-developed countries of the Western Hemisphere . . . an opportunity to participate in revising the 1928 model

[155] 'Suggestions of Studies for the Fiscal Commission of the UNO in the Field of International Tax Problems: Rough Draft', undated (around April 1946), 4, UNOG:PO—C.1684/68/1.
[156] Ibid.
[157] Ibid.
[158] Fiscal Committee, *Tenth Session Report*, 8.
[159] Stephen S Goodspeed, *The Nature and Function of International Organization* (Oxford University Press, 2nd ed, 1967) 93; see also Chapter 4, Section 4.1.1.
[160] See Chapter 3, Section 3.3.1.

Conventions' as they 'would be interested in industrial and commercial expansion when the war was over',[161] and having

> formulated a model convention which took into account the League model conventions of 1928 and that on allocation of business income of 1935, as well as the most up-to-date provisions in the more than sixty general bilateral conventions which had been concluded during the years in which the League meetings were held and reflected their recommendations.[162]

Moreover, despite the Committee having ceased to function, Carroll wrote that the Committee had 'transferred its activities to the Western Hemisphere ... headquartered at Princeton'[163] and that Suarez had 'invited the committee' to continue its work through the 1940 and 1943 regional tax conferences.[164] Carroll characterised the broad participation of Western Hemisphere governments in the 1943 meeting as signifying 'the importance they attributed to keeping alive the pioneer work of the League committee' despite the 'mounting burdens' faced by wartime tax systems.[165] He also stated that the Mexico Model had been drafted 'with a view toward encouraging economic development in the less-developed countries of the Western Hemisphere',[166] and was 'the expression of the views of less-developed countries'.[167] The League itself publicised that the 1943 meeting consisted of 'members of the Fiscal Committee ... and other experts',[168] and the *Tenth Session Report* and *Mexico/London Models Commentary* stated that the wartime work and conferences had been conducted 'under the auspices of the Fiscal Committee'.[169] The League had also earlier publicised that the 'outstandingly successful' 1940 meeting had contributed to 'a new draft model convention ... drawn up which brings up to date the model conventions for the prevention of

161 Carroll, 'ITL (1968)', 707.

162 Mitchell B Carroll, 'Report of the Committee on International Double Taxation' [1946] *Proceedings of the Section of International and Comparative Law (American Bar Association)* 40, 43 ('IDT Committee Report').

163 Carroll, 'ITL in Americas', 801; Carroll, 'Tax Trends', 14.

164 Carroll, 'IDT Committee Report', 43.

165 Carroll, 'IDT (1944)', 174.

166 Carroll, 'Germany', 199.

167 Carroll, 'ITL (1968)', 709. See also Carroll, 'Income Tax Conventions as an Aid', 18.

168 'Tax Conference in Mexico City', League (Princeton) Press Release, 19 July 1943, UNOG: PO—C.1645/29/2.

169 Fiscal Committee, *Tenth Session Report*, 7; Fiscal Committee, *London and Mexico Model Tax Conventions: Commentary and Text*, League Doc C.88.M.88.1946.II.A (November 1946) 6.

double taxation in the field of income and property taxes framed by the Conference of Governmental Experts of 1928' and to 'negotiations for several treaties between countries of the Western Hemisphere ... initiated on the basis of the new model convention'.[170]

The archival records indicate, however, that the wartime double taxation work was mainly driven by the League Secretariat and Carroll with the support of the US government and had ambiguous status in the absence of a functioning Fiscal Committee. In summary, the 1940 meeting had represented a propitious opportunity for the League to have the 1940 work of the Sub-Committee and Carroll approved in a gathering of governments when Europe was paralysed by war.[171] Despite the lacklustre interest shown by the Latin Americans in the double taxation work, the Mission (and Carroll) pursued its progress, even viewing efforts to develop Latin America's fiscal systems and administrations as a prelude to the conclusion of DTAs, sending Deperon on a mission to the region, and persevering in organising the 1943 meeting on Latin American soil and bearing its costs. Rather than having any keen desire for DTAs, the Latin Americans appeared to have been more swayed by the League's persistence (especially enabled by the Spanish-fluent Carroll and Deperon), its apparent concern for their socio-economic development and its facilitation of US interest in their region. They often displayed inertia, and while they occasionally made commitments in the moment, they habitually did not follow through on them.

The League itself had ongoing misgivings about the status of the Mexico drafts and the tenuous connection of its work in the Western Hemisphere to the Fiscal Committee: technically, with the League Council and Assembly defunct since 1939, there was no official approval for the 'regional tax conferences' or the resulting work; most of the participants of the conferences were from non-League member states[172] or member states in arrears; and the Secretariat itself was not a principal organ in its own right with independent ability to carry out its own agenda.[173] Although the publication of the Mexico Model alongside the London

[170] League of Nations, *Brief Statement on 1940 and 1941 Activities*, 8–9.

[171] Most of the League's technical committees in fact could not meet in 1940, so the 1940 Mexico meeting enabled the League to report that '[n]otwithstanding the difficulties of the moment, it was possible to carry through an appreciable part of the programme that the Fiscal Committee had drawn up at its session in June 1939': Ibid 8.

[172] These included the only fully fledged Committee members, Carroll and Jimenez; the latter's country, Peru, having withdrawn from the League in 1939.

[173] Myint-U and Amy Scott, *UN Secretariat*, 2. Even with the outbreak of the war, the Assembly had only empowered the Secretariat in September 1939 to take exceptional

Model in the *Tenth Session Report* legitimised the former, and both are today regarded as 'the Fiscal Committee's legacy to the international fiscal community',[174] in reality, two-thirds of the Committee were not formally appointed members,[175] and the *Tenth Session Report* and *Mexico/London Models Commentary* were never approved by the Council or Assembly.

There are many problematic aspects concerning the motivations and legitimacy of the League's efforts during this period, especially concerning its engagement with Latin America. On the one hand, the League had understandably sought to continue its raison d'être by extending its relevance to the Western Hemisphere when its work in Europe was no longer possible. It appeared to genuinely regard DTAs as universally beneficial for all countries, whatever the stage of development or state of their tax systems,[176] and that the experience of Europe, in terms of tax treaty proliferation and development, was transplantable. There were also impetuses for the Mission to support DTAs as a form of US development assistance to its poorer neighbours in their encouragement of trade and investment flows:[177] the League itself had, since 1939, espoused views supporting the industrialisation of underdeveloped countries as pivotal to world economic development;[178] and the Rockefeller Foundation was purposed to promote global welfare through developing solutions for, inter alia, underdevelopment.[179]

On the other hand, there is compelling evidence that suggests that the League overstepped its boundaries as an international civil service in its ulterior motives, overtures and methods to secure its institutional survival, especially in taking advantage of Latin America's economic needs and

and necessary administrative or financial measures or decisions: League of Nations, *The League Hands Over* (1946) 7–9.

174 Picciotto, *International Business Taxation*, 49.

175 As the Geneva League functioned under the Supervisory Committee which had been appointed as caretaker after the Assembly and Council were dissolved in 1939, and which only had charge over financial and administrative matters, issues such as the appointment of members to technical bodies were left in limbo: see, for example, correspondences in UNOG:PO—C.1630/526/14/2-4.

176 See Chapter 1, Section 1.3.1 regarding the League's traditional approach to double taxation solutions that generally did not consider underdeveloped countries as qualitatively distinct from developed countries.

177 Such a view appears indicated in Elliot's correspondence with Deperon (see Section 2.1.4). See also Letter from Elliott to Deperon, 2 October 1943, UNOG:PO—C.1646/30/6-5.

178 See Section 2.2.1.3.

179 Inderjeet Parmar, *Foundations of the American Century: The Ford, Carnegie, & Rockefeller Foundations in the Rise of American Power* (Columbia University Press, 2012) 40.

marginal status in international relations. In particular, the League capitalised on its technical principles of taxation work to gain a foothold in Latin America for its double taxation work; it used its 'study tour' to advance its other non-fiscal work and to procure League contributions; and it acted to further the US government's commercial interests in the region despite the region's relative lack of expertise in international negotiations or economic questions,[180] and the tense relations that existed between the two continents. The Mission also engaged Carroll, but without official authorisation, to advance its agenda during his trips to Latin America in March 1943 and February 1944 for other purposes (including for the US trade association, the National Foreign Trade Council (NFTC)).[181]

Moreover, the Mission was aware that Carroll's efforts to publicise the League's work in the United States often overstated Latin America's interest in double taxation and the relevance of the 1940 draft to the region.[182] In fact, the Mission worked together with Carroll in the Americas to bring about movement for DTAs from the private business sphere.[183] Their manifold efforts came to fruition, and the Mission used its record of achievement and the interest generated by its work to support a new grant request in favour of the Fiscal Committee,[184] to endorse the Mexico Model,[185] and to support proposals for the

[180] See also Memorandum by Loveday to Deperon, 29 August 1941, UNOG:PO—C.1643/27/5 (where Loveday notes that 'in Latin America there are few of them [ex-officials with information on postwar economic questions], fewer still who know anything about economic questions and fewer still whose opinions one would highly value').

[181] During the 1943 trip, Carroll worked to progress the stalled 1943 meeting (see Section 2.1.3). During the 1944 trip, at Deperon's request, Carroll discussed double taxation and the promotion of FDI as a follow-up on the 1943 Mexico meeting and to gather material for the study on foreign private investment. This was done on the basis that Carroll 'of course understood that you [he] would be acting in a personal and unofficial capacity': Letter from Deperon to Carroll, 18 January 1944, UNOG:PO—C.1645/29/16.

[182] Such representations were made at conferences organised by the Mission and were contained in draft speeches and publications Carroll frequently sent to the Mission for comment. In his memoir, Carroll mentioned that his governmental and League positions enabled him to avoid criticism for representing US corporations: Mitchell B Carroll, *Global Perspectives of an International Tax Lawyer* (Exposition Press, 1978) 78–9.

[183] These endeavours and their outcomes are detailed in Section 2.2.2.

[184] Deperon, 'Report on Attendance', 4.

[185] See Paul Deperon, *International Double Taxation* (Committee on International Economic Policy in Cooperation with Carnegie Endowment for International Peace, 1945) 2 (in which he appends the 1944 Inter-American Bar Association (IABA) resolution that he himself authored (see Section 2.2.2) as annex A as evidence of broad affirmation of the Mexico Model). See n 335 regarding how this publication came to be funded by the Carnegie Endowment for International Peace (CEIP).

Committee to be continued in the new UN.[186] Unbeknown to Latin America,[187] the fiscal work was facilitated by the patronage of a private foundation[188] that was ultimately interested in the growth of American business as well as a world trading system within a multilateral framework of international institutions.[189]

Unlike its more freewheeling operations in Latin America, the Mission does appear to have been somewhat more circumspect in its conduct in the United States. For example, Deperon, in determining how to organise 'a rather wide but selected distribution' of the 1940 reports, noted:

> At the same time, we are well aware of the discretion and reserve we should observe as guests of this country, and it would be most unfortunate if any action taken on behalf of the Fiscal Committee might be misconstrued either as a measure of publicity or as an interference in the affairs of this country.[190]

[186] Carroll, 'Future Work', 3 (in which he cited the work of the Mexico conferences and the tax resolution of the 1943 IABA conference (see Section 2.2.2) as evidence of the Fiscal Committee's desirability as 'a permanent continuance of the League of Nations or any institution which might be established to take its place'). See also Economic, Financial and Transit Department, *The Question of the Transfer of the Economic and Financial Organization of the League to a New United Nations Organization*, League Doc H.S.9 (November 1944) 9, UNOG:PO—C.1633/529/17/4-1.

[187] The Mission's archival records do not indicate any acknowledgement of the Rockefeller funding among the documents distributed to, and communications with, Latin American officials.

[188] Deperon credited the Rockefeller Foundation funding as having enabled the Committee 'to carry out its investigations, on larger and more methodical bases than it would otherwise have been possible' and being 'due a great deal of the practical and permanent value of the Committee work': Deperon, 'Note on the Fiscal Committee', 2.

[189] Parmar, *Foundations*, 64 (Parmar's work generally provides an archive-based critique revealing the pivotal (and not disinterested) role the three richest American private foundations, including Rockefeller and Carnegie, have played in US foreign policy through their financial initiatives which, inter alia, built the intellectual and political basis behind the advancement of US hegemony). See also Tournès, 'Rockefeller Foundation'; Domhoff, 'Council on Foreign Relations'. Note, however, that Nelson Rockefeller is also known to have been a staunch Latin Americanist keen on 'transforming the historically indifferent, extractive, and interventionist US business presence overseas into an "enlightened" capitalism' that could facilitate rather than 'simply stunt' Latin America's national development: Elizabeth A Cobbs, 'Entrepreneurship as Diplomacy: Nelson Rockefeller and the Development of the Brazilian Capital Market' (1989) 63(1) *Business History Review* 88, 93.

[190] Deperon letter, 22 November 1940, 1. See also Clavin, *Reinvention of the League*, 272, noting that as

> Loveday and his colleagues were the focus of suspicion in circles beyond the elite of Democrat internationalists and outward-looking Republicans, they did not want to look as though they were telling FDR what to do, and were mindful that [postwar] 'planning' had potentially unwelcome associations with the New Deal, and with National Socialism and Communism.

In promoting the League's double taxation work at a US tax conference, Deperon stated that he had 'no mandate to speak on behalf of the League . . ., or even of its Fiscal Committee' and that his 'remarks . . . [were] merely . . . the views of an individual who . . . had an opportunity to follow for a number of years the technical work of the international bodies in Geneva'.[191] Carroll would also refer to himself as 'former member of the League Secretariat'.[192] Such formalities, nevertheless, were sometimes relaxed for promotional purposes. For example, Loveday requested Carroll 'act as "Acting Chairman" of the Committee' on the basis that 'it would be a great convenience to us'.[193] In the case of Deperon's position title on his 1945 pamphlet *International Double Taxation*,[194] Loveday suggested that the publisher 'add, if you felt that it would be appropriate, "Secretary of the Fiscal Committee"' after 'Member of the Secretariat of the League of Nations'.[195] Carroll also went by the titles of President[196] or Chairman[197] of the Fiscal Committee. In 1946, after the war, Carroll referred to himself only having been Chairman of the Committee in 1938–9.[198]

The accomplishment of the Mexico Model within three years of the subject's initial presentation to Latin America was a remarkable feat given the region's almost negligible past participation and its relative disinterest in and unfamiliarity with the subject. Much of this

191 Paul Deperon, 'The Work of the League of Nations on Tax Problems' (Speech prepared for the Tax Institute Meeting, Chicago, 2–3 December 1940, document undated) 1, UNOG:PO—C.1774/159/3–1.

192 Carroll, 'Future Work', 1.

193 Letter from the Secretary of the Economic, Financial and Transit Department to Carroll, 1 October 1940, UNOG:PO—C.1643/27/5 (also indicating that Deperon was 'writing Kuylenstierna, for his formal approval').

194 See n 185.

195 Letter from Loveday to Gullick, 2 January 1945, UNOG:PO—C.1774/159/3–3. This was decided as 'Member of the Secretariat of the League of Nations and Secretary of the Fiscal Committee'.

196 Carroll, 'Removal of Tax Barriers', 616 n ** [author's details] (This article was Carroll's speech delivered at the National Foreign Trade Convention, San Francisco, in July 1940). Carroll had expressed doubt to the programme drafter whether he still occupied that position; the drafter was reported to have responded that 'he would resolve the doubt in my [Carroll's] favour as it would make a better impression': Letter from Carroll to Loveday, 2 October 1940, UNOG:PO—C.1643/27/5.

197 Carnegie Endowment for International Peace, 'The United States and World Organization during 1939' (1940) 20(June) *International Conciliation* 209, 220; Carroll, 'ITL in Americas', 801 n 44.

198 Mitchell B Carroll, 'Tax Inducements to Foreign Trade' (1946) 11(4) *Law and Contemporary Problems* 760, 760. Cf Carroll, 'ITL (1968)', 707 n 28 (where he states that he 'continued to serve in that capacity [of Chairman] through World War II until the opening of the final meeting in London in 1946').

achievement was undoubtedly brought about by the League's propaganda and persistence. Yet by mid-1945, the importance of Latin America and even Canada had diminished to the point that their participation on the Fiscal Committee was based on their strategic usefulness in furthering its continued existence. Why this abrupt loss of interest given that the League appeared to have held some conviction that the European experience in relation to tax treaty proliferation and development could be replicated in the Western Hemisphere; that tax law uniformity could be attained; and that Latin American cooperation was significant enough to merit a foreign investment study that considered their concerns? What had spurred the sudden governmental openness towards DTAs that had briefly drawn the economically powerful US and wary Latin Americans together to cooperate? To what extent had the League perceived a larger role for Latin America, or developing countries generally, in the postwar world economy? Why were no US–Latin America treaties concluded despite the many negotiations begun at this time?[199] To find these answers, it is necessary to turn to the broader external political and economic influences that enveloped and interacted with the Mission's wartime operations in the Americas.

2.2 Interplay between Inter-American Relations and the League's Inroads into Latin America

2.2.1 Wartime Interdependence and Postwar Planning

2.2.1.1 Inter-American Relations Prior to 1939

Inter-American relations had for a century prior to the 1930s been characterised by US neglect, apathy and, from the 1880s to 1920s, intervention and military occupation to protect America's commercial interests as well as its political pre-eminence against the European powers.[200] Between 1929 and 1943, however, US foreign policy sought to repair America's relations with its southern neighbours for two key reasons.[201]

199 These include Argentina, Brazil, Colombia, Cuba, Mexico and Uruguay: see DEA, Fiscal Division, *International Tax Agreements*, UN Doc ST/ECA/SER.C/3 (UN, 1951) vol 3: World Guide to International Tax Agreements 1943–1951, 328–31. Paraguay is not listed here despite the 'advanced stage' negotiations had reached in 1943 (see Section 2.1.3). The first US treaty with a Latin American country was concluded with Honduras in 1956 but which was denounced by the latter in 1964 (Carroll, 'Germany', 202).

200 Smith, *American Diplomacy*, chs 2–4.

201 Ibid ch 5; Rivas, *Missionary Capitalist*, 36–8; David Rock, 'War and Postwar Intersections: Latin America and the United States' in David Rock (ed), *Latin America in the 1940s* (University of California Press, 1994) 15, 22–3.

Firstly, the United States was shifting from protectionism, unilateralism and isolation towards more liberal trade policies as policymakers began to believe that restrictive practices led to international conflict. The increased trade from economic integration was also intended to help the recovery of the US economy from the Great Depression. Secondly, bolstering hemispheric defence and economic security had become a primary goal in view of the looming partitioning of the world with Nazi Germany's rise and the growing trade, political and economic penetration by the Axis powers into Latin America.[202]

Meanwhile, Latin America, which was most involved in the international economy through primary products,[203] had suffered greatly from the 1929 collapse of the multilateral trade and payments system and resultant tariff barriers of Europe and the United States, leaving the region's countries with inadequate foreign exchange to purchase needed imports of manufactures and food, and with declining revenues as a result of their dependence on export taxes and tariffs.[204] Private capital markets dried up almost entirely with only short-term, high-interest credits available from New York and European banks, leading many Latin American countries into increasing debt and default.[205] In a bid to move away from their traditional staple industries and export-led economies, the region's governments turned towards import-substitution, protectionist and often discriminatory commercial policies, the development of local manufacturing industries, and economic diversification.[206] Some countries expropriated foreign-owned industries while others turned to trade and barter agreements with Nazi Germany to

202 America's improved relations with its neighbours would enable it to implement a Western Hemispheric defence policy that included a 300-mile security perimeter around the hemisphere to exclude any extra-hemispheric intervention from belligerents: Rivas, 'US–LA Relations', 232; Smith, *American Diplomacy*, 102.

203 Primary products accounted for virtually all export earnings and almost 70 per cent of the region's external trade was conducted with just four countries, namely America, Britain, France and Germany: Victor Bulmer-Thomas, *The Economic History of Latin America since Independence* (Cambridge University Press, 2014) 209.

204 Ibid 210–16; Rivas, *Missionary Capitalist*, 37.

205 In 1940, 14 Latin American countries were in partial or total default on their external debt repayments: Eric Toussaint, *The World Bank: A Critical Primer*, tr Elizabeth Anne et al, ed Sylvain Dropsy (Pluto Press, 2008) 11.

206 André A Hofman, *The Economic Development of Latin America in the Twentieth Century* (Edward Elgar, 2000) 24; Norma Breda dos Santos, 'Latin American Countries and the Establishment of the Multilateral Trading System: The Havana Conference' (2016) 36(2) *Brazilian Journal of Political Economy* 309, 318; Rivas, *Missionary Capitalist*, 37; Bulmer-Thomas, *Economic History*, 256–7; Rock, 'War and Postwar Intersections', 15–16.

meet shortfalls in capital and foreign exchange.[207] The economic unrest would lead to many regimes being overturned between 1930 and 1931, which took the United States by surprise.[208]

In 1933, the 'Good Neighbor Policy' was launched with the inauguration of the Roosevelt Administration; it would lead to many conciliatory US efforts and commitments to forge greater economic and political ties within the hemisphere.[209] As the United States began to meet some of Latin America's economic demands, the latter's governments began 'to perceive a permanent change in their hemispheric status' and the potential to develop economies less reliant on the United States and Europe and on changing world conditions.[210] Larger nations (e.g. Argentina, Brazil, Chile and Mexico) increasingly pressed for industrial development, which required investment rather than export-led growth.[211] Latin America's positive outlook would be seemingly affirmed with the outbreak of World War II as the region's old ties with Europe crumbled while relations with the United States assumed increasing importance.[212]

2.2.1.2 Wartime Hemispheric Economic Solidarity (1939–1943)

In 1938, almost 55 per cent of all Latin American exports were purchased by Europe, the latter supplying around 45 per cent of the former's imports.[213] The outbreak of hostilities in September 1939 and resultant British blockade

207 Rivas, *Missionary Capitalist*, 37; Bulmer-Thomas, *Economic History*, 256; Hofman, *Economic Development*, 31.

208 Smith, *American Diplomacy*, 92–3.

209 These included the announcement of the demise of 'dollar diplomacy' and cessation of heavy-handed military intervention policies in Latin American affairs, increase of trade and commercial relations through bilateral reciprocal treaties, growing emphasis on multilateral cooperation and consultation on issues of inter-American concern, creation of a second Export-Import Bank, and commitment to industrial investment in Latin America: see EVK FitzGerald, 'ECLA and the Formation of Latin American Economic Doctrine' in David Rock (ed), *Latin America in the 1940s: War and Postwar Transitions* (University of California Press, 1994) 89, 91; Smith, *American Diplomacy*, 94–103; Rivas, *Missionary Capitalist*, 36–7; Rock, 'War and Postwar Intersections', 22–3; State Department, *Report of the Inter-Departmental Committee on Cooperation with the American Republics, Together with the Program of Cooperation Endorsed by the Committee* (10 November 1938), UNOG:OSG—S.562/12/3.

210 FitzGerald, 'ECLA', 91. See also Rivas, *Missionary Capitalist*, 36–7.

211 Rivas, 'US–LA Relations', 234; Rock, 'War and Postwar Intersections', 18–19.

212 Rock, 'War and Postwar Intersections', 15, 17, 22–4; Santos, 'Latin American Countries', 319; Stephen G Rabe, 'The Elusive Conference: United States Economic Relations with Latin America, 1945–1952' (1978) 2(3) *Diplomatic History* 279, 279–80.

213 Bulmer-Thomas, *Economic History*, 257.

and war economies devastated the former's access to its traditional markets and the demand for its commodities.[214] Moreover, three of the four main pre-war lenders of funds (i.e. Britain, France and Germany) 'ceased . . . to be significant net investors abroad' as foreign investment was sold off or became worthless due to, inter alia, destruction or expropriation.[215] Consequently, the United States, which had already become Latin America's largest total investor since the late 1920s,[216] was now 'more than ever the dominant investor'.[217] The Roosevelt Administration subsequently attempted to absorb commodities previously purchased by Europe in order to, firstly, prevent economic collapse in the region that would set in motion political destabilisation at a time when certain political groups were stirring for fascism and national socialism; secondly, reduce availability to enemy nations;[218] and thirdly, secure wartime alliances, especially for raw materials as its own sources of supply from outside the continent became disrupted.[219] Japan was threatening to control the Pacific, and a German conquest of Europe could have led to Latin American dependence on Germany if Europe were to be organised into an economic union.[220] The strengthening and expansion of inter-American economic relations was hence part of US national security, economic rehabilitation and long-term policy in the event of a victorious Germany.[221]

Many new initiatives and bodies were established to cultivate positive economic relations with Latin America, including the 1939 Pan American Union (PAU) Inter-American Financial and Economic Advisory Committee as an emergency agency,[222] the 1940 Inter-American Bank as a multilateral financial institution,[223] the 1940 PAU

[214] Ibid 255.

[215] Evan Luard, *The Management of the World Economy* (Macmillan Press, 1983) 37.

[216] Smith, *American Diplomacy*, 88.

[217] Luard, *Management*, 37.

[218] Nazi Germany, which now dominated Europe, was actively buying Latin American exports and investing in the region: Toussaint, *World Bank*, 12.

[219] Bulmer-Thomas, *Economic History*, 258–9; Gisela Cramer and Ursula Prutsch, 'Nelson A Rockefeller's Office of Inter-American Affairs (1940–1946) and Record Group 229' (2006) 86(4) *Hispanic American Historical Review* 785, 786; Rivas, 'US–LA Relations', 234; Smith, *American Diplomacy*, 101–3, 106–8; Rock, 'War and Postwar Intersections', 23–4; Rivas, *Missionary Capitalist*, 38–44.

[220] State Department, *Postwar Foreign Policy*, 30–2.

[221] Ibid 32–5.

[222] Pan American Union, *Report on the Meeting of the Ministers of Foreign Affairs of the American Republics, Panama, September 23–October 3, 1939* (1939) 6–7, 11–13, UNOG: OSG—S.562/12/3.

[223] Eugenio Díaz-Bonilla and María Victoria del Campo, *A Long and Winding Road: The Creation of the Inter-American Development Bank* (Lulu, 2010) 32–41.

Inter-American Development Commission as a venue for discussion of development projects and cooperation between the public and private sectors,[224] and the 1940 Office of the Coordinator of Inter-American Affairs (OCIAA).[225] The US Treasury had also organised a plan of cooperation enabling an official from the Brazilian Tax Bureau to make a survey of the US tax system in 1939 and 1940, and officials of the tax bureaus of Argentina and Peru to carry out similar studies following their attendance of the League's 1940 Mexico regional tax conference.[226]

With the bombing of Pearl Harbour in December 1941, the United States formally entered the war and began frenetically stockpiling strategic materials, mainly from Latin America, to preclude Axis purchasing and because Japanese occupation soon barred access to Asian markets.[227] The nation also stepped up its economic policies that would isolate the continent to protect it from Nazi aggression or penetration. In particular, at the Rio de Janeiro Meeting of Ministers of Foreign Affairs of the American Republics in January 1942 ('Rio Conference'), the US government, represented by Assistant Secretary of State Sumner Welles, made commitments to support the economic development of Latin America, with the foreign ministers agreeing on equitable allocations of basic and strategic materials; a feasibility study for the proposed Inter-American Bank; and the industrialisation of Latin American nations to raise standards of living and generate equitable and lasting trade and equal opportunities – goals which would be pursued even after the war.[228] Latin America was buoyed

[224] Rivas, 'US–LA Relations', 234 (noting that this Commission accomplished little in terms of actual projects).

[225] The OCIAA (originally named the Office for Coordination of Commercial and Cultural Relations between the American Republics) was designed to help stabilise the Latin American economies, secure and deepen US influence, and to combat Axis influence in the hemisphere, particularly in the commercial and cultural spheres. It executed its task through a comprehensive programme of 'forceful and well-coordinated policies' as well as 'thorough mobilization of the nation's resources' using various entities of government and the public and private sectors to operate in the fields of 'economic warfare, economic cooperation, transportation, health and sanitation, food supply, information and propaganda, and cultural and educational activities': Cramer and Prutsch, 'Nelson', 785–8, 791; Rivas, 'US–LA Relations', 234–5; Smith, *American Diplomacy*, 108–9.

[226] Letter from Reber to Loveday, 29 April 1941, UNOG:PO—C.1774/159/3-2.

[227] Rivas, *Missionary Capitalist*, 48–9; Rivas, 'US–LA Relations', 234.

[228] Rabe, 'Elusive Conference', 279. After Pearl Harbour, all Central American and Caribbean nations declared war against the Axis almost simultaneously while the more cautious Colombia, Mexico and Venezuela broke diplomatic relations. Consultation at the Rio Conference led to six South American nations severing relations with the Axis or maintaining technical neutrality but signifying their intention to cooperate with the United States: see Rivas, 'US–LA Relations', 232; Smith, *American Diplomacy*, 103–4.

by such pledges of US reward for its cooperation in the war effort.[229] Deperon's mission in Latin America coincided fortuitously with the invigorated hemispheric activity; he reported that:

> Double taxation and fiscal evasion are, however, the problems that now attract great interest and I may say that the mistrust which we feared about two years ago has now entirely disappeared. I think therefore that the next meeting should mainly deal with these two connected subjects. The preparatory work would be relatively small, though a number of new documents would have to be drafted and translated into Spanish.[230]

In his subsequent mission to Washington, Deperon reported that:

> The [Rio] conference had been a real success, he [the Colombian ambassador (Turbay)] told me, the countries of this Hemisphere have never been so united, the work contemplated as regards economic and juridical problems of continental organisation should prove useful. In Dr Turbay's view only the juridical problems should be regarded as post-war problems, and international economic organisation should be studied as a present problem as the war is to last a long time.[231]

New and favourable commercial treaties were signed, US loans (including for 'economic development') through the Export-Import Bank and Lend-Lease flowed[232] and the United States considered creating a hemisphere body (in contrast to a universal system).[233]

Latin America became an integral supplier of strategic materials for the Allies,[234] even 'cooperat[ing] in a major effort to provide alternative sources of supply [for commodities previously sourced from Asia]', and US public and private investments in the region soared in sectors that

229 Rivas, 'US–LA Relations', 234.

230 Letter from Deperon to Loveday, 18 December 1941, UNOG:PO—C.1643/27/4/1. At this stage, no Latin American country had yet expressed a position on double taxation, so Deperon's comment regarding minimal 'preparatory work' indicated an intention to rely on the work achieved by the League up to that point: see, for example, Letter from Deperon to Loveday, 7 January 1942, with attached note on 'Chile', UNOG:PO—C.1643/27/4/1 (in which Deperon contemplated 'the model convention of 1928 on that subject [fiscal evasion] should be resurrected, and brought up to date before being submitted to the meeting' ('Chile' note, 2)).

231 Deperon, 'Washington Mission', 1.

232 Smith, *American Diplomacy*, 106–8; Bulmer-Thomas, *Economic History*, 259; Rivas, *Missionary Capitalist*, 37–8.

233 Telegram by Loveday to Deperon, 25 March 1942, UNOG:PO—C.1645/29/19.

234 Rabe, 'Elusive Conference', 280 (quoting the Allied military officials as having agreed: 'Nobody knows how much we relied on the South American and Central American countries for commodities and things that we simply had to have').

produced or facilitated such exports, including the critical fields of transport and communications.[235] A similar pattern had occurred during World War I when the economic situation and industrial expansion of Latin America improved due to the demands of raw material exports from the continent; however, this development was not sustained as Western Europe and the United States discontinued their huge acquisitions in peacetime.[236] Once again, in the new world war, the Latin America economy became subordinated to that of the United States.[237] Although the region's share of world trade increased from 8 per cent in 1938 to 13 per cent in 1946, this was largely due to the collapse of European trade and growth in intra-region wartime commerce.[238]

On the other hand, while the United States had been a net debtor of capital flows during the 1930s, by 1939 it had reacquired its position as the lead actor in the world economy through armaments production and the safeguarding of strategic materials, activities of which would remain of central importance in the ensuing years.[239] Throughout the war, the US economy grew at an unprecedented rate with its productive capacity rising by 50 per cent and accounting for one-third of the world's exports but only one-tenth of imports.[240] Close inter-American cooperation was envisaged as long-term and inescapable as exploratory postwar proposals predicted a surge in scientific progress and industrial production that would require the United States to secure access to important raw materials, especially seeing that Britain and other European metropoles had such needs met from their colonies.[241] This led to calls to secure such supplies by investing in foreign countries where future reserves were available.[242] Reduced US foreign trade to other markets, especially Europe, also encouraged inter-American trade expansion on the grounds that the exports

[235] Bulmer-Thomas, *Economic History*, 259. See also Santos, 'Latin American Countries', 319. In 1943, US investment accounted for 31 per cent of total direct investment compared to 15 per cent in 1924. Despite the increase, however, this overall amount was still low compared to investments in other countries that held greater interest for the United States: Rosemary Thorp, 'The Latin American Economies in the 1940s' in David Rock (ed), *Latin America in the 1940s* (University of California Press, 1994) 41, 43.

[236] Bulmer-Thomas, *Economic History*, 167–74; Hofman, *Economic Development*, 21.

[237] Santos, 'Latin American Countries', 318; Smith, *American Diplomacy*, 114.

[238] FitzGerald, 'ECLA', 92.

[239] Thorp, 'Latin American Economies', 42–3.

[240] Ibid 43; Santos, 'Latin American Countries', 318.

[241] JB Condliffe, 'The Political Economy of Welfare', 25 August 1943, 21–3, UNOG:PO—C.1756/140/1-1.

[242] Ibid 23.

would help pay for Latin American imports.[243] Under Rockefeller's leadership, the OCIAA developed into one of the most high-profile agencies during the war, creating a newly emerging field of US foreign economic development aid to Latin American economies under the banner of hemispheric economic defence and helping to 'raise PanAmericanism to a fever pitch'.[244] Rockefeller used his influence to foster greater collaboration between the government and private sectors to facilitate capital flows to the region at a time when the 'ill-defined space' between the public and private sectors was 'significant' and 'overlapped more than at any earlier time in American history'.[245] The Rockefeller Foundation funding to the Princeton Mission was made flexible to accommodate activities that broadly fostered 'closer hemispheral [sic] relations'.[246]

The economic programme advocated by the OCIAA, nevertheless, was only partially successful as many congressmen opposed the lack of contribution of the development programmes to the emergency war effort.[247] Many of Latin America's economic requirements were unmet, and despite the wartime boom in the export of strategic materials and increased intercontinental activities, the region appeared headed towards a severe economic downturn due to the war-related disruptions to its international trade and capital flows: its terms of trade were deteriorating drastically, it faced shortages of imported manufactured products, its supply of strategic materials fuelled inflationary pressure and critically obstructed economic restructuring efforts, its capital technology required desperate repair but US exports of capital goods (e.g. machinery, transport equipment, spare parts) were obstructed, and there was little investment in sectors other than those producing strategic exports.[248] The

243 Stella K Margold, 'The National Foreign Trade Council Convention, 1939' (1939) 102(4) *World Affairs* 208, 210 ('NFTC Convention').

244 Rivas, *Missionary Capitalist*, 45, 51–2. See also Cramer and Prutsch, 'Nelson', 790–7. The League kept the OCIAA informed of its work, which included sending it the Spanish translation of the report of the 1943 conference: Letter from Waring to Deperon, 30 October 1943, UNOG:PO—C.1643/27/5.

245 Rivas, *Missionary Capitalist*, 3. See also Cramer and Prutsch, 'Nelson', 792, 805.

246 Memorandum by Loveday to Rosenborg and Deperon, 11 December 1940, UNOG:PO—C.1625/522/9/3. Before the Mission departed for Princeton, the Secretary-General advised that he tentatively had 'no objection to the acceptance of' any 'monetary grants [that might] ... be made by public-spirited bodies for the special purposes of your mission': Avenol letter, 30 July 1940, 2.

247 Rivas, *Missionary Capitalist*, 48–50, 53–4.

248 FitzGerald, 'ECLA', 91–2; Cramer and Prutsch, 'Nelson', 785, 792; Bulmer-Thomas, *Economic History*, 269; Rivas, *Missionary Capitalist*, 49; Smith, *American Diplomacy*, 108; Thorp, 'Latin American Economies', 46–8.

vulnerable commodity-exporting continent was thus principally concerned with economic cooperation and durable industrialisation at inter-American meetings.[249] The Mission noted the uneasy liaison and underlying tensions: the Latin American countries feared that the United States would cease its buying after the war when it no longer required their political and economic support, and that Europe might not be restored to the good buyer that it was previously.[250] They were also 'jealous of the loss of their natural resources . . . and, moreover, did not consider that these [US mining] companies had created adequate social conditions for their workers'.[251]

2.2.1.3 Latin America's Development Expectations in the Future World Economy

World War II was far more devastating than World War I in all respects, and efforts to avoid a recurrence of the economic chaos, errors and beggar-thy-neighbour policies of the interwar years began at an early stage.[252] In the context of the Atlantic Charter of August 1941, the United States, as the world's largest economy and greatest creditor nation, led and dictated discussions on the outlines of a new global economic order that would secure more lasting peace and prosperity.[253] The United States and the United Kingdom formed cooperative commitments under the Mutual Aid Agreement, which not only brokered the Lend-Lease agreements to help Britain and other Allied states finance the war against the Axis powers but also committed both countries to cooperating in postwar international economic affairs.[254] During 1941–3, US policymakers began to realise 'the necessity of the US assuming economic leadership' over Britain in postwar arrangements and that 'a return to

[249] Santos, 'Latin American Countries', 319; Rabe, 'Elusive Conference', 281.

[250] Deperon, 'LA Mission', 23.

[251] Memorandum by Loveday to Rosenborg, Deperon and Lutz, 22 February 1944, UNOG: PO—C.1648/32/1-1.

[252] Bulmer-Thomas, *Economic History*, 285; Michael Graff, AG Kenwood and AL Lougheed, *Growth of the International Economy, 1820–2015* (Routledge, 5th ed, 2014) 224 (see also 207–12 for an overview of the causes and events of the Great Depression).

[253] See Bulmer-Thomas, *Economic History*, 285–6; Joan E Spero and Jeffrey A Hart, *The Politics of International Economic Relations* (Routledge, 5th ed, 1997) 3–4. The economic policies in these developments 'showed a high degree of continuity' in '[t]he essential elements on which US economic foreign policy' had been based since the 1930s: State Department, *Postwar Foreign Policy*, 133.

[254] Graff, Kenwood and Lougheed, *Growth*, 224; WM Scammell, *The International Economy since 1945* (Macmillan Press, 2nd ed, 1983) 9–10.

strictly nationalistic economic policies should be prevented, as these could give rise to renewed militarism'.[255] US policy in particular was directed against the discriminatory imperial preference systems of the British Commonwealth and European empires,[256] and pursued an economic interdependence between states based on collective consultation and action.[257] Subsequent discussions between the two resulted in the US plan to set up international institutions under the control of member countries to supervise ideal conditions in financial, monetary and commercial relations,[258] guided by the principles of capitalism, liberalisation, multilateralism, non-discrimination and full employment.[259] By mid-1943, the United States began pressing forward in converting the wartime coalition into an international organisation to preserve postwar peace,[260] and in October, the United States, the United Kingdom, the USSR and China 'issue[d] a clear statement of resolve to create a general international organization'.[261] Proposals that had failed since World War I to encourage the reopening of channels of international trade were now revived and more favourably received.[262] The Mission itself embarked on

255 Reinalda, *International Organizations*, 276.

256 Robert Gilpin, *US Power and the Multinational Corporation: The Political Economy of Foreign Direct Investment* (Macmillan Press, 1975) 101–2; Alasdair Blair, *Britain and the World since 1945* (Routledge, 2015) 27.

257 See Luard, *Management*, 25–6; Thomas C Mills, 'British Industry and US–UK Economic Diplomacy during the Second World War' in John Fisher, Effie GH Pedaliu and Richard Smith (eds), *The Foreign Office, Commerce and British Foreign Policy in the Twentieth Century* (Palgrave Macmillan, 2016) 233, 233.

258 Graff, Kenwood and Lougheed, *Growth*, 224–9. Britain was by now 'crippled by the debt and war damage' and 'unable to win support for the radical ideas preferred by John Maynard Keynes', leaving the IMF and the World Bank clear reflections of 'US preferences and priorities', including being 'based in Washington to reflect the new global balance of power': Bulmer-Thomas, *Economic History*, 285–6.

259 Scammell, *International Economy*, 13–14; Luard, *Management*, xiii–xv. Note, however, that the liberalisation promoted by developed countries was highly selective, benefitting trade with each other but omitting (or upholding strong protectionist policies against) the areas vital to developing countries, such as in agricultural and manufactured exports. See also Hans W Singer and Javed A Ansari, *Rich and Poor Countries* (Allen & Unwin, 2nd ed, 1978) 98.

260 State Department, *Postwar Foreign Policy*, 163.

261 Inis L Claude Jr, *Swords into Plowshares: The Problems and Progress of International Organization* (Random House, 4th ed, 1971) 57.

262 See Henry F Grady, 'World Economics' in Harriet Eager Davis (ed), *Pioneers in World Order: An American Appraisal of the League of Nations* (Columbia University Press, 1944) 156, 167–8; Fritz Machlup, *A History of Thought on Economic Integration* (Macmillan Press, 1977) 8–9. See also Excerpt from ICC, *World Trade, Report to the British National Committee by a Sub-Committee on Post-War International Trade* (1944) [73], UNOG:PO—C.1756/140/1-1 (which listed double taxation as among the

an extensive programme of studies in international trade and commercial policies[263] and consulted for the State Department regarding plans for a future world organisation.[264] It also began to consider the League's future status among the proposed plans for a future international organisation and set about improving public education concerning the League's work to improve the likelihood of the continuance of the League's non-political sections and acceptance of the postwar policies that had been formulated.[265]

In the context of US hemispheric commitments and their solidarity and material contribution to the Allied war effort, Latin America nourished expectations that the new global interdependent economy would provide them with access to US markets, a programme of economic assistance and the chance to become less reliant on US capital.[266] Their assumptions seemed justified – the region had sold its commodities in a US price-controlled market during the war as a '$3 billion non-interest-bearing loan to the United States' and they expected to be rewarded.[267] The Mission's engagement of Latin America in discussions of postwar problems would have seemed to confirm to the region its certain place in future world affairs.[268] Such representations by the Mission, and the region's expectations, had some genuine reason for encouragement. In the League itself, views that supported the industrialisation of non-colonial, non-European developing countries as integral to world economic development had been circulated from 1939, stemming from recommendations for the reform of its economic and social work by the Special Committee on the Development of International Cooperation in Economic and Social Affairs.[269] This

'international sore points of long standing' that should be governed by an Economic Charter or code of good neighbour conduct).

263 Grady, 'World Economics', 168.

264 Archival documents dated between March 1943 and December 1944 concerning the Mission's involvement with and contribution to the State Department regarding plans for the new world organisation may be found in UNOG:PO—C.1633/529/17/3.

265 See various correspondences and preliminary reports in UNOG:PO—C.1756/140/1-1 and C.1756/140/1-3.

266 FitzGerald, 'ECLA', 90–1; Rabe, 'Elusive Conference', 281; Santos, 'Latin American Countries', 319.

267 Rabe, 'Elusive Conference', 284–5 (citing Laurence Duggan, Adviser of Political Relations, head of the Division of Latin American Affairs, State Department, during the war). See also Santos, 'Latin American Countries', 319.

268 See Sections 2.1.3 and 2.1.4.

269 Martin D Dubin, 'Towards the Bruce Report' in UN Library/Graduate Institute of International Studies, *The League of Nations in Retrospect: Proceedings of the Symposium* (Walter de Gruyter, 1983) 59, 63; FitzGerald, 'ECLA', 90–1.

dialogue was continued in various forms by the Mission during the war: for example, the Mission began inquiries into the needed industrialisation of underdeveloped countries and its repercussions on the trade of older industrial states;[270] developing countries such as Indonesia (then the Dutch East Indies), China and India were seen to have enhanced status in the new world order and were hence being considered for representation at 'a meeting of a reconstructed Economic Committee';[271] and exploratory proposals for the new UN strongly advocated a global economic system underpinned by welfare policies.[272] As early as 1942, in fact, the League had widely distributed among Allied and exile governments its report entitled *The Transition from War to Peace Economy* which advanced the groundbreaking post-war economic policy objective for the world to be unified towards the common goal of achieving and maintaining stable economies and rising living standards in all countries that global prosperity and security might best be served.[273] Such views and work of the Mission showed strong linkages to ideas generally being sponsored by Rockefeller or the Rockefeller Foundation.[274]

[270] This issue was thought to be important with 'the views held on it likely to have considerable political influence': Economic and Financial Committees, *Report to the Council on the Work of the 1943 Joint Session, Princeton, December 1943*, League Doc C.I. M.I.1944.II.A (February 1944) 12. See also Economic and Financial Committees, *Industrialization and Trade*, League Doc PEF/11 (December 1943); Grady, 'World Economics', 169.

[271] Letter from Grady to Sweetser, 12 November 1941, UNOG:PO—C.1630/526/14/2-1. Note that India at that time was the second largest financial contributor to the League after Britain: Clavin, *Reinvention of the League*, 273.

[272] Condliffe, 'Political Economy'; Letter from Hill to Gerig, 11 March 1943, 1, UNOG:PO—C.1633/529/17/3 (proposing that the 'World Economic Council' would supervise international agencies dealing with, inter alia, '[p]roblems of international investment, the development of backward areas, etc.').

[273] Clavin, *Reinvention of the League*, 285–6. This report, which showcased that the League's experts 'had come to place all societies of the world on a single continuum from the least to the most developed' in contrast to the prevailing Western view that perceived 'their own societies as distinct from those of Africa or Asia' (at 286), was circulated in draft form throughout 1942 before its publication in May 1943. It would become 'one of the most consulted and sought-after publications of the League' (at 285), be cited by the White House, the Departments of State, Commerce and Agriculture, as well as the NFTC in their own works, and have 'English and Spanish editions dispatched under a distribution list put together by the State Department' (at 289).

[274] See generally Tournès' 'Rockefeller Foundation' for a discussion on the Foundation's role in enabling the League 'to make major intellectual contribution to the reorganisation of the global economic order after 1945' (at 324) and in 'involv[ing] the United States in the LoN [League] system to the maximum degree possible' (at 323).

Through the OCIAA, Rockefeller worked 'to generate discussions of action to promote economic development' and, during his tour of the region in the autumn of 1942, he signed several agreements with various governments 'for health and sanitation and food supply programs', to the wariness of the State Department.[275] At the directive of Roosevelt in March 1943, who believed that US economic development assistance was in the US interest, the OCIAA produced a report arguing that the promotion of foreign living standards, particularly in Latin America, would not impair the United States' finances but would in fact stimulate its economic progress, prosperity and security by enhancing the purchasing power of other nations, thereby facilitating mutually beneficial trade which was a prerequisite for economic stability and peace.[276] From October 1943, Rockefeller urged the government to 'foster the creation of "a framework for stability" to encourage private capital to invest abroad', which included addressing 'minimum safeguards ... required to secure the maximum common benefit and the minimum of detrimental effect on ourselves and the aided countries'.[277] It appears no coincidence that the Mission in December 1943 began discussions on formulating 'some code of basic principles of a foreign investment policy' to address the legal and institutional deterrents to foreign capital, it being forecast that postwar demand for foreign capital would be great and necessary to promote economic progress,[278] but that private funds would only be channelled to countries which offered both security and adequate business opportunities.[279] Throughout 1944 and 1945, the Mission worked on drafting a report on conditions conducive to capital export and the acceptance of foreign capital which set out a code of conduct for economic and financial relations between borrower and lender countries to bring about a revival of private foreign

[275] Rivas, *Missionary Capitalist*, 58.

[276] Ibid 58–9. Note that this directive was also given to four other agencies (the Federal Trade Commission, Tariff Commission, State Department and Department of Commerce) which produced their own reports.

[277] Ibid 59–60.

[278] The future of international long-term investment was considered very 'problematical' because of 'the economic and political events of the thirties, which so damaged the framework of international credit as materially to reduce the prospects for international lending on anything like the scale that had prevailed previously': V Lutz, Draft Note on 'Outline of Discussion on Problems Connected with International Long-Term Investment after the War', undated (around January 1944), 1, UNOG:PO—C.1648/32/1-3.

[279] League Doc PEF/12, 1–2.

investment.[280] The preparatory work included informal consultative meetings in 1944 with experts from capital-exporting and borrowing countries, including Latin American countries,[281] and four months of investigative tours by Deperon in Canada, the United States and Latin America in the winter of 1944–5.[282] This report was eventually discussed by the Special Joint Committee convened between October and November 1945, which finalised its *PFI Conditions* report in December.[283]

In addition, the United Nations Monetary and Financial Conference ('Bretton Woods Conference') in July 1944, which birthed the IMF and the World Bank, 'explicitly recognis[ed] the necessity for Western capital assistance to such [developing] countries',[284] and the World Bank's second mission, after helping to rebuild Europe, was to provide capital to promote the economic growth of backward regions under the banner of 'development'.[285] Such objectives may have indirectly originated from the ideas supported by the Rockefeller and Carnegie Foundations, seeing that both fully backed movements for the IMF, World Bank and UN,[286] and given that American and British leaders generally had patronising attitudes towards underdeveloped nations.[287] The eighteen participating Latin and Caribbean nations represented almost half the participating countries at the conference but had little influence.[288] All joined both institutions (then dubbed the 'heavenly twins') as founding members, even though they wound up with just over 8 per cent of the votes collectively.[289] Together with the planned International Trade Organization (ITO) , this trio of intergovernmental institutions was to regulate balance of payments corrections, secure exchange rate stability,

[280] See documents in UNOG:PO—C.1648/32/1-3 and 1-4.
[281] 'Notes on Department Meeting Held on June 6, 1944', 1, UNOG:PO—C.1624/521/8/3.
[282] Alexander Loveday, 'Annual Report: Mr P Deperon (January 1-December 31, 1945)', 4 January 1946, UNOG:PO—C.1626/523/10/1; Economic and Financial Organization, *PFI Conditions*, 6.
[283] See Section 2.1.5 (regarding the report's recommendations concerning international tax measures). Records concerning these discussions and drafts of the report are contained in UNOG:PO—C.1648/32/1-4 and C.1649/33/4.
[284] Scammell, *International Economy*, 73. See also Rivas, *Missionary Capitalist*, 186.
[285] Toussaint, *World Bank*, 13–14.
[286] Parmar, *Foundations*, 57, 64, 93, 226.
[287] See Chapter 4, Section 4.3 n 187.
[288] Bulmer-Thomas, *Economic History*, 286; Claudia Kedar, *The International Monetary Fund and Latin America: The Argentine Puzzle in Context* (Temple University Press, 2013) 20.
[289] Toussaint, *World Bank*, 16.

promote international capital flows, eliminate trade barriers and stabilise primary commodity prices.[290] When trade discussions were deferred to a later conference, being of secondary importance to the United States, Latin America was not then 'unduly concerned' in its hopes for what the Bretton Woods twins purportedly offered.[291]

2.2.1.4 The Cooling of US Interest in Latin America: The Transitional Period from War to Peace (1944–1945)

From mid-1943, confidence of an Allied victory in Europe and Asia began to grow,[292] and by the end of the year, it was evident that the Allies would win the war.[293] During this time frame, the Latin Americanists in the State Department lost power and influence to the internationalists led by Secretary of State Cordell Hull,[294] and US attention correspondingly shifted towards postwar planning for devastated Europe and globalist views for postwar order.[295] Little policy effort was now directed to Latin America; in fact, 'US diplomats were ordered not to exchange ideas on postwar problems with Latin officials'.[296] Just one month after the D-Day landing in Normandy, the new international economic order began to materialise with the establishment of the IMF and the World Bank.[297] By September 1944, the United States was focused on international negotiations of the postwar economic policies it had been designing, and especially on the development of economic and social specialised agencies.[298] By the end of 1944, the inter-American economic conference that had been scheduled at the 1942 Rio Conference to take place in 1944 had been postponed twice.[299] Many Latin American governments began to suspect

[290] Graff, Kenwood and Lougheed, *Growth*, 225–9.

[291] Bulmer-Thomas, *Economic History*, 286.

[292] The Allies landed in Sicily in July 1943 and on the Italian mainland in September 1943: Graff, Kenwood and Lougheed, *Growth*, 219.

[293] Rivas, 'US–LA Relations', 235.

[294] Randall B Woods, 'Conflict or Community? The United States and Argentina's Admission to the United Nations' (1977) 46(3) *Pacific Historical Review* 361, 367–9; Roger R Trask, 'Spruille Braden versus George Messersmith: World War II, the Cold War, and Argentine Policy, 1945–1947' (1984) 26(1) *Journal of Interamerican Studies and World Affairs* 69, 70–2.

[295] Rivas, *Missionary Capitalist*, 63. See also State Department, *Postwar Foreign Policy*, 207–366.

[296] Rabe, 'Elusive Conference', 280.

[297] Bulmer-Thomas, *Economic History*, 285.

[298] State Department, *Postwar Foreign Policy*, 343, 353–6.

[299] Rabe, 'Elusive Conference', 280. See also Smith, *American Diplomacy*, 103 (noting that after Rio, the State Department 'discouraged any further Pan-American meetings for the

that inter-American cooperation would wane with the ending of the war, particularly as US meetings with the United Kingdom, the USSR and China increased regarding discussions on the new UN organisation.[300] As access to Asian supplies was restored, the United States not only decreased its purchases of primary materials from Latin America but also curbed its inter-American cooperative programmes channelling capital, goods and technical assistance to the region.[301] Even as the League made inquiries concerning its proposed *PFI Conditions* study in early 1944, expert opinion predicted that there would be little US investment in public utilities or the extractive industries in Latin America.[302] Any US help would likely be in the form of sale of machinery and technical assistance, and future foreign investment would mainly lie in the manufacturing industry for indigenous raw materials.[303]

In February–March 1945, tensions emerged at the Inter-American Conference on Problems of War and Peace in Chapultepec ('Chapultepec Conference'), when the United States announced its expectations and policies for world economic arrangements: reliance on private enterprise for economic development; the elimination of economic nationalism, protectionism and trade barriers; non-discrimination; and equitable treatment of foreign enterprise and capital.[304] The advice was little welcomed by the sceptical Latin Americans who, concerned about falling commodity prices and diminishing markets, desired assurances of long-term economic assistance for their industrial development, flexibility for state intervention to protect their infant industries, transfer of technology and continuation of high trade levels and fixed commodity prices.[305] However, Washington

duration of the war' as they 'were regarded as unnecessary and a diversion of diplomatic resources' while the US focused on Europe and Asia).

300 Rivas, *Missionary Capitalist*, 63–4; Smith, *American Diplomacy*, 112–13.

301 Bulmer-Thomas, *Economic History*, 276.

302 Loveday memo, 22 February 1944, 1.

303 Ibid.

304 Rivas, 'US–LA Relations', 235; RA Humphreys, *Latin America and the Second World War* (Athlone Press, 1982) vol 2: 1942–1945, 215–16; Thorp, 'Latin American Economies', 53. It is worth noting that key senior State Department officials responsible for postwar foreign economic policy themselves either came from giant multinational private enterprise or were major investors in Latin America: Gabriel Kolko, *Confronting the Third World: United States Foreign Policy, 1945–1980* (Pantheon Books, 1988) 37 (further quoting Assistant Secretary of State Spruille Baden who made clear in September 1946 that US loans to Latin America 'would only be for projects that "blaze the trail for private capital," especially in those nations that were not "exaggeratedly nationalistic"').

305 See also Rabe, 'Elusive Conference', 282. Many of Latin America's wartime industries in fact had little chance of survival without heavy protection: see DEA, Secretariat of the

refused commitments on aid or tariff preferences, and 'condemned Latin American proposals for development planning'.[306] The United States now regarded relations with the region as no longer 'vitally significant'[307] and considered the latter's economic woes as 'essentially internal rather than bound up with the international trade system'.[308] Latin America nevertheless held on to the United States' promises of ongoing economic support (including regarding commodity agreements, development loans and 'fair allocation of capital goods'),[309] and 'still widely assumed' that the United States would reinstitute the concessionary credits necessary for it to purchase US technology.[310] As their aspiration to participate on an equal juridical basis extended to the global stage and not just inter-American relations, they agreed to continue supporting US plans and preparations regarding the UN organisation based on US assurances of a major role for the inter-American system within the framework.[311]

Roosevelt's sudden death in April 1945 foreshadowed the end of the Good Neighbor Policy[312] and inter-American relations in the coming years would be plagued by, among other things, a lack of economic cooperation.[313] At the United Nations Conference on International Organization held between 25 April and 26 June at San Francisco ('San Francisco Conference'), the Latin American delegates fought doggedly, but unsuccessfully, to hold the United States to preserving the viability of the inter-American system within the UN organisation.[314] Expecting bitter confrontation to arise at any future inter-American economic conference, the United States postponed indefinitely the conference scheduled for the latter half of 1945.[315] After the end of the war, the

Economic Commission for Latin America, *Economic Survey of Latin America 1948* (UN, 1949).

306 FitzGerald, 'ECLA', 93.

307 Rabe, 'Elusive Conference', 279.

308 FitzGerald, 'ECLA', 93. See also Smith, *American Diplomacy*, 115.

309 Rabe, 'Elusive Conference', 282–3; Humphreys, *Latin America*, 216–17.

310 FitzGerald, 'ECLA', 93.

311 Smith, *American Diplomacy*, 113; Humphreys, *Latin America*, 213–15.

312 Amy Spellacy, 'Mapping the Metaphor of the Good Neighbor: Geography, Globalism, and Pan-Americanism during the 1940s' (2006) 47(2) *American Studies* 39, 59. It is worth noting that most scholars of American World War II policies have criticised the Roosevelt Administration for its lack of realistic long-term postwar plans: Warren F Kimball, 'Lend-Lease and the Open Door: The Temptation of British Opulence, 1937–1942' (1971) 86(2) *Political Science Quarterly* 232, 233.

313 Rabe, 'Elusive Conference', 283–94.

314 Rivas, *Missionary Capitalist*, 65; Humphreys, *Latin America*, 219–21.

315 Rabe, 'Elusive Conference', 283–91; Rivas, 'US–LA Relations', 238.

United States not only 'showed little economic favour to Latin America' but also facilitated its exploitation by private business by leveraging America's economic strength and the region's dependence on the US market to reduce prices of raw materials and primary products as well as taxes.[316]

2.2.2 Inter-American Activity over the Double Taxation Question

Prior to 1940, it is unclear whether many in the United States viewed double taxation as an issue of concern, although from 1934 the US government had begun to pursue more liberal policies, including tariff reductions and monetary stabilising agreements, to overcome discrimination against American exports.[317] Business interests, represented by the US Council of the ICC, naturally saw the subject as a serious burden and approached Carroll to help defend their cause in condemning its evils in political, scholarly and practitioner circles based on his positions in Treasury, the Fiscal Committee and various industry associations.[318] The mid-1930s saw a range of US positions on the subject: legislative amendments and court decisions that indirectly reduced the FTC,[319] a Democrat tax bill proposing to repeal the FTC,[320] and a trend by the US government towards active DTA negotiation starting with the US–France Treaty and the limited scope US–Canada Treaty (confined to investment income), both entering into force in 1936.[321] Between 1936 and 1937, certain government branches 'made considerable investigation on the subject of income tax conventions[,] . . . prompted by approaches made to the Department of State' from interested parties, including Britain and the Netherlands for a DTA as well as France and Canada for a new treaty that resolved

[316] Smith, *American Diplomacy*, 114. See also Kolko, *Confronting the Third World*, 37–8 (noting that the United States would 'both publicly and privately . . . unceasingly reiterate . . . the need to welcome US private investment on its own terms to develop the continent', emphasising that 'there would be no growth unless everything were to attract US corporations and freely allow them to make high profits with low tax rates').

[317] See Gilpin, *US Power*, 100–1.

[318] Carroll, *Global Perspectives*, 78–9.

[319] Mitchell B Carroll, 'International Double Taxation' (1938) 16(10) *The Tax Magazine* 588, 588–90, 608–10 ('IDT (1938)').

[320] Carroll, *Global Perspectives*, 78–9, 133. Carroll indicates that he played an instrumental role in defeating the bill and in restoring the entire FTC.

[321] Mitchell B Carroll, 'Developments in International Tax Law in 1937 – and Suggestions to Protect American Foreign Trade' (1938) 16(2) *The Tax Magazine* 75 ('1937 Developments').

'other outstanding questions'.[322] Secretary of State Hull, who was spearheading America's trade policy towards trade liberalisation,[323] became 'highly interested in exploring the use of double taxation conventions as one phase of his trade policies' and conferences were subsequently 'held between representatives of the Departments of State, Treasury and Commerce in order to debate the merits of a tax treaty program and to formulate American policy on the subject'.[324] By September 1937, the policy determined was to enter into DTAs 'on a large scale' using the 'the broad-scope formula . . . as opposed to the narrow, single-subject approach'.[325] The following month, King, as an Internal Revenue expert, went to Geneva to observe the League's Fiscal Committee meeting.[326]

Around this time, Carroll wrote in various publications that, through these treaties, the United States was helping to develop the new field of international tax law which was important to international trade in securing the position of American foreign enterprises by removing the trade impediments of discriminatory, extraterritorial and excessive taxation, and in assuring 'an equitable régime of taxation'.[327] He nevertheless also indicated that the general principle adopted in Europe for double taxation relief was for residence-country exemption from taxation of income arising in the source country, and that this system was competitively advantageous for American enterprises over the US FTC in promoting foreign trade and encouraging remittance of income.[328] He suggested that the US government would not lose much, if any, revenue

322 Richard E Titlow, 'International Double Taxation and the United States' (1968) 46(3) *Taxes – The Tax Magazine* 135, 138.

323 Susan Aaronson, 'How Cordell Hull and the Postwar Planners Designed a New Trade Policy' (1991) 20 *Business and Economic History* 171, 171.

324 Titlow, 'International Double Taxation', 138–9.

325 Ibid 139.

326 Ibid. King found 'the most immediate prospects' for comprehensive DTAs with Sweden, the Netherlands, Belgium, France and Canada, but the least with Britain and Switzerland. Although South Africa, Ireland and several Latin American countries had indicated interest in such treaties, the United States saw no urgency to approach them as they 'were of less commercial and tax interest'.

327 Mitchell B Carroll, 'The Development of International Tax Law: Franco-American Treaty on Double Taxation – Draft Convention on Allocation of Business Income' (1935) 29(4) *The American Journal of International Law* 586, 596–7; Carroll, '1937 Developments', 75.

328 Carroll, '1937 Developments', 78, 116, 118–19. Specifically, the 'liberal treatment' of exemption systems placed their nationals and corporations 'in a better position to undersell American exporters' (at 78). However, Carroll also noted that the US FTC had more advantages over certain other systems in the sense that relief was 'predicated

in adopting the exemption system as this would be offset by, firstly, the inflow of foreign income and resultant taxes stemming from the rise in exports and reduced unemployment, and, secondly, reduced administration costs of computing the FTC in conformity with restrictions imposed by statutory amendments and developments in case law.[329]

In 1938, the Section of International and Comparative Law of the American Bar Association (ABA) adopted a report by its Committee on International Double Taxation (of which Carroll was Chairman), which took the view that the exemption system of 'numerous foreign countries' was more generous and encouraging to the foreign trade of their enterprises than the FTC.[330] Around this time, Carroll was also serving as Special Counsel for the Tax Committee of the NFTC.[331] Between 1938 and 1939, the ABA and NFTC adopted resolutions that held double taxation relief as an integral part of the government's programme for encouraging foreign trade and helping American enterprise to compete in foreign markets; accordingly the FTC should be relieved of any encroachments or indirect limitations, and DTAs should supplement US trade agreements.[332] Carroll also prepared a speech advocating DTAs for use by the US representative on the PAU Inter-American Financial and Economic Advisory Committee.[333]

At the start of the Mission, there appeared to be little knowledge concerning the Fiscal Committee in tax circles, which was attributed to poor publicity of the League's work.[334] Deperon, Carroll and even Loveday set about growing the League's contacts and networks among individuals and various organisations dealing in taxation and promoting the League's fiscal work in the United States through publications,

upon a world market for American products, and our exporters receive equal treatment regardless of the foreign country in which they sell their goods' (at 118–19).

329 Ibid 119. See also Carroll, 'IDT (1938)', 588–90, 608–10; Mitchell B Carroll, 'Postwar International Organization and the Work of the Section of International and Comparative Law of the American Bar Association' (1945) 39(1) *The American Journal of International Law* 20, 31.

330 See Carroll, 'IDT (1938)', 588.

331 Carroll, *Global Perspectives*, 79. Carroll still held this position in December 1943: see Carroll, 'Tax Trends', 5.

332 Carroll, 'IDT (1938)', 610; Margold, 'NFTC Convention', 209.

333 Mitchell B Carroll, 'Preliminary and Provisional Memorandum for the Use of the US Representative on the Inter-American Economic and Financial Advisory Committee: Encouragement of Inter-American Trade through Removal of Tax Obstructions', 9 November 1939, UNOG:PO—C.1646/30/6-4.

334 Deperon, 'Report on Attendance', 2, 4; Letter from Walker to Loveday, 27 November 1940, UNOG:PO—C.1774/159/3-1.

conferences and private sector meetings,[335] as well as in Latin America through publications,[336] bar associations, local Chambers of Commerce and sections of the ICC.[337] The ICC was accredited as being 'outstanding in the help ... [it] extended' by '[carrying] on a most useful form of propaganda in favour of the Committee's recommendations in respect to the prevention of double taxation'.[338] The League particularly sought to

335 Deperon and Carroll's efforts were also publicly supported by King, Charles R Carroll (Chairman of the NFTC Law Committee; unknown if related to MB Carroll) and Henry Fernald (vice-chairman of the ICC Fiscal Commission). See Deperon, 'Report on Attendance'; Letters from Carroll to Loveday, 27 November and 4 December 1940, UNOG:PO—C.1774/159/3-1; Letter from Carroll to Loveday, 26 September 1941, UNOG:PO—C.1645/29/20; Letter from Deperon to Manning, 1 November 1943, UNOG:PO—C.1643/27/5; Letter from Carroll to Deperon, 15 June 1944, with attached Mitchell B Carroll, 'Outline of Post-War Programs on Prevention of Double Taxation' (Speech, National Association for Manufacturers (NAM), document dated 5 June 1944) UNOG:PO—C.1646/30/1. It is worth pointing out that the Mission's promotional efforts owed much to Carroll's connections with business organisations, such as the ICC, NFTC and NAM. Carroll had long had association with the ICC: Carroll's survey for the League's *Taxation of Foreign and National Enterprises* volumes was credited as having been carried out with the close collaboration of the ICC (George L Ridgeway, *Merchants of Peace: Twenty Years of Business Diplomacy through the International Chamber of Commerce, 1919–1938* (Columbia University Press, 1938) 283); and Carroll had helped the ICC defeat the Democrat tax bill to repeal the FTC in the mid-1930s, and had also been part of the ICC's Tax Committee from the late 1930s (Carroll, *Global Perspectives*, 78–9). Also, Deperon's *International Double Taxation* pamphlet published in 1945 by CEIP originated at the suggestion of the ICC's Advisory Council to CEIP to publicise the League's double taxation work: Letter from Condliffe to Loveday, 6 December 1943, UNOG:PO—C.1774/159/3-3. For CEIP's linkages with the ICC, NAM, the NFTC and the US Chamber of Commerce , see Parmar, *Foundations*, 51 (indicating the role a CEIP trustee had in these organisations). Regarding Carroll's association with NAM, see Chapter 4, Section 4.2.3; see also 'Note on National Association of Manufacturers', undated, UNARMS:AG-025-002—S-0441-0051-09 (stating that NAM was founded for the general purpose of promoting US industrial interests and fostering US domestic and foreign commerce, and had close ties with the US Chamber of Commerce, the NFTC and the American Section of the ICC).

336 The League saw 'Spanish blurbs and periodic bulletins giving information concerning recent and future publications' as bringing about an 'improvement which may have a propaganda value even though it is not immediately translated in an increase in sales [of League publications]': Deperon, 'LA Mission', 10–12. See also Letter from Deperon to Jimenez, 16 April 1941, UNOG:PO—C.1644/28/1; Letters by Deperon to Carroll, 18 February 1941, 21 April and 30 April 1942; Letter from Martinez Sáenz to Carroll, 8 April 1942, UNOG:PO—C.1643/27/5.

337 In giving a speech to IABA in Havana on DTAs, Deperon asked Carroll to make 'suggestions in personal conversations' concerning the creation of 'ad hoc committees or study groups within' such private groups: Deperon letter, 18 February 1941; Letter from Carroll to Deperon, 14 February 1941, UNOG:PO—C.1643/27/5.

338 Deperon, 'Note on the Fiscal Committee', 1–2. This connection contradicts the general opinion that 'the League [in its latter years] appeared to withdraw from collaboration

bring about movement from the private sphere as this was 'most desirable ... even if at the start it ... [was] not very efficient'.[339] Hambro himself instructed the Mission to give 'full publicity ... to the [1943 Mexico] meeting, though it is realized that the problems to be dealt with have little appeal for the general public'.[340]

Double taxation was presented as a form of protectionist impediment to trade and the opening of commercial establishments.[341] To the US audience, the 1940 Mexico Draft was promoted, firstly, as being integral to the removal of barriers to commercial relations and greater economic solidarity with Latin America,[342] and, secondly, as promising a future network of bilateral treaties within the Americas replicating that which had occurred in Europe after World War I to revive flows of capital, trade and commerce.[343] Carroll and Deperon projected that DTAs would generally be concluded on an even wider scale after World War II as they would not only deal with high national debts and accompanying high tax rates,[344] but also provide certainty to commercial intercourse through uniform basic principles of law 'applied practically throughout the hemisphere'.[345] This prediction appeared confirmed by the invigorated US interest in DTAs: by early March 1942, the United States had concluded DTAs with Sweden (1939), France (1939) and Canada (1942). The League promoted its work as being integral to this movement in improving and completing model conventions, and in creating opportunities for tax administrators to establish personal contacts through its meetings, as had proven fruitful in Europe.[346] Through the NFTC, Carroll also sought, inter alia, to have the Internal Revenue Code

and cooperation with NGOs, including the ICC' (Pei-heng Chiang, *Non-Governmental Organizations at the United Nations: Identity, Role, and Function* (Praeger, 1981) 38).

339 Deperon letter, 18 February 1941. Private action was petitioned on the basis that the League's efforts in fostering DTAs in the Western Hemisphere were 'not self-propelling, but need[ed] the active support and encouragement of the enterprises that are to be benefited': Carroll, 'Outline of Post-War Programs' speech, 9.

340 Deperon memo, 19 March 1943, 1.

341 Deperon, 'Work of the League' speech, 2; Carroll, 'History of Movement' speech, 16; Carroll, 'Removal of Tax Barriers', 616–17. See also, Carroll, 'Postwar International Organization', 31–2.

342 Carroll, 'Removal of Tax Barriers', 617; Carroll, 'History of Movement' speech, 16.

343 Deperon, 'Work of the League' speech, 2; Carroll, 'Future Work', 1–2. See also Carroll, 'ITL in Americas', 800–1.

344 Deperon, 'Work of the League' speech, 1–2; Economic, Financial and Transit Department, *Future International Economic Organisation*, League Doc H.S.10 (December 1944) 12, UNOG:PO—C.1623/520/7/11.

345 Carroll, 'ITL in Americas', 801.

346 Deperon, 'Report on Attendance', 2.

amended so that the reduced withholding rate on dividends, interest and certain other income allowed to contiguous countries (e.g. Mexico, Canada) could be extended to the other countries of the Western Hemisphere by treaty, and that credit would be allowed for foreign taxes paid in lieu of income taxes and foreign taxes deducted at source.[347]

Knowledge of double taxation spread. In 1940, a group of ABA's Section on International and Comparative Law members participated in the organisation of the Inter-American Bar Association (IABA).[348] Carroll became a member of the IABA Committee on Taxation and was a delegate to the subsequent IABA conferences in which double taxation was raised.[349] Deperon also contributed significantly to this Committee's output[350] and IABA conferences were used to spread 'good propaganda' for the Fiscal Committee[351] and to establish contacts with Latin American lawyers.[352] At the opening congress of the first IABA conference in Havana in March 1941, Carroll presented a talk which was primarily aimed at 'acquaint[ing] Latin Americans with what has been done in the field of treaties to prevent double taxation and to help prepare the way for the negotiation of treaties between the United States and the leading Latin American countries'.[353] This led to the creation of

347 Mitchell B Carroll, 'Amendments to the Internal Revenue Code' proposed on behalf of the NFTC, 1941; 'Statement of Mr Mitchell B. Carroll' on behalf of the NFTC, Presented to the Ways and Means Committee of the House of Representatives at hearings on revenue proposals on 1 May 1941, undated, UNOG:PO—C.1646/30/6–4.

348 Carroll, 'Postwar International Organization', 34. IABA was founded by a group of lawyers and jurists representing forty-four professional organisations and seventeen nations in the Western Hemisphere. It held conferences every eighteen months to, inter alia, promote uniformity of laws, and issued resolutions on what were considered urgent matters of legal interest within the Americas: 'The Inter-American Bar Association: Resolutions of the XXX Conference' (1993) 25(1) *The University of Miami Inter-American Law Review* 161, 161. The ABA continued relations with IABA through the former's Committee on Cooperation and Carroll's connection to the two organisations.

349 Carroll, 'Tax Inducements', 760.

350 See, for example, n 358.

351 Letters from Carroll to Deperon, 22 April 1942 and 10 June 1941, UNOG:PO—C.1643/27/5.

352 Letter from Deperon to Carroll, 28 June 1943, UNOG:PO—C.1645/29/2.

353 Carroll letter, 14 February 1941, UNOG:PO—C.1643/27/5. Deperon, in providing comments on Carroll's draft for his talk, suggested that Carroll inject 'some economical argumentation', which included that the growth of manufacturers in Latin America was normally 'expected to lead to an increased trade not only between those countries of that continent with one another, but also with other countries'; that 'practices placing an excessive tax burden on foreign capital or investments should be discontinued or avoided' for their 'negative' effect; that 'private borrowing of foreign capital and establishment of

a committee to study instances of double, extraterritorial and discriminatory taxation between the Western Hemisphere countries and to help promote the conclusion of treaties to eliminate such tax obstacles to inter-American trade.[354] At the second IABA conference in Rio de Janeiro in August 1943, this Committee on Taxation reportedly 'reviewed' the work of the 1943 Mexico meeting[355] and issued its first resolution, which, inter alia, recommended the study of means of achieving uniformity in income tax legislation across the various countries with a view to avoiding double and extraterritorial taxation.[356] In a trade publication, Carroll wrote that this IABA resolution gave '[i]mpetus ... to the conclusion of [DTAs]', adding that it would 'indeed be fortunate if the treaty movement ... [could] be supplemented by ... amending internal legislation ... to ... provide uniform territorial limits on fiscal jurisdiction over foreign enterprises and investors'.[357] At its third conference in August 1944, IABA adopted the Resolution on International Tax Problems (Resolution I) by its Committee on Taxation which recommended that governments of the Western Continent, through treaties or internal regulations, 'adopt measures for the equitable treatment of taxpayers' to prevent double, discriminatory and extraterritorial taxation, pursuant to the principles embodied in the Fiscal Committee's recommendations at the 1943 Mexico conference (a summary of which was provided).[358]

The importance of DTAs to inter-American trade and investment was also recognised at the Conference of Commissions of Inter-American Development[359] held in May 1944, New York, which recommended the

branches of foreign enterprises should be encouraged to speed up ... industrial development'; and that export duties should be discouraged as they were often 'likely to be paid chiefly by the exporting country itself': Deperon letter, 18 February 1941, 2.

354 Carroll, 'ITL in Americas', 801.

355 Carroll, 'Tax Trends', 14.

356 Carroll, 'Future Work', 3.

357 Carroll, 'Tax Trends', 14.

358 This resolution had been drafted by Deperon and sent by Carroll to the Mexican delegate to present to the IABA Tax Committee with Carroll stating 'it would be most appropriate for you [Alfonso Cortina], as a Mexican, to offer it': Letter from Carroll to Cortina, 18 July 1944, UNOG:PO—C.1643/27/5. Carroll noted to Loveday that '[i]n any case, Deperon should be congratulated for his clear statement of the principles underlying the draft conventions formulated by the Fiscal Committee': Letter from Carroll to Loveday, 17 August 1945, UNOG:PO—C.1774/159/3-3.

359 This was a system of twenty-one national commissions coordinated and directed by the PAU Inter-American Development Commission: 'The Inter-American Economic and Social Council' (1946) 80(1) *Bulletin of the Pan American Union* 12, 14.

Western Hemisphere governments 'consult and collaborate in the negotiation of bilateral treaties for the elimination of double taxation of income and capital, including extraterritorial and discriminatory taxation, and for the exchange of information between the governments concerned'.[360] Around this time, Carroll began appealing to private enterprises on the need to remove 'unnecessary tax obstructions' to assist in postwar reconstruction.[361] In particular, he projected that the reduced purchasing power of nations, especially throughout Europe, would force costs of goods to be kept at rock-bottom prices even though demand would be vast. Any profits realised would have narrow margins, and should these be 'consumed by taxes, there . . . [would] be little incentive to rehabilitate or expand existing enterprises or to launch new ones', thereby making it difficult to attract investment, especially from foreigners, when the need for new capital to facilitate 'the conversion from war to peace-time production' was 'enormous'.[362] The League advised the necessity of keeping tax rates to a minimum 'on the yield of such capital and on the profits themselves', restricting 'taxes to a territorial basis' and preventing double taxation.[363]

2.3 Commentary

The dynamic correlation between the success of the League's fiscal activities in the Americas and conducive US foreign policies concerning free trade and inter-American interdependence, the burst of corporate liberalism[364] and the quasi-political efforts of the Mission (and Carroll) provide a richer understanding of the actual propelling forces that begot the Mexico Model. Latin America's receptivity towards DTAs was palpably tied to the highpoint of Pan-Americanism, ceasing once US commitments and goodwill to the region waned, despite ongoing US attempts to conclude such treaties.[365] Of course, the downgraded US priorities towards its southern neighbours presumably also affected its willingness to negotiate terms based on the pro-source country

[360] Carroll, 'Postwar International Organization', 32.

[361] Carroll, 'Outline of Post-War Programs' speech, 3.

[362] Ibid 2–3.

[363] Ibid 3.

[364] See Kim McQuaid, 'Corporate Liberalism in the American Business Community, 1920–1940' (1978) 52(3) *Business History Review* 342, 364–6 (explaining the permeation of big business into government positions to staff specialised war agencies which gave them extreme influence in wartime policies, including taxation).

[365] See, for example, Chapter 7, Section 7.5; Chapter 8, Section 8.3; Chapter 9, Section 9.4.

concessions agreed to at Mexico. There is some suggestion that the Mission was aware of these shifts in inter-American relations in view of the more traditional allocation positions for business income adopted in the *PFI Conditions* report. Certainly, by the time of the London meeting, there was no consideration given to inviting Latin American countries purely on the grounds of their importance to trade relations.

The activities and events of the Princeton years provide invaluable insights into the drivers of early international tax coordination between developed and developing countries. They demonstrate the importance of understanding the impact of broader political, economic, business and even institutional forces in creating conducive conditions for international tax coordination. They show that politics were an inherent, although largely hidden, feature of the progress of the international tax work and that the League Secretariat recognised the importance of approaching double taxation not just as a purely technical problem. They reveal the crucial role that a few key people with vested interests (in particular Deperon, who had a strong incentive to preserve the League's continuity, and Carroll, who primarily represented the private business community) played in advancing the double taxation work, especially to nations that had little interest or need to address the subject. The Mission's efforts, in this regard, have never been revealed in the literature, and there is some question as to whether it acted beyond its mandate by engaging in political and propaganda activities, urging treaty negotiations between governments,[366] sidestepping procedural formalities and collaborating with the US government as well as with US business interests. This is particularly so in view of, firstly, the fact that League was ostensibly 'not an institution with an existence separate from . . . the totality of States which are its Members',[367] and, secondly, the 'ambiguous and complex'[368] character of inter-American relations, shaped by intense co-dependence, mistrust and uncertainty concerning the future world economy and security.

The League's wartime engagement of developing countries into its double taxation work stands in stark contrast to the situation applying to the League in 1921 and the OEEC in 1954 when the ICC formally petitioned these Eurocentric organisations to take up the study of double taxation. In the two latter instances, DTAs had been multilaterally

366 In theory at least, negotiation was 'no business of the Secretariat': JW Wilson, 'Problems of an International Secretariat', 9 December 1944, 3, UNOG:PO—C.1756/140/1(2).

367 See League of Nations, *Ten Years of World Co-Operation* (1930) 401.

368 Rivas, *Missionary Capitalist*, 4.

encouraged after the world wars at a time of rising tax rates and the spread of income taxes as a solution for restoring interrupted trade between countries with similar stages of development and a strong history of reciprocal trade relations. Conversely, in the former instance, DTAs were unilaterally promoted to Latin American countries during World War II as a way of stimulating US investment for their development when they had a history of inconsistent, nonreciprocal and even exploitative trade relations with the United States, when their economies and tax systems were so relatively underdeveloped that equality of sacrifice was unachievable, and when their wartime economies were virtually subordinated to that of the United States. External expert consultants were not engaged to study the specific double taxation problems or the tax systems and laws of the American countries in the way that the four economists first studied the double taxation problem in 1923. As was evident at the London meeting, the Western countries (several of them colonial metropoles) certainly did not have the development of Latin America, or any developing country for that matter, on their list of priorities. The Mexico Model (i.e. the so-called first model convention to consider the concerns of developing countries) was thus a highly crisis-related, regional solution forged in the abnormal conditions of World War II, and the impetus behind it was not sustainable once interregional dependence diminished with the reopening of global markets.

While a strong case arguably exists to separate the Mexico Model, perhaps even the London Model, from the pre-World War II work of the Fiscal Committee in view of the League's questionable conduct and operations, it is worth noting that the League's zeal to facilitate DTAs between developed and developing countries appears more premature and naïve than scheming. There was scant knowledge then of developing countries' economies,[369] of the role of taxation in developing economies[370] and even of concepts of economic development.[371] The

369 No reliable statistics concerning rates of growth or standards of living for most developing countries exist prior to World War II: Luard, *Management*, 11.

370 Literature filling this gap started with Bird and Oldman's volumes on *Readings on Taxation in Developing Countries*, first edition published in 1964, and subsequent revisions in 1967, 1975 and 1990: see Richard M Bird and Oliver Oldman, *Taxation in Developing Countries* (Johns Hopkins University Press, 4th ed, 1990) preface.

371 Economic development at this stage was primarily conceptualised in terms of quantitative economic growth and 'even greater vagueness' surrounded the process to achieve it: Scammell, *International Economy*, 72. Contemporary studies were exceedingly rare, and even the first generation of development models formulated in the early post–World

Mission envisaged that tax law uniformity was attainable, and that Western Hemisphere economic regionalism might be permanent. Carroll himself contemplated that the European countries might find the Mexico Model applicable for DTA negotiations with Latin America, Asia and Africa.[372] Moreover, the ideas and proposals prevalent in the United States, which espoused the free market, privatisation and export expansion (and which the private foundations were involved in promoting), were based on a belief, even if self-serving, in a significant and predominant role for private enterprise in economic development, especially in view of the knowledge that the United States would be the only country in a position to provide FDI immediately following the war.[373]

While no US–Latin American DTAs ensued from the League's wartime international tax coordination in the Americas, these efforts were not without consequence. As will be seen in the forthcoming chapters, the introduction of double taxation problems and solutions to Latin America as a component of economic development in attracting FDI laid the groundwork for pro-source positions that the region would hold fast to during the Fiscal Commission years. In addition, the publication of the Mexico and London Models as the work of the Fiscal Committee would lead to their use by developed countries to indicate the widespread acceptance of certain principles to the detriment of developing countries.

War II years were focused only on massive capital injections as the sole panacea for underdevelopment: Giang Dang and Low Sui Pheng, *Infrastructure Investments in Developing Economies: The Case of Vietnam* (Springer, 2015) 16, 22; Richard Jolly, Louis Emmerij and Dharam Ghai, *UN Contributions to Development Thinking and Practice* (Indiana University Press, 2004) 50–1. See also Chapter 1, Section 1.3.1 (regarding early theories of economic development).

372 See Section 2.1.5.

373 See Rivas, *Missionary Capitalist*, 60–1; Parmar, *Foundations*, 97–8.

3

Creation of the Fiscal Commission (1943–1946)

This chapter narrates how the Fiscal Commission was brought into existence from the time of its planning by the Princeton Mission through to its establishment by ECOSOC. It reveals the movers behind the Commission's creation, its intended blueprint and the key changes wrought that would make it fundamentally different from its League predecessor. It also situates the Commission's role and place within the newly fashioned world order of institutions and highlights the cross-purposes of the Commission's designers and various UN member states for the Commission's work and priorities.

3.1 Princeton (March 1943–May 1945)

As early as March 1943, the Mission began planning for the Fiscal Committee's postwar continuance in the context of exploratory discussions with the State Department for a world economic authority.[1] By March 1944, initial proposals projected that the existence of the Committee would be necessary to deal with two classes of tax questions (i.e. double taxation and fiscal systems).[2] The proposals envisaged a Committee structured like that of the Fiscal Committee in its heyday, namely: comprising mainly, if not wholly, of senior fiscal officials to facilitate successful inter-administrative cooperation; involving up to two international tax lawyers 'familiar with the difficulties as they present themselves to their business clients'; and having corresponding

[1] Letter from Hill to Gerig, 11 March 1943, UNOG:PO—C.1633/529/17/3 (proposing that the 'World Economic Council' would have the scope to deal with, inter alia, 'double taxation, fiscal evasion and other fiscal problems').

[2] A Loveday, 'Future International Economic Organization', March 1944, 12, UNOG:PO—C.1755/139/2-4. This was rationalised on the prediction that universal increase in taxes would require DTAs to be concluded on a much wider scale than before for international business to revive, and that many national fiscal systems would have to be reorganised to manage high rates and inflation.

members in all countries who would keep their governments informed of developments and attend any special meetings they were invited to.[3] However, the proposals also envisaged a larger role for the Committee to deal with a range of fiscal and interrelated subjects[4] and to have power, like the League's Economic Committee, to appoint ad hoc committees.

In late 1944, Deperon advised Loveday to advocate that the future Committee be given 'a somewhat broader mandate' that encompassed giving advice and technical assistance to the future ECOSOC and to governments 'on all matters presenting taxation', and conducting research and publishing information on such matters 'for the benefit of public authorities'.[5] The Committee was to comprise some fifteen to twenty national members to ensure continuity in the work and rotation, and could appoint up to three corresponding members in all countries (including non-sovereign territories with autonomous tax administrations). It was to have plenary meetings everyone to two years, but in the interval hold, when required, special regional or technical meetings to which members and correspondents would be invited. When not in session, the Committee would have 'a standing bureau composed of the chairman, a member and the secretary, which would convene meetings and take all necessary measures in connection with the work'.[6] In December 1944, discussions within the Mission considered it of 'essential importance' for the Mission to 'expand and intensify' its work and to establish 'direct and close contacts' with France, Belgium and Holland in order to secure a place at the UN.[7]

In February–March 1945, at the Chapultepec Conference, Deperon, at Loveday's instruction, circulated confidential documents concerning the economic organisation of the future international body and its intended

[3] Ibid 12–13.

[4] Double taxation was considered as just 'one of many administrative and legal obstructions to the international movement of capital', others of which included the status of foreigners and foreign corporations, shareholders and creditors; the right to participate in local enterprises; concessions; legal requirements to company organisation; etc.: Ibid 12.

[5] Letter from Deperon to Loveday, 13 November 1944, 1–2, UNOG:PO—C.1643/27/5.

[6] Ibid 2.

[7] Memorandum by KN to Loveday, 5 December 1944, UNOG:PO—C.1633/529/17/4–1. It was advised that the Mission 'get credit for the documents it prepared' and that the 'most efficient, if not the only, way' to establish contact with governments was through visits to, inter alia, outline the League's past and current work, obtain information on factual conditions and policies, gather ideas for future work, and ascertain tendencies regarding the UN.

continuation of the League's economic and financial work.[8] In the months that followed, Deperon sent copies of his *International Double Taxation* pamphlet[9] and a paper entitled 'Model Bilateral Conventions for the Prevention of International Double Taxation and Fiscal Evasion' to Latin American embassies[10] and to managers of bank branches in Latin American capitals on the basis that these officials were 'generally quite active in their local American or British Chambers of Commerce'.[11]

3.2 The Preparatory Commission and Its Executive Committee (September–December 1945)

When the UN Charter was signed at the San Francisco Conference in June 1945, the Preparatory Commission and its Executive Committee were entrusted to draw up detailed plans for the working of the new organisation, pending sufficient ratifications to bring the Charter into force. The Preparatory Commission comprised a representative from each of the fifty-one Charter signatories, while its Executive Committee comprised representatives from the fourteen governments which had been on the Executive Committee of the San Francisco Conference. These deliberations took place in London with the Executive Committee effectively completing its work in seven weeks before submitting its report[12] in November to the Preparatory Commission, which in turn completed its review in four weeks before issuing its report on 23 December.[13] The work was rushed[14] as the United States hastened to establish the UN.[15] Importantly, in these deliberations, the USSR rejected the general transfer of the League to the UN, accepting instead

[8] Paul Deperon, Note on 'Action Taken at the Inter-American Conference on Problems of War and Peace, Mexico, February 21–March 8, 1945', undated, UNOG:PO—C.1647/31/7. The League originally 'had been intentionally left out' of the conference but as Deperon was coincidentally in Mexico on his investigative tour for the *PFI Conditions* study, he managed to procure an invitation through his contacts with Mexican officials.

[9] See Chapter 2, Section 2.1.6 n 185 and Section 2.2.2 n 335 for details about this publication.

[10] Letter from Deperon to Chavez, 30 May 1945, UNOG:PO—C.1774/159/3-4.

[11] Letter from Deperon to Gullick, 12 May 1945, UNOG:PO—C.1774/159/3-4.

[12] Preparatory Commission of the United Nations, *Report by the Executive Committee to the Preparatory Commission*, UN Doc PC/EX/113/Rev.1 (12 November 1945).

[13] Preparatory Commission of the United Nations, *Report of the Preparatory Committee*, UN Doc PC/20 (23 December 1945).

[14] PC/EX/113/Rev.1, 51.

[15] See Chapter 4, Section 4.1.2.

a piecemeal transfer.[16] Accordingly, each piece of work or department had to be separately considered to determine which assets and non-political functions and activities would be transferred, and the question of the transfer of staff was now in limbo.[17] While the Executive Committee deliberated, Carroll continued to promote the Mexico Model at IABA's Fourth Conference held in Santiago, Chile, in October 1945, for the purpose of showing 'the continued usefulness of the work of the Fiscal Committee'.[18]

The Executive Committee's paramount consideration in designing ECOSOC's subordinate machinery was to avoid duplication of work with the existing or contemplated specialised agencies, which had ambulatory purposes and virtually 'complete freedom of action with respect to their operations'.[19] Accordingly, in the economic sphere, the Executive Committee 'necessarily somewhat arbitrar[il]y' assigned monetary cooperation, international investment, trade, food and agriculture and international aviation to the IMF, World Bank, Food and Agriculture Organization (FAO), ICAO and ITO.[20] In determining the ECOSOC commissions to be prioritised for establishment, the Executive Committee considered the postwar problems that required immediate attention and the continuation of the League's functions and activities.[21] Among the delegations supporting the creation of the Fiscal Commission, Britain[22] and Australia[23] made similar submissions, proposing that, in addition to continuing the League's work, it should have a broader mandate that included functioning as an international clearing house of information on the techniques of government finance (e.g. taxation, forced saving, subsidisation and borrowing and their effects on income distribution and production incentives), and fiscal techniques to offset depressions and controlling inflation. However, as support for

16 Letters by Loveday to Rosenborg, 5 and 16 October 1945, UNOG:PO—C.1633/529/17/4-1.

17 Loveday letter, 5 October 1945.

18 Letter from Carroll to Loveday, 17 August 1945; Mitchell B Carroll, 'Allocation of Income for Tax Purposes', Paper prepared for IABA Fourth Conference, 2 August 1945, 13, UNOG:PO—C.1774/159/3-3.

19 PC/EX/113/Rev.1, 50.

20 Ibid 50. These agencies had been established in 1944, except for the ITO, which was still in the making.

21 Ibid 51.

22 Executive Committee of the Preparatory Commission, *Submission by the UK to Committee 3*, UN Doc PC/EX/ES/8 (6 September 1945).

23 Executive Committee of the Preparatory Commission, *Submission by Australia to Committee 3*, UN Doc PC/EX/ES/22 (25 September 1945).

the Commission was not unanimous, the Executive Committee 'felt that the time had not come to make a decision', listing it instead among the commissions which were 'desirable' to be established 'at an early date'.[24] The Commission's terms of reference were to make studies and advise the ECOSOC on matters concerning:

> (a) international taxation problems;
> (b) exchange of information among states on the technique of government finance and on their social and economic effects;
> (c) fiscal techniques to assist the prevention of depressions or inflation;
> (d) such functions of the Fiscal Committee of the League of Nations as the Organisation may decide.[25]

In the Preparatory Commission, Canada, supported by Britain, advocated for the Commission to be designated for 'immediate establishment'.[26] Canada stated that the present state of world affairs demanded its necessity 'more ... than ever before', especially in the fields of preventing depressions and inflations, and double taxation given the 'many rises and advances and increases in [corporate and personal] taxation'.[27] Britain considered, firstly, that the Commission would most usefully address comparative study and interchange of information on fiscal technique as an important 'weapon' in fighting inflation; and secondly, that as the Fiscal Committee had been 'one of the most active and successful of the [League's] Committees', the failure to continue its functions would cause 'doubt and confusion' and work accomplished thus far to suffer.[28] However, several countries, including Czechoslovakia, Liberia, Mexico, Poland and the USSR, opposed the proposal[29] and it failed by a split

[24] PC/EX/113/Rev.1, 51–4.

[25] Ibid 54.

[26] 'Telegram from Stevenson to Acting Secretary of State', 23 December 1945, in State Department, *Foreign Relations of the United States: Diplomatic Papers, 1945* (USGPO, 1967) vol 1: General: The United Nations, Doc 355; Fiscal Commission, *Documentary Material Concerning the Terms of Reference of the Commission*, UN Doc E/CN.8/4 (20 March 1947) 3–4.

[27] Preparatory Commission, *Verbatim Report of the 6th Meeting of the Third Committee (Economic and Social)* (5 December 1945) 21–31, in *UN Preparatory Commission 1945–1946*, Bound vol V, UNARMS:AG-009—S-0931-0002-03.

[28] Ibid 22, 23.

[29] Mexico and the USSR considered that the decision should be left to ECOSOC, Czechoslovakia considered other economic and financial problems had priority, and Liberia and Poland considered that the Commission should be created by the Economic and Employment Commission as fiscal and financial problems were 'closely connected' with economic problems and because their terms of reference overlapped.

vote. A compromise suggested by the United States was instead adopted by a majority for the Commission to be included among the category of possible commissions for early establishment.[30] In the subsequent weeks, Loveday would take the matter up with the State Department and British authorities, the latter replying that 'they were completely in agreement' with 'the retention of a Fiscal Committee'.[31]

3.3 ECOSOC (1946)

3.3.1 *First Session (January–February 1946, London)*

ECOSOC was established in January 1946 and would spend its first few sessions 'dogged by organizational quibbling as ... [it] attempted to define the composition and functions of its commissions'.[32] It formed five 'nuclear commissions' in the 'urgent' fields of economic and employment, statistics, transport and communications, human rights and narcotics to plan for their permanent counterparts regarding their terms of reference, functions, work programme and composition.[33] Colombia argued for the immediate establishment of the Fiscal Commission to continue the League's Fiscal Committee which 'had done extremely useful work on important and highly technical questions, and had provided valuable help to countries in need', and because its functions 'had a bearing on those of several other Commissions and on the proposed International Conference on Trade'.[34] Belgium, nevertheless, considered

[30] Stevenson telegram, 23 December 1945; PC/20, 28, 39.

[31] 'Note on Department Meeting Held on 14 January 1946', undated, UNOG:PO—C.1624/521/8/3. The League was planning to print its new collection of 'International Treaties on Double Taxation and Fiscal Evasion' but eventually decided to leave this to the UN as this 'would indicate to the world that it was taking seriously its general instruction to carry on the [League's] work ... promptly': Letter from Loveday to Lester, 15 January 1946, UNOG:PO—C.1757/141/13-2.

[32] John Toye and Richard Toye, *UN and Global Political Economy: Trade, Finance, and Development* (Indiana University Press, 2004) 29. The issues lengthily debated included the type of membership (i.e. independent experts or government representatives), basis for selection, size of the commissions, and appointment of corresponding members: see Committee on the Organization of ECOSOC, *First Meeting, Held 30 January 1946*, UN Doc E/ORG/3 (22 February 1946); *Fourth Meeting, Held 2 February 1946*, UN Doc E/ORG/6 (22 February 1946); *Fifth Meeting, Held 4 February 1946*, UN Doc E/ORG/7 (23 February 1946).

[33] Committee on the Organization of ECOSOC, *Draft Report of the Committee on the Organization of the Economic and Social Council*, UN Doc E/ORG/2 (14 February 1946); Eugene Parker Chase, *The United Nations in Action* (McGraw-Hill, 1950) 237.

[34] Committee on the Organization of ECOSOC, *Sixth Meeting, Held 6 February 1946*, UN Doc E/ORG/8 (23 February 1946) 4.

there was neither urgency nor necessity for the Commission as it 'could do little effective work until international trade was put back on a stable and normal basis'.[35] At the proposal of Canada, it was eventually decided that the Commission (along with other 'desirable' commissions) would be established in principle, with its terms of reference and composition to be decided later.[36] The UN Secretariat was tasked to undertake the preparatory work.

ECOSOC's foot-dragging as well as the League's piecemeal transfer created uncertainties for the League, especially regarding where and how the Mission could carry on its work, or whether it would even be maintained.[37] In April, the League held its final Assembly to dissolve the organisation and transfer its property to the UN; staff contracts were to terminate from 31 July.[38] Over the ensuing months, it became increasingly difficult 'to keep things and people together'[39] as senior staff accepted outside offers,[40] sections were liquidated[41] and contracts terminated.[42] Deperon continued in his efforts to establish the Commission, holding conferences with US State Department and Treasury officials,[43] and requesting Elliott to talk with the Canadian

35 Ibid 5.

36 Ibid 2–3, 6–7.

37 Letter from Lester to Loveday, 20 February 1946, UNOG:PO—C.1633/529/17/4–1. The League contemplated reuniting the whole department in Geneva for a period or trying to arrange temporary quarters at the UN. By this time, the League's Supervisory Commission was already looking into liquidating the League's contracts with its Latin American correspondents and Indian Office which were integral to the League's collection of materials, sale of publications, translation work and publicity: Letter from Loveday to Lester, 9 February 1946, UNOG:PO—C.1631/527/15/4–3. See also Chapter 2, Section 2.1.5 (regarding the Mission's efforts to influence the Commission's establishment with the Fiscal Committee's London Meeting).

38 *Resolution for the Dissolution of the League of Nations*, League Assembly, League Doc A.32(1).1946.X (18 April 1946) 12–16.

39 Note by Frumkin to Acting Secretary-General, 21 May 1946, UNOG:PO—C.1633/529/17/4–1.

40 See Letter from Rosenborg to Lester, 18 July 1946, UNOG:PO—C.1633/529/17/4–1 (stating that the Mission tried to secure UN positions for its members, but this was 'not dealt with expeditiously' by the UN (at 1)). See also Letter from Rosenborg to Aglion, 7 June 1946, UNOG:PO—C.1633/529/17/4–1. This threatened the near-breakdown of the Princeton work: Telegram from Rosenborg to Lester, 19 July 1946, UNOG:PO—C.1633/529/17/4–1.

41 Telegram from Stencek to Rosenborg, 26 June 1946, UNOG:PO—C.1633/529/17/4–1.

42 Rosenborg letter, 18 July 1946; Telegram from Lester, 18 July 1946, UNOG:PO—C.1633/529/17/4–1.

43 Letter from Deperon to Rosenborg, 8 June 1946, UNOG:PO—C.1631/527/15/4–3; Letter from Deperon to Fales, 15 May 1946, UNOG:PO—C.1777/162/3–13. Deperon came away assured of a good chance for the Commission's establishment.

ECOSOC representatives.[44] Carroll also engaged in talks with Washington officials.[45] At the end of May, Deperon was seconded to the UN to provide assistance to the Secretariat in preparing a paper for ECOSOC concerning the Commission's establishment and in outlining a programme of work for the Fiscal Division, which was (informally then) to come under his charge, as indicated by Assistant Secretary-General David Owen of the Department of Economic Affairs (DEA).[46] The Mission had 'strongly recommend[ed]' to Geneva to approve the secondment as Deperon's assistance was 'urged by American authorities' who were 'anxious' to 'assure continuity [in the] fiscal work and proper orientation [of the] new commission'.[47] The United States was then planning a DTA with the Philippines, and Belgium had indicated interest in negotiating one with the United States.[48] The Mission saw the secondment 'as a means of securing the fruitful continuation within the new organization of the international work so successfully begun by the Fiscal Committee of the League'.[49]

Deperon's early plans for the Commission's establishment were elaborate. In brief, he intended the Commission to assume the work of the League's Fiscal Committee and Economic, Financial and Transit Department over 'tax problems, fiscal systems and public finance in general'.[50] Its functions included making studies, publishing information, advising and making recommendations, and rendering technical assistance. Its objectives covered developmental, educational and ideological goals, including trade and investment liberalisation; standard-setting to improve and achieve uniformity in revenue administrations, especially in less-developed and younger nations; becoming an information clearinghouse for administrations, lawyers and students; and promoting 'democratic and sound economic principles'.[51] The

44 Letter from Deperon to Elliott, 14 May 1946, UNOG:PO—C.1777/162/3-13.

45 Letter from Carroll to Deperon, 2 May 1946, UNOG:PO—C.1777/162/3-13.

46 Telegram from Rosenborg to Lester, 23 May 1946, UNOG:PO—C.1631/527/15/4-3; Deperon letter, 8 June 1946.

47 Rosenborg telegram, 23 May 1946.

48 Deperon letter, 15 May 1946. The treaty with the Philippines was in fact the 'first on ... [the US] list' and was to have priority over the Belgium treaty.

49 Letter from Rosenborg to Lester, 10 June 1946, 2, UNOG:PO—C.1631/527/15/4-3.

50 'United Nations – Economic and Social Council: Fiscal Commission (Draft)', undated (around early 1946), 1, attached to envelope marked 'Deperon papers', UNOG:PO—C.1633/529/17/4-2.

51 Ibid 5–6. This reference to democracy suggests an attempt to align the Commission with American foreign policy goals.

Commission would comprise some fifteen members acting in their individual capacity, selected on a wide geographical basis, with 'very high national and international standing ... [and] authoritative experience in matters of taxation, government finance, public administration and international law'.[52] It was to have a Tax Sub-Commission and a Public Finance Sub-Commission, with members drawn partly from the Commission and partly from the outside.[53] The Commission and its Sub-Commissions could have corresponding members and associates in countries not represented on these bodies to ensure continuous liaison with the administrations of those countries. The Secretariat would be represented by the Fiscal Division, which, when fully constituted, 'might include some ten officials with professional training and experience in taxation, law, public administration, accountancy, and taken together possessing a wide knowledge of languages', supported by adequate junior staff of technical and statistical assistants.[54] Towards the end of May, Deperon greatly simplified the Commission's terms of reference, firstly, to increase its likelihood of going through by emphasising that the Commission would have no jurisdictional overlaps with other bodies, and secondly, because he envisaged that much of the omitted content would be dealt with by a 'nuclear' Fiscal Commission.[55] He circulated his preparatory proposals and the Report of the Fiscal Committee's London meeting to various ECOSOC delegations, stating that:

> if the Fiscal Commission is constituted along the lines now suggested, it could be in its sphere a useful instrument for economic development, financial stability, administrative efficiency and integrity in the various countries of the world, and especially among the smaller and younger nations.[56]

[52] Ibid 3.

[53] Members of the Tax Sub-Commission were to be actual or former heads of tax administrations or 'individuals with an outstanding knowledge of the legal, administrative and economic aspects of taxation'; members of the Public Finance Sub-Commission were to comprise actual or former high budgetary officials or other persons with similar experience: Ibid 3–4.

[54] Ibid 4.

[55] Letter from Deperon to Williams, 21 May 1946; Letter from Deperon to Elliott, 21 May 1946; Letter from Deperon to Fong, 23 May 1946, UNOG:PO—C.1777/162/3-13.

[56] Letter from Deperon to Perez-Guerrero, 23 May 1946, 2, UNOG:PO—C.1684/68/5-14. This folder contains identical/similar correspondence to other officials.

3.3.2 *Second Session (May–June 1946, New York)*

Now based at the UN, Deperon arranged for Emilio Toro (the Colombian representative)[57] to present the document to ECOSOC along with a speech.[58] Deperon also 'carried out consultations with various delegations ... concerning appointments to be made on the "nuclear" Fiscal Commission'.[59] He wrote optimistically to Princeton of the Commission's likely establishment, and that its membership would 'probably include several members of the old League Fiscal Committee, thus assuring continuity of work', albeit with an enlarged competence that 'embrace[d] the entire field of public finance'.[60] Deperon began planning the Division's programme of activities and made proposals for the recruitment of staff.[61] He simultaneously continued working on, inter alia, the *Mexico/London Models Commentary*, which the League desired to have 'published as a League document' and 'to be circulated for rapid approval by the Fiscal Committee members concerned'.[62]

Toro introduced the document for the Commission's establishment[63] to ECOSOC, along with the speech.[64] The speech called for the Commission's creation on the grounds that taxation and public finance formed 'the economic basis of life of ... organized society', being a 'powerful means to eradicate the evils of excessive economic and social inequality', stabilise business activity, maintain employment and promote economic development, 'especially in younger countries'.[65] It also referred to the League's Fiscal Committee as having 'made a valuable contribution to the elimination of double taxation, extraterritorial taxation and discriminatory taxation' and having rendered 'great services' to Latin American countries regarding 'the organization of their fiscal

57 Toro had been a member of the League's Special Joint Committee that produced the *PFI Conditions* report (see Chapter 2, Section 2.1.5).

58 Deperon letter, 8 June 1946.

59 Ibid.

60 Deperon stated that '[t]his will be in harmony with the process of growth which the League Fiscal Committee went through starting as a mere double taxation committee, and gradually developing into a genuine tax Committee, and now is doing [sic] a third step further': Ibid.

61 Ibid.

62 Rosenborg letter, 10 June 1946. An agreement was made enabling Deperon to perform these tasks at the UN headquarters and with the help of UN secretarial staff.

63 *Proposal Submitted by the Representative of Colombia Concerning the Establishment of a Fiscal Commission*, UN ESC, 2nd sess, UN Docs E/54 and Corr.1 (4 June 1947).

64 E/CN.8/4, 5 (reproducing extracts from the *Verbatim Report of the Twelfth Meeting*, UN ESC, 2nd sess, 12th mtg, UN Doc E/PV.12 (11 June 1946)).

65 Ibid 5–6.

systems'.[66] The Commission's terms of reference encompassed 'all legislative, juridical and administrative, economic and other technical aspects of taxation and public finance', including (a) international tax problems; (b) structure and administration of tax systems; (c) relationships between general economic and social policies and taxation; (d) budgetary and public accountancy standards and practices; (e) methods of financing various types of public expenditures; and (f) coordination of central and local governmental fiscal systems.[67] Its activities were to be coordinated with other UN commissions and specialised agencies, and it was to be 'primarily concerned not with policy planning'.[68] Toro's proposal was supported by China and Peru;[69] however, ECOSOC did not establish the Commission, Deperon reporting because it 'did not have sufficient time' but that this would hopefully be achieved at the third session.[70]

Meanwhile, ECOSOC had deliberated on reports of the nuclear commissions and established their permanent counterparts as well as two further commissions (the Social Commission and Commission on the Status of Women).[71] More importantly, it also decided on the general composition of ECOSOC commissions after protracted and contentious debate – outcomes of which would have significant repercussions for the Fiscal Commission as with the other commissions. Firstly, the majority sided with the Soviet view to wholly constitute the commissions of representatives acting upon government instructions rather than in their individual capacity.[72] Although the Soviet proposal was motivated by communist ideology, other ECOSOC members considered that the

66 Ibid 6.

67 E/54, 4.

68 Ibid.

69 *Proposal by the Representative of Colombia for the Establishment of a Fiscal Commission (Document E/54)*, UN ESCOR, 1st yr: 2nd sess, 12th mtg (11 June 1946) para 33. At the suggestion of the ECOSOC's president, the Council decided to refer the matter to its 'Committee ... dealing with economic questions' for recommendations regarding the Fiscal Commission's terms of reference and composition. No such recommendations were produced by the time of the Council's last meeting of the session (15th mtg, 21 June 1946).

70 Letter from Deperon to Elliott, 2 August 1946, UNARMS:AG-025-002—S-0441-0463-23407.

71 Trygve Lie, 'Full Text of Trygve Lie's Summary of Work of the United Nations' (1946) 32 (9) *American Bar Association Journal* 553, 553.

72 Joint Committee of ECOSOC on Composition of Commissions, *Summary Record of the First Meeting, 17 June 1946*, UN ESC, 2nd sess, UN Doc E/JC/1 (19 June 1946). Britain (and the Executive Committee and Preparatory Commission) had favoured a mixed composition approach of government representatives and individual experts:

approach could improve implementation by enabling the representatives to commit their governments rather than the commissions becoming mere talk shops.[73] Secondly, the majority also decided to compose the commissions with an average of fifteen members from different member states according to a formula of equitable representation that reflected the geopolitical grouping system used to assign countries to General Assembly committees.[74] The memberships of each commission would thus only be determined when the last of ECOSOC's commissions were established.

By mid-July, Deperon had secured employment on the UN staff.[75] He completed the *Mexico/London Models Commentary*, amended the Commission's terms of reference and continued with preparatory work concerning the Fiscal Division.[76] He was unable to submit the *Commentary* for Carroll's review as intended due to printing deadlines in Geneva, but he assured Carroll that the foreword had been 'written in such terms that ... clearly disengage[d] the responsibility of the Fiscal Committee or any of its members'.[77] He added that '[i]n any case, in my opinion at least, the whole work will have to be overhauled by the Fiscal Commission'.[78] He consulted with Carroll, Elliott and Britain's Inland Revenue on the planned functions and studies of the Commission.[79]

Submission of the UK Delegation on the Composition of ECOSOC Commissions, UN ESC, 2nd sess, UN Doc E/Commissions/2 (30 April 1946); PC/EX/113/Rev.1, 54; PC/20, 39. The United States (and the nuclear commissions) had preferred the appointment of non-officials based on technical competence: *Memorandum Submitted by the US Delegation on the Composition of ECOSOC Commissions*, UN ESC, 2nd sess, UN Doc E/Commissions/3 (6 May 1946); 'State Department Briefing Paper', 4 September 1946, n 6, in State Department, *Foreign Relations of the United States, 1946* (USGPO, 1972) vol 1: General: The United Nations, Doc 96 ('*FRUS, 1946*'). Following ECOSOC's decision, the State Department briefed US representatives on ECOSOC commissions on how to conduct themselves in speaking for the government, which included having to be familiar with government policies; being allowed to collaborate in the preparation of their instructions; to rarely speak as individuals; and having 'the right, for tactical as well as other reasons, to seek special instructions': 'State Department Briefing Paper', 4 September 1946.

73 Alexander Loveday, 'An Unfortunate Decision' (1947) 1(2) *International Organization* 279, 280; Chase, *United Nations*, 237.

74 Robert W Gregg, 'UN Economic, Social, and Technical Activities' in James Barros (ed), *The United Nations: Past, Present and Future* (The Free Press, 1972) 218, 241.

75 Lester telegram, 18 July 1946.

76 Deperon letter to Elliot, 2 August 1946.

77 Letter from Deperon to Carroll, 2 August 1946, UNARMS:AG-004-001—S-0979-0002-26.

78 Ibid.

79 Carroll was 'greatly impressed with the world-embracing scope and depth of the studies ... envisage[d]': Letter from Carroll to Deperon, 12 August 1946, UNARMS:

Meanwhile, Carroll continued to promote the Commission's establishment in professional journals, reporting on details of the envisaged work programme, including 'the continuous perfecting of the model bilateral conventions and the resumption of the study of principles and methods of allocating taxable income to permanent establishments as provided in conventions'.[80]

3.3.3 *Third Session of ECOSOC (September–October 1946, New York)*

At ECOSOC's third session, Colombia presented its modified proposal concerning the creation of the Commission, which contained Deperon's greatly scaled-down terms of reference.[81] In the ensuing discussions, several countries (including Peru, Chile and the United States) stated that the Commission's creation had been overly delayed.[82] The USSR sought to narrow the Commission's study and advisory functions to technical aspects concerning 'the organization of the interchange of information on the fiscal subjects between various countries' as well as international investments and tariff barriers.[83] This was, however, opposed by Norway, India, Greece, France and Britain for various reasons, including the importance of: technical assistance (India), the study of social and economic problems incident to taxation (Norway) and the study of underlying economic foundations of depressions and deflations (France). Britain highlighted that the terms of reference had been drafted in view of the League's wide practice and experience continued in Mexico during the war and in London earlier in March. France argued that the work of mere compilation, even codification,

AG-004-001—S-0441-0054-01. Conversely, Inland Revenue felt that 'the real work of the [League's] Committee – the model conventions – ha[d] been taken pretty well as far as it can be' and that '[t]he broad questions which remain for study belong more . . . to the economists and the experts in public finance generally' rather than to 'pure tax experts': Letter from Willis to Deperon, 12 August 1946, UNARMS:AG-004-001—S-0979-0003-17. To the British, the 'most important feature' to 'be found in the tax expert's field . . . [would] be the secretariat's work, the collection and distribution of information about national tax laws and so on': Ibid.

80 Mitchell B Carroll, 'Report of Committee on International Double Taxation' [1946] *Proceedings of the Section of International and Comparative Law (American Bar Association)* 40, 44.

81 *Proposal Submitted by the Representative of Colombia Concerning the Establishment of a Fiscal Commission*, UN ESC, 3rd sess, UN Doc E/54/Rev.1 (21 September 1946).

82 *Consideration of the Amended Proposal by the Representative of Colombia for the Establishment of a Fiscal Commission (Document E/54/Rev.1)*, UN ESCOR, 1st yr:3rd sess, 15th mtg (1 October 1946) para 31.

83 E/CN.8/4/Add.1, 5 (reproducing extracts from the *Verbatim Report of the Fifteenth Meeting*, UN ESC, 3rd sess, 15th mtg, UN Doc E/PV.30 (1 October 1946)).

was of no practical value but only of scientific interest. France nevertheless wanted to define the Commission's precise role given its potential for overlap with other commissions for economic development or population, but Peru, supported by Colombia, Norway, France and Greece, considered that the Commission's scope should be widened instead to provide for close coordination and collaboration with other UN bodies in view of the interconnections among economic, social trends and fiscal policy. A compromise was made to adopt the proposed Colombian resolution and to leave it to the Commission to consider any modifications.

The Commission was thus established in October, along with the Population Commission, as ECOSOC's final two commissions. Its terms of reference simply covered (a) studying and advising ECOSOC and providing technical assistance to member states 'in the field of public finance, particularly in its legal, administrative and technical aspects'; and (b) advising ECOSOC and its commissions 'on the fiscal implications of recommendations made by the Commissions in their fields', and cooperating 'in matters of common interest' with other UN bodies and specialised agencies.[84] A further paragraph stated that the Commission could, '[s]hortly after its creation, and thereafter when appropriate', make recommendations and reports to ECOSOC concerning 'its terms of reference, organization and programme of work'.[85]

ECOSOC proceeded to appoint the country compositions of eight of its commissions.[86] These allocations had in general already been worked out in private between the United States, the USSR and the United Kingdom (the 'Big Three') so that their unified formulation could be presented and voted upon without delay or acrimonious debate.[87] The outcome gave to the Big Five representation on each of the eight 15-membered commissions, which in effect took up 40 of the available 120 seats, leaving the remaining 80 seats to be distributed among the other 46 UN member states. While initial attempt had been made to give every UN member a seat on at least one commission, the Big Three subsequently wrangled to increase the representation of their supposed respective adherents so that each would have more

84 See *Fiscal Commission*, ESC Res 2 (III), UN ESCOR, UN Doc E/245/Rev.1 (3 May 1947, adopted 1 October 1946, supplemented by action taken by the Council on 2 and 3 October 1946) para 1(b).

85 Ibid para 7.

86 Membership of the Narcotics Commission had already been determined separately under international arrangements.

87 'Memorandum by David H Popper on Selection of ECOSOC Commissions', 9 October 1946, in State Department, *FRUS, 1946*, Doc 102.

support, particularly on the 'more important Commissions' (which for the United States and the United Kingdom included the Fiscal Commission).[88] The United States thus contended for Latin America and the Philippines; the USSR for the Soviet Bloc; and Britain for the British dominions. The USSR, moreover, demanded fewer seats for the Western European countries. The eventual compromise left twelve member states without a seat on any commission[89] and gave a disproportionate number of seats to the Eastern bloc more than any other regional group.

The original US designations for the Fiscal Commission had included two or three smaller Eastern European states, two Latin American states, Denmark and the Philippines.[90] Meanwhile Chile, Colombia, Cuba and Peru proposed Colombia, Paraguay and Panama for membership on the Commission.[91] The list of candidates for election comprised Belgium, Bolivia, Brazil, Canada, China, Colombia, Cuba, Czechoslovakia, Denmark, France, India, Lebanon, Mexico, New Zealand, Norway, Paraguay, the Philippines, Poland, Turkey, South Africa, Ukraine SSR, the United Kingdom, the United States and the USSR.[92] The final election left the following states represented on the Commission: the Big Five, three Soviet Eastern European states (Czechoslovakia, Ukraine SSR, Poland); two Latin American states (Colombia and Cuba); two British Dominions (South Africa and New Zealand); another Western European state (Belgium); another Asian state (India); and one Near East-African state (Lebanon).[93]

3.4 Commentary

The rebirth of the League's Fiscal Committee in the UN owed much to Deperon's efforts as well as the networks the Mission had formed or maintained with American, British, Canadian and Latin American

[88] Ibid.

[89] These comprised eight Latin American states (Argentina, Bolivia, Dominican Republic, El Salvador, Haiti, Honduras, Nicaragua and Paraguay); three states of the Near East-African regional group (Ethiopia, Liberia and Saudi Arabia); and one Western European state (Luxembourg).

[90] 'Memorandum Prepared in the Division of International Organization Affairs', 6 September 1946, in State Department, *FRUS, 1946*, Doc 97, Section 2(d) (re discussion of the Philippine representation).

[91] *Commissions of the Economic and Social Council: List of Candidates, Proposal of the Delegations of Chile, Columbia* [sic], *Cuba and Peru*, UN ESC, 3rd sess, UN Doc E/209 (2 October 1946).

[92] *Fiscal Commission*, UN ESC, 3rd sess, UN Docs E/214 and Corr.1 (2 October 1946).

[93] *Election of Commissions*, UN ESC, 3rd sess, UN Doc E/223 (2 October 1946).

officials. Deperon's plans were greatly ambitious: in addition to continuing the fields of work that had been covered or contemplated by the Fiscal Committee and the Mission, he intended the Commission to encompass the entire field of public finance as well as to provide technical assistance. The evolution of these plans to cover the additional spheres indicate his incorporation of works of interest or matters of concern gathered from his consultations with various governments. Such ideas, which were effectively the blueprint for the Fiscal Commission to become the world authority on taxation and public finance, received overall support from US officials, who not only appeared instrumental in facilitating Deperon's joining of the UN Secretariat but were also privy to Deperon's draft designs. The emphasis on development objectives among Deperon's plans suggests that he saw a significant role for the UN's fiscal work in developing nations, and that this had not merely been a propaganda effort to link the Commission's purposes with the UN Charter's ideals[94] as evidenced in the forthcoming chapters regarding his subsequent technical assistance work and changing views concerning the suitability of DTAs for underdeveloped countries.[95] Perhaps such concerns were why he considered, even at the time of writing the *Mexico/London Models Commentary*, that the 'whole work' would need overhauling by the Commission.

The successful establishment of the Commission as designed was nevertheless marred by ECOSOC's decision to constitute its commissions with government representatives distributed according to geopolitical groupings of UN member states.[96] This thwarted the expectation that Carroll would be part of the Commission and that the Secretariat would have discretion in determining the Commission's composition. The Commission's membership was now limited to UN members and its discussions and work were open to overt political interference, national interest and prejudice, rather than being guided, at least in principle, by the collective interest of the international community. The Commission would also begin its existence with a composition of countries which, while diverse, entailed few commonalities (e.g. close trade ties, shared beliefs on free trade) and was disproportionate and fragmented (e.g. few

[94] For example, to promote 'higher standards of living' or 'conditions of economic and social progress and development': *Charter of the United Nations* art 55.

[95] See Chapter 5, Section 5.6 and Chapter 7, Section 7.4.

[96] See Toye and Toye, *UN*, 29 (revealing a Canadian delegate's remark of ECOSOC's 'apparent conviction that its commissions would be composed of morons who had to have everything spelled out for them').

Western European, large Soviet presence). Most of these countries had not been League members, let alone involved in the Fiscal Committee's work. There was, in short, little continuity between the League's Committee and the UN Commission in these fundamental ways.

Other aspects evident in the Commission's establishment which are worth noting here for the future problems they would pose to Deperon's plans for the body include the Commission's vague and potentially overlapping terms of reference which were never fine-tuned by a nuclear commission; the lack of Soviet enthusiasm for the Commission; the existence of specialised agencies with ambulatory jurisdiction; and that most countries supporting the Commission's creation did not express double taxation as a priority for the Commission's work (Britain in fact indicating that little remained to be accomplished concerning the League's work on the model conventions).

4

Pax Americana, Cold War and Decolonisation

Impact on the UN Institutional Machinery for Fiscal Activities and Postwar International Financial Flows

This chapter outlines key developments in the global political economy and governance of the first postwar decade that affected the UN's capacity for international tax coordination, highlighting the shifts in the global balance of power and institutional order that prevented the Commission from functioning in the manner that the League's Fiscal Committee had. This background is critical to framing the impetus and facilitators behind the direction of the international tax work during this period and the subsequent erosion of the Commission's sole competence over fiscal matters. Section 4.1 introduces the key features of the UN's framework for fiscal activities that diverged from that of the League's and outlines the main reasons for these departures. Section 4.2 highlights broad impacts of these developments on the Fiscal Commission and Fiscal Division. Section 4.3 explains the critical role FDI assumed in the postwar economy for developing countries and the consequential significance source-taxing rights presented to bolstering capital flows and revenue for their development.

4.1 The UN's Framework for Fiscal Activities

As outlined in the previous chapter, Deperon had envisaged a Fiscal Commission and Fiscal Division that were essentially enlarged and fortified versions of their predecessors. It was also presumed that they would carry on their activities in the same flexible manner as had occurred under the League, namely: in close collaboration with each other and without interference from the governing political bodies of the Assembly and Council.[1] At the outset, these plans were at risk of

[1] In general, the League's various committees had performed the main expert work in close collaboration with a small Secretariat which was responsible for the preparatory and implementing work. The work produced was considered the fruit of both the committees

frustration by the constituting of the Commission as a political body. In the ensuing years, further departures from League practices would develop in the following key respects: a more rigid and formal relationship between the Commission and the Division; a Secretariat of less calibre and independence; the weighing in by ECOSOC and the General Assembly on double taxation proposals and work; and the encroaching reach of specialised agencies and regional bodies on the Commission's sphere of fiscal activities. These divergences had a root cause in the very different contours of world power in operation at the UN's formation, which would themselves dramatically and unexpectedly evolve over the ensuing years due to the Cold War and decolonisation of the Third World. These geopolitical shifts inevitably bore upon every global concern and the new international institutional machinery that had been created and deployed to govern the economic and political interdependence of the American-led liberal world order.

4.1.1 UN Membership and the Global Balance of Power: Rise of the East–West, North–South Divisions

A very different world and global balance of power emerged after World War II in contrast to the League era when Europe still dominated much of the world, the British Empire reached its largest territorial extent and international politics mainly took place between the European powers (the United States having retreated into isolationism and Russia becoming an outsider after the revolution of 1917 that would see it morph into the USSR).[2] In 1945, the Big Three were the only surviving great powers, the war having vanquished France, Germany, Italy and Japan. As the principal Allied powers, the three were the key architects of the UN's

and Secretariat. The Assembly and Council typically accepted the committees' reports and endorsed their proposals: Arthur Sweetser, 'The Non-Political Achievements of the League' (1940) 19(1) *Foreign Affairs* 179, 182; League of Nations, *Ten Years of World Co-Operation* (1930) 189. By 1930, the Economic and Financial Committees were able to, inter alia, decide their agenda, publish and disseminate their reports to governments, consult experts, establish special committees and initiate research without first consulting the Council: Bob Reinalda, *Routledge History of International Organizations: From 1815 to the Present Day* (Routledge, 2009) 246–7. Also, from 1931, many committee experts and Secretariat officials were interchangeable: Ursula Phalla Hubbard, 'The Cooperation of the United States with the League of Nations, 1931–1936' (1937) 18(April) *International Conciliation* 295, 319.

[2] Geir Lundestad, *East, West, North, South: International Relations since 1945* (Sage, 7th ed, 2014) 3.

formation, and while they admitted China and France to their circle to form the Big Five, they would continue to decide most of the important issues behind the scenes.[3] Geopolitically, the Big Five represented the two superpowers, the two largest colonial powers and the most populous country, thereby accounting for two-thirds of the world's population.[4] The European colonial empires were then still intact and the Third World had yet to appear on the world scene.[5] In reality, however, the United States and the USSR were the only two superpowers: the United States by far the mammoth power in military, economic and political might, while the USSR was primarily a military power.[6] Between the two lay long-standing tense relations grounded in a fundamental ideological chasm: the United States as the greatest capitalist state, and the USSR as the leading communist state.[7] Britain was now weak and impoverished, dependent on US aid and its Empire collapsing,[8] although it was able to

[3] Eugene Parker Chase, *The United Nations in Action* (McGraw-Hill, 1950) 11, 15; Evan Luard, *A History of the United Nations* (Macmillan Press, 1982) vol 1: The Years of Western Domination, 1945–1955, 17–36.

[4] Panos Tsakaloyannis 'International Society at a Crossroads: The Problem of Conceptualization' in Dimitris Bourantonis and Marios Evriviades (eds), *A United Nations for the Twenty-First Century: Peace, Security and Development* (Kluwer Law International, 1996) 19, 33–4.

[5] Ibid.

[6] Lundestad, *East*, 3–5; Thomas G Paterson, *Soviet–American Confrontation: Postwar Reconstruction and the Origins of the Cold War* (Johns Hopkins University Press, 1973) 8–14.

[7] Lundestad, *East*, 5, 14; Heather Streets-Salter and Trevor R Getz, *Empires and Colonies in the Modern World: A Global Perspective* (Oxford University Press, 2016) 474.

[8] Britain was no longer a trading power or global financial centre, and was in fact 'the world's leading debtor country' facing, in Keynes words, an imminent 'financial Dunkirk', although its financial ruin was not widely known, which complicated its struggles from mid-1944 to wring postwar aid from Washington as the cessation of Lend-Lease loomed (George C Herring Jr, 'The United States and British Bankruptcy, 1944–1945: Responsibilities Deferred' (1971) 86(2) *Political Science Quarterly* 260, 260–80). The various camouflaging factors included the perception of Britain's political and economic superiority over the European nations and Japan, the belief that it was buttressed by the economic entity of the Commonwealth and Britain's public pretence as a first-class power: Stephen Blank, 'Britain: The Politics of Foreign Economic Policy, the Domestic Economy, and the Problem of Pluralistic Stagnation' (1977) 31(4) *International Organization* 673, 681; Alasdair Blair, *Britain and the World since 1945* (Routledge, 2015) 28. Sir Basil Newton of the UK Foreign Office noted of the geopolitical rankings after the war that 'individually the UK would be a second-class power and the Dominions only third class': Francine McKenzie, 'Imperial Solutions to International Crises: Alliances, Trade and the Ottawa Imperial Economic Conference of 1932' in John Fisher, Effie GH Pedaliu and Richard Smith (eds), *The Foreign Office, Commerce and British Foreign Policy in the Twentieth Century* (Palgrave Macmillan, 2016) 165, 181.

sustain a great power masquerade as head of its Empire and through its close relations with the United States and strong political clout among the Western European states.[9] France 'had little influence' and was preoccupied with domestic problems; China 'similarly . . . remained more or less on the sidelines . . . when there were policy conflicts among the Big Five'.[10]

The establishment of the Big Five in the UN Charter as permanent members of the Security Council was premised on the rationale that countries that had made the most contribution to the war effort had the most potential to contribute to collective peace and security and should hence have ascendancy in postwar arrangements.[11] The prevalence of these views while the organisation was set up between 1945 and 1946 quickly led to the development of a precedent for the Big Five to be overly represented throughout the UN structure as a whole. In addition, an unofficial category of 'middle powers' (generally Australia, Belgium, Brazil, Canada, India, Mexico and the Netherlands) also emerged which were able to contend for special privileges, including more frequent representation on the various UN bodies.[12] Hopes for peacetime solidarity and cooperation under this governance structure, however, soon evaporated with the outbreak of the Cold War and the great wave of decolonisation.[13] These two confrontations of East–West and North–South, moreover, became intertwined,[14] the former empowering the Third World's rise to alter the balance of power on the global economic playing field under the UN system of majority voting (versus the League's unanimity rule) and equality of voting rights. They would also

[9] Lundestad, *East*, 7.

[10] Stephen S Goodspeed, *The Nature and Function of International Organization* (Oxford University Press, 2nd ed, 1967) 92.

[11] Inis L Claude Jr, *Swords into Plowshares: The Problems and Progress of International Organization* (Random House, 4th ed, 1971) 62; DW Bowett, *The Law of International Institutions* (Steven, 4th ed, 1982) 28; Luard, *History*, 18–19.

[12] Bernard Wood, 'Towards North–South Middle Power Coalitions' in Cranford Pratt (ed), *Middle Power Internationalism: The North–South Dimension* (McGill-Queen's University Press, 1990) 69, 75, 78–9; G deT Glazebrook, 'The Middle Powers in the United Nations System' (1947) 1 *International Organization* 307; David Armstrong, *The Rise of the International Organisation: A Short History* (Macmillan Press, 1982) 52.

[13] John Toye and Richard Toye, *UN and Global Political Economy: Trade, Finance, and Development* (Indiana University Press, 2004) 1.

[14] Adam Szirmai, *The Dynamics of Socio-Economic Development: An Introduction* (Cambridge University Press, 2005) 525. Szirmai notes that international conflicts between 1945 and 1991 mainly occurred in developing countries and that most of these 'had an East–West dimension' with the superpowers fighting 'wars by proxy within and between developing countries'.

subsequently alter the functioning and structure of the UN, excessively politicising almost every issue under its sphere.[15]

In the immediate postwar years, East–West tensions escalated, the Chinese Revolution was underway and anti-colonialism movements were breaking out across the developing world.[16] The two superpowers, which had come to view their bipolarity as 'mutually incompatible and that each represented a dire threat to the survival of the other', set about dividing the world between the American and communist ways of life in their manoeuvrings for world hegemony, allies and access to critical raw materials.[17] As part of the Truman Doctrine articulated in March 1947,[18] the United States took charge of Western Europe, and later Japan, by supplying massive reconstruction aid, while the USSR dominated Eastern Europe by installing communist regimes. Meanwhile, in the colonial world, several of the fifty-one UN founders (Egypt, India (which was later partitioned), Lebanon, the Philippines and Syria) attained independence just prior to or within seven years of the UN's establishment. While many other colonies would achieve independence within the first postwar decade, only nine elective members[19] were admitted to UN membership due to the blocking by Cold War protagonists of over twenty states based on their governments' communist or Western leanings.[20]

The sweeping rise against Western imperialism was a rude awakening for the colonial powers which had intended, although poorly equipped, to revive their empires through reconquest and expansion.[21] At San Francisco, Britain, France, Belgium and the Netherlands were forced to concede to the demands of the small powers, supported by China and the USSR, to extend the Trusteeship system to dependent territories and to commit to a wide range of undertakings in their colonies, including the

15 Inis L Claude Jr, *The Changing United Nations* (Random House, 1967) 35, 54.

16 Streets-Salter and Getz, *Empires and Colonies*, ch 15.

17 Ibid 474–6. See also Lundestad, *East*, 20–34, 39; Reinalda, *International Organizations*, 406–9. See generally Paterson, *Soviet–American Confrontation*.

18 The Truman Doctrine represented the containment policy of Soviet expansionism in which the United States pledged political, military and economic assistance to democratic governments threatened by communist insurrection: see State Department, 'The Truman Doctrine, 1947', *Office of the Historian* (Web Page) <https://history.state.gov/milestones/1945-1952/truman-doctrine>.

19 Afghanistan, Iceland, Siam (later Thailand), Sweden, Pakistan, Yemen, Burma, Israel, Indonesia: 'Growth in United Nations Membership, 1945–Present', *United Nations* (Web Page) <www.un.org/en/about-us/growth-in-un-membership>.

20 Claude, *Swords into Plowshares*, 88–92.

21 Streets-Salter and Getz, *Empires and Colonies*, 440–4.

promotion of self-government and political and economic development, as well as to regularly report on such conditions to the Secretary-General.[22] In need of powerful sponsors, liberation movements courted the United States and the USSR, setting the stage for East–West conflicts in other parts of the world.[23] Ideologically, American liberalism and Soviet socialism supported self-determination, but both superpowers were also broadly anti-colonial for pragmatic reasons: for the United States, decolonisation offered new markets and the expansion of trade links for emergent transnational American corporations otherwise excluded by imperial preference systems; for the USSR, it offered the potential to dismantle Western capitalist empires, threaten the power of the West and promote the Communist bloc.[24] The United States alternated between supporting and opposing independence struggles based on their political-global orientation as it balanced containing the spread of communism and maintaining good relations with its European allies.[25] The USSR in turn supported communist-oriented nationalist movements and attempted to create a Northwestern–Southeast division.

In 1950, the Cold War was in high gear: the USSR had carried out its first nuclear test; the Red Army had been victorious in China; the Korean War had broken out; and the global South, specifically Asia and the Middle East, had become a key battleground.[26] The UN became a tool in these political confrontations, the United States using its influence in the Security Council and Assembly to recognise Chiang Kai-Shek's exiled Nationalist regime in Taiwan as the legitimate Chinese government over Mao Zedong's People's Republic of China (PRC),[27] while the Soviet bloc would contest such representation in virtually every UN body.[28] Gone

[22] Armstrong, *Rise*, 52–3; Luard, *History*, 61–2; Reinalda, *International Organizations*, 284.

[23] Streets-Salter and Getz, *Empires and Colonies*, 442–4; Lundestad, *East*, 13–14.

[24] Streets-Salter and Getz, *Empires and Colonies*, 442; Luard, *History*, 377. See Paterson, *Soviet-American Confrontation*, 7–8 (regarding US deficiencies in critical minerals for industry and military necessities, and hence its emphasis on free trade and the 'open door' policy).

[25] Streets-Salter and Getz, *Empires and Colonies*, 442–3; Lundestad, *East*, 43–5, 255–6. See also PJ Cain and AG Hopkins, *British Imperialism: 1688-2015* (Routledge, 2016) 667.

[26] Africa and Latin America then had little significance for either superpower as the least-conflict prone regions of the international system: Lundestad, *East*, 46–7, 53, 58–60; Rosemary Thorp, 'The Latin American Economies in the 1940s' in David Rock (ed), *Latin America in the 1940s* (University of California Press, 1994) 41, 51.

[27] Reinalda, *International Organizations*, 292.

[28] The question of China's representation was raised in the General Assembly as early as September 1950 when India proposed the admission of PRC representatives. The proposal was defeated by thirty-three votes with sixteen in favour and ten abstentions. The

were the previously popular 'idealist' notions of world government that had led to the mushrooming of international organisations based on the belief that such institutions had transformative power to solve common problems.[29] 'Realist' theories now rose in the West as the dominant approach to international relations which saw international organisations as relatively insignificant actors, being tools of great powers to further their own interests.[30] The UN began to suffer various reputational losses as its autonomy and effectiveness were weakened by efforts by the majority West to further its interests and the minority East to neutralise the organisation.[31]

As the Cold War intensified, the superpowers began to align themselves with developing county issues to gain voting victories for their own proposals regarding political issues.[32] Developing countries in turn began to use the UN forum to articulate their economic and industrialisation goals.[33] This was achieved by, firstly, the growing alliance between developing countries, led by Latin America, India and Pakistan,[34] and secondly, the use of the Assembly as an alternative, and importantly more authoritative, forum for decision-making. The latter arose because

Soviet bloc would subsequently submit resolutions in the various other UN bodies to change China's representation. Regarding such submissions raised in ECOSOC subsidiary bodies, the American general response was to state that it was undesirable for a functional commission to determine political issues, while the British approach was to state that commissions were not competent to decide the question as representatives had been appointed in their personal capacity: Foreign Office Intel No 68, 27 March 1951; Foreign Office, Memorandum on 'Chinese Representation', 14 April 1950, TNA:IR40/9959(1).

29 Paul F Diehl and Brian Frederking, 'Introduction' in Paul F Diehl and Brian Frederking (eds), *The Politics of Global Governance: International Organizations in an Interdependent World* (Lynne Rienner, 4th ed, 2010) 1, 1–2, 5.

30 Ibid; Campbell Craig, 'The Resurgent Idea of World Government' in Paul F Diehl and Brian Frederking (eds), *The Politics of Global Governance: International Organizations in an Interdependent World* (Lynne Rienner, 4th ed, 2010) 397, 398.

31 Paterson, *Soviet–American Confrontation*, 10–11; Evan Luard, *The United Nations: How It Works and What It Does* (Palgrave Macmillan, 1979) 139, 141. In the first UN decade, the West had dominance with the majority of UN members favourable to, or dependent on, America, allowing it frequent victories in bloc voting.

32 See Luard, *History*, 377–8.

33 Toye and Toye, *UN*, 110.

34 Luard, *How It Works*, 143; John A Houston, *Latin America in the United Nations* (CEIP, 1956) 222. The leadership role assumed by these countries correlates to the length of their self-governance and hence longer history of building up economic and political infrastructure, as well as a solid class of intellectuals and leaders in contrast to the other European colonial territories in Africa and Asia: see Christopher M White, *A Global History of the Developing World* (Routledge, 2014) 17, 41, 48, 107–9, 130.

debates on economic questions in ECOSOC were often frustrated by 'stonewalling' tactics used by the richer countries of America, Britain and France, as any action recommended usually required them to undertake economically burdensome obligations.[35] Meanwhile, the Soviet economies, which were effectively insulated from the world economy, voted unpredictably, either siding with the poorer countries or abstaining; while the north-west European countries took 'neutral' positions in voting 'according to interest and to conscience'.[36] With the eighteen-membered ECOSOC comprising approximately one-third of UN members, developing countries consequently struggled to secure voting majorities. In the Assembly, however, the Third World represented almost half of the UN membership, with Latin America forming the single largest group with twenty members.[37] Within the first few years of the UN's life, the Assembly became the preeminent forum for a second chance at discussions or to bypass the other Councils as the numerous cross-currents of issues under discussion enabled countries to bargain for votes for their individual proposals in both formal consultations and corridor conversations.[38] These factors gave developing countries a chance to press for decisions in their interests and to influence the direction of economic work, particularly by taking their case to the Assembly when they were outnumbered in ECOSOC.[39] From 1950 onwards, development problems began to dominate while European problems, which had previously been the emphasis, diminished and were eventually 'rarely discussed'.[40]

At the time of the Commission's dissolution, developing countries had not been overtly successful in pressing for international responsibility towards underdeveloped countries. They had only obtained relatively meagre levels of assistance compared to the reconstruction financing which had been provided to Europe and Japan.[41] This comprised largely of technical assistance and special studies by groups of experts on development proposals, the latter of which, inter alia, recommended the establishment of an international development authority and a Special

[35] W Arthur Lewis, 'The Economic and Security Council' in BA Wortley (ed), *The United Nations: The First Ten Years* (Oceana, 1957) 34, 44.

[36] Ibid 45.

[37] Luard, *How It Works*, 47.

[38] Goodspeed, *Nature and Function*, 159–60; Luard, *How It Works*, 45, 48; Paterson, *Soviet–American Confrontation*, 11.

[39] Lewis, 'Economic and Security Council', 45; Goodspeed, *Nature and Function*, 160.

[40] Luard, *How It Works*, 47.

[41] Lundestad, *East*, 278–9; Houston, *Latin America*, 233, 236–46.

United Nations Fund for Development (SUNFED) for grants-in-aid and low-interest, long-term loans financed out of compulsory contributions by rich countries.[42] Developed countries, however, opposed calls for public capital as fundamental to developing countries' development, advancing instead the view that the Third World should promote its own growth through domestic capital and savings from trade expansion, supplemented by private capital.[43] The First World also contested the Third World's attempts at economic nationalism.[44] Outside of the core UN system, the Third World faced a similar difficulty obtaining financial aid. From 1950, the United States and the British Commonwealth had offered modest bilateral assistance through the transfer of physical capital, technology and experience, while colonial powers undertook certain investments and development programmes in their colonies and former colonies.[45] Such aid was largely linked to security, political and military strategies to contain communism and limit Soviet influence as the USSR began using aid as a tool in the Cold War.[46] The World Bank, which funded reconstruction primarily through guaranteed private investment, concentrated its efforts in industrialised nations.[47] The Havana Charter for the ITO, which contained path-breaking provisions addressing the special difficulties faced by countries in the early stages of industrial development,[48] failed of ratification, resulting in a trading system under the General Agreement

[42] Luard, *How It Works*, 57, 143–4. The SUNFED sought by developing countries was essentially a special fund controlled by the UN that was separate from the World Bank, which would effectively force developed countries into minority votes under the UN 'one country, one vote' rule: Eric Toussaint, *The World Bank: A Critical Primer*, tr Elizabeth Anne et al, ed Sylvain Dropsy (Pluto Press, 2008) 32–3.

[43] Joan E Spero and Jeffrey A Hart, *The Politics of International Economic Relations* (Routledge, 5th ed, 1997) 168, 215; Lundestad, *East*, 278; Evan Luard, *The Management of the World Economy* (Macmillan Press, 1983) 45.

[44] Toye and Toye, *UN*, 110–11.

[45] Lundestad, *East*, 278–9; WM Scammell, *The International Economy since 1945* (Macmillan, 2nd ed, 1983) 75–6; Szirmai, *Socio-Economic Development*, 585–6. Much of this aid not only 'would not be classified today as development assistance at all' as they 'took the form of loans at market rates of interest': Luard, *Management*, 46. For a history of international aid covering this period, see IMD Little and JM Clifford, *International Aid: The Flow of Public Resources from Rich to Poor Countries* (Routledge, 2017) ch 1.

[46] Scammell, *International Economy*, 73–7; Spero and Hart, *Politics*, 169–70.

[47] John W McArthur and Eric Werker, 'Developing Countries and International Organizations: Introduction to the Special Issue' (2016) 11(2) *Review of International Organizations* 155, 156.

[48] This included price stability of production and trade in primary commodities, effective support of the agricultural sector, and recognition of the right of expropriation and restriction by host countries on foreign direct investment: Sidney Wells, 'The Developing Countries GATT and UNCTAD' (1969) 45(1) *International Affairs* 64;

on Tariffs and Trade (GATT), which almost wholly emphasised the needs of the developed countries. Deprived of such key avenues for advancing their development, developing countries sought to increase private foreign investment to facilitate structural changes and economic stability, pressing in the UN for favourable principles (including tax measures) to be adopted by industrialised governments to stimulate the flow of private capital to underdeveloped countries.[49] Developed countries staved off these various efforts with alternative proposals or watered-down resolutions that kept the subjects as ongoing studies pending further consultation and review.[50]

4.1.2 *Structural and Functional Changes*

The UN was the second great experiment in world organisation with its two superpowers, previously outsiders in the international political arena, keen to portray it as an entirely new and different organisation from the discredited League.[51] The UN structure was thus formed and in great haste to take advantage of the cooperative Allied atmosphere that was still strong in the final months of the war.[52] The world was in a state of colossal upheaval and its economy disrupted; fifty million people had perished and millions of refugees displaced; tens of thousands of cities

Daniel Crache, 'The Short but Significant Life of the International Trade Organization: Lessons for Our Time' (Working Paper No 62/00, Centre for the Study of Globalisation and Regionalisation, University of Warwick, November 2000) 20. Export instability, in particular, was a far greater problem for developing rather than developed countries, the former suffering, between 1945 and 1958, around 30 per cent more frequent fluctuations in their export earnings than the latter, whose exports grew steadily in manufactured goods: Hans W Singer and Javed A Ansari, *Rich and Poor Countries* (Allen & Unwin, 2nd ed, 1978) 78–9.

49 See Houston, *Latin America*, 236–7.

50 See ibid 236–46; Luard, *How It Works*, 144.

51 Claude, *Swords into Plowshares*, 66. As the League had never gained US membership and had expelled the USSR, the United States desired 'the League [to] pass away quietly and with dignity', while the USSR preferred for the 'the League to liquidate itself': 'Telegram by Stettinus to Acting Secretary of State', 14 September 1945, in State Department, *Foreign Relations of the United States: Diplomatic Papers, 1945* (USGPO, 1967) vol 1: General: The United Nations, Doc 329.

52 Goodspeed, *Nature and Function*, 91. British correspondence indicates that even US interest in the organisation was 'flagging and its proprietary pride dissipating' by September 1945: Letter from Mackenzie to Gore-Booth, 1 September 1945, TNA: FO371/50879. Britain itself was turning towards a greater focus on domestic affairs with less emphasis on world politics under Prime Minister Attlee, who replaced Churchill in July 1945: Lundestad, *East*, 7.

across Europe, Asia and North Africa lay devastated; many governments were in ruin or provisional; unemployment was at record high level; famine threatened; and the peace settlement was yet undecided.[53] Britain and Western Europe needed US support for economic aid and reconstruction and to counter the local Soviet dominance, and they feared a US return to isolation.[54] For the United States, which had assumed leadership for the new organisation, national pride and confidence were at stake as much of the world looked to the superpower to restore international order and to create a new foundation for peace and cooperation between nations.[55] Compromises were hence swiftly made amid high enthusiasm, expectations, confusion and hypocrisy even as the wartime alliance began to disintegrate in the closing days of World War II as a result of rising East–West suspicions and Soviet intransigence.[56] The UN Charter[57] was signed by fifty countries in the month following Nazi Germany's surrender, and, after ratification by just over half of its signatories, entered into force in the month following Japan's surrender.

Importantly, the various founders had different aspirations for the world order being created, thereby perpetuating the uncertainty of the UN's true purpose. The Big Three were anxious not to construct an organisation that could endanger their control of world affairs, while the lesser states were bent on weakening the privileged power of the major powers to advance the principle of sovereign equality of nations enshrined in the Charter.[58] The United States, moreover, was bent on using its overwhelming economic power as diplomatic leverage to 'fashion a United States-oriented world order'.[59] Following the December 1945 decision to base the organisation in the United States, the UN would carry out its work in various improvised accommodations in different locations around New York until construction of its

[53] White, *Developing World*, 103; Trygve Lie, 'Full Text of Trygve Lie's Summary of Work of the United Nations' (1946) 32(9) *American Bar Association Journal* 553, 557.

[54] Scammell, *International Economy*, 11; Lundestad, *East*, 7.

[55] Maurice Bertrand, *The United Nations: Past, Present and Future* (Kluwer Law International, 1997) 32–3; Goodspeed, *Nature and Function*, 91.

[56] See Goodspeed, *Nature and Function*, 90–100; Thant Myint-U and Amy Scott, *The UN Secretariat: A Brief History (1945–2006)* (International Peace Academy, 2007) 18; Paterson, *Soviet–American Confrontation*, 22–4.

[57] *Charter of the United Nations*, opened for signature 26 June 1945, 1 UNTS XVI (entered into force 24 October 1945) ('*UN Charter*'). Poland later signed the Charter on 15 October 1945.

[58] See Luard, *How It Works*, 143; Goodspeed, *Nature and Function*, 93, 160; Paterson, *Soviet–American Confrontation*, 10.

[59] Paterson, *Soviet–American Confrontation*, 12–13, 22.

permanent headquarters was completed in October 1952.[60] Proper facilities or support staff were thus hardly in place when the ECOSOC structure was more or less established by end 1946, and when the Fiscal Commission held its First Session in May 1947.

These cross purposes and the UN's hectic, disorderly start would have long-lasting repercussions for the organisation's work.[61] The key structural and functional impacts relevant to the Fiscal Commission story may be summarised in the following. Firstly, different views concerning economic development and the UN's role in this regard surfaced. The United States stressed free trade and the role of the private sector, the Soviets advanced government control and socialist economy, while developing countries sought, inter alia, fair prices for primary commodities, development aid and long-term private capital injection.[62] The North saw development as secondary to peace and security issues, while the South saw it as the UN's primary task.[63] With few alternative forums to advance their interests, they were strident and persistent in the aim of persuading the United States, in particular, to agree to their proposals.[64] However, as the wealthy capitalist states had not envisaged the Assembly or ECOSOC to have any major role in advancing development and had already provided for the chief global economic concerns to be governed by specialised agencies, they resisted many Third World resolutions and giving too much competence to the UN.[65] The North's domination over activities and policies that could be pursued left ECOSOC to evolve to become a relatively powerless structure,[66] which also 'weakened the DEA that was designed to serve it'.[67] The reporting structure for economic activities was rigidly applied and the operations became more regimented and procedurally burdened. Moreover, ECOSOC and the Assembly were not able to perform their intended leadership and coordination roles for reasons that included the difficulties in the relationship between the two organs, their politicised nature,

60 Luard, *History*, 78–85; Myint-U and Scott, *UN Secretariat*, 10–12.

61 See Myint-U and Scott, *UN Secretariat*, 16.

62 Jussi M Hanhimäki, *The United Nations: A Very Short Introduction* (Oxford University Press, 2008) 93–4; Luard, *How It Works*, 57, 143–4.

63 Reinalda, *International Organizations*, 314.

64 Lewis, 'Economic and Security Council', 44.

65 Thomas G Weiss et al, *The United Nations and Changing World Politics* (Routledge, 8th ed, 2017) 249; Reinalda, *International Organizations*, 314.

66 Reinalda, *International Organizations*, 314; Hanhimäki, *Short Introduction*, 41.

67 Toye and Toye, *UN*, 66.

ECOSOC's lack of a budgetary role, and the independence and assertiveness of the specialised agencies and regional bodies (see Section 4.1.3).[68]

Secondly, the Secretariat faced struggles of 'autonomy, competence, and member state control'[69] and never fulfilled its original design of replicating the League's first-rate career international civil servants in quality, efficiency, independence and geographical diversity,[70] and of becoming a political and intellectual actor in its own right.[71] These struggles were attributable to the vast logistical, geographical and political problems experienced by the UN in its formative years, as well as the poor administrative leadership of first Secretary-General Trygve Lie over staffing and his betrayal of the Secretariat's independent character.[72] In brief, the UN Secretariat had to be built from scratch while confronting a 'full plate of activities' from the start with the weight of new ideals, leadership and expectations in addition to assuming most of the League's functions and developing liaisons with the specialised agencies.[73] Unlike the League which had taken two years to properly establish its bureaucratic machinery and recruit the most suitable staff before beginning its business, some 2,500 staff were added to the UN Secretariat over 1946–7 alone under 'less than ideal' recruitment procedures amid the fledging organisation's move from London to a temporary New York base with a permanent site only settled upon at end 1946.[74] Staff were predominantly recruited from America, Britain, Western Europe and Canada, with developing countries heavily underrepresented.[75] The UN struggled to attract high-calibre personnel with salaries lower than those of the League in its heyday and even of comparable international organisations,

[68] Armstrong, *Rise*, 68.

[69] Myint-U and Scott, *UN Secretariat*, 6.

[70] *UN Charter* ch XV; Dag Hammarskjöld, 'The International Civil Servant in Law and Fact' in Robert W Gregg and Michael Barkun (eds), *The United Nations System and Its Functions: Selected Readings* (D Van Nostrand, 1968) 215, 217; Myint-U and Scott, *UN Secretariat*, 1–2, 4–6.

[71] *UN Charter* arts 98, 99; Luard, *How It Works*, 96. The League Secretariat had not been an independent organ with the autonomy to advocate views or take sides. The UN planners had sought to redress this by making the Secretariat into a principal organ in order that it would have its own voice and independent agency to steer the organisation: Myint-U and Scott, *UN Secretariat*, 3–4; Preparatory Commission of the United Nations, *Report of the Preparatory Committee*, UN Doc PC/20 (23 December 1945) 81.

[72] Bob Reinalda, 'Institutional Development of the United Nations Secretariat' (2020) 26(2) *Global Governance* 325, 337.

[73] Myint-U and Scott, *UN Secretariat*, 16.

[74] Ibid 3, 16–17.

[75] Ibid 17–18, 122–3; Alan Ford, 'The Secretariat' in BA Wortley (ed), *The United Nations: The First Ten Years* (Oceana, 1957) 81, 97.

such as the IMF or World Bank, which was aggravated by the costs of New York housing and living.[76] Senior positions were politicised with the highest-ranking posts distributed to the Big Five based on government nominations.[77] In 1947, a mass employee protest arose over salaries and working conditions,[78] and in 1948, strong demands for the distribution of staff to correspond with the balance of membership led to a system of accepting temporary secondments, resulting in the prioritising of geographical diversity over the Charter's conditions of 'efficiency, competence and integrity'.[79] The practice of engaging staff based on pressures exerted by member states affected the upward mobility of career officials, resulting in a decline in their number.[80] Staff from developing states frequently had little expertise or experience, while the 'more industrialised states . . . saw the UN as a useful place to "dump" their less successful politicians'.[81] In the early 1950s, the Secretariat's fairness, impartiality and morale were further damaged when a precedent for the interference by member states in the UN's administrative affairs was set by the McCarthy witch-hunts which led Lie to dismiss staff who were allegedly communist sympathisers.[82]

Notwithstanding these challenges, DEA worked to address the 'aspirations of the underdeveloped countries at a time when it was not at all clear how Keynes's theory could throw light on the problem of economic development, as opposed to that of economic stability'.[83] DEA in fact attracted 'some of the brightest economic lights of the day' who would introduce unorthodox economic ideas forming the 'main intellectual substance of the South's point of view', including that primary producing nations stood to lose in the growth and terms of trade of the prevailing world economy.[84] The Cold War era, however, imposed limitations on the type of 'objective' research the Secretariat could undertake in house,

[76] Myint-U and Scott, *UN Secretariat*, 21.

[77] Ibid 15–16, 122; J Russell Bulkeley, 'Depoliticizing United Nations Recruitment: Establishing a Genuinely International Civil Service' in Paul Taylor, Sam Daws and Ute Adamczick-Gerteis (eds), *Documents on Reform of the United Nations* (Dartmouth, 1997) 267, 278–9.

[78] Reinalda, 'Institutional Development', 331.

[79] *UN Charter* art 101, para 3; Luard, *How It Works*, 106–7.

[80] Bulkeley, 'Depoliticizing', 278–9.

[81] Reinalda, *International Organizations*, 323.

[82] Ford, 'Secretariat', 102–6; Abdelaziz Megzari, *The Internal Justice of the United Nations: A Critical History 1945–2015* (Brill Nijhoff, 2015) 129–90.

[83] Toye and Toye, *UN*, 89.

[84] Ibid 54, 10; see also ch 5. Hans Singer, one of the first UN economists to work on developing countries' problems, is noted to have been 'delighted to be in the Secretariat in those days, when it was an intellectual hothouse' as the UN seemed, in Singer's words,

which led to its use of other methods (frequently the engagement of expert consultants) to produce output involving value judgements that might attract political controversy.[85] Under Lie, a practice also developed for the Secretariat to engage in 'private, behind-the-scenes consultations with member nations' to influence policymaking rather than risk offending member states in the overt exercise of its Charter powers.[86]

Thirdly, the UN faced scarce and unpredictable funding, with the more powerful and prominent financial contributors (the United States in particular) having disproportionate control over the financial and budgetary policy as well as overall organisation of the Secretariat through the administrative and budgetary committees of the Assembly.[87] The underdeveloped countries wanted larger budgets for international redistribution, the richer countries opposed this, while the Soviets 'were particularly fervent budget cutters'.[88] Meanwhile, the larger contributors kept the Secretariat on a short financial leash to control, even 'micromanage',[89] the direction of its operations.[90] In the early years, the financial problems were compounded by ECOSOC's rapidly expanding mandate, continual adoption of subjects to be studied, poor programme coordination and failure to establish and maintain clear priorities.[91] The Secretariat was consequently engaged in hundreds of

to be 'at the center of things ... the home of mankind ... at the center of international organizations, the Bank and Fund [then] ... very much on the periphery': Thomas G Weiss, Ramesh Thakur and John Gerard Ruggie, *Global Governance and the UN: An Unfinished Journey* (Indiana University Press, 2010) 159. Note that US approval does appear to have been necessary before important hiring decisions were made: see, for example, Edgar J Dosman, *The Life and Times of Raúl Prebisch, 1901–1986* (McGill-Queen's UniversityPress, 2008) 265 (stating that the Secretary-General 'checked with Washington' before engaging DEA's favoured candidate to head ECLA).

85 Toye and Toye, *UN*, 47.

86 Ford, 'Secretariat', 86–7. See also Luard, *How It Works*, 109.

87 Myint-U and Scott, *UN Secretariat*, 15, 119; Luard, *How It Works*, 116–18, 125–9; Hanhimäki, *Short Introduction*, 48–9.

88 Luard, *How It Works*, 40.

89 Myint-U and Scott, *UN Secretariat*, 15.

90 This was achieved through delays or refusals to pay contributions, or threats of such: Richard Falk, 'Explaining the UN's Unhappy 50th Anniversary: Toward Reclaiming the Next Half-Century' in Dimitris Bourantonis and Marios Evriviades (eds), *A United Nations for the Twenty-First Century: Peace, Security and Development* (Kluwer Law International, 1996) 89, 100; Paterson, *Soviet–American Confrontation*, 11; Bertrand, *United Nations*, 81, 84.

91 Emilio J Cárdenas, R Carlos Sersale di Cerisano and Oscar A Avalle, 'Financing the United Nations' Operations: A Frustrating Nightmare' in Harlan Cleveland, Hazel Henderson and Inge Kaul (eds), *The United Nations: Policy and Financing Alternatives: Innovative Proposals by Visionary Leaders* (Elsevier Science, 1995) 145,

reports, accommodating myriad conferences with negligible 'net addition to knowledge or policy action'.[92] The situation was hence markedly different to that of the League, whose economic activities benefitted from external sources of funding (e.g. the Rockefeller grants[93]) and from the diversion of available resources to the technical work as the League's political activities became defunct.[94]

4.1.3 *Decentralisation of the UN System*

The UN's competence over economic activities would also be challenged through institutional choice and forum shopping facilitated by newly established specialised agencies and regional institutions. While the UN planners had designed ECOSOC's subordinate machinery to have mutually exclusive jurisdiction in the residual fields not occupied by existing or envisaged specialised agencies, by 1950, these agencies, which had fluid purposes and operational freedom, had already intruded into the UN's spheres of competence.[95] The creation of regional economic commissions for Europe, Asia Pacific and Latin America within ECOSOC and the growth of other independent regional organisations, such as the OEEC, would only serve to exacerbate the chronic overlap, duplication and fragmentation.

147; Lewis, 'Economic and Security Council', 44; Edward C Luck, 'Reforming the United Nations: Lessons from a History of Progress' in Paul F Diehl and Brian Frederking (eds), *The Politics of Global Governance: International Organizations in an Interdependent World* (Lynne Rienner, 4th ed, 2010) 370, 371.

92 Lewis, 'Economic and Security Council', 44.

93 See Fiscal Committee, *Report to the Council on the Work of the Second Session of the Committee*, League Doc C.340.M.140.1930.II (31 May 1930) 7–8; Fiscal Committee, *Report to the Council on the Work of the Third Session of the Committee*, League Doc C.415.M.171.1931.II.A (6 June 1931) 5; Fiscal Committee, *Report to the Council on the Work of the Fourth Session of the Committee*, League Doc C.399.M.204.1933.II.A (26 June 1933) 1; Fiscal Committee, *Report to the Council on the Seventh Session of the Committee*, League Doc C.490.M.331.1937.II.A (16 October 1937) 5. See also Ludovic Tournès, 'The Rockefeller Foundation and the Transition from the League of Nations to the UN (1939–1946)' (2014) 12(3) *Journal of Modern European History* 323, 325 (noting that the Rockefeller financial support, which could cover up to 40 per cent of the budget of the League's technical sections as well as the implementation of their projects, was aimed at promoting the autonomy of these sections to allow 'various parts of the American federal administration ... [to] participate without any risk of interfering in the political activities of the League').

94 By 1939, over 60 per cent of the League's budget was allocated for economic and social activities: Armstrong, *Rise*, 41.

95 Luck, 'Reforming', 370–1. See also Myint-U and Scott, *UN Secretariat*, 14.

The West preferred the autonomous and self-governing specialised agencies not only because their voting power, membership and rules of governance concentrated power in their major donors, but also because they had limited Soviet involvement, thus providing the wealthy industrialised countries control and dominance in the global marketplace.[96] The United States accordingly 'participated enthusiastically' in such institutions while 'circumvent[ing] or weaken[ing] those [in particular, the UN] which did not serve its purposes'.[97] On the other hand, developing countries favoured the regional commissions as vehicles for articulating their claims for development.[98] Such commissions were quasi-autonomous. They had their own secretariats located in their respective regions, more capacity to take initiatives independent of New York and competence over all economic matters. Nevertheless, their budgets were financed from UN funds, their secretariats formed part of the UN Secretariat's economic and social departments and they acted under the general supervision of ECOSOC.[99] These commissions enjoyed closed and inclusive membership within their respective regions, regional solidarity and a tendency to act by agreement rather than voting.[100]

The regional commissions created during the Commission years comprised the Economic Commission for Europe (ECE) and Economic Commission for Asia and the Far East (ECAFE) established in March 1947, and Economic Commission for Latin America (ECLA) in February 1948. The former two were purposed to address war reconstruction, but ECE was eventually eclipsed by the OEEC birthed in 1948 to bypass ECE to administer the $14.1 billion US Marshall Plan.[101] The OEEC

[96] See Weiss et al, *United Nations*, 249–53; Hanhimäki, *Short Introduction*, 41–3; Luck, 'Reforming', 370–1.

[97] Paterson, *Soviet–American Confrontation*, 147. In particular, the US vote in the Bretton Woods institutions approximated a third of the total weighted voting, enabling America to wield these agencies to execute its foreign policy (at 151–2).

[98] WR Malinowski, 'Centralization and Decentralization in the United Nations Economic and Social Activities' (1962) 16(3) *International Organization* 521, 540; Robert W Gregg, 'The UN Regional Economic Commissions and Integration in the Underdeveloped Regions' (1966) 20(2) *International Organization* 208, 209, 212.

[99] Malinowski, 'Centralization', 525; Gregg, 'Regional Economic Commissions', 210; Lewis, 'Economic and Security Council', 42.

[100] Malinowski, 'Centralization', 523.

[101] Lewis, 'Economic and Security Council', 42–3; Daniel Stinsky, 'Western European vs All-European Cooperation? The OEEC, the European Recovery Program, and the United Nations Economic Commission for Europe (ECE), 1947–1952' in Matthieu Leimgruber and Matthias Schmelzer (eds), *The OECD and the International Political Economy since 1948* (Palgrave Macmillan, 2017) 65, 70–2; Paterson, *Soviet–American Confrontation*, 208, 228–30. Prior to the Marshall Plan, Europe had already received $8.3 billion from the United

would pave the way for economic cooperation concerning Western Europe to leave the UN framework.[102] ECAFE had negligible impact, being dominated by non-Asian states in its early years, lacking in ideological thrust and covering too vast a geographic expanse.[103] Meanwhile, ECLA became 'a force to be reckoned with in the Western Hemisphere'[104] in pioneering industrialisation and development policies, especially to attract both public and private investments.[105] In it, the United States was typically a minor and frequently dissenting member.[106] US–Latin American relations were strained at the time of ECLA's creation. With the UN's formation, Latin America had been hopeful of another means to advance its development goals, which it considered its entitlement for its Allied war contribution.[107] The announcement of the Marshall Plan in mid-1947 however made clear that no counterpart would be offered to Latin America: the region had been sidelined as 'a poor third' in US overseas aid to Europe and Asia.[108] The World Bank also failed to provide a counterweight to exclusive dependency on US capital as its major contributors, the United States and the United Kingdom, gave greater priority to rebuilding Europe to become an important power alongside them.[109] Frustrated and fearful that the United States would subordinate inter-American cooperation to its global interests, the growingly resentful and disillusioned Latin American countries began activism in all possible spheres and means to have their developmental and balance of payments requirements met.[110] At the ITO Havana Conference

States in bilateral aid: Geir Lundestad, '"Empire by Invitation" in the American Century' in Michael J Hogan (ed), *The Ambiguous Legacy: US Foreign Relations in the "American Century"* (Cambridge University Press, 1999) 52, 62.

102 Stinsky, 'Western European', 68, 72, 81.

103 Gregg, 'Regional Economic Commissions', 220–1.

104 Ibid 218. See also Dosman, *Prebisch*, 287–90, 295–6.

105 EVK FitzGerald, 'ECLA and the Formation of Latin American Economic Doctrine' in David Rock (ed), *Latin America in the 1940s* (University of California Press, 1994) 89, 96; Dosman, *Prebisch*, 273.

106 Gregg, 'Regional Economic Commissions', 216.

107 Dosman, *Prebisch*, 236.

108 Houston, *Latin America*, 222–3, 233; Stephen G Rabe, 'The Elusive Conference: United States Economic Relations with Latin America, 1945–1952' (1978) 2(3) *Diplomatic History* 279, 279.

109 Victor Bulmer-Thomas, *The Economic History of Latin America since Independence* (Cambridge University Press, 2014) 287. By 1947, the United States and the United Kingdom together held almost 50 per cent of the voting rights in the World Bank, with the eleven most industrialised countries holding over 70 per cent of the votes altogether: Toussaint, *World Bank*, 15–16.

110 Norma Breda Dos Santos, 'Latin American Countries and the Establishment of the Multilateral Trading System: The Havana Conference' (2016) 36(2) *Brazilian Journal of Political Economy* 309, 319–20.

on Trade and Employment ('Havana Conference'), they sought favourable policies that would, inter alia, facilitate their acquisition of capital for industrialisation.[111] In the UN, they fought to establish ECLA but this was resisted by the industrialised countries led by the United States.[112] ECLA was grudgingly founded in February 1948 on a three-year probationary basis and had a slow, troubled start to its operations.[113] In the meantime, at the PAU Ninth International Conference of American States held in Bogotá in April 1948 ('Bogotá Conference'), the United States led the recreation of the Washington-based, mostly US-funded and US-dominated PAU into the Organization for American States (OAS), equipping its Inter-American Economic and Social Council with a budget equal to ECLA's to provide a competing economic commission that it could more fully control.[114] Despite heavy US campaigning for the latter's termination or merger with the Inter-American Economic and Social Council, ECLA nevertheless became a permanent body in 1951 with an expanded and strengthened mandate in practical activities and policy work.[115] It would become a main avenue for Latin America to contend with the United States on economic issues, which would give rise to more controversies than any other source of dissension in the UN.[116]

4.2 The Workings of the Fiscal Commission and Fiscal Division

The aforementioned dynamics and dilemmas taking place generally in the UN would pervade almost all the workings of the Fiscal Commission and Fiscal Division. As a background to the forthcoming chapters, the following provides an overview of these impacts on the Commission's and Division's structure, operations and relations with non-governmental organisations (NGOs).

[111] Bulmer-Thomas, *Economic History*, 287. The United States perceived the region as being the cause of many complications at the conference and was annoyed with its opposition to US positions: Santos, 'Latin American Countries', 322.

[112] Houston, *Latin America*, 223–7; Dosman, *Prebisch*, 236–7.

[113] Dosman, *Prebisch*, 236–9, 246, 252–71.

[114] Ibid 237, 254, 258–60.

[115] Ibid 237, 259–60, 262–4, 269–72. This merger was also resisted strongly by the UN Secretariat (at 254).

[116] Houston, *Latin America*, 223. See also Dosman, *Prebisch*, 247, 250–1.

4.2.1 Structure

4.2.1.1 The Fiscal Commission

As with all other ECOSOC functional commissions, the Fiscal Commission's fifteen members were elected for a term of three years, with a third retiring at the end of each year to allow opportunity for participation by other countries while retaining smooth succession.[117] However, the Big Five's de facto permanent seats, the eligibility of retiring members for re-election and the pressure to ensure representation of geopolitical blocs and middle powers[118] resulted in eight of the ten original non-Big-Five members serving on the Commission for most of its short life: Czechoslovakia and Cuba for the entire eight years; Belgium for seven years; Colombia, India and Pakistan for six years; and Canada, South Africa and New Zealand for five years. Only five countries (Sweden, Chile, Venezuela, Lebanon and Turkey) served for a single term. Despite this ostensible continuity, only Cuba, France and the United States would send the same representative to all four of the Commission's sessions, followed by the USSR for three sessions, and Britain, Canada, China, Colombia, Czechoslovakia, Pakistan and South Africa for two sessions.

The State Department played a major role in reviewing the membership and determining which country would be nominated for election. In 1951, its policy, apart from the aforementioned considerations and in view of its 'general overall economic philosophy ... [and the] free world ... [it] was trying to encourage', was to prefer: (1) countries with similar fiscal policies and programmes; (2) new or underdeveloped countries 'whose fiscal policies ... [were] embryonic and in a state of flux', which stood to greatly learn 'about the use and development of fiscal policy' and which were 'less likely to use the administrative techniques common to dictatorships'; and (3) countries which had 'shown energetic and constructive interest in the Commission'.[119] The United States' insistence of China's representation by a Nationalist Party member would give rise to tensions at the Commission's Third and Fourth Sessions as the Soviet Bloc sought to have the seat replaced by a member of the PRC government.

[117] To bring the rotation into operation, a third of the original members were to serve for two years, a third for three years and the remaining third for four years.

[118] See Memorandum by Evans to Bartelt, 27 April 1949, NARAII:RG56-199-2; Letter from Nicholas to Butler, 16 April 1952, TNA:IR40/11173(2).

[119] Memorandum by Hayes to Bartelt, 18 May 1951, NARAII:RG56-199-3.

Although ECOSOC had provided for the Secretariat to consult with governments to ensure that suitably competent representatives were nominated,[120] in practice the Secretariat had no say in the government nominations and ECOSOC confirmed all nominations that were put to it. While these official representatives typically comprised high-ranking members of their respective Treasury or Ministry of Finance,[121] countries often sent alternates to substitute or stand in for their official representatives, such alternates being frequently diplomatic members of their countries' permanent UN delegations.[122] This resulted in a Commission that tended to comprise a combination of 'general men ... [who were] not expert in the subjects', Treasury or Finance officials who were 'expert in Budgetary matters but not in fiscal matters', and 'fiscal experts who ... [were] not necessarily budgetary experts'.[123] Attendance records of the meetings of each session as well as voting numbers on decisions moreover indicate that countries' delegates were absent for some meetings. Also, while only a handful of countries sent one, or in the rare instance two, adviser(s) to accompany their representative/alternate, the United States had such an overwhelmingly sized delegation[124] that the American UN Ambassador Warren Austin in 1951 would express his embarrassment, leading the delegation to list only four names as advisers, with the rest to remain as 'observers to be called up at instance of Mr Bartelt [the US representative]'.[125] (See Appendix B, Table B.1, for the list of members of countries' delegations to the Commission's sessions.)

120 *Fiscal Commission*, ESC Res 2 (III), UN ESCOR, UN Doc E/245/Rev.1 (3 May 1947, adopted 1 October 1946, supplemented by action taken by the Council on 2 and 3 October 1946) para 4.

121 See *Biographical Data on the Members of the Fiscal Commission*, UN ESC, UN Doc E/453 (8 July 1947).

122 Travel constraints, such as the length of time needed for steamship travel and the exclusivity of air travel due to its prohibitive cost and limited routes, were likely major contributory factors to the use of alternates.

123 Frank Bower, 'Confidential Note by the ICC Representative on the Fiscal Commission's Second Session', 2, attached to Letter from Bower to Bartelt, 28 January 1949, NARAII: RG56–199–4. Britain also considered that the Commission was divided between 'fiscal officials who were interested in points of taxation principle and so on' and 'members of permanent delegations, who were more interested in political and diplomatic questions', and that '[e]ither group left to themselves might perhaps have achieved something; but the mixture rendered useful discussion almost impossible': Letter from MHC (on behalf of JMG) to Bartlett, 15 February 1954, TNA:IR40/11173(1).

124 This encompassed officials from various Treasury agencies, including the Tax Research Division, Tax Legislative Counsel, Internal Revenue Bureau and Office of International Finance.

125 File Note by McKenna for Bartelt, 4 May 1951, NARAII:RG56–199–6.

4.2.1.2 The Fiscal Division

The Fiscal Division formed part of DEA, which was initially headed by Owen.[126] Deperon served as Director of the Division until 1949, after which the seat was filled by Henry Bloch.[127] By March 1948, the Division had an International Tax Section and a Budgetary Research Section,[128] each headed by Chiefs: the former by Karl Lachmann; the latter by Wladimir Karakacheff and after 1951, Stein Rossen. By mid-1947, the Division had a permanent staff of seven professionals and had plans to increase this total to a minimum of thirteen professionals.[129] By end 1948, however, it was still struggling to fill these positions,[130] and there was some indication of political appointments having been made (e.g. Benedicto Silva [Brazil] as Deputy Director).[131] In November 1951, the Division's professional staff of lawyers and economists numbered thirteen and those that had particular expertise included Bloch, Lachmann and Karol Kremery, a Czech lawyer who studied at London School of Economics during the war.[132] Other unnamed members of the International Tax Section included a French Lawyer who had a PhD in economics (public finance), a Dutch Lawyer who had an LLM from Indiana University Law School and was a teaching fellow at the University of Chicago Law School, and an Iranian Lawyer who studied at the University of Paris Law School. Altogether, the team was reportedly 'in a position to deal with legal materials of a great variety of systems and languages, including Anglo-Saxon, Latin American, French,

[126] 'The Secretariat' [1946–7] *Yearbook of the United Nations* 613, 657. Owen was 'the first economist to be appointed to the UN': Richard Jolly, Louis Emmerij and Dharam Ghai, *UN Contributions to Development Thinking and Practice* (Indiana University Press, 2004) 70. For accounts of Owen's major role in recruiting formidable economists to DEA, see Toye and Toye, *UN*, ch 2; Dosman, *Prebisch*, 251.

[127] 'The Secretariat' [1948–9] *Yearbook of the United Nations* 152, 164.

[128] The Division also had a third unit, the Office of the Director, which, inter alia, formulated policies and programmes, approved and released documents and correspondence, reported to the more senior sections of DEA and dealt generally with liaison matters: 'Note on Fiscal Division: Allocation of Functions', 24 March 1948, UNARMS:AG-004-001—S-0979-0001-01.

[129] 'UN Secretariat DEA: Fiscal Division', undated (around July 1947), chs 2, 6, NARAII: RG56-199-3. Lachmann is recorded here as the only professional working on international tax matters (at 4).

[130] See Chapter 5, Section 5.6.

[131] Silva is referred to as having a liaison role (see Chapter 6, Section 6.1). He is not found among the UN archival records to have worked on any substantive matters.

[132] KE Lachmann, Memorandum on 'References in Published Materials to the Fiscal Division: Its Functions, Operations and Staff', 20 November 1951, 1, UNARMS:AG-025-002—S-0441-0468-23886(A).

Scandinavian, Italian and those of most other European countries, Russian, Arabic, Turkish and Persian'.[133]

4.2.2 Operations

The Commission had been intended to hold sessions annually and even more frequent meetings if necessary;[134] however, budgetary restrictions by the relevant committees of the Assembly would lead to the sessions being held biennially. The session dates were determined by ECOSOC (with strong US influence[135]):

First Session	19–29 May 1947
Second Session	10–25 January 1949
Third Session	7–17 May 1951
Fourth Session	27 April–8 May 1953

At each session, a chairman, two vice-chairmen and a general rapporteur were elected as officers. These elections appeared heavily predetermined by the United States based on considerations of geopolitics,[136] competence and stature in fiscal matters,[137] and command of English (although

[133] Ibid.

[134] *Sessions of the Council and of Its Commissions and Sub-Commissions*, ESC Res 55 (IV), UN ESCOR, UN Doc E/437 (1947, adopted 28 March 1947). Conversely, four other commissions, including the Economic and Employment Commission, were to hold biannual sessions.

[135] See Chapter 9, Sections 9.4 and 9.5.

[136] This included considerations of overall geographic balance in the officers elected across the other ECOSOC commissions; the number of states of a regional group represented on each commission; and favouring certain allies. For example, in 1947, the United States instructed that the four eastern European states represented on the Commission purportedly entitled them to one officer; however, this was subject to the reservation that the United States should support the UK representative if the British government proposed him for an office. An 'additional officership for a Latin American' was also contemplated. The United States did not propose the US representative for an office as US members were already being advanced for the chairmanship of two other commissions. Belgium's candidacy for Chairmanship, even though its representative (Putnam) was the 'most suitable' choice, was briefly considered to be objectionable because Deperon was also Belgian: Telegram from State Department to US–UN Mission, 16 May 1947; Memorandum by Olsen to Bartelt, 15 January 1947; Memorandum by Kellogg to Cooley and Popper, 2 May 1947, NARAII:RG56–199–3.

[137] Olsen memo, 15 January 1947. For the Third Session, possibly due to the Cold War, the State Department ceased to propose Soviet members to officership, desiring instead 'to pass the "plums" around as widely as possible': Memorandum by Hayes to Bartelt, 5 May 1951, NARAII:RG56–199–6. Even so, Czechoslovakia was

this was not a controlling factor).[138] By 1949, the State Department's policy was 'always . . . that no US representative should allow himself to be elected'[139] and, after 1949, for the United States to not 'take the lead in sponsoring the Chinese representative for any office' to avoid friction.[140] It also considered that there were 'several undesirable aspects of having a Russian as Chairman on this particular Commission'[141] and envisaged 'that any representative of an Iron Curtain country might use his office to hamstring the Commission'.[142] The Commission's elected officers for each session showed close alignment with the United States', and to some extent Britain's, preferred candidates and political compromises: a Soviet state was always appointed as vice-chairman; the rapporteur came from a Western English-speaking country; and members not fluent in English would serve as chairmen, their language skills affecting their effectiveness, especially as the discussions became more politically and procedurally burdened.

Deperon's planned Tax and Public Finance Sub-Commissions were never established. Procedurally, these subordinate bodies could only be created by ECOSOC and to avoid the bureaucracy, Deperon suggested the use of temporary ad hoc working committees as a more 'expeditious and flexible' device,[143] which was accepted by the Commission at its First Session. A committee (or working group) on international tax issues was set up at every session, while one concerning public finance was only

appointed as vice-chairman despite the United States believing there was 'no good reason' for favouring the official candidate.

138 Olsen memo, 15 January 1947; Kellogg memo, 2 May 1947; Hayes memo, 5 May 1951. Deperon was also involved in recommending candidates for office: Memorandum by Evans to Bartelt, 4 October 1948, NARAII:RG56–199–4; Telegram No 1406 from Foreign Office to New York (UK Delegation to UN), 12 May 1947, TNA:IR40/8946. Britain itself exerted some influence in 'impress[ing] upon the Secretariat the importance of an English-speaking rapporteur': Telegram No 1406 from New York (UK Delegation to UN) to Foreign Office, 16 May 1947, TNA:IR40/8946.

139 Memorandum by Evans to Bartelt, 23 November 1948, NARAII:RG56–199–4.

140 Hayes memo, 5 May 1951.

141 Olsen memo, 15 January 1947.

142 Hayes memo, 5 May 1951.

143 Fiscal Commission, *Remarks Concerning the Tasks of the Fiscal Commission*, Note by the Secretariat, 1st sess, Provisional Agenda items 6 and 9, UN Doc E/CN.8/6 (10 April 1947) 9. Britain may also have influenced this change, having indicated 'it premature to appoint a permanent standing committee. If an interim committee is needed, we would prefer a committee with terms of reference limited to matters which Commission will have discussed. We would not like to have a body composed on factitious criterion of residence in United States': Foreign Office, Telegram No 1406, 12 May 1947.

established at the First and Third Sessions. Theoretically, these committees could comprise commission members, other government representatives and private persons. However, in practice, they were only ever composed of a few interested members of the Commission. Moreover, unlike the subcommittees of the League's Fiscal Committee, the Commission's committees only ever met during the Commission's sessions, typically completing their work within three days. The ICC observed that the Commission members had 'an aversion' to dividing into these committees 'to deal with the . . . separate facets of the work for fear . . . [that] someone . . . [might be] missing something'.[144]

As a political body, not to mention one composed of participants with little commonality, the Commission's sessions produced only the lowest common denominator of agreement on policies to be pursued and the work programme to be undertaken. In fact, the discussions often indicated that few participants read the Division's preparatory documents for each session. Procedural rules, including those related to working methods as well as interpretation and translation,[145] grew unwieldy, adding to costs and delays in the proceedings.[146] Substantive debates on controversial subjects (i.e. those related to double taxation) were disrupted by procedural arguments, frequently as a tactic employed by countries to direct or divert discussions on a path favourable to their respective interests. As the divisions between the political factions intensified and the discussions became more contentious, the Commission's reports to ECOSOC progressively contained little technical matter, cursory and skewed narratives by the rapporteurs and specific views of countries which insisted upon the inclusion of their minority positions. As such reporting provided little background or context to the Commission's recommendations for adoption, members of ECOSOC,

[144] Bower, 'Confidential Note', 2.

[145] The UN's official languages then comprised Chinese, English, French, Russian and Spanish, with its working languages comprising English, French and, from December 1948 in the Assembly, Spanish: 'What Are the Official Languages of the United Nations', *Dag Hammarskjöld Library* (Web Page) <https://ask.un.org/faq/14463>. Documents, summary records and speeches in any official language were drawn-up or made available in the working languages. All official UN documents were made available in the official languages.

[146] Few rules of procedures were in place in the beginning, but these were adopted over time, often in response to problems that arose among ECOSOC's commissions: see *Rules of Procedure of ECOSOC Commissions*, UN ESC, UN Doc E/460 (10 July 1947). Cf *Rules of Procedure of ECOSOC Functional Commissions*, UN ESC, UN Doc E/2425 (12 May 1953).

particularly developing countries, who were not knowledgeable about the issues at point or competing technical arguments were hence disadvantaged in determining which way to vote. Meanwhile, those who were better informed and more geopolitically connected were able to sway the proceedings towards their preferred outcome.

The Division was perpetually resource-strapped, understaffed and affected by politics. In addition to its technical work, it accommodated requests by member states for technical assistance and collaborated on projects of mutual interest with other UN bodies, including the Statistical Commission, Trusteeship Council, IMF and FAO. By end 1949, it was running a 'consultants program', which included seminars by technical assistance experts, to enable it to learn about existing technical assistance experience and to accomplish certain ad hoc assignments requested of it.[147] It drew on DEA's general and travel funds for hiring consultants and temporary assistants,[148] and DEA's needs also determined the timing and order of priority of its publications.[149] While the Division produced much factual and statistical output, many of its in-house studies remained in a state of work-in-progress throughout the Commission's life, in part due to the magnitude of the projects, their need for applicability to the broad UN membership and the difficulty the Division faced in obtaining data from countries. Importantly, projects were abandoned, evolved or taken up to meet US preferences, views and demands. The Division regularly reported to the United States and kept it informed of its work and related developments. In the early years, and on matters which had US support, the Division was able to seek US intervention when its work was being held up by another body in the UN (e.g. an Assembly committee).[150] However, as the Division moved in a more independent direction in its work, US support for its work, even its existence, waned.[151] The Division resorted to utilising external experts to produce reports containing controversial policy positions (which it itself held), but such research was ultimately suppressed either by the Division for having offended countries[152] or by countries' manoeuvring to have the work disregarded.[153] In 1949, Deperon departed the Division

[147] Note (untitled) on work plan of the Fiscal Division, 20 December 1949, 9, UNOG: UNOGRFP—G.X.25/1.
[148] Lachmann memo, 20 November 1951, 2.
[149] Note on work plan, 1.
[150] See Chapter 5, Section 5.4.
[151] See Chapter 8, Section 8.1.
[152] See Chapter 7, Sections 7.2.4, 7.4 and 7.5.
[153] See Chapter 11, Sections 11.5–11.10.

under mysterious circumstances,[154] and after 1951, which coincided with McCarthyism in the UN,[155] the Division produced no more contentious intellectual work.

4.2.3 Relations with NGOs

The ICC is generally famed in the literature for having played an influential role in the League's double taxation work.[156] Its involvement was facilitated by the silence in the League Covenant concerning relations with NGOs, which led to the development of an informal practice allowing interested NGOs a consultative role in relevant League committees.[157] Such participation was placed on an equal footing with that of intergovernmental organisations and even governmental representatives 'in all but voting', with NGO representatives 'allowed to speak, present reports, initiate discussions, propose resolutions and amendments, and be assigned to subcommittees'.[158] The League's practice was codified in the UN Charter which provided for ECOSOC to 'make suitable arrangements for consultation' with NGOs.[159] However, this relationship was fundamentally distinguished from the participation without vote granted to specialised agencies[160] due to Soviet suspicion as well as Third World wariness of NGOs, which were predominantly Western-oriented.[161] Relations with NGOs thus developed considerably more formally with a special ECOSOC committee established to draft regulations and procedural rules concerning criteria for admission to consultative status, and the type and degree of participation to be

[154] See Chapter 7, Section 7.2.

[155] See Chapter 9, Section 9.5.

[156] See, for example Ke Chin Wang, 'International Double Taxation of Income: Relief through International Agreement 1921–1945' (1945) 59(1) *Harvard Law Review* 73, 73; Michael J Graetz and Michael M O'Hear, 'The "Original Intent" of US International Taxation' (1997) 46(5) *Duke Law Journal* 1021, 1066–82. Recent scholarship, however, reveals that the ICC had relatively little impact on the development of the 1928 Models: Sunita Jogarajan, *Double Taxation and the League of Nations* (Cambridge University Press, 2018) ch 4.

[157] Pei-heng Chiang, *Non-Governmental Organizations at the United Nations: Identity, Role, and Function* (Praeger, 1981) 34–5; Interim Committee to Consultative Non-Governmental Organizations, *Consultation between the United Nations and Non-Governmental Organizations*, United Nations Studies 3 (CEIP, December, 1949) 11–12 ('*UN and NGOs*').

[158] Chiang, *Non-Governmental Organizations*, 34–8.

[159] *UN Charter* art 71; Reinalda, *International Organizations*, 316.

[160] *UN Charter* art 70; Chiang, *Non-Governmental Organizations*, 35.

[161] Chiang, *Non-Governmental Organizations*, 4.

granted.[162] The initial hopes, at least of the Western nations, were that NGO consultation would enable (1) ECOSOC and its commissions to secure expert assistance, particularly through informal relations with the Secretariat, working parties or sub-commissions in the initial scoping of problems for discussion;[163] and (2) global organised movements, which represented important elements of public opinion, to express their views and be in close contact with ECOSOC as it was believed that the UN would fail in the long run without public support.[164] The Secretariat itself hoped that coordination with NGOs, as with other UN bodies and specialised agencies, would assist the Fiscal Commission by providing needed information or preventing 'duplication of effort or omissions in important activities'.[165]

The key NGOs which attempted to play a role in the Commission's fiscal work were the ICC, which obtained Category A status (i.e. NGO with basic interest in most of ECOSOC's activities) in October 1946, and the National Association for Manufacturers (NAM) and the International Fiscal Association (IFA), which obtained Category B status (i.e. NGO with special competence in a particular field of ECOSOC's activities) in August 1947 and February 1949, respectively.[166] These business organisations communicated documents to the Commission and sent representatives to its sessions who contributed to the discussions, especially

[162] Committee on Arrangements for Consultation with Non-Governmental Organizations, *Report of the Committee*, UN ESC, UN Doc E/43/Rev.2 (1 July 1946); Reinalda, *International Organizations*, 317–18.

[163] Interim Committee to Consultative Non-Governmental Organizations, *UN and NGOs*, 28–30.

[164] Ibid 19–20.

[165] Fiscal Commission, *Remarks by ADK Owen, Assistant Secretary-General for Economic Affairs, at the Opening of the First Session of the Fiscal Commission, at Lake Success, NY on 19 May 1947*, 1st sess, UN Doc E/CN.8/12 (19 May 1947).

[166] Fiscal Commission, *Documentary Material on Relations with Non-Governmental Organizations*, 1st sess, Provisional Agenda item 12, UN Doc E/CN.8/9 (29 April 1947); Committee on Arrangements for Consultation with Non-Governmental Organizations, *Report of the Committee on Applications of Non-Governmental Organizations for Consultative Status with the Economic and Social Council*, UN ESC, UN Doc E/500 (29 July 1947); *Report of Committee of the Whole of the Economic and Social Council: Recommendations Concerning the Applications of Non-Governmental Organizations for Consultative Status with the Economic and Social Council, 7 August 1947*, UN ESC, UN Doc E/543 (9 August 1947). All categories could consult directly with the relevant commission, but only Category A NGOs had the right to propose items for the provisional agenda: Bowett, *Law of International Institutions*, 69–70.

concerning double taxation.[167] (See Appendix B, Table B.2 for the members of NGO delegations to the Commission's sessions.)

The ICC proved the most active, continually advocating for the elimination of double taxation and expressing a preference for the exemption method of relief, DTAs based on the London Model, and even a multilateral tax treaty. In 1949, nevertheless, it had deemed the Commission's composition to 'not lend itself to progress in study',[168] and by July 1954, it had abandoned the Commission by appealing to the OEEC to take up the reins of double taxation.[169] The consultative status of NAM and IFA was mainly achieved as a result of Carroll's efforts and connections, conducted with the aim of participating as a consultant to the Commission.[170] As a US association,[171] NAM's application was initially rejected;[172] however, the US delegation successfully intervened to support NAM's request.[173] Meanwhile, Deperon assisted Carroll in making IFA's application for consultative status.[174] He also circulated the resolutions adopted at IFA's 1947 Congress to the Commission[175] but was reprimanded by the Secretariat's Division of Coordination and Liaison for having given 'better treatment' to an organisation without

[167] Although the Commission's records do not indicate that such participation was welcomed, positive accounts were reported by the NGOs themselves: for example, Franck Bower (ICC) reported that at the Second Session, the Soviet Chairman had initially treated him as a 'poor relation' in comparison to the government delegates but that this 'soon disappeared'; he had 'every opportunity to speak' and had 'intervened in plenary session and in working committee'; his remarks influenced decisions; and the ICC's documents 'were noted with appreciation': Bower, 'Confidential Note', 2. See also Chapter 10, Section 10.1 (regarding Carroll's reporting of the reception of his views). In general, scholars note that NGO contributions to ECOSOC's work have been unremarkable and viewed with scepticism: Bowett, *Law of International Institutions*, 70.

[168] Bower, 'Confidential Note', 1.

[169] See Chapter 13, Section 13.2.

[170] Carroll would officially attend all the Commission's sessions as NAM's representative, although he would in some meetings be recorded as representing IFA (i.e. the Working Party's meetings of the Second Session and in one plenary meeting of the Fourth Session).

[171] See Chapter 2, Section 2.2.2 n 335 for a background on NAM.

[172] E/500, 5.

[173] Committee on Arrangements for Consultation with Non-Governmental Organizations, *Proposal of the Delegation of the United States to Bring the National Association of Manufacturers into Consultative Relationship with the Economic and Social Council*, UN ESC, Agenda item 28, UN Doc E/502 (30 July 1947); E/543, 4.

[174] Letters by Carroll to Deperon, 17 and 28 April 1947; Memorandum by Deperon to White, 30 April 1948, UNARMS:AG-025-002—S-0441-0054-01.

[175] Fiscal Commission, *Resolutions and Themes for Study 1947/48 Adopted by the International Fiscal Association Congress 1947*, Note by the Secretariat, UN Doc E/CN.8/W.14 (25 February 1948).

consultative status when no Commission member had specifically requested for such treatment.[176]

Despite the cool reception by the Commission, the Fiscal Division under Deperon did attempt to form ties with these NGOs. The ICC, however, declined his request for it to call upon its national committees in various countries to prepare replies to the Division's questionnaires for information.[177] Deperon had more success with IFA due to his personal ties with Carroll: Carroll invited Deperon to speak about the Commission's work at IFA (and also the International Bar Association)[178] and called upon IFA's national groups to reply to the Division's questionnaire for information;[179] and Deperon helped to promote IFA to, and connect Carroll with, the UN's growing government contacts, including those formed during technical assistance missions.[180] Deperon and Carroll also continued to consult and mutually assist each other on their double taxation work as well as inform on tax treaty developments,[181] which included Deperon (and Lachmann) proofing Carroll's articles for IFA to boost its tax treaty programme,[182] and Carroll's assistance in distributing the *Mexico/London Models Commentary*.[183] After Deperon's departure, relations between the

[176] Memorandum by White to Deperon, 26 April 1948, UNARMS:AG-025-002—S-0441-0054-01. ECOSOC later adopted procedures requiring NGOs to first consult the Secretariat's NGO Section to submit any proposed statements: *Arrangements for Consultation with Non-Governmental Organizations*, ESC Res 288B (X), UN ESCOR, UN Doc E/1661 (19 April 1950, adopted 27 February 1950) paras 28–29.

[177] Letter from ICC Secretary-General to Deperon, 20 September 1948, UNARMS:AG-025-002—S-0441-0464-23412. The ICC considered that it wasn't within its 'competence . . . to supply factual data on existing legislation . . ., especially as such data would inevitably duplicate data from government sources'.

[178] Letter from Carroll to Deperon, 16 June 1948, UNARMS:AG-025-002—S-0441-0054-01.

[179] Letter from Kremery to Carroll, 30 August 1948; Letter from Deperon to Carroll, 5 August 1948; Letter from IFA Secretary-General to Deperon, 31 December 1948, UNARMS:AG-025-002—S-0441-0464-23412. See also Willem Dirksen, *IFA: International Fiscal Association, 1938–1988* (Kluwer Law and Taxation, 1988) 29–30, 45–6 (indicating that IFA's expectations of continuing collaboration led it, in 1949, to appoint 'a secretary for UN matters to study ECOSOC documents for IFA purposes' and to change the institution's original 1938 name (International Association for Financial and Fiscal Law) to IFA 'to show the relation between the objectives of IFA and those of the Fiscal Commission').

[180] See, for example, Letters by Deperon to Carroll, 26 September 1947 and 28 January 1948, UNARMS:AG-025-002—S-0441-0054-01.

[181] See, for example, Letters between Carroll and Deperon, 12 and 21 August 1946 and 5 August 1947, UNARMS:AG-025-002—S-0441-0054-01.

[182] Letter from Deperon to Carroll, 9 July 1948; Memorandum by Lachmann to Deperon, 9 July 1948, UNARMS:AG-025-002—S-0979-0004-10.

[183] Letter from Carroll to Deperon, 19 March 1947, UNARMS:AG-025-002—S-0441-0054-01.

Division and IFA proceeded on more formal terms. The new Division head, Bloch, declined IFA's requests to place the topics of judicial interpretation of DTAs and international fiscal jurisdiction on the Commission's agenda,[184] and to circulate older IFA discussions and resolutions to the Commission which had been belatedly communicated to the Division.[185]

4.3 The Role of Private Investment in Developing Countries

The entry of a Third World onto the international scene that was hungry for development and self-determination had not been catered for in the new international economic order launched and controlled by the Western nations in its coverage of monetary questions, trade and commercial policy, development assistance, and capital flows and restrictions.[186] Such a system had been predicated not only on developing countries' continuing role as suppliers of (underpriced) raw materials,[187] but also on the enormous role of private foreign capital in funding the postwar economy.

The emphasis on private investment was a marked shift from the typical pre-World War I international financial flows that had consisted of loans by individuals through portfolio investment, and bonds sold by governments and public utilities.[188] Such capital enabled wealth to spread from the most developed economies to the less developed, especially those that supplied commodities to Europe.[189] In colonial territories, metropoles undertook

184 Letter from Helders to Bloch, 12 September 1953; Letter from Bloch to Helders, 23 September 1953, UNARMS:AG-025-002—S-0441-0463-23403. Bloch explained that this was a right reserved for Category A NGOs.

185 Memorandum by Bloch to Hogan, 3 March 1954, UNARMS:AG-025-002—S-0441-0463-23403. Bloch explained that the material was either obsolete because the Commission had already disposed of the subjects or of 'limited interest' to the UN 'as a whole'.

186 Jeff Haynes, *Third World Politics: A Concise Introduction* (Blackwell, 1996) 65–6; Toye and Toye, *UN*, 23.

187 British and American hierarchical attitudes towards underdeveloped countries are perceived in Keynes' reference to such countries' participation at Bretton Woods 'as [t]he most monstrous monkey-house assembled for years', while Harry Dexter White remarked that Cuba's role was merely to supply the cigars: see Claudia Kedar, *The International Monetary Fund and Latin America: The Argentine Puzzle in Context* (Temple University Press, 2013) 20; Toye and Toye, *UN*, 23. Also, at the ITO Charter negotiations at Havana, underdeveloped country delegations were referred to as '"desarrollo [developing] boys" as WW calls them': Letter from Kremery to Deperon, 20 January 1948, 3, UNARMS:AG-004-001—S-0979-0002-12 (the initials likely stand for British Wyndham White, DEA's Director of the ITO Interim Commission).

188 Luard, *Management*, 37–9, 45; Singer and Ansari, *Rich and Poor*, 194.

189 Luard, *Management*, 38–9.

significant investment. These investments in poorer regions and colonies, however, were focused on infrastructure, communications, and production and commercial structures connected with the export market or the investor's economy.[190] Consequently, most Third World countries achieved little industrialisation before World War II and that which had taken place had largely been determined outside of their control.[191] Their economies were dualistic, their proportion of subsistence activity exceedingly high and they were unable to absorb and assimilate technology transfers as their investors, preoccupied with maximising export output and earnings, kept costs down by using outmoded technology that 'was primitive by Western standards'.[192]

In the interwar years, the aforementioned investments generally ceased and a new type of investment emerged: companies, especially American ones, began to invest directly into expanding their foreign operations, principally in Latin America.[193] This brought about a 'higher proportion of genuine investment in production facilities, including manufacturing' in place of the government borrowings, which had been mostly used to meet day-to-day expenditure or to repay loans.[194] After World War II, the United States was not only 'virtually the only major source of credit'[195] but also the only potential foreign investor possessing substantial capital surpluses ripe 'for suitable investment outlets'.[196] FDI by developed countries' multinationals (mostly American) in manufacturing facilities rose as the main foreign investment in the reviving world economy; however, this flowed 'to countries that were equally or almost equally developed'.[197] From 1947, direct lending by governments (principally the United States) to other governments and lending by international institutions to governments also emerged, but, again, such investments were initially concentrated on the First World's reconstruction.[198]

As Western industrial capitalism promoted underdevelopment 'merely as a state of capital scarcity'[199] with trade as the main driver for

190 Singer and Ansari, *Rich and Poor*, 194.

191 Luard, *Management*, 10–11.

192 Singer and Ansari, *Rich and Poor*, 195. See also Michael P Todaro and Stephen C Smith, *Economic Development* (Pearson, 12th ed, 2015) 133–4.

193 Luard, *Management*, 37.

194 Ibid.

195 Lundestad, '"Empire by Invitation"', 62.

196 Inderjeet Parmar, *Foundations of the American Century: The Ford, Carnegie, & Rockefeller Foundations in the Rise of American Power* (Columbia University Press, 2012) 97.

197 Luard, *Management*, 39, see also 38, 40.

198 Ibid 45.

199 Singer and Ansari, *Rich and Poor*, 56–7.

growth, poor countries were urged to cultivate a strong raw material export sector from which savings from profits could finance emergent industrial sectors.[200] Many developing country governments consequently 'did everything possible' to attract private investment, including 'through tax holidays, investment grants, rapid depreciation, [and] regional means', even in 'mutually destructive competition'.[201] However, most governments of both developing and developed countries were ambivalent about the role of multinational investment in poor countries.[202] For developing countries, the benefits of vital resources and technological inflows also exposed them to considerable costs involved in subjugating their domestic economy to foreign domination that was only interested in profit maximisation rather that the host country's long-term development. Some governments became hostile and expropriated such firms. While most developed countries favoured the global spread of their firms in principle, in practice they imposed controls on outward investment for various reasons, including balance of payments, or ideological or political grounds. Multinationals themselves considered developing countries to be riskier and inferior investment choices. In newly independent colonies, private enterprises faced a dramatic change of environment as the national government focused on building the nation state rather than supporting the commercial and economic policies and interests of the former metropole.[203] Such disincentives led FDI in developing countries to be 'uncertain in volume and unpredictable in effect'.[204]

These complex circumstances set the scene for developing countries' assertion for double taxation relief principles to be skewed in their favour to incentivise FDI flows and reduce revenue sacrifice. Such assertions would intensify from 1950 as other potential key sources of stimulation for, or protection of, their economic development were either hindered or not forthcoming, namely: the stillbirth of the ITO and the flow of financial aid only to countries of established political and economic status.

It is worth noting that on the other side of the coin, the international spread of private enterprise was as intrinsic to the economies of developed countries, especially the United States, as it was to those of

200 Ibid 64; Luard, *Management*, 45. See also Haynes, *Third World*, 15, 72–3.
201 Luard, *Management*, 44.
202 Ibid 43–5.
203 Singer and Ansari, *Rich and Poor*, 195–6.
204 Luard, *Management*, 45.

developing countries. In 1945, America's economic power was singularly peerless with '[a] stunning half of the world's economic activity occur[ing] in or with the United States, a figure never equaled by one country before or since', due to the vast expansion of industrial production, employment and wealth generated during World War II.[205] Sustaining an economy of such magnitude, however, was projected to necessitate open access to overseas markets less 'a postwar crisis of surplus production . . . create a depression perhaps even worse than that of the 1930s'.[206] The American liberal trading order (including the establishment of standards of currency convertibility under the IMF, dismantling of non-US colonial preference systems, and US foreign aid that tied the reconstruction of Europe and Japan to US imports and exports) was hence designed to place the United States at the centre of the postwar world economy. The sheer dominance of American enterprise, the sense of unique entitlement to global leadership and power,[207] and the desperate need for foreign trade opportunities to maintain its unmatched resources, prosperity and military might, particular as the costs of the Cold War mounted, gave strong incentive for American policymakers to hold fast to residence-based taxation and to reduce the source taxation of other countries that ostensibly impeded the spread of private business. The ascendency of American corporations does not appear to have concerned Britain and the Western European powers into reserving more source taxing rights in view of their depleted financial resources, although the weight of their historical tax practices, and more importantly the pressure to align with US policies to obtain economic aid and attract private investment, may have deterred any such inclinations. Most certainly, the expectation of being restored to the status of creditor nations, not to mention their diminishing imperial privilege and the costs of colonial maintenance and wars, likely made for a continued adherence to residence principles, at least vis-à-vis the Third World.

[205] Jeffrey A Engel, *Cold War at 30,000 Feet: The Anglo-American Fight for Aviation Supremacy* (Harvard University Press, 2007) 2. See also Christopher J Tassava, 'The American Economy during World War II', *EH.Net Encyclopedia*, edited by Robert Whaples (Web Page, 10 February 2008) <https://eh.net/encyclopedia/the-american-economy-during-world-war-ii/>.

[206] Jenifer Van Vleck, *Empire of the Air: Aviation and the American Ascendency* (Harvard University Press, 2013) 169.

[207] See Ibid 90; Engel, Aviation Supremacy, 1.

5

First Session of the Fiscal Commission and Aftermath (1947)

5.1 Preparatory Documents of the Fiscal Division

The First Session was mostly introductory in nature with the Commission mainly concerned with establishing a future programme of work for the Division. Prior to its start, Deperon consulted with the US representative (Edward Bartelt) in March and April 1947 regarding the agenda for the session.[1] The United States, with reference to its active tax treaty programme and policy of the past decade to eliminate double taxation as far as possible,[2] wanted the Commission's programme to include intensive study of double taxation so it could be prepared to advise member governments interested in concluding DTAs. In this connection, the United States intended the Division to 'collect, assemble and publish all tax treaties which have been negotiated for use and assistance of all [UN] members'.[3]

The Division's preparatory documents circulated to the Commission mainly addressed organisational matters (i.e. procedural rules, terms of reference, material concerning relations with other UN bodies, specialised agencies and NGOs) and an extensive proposed work programme for the Commission[4] that was supplemented by four background studies (three concerning public finance and one on international tax).[5] In brief, the work programme incorporated Deperon's suggestions for future work that had been addressed in the

[1] Letter from Bartelt to Deperon, 29 April 1947, NARAII:RG56–199–3.

[2] See Chapter 2, Section 2.2.2.

[3] Notes on US Position to the Fiscal Commission: 'Comment Paper H', undated (possibly 7 May 1947), NARAII:RG56–199–3.

[4] Fiscal Commission, *Remarks Concerning the Tasks of the Fiscal Commission*, Note by the Secretariat, 1st sess, Provisional Agenda items 6 and 9, UN Doc E/CN.8/6 (10 April 1947). See Appendix C, which reproduces the annexes containing Deperon's illustrative lists of problems for the Commission's consideration.

[5] See Fiscal Commission, *List of Documents Distributed before the Opening of the First Session*, 1st sess, UN Doc E/CN.8/20 (17 May 1947).

League's Fiscal Committee's *Tenth Session Report*, plans for the continuation of the League's public finance and tax treaty publications, and a comprehensive list of problems in the field of public finance (under which international tax problems were included). The background study on international tax, entitled 'International Tax Relations', presented 'two principal types of tax problems' for work to be undertaken concerning international economic and financial relations, namely: the removal of tax obstacles to international trade and finance, and reciprocal assistance among national fiscal administrations to deal with tax evasion.[6] The Division's four recommended actions regarding this work comprised (1) examining tax barriers to international trade and investment; (2) becoming an international clearing house of information concerning national tax laws with international implications; (3) promoting tax treaties (which included revising the League's draft models to eliminate gaps and inconsistencies); and (4) liaising with national tax administrations to facilitate the elimination of tax conflicts and practices restricting international economic initiatives.

The Division also circulated communications from the ICC comprising resolutions adopted by the ICC's Executive Committee in April[7] and a report entitled *International Double Taxation* approved by the ICC's Committee on Taxation in February.[8] The resolutions and report, inter alia, endorsed the three London models and presented the following three recommendations regarding preferred mechanisms for preventing double taxation: the exemption method as the 'only one perfect method of avoiding double taxation of income and property' (hence the exclusive jurisdiction of countries of origin of income or situation or property); unilateral relief through a foreign tax credit system as 'a second-best solution'; and comprehensive bilateral conventions as a third solution, with a preference for plurilateral conventions or progress towards uniformity of all bilateral conventions with the London models.[9]

[6] Fiscal Commission, *International Tax Relations: Fourth Additional Memorandum on Programme of Work*, Note by the Secretariat, 1st sess, UN Doc E/CN.8/16 (16 May 1947).

[7] NGO Consultation Committee, *Resolution of the ICC on Taxation*, UN Doc E/C.2/38 (14 April 1947).

[8] Fiscal Commission, *Communications from the International Chamber of Commerce*, UN Doc E/CN.8/24 (22 May 1947) (the report was prepared by Bower, British member of the Committee of Taxation).

[9] The resolutions also opposed the linking of information exchange and enforcement of the collection of taxes in DTA negotiations.

5.2 Deliberations in the Fiscal Commission (19–29 May 1947)

The First Session was attended by fourteen participant countries: Belgium, Cuba, China, Colombia, Czechoslovakia, France, India, Lebanon, New Zealand, Poland, Ukraine SSR, the United Kingdom, the United States and the USSR.[10] The remaining country, South Africa, was unrepresented at the session.[11] The Commission elected Putnam (Belgium) as Chairman given his long experience as a member of the League's Fiscal Committee,[12] Pavel Chernyshev (USSR) and Jorge Ortiz (Colombia) as Vice-Chairmen, and ARF Mackay (New Zealand) as Rapporteur.[13] Putnam became ill after the opening meeting and the Chairmanship passed to Chernyshev.[14] Deperon acted as Secretary of the Commission. Observers comprised representatives from ICAO, FAO, the IMF, the World Bank and the ICC.

The Commission held its first plenary meeting, then divided into two working groups. Committee II was tasked with 'International Tax Relations and Allied Problems' and comprised ten members: Belgium, China, Colombia, Cuba, Czechoslovakia, France, New Zealand, the United Kingdom, the United States and the USSR.[15] Chernyshev was elected Chairman, and Jacques Certeux (France) as Rapporteur. Committee II met three times and at its first meeting, the United States and Cuba submitted proposals concerning the focus of the Commission's work. The United States desired the Commission to confine itself to two main projects: (1) double taxation and mutual administrative assistance in collection of taxes and information exchange (which included sponsoring

[10] Fiscal Commission, *Provisional List of Participants*, 1st sess, UN Doc E/CN.8/19/Rev.2 (21 May 1947). See Appendix B, Table B.1.

[11] As of 17 March 1947, South Africa had nominated a representative, but he had yet to be confirmed by ECOSOC. The representative did not attend the session, nor was an alternate or observer designated in his place.

[12] The United States considered Putnam to have 'an excellent background of experience' for the Commission's Chairmanship, 'particularly if a large bulk of its work should be in the field of taxation': Memorandum by Olsen to Bartelt, 15 January 1947, NARAII:RG56-199-3.

[13] Fiscal Commission, *Report to the Economic and Social Council on the Work of the First Session of the Commission by Dr ARF Mackay, Representative for New Zealand, General Rapporteur*, UN Doc E/440 (29 May 1947) 1–2.

[14] RG Hawtrey, *UN Fiscal Commission, Meetings 19th–29th May 1947: Report by UK Representative*, 8 July 1947, 1, TNA:IR40/9959(1) ('*Hawtrey Report*'). Putnam's place as Belgium's representative was taken up by his adviser.

[15] Fiscal Commission, *Composition of Committee I and Committee II*, 1st sess, UN Doc E/CN.8/21/Rev.1 (20 May 1947). Committee I comprised eleven members and was tasked with questions on public finance and information required by the Commission to accomplish its tasks. It had Cuba as Chairman and Britain as Rapporteur.

regional conferences of tax experts, particularly among countries unfamiliar with such treaties); and (2) tax obstacles to international trade and investment (which included making recommendations of model treaty provisions or statutes to meet these problems).[16] Meanwhile, Cuba proposed the following as studies to be prioritised: double taxation, discrimination between nationals and foreigners from the fiscal point of view, taxes on foreign capital, and fiscal problems arising from migration as well as foreign-held public debt.[17] During the discussions, the United States, supported by France and China, advocated 'a thorough study of taxation problems, including the full publication of all relevant tax treaties' and the elimination of double taxation.[18] On the other hand, the USSR put forward that the Commission's 'main duty should be to aid the economic development of underdeveloped countries'.[19] It viewed the Division's preparatory documents as having 'been prepared in the interest of exporting and investing countries' and that the ICC's proposals 'were similarly directed'.[20] It also cautioned that the reduction of taxation on the part of an underdeveloped country to achieve the elimination of double taxation 'might mean a heavier tax burden on that country's people'.[21] It called for, firstly, the Commission to make a recommendation for a system of safeguarding underdeveloped countries against political loans and investments, and secondly, the financing of development of underdeveloped countries by loans and credits free of political conditions rather than by foreign investment.[22] The United States opposed these proposals on the basis that such questions were outside the Commission's scope and belonged to the Economic and Employment Commission.

The Committee II's report mostly approved, with few amendments, the US proposals for the direction of the Commission's work.[23] The category of 'General Remarks' contained recommendations concerning[24] (a) the general

[16] Fiscal Commission, *Committee II – Proposal Submitted by the Delegate for the United States*, 1st sess, UN Doc E/CN.8/22/Rev.1 (20 May 1947).
[17] Fiscal Commission, *Committee II – Proposal of Dr Jose Perez Cubillas (Cuba)*, 1st sess, UN Doc E/CN.8/23 (20 May 1947).
[18] 'Summary Report of the First Session of the Fiscal Commission' [by the US delegation], undated, 2, NARAII:RG56–199–3 ('Summary Report (US)').
[19] Ibid.
[20] Ibid.
[21] Ibid.
[22] Ibid 2–3, 5.
[23] Ibid 5.
[24] Fiscal Commission, *Report Submitted by Mr Jacques Certeux, Representative for France, Rapporteur of Committee II*, 1st sess, UN Doc E/CN.8/W.1 (25 May 1947) 2.

desirability of broad-based DTAs;[25] (b) the desirability of mutual administrative assistance agreements; (c) the elimination of all forms of discriminatory measures on the taxation of nationals and foreigners; and (d) the Commission's consideration, in formulating its technical recommendations on DTAs, of the different stages of development of countries to avoid the inclusion of any provision which might deprive underdeveloped countries of fiscal resources on which they might legitimately rely on in order to assure their economic development and social progress.[26] The category of 'Proposals' mainly elaborated the various materials the Division was to collect.[27] The Division was also to synthesise the work accomplished by the League on international tax problems. Finally, the category of 'Additional Remarks' listed the US and USSR proposals that had not found consensus. The US proposals for regional tax conferences and '"model treaty provisions or statutes" regarding international tax relations' were stated as to be deferred for later consideration by the Commission.[28] Meanwhile, the USSR proposals concerning (1) the financing of underdeveloped countries by loans and credits provided to governments rather than direct investment in domestic private enterprises, and (2) the provision of advice and technical assistance to underdeveloped countries on fiscal methods to aid their development and procurement of foreign capital 'on the best possible terms' were stated as 'call[ing] for special mention' but which were possibly beyond the Commission's competence.[29] Britain subsequently submitted a memorandum objecting to the report on the grounds that the Committee had neglected to address the Commission's research function and to make a selection out of the special studies proposed by the Secretariat.[30]

During the Commission's plenary discussions of Committee II's report, France proposed that General Remarks (a) and (b) be framed as

[25] The USSR and Ukraine voted against this recommendation: 'Summary Report (US)', 3.

[26] Recommendation (d) had been championed by the USSR and Cuba: Ibid 5.

[27] E/CN.8/W.1, 2–4. These materials included information on public debt, thus incorporating the Cuban proposal for such studies: 'Summary Report (US)', 6.

[28] E/CN.8/W.1, 4–5.

[29] Ibid 4.

[30] Fiscal Commission, *Memorandum by Mr RG Hawtrey, Representative of the United Kingdom, Rapporteur of Committee I*, 1st sess, UN Doc E/CN.8/W.3 (25 May 1947) (also containing Britain's similar complaint of Committee I's report). See also Fiscal Commission, *Committee Papers*, 1st sess, UN Doc E/CN.8/W.7 (10 June 1947) 4, 8 (containing Britain's submissions that the proposed work on public finance, economic depressions and technical assistance bordered closely with the competence of the Economic and Employment Commission).

concrete recommendations based on the League's experience in this field.[31] The USSR, however, opposed these formulations because they had 'important economic and political significance' and constituted 'protectionism for the powerful', being 'directed in the interests of the developed states, which were least in need of UN protection'.[32] The USSR argued that DTAs 'should be based on the interests of both parties, and should aim at the national development of undeveloped countries', adding that if the Commission was to express any views at all, 'it should express preference for loans over direct capital investment'.[33] The United States subsequently moved, seconded by the USSR, to delete of all the General Remarks on the basis that intensive debate and formulation of recommendations on double taxation be deferred to the Commission's next session. This action led the USSR to also call for the deletion of the points it 'had originally advocated as a "counter-balance" concerning the interests of the undeveloped States'.[34]

The Commission's report to ECOSOC consequently focused on detailing an extensive programme of work for the Division which, inter alia, addressed the building up of a fiscal information service; the provision of technical assistance, especially to underdeveloped countries; the continuation of the League's public finance publications and collection of tax treaties; establishing liaison and cooperation with governments and their national fiscal administrations to obtain information; and coordinating work with other UN bodies and NGOs.[35] The features of the work programme specifically related to international tax comprised (a) the review and revision of the League's work on international tax problems for further action to the solution of such problems; (b) the collection of countries' comments on the Mexico and London Models and the circulation of those comments to the Commission well in advance of the next session; (c) the collection of information on matters such as discriminatory taxation or treatment, extraterritorial taxation, tax legislation concerning foreign nationals or resources, mutual administrative assistance in information exchange and tax collection, and taxes on international travel, transport and communications; and (d) the study of tax

[31] Fiscal Commission, *Proposal by the Representative of France*, 1st sess, UN Doc E/CN.8/25 (27 May 1947). See also 'Summary Report (US)', 5–6.
[32] 'Summary Report (US)', 7.
[33] Ibid.
[34] Ibid.
[35] E/440, 3–5.

problems[36] from the point of view of their effects on international trade and investment.[37] The report's single draft resolution called for ECOSOC to take note of the Commission's report, for the Secretariat to take the action on the work programme outlined, and for UN members to assist the Secretariat in fulfilling its duties.[38] The report also called for the Commission's next session to be held 'as early as possible in 1948' and provided the Division's estimates totalling $133,080 for its 1948 expenditures to cover the costs of hiring additional staff and resuming work on and publishing the League's publications (including the tax treaties collection).[39]

5.3 Deliberations in ECOSOC (July 1947)

At ECOSOC's Fifth Session,[40] the Commission's report was considered at the Council's eighty-seventh and ninety-third plenary meetings on 21 and 24 July,[41] as well as at the fifth meeting of the Council's Economic Committee on 21 July.[42] There was general endorsement of the report;[43] however, various countries, including Canada, Czechoslovakia, Norway, the United States and the United Kingdom, called for a system of priorities to be established in view of the ambitious programme and expenditure involved. The United Kingdom and Norway questioned the desirability of continuing all the League's publications. Czechoslovakia remarked that the Commission's lack of direction confirmed its earlier views in the 1946 ECOSOC debates that the Commission's immediate establishment had been unnecessary as it was sufficient for the time being

[36] Committee II had substituted 'problems' for the word 'obstacles' used in the original US proposal 'to avoid prejudgment': 'Summary Report (US)', 6.

[37] E/440, 5–7.

[38] Ibid 8.

[39] Ibid 8–9; Fiscal Commission, *Report of the Fiscal Commission: Estimate Presented by the Secretary-General in Accordance with Rule No 30 of the Rules of Procedure of the Council*, 1st sess, UN Doc E/440/Add.1 (16 July 1947).

[40] ECOSOC membership in 1947 comprised Belgium, Byelorussian SSR, Canada, Chile, China, Cuba, Czechoslovakia, France, India, Lebanon, New Zealand, Norway, Peru, Turkey, the United Kingdom, the United States, the USSR and Venezuela.

[41] See *Verbatim Record of the 87th Meeting*, UN ESC, 5th sess, 87th mtg, UN Doc E/PV.87 (21 July 1947); *Summary Record of the 93rd Meeting*, UN ESC, 5th sess, 93rd mtg, UN Doc E/SR.93 (24 July 1947).

[42] See Economic Committee, *Summary Record of the 5th Meeting*, UN ESC, 5th sess, 5th mtg, UN Doc E/AC.6/SR.5 (21 July 1947).

[43] China, Lebanon and Venezuela in particular expressed their approval of the recommendations concerning the provision of technical assistance to economically less-advanced countries.

for the Secretariat to study and report on fiscal problems.[44] France, New Zealand and Norway specifically advocated the prioritisation of double taxation and fiscal evasion. The United States suggested the prioritisation of the service functions required by the Commission's terms of reference; the collection, compilation and publication of data; and the continuation of the League's work on double taxation.[45] Meanwhile, the USSR (represented by Chernyshev, the Fiscal Commission's Chairman) repeatedly defended the Commission's proposed programme, stating that the Commission had given full and careful consideration to the financial implications involved.

The discussion in the Economic Committee led to some agreement on the UK proposal for the work programme to be established as a long-term endeavour without time limit and for the Fifth Committee (Administrative and Budgetary Committee) of the General Assembly to have the final say in its determination of the allocable funds. The debate was finally settled by the US proposal to let the Secretariat have certain discretion to determine the priority of work to be undertaken within its resources. The Committee adopted the Commission's draft resolution and report with minor amendments comprising structural changes, rephrasing, and the addition of a citation to a recent ECOSOC resolution regarding the Secretariat's provision technical assistance.[46] ECOSOC in plenary meeting adopted, without discussion, the report as amended.[47]

5.4 Deliberations in the General Assembly (September–October 1947)

The Commission's report was raised by France in a meeting of the Second Committee (Economic and Financial Committee) of the Assembly in September. In general, France thought that the work embarked upon by ECOSOC in the past year was too vast, the

[44] See Chapter 3, Section 3.2.

[45] The US delegation had been briefed to suggest these priorities '[i]n the event' the 'consensus [of the State Department and Treasury] that the United States position ... to recommend strongly the adoption of the whole report, and the providing of sufficient resources to carry out properly the recommendations contained in the report ... [was] not considered possible': Memorandum from Nisonger to Bartelt, 26 June 1947, NARAII: RG56-199-3.

[46] Economic Committee, *Draft Resolution on Report of Fiscal Commission*, UN ESC, 5th sess, UN Doc E/AC.6/W.3/Rev.1 (22 July 1947).

[47] *Fiscal Questions*, ESC Res 67 (V), UN ESCOR, UN Doc E/573 (2 September 1947, adopted 24 July 1947).

assignments given to the various commissions were too vague and extensive, and that inadequate consideration had been given to establishing priorities.[48] Consequently, there were overlaps in jurisdiction with the IMF and the World Bank as well as between the functional and regional commissions. These overlaps gave rise to duplication and even quadruplication of work in view of the propensity of commissions and specialised agencies to create sub-commissions. Concerning the Fiscal Commission specifically, France considered that it had been assigned a work programme that 'require[d] the efforts of a very large number of specialists for a period of 10 to 20 years', which meant that it would 'study almost every problem without solving any one of them' given the indeterminate time needed to arrive at substantial recommendations.[49] France considered it preferable to assign the Commission 'well-defined studies' concerning 'problems of immediate international interest', such as capital evasion and double taxation, 'in the expectation that it could arrive at acceptable recommendations to governments'.[50] It proposed that the Assembly request ECOSOC to specifically define the tasks of the Commission and establish a scale of priorities with strict regard to the UN's most pressing needs.[51]

The Secretariat defended its work programme on the grounds that its fiscal information service would enable the Commission to not only give advice and expert assistance to governments but also provide comprehensive, specialised and internationally comparable information to ECOSOC, other UN bodies and specialised agencies 'with considerably less expenditure of time and money than if each commission or agency were to do its own fiscal research'.[52] It was moreover continuing the role and work of the League's Fiscal Committee in accordance with the Assembly's resolutions to assume the League's non-political functions. It stated that ECOSOC had refrained from establishing a system of priorities given that this was dependent on the final budget approved, the progress of work made and the time required to respond to technical assistance requests. Furthermore, a management survey undertaken

[48] 'Statement of Mr Jules Moch, French Delegate to Economic and Social Committee (Committee 2)', 27 September 1947, 1, NARAII:RG56-199-4.

[49] Ibid 3.

[50] Ibid.

[51] *Resolution Proposed by the French Delegation*, UN GA, 2nd Comm, 2nd sess, UN Doc A/C.2/111 (30 September 1947).

[52] Fiscal Division, 'Note Concerning the Functions and Programme of the Fiscal Commission', 3 October 1947, NARAII:RG56-199-4.

recently for the Division provided specific methods of close and continuous liaison with other UN bodies, and the Division had already established correspondence and exchange programmes with ECE, FAO and ICAO. Presumably because of the Secretariat's arguments, the Second Committee did not take action on the French proposal.

In the Fifth Committee, the budget for the publication of tax treaties was reduced on the grounds of 'apparent duplication' with the general publication of treaties contemplated by the Secretariat's Legal Division.[53] Deperon raised his concerns with Bartelt that the reduction 'would result in the discontinuance of the publication of tax treaties in usable form, and would impair the services performed by the Fiscal Division for the Fiscal Commission'.[54] The matter was discussed among US Treasury (including the Tax Research Division and Budget Bureau) and State Department officials, who considered the separate publication of tax treaties 'convenient', 'useful' and 'desirable', but not 'of such importance to justify making an issue out of it'.[55] According to King, the United States only referred to the old League publications when negotiating current treaties 'as a guide to the nature of provisions of' the other negotiating party's existing treaties, and the fact that the League's last publication only covered treaties up to 1936 had not appeared to 'impair seriously' US negotiations.[56] Bartelt informed the Division that he thought 'it best we not do anything for the present'; however, Deperon pursued the matter further with Bartelt and the US representative (Stone) on the Fifth Committee[57] and appears to have been successful as this publication was printed in 1948.[58]

In an economy move led by Belgium, the United Kingdom and the USSR, the Fifth Committee deferred the Commission's 1948 session to early 1949 on the grounds of providing time for the Secretariat to prepare and complete its studies.[59] The Division welcomed the cancellation,

53 Memorandum by Nisonger to Bartelt, 25 September 1947, 1, NARAII:RG56-199-4. Note that this decision was part of general reduction in the amount provided to ECOSOC for contract printing.

54 Ibid.

55 Ibid.

56 Ibid.

57 File Note by Vassar to Nisonger, 26 September 1947 (also containing Nisonger's handwritten notes concerning telephone conversations with Deperon on 29 and 30 September 1947), NARAII:RG56-199-4.

58 See Chapter 7, Section 7.1.

59 *Summary Record of the 56th Meeting*, UN GAOR, 5th Comm, 2nd sess, 56th mtg, UN Doc A/C.5/SR.56 (6 October 1947) 4–5. The Fifth Committee also reduced the budget for four other ECOSOC sub-organs, entailing that these bodies would only convene once instead of twice in 1948.

Deperon having earlier advised the United States that the Division was unlikely to be prepared for the session due to delays in the approval of staff increases and in recruitment.[60] When Lachmann visited Washington in November, he reported Bartelt as having 'emphasized several times his great interest in our work and his desire to help us in every way' and being 'somewhat apologetic about his failure to take direct action in our defense during the Assembly' due to 'the delicate relationship between him as delegate and the State Department'.[61]

5.5 Commentary

The discussions of the Commission's First Session reveal that Cold War tensions were already flaring and that views concerning the economic development of underdeveloped areas which were contrary to liberal capitalism were being expressed by the USSR and developing countries. The United States' tactical intervention in the drafting of the Commission's report, however, ensured that the official reporting betrayed no such disharmony,[62] although at the expense of no Western-sponsored policies being recommended either. The Commission's inability to define its concentration of work appeared an endemic problem faced by other ECOSOC commissions, suggesting that the geopolitical and economic diversity of the UN membership made for little agreement and progress at the start of ECOSOC's operations. US dominance was overwhelmingly palpable in the Commission's discussions: most of its proposals were adopted in the recommendations of Committee II. The USSR was its only counterweight, and while its arguments were evidently in response to the Truman Doctrine announced in March,[63] the superpower may have voiced some of developing countries' own hopes for obtaining (politically unencumbered) capital aid, as well as suspicions concerning their potential exploitation by private enterprise and unwarranted revenue sacrifice under DTAs. Committee II's report showed the deference that had to be paid to the two superpowers: even proposals

[60] File Note by Nisonger to Bartelt, 7 October 1947, NARAII:RG56–199–4.

[61] Memorandum by Lachmann to Deperon, 18 November 1947, 1, UNARMS:AG-004-001—S-0979–0004–01.

[62] This allowed the US government to report to Congress that the Commission had 'had a successful session': State Department, *Report by the President to the Congress for the Year 1947; Second Annual Report on Activities of the United Nations and the Participation of the United States Therein* (USGPO, 1948), 120, NARAII:RG56–199–2.

[63] See Chapter 4, Section 4.1.1, n 18 for a brief description of the Doctrine.

which had not obtained consensus were given mention. Just one week after the conclusion of the First Session, the United States would announce its Marshall Plan for Europe, solidifying the ignition of the Cold War and Latin America's anxieties of being overlooked in the postwar economic order.[64] At the time of the ECOSOC meeting, nevertheless, the USSR was still defensive of the Commission's report, the political pride of having presided as Chairman of the Commission appearing a key factor in its stance. Meanwhile, Britain's and the United States' tactical persuasion of ECOSOC to defer the determination of work prioritisation to the Assembly's Fifth Committee and to the Secretariat reflected an intention to indirectly steer the Commission's work through their influence (particularly the United States') in the Fifth Committee and with the Secretariat.

The early concerns over budget and the capacity for overlapping jurisdictions and repetitive discussion throughout the UN system highlight fundamental problems that would recurringly haunt the Commission's work and be catalysts for its downfall as well as the curbing of the Division's activities. At this stage at least, it was evident that the United States (and most certainly the Division) intended the Fiscal Commission to have a central role over fiscal matters in the UN system. Bartelt would in fact report to the Secretary of State that 'all of the decisions reached by the Commission are in conformity with the policies of the United States Government'.[65] Not only did the United States have high hopes for the Commission to further free trade and private enterprise, including through regional tax conferences to promote DTAs in underdeveloped areas and the formulation of a model treaty that would eliminate tax obstacles to trade and investment, but it was also unwilling to define the exclusive jurisdiction of the Commission 'because of the manifold and extensive ramifications which public finance and fiscal policy have upon all economic activity'.[66] The ICC itself appeared to have come away from the First Session with an impression of the Commission's paramount fiscal jurisdiction. Just the month prior to the session, the ICC's Executive Committee had adopted resolutions that, inter alia, indicated its anticipation of the Commission's collaboration with the ITO to progress the work on bilateral treaties 'towards uniformity and liberality in

[64] See Chapter 4, Section 4.1.3 concerning Latin America's upsurge of activism from this point onwards.

[65] EF Bartelt, 'Memorandum to the Secretary [of State]', 3 June 1947, 1, NARAII:RG56-199-3.

[66] Note (untitled) on the Fiscal Commission's terms of reference, undated (around July 1947), 3, NARAII:RG56-199-3.

the provisions' and 'towards the effective adoption by all countries of an international code'.[67] However, when the ICC adopted its Executive Committee's draft resolutions in June 1947, it removed the reference to the ITO and instead commended the Commission's work programme and pledged its complete cooperation with the Commission.[68]

It was also evident that US support, in particular State Department approval, was vital to any of the Commission's endeavours: the Division reported directly to US officials who steered its programme and work, and the United States could single-handedly sway the course of decisions, particularly in the 'highest legislative body in matters of financial control and administration in the UN' (i.e. the Fifth Committee).[69] While Deperon appeared to have some degree of influence in persuading the United States to back projects of importance to the Division (i.e. the publication of the tax treaty collection), this was likely more attributable to the publication's supplementing of the US agenda to promote DTAs. Britain's own colonialist attitude is glimpsed in the UK representative's report to his government in which he remarked on Colombia's indicated reservations regarding tax discrimination as representing the view 'that a weak country ought to be free both to attract foreign enterprise and to fleece it when it has come'.[70]

5.6 Subsequent Secretariat Work

In early September, Lachmann visited Bartelt to inquire of the US view on the 'attitude to be adopted' towards the work programme listed in the Commission's report.[71] While it is not known what was relayed at this discussion, the US position around this time indicated four priority items: (1) an examination of the effects of taxation on international flow of trade and capital; (2) the collection of statistics and information on national finances and a survey of tax systems; (3) a study on mutual administrative assistance; and (4) double taxation problems.[72] Item 1 'rank[ed] first' because of 'the importance of this subject and the vast

[67] E/C.2/38. The Executive Committee had made this statement in view of the inclusion in the ITO draft charter of the promotion of DTAs as a function of the organisation.

[68] Fiscal Commission, *Resolution 12 Adopted by the International Chamber of Commerce at its XIth Congress, Montreux, 2–7 June 1947*, UN Doc E/CN.8/29 (23 July 1947).

[69] This status was acknowledged by the Fifth Committee itself: see A/C.5/SR.56, 1.

[70] *Hawtrey Report*, 5.

[71] Memorandum by Vassar to Bartelt, 2 September 1947, NARAII:RG56–199–3.

[72] Note (untitled) on priority items concerning the Fiscal Commission's programme of work, undated (around July 1947), NARAII:RG56–199–3 (pencil edits in this document reversed the rank order of Items 1 and 2, and added a fifth item on 'Information on fiscal administration').

extent to which it remain[ed] unexplored'; however, the project was dependent on the assembling of information, that is, Item 2.[73] The United States considered certain areas of Item 3, particularly the comparison of administrative procedures available, could be studied 'with profit' but that 'the greatest effectiveness of the Commission in this field lies not in study which it may undertake but in the moral force which it may exert on countries to negotiate [mutual administrative assistance] treaties'.[74] Regarding Item 4, the United States believed that the League's 'extensive work ... has pretty well exhausted the field so far as new developments are likely' and that the Commission's 'effectiveness' was 'principally in advising member countries which wish to learn from the existing experience in the field and as a force which pushes the subject the Commission can interest member governments in negotiating bilateral or multi-lateral treaties to prevent double taxation'.[75]

The Fiscal Division appeared to embark on work that more or less reflected the US priorities.[76] It sought information collection through circular letters and questionnaires to member governments, which included requests for their views on the Mexico and London Models as well as on methods to prevent double taxation and fiscal evasion and to grant administrative assistance;[77] correspondence with national officials and contacts provided by member delegations; missions to Europe, South America and the Middle East;[78] and trips to public libraries. It reviewed the League's work on international tax problems regarding tax obstacles to international economic activity and began studying the impact of taxation on foreign trade and investment.[79] In addition, it continued

[73] Ibid 2.

[74] Ibid.

[75] Ibid 1–2. In contrast, Britain had come away from the First Session expecting that the 'question of double taxation ... [had] by no means reached finality' and that an expert conference composed of experts from both developed and developing countries, as recommended in the Fiscal Committee's *Tenth Session Report*, would be held to review the Mexico and London drafts: *Hawtrey Report*, 4.

[76] Fiscal Commission, *References of Interest to the Fiscal Commission Contained in Documents Prepared for the Sixth Session of the Economic and Social Council*, Note by the Secretariat, UN Doc E/CN.8/W.15 (10 March 1948) 1–2.

[77] Circular letter 503-4-1/KL (later 503-10/KL) of 2 September 1947 (incorporated in Fiscal Commission, *Circular Letter to Member Governments Dated 2 September 1947*, Note by the Secretariat, UN Doc E/CN.8/W.11 (25 September 1947)); Circular letter 503-10/PD on 19 January 1948 (incorporated in Fiscal Commission, *Circular Letter to Governments Dated 19 January 1948*, Note by the Secretariat, UN Doc E/CN.8/W.13 (28 January 1948)).

[78] Memorandum by Nisonger to Bartelt, 21 January 1948, NARAII:RG56-199-2.

[79] See Outline for Paper on 'International Tax Problems in Their Relation to Foreign Trade and Investment', 11 December 1947, UNARMS:AG-025-002—S-0441-0468-23889(A).

work on the League's publications; provided technical assistance or advice to Venezuela,[80] Haiti and Brazil;[81] cooperated with the Trusteeship Council;[82] and established liaison with specialised agencies (i.e. the IMF, the World Bank, FAO, the ILO and ICAO) to collect and exchange information and to discuss certain studies.[83] It is worth noting here that in January 1948, ECOSOC's Coordination Committee, which had been created to facilitate relations between specialised agencies and the UN to ensure cooperation and avoidance of duplication, reported that it had found no overlap between the work of the Fiscal Division and specialised agencies, and had made informal arrangements to assure close liaison between those bodies with regard to the planning of research, and the exchange of available information and completed studies in the field of public finance.[84] The Division regularly reported on its progress to Bartelt, who was 'most receptive' to the former's idea of holding informal meetings of Commission delegates stationed in the United States.[85] Deperon was also attempting to have ECOSOC establish an international centre for training in public administration.[86]

The replies received from governments were, in general, considered 'unsatisfactory' by the Division due to their impreciseness and incompleteness.[87] In December 1947, Deperon dispatched a Division member (Elba Gómez del Rey) on mission to nine Latin American countries[88] to make contacts and gather information, especially regarding views on double taxation.[89] Gómez reported that much of the interest in double taxation had arisen out of conferences held by the League and industry bodies, including

[80] Deperon had several sessions on double taxation with relevant officials during his mission to Venezuela: Letter from Deperon to Carroll, 26 September 1947, UNARMS:AG-025-002—S-0441-0054-01.

[81] 'Fiscal Questions' [1947–8] *Yearbook of the United Nations* 559, 560.

[82] Fiscal Commission, *Provisional Questionnaire of the Trusteeship Council*, Note by the Secretariat, UN Doc E/CN.8/W.12 (1 October 1947); Memorandum to Bartelt, 17 December 1948, NARAII:56-199-4.

[83] E/CN.8/W.15, 3.

[84] Ibid.

[85] Lachmann memo, 18 November 1947. See also Memorandum by Lachmann to Deperon, 10 December 1947, UNARMS:AG-004-001—S-0979-0004-01 (reporting on Lachmann's progress meeting with Treasury in December).

[86] Letter from Kremery to Deperon, 14 February 1948, UNARMS:AG-004-001—S-0979-0002-22.

[87] Nisonger memo, 21 January 1948.

[88] Argentina, Brazil, Chile, Colombia, Costa Rica, Guatemala, Peru, Mexico and Uruguay.

[89] Elba Gómez del Rey, Note (untitled) on mission to Latin America, 19 April 1948; Memorandum by Gómez del Rey to Lachmann, 6 May 1948, UNARMS:AG-004-001—S-0979-0003-22.

IABA and the Inter-American Trade Council. Gómez considered that the Latin American positions were of such mixture that regional conferences were needed to enable an exchange of views and free discussions to 'throw more light on the subject and make the outline of the problems involved clearly outstanding'.[90] In brief, Argentina, Brazil and Chile were not interested in DTAs for different reasons;[91] Mexico, Peru and Uruguay were keen to consider DTA negotiations;[92] while Colombia and Costa Rica had the more ambitious aim of using double taxation measures not just to prevent double taxation but 'as a fiscal device to stimulate the flow of US private investments into Latin America' through the abolition by the United States and other countries of taxes levied on foreign investment income of their nationals.[93] Colombia in particular considered that, in the event of the failure of direct assistance from the United States (i.e. 'a sort of Marshall Plan for Latin America'), 'a multilateral agreement on double taxation would be an excellent form of indirect assistance'.[94] Gómez reported that 'public opinion' in the countries she visited indicated that 'with the exception of Uruguay – there is no country ready to receive private foreign capital freely'.[95] Gómez appears to have promoted FDI as 'far better for Inter-American relations' based on such capital 'being almost as useful as material assistance in the form of dollar loans, without the complicating effects of such [intergovernmental] loans on national budgets' and the 'subordination' of the borrowing country to 'pressures' exercised by the lender 'in international political assemblies'.[96] Gómez also attempted to procure 'very tactfully' an invitation for the Division to be represented at the upcoming PAU/OAS Bogotá Conference[97] on the grounds of the Division being 'the only

90 Gómez del Rey note, ch 2, 4–5.

91 The Argentinian system presented few instances of international double taxation, while Brazil was more concerned with internal double taxation. Chile saw DTAs as disadvantageous to the country and was only willing to sign conventions with countries that did not have much investment in Chile.

92 Peru favoured the Mexico Model, while Uruguay had engaged in a policy to attract foreign investments and was prepared to remove all obstacles preventing such inflows.

93 Guatemala's views were not reported.

94 Gómez del Rey memo, 6 May 1948, 10. Colombia also reported that Carroll had come as a representative of American shipping companies to propose a bilateral convention or to negotiate for an amendment of Colombian tax laws with respect to foreign companies. Colombia declined as it did not consider it desirable to discuss double taxation matters 'piecemeal' and because a treaty on the taxation of shipping companies based on the principle of reciprocity would only benefit the United States as Colombia had no merchant fleet (at 11).

95 Ibid 8.

96 Ibid.

97 See Chapter 6, Section 6.1.

organization in the world with such a wealth of experience in this subject' and 'because the problem of double taxation . . . presented very interesting features such as: the question whether it would be possible to reach international agreements on the subject with the one purpose of attracting capital for the economic development of Latin America'.[98]

By March 1948, the Division had noted that economically less-developed countries appeared to have 'become more articulate on international double taxation problems' and there was 'a feeling that an excessive share of the profits realized by foreign companies in their territories . . . [was going] back to the home country of those companies'.[99] Such countries had expressed the desirability for (1) forms of taxation penalising foreign companies which withdrew their profits to their home country; (2) exclusive source-country taxation of business profits, dividends and interest, and corresponding exemption by residence countries on the grounds of fairness to underdeveloped countries whose resources were 'exploited by foreign capital'; (3) British precedents in which foreign earnings were only taxable in the home country when remitted; (4) the refraining by residence countries from taxing of profits reinvested in the source country; and (5) the moderation by capital-exporting countries of their tax rates on foreign income as opposed to profits earned domestically to equalise incentives and offset differences in their evaluation that foreign investments were more risky than domestic counterparts. Such countries also indicated that the Mexico Model, under which income was taxed by both source and residence countries with the latter giving credit for taxes paid in the former, was only acceptable in the case of individuals but not in the case of corporations whose only link to the capital-exporting country was due to the place of incorporation or formal seat.

By May 1948, the Division was pressured to consider the situation of decolonised new states in its study on the influence of taxation on foreign investments.[100] It realised that it would 'not be easy to apply the simple

98 Gómez del Rey memo, 6 May 1948, 7–8.

99 Confidential note on 'Recent Views on International Double Taxation', 20 February 1948, UNARMS:AG-025-002—S-0979-0004-11.

100 This was specifically pressed upon by Indonesia's segregation from the Netherlands Empire: Memorandum by Kremery to Deperon, 19 April 1948, UNARMS:AG-025-002—S-0441-0468-23889(A). The UN was also at this point under some criticism for not giving 'enough attention . . . to the problems of Asiatic countries . . . [even though they were] perhaps, in greatest need for expert assistance' (at 4). Another strong source of pressure was likely the Secretariat's general activism on the subject of decolonisation: Thant Myint-U and Amy Scott, *The UN Secretariat: A Brief History (1945–2006)* (International Peace Academy, 2007) 19.

provisions of the Model Conventions' to find a 'compromise ... between the conflicting interests' of the capital-exporting and capital-importing countries as 'a thorough survey of the ... tax system [of new states had] ... to be undertaken before any equitable and just recommendations could be made'.[101] Around September, the Division engaged consultant J Wilner Sundelson[102] to supervise the preparation of its report.[103] The Division now appeared to be moving away from a narrower study that sought to improve and refine the League's study on the incidence and burden of taxation (and hence the London and Mexico Models) to more broadly 'situate ... the problems of private investment and taxation in the complete framework of the post-war economic situation'.[104] Using this approach, it was investigating private contracts concluded between local governments of underdeveloped countries and foreign investing firms that assured such companies of favourable tax treatment.[105] The Division, however, failed to provide Sundelson with adequate staff,[106] and consequently, by the end of December, critical areas of study had yet to be

[101] Kremery memo, 19 April 1948, 2.

[102] Sundelson was an American professor of public finance in the 1930s. The archival correspondence, however, indicates that he was at this time part of Ford International, Ford Motor Co. This position may have best placed Sundelson in the know of private business practices as Ford had been one of the giant American corporations investing in Latin America as well as Asia since the early 1900s for markets, manufacturing plant and raw materials: Joseph Smith, *The United States and Latin America: A History of American Diplomacy, 1776–2000* (Routledge, 2005) 89; Mira Wilkins and Frank Ernest Hill, *American Business Abroad: Ford on Six Continents* (Wayne State University Press, 1964) 56–7, 94–5.

[103] See Memorandum by Sundelson to Deperon, 30 December 1948; Memorandum by Gómez del Rey to Sundelson, 16 September 1948, UNARMS:AG-025-002—S-0441-0468-23889(A).

[104] See Memorandum by Hedervary to Deperon, 14 October 1948, UNARMS:AG-025-002—S-0441-0468-23889(A).

[105] Staff working on the study had come to regard DTAs as 'work[ing] well enough between governments on a similar level of economic development but not so well in cases involving highly developed and underdeveloped countries': Letter from Cruickshank to O'Connor, 22 November 1948, UNARMS:AG-025-002—S-0441-0468-23889(A). They instead considered '[a]greements between governments of backward countries and private foreign companies ... to be practical arrangements which take into account the special difficulties under which the companies operate'. The Division had knowledge of such agreements existing in Latin America in the fruit, oil, tin and nitrates industries as such texts had either been published or had been disclosed as a result of disputes. The Division was consulting various agencies, including the US Chamber of Commerce and US Treasury, in gathering further information. See also Memorandum by Hedervary to Deperon, 11 October 1948, 2, UNARMS:AG-025-002—S-0441-0468-23889(A).

[106] The initial full-time staff officer assigned to Sundelson was not sufficiently competent and other staff members later assigned to assist him were involved with other priorities of the Division.

completed, and only a small amount of work in preliminary form was made available to him in the closing days of 1948.[107] He would thus undertake to write a preliminary report 'based on such materials as I have been able to collect chiefly by myself' through discussion with 'experts in varying governmental, business and academic capacities as well as with some competent students of international trade and investment at the [UN]', believing 'that the approach I have taken and the conclusions I will reach have been greatly benefited by these contacts'.[108]

In October 1948, the Commission's Second Session, which had been previously scheduled for April 1949,[109] was brought forward to January.[110] Deperon would report to the United States that the Division's work was handicapped by insufficient personnel and the diverting of available personnel to respond to specific inquiries and requests for technical assistance and information.[111] Deperon considered 'that to some extent the highly qualified personnel of the Division had been, of necessity, required to perform work below their level of competence' and 'that the program of work recommended by the Commission ... was much too "timid"'.[112] He felt that the Division's scope of work 'should be broadened' and that it be 'given the necessary personnel to effectively perform the tasks assigned to it'.[113] US officials considered that the Division's slow progress entailed that it would not 'be necessary to extensively determine US policy and prepare US position papers' as no new projects were likely to be submitted for consideration.[114] In December 1948, Deperon met with Bartelt and other officials from the State Department and Treasury's Tax Research Division, Internal Revenue Bureau and Office of International Finance to discuss the Fiscal Division's implementation work, the provisional agenda for the Second Session and the proposed recommendations to be made by the Commission.[115]

107 Sundelson memo, 30 December 1948, 1.

108 Ibid. Sundelson's contract, moreover, had ended on 30 November and he indicated that 'to assure completion of the report ... I will be very happy to contribute my services to the Division' in the event he would not be compensated for the work (at 2).

109 Memorandum by Evans to Bartelt, 3 September 1948, NARAII:RG56–199–4.

110 Letter from Kotschnig to Bartelt, 8 October 1948, NARAII:RG56–199–4.

111 Memorandum by Evans to Bartelt, 23 November 1948, 1, NARAII:RG56–199–4; Fiscal Commission, *Report on the Implementation of the Recommendations Made by the Fiscal Commission at Its First Session*, 2nd sess, UN Doc E/CN.8/33/Rev.1 (30 December 1948) 4.

112 Evans memo, 23 November 1948, 1.

113 Ibid.

114 Ibid 2.

115 Bartelt memo, 17 December 1948.

6

Related Intervening Developments (September 1947–November 1948)

6.1 Double Taxation Discussions at the Havana ITO Conference and PAU/OAS Bogotá Conference

Towards the end of 1947, Latin America began to pursue strong source-country taxation rights at the Havana Conference held between November 1947 and March 1948 that adopted the ITO Charter,[1] and the PAU/OAS Bogotá Conference held between March and May 1948 that adopted the OAS Charter.[2] The Fiscal Division would lobby behind the scenes at both conferences to ensure that the double taxation field was left solely to the competence of the Commission, even managing to dissuade at least one newly independent developing country from aligning with the Latin American argument.

At Havana, during discussions considering international tax problems in their connection to economic development,[3] Colombia and Costa Rica proposed for inclusion in the ITO Charter provisions that collectively espoused exclusive source-country taxation of capital and property (i.e. the source country being the country where the capital is employed and the property situated), and profits and dividends derived from industrial or agricultural enterprises in which such capital had been invested.[4]

[1] *Final Act of the United Nations Conference on Trade and Employment: Havana Charter for an International Trade Organization*, opened for signature 24 March 1948, UN Doc E/CONF.2/78 (never entered into force) ('*Havana Charter*').

[2] *Charter of the Organization of American States*, opened for signature 30 April 1948, 119 UNTS 3 (entered into force 13 December 1951).

[3] Fiscal Commission, *References of Interest to the Fiscal Commission Contained in the Proceedings of the International Conference on Trade and Employment, Havana (21 November 1947–24 March 1948)*, UN Doc E/CN.8/W.17 (1 August 1948). For an account of the debate as well as the interchange concerning cross-competencies between ITO delegates and UN representatives based on ITO records, see Jennifer E Farrell, *The Interface of International Trade Law and Taxation* (IBFD, 2013) 15–23.

[4] E/CN.8/W.17, 2.

While these proposals were supported by several underdeveloped countries for giving 'maximum stimulus ... to international investment' should capital-exporting countries 'refrain from taxing capital invested abroad', they were not generally accepted; the 'prevailing opinion' being that the prevention of double taxation 'should be sought in a compromise of the interests of capital-exporting and capital-importing countries'.[5] Opposition also arose against the inclusion of any specific formula allocating tax jurisdiction in the Charter because 'experience had shown that solutions ... were arrived at only after long and difficult negotiations which had to take into account the different conditions existing in the negotiating countries' and because the principles embodied in the Latin American proposals 'might run counter to existing tax treaties'.[6]

Kremery, and briefly Deperon, attended the conference, making strong representations mainly through informal discussions and by distributing the Fiscal Division's documents[7] concerning the Fiscal Commission's role and work.[8] Deperon instructed Kremery to direct his 'efforts on both lines [of international tax problems and technical assistance]' to 'various countries on which the Division could work', and to advise the Brazilian delegation 'that their compatriot Benedicto Silva has been appointed Deputy Director of the Division' and would, inter alia, 'have the overall responsibility for liaison with Latin America, Asia and Africa, as well as Oceania'.[9] Kremery had to work carefully so as:

> not to rush the things unreasonably and not to give any foundation to suspicions that my approach could be a part of a well designed attempt to atract [sic] attention to the work of a body which in eyes [sic] of some

[5] Ibid 2–3.

[6] Ibid 3.

[7] These included the Division's preparatory documents; questionnaires; technical mission reports; plans regarding the international centre of public administration; the Commission's report; certain League literature; and the Mexico and London Models in English, French and Spanish.

[8] Letters by Kremery to Deperon, 20, 24 and 29 January 1948, UNARMS:AG-004-001—S-0979-0002-12. This approach 'proved to be a rather time-consuming business' as '[s]mall delegations had very crowded schedules of meetings and it was quite difficult to reach them', while '[o]ther delegates had very little knowledge about the functions and tasks of the United Nations in the fiscal field and it took several conversations to give them a comprehensive picture': Kremery letter, 24 January 1948, 2.

[9] Letter from Deperon to Kremery, 26 January 1948, UNARMS:AG-004-001—S-0979-0002-12.

> delegates still had certain connotation of a rival to the Trade Organization and the proposed Economic Development Committee in the field of double taxation.[10]

Their endeavours proved persuasive: Kremery reported that their 'tactic worked out quite nicely'; that he had 'very friendly and undisguised conversations' with delegates; and that some representatives, including the Chilean representative, 'were even apologetical about the stand they took on double taxation'.[11] Kremery also convinced the recently independent Indonesia (not then a UN member) to 'not press for [the] adoption of the principle of exclusive taxation of the capital by the country where the capital is employed' and to 'take into account the interests of capital exporting countries'.[12] Kremery's Czech nationality also appeared to have engaged the help of the Czech delegation: Czechoslovakia made a formal request for the Division to submit a paper containing information concerning the Commission's work to the ITO delegates,[13] and at Czechoslovakia's suggestion, the delegates agreed to leave further work to future cooperation between the Commission and the ITO, once the latter was brought into being and into relationship with the UN.[14] Ultimately, watered-down, generalised provisions were incorporated into the Charter that provided for the ITO, in collaboration with other intergovernmental organisations as appropriate, to study, make recommendations or promote agreements on measures to prevent double taxation in order to stimulate foreign private investment.[15]

The Division's success is notable considering that the Havana Conference 'ran into virtual deadlock on several important issues' due to the 'uncompromising attitude of Latin Americans' and because 'everything ... [was then] still in a very fluid stage and changing from day to day – even from hour to hour in the enormous confusion

10 Kremery letter, 24 January 1948, 2. This approach meant 'leav[ing] out at least for a limited time, representatives who took issue on double taxation in the Joint Committee, though some of them, specially Latin Americans, would have been of greatest interest to us' (at 3).

11 Ibid 3.

12 Memorandum by Kremery to Deperon (on Conversation with Dr Gani, Representative of Indonesian Republic), 21 April 1948, UNARMS:AG-004-001—S-0979-0002-22.

13 UN Conference on Trade and Employment, *Information Requested by the Delegate of Czechoslovakia Concerning the Fiscal Commission of the Economic and Social Council*, Note by the Secretariat, 6th Comm, UN Doc E/CONF.2/C.6/27 (18 December 1947) (prepared by Deperon); see also E/CN.8/W.17, 3–4.

14 E/CN.8/W.17, 4.

15 *Havana Charter* arts 11, 72.

of Committees, Sub-committees and Working parties'.[16] The Division had viewed the conference as 'an excellent opportunity' to gain 'easy access to fiscal experts and heads of respective departments in Ministries of Finance of 58 countries'[17] with the aim of establishing contacts to procure 'authentic' and 'complete' country information required by the Division.[18] Kremery reported that 'a great task' still awaited them 'to gain goodwill, co-operation and interest of all these officials', which the Division perceived as being necessary for the success of its work.[19] He considered that the crisis brought about by the 'ten year "interregnum" in international relations', the '[magnitude of] changes in political and economic structures', and 'even the changes in posts of high officials ... [who had been] acquainted with the League's work' presented 'many difficulties in the attempt of taking up where the League's work ended in a smooth continuation of its work'.[20]

Anticipating that some Latin American delegations would raise double taxation at the upcoming Bogotá Conference,[21] Deperon had discussions with the influential Uruguayan Deputy-Executive Secretary of the Interim Commission of the ITO (Julio A Lacarte-Muró), forwarding him numerous documents concerning the UN's international tax and technical assistance work, the League's 1945–6 documents addressing international tax matters, and even the IABA resolutions adopted at its 1946 Santiago and 1947 Lima Conferences supporting the continuation of the League's work.[22] Deperon considered that 'the most useful contribution' that the UN representative to Bogotá 'could make' was to promote the work of the Commission and Division and to suggest that the Commission be left 'to propose practical remedies and procedures ... [for eliminating tax obstacles] to the desired flow of foreign investment and expansion of world and regional trade'.[23]

[16] Kremery letter, 20 January 1948, 1. See also Stephen G Rabe, 'The Elusive Conference: United States Economic Relations with Latin America, 1945–1952' (1978) 2(3) *Diplomatic History* 279, 287 (noting that the US delegation at Havana 'found that Latin America offered the "most consistent and difficult" opposition to its positions on trade and investment').

[17] Kremery letter, 24 January 1948, 2.

[18] Ibid. Kremery also met with the IMF delegation which shared their experience in approaching governments for information and data: Letter from Kremery to Deperon, 14 February 1948, 3, UNARMS:AG-004-001—S-0979-0002-22.

[19] Kremery letter, 24 January 1948, 2.

[20] Ibid.

[21] P Deperon, 'Bogotá Conference: International Tax Problems', 31 March 1948, 1, UNARMS:AG-025-002—S-0441-0463-23403.

[22] Memorandum by Deperon to Lacarte, 2 April 1948, UNARMS:AG-025-002—S-0441-0463-23403.

[23] Deperon, 'Bogotá Conference', 3.

At Bogotá, Colombia submitted 'an elaborate and detailed proposal' for complete tax exemption by each signatory country of foreign income derived by its taxpayers in other signatory countries 'in connection with general problems of economic development, and those of international investment'; however, the proposal was not accepted by the United States.[24] The following views were put forward in the debates on international tax problems: (1) the United States supported measures to liberalise taxes on foreign capital invested to encourage not only initial investment and the retention and reinvestment of earnings derived from such capital, but also US citizens to accept foreign employment as technical experts; (2) Mexico supported the call to conclude DTAs and to try to resolve other problems of a taxation character through such agreements; (3) Guatemala considered that capital-exporting countries should stimulate foreign investment, while capital-receiving countries should afford guarantees to such investment, and that the equitable tax treatment of capital should be dealt with on a basis of reciprocity; and (4) Uruguay and Peru felt that foreign capital should be treated on a non-discriminatory basis and should not require special tax privileges.[25] The text of the provision finally adopted as Article 27 in the Economic Agreement of Bogotá, signed on 2 May, was the US proposal which called for:

> Each State, in order to stimulate private investment for the purpose of economic development, shall, within the framework of its own institutions, seek to liberalize its tax laws so as progressively to reduce or even eliminate double taxation as regards income from foreign sources and to avoid unduly burdensome and discriminatory taxation, without, however, creating international avenues for tax avoidance.

[24] Colombia indicated that as far as Latin American countries were concerned, the United States was 'justly expected to contribute to the economic development' of the continent 'by furthering investment in those countries' and that the United States 'would give a strong impulse to those countries by sacrificing on their part certain sources of revenue and by undertaking to adopt the principle of taxation of the income from invested capital by countries in which the capital is invested': 'Short Outline of Conversations with Mr Lleras Restrepo', 6 April 1948, UNARMS:AG-025-002—S-0441-0463-23407. See also Executive Committee on Economic Foreign Policy, *Encouragement of International Investment through Tax Incentives*, 22 March 1948 (ECEFP D-25/48/Rev.1), 3–4, 19–24, NARAII:RG56-199-9 (regarding US positions).

[25] Fiscal Commission, *References of Interest to the Fiscal Commission Contained in the Proceedings of the Ninth Inter-American Conference, Bogota, 1–30 April 1948*, Note by the Secretary, UN Doc E/CN.8/W.16 (1 August 1948) 1–2.

The States shall also seek to conclude as soon as possible agreements to prevent double taxation.[26]

6.2 Double Taxation Movement among Private Sector Associations

At IFA's Hague Congress in September 1947, resolutions were adopted that generally welcomed the Commission's work, urging it to study whether 'tax appeals arising from different interpretations of tax treaties' should be handled by an international tax tribunal rather than by national courts.[27] These resolutions also recommended that 'any secondary object' of DTA negotiations (specifically mutual administrative assistance) be 'negotiated on its own merits' so as not to delay the 'urgency of concluding' DTAs as double taxation was 'an evil of main importance . . . [and] ever-increasing obstacle for the development of international trade with, and recovery of, war-stricken countries'.[28] At its 1948 Rome Congress, IFA 'call[ed] special attention' to France's exemption of source taxation of 'any profits that might be attributed to the activity of merely purchasing goods by an establishment of a foreign enterprise'.[29]

In June 1948, the ICC Council adopted a resolution on double taxation and endorsed the Committee of Taxation's *Report on the Administrative Assistance for Tax Collection and Assessment* (Brochure No 126).[30] The resolution urged the 'movement for the removal of double taxation' to

[26] *Economic Agreement of Bogotá*, opened for signature 2 May1948 (never entered into force), available at *OAS* (Web Page) <www.oas.org/juridico/english/treaties/a-43.html>.

[27] IFA, *International Fiscal Association Resolutions Book* (IBFD, 1988) 3; Fiscal Commission, *References of Interest to the Fiscal Commission Contained in the Report of the International Fiscal Association on Its Tax Symposium and Its Tax Congress of 1948*, Note by the Secretariat, UN Doc E/CN.8/44 (23 December 1948). The Netherlands (where IFA was based) would subsequently propose this study for consideration at the Commission's Second Session where it was not taken up: see Chapter 7, Section 7.2.2 n 39. IFA would nevertheless issue a resolution at its 1951 Congress recommending, inter alia, the creation 'of a permanent juridical committee which would have as its aim to bring to the attention of the Fiscal Committee of the UN the claims [concerning the interpretation of DTAs] presented to them', and the establishment of 'a supernational tribunal embodying, in principle, bilateral tribunals . . . a Supreme Court which would be competent to receive the complaint of any interested person, after exhausting the provision for applying internal legislation': IFA, *Resolutions Book*, 18.

[28] IFA, *Resolutions Book*, 3–4.

[29] Ibid 8.

[30] Committee on Arrangements for Consultation with Non-Governmental Organizations, *Communication from the International Chamber of Commerce Dated 22 September 1948*, UN ESC, UN Doc E/C.2/126 (14 October 1948). The report (approved by the Committee

'spread widely and rapidly through the conclusion of [DTAs]' based on the League's two London Models concerning income and property, and estates and successions.[31] The resolution, however, deplored 'the recent tendency to combine negotiations' for double taxation relief with negotiations for mutual administrative assistance in the assessment and collection of taxes on the basis that they were 'entirely separate problems' and that the latter was an 'irrelevant' consideration that obstructed the former.[32]

In September 1948, the Inter-American Council of Commerce and Production (IACCP)[33] adopted resolutions regarding the 'Mutual Beneficial Development of Foreign Investments', which included recommendations for capital-exporting countries to provide effective tax incentives for FDI in undeveloped countries, and for the Western Hemisphere countries to actively negotiate DTAs.[34]

6.3 US Foreign Policy on Private Investment and DTAs

US policy guidance relating to private investment issued in August 1948 to US government agencies, overseas missions and representatives on international bodies indicates the integral role American private foreign investment held in US foreign policy for the purposes of facilitating 'adequate amounts' of capital flows 'to foreign countries' in order 'to see a world trading system established on a multi-lateral and

on Taxation in January 1948 based on a draft prepared by Bower) viewed that the League's London Model concerning mutual administrative assistance was 'inappropriate to present fiscal conditions', 'superfluous' where administration was efficient, not 'a corollary of' DTAs, gave rise to 'political and financial problems of great difficulty' and impeded the conclusion of DTAs. The report instead recommended that it was 'sufficient simply to include . . . a single paragraph' in DTAs providing for information exchange that was limited to examining claims for double taxation relief submitted by claimants of the other contracting state (at 2, 13).

31 Ibid 2.

32 Ibid.

33 The IACCP, purposed, inter alia, to 'defend free private enterprise and the competitive system' and 'serve . . . all commercial interests of the Hemisphere', was originally formed in 1941 among the many wartime bodies created to foster wartime inter-American relations: see 'Inter-American Council of Commerce and Production' in Union of International Associations, *Yearbook of International Organizations* (Brill, 2007) [e-Resource].

34 Fiscal Commission, *References of Interest to the Fiscal Commission Contained in the Proceedings of the Fourth Plenary Meeting of the Inter-American Council of Commerce and Production, Chicago, 19–22 September 1948*, Note by the Secretary, UN Doc E/CN.8/43 (6 December 1948).

nondiscriminatory basis'.[35] Foreign investment was to 'be provided as far as possible by private capital' and the US government sought 'maximum private participation in its new and outstanding foreign loans', even signalling a willingness to 'issue guaranties in connection with private foreign credits and investments'.[36] To facilitate and encourage such investment, the government was undertaking measures to, inter alia, negotiate DTAs and eliminate 'inequitable tax burdens on income derived from investments abroad'.[37]

By November 1948, the US tax treaty programme had advanced steadily, although only with First World countries. Since 1946, DTAs had been signed with the Netherlands, Denmark, France,[38] South Africa, New Zealand and Belgium; an agreement with Luxembourg was close to being finalised, and negotiations were set to begin with Italy, Greece, Norway and Ireland.[39] While informal discussions regarding the negotiation of a DTA with Australia had 'been conducted . . . over a considerable period of time', the Australian Cabinet had preliminarily determined 'that there was little need or basis for a treaty on income tax'.[40] Regarding DTAs with the Third World, negotiations with the Philippines that had been underway in 1947 had 'been suspended' with no indication of 'whether they will be resumed'.[41] Meanwhile, negotiations with Mexico, which had reached 'an advanced drafting stage by mid-1947', had made 'no further progress' since and the United States was planning their recommencement 'with the hope that a convention can be concluded'.[42] The State Department noted that despite the existence of Article 27 of the yet-to-be-ratified Economic Agreement of Bogotá, 'discussions with individual [Latin American] countries have not yet ripened into the negotiation stage, except in the case of Mexico'.[43]

[35] 'Memorandum by the Secretary of State to the President', 20 August 1948, in State Department, *Foreign Relations of the United States, 1948* (USGPO, 1976) vol 1, pt 2: General: The United Nations, Doc 222 ('*FRUS, 1948*').

[36] Ibid.

[37] Ibid.

[38] This agreement revised the 1939 US–France income tax treaty.

[39] 'Extract from Bulletin No 174: Tax Treaty Program Revealed', 25 October 1948, in State Department, *FRUS, 1948*, Doc 221.

[40] Ibid. Australia had nevertheless indicated the possibility of a tax treaty regarding estate taxes. The US response was to urge the authorisation of a technical mission to discuss both income and estate tax conventions.

[41] Ibid.

[42] Ibid. These stalled negotiations appear to coincide with the announcement of the Marshall Plan.

[43] Ibid.

7

Second Session of the Fiscal Commission and Aftermath (1949)

7.1 Preparatory Documents of the Fiscal Division

In early December 1948, the Division would begin to issue some twenty documents to the Commission,[1] several of which were only circulated well into the Second Session, including Sundelson's preliminary survey ('Sundelson's Report'). The nature of these documents varied greatly, consisting of the summary reporting of work done, preliminary reports, work that had already been made into publications, proposals for future work, reporting of double taxation activity in other organisations, and various communications by other organisations. The documents were repetitive, long-winded and poorly organized.

The Division reported having spent most of its time on its information service in collecting and disseminating data to many users (including other UN bodies, specialised agencies and member governments), and having been overwhelmed by requests for technical assistance and advice.[2] It had cooperated with other UN bodies, including with the Trusteeship Council on a detailed questionnaire on fiscal matters; the Economic and Employment Commission and its sub-commissions on a world economic survey and a study on inflation and deflation problems; and the IMF and UN Statistical Office on a questionnaire intended to remedy gaps in current national publications and develop standard methods in data reporting. In continuing the League's publications, the Division had completed its public debt project[3] and its collection of tax treaties (published as *International Tax Agreements*

[1] This figure includes revisions of the same documents.

[2] See Fiscal Commission, *Report on the Implementation of the Recommendations Made by the Fiscal Commission at Its First Session*, 2nd sess, UN Docs E/CN.8/33 and Rev.1 (15 December 1948).

[3] DEA, Fiscal Division, *Public Debt, 1914–1946* (UN, 1948).

(*ITA*)[4]) with plans for supplementary publications on the latter. Of the Division's remaining efforts that had been expended on international tax matters, it reported works-in-progress covering the review of the League's work on international tax problems; a study of the effects of taxation on international economic activity (which at this stage only consisted of Sundelson's Report); country's comments on the Mexico and London Models; an inquiry on national tax assessment and collection practices for the prevention of tax evasion; and an inquiry on countries' internal laws affecting the taxation of foreigners, foreign resources and international transactions.[5]

Many of the Division's documents communicated requests from other UN bodies and specialised agencies (including the IMF, the World Bank, FAO and the Transport and Communications Commission),[6] or reported relevant discussions or decisions raised in the proceedings of other organisations (e.g. the ICC, IFA, the PAU/OAS Bogotá Conference and the ITO Havana Conference).[7] The Division also communicated problems and studies that had been proposed by member governments for the Commission's consideration.[8]

7.2 Deliberations in the Fiscal Commission (10–25 January 1949)

The Commission members of the Second Session comprised the same countries as the First Session,[9] with two exceptions: South Africa was now represented, and Pakistan had officially replaced India on the Commission but was unrepresented.[10] Putnam again fell ill before the

[4] DEA, Fiscal Division, *International Tax Agreements*, UN Doc E/CN.8/30 (UN, 1948). This publication, eventually known as volume 1 of the *ITA* series, contained over 100 agreements concluded between 1936 and 1948.

[5] The progress of these projects is discussed in Sections 7.2.1 to 7.2.4.

[6] See Section 7.2.5 for details of these requests.

[7] Much of the content of this reporting is discussed in Chapter 6, Sections 6.1 and 6.2.

[8] Key proposals are addressed within the discussion in Sections 7.2.2 and 7.2.3.

[9] Fiscal Commission, *Provisional List of Participants*, 2nd sess, UN Doc E/CN.8/W.29/Rev.3 (10 January 1949). Of the individual delegates, only six had represented their country at the First Session, namely, Ortiz (Colombia), Perez (Cuba), K Czesany (Czechoslovakia), Certeux (France), Chernyshev (USSR) and Bartelt (United States): see Appendix B, Table B.1.

[10] India's seat was given to Pakistan due to the partitioning of British India in August 1947. India retained its representation on six other functional commissions. By the end of 1949, Pakistan had yet to nominate a candidate to the Commission ('Members of Subsidiary Organs' [1948–9] *Yearbook of the United Nations* 120, 121). Although it sent an alternate and adviser to the Second Session, these persons barely attended the meetings of the session.

start of the session and Chernyshev was again elected as Chairman.[11] José Perez (Cuba) and Jules Woulbroun (Belgium) were elected as Vice-Chairmen, and WW Morton (United Kingdom) as Rapporteur. Just before the session opened, the Division was reportedly 'thrown into chaos' by the 'nervous breakdown' of Deperon,[12] who permanently left his position on 7 January.[13] Silva (Acting Director of the Division) and Shahbaz (Chief of the Division's General Section) acted as Secretary and Assistant Secretary of the Commission, respectively. Karakacheff and Lachmann also attended the plenary meetings involving substantive discussions.

The Commission held ten plenary meetings, with the first nine conducted in the first six working days of the session.[14] At the ninth meeting, it appointed a Working Party on International Tax Problems ('Working Party') and then suspended its meetings to enable the latter to deliberate.[15] The Working Party held five meetings over three days and was attended by Belgium (Chairman), Cuba, South Africa, Ukraine SSR, the United Kingdom and the United States, with Lachmann acting as Secretary. The Commission subsequently reassembled for its tenth meeting on the final day of the session. Observers to the session included representatives from FAO, ICAO, the ILO, the IMF, the ICC and NAM (Carroll).

Broadly, the greater part of the substantive plenary discussions was spent on international tax problems. Aside from discussions on the Trusteeship questionnaire, the Commission made little contribution to, but was encouraging of, the work on the information service, public

[11] The nomination was made by the United States: Letter from Bartelt to Secretary of State, 2 March 1949, 1, NARAII:RG56-199-4.

[12] The United States suspected that Deperon's illness was 'a cover for a more underlying personal difficulty': Memorandum by Kellogg to Rusk et al, 26 January 1949, 2, NARAII: RG59-UD-07D_73B(Lot56D479)-4. The official reason given was 'ill-health': Fiscal Commission, *Summary Record of the 1st Meeting*, 2nd sess, 1st mtg, UN Doc E/CN.8/SR.1 (13 January 1949) 1.

[13] Memorandum by Owen to Yates, 11 January 1949, UNARMS:AG-004-001—S-0991-0005-04.

[14] Unless otherwise stated, the material regarding these discussions has been drawn from the Division's summary report on its work accomplished (E/CN.8/33 and Rev.1); the *Summary Records* of the Commission's Second Session (UN Docs E/CN.8/SR.1–SR.10 (11–31 January 1949)); and the *Summary Records* of the Working Party (UN Docs E/CN.8/AC.1/SR.1–SR.5 (19–25 January 1949)).

[15] A Working Group to discuss the Trusteeship Questionnaire was also appointed and was attended by Cuba (Chairman), Czechoslovakia, France, New Zealand and the United States.

finance and technical assistance.[16] The deliberations on international tax problems were themselves repetitious and cursory due to, firstly, the poor organisation of, and overlapping relationships between, the many agenda items and Secretariat documents presented;[17] secondly, the preliminary nature of much of the Division's work; and thirdly, conflict avoidance by Commission members when disagreements arose.[18] The late circulation of certain Secretariat documents also delayed discussions on three occasions, either to give members time to study the relevant paper or to wait for working-language translations. Sections 7.2.1 to 7.2.5 summarise the deliberations on key discussion items that were connected to double taxation.[19] Only nine members of the Commission (Belgium, Cuba, France, New Zealand, South Africa, Ukraine SSR, the United Kingdom, the United States and the USSR) were active participants in these international tax discussions.[20]

There were two important developments giving rise to some tension in the discussions which are worth noting upfront here. The first concerned criticism by several Commission members of the Division's documents and progress. Such criticisms included[21] the large volume, repetition and

[16] Two points relating to technical assistance discussions are worth highlighting in their connection with crossover competencies and the expectations of Latin American countries. Firstly, Bartelt cautioned the Division to coordinate its work with the IMF to avoid overlap between their closely related programmes. The Division clarified that it performed the greater part of its work in close cooperation with specialised agencies and held daily conversations with IMF representatives when working in a field of similar interest. Secondly, Cuba argued for the UN to bear the costs of technical assistance, but the USSR, Ukraine SSR and China conversely argued for every effort to be made to minimise UN expenses.

[17] The Commission initially grouped agenda items together and, during some debates, deferred items for later related discussions; however, this frequently led to issues being overlooked. The ICC reported 'complete confusion in the minds of the delegates' as the documents were not referenced to their subject matter: Frank Bower, 'Confidential Note by the ICC Representative on the Fiscal Commission's Second Session', 1, attached to Letter from Bower to Bartelt, 28 January 1949, NARAII:RG56-199-4.

[18] Bower also noted that the Chairman was not 'sufficiently versed' in international tax matters 'to follow or appreciate the significance of contributions to the debate', which led him to 'dry up discussion rather than guide it when the subject became technical': Ibid.

[19] The projects concerning tax assessment and collection practices, and the taxation of foreign nationals, transactions and resources are not discussed here as these were only at the information-gathering stages and the Commission merely noted them.

[20] China, Czechoslovakia and Poland either did not participate in or materially contribute to the discussions, while Colombia and Lebanon only spoke when the issue was perceived to have benefit for underdeveloped countries.

[21] These discussions took place in the second and third plenary meetings. Note that some members, especially Belgium, commended the Division's work.

excessive scope of the documents (the USSR and Lebanon); 'badly presented', 'unevenly done' and 'overly academic' work (the United Kingdom);[22] objection to Sundelson's Report (the United States, the United Kingdom and Cuba) and the review of the League's work (the USSR); and the suitability of many documents for use by technical experts rather than for the Commission's study (Belgium and the United Kingdom). The United States proposed the creation of a small consultative group to liaise between the Division and the Commission in between sessions by reporting on the Secretariat's work to the Commission.[23] Although this was a departure from normal UN practice[24] and the motion was resisted by the Secretariat, the USSR, Ukraine SSR and France for its potential encroachment on the prerogatives of the Secretariat, the US proposal was eventually adopted by nine votes to three. The consultative group was constituted of the Belgium, Lebanon and Ukraine SSR representatives on the basis that they were permanently based in New York, thus limiting any expenses involved.[25]

The second development concerned lengthy Soviet views (hereinafter referred to as 'general Soviet positions') expressed by the USSR and Ukraine SSR, supported by Czechoslovakia,[26] on agenda items related to international tax. These representations, to some extent, disrupted the flow and depth of the discussions, but the Soviet opposition was generally considered 'half-hearted' and Chernyshev a 'good' and 'fair' Chairman by the United States, the United Kingdom and the ICC.[27] In brief, the Soviet arguments were that the documents submitted to the Commission detailing the work and recommendations of the Secretariat, specialised agencies and NGOs attempted to require the Commission to exceed its competence in, inter alia, interfering with countries' right to determine their fiscal policies, bringing the pressure of the UN to bear against small

[22] WW Morton, *Report of UK Delegate to the Fiscal Commission, Second Session: 10th–25th January*, undated, 1, TNA:IR40/9959(1).

[23] While the US intention was for this group to study the Secretariat's work in advance to give the Commission 'a better idea of the work carried out' (E/CN.8/SR.2 (11 January 1949) 4), other countries had different agendas, including for the committee to ensure the budget was being used most effectively (Colombia and the United Kingdom), and to supervise the Division and establish its work priorities (Cuba).

[24] Morton, *Report*, 1.

[25] Morton reported to his government that these three were persons without 'any expertise in fiscal matters' and thus were not considered to have valuable influence: Ibid.

[26] Despite being under Communist rule, Poland did not indicate support for the Soviet views expressed.

[27] Kellogg memo, 26 January 1949, 2; Morton, *Report*, 3; Bower, 'Confidential Note', 1.

countries, and weakening their bargaining position vis-à-vis big countries. Such recommendations (including the imposition of unified model conventions on all countries, without consideration of variations in the level of economic development) attempted to revive the system advanced by the League. Not only were they based on theories that tax barriers were obstacles to economic expansion and that double taxation made the position of foreign investors worse than that of domestic investors, but they were also designed to further the interests of foreign investors and capital-exporting countries by influencing capital-receiving states to modify their fiscal laws to the detriment of their own national interests. The adoption of such recommendations, while inevitably promoting capital flows, would only result in the expansion of large monopolies, absorption of local enterprises by powerful foreign companies, infiltration by economically powerful states into the national economy and domestic affairs of weaker states, and the brunt of the tax burden being borne by the working masses.[28]

The general Soviet positions were rejected by Belgium, Cuba, France, New Zealand, South Africa, the United Kingdom,[29] the United States, the American Federation of Labor, FAO and Carroll on the following basis: double taxation measures were designed to assist underdeveloped countries given that increased capital investment helped raise depressed standards of living, relief was generally borne by the residence country of the investor and the Mexico Model indicated that most Latin American countries considered such work to be of importance and benefit to less-developed countries. Moreover, New Zealand and South Africa believed that the function of the Commission was to study and provide information to assist countries in concluding fair agreements.

7.2.1 The Tax Treaties Collection

Discussions on this item were amicable and began with Lachmann's explanation of the *ITA* publication and the projects it planned to embark on, ideally with the collaboration of universities and scientific institutions in various countries, as the League had done. These projects included analytical studies into the 'nature, meaning and import of trends and

[28] The USSR also attributed the rising tax burden of many countries, particularly the United States, to the increase of non-productive expenditures, such as armaments and the Marshall Plan.

[29] Morton speculated that the Soviet line might have been due, in part, to its 'dislike of seeing . . . [the League's work] continued': Morton, *Report*, 3.

provisions' of the agreements collected, which would 'also emphasize the similarities among groups of agreements entered into between countries of the same region or of a comparable level of economic development'.[30] Comparative study of common traits in DTAs notwithstanding the diversity of national tax laws were also envisaged, as were supplements to the tax treaties collection comprising, firstly, a volume entitled Collection of Laws Affecting International Tax Relations, and secondly, a compilation of extracts of tax clauses in friendship and navigation treaties and other agreements related to international economic relations.

The following requests and comments were made in the Commission's plenary sessions: (1) the ICC, supported by Britain and Belgium, requested the Secretariat to prepare a paper regarding which DTAs were still in effect to ensure that the work was brought up to date; (2) Belgium suggested future editions of the volume be issued in loose-leaf form to facilitate the removal of out-of-date agreements, and for the volume to contain a summary of current administrative regulations on international taxation as this would be of additional assistance to governments and specialists; (3) Britain, supported by the United States, requested that the Secretariat revise statements made in its introduction to the volume regarding the nature of Anglo-American agreements; and (4) Cuba, supported by the United States and Belgium, proposed that the Commission recommend to ECOSOC to allocate an additional sum of $5,000 for the Spanish publication of *ITA*.[31]

When Lachmann raised the Secretariat's recommendations concerning planned projects and cooperation with external institutions, the USSR (as Chairman) instructed him to refrain from making proposals for future work. On the last day of the session, nevertheless, South Africa submitted a resolution recommending that the Secretariat engage with universities, scientific institutions or learned societies to assign them individual research projects of a more regional or specialised nature to ease the Secretariat's task, and that the costs be borne either by these institutions or by the UN, in whole or in part, through research funds to be assigned from the UN

[30] Fiscal Commission, *Introductory Survey of Some Trends in Recent Tax Agreements*, Note by the Secretariat, 2nd sess, UN Doc E/CN.8/41 (30 December 1948). So far, the Division had only prepared an introductory survey on the General Clause of the various bilateral treaties on income and property.

[31] This sum was based on the Secretariat's estimates for 2,000 Spanish copies: Fiscal Commission, *Financial Implications of the Proposal Submitted by the Representative of the United States to Print a Spanish Edition of the Volume 'International Tax Agreements' (E/CN.8/30)*, Note by the Secretariat, 2nd sess, UN Doc E/CN.8/W.32 (7 February 1949).

budget.[32] The USSR and the United Kingdom objected to the increase in UN expenses; however, Colombia endorsed the proposal as it would help address problems of special interest to 'the small Powers'.[33] The United States considered that the proposal would likely save money rather than impose additional costs since universities could perform a certain amount of work and lighten the Secretariat's burden. At Britain's suggestion to remove the financial reference from the resolution, which was accepted by South Africa, the Commission adopted the resolution as amended.

7.2.2 Progress on the Mexico and London Models

The Division's compilation of governments' views on the Mexico and London Models so far comprised replies received from nine governments, namely: Australia, Ecuador, India, Luxembourg, the Philippines, the Netherlands, New Zealand, the United Kingdom and the United States.[34] Prior to the session, the United Kingdom had submitted a proposal for the two models to be consolidated to minimise deviations from the Models arising when countries negotiated DTAs.[35] It advanced that this could 'be largely achieved without great controversy . . . [f]or instance, the treatment of patent royalties in the London draft might prove generally acceptable when it becomes appreciated that this treatment accords with realities', although 'other matters might prove more intractable, e.g., the definition of "fiscal domicile" in relation to companies'.[36]

32 Fiscal Commission, *Proposed Amendment to Part A of the Economic and Social Council Draft Resolution on the Report of the Second Session of the Fiscal Commission Submitted by the Delegate of the Union of South Africa*, 2nd sess, UN Doc E/CN.8/W.31 (24 January 1949).

33 Colombia accused 'the great Powers' of being prepared to undertake expenses to find solutions for major political problems in parts of the world of special interest to them (e.g. Greece, Palestine or China), and while 'the small Powers' had 'not hesitate[d] to follow them', the latter's problems also needed to be addressed: E/CN.8/SR.10 (31 January 1949) 9.

34 Fiscal Commission, *Statements of Views of Member Governments on Mexico and London Model Tax Conventions 1943–1946*, Note by the Secretariat, 2nd sess, UN Docs E/CN.8/W.22 and Add.1 (15 November 1948). These replies provided the countries' views, to varying depth, on the articles of the model conventions, including the model conventions on estates and successions. Only a few countries had expressly indicated their preference for one model over the other: Australia and Ecuador in favour of the Mexico Model, and Luxembourg and Britain in favour of the London Model.

35 Fiscal Commission, *Items Proposed by Member Governments for Consideration by the Fiscal Commission*, Note by the Secretariat, 2nd sess, UN Doc E/CN.8/W.20 (1 November 1949) 3.

36 Ibid.

In the discussions of the Commission in plenary and the Working Party, Cuba, France, Ukraine SSR, the United States and the ICC considered that the consolidation of the two models was undesirable, difficult or not an urgent consideration. France, Cuba and the ICC favoured having two, or several, models to allow negotiators to choose between them. Belgium, Cuba and the United States considered that member governments should continue to conclude DTAs following the principles of the present model conventions. Belgium, supported by Cuba, suggested that the Secretariat consider consolidating some of the important parts of the model conventions. The USSR, supported by Czechoslovakia and Ukraine SSR, expressed their general approval for bilateral negotiations of DTAs but argued against international action in this field by the Commission or any other UN bodies as the initiative to conclude DTAs had to emanate from states and not through exhortation by an international body. Discussions were concluded with the US submission of a draft resolution recommending the conclusion of bilateral agreements.[37]

In addition, the Working Party also considered various proposals of member states that had been submitted to the Division prior to the session and which were related to extending the scope of the model conventions to (1) cover certain forms of extraterritorial taxation (the United Kingdom),[38] (2) include provisions regulating the procedure to be followed to settle differences arising between governments regarding compliance with treaty provisions (the Netherlands),[39] (3) include social security taxes but exclude penal taxes (New Zealand),[40] (4) grant credits for taxes paid abroad for dividends and the dual domicile of trustees (New Zealand),[41] and (5)

[37] See Section 7.2.6.

[38] E/CN.8/W.20, 3. This was resolved on the basis that it was relevant to the study of tax barriers to trade and investment and that the Secretariat be instructed to include extraterritorial taxation in its inquiry.

[39] Ibid 2. The Working Party agreed to recommend that DTAs include such provisions. Relatedly, the Netherlands had also proposed that tax disputes be dealt with by a special fiscal chamber set up within the International Court of Justice, or by a special international court, however, the proposal was not supported by Cuba, South Africa, the United Kingdom, the United States or the ICC.

[40] Ibid 1. The United States opposed the inclusion of social security contributions (supported by Belgium, Cuba, France, the United Kingdom and the ICC) but favoured the exclusion of penal taxes (supported by Belgium and Cuba).

[41] Ibid 2. While the United States, France, South Africa and the ICC supported the Division's study of such questions, Britain's response was largely unenthusiastic. The matter was resolved by an agreement to simply indicate the various members' remarks in the Working Party's report.

cover mutual administrative assistance to prevent tax evasion (Belgium and El Salvador).[42]

7.2.3 *Review of the League's Work on International Tax Problems*

The Division's document regarding this subject was an extensive review that covered all the League's fiscal work, not just that concerning international tax ('League Review').[43] The explanation given was that national tax problems formed part and parcel of the international tax work as they enabled the search for solutions to international double taxation and fiscal evasion. In the Review, the Division indicated that it intended to continue the League's work in studying and settling differences arising between national fiscal legislations (i.e. international tax work); studying and promoting information exchange on developments in fiscal methods and techniques on national fiscal problems;[44] and addressing economic, social, political and administrative aspects of barriers to investment and trade.

Under a chapter headed 'Work remaining to be done', the Division explained the work already underway to further the League's work and outlined projects it intended to undertake. The work that remained 'in the field of international fiscal relations' was grouped into three categories: (1) study of existing legislation and conventions; (2) study of the influence of taxes on world economic relations; and (3) formulation of

[42] Ibid 3. El Salvador's proposal appeared broadly intended to obtain information on how a country taxed the income and capital of its nationals who resided in another country, but it was dealt together with the Belgian proposal for information exchange to combat tax evasion as the United States, the United Kingdom, France and the ICC were only interested in discussing mutual administrative assistance in connection with tax treaties. Disagreement arose over the type of information that should and could be exchanged and whether the proposals encompassed the collection and assessment of taxes. Ultimately, the Working Party reached no conclusion and simply instructed the Secretariat to assemble 'all possible information' for the Commission's Third Session: E/CN.8/AC.1/SR.4 (24 January 1949) 5.

[43] Fiscal Commission, *Preliminary Report on the Work Accomplished by the League of Nations in Fiscal Matters*, 2nd sess, UN Doc E/CN.8/37 (5 January 1949). The authorship appears attributable to Deperon based on the Review's breadth and depth of coverage of the League's work; the ascribing of the *PFI Conditions* study, which Deperon had been responsible for, as 'mainly' the work of the Fiscal Committee (at 20); and the verbatim incorporation of the studies Deperon had contemplated for the Commission as listed in annex B of the Fiscal Committee's *Tenth Session Report* (at 30).

[44] The Review described this function as purposed at 'assist[ing] under-developed countries', 'facilitat[ing] the negotiation of fiscal conventions' and 'secur[ing] some international unification of fiscal systems': Ibid 9.

practical recommendations concerning 'the best techniques to adopt and the best policies to follow'.[45] Category 1 was composed of two main projects that would enable 'the organ set up within the United Nations . . . [to] really become the highest authority on international fiscal questions': firstly, the '[c]entralization of adequate documentation' relating to international fiscal laws; and secondly, based on such documentation assembled, 'analytical and comparative studies of various international fiscal problems that have so far been insufficiently considered' and the continuation of 'studies made on double taxation and fiscal evasion'.[46] Category 2 supplemented the aforementioned 'technical analyses' by assessing the 'real influence [of these fiscal problems] on world economic relations'.[47] To this end, the Division sought 'a new and general analysis' to take into account increased fiscal burdens and changes 'in world economic currents'.[48] This was proposed to be accomplished through, firstly, resuming and developing the 1923 'partial study' of the four economists on fiscal barriers to international economic relations within the present framework of economic problems, and secondly, expanding the *PFI Conditions* study.[49] Category 3 was to come about through the work of Categories 1 and 2. Through it, the Commission was to '[a]bove all . . . endeavour to improve on the model Conventions of Mexico and London', and would 'succeed in accomplishing really creative work in international fiscal matters'.[50] The Division also advised the Commission to arrange 'regional fiscal conferences to deal with regional fiscal problems of particular importance' (e.g. reciprocal adjustment of national fiscal systems within the economic unions being set up in Europe).[51]

In the Commission's discussions, Belgium, Cuba and the United States commended the League Review; the United States praised the Division's thoroughness, while Belgium considered the review to be of 'great historic value' and to contain helpful suggestions for the Commission's

45 Ibid 27–31.

46 Ibid 28–9.

47 Ibid 29.

48 Ibid.

49 Ibid.

50 Ibid 31. In this regard, the Division stated that '[t]wo problems in particular require rapid solution': (1) the manner in which to apply the rules regarding the allocation of taxable income of multinational enterprises that had been drawn up by the Fiscal Committee, and (2) the 'serious divergences between the two model texts' on taxation of interest and dividends.

51 Ibid.

future work.[52] The USSR, however, considered these tributes premature and that the document, among others, went beyond the Secretariat's competence in suggesting future programmes of work. Ultimately, the review was never systematically examined because, firstly, the Commission decided, after some debate, to discuss the review's recommendations jointly and generally with other relevant agenda items. And secondly, whenever the review was mentioned again, the Soviet members often interrupted by outlining their general Soviet positions, which tended to discourage further discussion. The following three proposals mentioned in the Review were nevertheless debated either because they were pursued by certain Commission members or had been formally suggested by member governments for the Division's studies.

The first proposal concerned the insistence by Cuba and Belgium, albeit for different reasons, on convening regional fiscal conferences. Belgium desired regional conferences to be convened in Europe to deal with the reciprocal adjustment of national fiscal systems within the European customs union. No discussion was recorded on this proposal. Conversely, Cuba, supported by Lebanon, advanced the importance of such conferences for economically less-developed areas, such as Latin America, where international fiscal problems were still largely unknown. However, France and the United States disagreed. France pointed out the potential for overlap with the regional economic commissions already in existence. The United States considered such conferences of little value and was unwilling to attend any because experience had shown that DTAs were most effectively arranged through bilateral negotiations; double taxation was a question of general, rather than regional, interest; and such conferences incurred considerable expense, whereas the Secretariat could carry out work that was just as useful. Cuba expressed surprise at the American attitude given that the Mexico Model had been adopted at such a conference and pointed out that a regional American conference could not bring profitable results unless it were attended by the United States and Canada. When questioned by the United States, Lachmann indicated that several Latin American governments had repeatedly shown interest in such conferences. He then explained that such a conference would be devoted to technical assistance given that countries encountering similar difficulties in their internal tax systems would profit from the experience of others. Double taxation would only be discussed to the degree that national legislation impinged on it. The

52 Ibid.

United States, nevertheless, remained unenthused, and at the suggestion of France, Belgium and Britain for an American conference to be held under the auspices of ECLA or the OAS, Cuba withdrew its proposal, reserving the right to raise the question at the Commission's Third Session after preliminary consultation with the American states.

The second recommendation concerned Britain's formal submission for the Commission to consider tax problems amounting to trade barriers which had been listed in Annex B of the League Committee's *Tenth Session Report* for recommended study by the Commission.[53] Discussions on this proposal were brief as most of the listed problems were already being addressed by the Secretariat in connection with other headings (e.g. the treatment of foreign nationals, assets and transactions) and the Working Party simply recommended that the Secretariat continue its study based on the replies received from governments to its questionnaire. The United States, Cuba and the ICC indicated their keen interest in the subject and urged that the Division complete its work in time for the Third Session. Cuba considered the whole question extremely complicated, especially from the standpoint of economically underdeveloped countries, and that it should not be examined superficially, particularly in view of the proposal for DTAs to incorporate the most-favoured-nation clause, which itself was interpreted differently in different countries.

The third recommendation concerned Ecuador's proposal for a study on fiscal measures to prevent depressions, with special regard for the situation of underdeveloped countries.[54] Ecuador indicated that the subject had been discussed at the 1943 Mexico conference but that no concrete conclusions had been reached beyond the recommendation that the subject be studied by tax administrators and experts. New Zealand indicated strong interest in the proposal, but the United States was unsupportive, stating that the question was beyond the Commission's scope. In the Working Party, the ICC, Cuba and Belgium briefly debated how the study could be conducted without crossovers with the work of that Economic and Employment Commission, but they eventually decided not to undertake the study to avoid overburdening the Secretariat's workload. The United Kingdom (as Rapporteur), nevertheless, included the item as part of the long-term future work of the

[53] E/CN.8/W.20, 4–5.

[54] Ibid 5. This proposal was supported by the American Federation of Labor: Fiscal Commission, *Memorandum by the American Federation of Labor*, 2nd sess, UN Doc E/CN.8/W.20/Add.1 (10 January 1949).

Commission. In the plenary discussions, the United States adamantly objected to this inclusion while Belgium, Britain, New Zealand, the Secretariat and ICC defended it. The matter was resolved by Britain's suggestion to redraft the reference to emphasise cooperation with other organs rather than as part of the Commission's prerogative to conduct independent studies.

7.2.4 *Effects of Taxation on International Trade and Investment*

The Division's main document supplied on the subject consisted of Sundelson's Report, which was issued only a few days into the session (on or just after 13 January).[55] In another document (i.e. the Division's summary report of its implementation work since the First Session [dated 30 December]), the Division explained that its study of the subject was purposed at formulating recommendations on the removal of tax obstacles to international trade and investment 'in the light of most recent knowledge on economics'.[56] The Division further indicated that most of 'the numerous tax treaties and unilateral tax measures . . . passed since 1920, and in particular, during the last ten years' in response to revenue authorities' increasing concerns since World War I to address 'practical aspects of this problem', had been 'based on purely empirical considerations'.[57] Also, no 'scientific analysis of the economic aspects of international tax problems' had been undertaken since the four economists' report, which only covered double taxation, and since then 'new developments in general economic theory' and 'deep changes' in 'the institutional machinery and geographical pattern of world trade and investment' had occurred.[58] An earlier issued version of this summary report (dated 15 December) provided a different synopsis, indicating a narrower study purposed at (1) formulating recommendations on tax treaty provisions and governmental tax policies 'to derive greater benefits from trade and international investment, both from the viewpoint of buyers and sellers, creditors and debtors'; and (2) assisting the reconciliation of the London and Mexico Models.[59] To these ends, the study investigated 'devices' used by governments 'to correct the most obvious

[55] Fiscal Commission, *The Influence of Taxation on the Flow of International Trade and Investment*, 2nd sess, UN Doc E/CN.8/38 (13 January 1949).
[56] E/CN.8/33/Rev.1 (30 December 1948) 13.
[57] Ibid.
[58] Ibid.
[59] E/CN.8/33, 11.

defects of their tax systems', namely: tax treaties, national tax laws and 'special agreements with individual firms and taxpayers'.[60] The study also took into account 'the economic incidence and effects of taxation', which in general had not been 'adequately considered among the factors affecting ... [tax] conventions' because of the tendency 'in drafting tax conventions' for consideration to be 'given primarily to the tax problems created in industrialized and developed areas'.[61]

Sundelson's Report was prefaced by a Secretariat note that stated that Sundelson's preliminary report 'contains the main elements which have been brought to light during the complex preparation of this study'; however, the views expressed therein 'do not represent the official opinions of the Secretariat', which would only be formulated when the study of the problem was completed in a few weeks' time to be discussed more 'fully' at the Commission's Third Session.[62] The note, nevertheless, stated that '[t]he Secretariat believes that the attached preliminary report of the Consultant will be very useful for the discussion of this problem at this session'.[63] In brief, Sundelson's Report set out 'a new approach' to establishing the role of international tax policy in contributing to 'the revival of multilateral trade and private international investment'.[64] It explained that a re-examination was necessary because 'no comprehensive study' had been undertaken since the first study carried out by Bruins, Einaudi, Seligman and Stamp in the 1920s, which was premised on the now outmoded methodology of fiscal neutrality. In addition, it was necessary to consider 'the influence of non-tax factors', importantly, the marked reduction of both portfolio and direct private international investment 'as the preponderant element in international long-term capital movements',[65] and 'the growing tendency to abandon taxation as the instrument for revenue, control and discrimination, and to substitute instead multiple currency devices'.[66] Accordingly, the re-examination required (1) '[a] realistic approach to the institutional factors and ... actual circumstances under which transactions take place ... to prevent some unwarranted generalisations made in the past' (including 'simplified

[60] Ibid.
[61] Ibid.
[62] E/CN.8/38, 1.
[63] Ibid.
[64] Ibid 2.
[65] Such reduction had been brought about by the 'unfavourable climate' created by 'currency questions' and 'such political factors as programmes of nationalization': Ibid.
[66] Ibid.

assumptions regarding incidence'); (2) distinguishing 'between industrialized and non-industrialized countries'; and (3) considerations of 'the political and economic philosophy of each jurisdiction' as this affected 'the extent to which the tax burdens on international business could be modified'.[67] The conclusions advanced in Sundelson's Report may be summarised as follows:[68]

- Tax provisions did not greatly affect foreign trade and investment except where they discriminated against businesses that earned foreign exchange[69] or enabled tax avoidance or evasion.[70]
- The best method of double taxation relief was through unilateral measures provided by creditor countries on foreign profits earned by their nationals.[71]
- The tendency at recent international conferences 'to over-emphasize the influence' of taxation on accelerating and directing international trade and capital flows had led less-industrialised countries to become 'excessively optimistic concerning the immediately stimulating effects of tax agreements on international capital movements'.[72]
- Model tax conventions and present-type DTAs had limited utility in assisting less-developed countries by producing marked results in enhanced trade and investment for the following reasons:
  - DTAs had 'no immediate value' where it was common practice for the non-industrialised country (especially in Latin America) 'to enter into specific arrangements with foreign business and investors which reflect the bargaining position of the foreigners' in their procurement of 'freedom from current burdens' and even 'future

[67] Ibid 2–3.

[68] Ibid 3–7.

[69] For example, postwar exchange and transfer taxes, which would eventually cease when currency stabilisation and convertibility were established.

[70] Tax havens and preferential tax regimes did not have the ability to stimulate trade and investment flows but were merely influential on the direction and nature of existing arrangements.

[71] Since such relief on a liberal scale was practised by the 'great creditor countries' and 'members of some of the important trading blocs', their nationals already had 'adequate [relief available] in most circumstances': (E/CN.8/38, 4). While some countries were extending credits to increase the measure of relief (e.g. the United Kingdom to its colonies, and the United States to its possessions and the Western Hemisphere), the value of the relief was diminished insofar as the taxes eligible for the deduction did not normally exist in underdeveloped areas.

[72] Ibid 7.

taxes or tax changes'.[73] Until 'this peculiar form of bilateral contract' was taken into consideration, no study of existing statutory tax provisions per se nor any relief proposals would be relevant.[74]

- Model conventions provided a useful framework for initiating agreements where countries lacked fixed relief policies, but they were unlikely to affect countries that had set attitudes towards relief that were exhibited in their national laws. They were also 'essentially suited to relations between industrialized countries' and hence of doubtful effectiveness in aiding the spread of DTAs to underdeveloped and capital-importing countries.[75]
- Reconciliation of the Mexico and London Models was futile as there '[could] be no universal agreement' between underdeveloped country viewpoints and creditor country or taxpayer viewpoints. Moreover, both Models failed to consider 'problems created by tax measures associated with currency difficulties, tax payments in kind, or the basic problems of making agreements between jurisdictions relying on different types of taxes'.[76]
- Non-industrialised debtor countries were in 'major need for revised policies' to which an extension of present-type DTAs had little contribution to make to their basic tax problems.[77]

Sundelson's Report concluded that further studies were necessary 'to shed light on the numerous problems raised' by (1) giving emphasis 'to a fuller analysis of the economic effects of tax policies and of the

[73] Ibid 4. Such bargains were sometimes 'supported by statutory authority' but were 'most frequently' made 'without the benefit of statutes' and, 'in some isolated cases, in spite of statutory prohibitions'. While 'a conspiracy of silence' had been created by the benefitting enterprises and contracting governments to such arrangements, there was 'ample evidence that they . . . [were] widespread and significant'.

[74] Ibid 5.

[75] Ibid 6.

[76] Ibid.

[77] These problems included underdeveloped countries' lack of broad-based income taxes; inability to successfully apply income taxes against extractive industries (i.e. the typical area into which FDI flowed), including due to difficulties in obtaining payments of foreign exchange from business enterprises with head offices or processing establishments abroad; and reliance on taxes (e.g. export or royalty taxes) on the raw or relatively unprocessed material as '[t]he only effective revenue-raising technique': Ibid 6–7. Conversely, the continental European agreements did not particularly reflect creditor or debtor perspectives, while the Anglo-American agreements (1) only addressed certain categories of income and were subordinate to unilateral tax relief policies in providing minor ancillary relief above that allowed under national laws, and (2) were premised on net income taxation being the chief instrument for taxing income from international trade and investment.

behaviour patterns of international business enterprise in response to tax changes'; (2) devoting effort 'to a study of the specific problems created by limitations on private enterprise in international trade and investment and on the problems of specific geographic areas where tax policy influences are recognized as significant'; and (3) making efforts 'to restate the objectives of international tax policy with regard to under-developed areas and to stress the basic needs and problems of such areas'.[78]

During the Commission and Working Party discussions, Silva acknowledged that 'there were certain contradictions' between the League Review and Sundelson's Report, stating that Sundelson 'had approached the problem from a new angle'.[79] Silva asserted that the document 'in no way expressed the Secretariat's views', whose own study would be completed in April 1949,[80] but that the Division 'had merely attempted to supply the Fiscal Commission initial data on which it could base its conclusions',[81] as 'it was unwilling to assume responsibility for the omission of a point of view which was the subject of numerous controversies'.[82]

This agenda item attracted the most contentious debates of the session. The plenary discussions centred on whether the report should be received by the Commission. The report was heavily criticised by Cuba, the United States, the United Kingdom, the ICC and Carroll, and to a lesser extent by Belgium and China, for containing inaccuracies or lacking substantiation. Britain and Cuba objected to particular statements in the document: the former regarding the assertion that selected capital-exporting countries granted tax exemptions outside of DTAs to facilitate investment abroad,[83] the latter regarding the claim that many governments, especially in Latin America, engaged in bargaining practices with foreign firms and capitalists that were statutorily prohibited.[84]

[78] Ibid 7.

[79] E/CN.8/SR.7 (18 January 1949) 3. Silva also stated Sundelson would explain certain aspects of his work to the Commission; however, there is no record of him speaking in, or attending, the discussions.

[80] Ibid 4.

[81] Ibid 4–5.

[82] E/CN.8/AC.1/SR.2 (25 January 1949) 7.

[83] Morton stated that the United Kingdom did not grant any special advantages to British businessmen who invested capital in the British Empire as opposed to other countries, and that British policy had never allowed tax exemption except pursuant to DTAs: E/CN.8/SR.7, 4.

[84] Cuba insisted that Cuba's negotiations with foreign investors had always been conducted publicly and denied 'a conspiracy of silence' ever having existed: Ibid 3.

Britain also maintained that the only means of avoiding double taxation was, and always had been, through bilateral negotiation rather than unilateral measures. The United States censured the Secretariat for failing to timely submit its own study and for presenting an incomplete report which contained views that it did not necessarily endorse, and which were inadequately substantiated. Carroll stated that the report contained many conclusions which were entirely unsupported by the facts. The ICC considered that the report revealed Sundelson's lack of familiarity with fiscal systems then in use, and thus was of no value to the discussion. China thought the report was poorly organised and the conclusions insufficiently substantiated. Belgium considered it impossible to open a meaningful discussion on a document which contained neither factual data nor concrete information. The United States, supported by Britain and Belgium, moved to have the document discredited altogether.

On the other hand, Cuba, South Africa, Ukraine SSR, the USSR and FAO defended the report's usefulness and opposed discounting it in its entirety. FAO considered that the report should be taken into consideration as it contained personal conclusions that might be of future interest, unlike the League Review which only indicated the remaining work to be undertaken. Cuba acknowledged that Sundelson's Report was not entirely without interest despite its criticisms. The USSR viewed the report 'less undesirable than' the League Review and felt that the US proposal was unnecessary as objections to Sundelson's Report would be noted in the summary records. The USSR reminded the Commission that the Secretariat itself considered the document constructive to the discussions and that disregarding the report would eliminate discussion of the agenda item since no other document was available to take its place. Ukraine SSR stated that, while Sundelson's Report had defects that were open to criticism, it was wrong to completely exclude it as it contained very pertinent notes which several delegations might wish to have elaborated. The USSR and Ukraine SSR both suggested postponing the discussion to allow the Secretariat time to recast the document to provide supplementary evidence. South Africa considered that the report should not be withdrawn from consideration for the sole reason that it was not backed by concrete data. At this point, Belgium indicated that the proposals to exclude Sundelson's Report could no longer stand as the exchange of views had raised arguments which amounted to an analysis of the document. The USSR (as Chairman) declared the matter closed and that the report was open for consideration by the Commission.

The Commission in plenary did not return to address Sundelson's Report likely because of the subsequent chaotic meetings in which discussions outstanding on agenda items related to international tax matters were merged but not resolved. FAO did nevertheless suggest that, as differences of opinion existed regarding the effects of DTAs within individual countries, particularly those with relatively primitive fiscal systems and tax structures, the Commission should broaden its inquiry to include the study of the internal effects of DTAs in under-developed countries and 'the ways in which those countries could raise the considerable revenue' that had been sacrificed.[85] The USSR also remarked that the elimination of barriers to trade was 'desirable in itself where two States were on an equal footing' but 'to be regretted where a powerful State and a weak State were concerned'.[86]

In the Working Party, Cuba requested that the Working Party take no note of Sundelson's Report and for the document to be marked as 'Restricted' to prevent journalists from publishing relevant passages as such could 'have an extremely unfortunate effect on the peoples of Latin America' if published without explanation.[87] Silva stated that only a very limited number of copies of the document were in circulation, while Ukraine SSR insisted that only the Commission could decide whether to place the document in the 'Restricted' category.[88] The United Kingdom, supported by South Africa, proposed that, as neither the Commission nor the Working Party had 'made any real study of the agenda item . . . and had been content to indulge in sharp criticism of the document', the Secretariat be requested to complete the document and that discussion be deferred to the Commission's Third Session.[89] The Working Party accepted this proposal.

7.2.5 Recommendations of Other UN Bodies, Specialised Agencies and NGOs

In general, the Commission and Working Party dealt superficially with the recommendations/discussions of other UN system organisations and

[85] E/CN.8/SR.8 (19 January 1949) 8.

[86] E/CN.8/SR.9 (20 January 1949) 8.

[87] E/CN.8/AC.1/SR.2, 6.

[88] There is no record of the Commission making this decision; however, the Division later refused to provide Sundelson's Report to an interested academic on the grounds that it was 'Restricted': Letter from Karakacheff to Petras, 5 April 1949, UNARMS:AG-025-002—S-0441–0468–23889(A).

[89] E/CN.8/AC.1/SR.2, 7.

NGOs by simply taking note of those communications.[90] This response was largely attributable to disagreements that arose over the subject matter, including objections raised by Soviet members based on general Soviet positions, or suggestions that the relevant communication was purely informational in purpose. The following details of certain discussions are nevertheless worthy of some mention:

- Cuba's opposition to the IACCP Resolution regarding the elimination of discriminatory treatment between national and foreign persons through tax legislation to encourage private foreign investment.[91]
- Cuba's interest in the IMF's and World Bank's recommendation for cooperation to study and formulate standards on fiscal organisation (e.g. budgetary matters and classification).[92] Belgium, however, considered the request purely informational as it did not contain a full statement of the official policy of the IMF and Bank. This topic would nevertheless later become part of the Commission's work programme at the United States' instigation.[93]
- Belgium's support of FAO's proposal for the Fiscal Commission and the Economic and Employment Commission (and its Sub-Commission on Employment and Economic Stability) to jointly study how fiscal policy could promote economic progress and living standards.[94] The Working Party approved Belgium's suggestion for the Secretariat to study the subject given its similarity with the Secretariat's intention to further the League's work covering the influence of taxes upon consumption, living standards and production. However, the United States in plenary discussion opposed this for being outside the Commission's scope. The matter was resolved with the stipulation that

[90] Such treatment must have disappointed the ICC and IFA, and perhaps even the Division which had laboured to secure the Commission's double taxation jurisdiction against the ITO and PAU/OAS.

[91] Fiscal Commission, *References of Interest to the Fiscal Commission Contained in the Proceedings of the Fourth Plenary Meeting of the Inter-American Council of Commerce and Production, Chicago, 19–22 September 1948*, Note by the Secretary, 2nd sess, UN Doc E/CN.8/43 (6 December 1948).

[92] Fiscal Commission, *References of Interest to the Fiscal Commission Contained in the Proceedings of the International Monetary Fund and the International Bank for Reconstruction and Development*, 2nd sess, UN Doc E/CN.8/W.17/Add.1 (17 December 1948).

[93] See Chapter 8, Section 8.1, n 11.

[94] E/CN.8/AC.1/SR.9 (20 January 1949) 6; Fiscal Commission, *Memorandum by Mr FL McDougall, Counselor, Food and Agriculture Organization*, UN Doc E/CN.8/26 (6 June 1947).

the Commission was only able to take up such studies at the instigation of and in cooperation with other UN bodies.

The Commission's handling of ICAO's interest in double taxation of international airlines is discussed in Chapter 11, Section 11.3.

7.2.6 The Commission's Report

The Commission's report[95] of its Second Session mainly consisted of its decisions on each agenda item[96] and its recommended draft resolutions for adoption by ECOSOC. The latter contained only one resolution of substance, namely: the US-originated resolution entitled 'Promotion and Adoption of Bilateral Agreements for the Avoidance of Double Taxation' (Resolution C).[97] The preamble to the resolution affirmed the utilisation of 'all appropriate means' to promote international trade and investment; the 'obstructions' to trade and investment flows that could result from 'uncoordinated' taxation by governments; the double taxation studies of the League's Fiscal Committee, private organizations 'in numerous conferences' and continuing work of the Fiscal Commission; and the 'important progress . . . already achieved' through DTAs and their 'special suitability' to achieving 'concrete co-ordination among the diverse national regimes of taxation'.[98] The operative part of the resolution recommended that governments 'actively pursue a policy of negotiating bilateral agreements wherever possible for the avoidance of double taxation'.[99]

The resolution concerning the Secretariat's future work programme listed the following items in the order of priority: technical assistance,

[95] Fiscal Commission, *Report to the Economic and Social Council on the Second Session of the Commission, Held at Lake Success, New York, 10 to 25 January 1949*, UN Docs E/1104 and Corr.1 (also E/CN.8/49/Rev.2) (3 February 1949).

[96] These included the call for the Secretariat to be more concise and organised in its reporting and for a consultative group to be established to maintain liaison between the Commission and the Secretariat (Ibid 5 [10]) and the recommendation that the Secretariat make available appropriate funds for the Spanish translation of *ITA* (at 9 [20]). In a follow-up response to the Commission's report, the Secretariat indicated that the translation cost of $2,600, but not the printing costs of $5,000, could be absorbed within the present budget: Fiscal Commission, *Report of the Second Session: Financial Estimates Presented by the Secretary-General in Accordance with Rule 30 of the Rules of Procedure of the Council*, 2nd sess, UN Doc E/1104/Add.1 (8 February 1949).

[97] E/1104, 16.

[98] Ibid.

[99] Ibid.

work of collation and synthesis,[100] study of the effects of taxation on international trade and investment, examination of the Mexico and London Models (especially the taxation of company profits and dividends, and dual domicile in estate taxes), study of the scope of mutual administrative assistance, cooperation with other UN bodies in continuing the League's work on the study of economic influences of taxation, and cooperation with scholarly institutions.[101]

7.3 Deliberations in ECOSOC (July 1949)

At ECOSOC's Ninth Session,[102] the Commission's report was considered by the Economic Committee over the course of its forty-eighth, forty-ninth and fifty-fourth meetings held on 6 and 19 July, during which Australia, Brazil, France, New Zealand, the United Kingdom and the United States stressed their strong endorsement of the work of the Commission.[103] However, the USSR submitted a motion for the Commission to be abolished on the grounds that it was redundant given that it did not meet in 1948; it 'could not be expected to yield positive results' except in fields which other regional and functional commissions were able to handle; and the sum of $15,120, representing the budget estimates for the Commission's 1950 session, would be saved.[104] The USSR clarified that

[100] This comprised work on (1) the fiscal information service; (2) public finance survey; (3) administrative practices relating to the assessment and collection of taxes; (4) taxation of foreign nationals, transactions and resources (with particular reference to extraterritorial taxation); and (5) the *ITA* series.

[101] Resolution A: E/1104, 14–15. The first draft of the report (UN Doc E/CN.8/49 (21 January 1949)), written by Morton as Rapporteur, made specific mention of subjects that Britain had advanced (e.g. extraterritorial taxation, fiscal measures to prevent depressions) but failed to mention certain proposals that it had opposed (e.g. regional conferences). This bias was somewhat readdressed during debates on the draft: see E/CN.8/AC.1/SR.5 (25 January 1949).

[102] ECOSOC membership in 1949 comprised Australia, Belgium, Brazil, Byelorussian SSR, Chile, China, Denmark, France, India, Lebanon, New Zealand, Peru, Poland, Turkey, the United Kingdom, the United States, the USSR and Venezuela.

[103] 'Fiscal Questions' [1948–9] *Yearbook of the United Nations* 490, 491; Fiscal Commission, *Action Taken by the Economic and Social Council at Its Ninth Session with regard to the Fiscal Commission*, UN Doc E/CN.8/W.33 (22 September 1949) (citing the *Summary Records* of the Economic Committee's relevant meetings (UN Docs E/AC.6/SR.48 (6 July 1949), E/AC.6/SR.49 (6 July 1949) and E/AC.6/SR.54 (19 July 1949)).

[104] Economic Committee, *Draft Resolution of the USSR*, UN ESC, 9th sess, Agenda item 13, UN Doc E/AC.6/W.41 (6 July 1949); Economic Committee, *Secretary-General's Statement of the Financial Implications of the USSR Draft Resolution*, UN ESC, 9th sess, Agenda item 13, UN Doc E/AC.6/W.41/Add.1 (16 July 1949).

the Division's work was 'in no way' to be curtailed with the discontinuation of the Commission.[105] The proposal was defeated by fifteen votes to two (the USSR and Byelorussian SSR) and one abstention (Poland).[106]

The Economic Committee adopted the Commission's report with minor textual changes. During the voting on the adoption of the report, Australia, Brazil, Chile, France and the United States spoke in favour of Resolution C; however, India stressed the difficulty of trying to uniformly follow the London and Mexico Models in concluding DTAs.[107] This ensued in the replacement of the phrase 'wherever possible' with 'wherever appropriate'[108] in the operative part of Resolution C. Resolution C, as amended, was adopted as ECOSOC Resolution 226D (IX) (22 July 1941).[109] ECOSOC adopted the Economic Committee's report[110] without debate.[111]

7.4 Commentary

The Second Session was ill-fated in many respects. The advancement of the date of the session had resulted in the resource-strapped Secretariat having to hastily compile its preparatory work and many Commission members having insufficient time to adequately study the material.[112] Deperon, the most capable Secretariat member with full knowledge and direction of the Division's work as well as familiarity with most of the Commission members, had left untimely.[113] The East–West and North–South divisions had emerged, the Cold War was in full swing on various fronts and the Latin American countries were manifestly aggrieved by the lack of economic aid or concern being shown for their region,[114]

[105] E/CN.8/W.33, 1.

[106] Memorandum by Livesey, 27 July 1949, 2, NARAII:RG56-199-4. During these discussions, the US representative (Stinebower) responded that the Commission was 'unglamourous but useful' (at 1).

[107] E/CN.8/W.33, 2.

[108] This was suggested by Australia: Livesey memo, 27 July 1949, 2.

[109] *Promotion and Adoption of Bilateral Agreements for the Avoidance of Double Taxation*, ESC Res 226D (IX), UN ESCOR, UN Doc E/1553 (15 August 1949, adopted 22 July 1949).This resolution is reproduced in Appendix D.

[110] Economic Committee, *Report of the Economic Committee*, UN ESC, 9th sess, Agenda item 13, UN Docs E/1438 and Corr.1 (20 July 1949).

[111] E/CN.8/W.33, 2.

[112] Bartelt letter, 2 March 1949, 2.

[113] As Deperon and Putnam never returned to their respective positions, this ended the personal connection with the League's Fiscal Committee.

[114] By this stage, 'a sense of injustice was boiling up' in US–Latin American relations with the Truman Administration having 'vetoed every Latin attempt to implement its [US] promises of economic partnership made during the war', including for stabilised

although this may have been blunted by Truman's Point Four Program announced on 20 January while the session was ongoing.[115] But unfortunate as these developments were, they merely exacerbated fundamental problems concerning how double taxation had been introduced to developing countries during the League years, the competing agendas various stakeholders had for the UN's fiscal work and the Commission's political nature.

Importantly, the League Review and the Division's efforts to safeguard the Commission's fiscal jurisdiction against other international organisations reveal Deperon's pursuit of the programme he had established for the Commission. He had, however, overestimated the Division's ability to produce timely results, in part due to the unexpected demands of its new technical assistance function, as well as unforeseen difficulties faced in recruiting competent staff and obtaining information at a time when many countries were rebuilding their governments, facing civil war, or simply lacked the resources, skill set or even fiscal system in place to answer the Division's questionnaires and inquiries. There are, moreover, strong suggestions that Deperon had come to an inflection point concerning the suitability of DTAs (at least those based on the Models) for developing countries. This is indicated by the Division's brief to ICAO advising of the inequality of the general reciprocal exemption tax treatment of international air transport in DTAs for debtor and underdeveloped countries;[116] the Division's study of tax bargaining contracts between governments and private firms; Deperon's engagement of Sundelson to write the report concerning the influence of taxation on

commodity prices and the creation of an inter-American development bank. Many Latin American countries, including Chile, Cuba and Venezuela, were 'on the verge of serious economic crisis': Edgar J Dosman, *The Life and Times of Raúl Prebisch, 1901–1986* (McGill-Queen's University Press, 2008) 240–1. See also Stephen G Rabe, 'The Elusive Conference: United States Economic Relations with Latin America, 1945–1952' (1978) 2 (3) *Diplomatic History* 279, 285–92.

115 The programme essentially piloted American technical assistance to underdeveloped areas profitable for investment to foster a domestic environment in which private capital and local labour could collaboratively facilitate economic growth and improved living standards. The aims were not humanitarian but stressed profit-making as the principal motive of corporate investment, containment of revolution or communism, replacement of 'old imperialism' and the creation of an open trading arena with the United States, Western Europe and Japan: see Herman Olden and Paul Phillips, 'The Point Four Program: Promise or Menace?' (1952) 16(3) *Science and Society* 222, 230; Stephen Macekura, 'The Point Four Program and US International Development Policy' (2013) 128(1) *Political Science Quarterly* 127.

116 See Chapter 11, Section 11.2.

foreign investments; Deperon's incorporation of national tax problems as part of the work on international tax problems; his recommendation for regional conferences to deal with regional fiscal problems, rather than to promote DTAs to underdeveloped countries;[117] and the more vague emphasis on improving, rather than reconciling, the Mexico and London Models. Such a reconsideration may have been the corollary of the Secretariat's growing knowledge of the multifaceted challenges and situations faced by the Latin American economies,[118] developing countries' growing articulation of double taxation problems and discontent with the Mexico Model, the Division's consideration of the situation of newly decolonised countries, and the realisation stemming from inadequate replies to the Division's questionnaires and the Division's own increasing participation in technical assistance and consultation with experts that many less-developed economies did not require or would not benefit from DTAs. Whatever the exact cause(s), Deperon's concern for developing countries' interests appeared to run deep – after his departure from the Division, an archival record reveals that he was still working for the UN on a technical assistance mission in Latin America.[119]

Accordingly, while the Division would claim before the Commission that Sundelson's Report did not necessarily represent the Secretariat's views, there is evidence that points otherwise. In particular, the League Review and the Division's summary reports (both of 15 and 30 December) indicate that the Division itself was advancing a major systematic approach to addressing tax obstacles to international trade and investment. Sundelson himself was based at the UN during his period of consultancy and would have been privy to the Division's views in addition to its research.[120] Significantly, literature on UN intellectual history indicates

[117] This was despite such double taxation conferences having been recommended by the United States at the First Session and by Gómez following her Latin American mission (see Chapter 5, Sections 5.2 and 5.6).

[118] For example, in January 1948, the preparatory committee for ECLA delivered a report which concluded, inter alia, that the continent was in 'need for an accelerated rate of recovery from the effects of the war and of economic development', faced 'serious economic maladjustments' and generally had '[f]iscal, budgetary and tax systems ... [that were] inadequate to meet the growing demands of the economies of these countries' as well as 'personnel of these systems ... [who were] inadequate in numbers and in some cases insufficiently trained': Fiscal Commission, *References of Interest to the Fiscal Commission Contained in Documents Prepared for the Sixth Session of the Economic and Social Council*, Note by the Secretariat, UN Doc E/CN.8/W.15 (10 March 1948) 4.

[119] See n 157.

[120] This is indicated by, inter alia, Sundelson's use of UN interoffice letterhead, the assigning of Division staff to him, and his reference to face-to-face discussions with various

that the Secretariat's 'choice of topic of economic research' was affected by 'the faster-flowing currents of nationalism outside North America and Europe' and that it was, at this time, still bold enough to spread 'unorthodox economic ideas that suited well the new nationalist mood of non-industrial countries', although it would often involve 'outside experts taking formal responsibility' in its production of potentially controversial research.[121] Sundelson's Report certainly offended Cuba, due to its reference to systemic corruption by Latin American governments, as well as those who were keen on pursuing a DTA agenda, especially the United States, the United Kingdom, the ICC and Carroll. It is moreover likely that the Report greatly embarrassed the United States in publicising ruthless practices of American corporations at a time when the superpower was not only contending with reputational attacks[122] but also launching its foreign policy programme that promoted private business and capital as the major source of economic aid for the Third World's development. Exploitative demands by US companies, including 'tax exemptions, land expropriation rights, and unfettered access to government facilities' had in fact been 'fairly typical for US companies operating in Latin America', particular during the 'years of American "gunboat diplomacy"'.[123] As of October 1948, as part of its foreign policy concerning American private investment, the US government had issued a directive

> discourag[ing] private investments which are accompanied by terms and conditions or are for purposes likely to become the subject of reasonable public resentment in either country or are otherwise detrimental to good relations between the United States and a foreign country ... [such as] investments accompanied by arrangements whereby the investor receives from a foreign government some special privilege such as tax or customs favors ..., exclusive concessions ..., investments directly strengthening and extending international private monopolies and cartels, and investments involving exploitation of labor.[124]

persons at the UN: see Memorandum by Sundelson to Deperon, 30 December 1948, UNARMS:AG-025-002—S-0441-0468-23889(A).

121 John Toye and Richard Toye, *UN and Global Political Economy: Trade, Finance, and Development* (Indiana University Press, 2004) 111, 47.

122 See also Chapter 8, Section 8.1 (regarding the State Department's concerns over allegations of America's use of its economic superiority to dominate smaller nations).

123 Erik Benson, 'The Chosen Instrument? Reconsidering the Early Relationship between Pan American Airways and the US Government' (2004) 22 *Essays in Economic and Business History* 97, 103. See also Chapter 11, Section 11.1.1 (for the specific application of such practices by American commercial aviation business in Latin America).

124 'Memorandum by the Secretary of State to the President', 20 August 1948, in State Department, *Foreign Relations of the United States, 1948* (USGPO, 1976) vol 1, pt 2:

Presumably because of the ire of the Commission's member states (especially the United States'), the ground-breaking arguments in the Report and the Division's own research concerning bargaining arrangements between underdeveloped country governments and foreign firms were suppressed and never debated.[125] The United States' Resolution C specifically worked to override any suggestion that free trade, the elimination of double taxation, or DTAs were questionable policies for underdeveloped economies. The mere existence of the Mexico Model was used to justify that DTAs were appropriate and even beneficial for developing countries. While it is difficult to ascertain what developing countries thought about Sundelson's conclusions, or even the general Soviet positions concerning developed countries' use of model conventions and private enterprise to exploit weak economies, such arguments would have, at the very least, heightened Latin American suspicions, especially given the US backpedalling on the convening of regional double taxation conferences[126] when it desired to negotiate DTAs and supported the Spanish translation of *ITA*.

Deperon's hopes for the Commission (and the Division) to become the foremost global fiscal authority was by now largely a pipedream. The Commission's small and political composition and effective control by the Big Three made technical or fair debate impossible. At this session, four of the members were Communist states and less than half of the remaining members present showed interest, or had sufficient technical expertise to engage, in the international tax discussions. China made no substantive contribution, likely because of Mao's accelerating conquest in the country's civil war. Key developing country representation, specifically India, was lacking.[127] In this regard, Deperon's efforts at Havana and Bogotá to prevent crossover competences with the Commission perhaps thwarted the potential development of pro-source country rules in intergovernmental assemblies with larger developing country representation,

General: The United Nations, Doc 222. See Chapter 6, Section 6.3 for further details of this policy guidance.

125 See Section 7.5 regarding the Division's shift in approach in continuing its work on the subject to produce a less-controversial publication.

126 See Chapter 5, Section 5.2. US backtracking on this activity most probably arose from the State Department's desire to avoid further confrontation with Latin America over economic issues, as had occurred at Havana and Bogotá, and its ongoing attempt to 'kill' the inter-American economic conference promised since the 1942 Rio Conference: Rabe, 'Elusive Conference', 284–90. See also Chapter 2, Section 2.2.1.4.

127 India's statements in ECOSOC indicated that it could have constructively contributed to the discussion in the Commission.

although how far such advancements might have reached is a moot point since the ITO and PAU/OAS failed to become anchor organisations in international economic relations due to US stalling.

Most importantly, as in most other international arenas, the United States dominated the direction of the Commission's work and, as with the United Kingdom,[128] did not intend for the UN to make any innovative contribution, at least in the international tax sphere.[129] For these two powers, the Commission's intrinsic purpose appeared as a means of facilitating economic expansionism; to this end, as indicated in the US and UK representatives' respective reports to their governments, the Commission was still considered a viable forum despite the little accomplishment of the session.[130] Bartelt reported that the Commission's future held 'considerable promise' in influencing member governments 'in the solution of practical fiscal problems' and that it was 'appropriate now to advance to a consideration of substantive fiscal problems', with Resolution C being 'a step in the right direction'.[131] Morton similarly advised that it would 'be worth the trouble taken' for 'continuing on the present lines' as the United Kingdom had 'particularly ... much to gain from the increasing adoption, particularly by under-developed countries of sound principles of income taxation and from the conclusion on sound lines of [DTAs]'.[132] Morton considered the Spanish publication of *ITA*, 'so far as the United Kingdom share is concerned, should be eminently worth while' as '[w]e are anxious to negotiate agreements with certain of the South American countries but so far interest on the other side is

[128] Morton considered that 'most of what can usefully be done' regarding double taxation relief principles had been completed by the League: Morton, *Report*, 4.

[129] Bartelt assured the State Department that 'studies on economic effects of taxation' were 'given the lowest priority ranking' despite 'strong outside pressure' by other governments, specialised agencies and NGOs, and that the 'the time and budgetary resources of the Fiscal Commission' could 'largely be pre-empted by specialised agencies'. He nevertheless considered that the Commission 'could be of great service', especially to underdeveloped countries, in 'developing standards for fiscal administration in its various phases' and 'in considering problems of fiscal policy': Bartelt letter, 2 March 1949, 3. Morton similarly was dubious of the Division's ideas of comparative and analytical studies but anticipated that the Secretariat's resources were unlikely 'to run beyond the labour of compiling and editing national statistics' and that the public finance 'encyclopaedic' work would be 'of value ... as a reference source for a variety of purposes', especially countries 'in an early stage of development': Morton, *Report*, 1, 4.

[130] The ICC, conversely, considered that the debates produced 'only the least common ground of agreement' and left 'too much to the Secretariat': Bower, 'Confidential Note', 2.

[131] Bartelt letter, 2 March 1949, 3.

[132] Morton, *Report*, 4.

slight' and '[a]nything that can be done to stimulate interest there should redound otour [sic] ultimate advantage'.[133]

The 'fate of Resolution C' would in fact appear very important to the United States – even before its adoption by ECOSOC, Livesey of the State Department's Office of Financial and Development Policy was 'constantly using this resolution in Departmental memoranda, in instructions, and in communications including communications direct or indirect to foreign governments', and he was eager to 'begin to describe it simply as an ECOSOC resolution' rather than 'refer[ring] to it by a long circumlocutory descriptive phrase as a resolution submitted by the Fiscal Commission for adoption by ECOSOC'.[134] He also considered that the 'wherever appropriate' amendment made by Australia 'does not entirely destroy the value of the resolution as a quotable international declaration in support of a line of action by the member states'.[135]

7.5 Subsequent Secretariat Work

Deperon's 'indefinite leave of absence' led the State Department to consider taking informal steps towards a 'complete re-organization and possible abolition of the Division'; however, Treasury expressed the Division's abolition as regrettable as it would 'deprive the Commission of its own service branch in the Secretariat'.[136] Nothing appears to have

133 Ibid 3. The importance of this to Britain is further evidenced by Morton's cordial enquiry with Chernyshev whether the latter's 'objections ... to the Commission working on problems of international double taxation could be expected to reappear at the meeting of [ECOSOC]', to which Chernyshev indicated 'that the Soviet representative on the Council would probably content himself with abstaining from any vote'. This must have been reassuring in view of Britain's then 'explicit desire to boost the country's trade with Latin America as much as possible' to recover its prewar share of Latin American imports: Rory M Miller, 'Economic Nationalism and British Investments in Post-War Latin America, 1945–1970' in Thomas C Mills and Rory M Miller (eds), *Britain and the Growth of US Hegemony in Twentieth-Century Latin America: Competition, Cooperation and Coexistence* (Palgrave Macmillan, 2020) 151, 153–4. By now, the stock of British capital in Latin America was half that in 1939 due to the latter's drawing down of their sterling balances to nationalise vital British-owned infrastructure after Britain's suspension of convertibility in 1947, and the continent was moreover wary of building up its balances through continued export to Britain: see Rory Miller, *Britain and Latin America in the Nineteenth and Twentieth Centuries* (Routledge, 1993) 228–30; Gerold Krozewski, *Money and the End of Empire: British International Economic Policy and the Colonies, 1947–58* (Palgrave, 2001) 65.

134 Livesey memo, 27 July 1949, 2.

135 Ibid.

136 Kellogg memo, 26 January 1949, 2.

come of this, perhaps due to the appointment of Bloch, an American and former Treasury official, as Acting Director of the Division, as well as the implementation of Truman's Point Four Program, which subsequently led to the August 1949 launch of the Expanded Programme of Technical Assistance comprising a large-scale, coordinated technical assistance programme through the UN and its specialised agencies.[137] The Commission's consultative group to liaise with the Division did not materialise,[138] and the Division under Bloch continued its tradition of meeting and corresponding with Treasury to report on the Division's work and to discuss the Commission's agenda.[139] Interestingly, some of Bloch's own early personal views came to be reflected in the Division's policies henceforth, in particular that (1) multiple taxation was neither 'obnoxious per se' nor 'always restrictive of international trade', (2) tax credit treaties were superior to outright exemption treaties due to the opportunities the latter afforded for tax avoidance, and (3) mutual administrative assistance agreements to secure tax enforcement were desirable.[140]

[137] See *Economic Development of Under-Developed Countries*, ESC Res 222 (IX), UN ESCOR, UN Doc 1553 (15 August 1949, adopted 14–15 August 1949); *Expanded Programme of Technical Assistance for Economic Development of Under-Developed Countries*, GA Res 304 (IV), UN Doc A/RES/304(IV) (16 November 1949). See also, US Congress, Senate Committee on Foreign Relations, Subcommittee on Technical Assistance Programs, *Development of Technical Assistance Programmes: Background Information and Documents*, 83rd Congress, 2nd sess (22 November 1954) 14; Olav Stokke, *The UN and Development: From Aid to Cooperation* (Indiana University Press, 2009) 50 (noting elsewhere that the United States itself launched its own bilateral programme of technical assistance 'that had a financial framework that far exceeded that of UN programs' (at 44)).

[138] This was due to the expiration of the terms of two of the three members shortly after the Second Session: E/CN.8/SR.12 (16 May 1951) 7.

[139] Letter from Ecker-Racz to Bartelt, 31 January 1950, NARAII:RG56–199–6; Letter from Bloch to Bartelt, 11 July 1950, NARAII:RG56–199–2.

[140] See Henry S Bloch and Cyril E Heilemann, 'International Tax Relations' (1946) 55(5) *Yale Law Journal* 1158, 1159, 1168–70. Bloch and Deperon incidentally became acquainted during the time of the Princeton Mission's work, the former (then a Research Assistant in Government Finance at the University of Chicago's Department of Economics) challenging some of the assertions put forward by the League in its 1940 Mexico report concerning TPT: Letter from Bloch to Deperon, 12 March 1941, UNOG:PO—C.1644/28/1. Specifically, Bloch argued, inter alia, that the League's view that excessive taxation of capital and business profits slowed a nation's economic development was 'true under certain conditions only' (at 1). He also refuted the League's claim that moderate taxation facilitated the adaptation of tax to taxpaying capacities, stating that this was 'certainly not to be proven by scientific methods' and that such adaption was instead 'easier if the range of progression is wide' (at 2).

The Division's public finance work, based on DEA's needs, now gave 'preference ... to under-developed areas' with relatively heavy emphasis on Asiatic and Latin American countries.[141] Its technical assistance activities as well as other considerable work arising from other ECOSOC resolutions, particularly as ECOSOC took on 'a more direct interest in financing development', reduced the importance of 'Fiscal Commission assignments' emanating from 'Fiscal Commission resolutions'.[142] The duties of the Division were now 'so manifold that it ... [was] necessary to establish a system of flexible specialization assigning to each staff member both a regional and functional field of primary interest'.[143] The Division was persisting in it cooperative efforts with ICAO.[144] It also decided to use 'a fundamentally different approach' to its study on the effects of taxation on international trade and investment to emphasise 'the role of public finance in the development of economically less advanced countries' by addressing 'the dual role of taxes on foreign investment as sources of revenue for financing government development projects and as barriers and incentives to foreign trade and investment'.[145] By November 1949, the Division had formed the following internal policies regarding developing country governments' financing of development schemes using revenues derived from their taxation of trade and investment:[146]

- It was necessary for developing countries to secure sufficient tax revenue from the operations of foreign traders and investors because of their low volume of savings and the importance of domestic financial resources to their economic development schemes.

141 See Note (untitled) on work plan of the Fiscal Division, 20 December 1949, 2, UNOG: UNOGRFP—G.X.25/1.

142 Ibid 8. This was also because 'the bulk of the Commission assignments involve[d] a continuous flow of work', the nature of which required 'close collaboration with other divisions of [DEA]'.

143 Ibid 9.

144 See Chapter 11, Sections 11.4 to 11.6.

145 Note on work plan, 7. Sundelson was still assisting in revising this study in September 1949: Letter from Sundelson to Lachmann, 13 September 1949, UNARMS: AG-025-002—S-0441-0468-23889(A).

146 Fiscal Division, Memorandum on 'International Tax Policy and Economic Development', 31 October 1949, UNARMS:AG-025-002—S-0441-0469-23893(A). These policies guided the Division's views against the reciprocal exemption system in the taxation of international airlines (see Chapter 11) and perhaps its technical assistance missions. Many of these policies in fact confirm that the Division held the positions that had been advanced in Sundelson's Report.

- There was 'nothing inherently obnoxious' about multiple taxation.[147] Such taxation 'might be considered legitimate within well-defined limits' as those extending their economic activities into foreign countries to expand profitability should contribute taxes to those countries proportionate with the importance of those activities.[148] Although foreign investments carried larger risks, 'mostly the expected profits are such that the risks can be undertaken without special tax concessions'.[149] The 'limits to such multiple taxation' were thus determinable 'not so much by general notions of tax justice and equality as by the maximum tax burden which can be usefully imposed on such assets or income'.[150]
- The continental European and Anglo-American systems of DTAs were not appropriate for application between advanced and underdeveloped countries as no quid pro quo could be expected in any renunciation of taxing authority. Specifically, the overriding taxing power of the home government was of little value in underdeveloped countries if investment income was taxable only in the capital-exporting country (which was the rule under the great majority of existing DTAs) as the capital-importing country would be deprived of an important source of tax revenue. Conversely, if DTAs were concluded on the basis that investment income was taxed only in the country in which it was earned, capital-exporting countries would draw no tax revenue from foreign-sourced income of its residents/nationals. Consequently, no DTA yet existed between advanced and underdeveloped countries.[151] Such DTAs could be 'useful only if' they considered 'the vast differences in the operation of the same provision in the two contracting parties'.[152] Accordingly, an important requirement was to reserve to each country primary taxing power over assets and profits properly

147 Ibid 3.

148 Ibid 3–4.

149 Ibid 4.

150 Ibid.

151 Note that from 1945 Britain was actively negotiating DTAs with the Commonwealth. Regarding newly independent former colonies, it was successful in concluding DTAs with Burma and Ceylon in 1950; however, negotiations took longer with India and Pakistan, with agreements only signed after 1954: see Richard Vann, 'Travellers, Tax Policy and Agency Permanent Establishments' [2010] (6) *British Tax Review* 538, 545 n 32; DESA, *International Tax Agreements*, UN Doc ST/ECA/SER.C/8, Suppl 3 (UN, 1968) vol 8: World Guide to International Tax Agreements, Country Table: United Kingdom, 9–23.

152 Fiscal Division, 'International Tax Policy', 6.

allocable to it, with the residence country retaining only an overriding taxing power subject to the tax credit rule. The reciprocal exemption principle was to be avoided as it necessarily caused 'uncompensated loss of revenue to the underdeveloped country whose citizens and residents have only small assets or establishments in the other country'.[153]

- While capital-exporting countries provided unilateral relief solutions, high tax rates applied to investment profits left only a slim margin for taxation by capital-importing countries, which was possibly contributing (in addition to economic and political pressures) to the latter's keeping of low tax rates, hence depriving themselves of much needed revenue. Since the American and British type of unilateral credit relief systems offered 'a wide margin for the taxing power of capital-importing countries', capital-importing countries 'should be encouraged to take full advantage' of such systems 'by raising their rates to the level of the tax credit granted'.[154] Meanwhile, capital-exporting countries could contribute to the economic development of underdeveloped countries 'by expanding the geographical scope and the size of their tax credit provisions'.[155]
- In view of the growing tax structure of underdeveloped countries, the extension of the DTA network to such countries could be instrumental in countering 'the individual tax arrangements with powerful private investment groups which were concluded in so many countries'.[156] Capital-importing countries should be urged against making unwarranted tax concessions to foreign investors.

In February 1950, the Division completed and published *The Effects of Taxation on Foreign Trade and Investment* ('*Effects of Taxation*').[157] The publication contained none of the inflammatory content of Sundelson's

[153] Ibid 7.

[154] Ibid 6. Note that at this time, while the US FTC granted its nationals and residents relief up to the portion of US tax allocable to the foreign income in question (s 131, *Internal Revenue Code*), Britain's Dominion Income Tax Relief system only applied within the Empire, with the credit limited to 50 per cent of the UK tax rate (s 27, *Finance Act 1920*). Just the following year, Britain would abolish this system with its introduction of a limited unilateral foreign tax credit, which itself would be short-lived: see Chapter 10, Section 10.5, n 90.

[155] Fiscal Division, 'International Tax Policy', 6–7.

[156] Ibid 7.

[157] DEA, *The Effects of Taxation on Foreign Trade and Investment*, UN Doc ST/ECA/1 (UN, 1950). The publication surveyed the possible trade and investment effects of a wide range of taxation issues for both developed and developing countries, including discriminatory

Report but set forth, inter alia, that capital-importing countries should not be the parties to offer tax concessions to attract trade and investment, and that the elimination of double taxation between countries at different levels of development was to be achieved through the renunciation of tax revenue by capital-exporting countries through unilateral legislation and bilateral agreements. Such absorption of tax losses was one of three methods by which capital-exporting countries were to implement their declared 'intention of contributing to the costs of the economic development of under-developed countries'.[158] The publication did not specifically recommend that underdeveloped countries negotiate DTAs, although it noted that the United States was negotiating such agreements with Argentina, Mexico, Brazil, Colombia and Cuba.[159] A preference for the credit method was also expressed over allocation or exemption.

taxes, tax incentives, tax havens, double taxation and tax evasion. Lachmann was credited with preparing and writing the study, using the background material collected by Sundelson and another consultant (Reder): Memorandum by Bloch to Goldet, 23 January 1950, UNARMS:AG-025-002—S-0441-0468-23889(A). Neither Sundelson nor Reder were acknowledged in the publication. The Division sent a copy to Deperon in March 1950, the address indicating that he was part of the UN technical mission in Ecuador: Letter from Bloch to Deperon, 9 March 1950, UNARMS:AG-025-002—S-0441-0468-23889(A).

158 DEA, *Effects of Taxation*, 38–9. The other two methods comprised contributions to technical assistance and grants of public funds, directly or indirectly through international organisations. Treasury criticised the Division for giving 'insufficient attention' to the 'large part of the burden' shouldered by capital-exporting countries 'in offering tax incentives to residents who wish to invest in under-developed countries': Letter from Lachmann to Gordon, 10 July 1950, 1, UNARMS:AG-025-002—S-0441-0468-23889(A).

159 Argentina's and Brazil's engagement in such negotiations is intriguing given that Gómez reported their lack of interest two years prior: see Chapter 5, Section 5.6. It is worth noting, however, that Britain's suspension of sterling convertibility and reimposition of exchange controls in August 1947, and its devaluation of the pound by almost one-third in September 1949 left Argentina and Brazil, Britain's 'leading creditors in Latin America', with substantial balances in their Special Accounts in London that they could neither use 'for purchases from the Sterling Area, for … [British industry had] little to export' nor convert 'to obtain dollars to purchase essential US products': Miller, *Britain and Latin America*, 227–8. The declining trade with Britain, coupled with US manifold efforts beginning around this time to foster economic collaboration with Latin America as part of its hemispheric defence arrangements in the Cold War emergency (see 'Policy Statement Prepared in the Department of State', 26 October 1951, in State Department, *Foreign Relations of the United States, 1951* (USGPO, 1979) vol 2: The United Nations; The Western Hemisphere, Doc 680), appear likely triggers for Argentina's and Brazil's sudden interest in DTAs. See further Chapter 8, Section 8.3, and Chapter 10, Section 10.3.

Although ECOSOC had, in August 1949, scheduled the Commission's Third Session for April 1950,[160] the Assembly's Fifth Committee recommended against a 1950 meeting in the interests of budgetary savings.[161] The session was eventually rescheduled to May 1951 so that the Commission's meetings would overlap with those of the Economic, Employment and Development Commission (originally Economic and Employment Commission) to enable direct consultation between the two given the latter's consideration of topics of interest to the former concerning problems of financing economic development and of full employment.[162] By this time, the Division had accomplished the following regarding its fiscal information service: it had published statistical budgetary data jointly with the IMF; prepared various public finance information papers and surveys on Iran, Colombia, India and Venezuela, as well as regional surveys for ECLA and ECAFE; published a volume entitled *Budgetary Structure and Classification of Government Accounts* (1951) ('*Budgetary Structure*'); and was about to publish two further volumes in its *ITA* series.[163] Regarding technical assistance, the Division had briefed external fiscal experts on missions to Bolivia, Chile, Colombia, Ecuador, Haiti and Iran; sent two personnel on mission to Haiti and Libya; and taken part in training technical assistance fellows and scholars in the fiscal programme.[164] It was also cooperating with the Transport and Communications Division on the study of the taxation of road transport for ECE.[165] Bartelt had advised the Division to take up the subject of accounting reforms but Bloch indicated in mid-1950 that there were no available personnel to take on the work.[166] From July 1949, the Division also attempted to progress its loose-leaf World Tax Service

[160] E/CN.8/W.33, 2–3.

[161] See Advisory Committee on Administrative and Budgetary Questions, *Second Report of 1949 to the General Assembly*, UN GAOR, Suppl 7, UN Doc A/934 (8 August 1949) 17.

[162] Report of the Interim Committee on Programme of Meetings, *Report Regarding Readjustment of the Calendar of 1951*, UN ESC, UN Doc E/1871 (6 December 1950) 2. This arrangement appears to have been desired by Bloch in the hope that 'a short joint session' between the two commissions 'might develop the broader economic framework for which appropriate fiscal policies have to be formulated': Ecker-Racz letter, 31 January 1950. Despite this scheduling, no records have been found indicating such a joint session as taking place.

[163] Volumes 2 and 3 were completed in December 1950 and April 1951, respectively.

[164] Fiscal Commission, *Improvement of Fiscal Techniques*, Note by the Secretary-General, 3rd sess, Provisional Agenda item 6, UN Doc E/CN.8/54 (20 April 1951) 7.

[165] Memorandum by Bloch and Lukac, 20 July 1950, UNARMS:AG-025-002—S-0441-0469-23894.

[166] Bloch letter, 11 July 1950, 2.

publication;[167] however, this would be held up by problems with the publisher, copyright and costs.[168] The situation only looked to being resolved when Harvard Law School (HLS) wrote to Bloch of its interest in establishing a world tax centre and its desire for cooperation with the UN in this regard.[169] HLS indicated its expectation that it could secure the necessary funding, and hence would underwrite the necessary financial obligations, including costs of editing, translating and publishing. Bloch accepted the offer given the mutual interests and complementarity of the plans with the Division's work.[170] Professor Stanley Surrey apprised his contacts in Treasury of these plans, which led to Bartelt's submission of a resolution at the Commission's Third Session to approve the collaboration on the World Tax Service.[171]

167 Coverage included the tax administration and procedures available for mutual administrative assistance; list of tax laws and regulations; list of authoritative treatises and articles; and texts of all DTAs in force, regulations issued thereunder, and tax provisions included in general treaties: Memorandum by Lachmann to Bloch, 4 August 1949, UNARMS:AG-025-002—S-0441-0468-23886(A).

168 See documents in UNARMS:AG-025-002—S-0441-0468-23886(A).

169 Letter from Cavers to Bloch, 20 April 1951, UNARMS:AG-025-002—S-0441-0468-23886(A). HLS' objectives included publishing surveys of countries' principal tax laws, research into appropriate laws and procedures for national tax systems at various stages of development, studying methods to remove tax impediments to foreign investment, providing facilities to train officials and lawyers in tax law and administration, and developing a staff of experts who could serve on technical missions. UN cooperation was considered essential for technical assistance work, its global correspondence network and developing a research programme directed at subjects of mutual interest.

170 Letter from Bloch to Cavers, 1 May 1951, UNARMS:AG-025-002—S-0441-0468-23886(A).

171 See Letter from Bartelt to Surrey, 4 June 1951, NARAII:RG56-199-2; Letter from Barnes to Lachmann, 3 May 1951, 2, UNARMS:AG-025-002—S-0441-0468-23886(A). This resolution would be approved by the Commission after amendment: Fiscal Commission, *Summary Record of the 22nd Meeting*, 3rd sess, 22nd mtg, UN Doc E/CN.8/SR.22 (14 June 1951) 2-5, 18.

8

Related Intervening Developments (January 1949–April 1951)

8.1 Near-Abolition of the Fiscal Commission and Fiscal Division

Events in 1950 ushered in repercussions that threatened the Division's and Commission's existence. In August, a separate Technical Assistance Administration (TAA) department within the Secretariat was created to handle the various UN technical assistance programmes. Several economic and social sections of the Secretariat previously responsible for conducting technical assistance were transferred to the TAA.[1] That same month, ECOSOC established an ad hoc Committee on the Organization of the Council and Its Commissions ('Organization Committee') to conduct a comprehensive review of the organ and its bodies.[2] By the year's end, US officials had formed the position to terminate the Fiscal Commission as a permanent standing body and to transfer its functions to other bodies, with the possibility of holding ad hoc meetings of experts or conferences of governmental representatives on fiscal matters as ECOSOC required.[3] Importantly, the State Department had been

[1] 'The Secretariat' [1950] *Yearbook of the United Nations* 125, 136–7.

[2] *Organization of the Economic and Employment Commission and Its Two Sub-Commissions*, ESC Res 295B (XI), UN ESCOR, UN Doc E/1849 (31 August 1950, adopted 12 and 16 August 1950). This move was likely led by the United States: in May 1950, the State Department had determined it 'imperative [that the] US take firm stand' to 'drive further reductions' in its contribution percentage to the UN (as well as to other specialised agencies) in the face of 'intense pressure' by other governments to increase its percentages: 'The Secretary of State to the Embassy in the United Kingdom', 5 May 1950, in State Department, *Foreign Relations of the United States, 1950* (USGPO, 1976) vol 2: The United Nations; The Western Hemisphere, Doc 36.

[3] See Memorandum by Gordon to Bartelt, 3 December 1950; Memorandum by Bartelt to Ecker-Racz, 11 December 1950; State Department, 'Draft Position Paper: Status of the Fiscal Commission', 19 December 1950; State Department, 'Preliminary Consideration Regarding the Reorganization of ECOSOC and Its Subsidiary Bodies', undated (for discussion at a 1 December 1950 meeting of US Members on UN Commissions, and US Representatives on ECOSOC, Specialized Agencies and Certain Inter-American Organizations), NARAII:RG56–199–2. The proposals were primarily purposed at

infuriated with the Fiscal Division, which it considered to be 'bent on "building an empire"' due to, firstly, the latter's intervention in the ICAO discussions on the taxation of international air navigation which had 'succeeded in delaying action on certain [US sponsored] proposals', and secondly, because the 'Division had a representative in Chile to review its fiscal position at the same time' an IMF mission was there and '[t]he recommendations of the two were not in harmony'.[4] Another consideration of 'special concern' to the State Department was that the IMF had 'only a minor job to do, and that the work of the Fiscal Division . . . appear[ed] to be within the Fund's field of competence',[5] so much so that it 'could, in its entirety, be taken over by the [Fund]'.[6] The State Department would conclude that there was little that the Commission could achieve.[7] While the Commission had 'devoted its principal attention to the question of double taxation', in the view of the United States, the negotiation of a multilateral tax treaty was futile, the Mexico and London Models had 'probably already served their purpose' and 'not much more good' could be accomplished in seeking to refine the Models 'through further multilateral discussions'.[8] Moreover, the Commission's existence and 'its continuing discussions of a multilateral treaty provide a basis for charges that the US wishes to work on a bilateral basis so that it may dominate the smaller countries through using its superior bargaining position'.[9] The State Department nevertheless had a reconsideration of the Division's functions in the public finance field, deeming them 'valid', and that they 'should be continued', although there was 'a continuing danger' of duplication of work with the IMF.[10]

reducing duplication of work and unnecessary expenses. Another six functional commissions/sub-commissions as well as the regional commissions were also considered for abolition or transformation.

4 Gordon memo, 3 December 1950, 3. Gordon (Treasury) advised it was possibly 'premature' to decide on the Commission's future before its Third Session as the Commission had only 'one working session since the initial organizational meeting' for which the preparation had been 'inadequate' due to staffing difficulties. He also indicated that the reallocation of the Division's work need not be necessarily accompanied by the Commission's abolition.

5 Ibid.

6 State Department, 'Preliminary Consideration', 6.

7 State Department, 'Draft Position Paper'.

8 Ibid 3.

9 Ibid.

10 Ibid 4.

In April 1951, the US position on the Commission's utility had changed in relation to its potential activities on municipal and provincial finances, specifically in the formulation of 'a model fiscal organization' for governments (e.g. government accounting and expenditures), as well as 'a body of recommendations in public finance' to guide governments.[11] It was now to 'strongly urge the continuation of the Fiscal Commission and a strengthening of its activities'; the abolition of the Commission was in fact considered

> a serious psychological and tactical mistake at a time when the world is more than ever urgently in need of adopting sound fiscal policies and when there is an apparent upsurge in that direction in many countries. For the US Government to acquiesce in the abolition of the Fiscal Commission would be construed in many quarters as a lack of interest on the part of this Government in the improvement of fiscal standards, and as a disinclination on our part to encourage them.[12]

At the meeting of the Organization Committee that month, voting was close or tied as Australia, China, the USSR and the United Kingdom stood

[11] 'Proposed Statement on the Fiscal Commission for Use before the Ad Hoc Committee of ECOSOC', undated (discussed at a 16 April 1951 meeting), 3, NARAII:RG56–199–6. See also various correspondence between relevant US departments between 4 and 14 April (same folder). This revised position appears to have come about by, firstly, the indication from the US representative on the IMF that while there were areas of overlap, and hence potential for conflicting recommendations on financial policy arising out of field missions, the IMF had 'no business getting involved in the great area of technical work that the Fiscal Commission is supposed to carry out', for example, public accounting, fiscal administration and debt management: EF Bartelt, 'Memorandum for the Files', 19 April 1951, NARAII:RG56–199–6. Secondly, the International Union of Local Authorities had raised a proposal for problems of municipal finances to be included in the Commission's work, and ECAFE had expressed an interest in uniform budgetary classifications, both subjects of which were welcomed by the Division. In a tactical move, Bartelt incorporated these subjects as part of the 'fiscal information service' agenda item rather than as a new item: see Memorandum by Ecker-Racz to Bartelt, 31 January 1951; Letter from Ascher to Lie, 8 February 1951; Letter from Emerich to Acheson, 20 February 1951; Letter from Bartelt to Ascher, 11 April 1951; Letter from Ascher to Bartelt, 14 April 1951, NARAII:RG56–199–6.

[12] 'US Position on Status of Fiscal Commission at "Ad Hoc" Committee on the Organization and Operation of the Economic and Social Council and its Commissions', UNEC D-47(a), 11 April 1951, 1, 2, NARAII: RG56–199–6. The alternative proposal of replacing the Commission with temporary or ad hoc committees of experts that had not 'the stature of a Commission' was thought 'would be to abandon a Commission which may develop into a body with considerable prestige and influence': 'Proposed Statement', 7. Among the proposals to strengthen the Commission was the encouragement of 'all governments represented on the Commission to send expert personnel rather than . . . individuals who lay no claim to expertness in fiscal matters' (at 7).

for abolition of most of the ECOSOC bodies, while Brazil, France and India fought for retention of almost all.[13] Opinion on the Fiscal Commission was evenly divided and was ultimately resolved by the 'compromise formula' put forward by the United States to continue the Commission (and other commissions) for a 'trial period' until 31 December 1953.[14]

8.2 The UN Agenda for Financing Economic Development in Underdeveloped Countries

From mid-1949, the problems and possibilities of financing economic development in underdeveloped countries emerged as a major ECOSOC agenda item as a deluge of related studies, reports and recommendations by the UN Secretariat and various specialised agencies (i.e. FAO, the ILO, the IMF and the World Bank) poured forth, presumably in response to the General Assembly's December 1948 resolution directing ECOSOC and the specialised agencies to 'give further and urgent consideration to the whole problem of the economic development of underdeveloped countries in all its aspects'.[15] This would importantly lead to Assembly resolutions on the subject which directed ECOSOC, in November 1949, to give further attention to questions of international economic and commercial policy that influenced such economic development,[16] and in November 1950, to consider practical methods, conditions and policies to achieve adequate expansion and a steadier flow of both public and private foreign capital, with special attention to non-self-liquidating projects that were basic to economic development.[17]

As fiscal measures formed part of the aspects being examined, this agenda item would open an expedient pathway for developing countries,

[13] Letter from Murden to Fields, 20 April 1951, NARAII:RG56–199–6.

[14] Ibid. Ad Hoc Committee on the Organization and Operation of the Council and Its Commissions, *First Report*, UN ESC, UN Doc E/1995 (also E/AC.34/23) (31 May 1951) 11, 23–4. See further Chapter 9, Section 9.5, n 105 regarding ECOSOC's resolutions stemming from its consideration of the Organization Committee's report.

[15] *Economic Development of Under-Developed Countries*, GA Res 198 (III), UN Doc A/RES/198(III) (4 December 1948) para 3. For the enumeration of the studies issued during 1949 and 1950, and the consideration of the subject by ECOSOC and the Sub-Commission on Economic Development, see 'Economic Development of Under-Developed Areas' [1950] *Yearbook of the United Nations* 438, 438–45. The *Effects of Taxation* was listed among such studies (at 438–9).

[16] *Economic Development and International Economic and Commercial Policy*, GA Res 307 (IV), UN Doc 307(IV) (16 November 1949).

[17] *Financing of Economic Development of Under-Developed Countries*, GA Res 400 (V), UN Doc A/RES/400(V) (20 November 1950).

especially Latin America, to raise double taxation issues before ECOSOC and the Assembly without first going through the Commission.[18] Some of the relevant findings or developments concerning double taxation that emerged during this time frame included the following:[19]

- An October 1949 report concerning government stimulation of private investment in Britain's dependent territories noted that Britain had not set up special incentives to encourage investment in its colonies, with the 'minor exception' of the system of double income tax relief operating within the Commonwealth which made investment inside the Commonwealth 'somewhat more attractive than investment in foreign countries'.[20]
- The May 1950 recommendation by the Sub-Commission on Economic Development that developed countries should encourage outbound private investment by concluding DTAs and offering unilateral tax incentives to help increase the presently inadequate sources of foreign financing available for the continued and accelerated economic development of underdeveloped countries.[21]
- ECLA's June 1950 request to the Secretariat to give special consideration to double taxation as part of its research into increasing the flow of foreign investment to Latin America.[22]

On the part of UN economists' analysis of development generally, the view was nevertheless 'pessimistic about the capacity of market forces to promote economic development' and 'the point [was emphasised] that if the industrialization of underdeveloped areas were to be left to private enterprise, the process would be slower, there would be less investment and lower national income, and the economic structure of the region would be different'.[23] Contrary to the US 'official discourse' of 'trade not aid', the

[18] See further Chapter 10, Section 10.2.

[19] See also Chapter 9, Section 9.1, for the Division's reporting to the Commission of other double taxation-related recommendations of the Secretariat and UN bodies of this period.

[20] Sidney Caine, 'Memorandum on Methods of Financing Development in United Kingdom Dependent Territories' (30 September 1949), UNARMS:AG-004-001—S-0991-0011-01. This paper was prepared for the Meeting of Experts on Financing of Economic Development at Lake Success, 24 October 1949, that was organised by DEA's Division of Economic Stability and Development.

[21] UN Yearbook, 'Economic Development of Under-Developed Areas', 439.

[22] ECLA, *Resolutions of the 11th Session*, 11th sess, UN Doc E/1762 (10 June 1950); ECLA, *Annual Report*, UN Doc E/1717 (20 June 1950).

[23] Richard Jolly, Louis Emmerij and Dharam Ghai, *UN Contributions to Development Thinking and Practice* (Indiana University Press, 2004) 52.

Secretariat would begin to promote 'revolutionary and subversive' approaches that, inter alia, called for soft financing, better terms of trade and for developing countries to 'remain in command' with '[a]ny foreign assistance that might flow to [them] ... retain[ing] the character of a supplement to the efforts and resources of the countries in question'.[24]

8.3 Inter-American Economic Relations and DTAs

In mid-1949, the State Department had 'abandoned all hope of either resolving differences in the economic charter or holding an economic conference' with Latin America.[25] It would instead not only increasingly advance that '[f]ailure to attract foreign capital [due to economic nationalism] was "the greatest single obstacle to economic development in Latin America"', but also declare that 'the United States had no obligation to aid Latin America'.[26] Latin American countries continued to face the central problem of 'dollar shortage' with Britain's and Europe's failure to return to full convertibility impeding their ability to finance the purchase of critical capital and intermediate goods that were only suppliable by the United States while Europe recovered.[27] In early November 1949, the United States was still actively attempting to negotiate tax treaties with Argentina, Cuba, Colombia and Venezuela.[28] The State Department's instructions to the Panama Embassy, however, were to only seek an agreement on aircraft earnings and not to seek a comprehensive DTA. Later that month, 'following detailed negotiations', '[a] treaty with Colombia was signed *ad referendum* at Bogotá ... contain[ing] tax

[24] Ibid.

[25] Stephen G Rabe, 'The Elusive Conference: United States Economic Relations with Latin America, 1945–1952' (1978) 2(3) *Diplomatic History* 279, 290.

[26] Ibid. 291. See also Frank D McCann, *Brazil and the United States during World War II and Its Aftermath: Negotiating Alliance and Balancing Giants* (Palgrave Macmillan, 2018) 253 (noting that while the White House 'always said soothing words of friendship', the actions of the US government displayed a 'hardness' towards Latin America's development, and that, in fact, 'American officials had little interest in or knowledge of Latin America').

[27] Gabriel Porcile, 'The Challenge of Cooperation: Argentina and Brazil, 1939–1955' (1995) 27(1) *Journal of Latin American Studies* 129, 138.

[28] Memorandum by Livesey to Young, 7 November 1949, NARAII:RG59–77. In the meantime, DTAs with Greece, Norway and Ireland were signed between June 1949 and February 1950: DESA, *International Tax Agreements*, UN Doc ST/ECA/SER.C/8, Suppl 3 (UN, 1968) vol 8: World Guide to International Tax Agreements, Country Table: United States, 9–10.

incentive provisions which would have eased United States income tax charges on the profits earned in Colombia by United States companies'.[29] These 'preferences', however, 'were opposed ... at high levels in ... Treasury', and consequently 'this treaty was not presented to Congress'.[30]

In February 1950, the State Department reported 'heightened interest' by foreign countries in negotiating DTAs with the United States in view of the role private US capital could play in their economic development and 'of the importance of tax assurances as an inducement to that investment'.[31] DTA discussions were set to begin with Uruguay; Pakistan, Austria, Switzerland and Israel had signalled their interest; formal negotiations with Australia were 'still under discussion'; while 'tax conversations with India', which had been held up, looked to resume.[32] Discussions had been initiated with Brazil, which 'desired even more liberal tax incentives than were provided in the Colombian draft ... [entailing] a virtual return to the pre-Bogotá [Conference] positions, in that United States capital invested in Brazil would be subject to income tax charges only at the source of profit'.[33]

In June 1950, the Cold War turned hot with the Korean War's outbreak, and the United States began to court Latin American governments in its need for strategic materials for the war effort.[34] Just the following month, however, the State Department would report that '[t]ax treaty negotiations with American republics are close to definite collapse', with Treasury 'firmly refusing to accept any treaty innovation designed to stimulate American private investment abroad by reductions in United States income tax rates on income derive by Americans and American corporations from investments abroad'.[35] The State Department tentatively concluded that:

> Failure with the American republics would probably mean failure with underdeveloped countries elsewhere, such as India and Pakistan. If we get

[29] 'Editorial Note', undated (around July 1950), in State Department, *Foreign Relations of the United States, 1950* (USGPO, 1977) vol 1: National Security Affairs; Foreign Economic Policy, Doc 236 ('*FRUS, 1950*, vol 1') (emphasis in original).

[30] Ibid.

[31] 'Extract from Bulletin No 242: Interest Increases in Tax Treaties with the United States', 20 February 1950, in State Department, *FRUS, 1950*, vol 1, Doc 234.

[32] Ibid.

[33] 'Editorial Note'. Discussions were also contemplated with Ecuador.

[34] Edgar J Dosman, *The Life and Times of Raúl Prebisch, 1901–1986* (McGill-Queen's University Press, 2008) 268.

[35] 'Memorandum by the Deputy Director of the Office of Financial and Development Policy (Spiegel) to the Assistant Secretary of State for Economic Affairs (Thorp)', 21 July 1950, in State Department, *FRUS, 1950*, vol 1, Doc 235.

> a treaty with Australia, it will result from Australia adopting a dynamic policy of economic expansion with the cooperation of American private investments.[36]

It also resolved not to hold further negotiations with any other American republic until Treasury 'decided what type of concessions it would approve', which resulted in 'an impasse' developing.[37] At the end of 1950, 'the program of concluding treaties for the avoidance of double taxation with underdeveloped countries went into abeyance'.[38] Furthermore, the establishment of the ITO was aborted after the Truman Administration announced it would not submit the ITO Charter for ratification by the Senate, leaving Latin Americans 'disappointed and frustrated'.[39] By 1951, Latin America was the only area in the non-communist world that was not under a US foreign aid programme, having been deemed 'safe from the grasp of Russia' and hence 'eligible for aid only from the meagerly funded Point Four technical assistance program'.[40]

[36] Ibid.

[37] 'Editorial Note'.

[38] Ibid.

[39] Dosman, *Prebisch*, 241.

[40] Rabe, 'Elusive Conference', 292. See also Mark T Gilderhus, 'An Emerging Synthesis? US–Latin American Relations since the Second World War' in Michael J Hogan (ed), *America in the World: The Historiography of American Foreign Relations since 1941* (Cambridge University Press, 1995) 424, 442 (quoting State Department official George F Kennan, who would be instrumental in shaping the US containment policy, in the context of his review of his 1950 trip to Latin America that, except for Cuba, Panama and parts of Central America, 'we have really no vital interests in that part of the world. Let us be generous in small things ... but not be greatly concerned for their opinion of us, and happy enough not to be an active factor in their affairs').

9

Third Session of the Fiscal Commission and Aftermath (1951)

9.1 Preparatory Documents of the Fiscal Division

Prior to the session, the Division issued fourteen documents to the Commission comprising summary reporting of its work and activities; two draft papers on international tax matters; and communications from, or information regarding, the fiscal-related work and actions of other UN bodies, specialised agencies and NGOs.[1] The two international tax papers comprised a background paper on the 'Evaluation of Recent Trends in International Tax Agreements' ('Recent ITA Trends') that had been included in volume II of the *ITA* series,[2] and a preliminary report entitled 'Comparative Approach to National and International Corporate Tax Problems' ('Corporate Tax Problems') on the comparative study of the taxation of corporate profits and dividends.[3]

The documents collectively indicated that the Division now largely saw all its work and activities as having primary application to underdeveloped countries under the broad label of 'Improvement of fiscal

[1] The Division had mainly streamlined its documents by not circulating material that had been made into publications, issuing only one document per subject, reporting most of the fiscal-related work or action of other bodies in one document and reporting much of the progress of its work in notes to the agenda (Fiscal Commission, *Note on the Agenda of the Third Session*, Note by the Secretariat, 3rd sess, UN Docs E/CN.8/52 and Corr.1–2 (21 February 1951)).

[2] Fiscal Commission, *Evaluation of Recent Trends in International Tax Agreements*, Note by the Secretary-General, 3rd sess, Provisional Agenda item 3, UN Doc E/CN.8/53 (12 April 1951).

[3] Fiscal Commission, *Comparative Approach to National and International Corporate Tax Problems*, Note by the Secretariat, 3rd sess, Agenda item 6(a), UN Doc E/CN.8/55 (3 May 1951). The study addressed the tax treatment of multinational enterprises and foreign stakeholders, and the role of corporate taxation at various levels of economic development. It included surveys of the relevant tax measures of seventeen 'principal tax systems' comprising eight First World countries and nine underdeveloped countries. The report was to be discussed at an expert conference evaluating technical assistance recommendations in the fiscal field to be held in July (see Section 9.5).

techniques'.[4] Specifically, the Secretariat had established an International Fiscal Information Centre which was, inter alia, purposed with publishing current information of special interest to underdeveloped countries, preparing studies of special relevance to technical assistance and providing general support for fiscal technical assistance activities. The international tax work (e.g. the *ITA* series and *Effects of Taxation* publication) was described as representing special studies used to brief technical assistance experts and to evaluate their recommendations. Work on new subject matter was similarly explained as being of special interest to technical assistance experts, for example, the *Budgetary Structure* publication and the study on administrative and judicial procedures for reviewing tax assessments.[5]

In both its international tax papers, the Division now recommended outright that underdeveloped countries adopt DTAs. In 'Recent ITA Trends', the Division noted that despite the unprecedented spread of DTAs between developed countries since the end of World War II, underdeveloped countries had not concluded agreements with a developed country apart from Britain's treaties with its former colonies/mandate of Burma, Ceylon and Israel (partitioned from Palestine). The Division cited four considerations as contributing to this dearth: (1) the economic imbalance between underdeveloped and developed countries; (2) the existence of unilateral tax credit legislation in the major capital-exporting countries;[6] (3) undeveloped countries' lesser need to relieve their residents of double taxation burdens on their foreign investments, and their preference to deter capital flight and encourage investment of scarce domestic savings in national enterprises; and (4) the favouring of the residence criterion in the distribution of tax jurisdiction in most DTAs. The Division noted that the Latin American countries especially espoused the source-of-income criterion and insisted on exclusive source tax jurisdiction; however, it warned against this, stating that the credit system possibly

4 Fiscal Commission, *Improvement of Fiscal Techniques*, Note by the Secretary-General, 3rd sess, Provisional Agenda item 6, UN Doc E/CN.8/54 (20 April 1951).

5 Fiscal Commission, *Procedures Available for the Review of Initial Tax Assessments*, 3rd sess, UN Doc E/CN.8/59 (7 May 1951). The Division also indicated this study as connected to the Secretariat's overall study on mutual administrative assistance.

6 Britain's DTAs with Burma, Ceylon and Israel were cited as examples of having been signed to gain the benefit of tax credit up to the full amount of UK tax, as against the lower maximum allowed under UK law in the absence of a DTA. Meanwhile, the Latin American countries, which expected largely US investment capital, were stated as not being similarly incentivised because of the US FTC rules.

offered 'a compromise between the two systems, even favouring the position of the underdeveloped countries',[7] and that the taxation-at-source rule left capital-importing countries vulnerable to demands for tax concessions by foreign investors. The paper then cited the potential scope of the tax credit mechanism[8] and mutual administrative assistance provisions as two features that should encourage underdeveloped countries to conclude DTAs. The paper concluded stating that:

> Up to now tax agreements have chiefly served the aims of fairness and simplification in international tax relations of developed countries and their dependencies: it is proper to expect of them, in the future, a still broader usefulness in giving effective tax support to the role of private trade and investment in the economic development of under-developed countries.[9]

In 'Corporate Tax Problems', the Division highlighted the dominant position of foreign corporations in underdeveloped economies and the need of such countries to maximise tax revenues while simultaneously guarding foreign investors 'against oppressive taxation' without granting them preferential tax treatment over their own nationals.[10] It put forward that it was not multiple taxation itself but excessive or oppressive taxation that was 'necessarily inequitable or injurious to the flow of international trade and investment', and that DTAs served to 'avoid those evils' while ensuring 'an equitable distribution of the total tax revenues from corporations and their stockholders among the contracting countries'.[11] Without DTAs, underdeveloped countries were left 'in a potentially disadvantageous position' as they, firstly, could not guarantee that foreign investors would 'receive credit' in their home country for the specific taxes imposed, and, secondly, were vulnerable to any reduction or elimination of 'expected tax credits' by capital-exporting countries in their unilateral relief mechanisms.[12]

[7] Specifically, underdeveloped countries could raise their taxes to the limit of the credit allowed without imposing any additional burden on the foreign investor.

[8] Specifically, tax credit DTAs offered 'powerful protection for the growth of an effective tax system in under-developed countries' and 'serve to add those refinements which are necessary to attune the general credit rule to the individual tax and trade relationships of the co-contracting countries': E/CN.8/53, 7–8.

[9] Ibid 8–9.

[10] E/CN.8/55, 37.

[11] Ibid 38.

[12] Ibid 39. The specific use of 'credit' terminology indicates the Division's preference for credit DTAs over exemption DTAs, although it did not explicitly state such in this document as it had in 'Recent ITA Trends'.

The Division's communications regarding the actions of other organisations that were related to double taxation comprised the following:[13]

- ICAO's referral of its draft resolution concerning the taxation of income and movable property of international air transport enterprises.[14]
- A resolution adopted by the Conference on the Freedom of Information, and subsequently by ECOSOC,[15] inviting governments to conclude bilateral or multilateral agreements to eliminate unreasonable or discriminatory taxes affecting the operations of foreign information agencies and news personnel, 'being guided, in particular, by the results of the work of the Fiscal Commission … concerning double taxation'.[16]
- The ICC's proposal for unilateral relief measures to be included in the Commission's agenda, and its statement of a proposed scheme of unilateral action to relieve double taxation that had been adopted by the ICC Council in January 1951.[17] This statement essentially advanced that 'double taxation remains a dead-weight on the expansion of international trade and investment'; 'income should bear one tax and one tax only'; the exemption system was 'far more advisable' than the tax credit

13 These communications would be dealt with by the Commission in discussions regarding their relevant subject matter within the greatly streamlined agenda, rather than under a separate agenda item as had occurred during the Second Session. Other communications included references to public finance publications by the IMF and various Secretariat divisions to the Statistical Commission and regional commissions, fiscal-related aspects of the work of the Economic and Employment Commission and FAO, and ECE's establishment of a working party to draft a convention on the taxation of commercial passenger and goods vehicles: Fiscal Commission, *References to Fiscal Matters in Actions of Other Organs of the United Nations and in Studies of the Secretariat*, Note by the Secretariat, 3rd sess, UN Doc E/CN.8/58 (3 May 1951). The ICC also submitted proposals for the subjects of 'National Accounting and Budgetary Practices' and 'Profit Taxes and Devaluation of Money' to be included in the Commission's agenda: Fiscal Commission, *National Accounting and Budgetary Practices: Item Proposed for the Agenda by the International Chamber of Commerce*, 3rd sess, UN Doc E/CN.8/NGO/1/Add.1 (4 April 1951); Fiscal Commission, *Profits Taxes and Depletion of Money: Item for the Provisional Agenda Proposed by the International Chamber of Commerce*, 3rd sess, UN Doc E/CN.8/NGO/3/Rev.1 (5 March 1951).

14 See Chapter 11, Sections 11.6 and 11.7.

15 *Freedom of Information: Resolutions from the Final Act of the United Nations Conference on Freedom of Information*, ESC Res 241H (IX), UN ESCOR, UN Doc E/1553 (15 August 1949, adopted 22 July 1949).

16 Fiscal Commission, *Taxes Affecting the Operation of Foreign Information Agencies and News Personnel*, Note by the Secretariat, 3rd sess, UN Doc E/CN.8/56 (2 May 1951).

17 Fiscal Commission, *Unilateral Relief from Double Taxation: Item Proposed for the Agenda by the International Chamber of Commerce*, 3rd sess, UN Doc E/CN.8/NGO/2 (21 February 1951). The ICC also attached the report of its Committee of Taxation which contained further detailed analysis.

system; and unilateral relief action should comprise residence countries' exempting residents from tax on foreign income, and source countries' exempting non-residents from tax of certain income items derived from sources within the country (e.g. royalties, interest on a reciprocal basis, business profits not attributable to a PE).[18]

The Division also reported various conclusions concerning the role of double taxation and foreign private capital in underdeveloped countries that had been advanced by other UN bodies and Secretariat studies under the Financing of Economic Development agenda.[19] These included:

- '[R]elief [to foreign investors] from double taxation should be granted ... in a form which will not deprive under-developed countries of revenue from taxation on economic activities, property and income within their territories': Report of the Sub-Commission on Economic Development (Third Session, 1949).[20]
- The elimination of double taxation by bilateral or multilateral agreements was a form of 'special inducement' to be offered to attract foreign funds: Report of the Economic and Employment Commission (Fourth Session, 1949).[21]
- It was 'particularly important' that underdeveloped countries 'receive substantial tax revenues from foreign investments without thereby discouraging them'. The tax credit method, especially if effected via DTAs, was 'much the superior method' in contrast to mutual exemption systems and special tax privileges granted by underdeveloped countries. Such a system allowed scope for underdeveloped countries, which had generally lower rates of taxation, 'to raise tax rates to the level prevailing in [capital-exporting countries] ... without a deterrent effect on investment'. Exclusive residence taxation of foreign assets and income was not recommended as underdeveloped countries, which had 'scant foreign establishments and investments', would 'lose important sources of revenue without equivalent compensation': DEA, *Domestic Financing of Economic Development* (UN, 1950).[22]

[18] Ibid 2, 3–5.

[19] E/CN.8/58, 7–16.

[20] Ibid 7.

[21] Ibid 8.

[22] Ibid 9–12 (reproducing extracts from UN Publication Sales No 1951.II.B.1, which had earlier been issued by the Secretariat as DEA, *Methods of Increasing Domestic Savings and of Ensuring Their Most Advantageous Use for the Purpose of Economic Development*, A Study by the Secretary-General, UN ESC, 10th sess, Agenda item 9(c), UN Doc E/1562 (16 December 1949), the relevant text found at 9–12, 39–40). This study was based

9.2 Deliberations in the Fiscal Commission (7–17 May 1951)

The Commission members of the Third Session were composed of Belgium, Canada, China, Cuba, Czechoslovakia, France, India, New Zealand, Pakistan, Poland, South Africa, Venezuela, the United Kingdom, the United States and the USSR (Canada, India and Venezuela having replaced Colombia, Lebanon and Ukraine SSR).[23] Membership thus comprised seven First World countries, four developing countries, three Soviet countries and China, which would lead to voting deadlocks on fractious debates when the Soviets aligned themselves with the developing countries' positions. The Commission appointed Perez as Chairman, J Nosek (Czechoslovakia) and Certeux as Vice-Chairmen, and Morton as Rapporteur. Bloch served as Secretary to the Commission.

The Commission held thirteen plenary meetings over nine days, with ten of the meetings spent on substantive matters.[24] It established a Working Group on International Tax Problems ('Working Group') at the end of the fourth meeting which met four times around the plenary sessions.[25] The Working Group was attended by six members: France, Pakistan, Poland, South Africa, the United Kingdom and the United States, with Certeux as the Chairman and Morton present in an ex officio capacity as the Commission's Rapporteur. This composition was appointed by the Commission at the suggestion of Cuba as Chairman.[26] Lachmann served as Secretary to the Working Group.

on the results of a meeting of seven consultant experts from the United Kingdom, Mexico, Philippines, Puerto-Rico, Chile, India and Egypt, which took place at Lake Success between October and November 1949 in response to GA Res 200 (III) (4 December 1948) (entitled *Technical Assistance for Economic Development*), UN Doc A/RES/200(III) (4 December 1948).

[23] Fiscal Commission, *Provisional List of Participants*, 3rd sess, UN Doc E/CN.8/INF.1/Rev.1 (15 May 1951). Of the individual delegates, only five had represented their country at the Second Session, namely: Morton (United Kingdom), Bartelt (United States), Certeux (France), Perez (Cuba) and Chernyshev (USSR): see Appendix B, Table B.1.

[24] Unless otherwise stated, the material regarding these discussions has been drawn from the *Summary Records* of the Commission's Third Session (UN Docs E/CN.8/SR.11–23 (16 May–14 June 1951); and the Commission's report (Fiscal Commission, *Report to the Economic and Social Council on the Third Session of the Commission, Held at Lake Success, New York, 7–17 May 1951*, UN Doc E/1993 (also E/CN.8/62) (31 May 1951)).

[25] A Working Group on Government Financial Reporting was also established and was attended by the United States (Chairman), Belgium, New Zealand, the United Kingdom and the USSR.

[26] It is not clear how the composition of the working groups of the previous sessions was achieved but considerations of having different viewpoints represented were likely involved.

Observers to the session included representatives from FAO, ICAO, the ILO, the IMF, the ICC, IFA and NAM (Carroll).

Broadly, the substantive plenary discussions were equally split between international tax issues and public finance matters. Of the time spent on the former, over half was taken up with the taxation of international air transport with the remainder spent on DTAs, unilateral relief methods and double taxation principles to apply in relations between underdeveloped and developed countries. These debates saw East–West as well as North–South tensions rise and some meetings ran for an unprecedented length of time, with the longest meeting spanning 4.5 hours. There was overall broad participation among participants[27] but while full attendance was recorded across all meetings, this was not always reflected in the voting. The level of discussion also remained superficial.

The Soviet members, led by the USSR, raised arguments on the following matters that gave rise to some friction. Firstly, they stated that China's representation by a Kuomintang member (Lee) was illegal and raised a motion for the Commission to exclude Lee from the debates and to invite a PRC representative to take his place.[28] The motion was defeated by eleven to three, with India abstaining on the grounds that the Commission had no competence in the matter as Lee's appointment had been confirmed by ECOSOC. Lee nevertheless indicated that he had no intention of speaking on matters of substance, only on procedure. The Soviets declared that they would pay no heed to Lee's views and votes. Secondly, throughout the discussions, they argued similar positions as had been expressed in the Second Session.[29] They also accused the United States of influence over the Secretariat and were critical of the ICC's and NAM's submissions. They would vote against, or abstain from voting on, all draft resolutions proposed by the United States, but their obstructiveness against US or UK positions would lead them to support the developing countries, thus facilitating resolutions favouring the latter's interests. Morton and Bartelt nevertheless did not consider the Commission's discussions to have been affected by the Soviet lines of argument, reporting to their respective governments that

[27] US participation, however, surpassed the others with lengthy speeches and draft resolutions introduced on each agenda item, including the priorities for the Secretariat's concentration of work.

[28] See Chapter 4, Section 4.1.1, n 28 (regarding the Soviets' submission of this matter in other bodies).

[29] See Chapter 7, Section 7.2.

the Soviet group had 'not pressed too hard'[30] and their 'attempts at political coloration of the proceedings did not appear to have any influence on other delegations'.[31]

The following presents the Commission's and Working Group's discussions on the main international tax items other than the taxation of international air transport.[32]

9.2.1 *The* International Tax Agreements *Series*

This topic was retitled 'Comparative review of international tax agreements' at France's suggestion to direct the discussions towards drawing out the general features of DTAs that 'would be helpful to public as well as private enterprises, governments, tax departments and those engaged in tax negotiations';[33] however, this objective was not ultimately achieved. Discussion began with Bloch providing an explanation of volumes 2 and 3 of the *ITA* series and proposing that future work give emphasis to measures likely to promote the economic development of underdeveloped countries. France and Pakistan agreed with the continuation of efforts along these lines. France also suggested making the study more comprehensive by illustrating treaties between countries in approximately the same stage of development to exemplify how the tax-credit and tax-reduction systems could be employed concurrently, separately or in combination, such as the treaties that had been concluded recently among European countries.

A debate ensued among Cuba, India, the United Kingdom and the ICC on practical proposals the Commission could now make regarding measures that would encourage the development of underdeveloped countries. Cuba and the ICC considered that analysing the text of different DTAs would unduly protract the debates. Cuba suggested that the Commission should decide whether double taxation should be combated via DTAs,

30 Cabinet Steering Committee on International Organisations ('CSCIO'), *Draft Brief for United Kingdom Delegation to the 13th Session of the Economic and Social Council: Report on the Third Session of the Fiscal Commission*, IOC(51)110 (25 July 1951) 2, TNA:IR40/9959(1).

31 Letter from Bartelt to Secretary of State, 19 June 1951, 1, NARAII:RG56–199–6.

32 The discussion regarding two other items was inconsequential: (1) the Commission merely acknowledged the receipt of the referral regarding the unreasonable or discriminatory taxation affecting the operations of foreign information agencies and news personnel, and (2) by majority vote, the Commission adopted a French proposal calling for the Secretariat to study the fiscal status of international civil servants. The discussion on the taxation of international air transport is presented in Chapter 11, Section 11.7.

33 E/CN.8/SR.13 (17 May 1951) 8.

unilateral measures or a combination of both. If DTAs were favoured, the Commission should then consider what basic measures were appropriate and ideally find common ground between the standpoints of the Mexico and London Models. The ICC, however, thought that little would be accomplished by re-examining the two models and it was best to leave it to states to choose between the various solutions. It also felt that there was 'a certain tendency to exaggerate the differences between capital-exporting and capital-importing countries' and that '[a] good technical solution should suit both categories'.[34] The ICC considered the most important task was to determine the circumstances under which governments should take unilateral action and the principles on which such action should be based. In this regard, it stated that while theoretically a choice existed between the tax-credit and tax-reduction method, the former presented 'serious difficulties' regarding definitions.[35] India, supported by Britain, considered that the Commission merely had to decide whether the Secretariat should continue the series and whether to continue them in the same form. India also stated that, as double taxation relief by DTAs or unilateral measures were not mutually exclusive, the Commission should simply try to determine the conditions under which one method was preferable over the other, for example, that unilateral action depended on internal financial conditions while the adoption of DTAs depended on the advantages each contracting party hoped to receive from the other.

The discussion was eventually resolved with Britain's submission of a resolution that commended the Secretariat on its *ITA* series, recommending that it continue its studies in the field.[36] Britain also further suggested that the question of relief methods be examined during the discussion on the agenda item concerning effects of taxation on foreign trade and investment, and that consideration of the Mexico and London Models be postponed. The UK resolution was adopted by twelve votes to none with the Soviet members abstaining.

9.2.2 *Effects of Taxation on Foreign Trade and Investment; Unilateral Relief from Double Taxation*

Early plenary discussions on the topic commenced with Bloch providing an outline of the *Effects of Taxation* publication. The USSR criticised the

[34] Ibid 10.
[35] Ibid.
[36] Fiscal Commission, 'United Kingdom: Draft Resolution', 3rd sess, Agenda item 3(a), Conference Room Paper No 1 (8 May 1951), NARAII:RG56–199–6.

study for its bias in reflecting the views of capital-exporting countries seeking foreign markets, and the recommendations of organisations representing 'the interests of private monopolies', specifically NAM[37] and the ICC.[38] The USSR called for (1) the recognition of states' right to grant preferential fiscal treatment for the development of national industries (the practice of which had been criticised in the publication); (2) the UN not to interfere in taxation questions, specifically in providing uniform solutions that only benefited the capital-exporting countries; and (3) underdeveloped countries to develop their economies by relying on their own domestic resources and national production in order to become increasingly independent of more advanced economies. China, the United Kingdom and the United States rebutted these statements by putting their own views forward.

China stated that as an underdeveloped country, it hoped to be able to develop its industry much more rapidly with the aid of the capital-exporting countries and that the question of competition between domestic and foreign capital would only arise later. China suggested that as the Secretariat's study only dealt with how underdeveloped countries could attract capital, it should expand the report to consider the problem of reconciling the interests of foreign and domestic capital after the initial period of economic development. The United States commended the Secretariat study for, firstly, its timeliness given the growing interest among underdeveloped countries in tax incentives as a method for attracting foreign capital, and, secondly, its valuable contribution in emphasising to governments that tax incentive schemes were not cost-free. The United States subsequently delivered a lengthy speech on how its policy of tax neutrality and its FTC system enabled underdeveloped countries' application of a uniform income tax and encouraged the flow of US capital to such countries, particularly because they could increasingly rely on income taxes without fear of discouraging potential US investors. The disadvantages of a system that exempted nationals/residents from the taxation of foreign-source income were then outlined.[39] The United States concluded stating that the FTC

[37] NAM's recommendation concerned the lowering of tariff barriers: E/CN.8/SR.13, 4.

[38] Ibid. The USSR also explained 'why capitalist concerns made investments abroad (underpaid labour, cheap raw materials, low-priced land, etc.)' and quoted US State Department statistics that indicated that foreign investments provided a higher return than domestic investments and were on the increase.

[39] Reasons provided included that such a system was costly, could encourage governments seeking American capital to exempt or reduce income taxes on American investors and

system, together with a programme of DTAs, 'constituted a flexible, effective and equitable method' for removing tax barriers to FDI.[40]

Britain stated its agreement with the United States and Secretariat's views that 'there was no justification in law or in practice for reducing taxes on foreign capital as a means of stimulating foreign investment'.[41] It nevertheless argued that 'discriminatory taxation of foreign capital was equally inequitable and apt to deter foreign investors', and that the fiscal needs of a country sometimes had to be sacrificed for its economic needs.[42] It advanced that 'a fair, complete and sound system of taxation, especially as regards business profits' as well as DTAs, 'could do much to help under-developed countries', the most important items in such agreements being the prevention of tax discrimination and the definition of taxable profits.[43] It claimed that DTAs did not require a greater sacrifice by underdeveloped countries than developed countries, the credit system enabled tax policies and revenues of underdeveloped countries to remain unaffected and there was no reason for a government to exempt its nationals from taxes on foreign-sourced income.

Britain proposed establishing a small working group of no more than five members to examine the technical aspects of the problem, but the USSR considered that the matter should be debated in plenary. The UK proposal was adopted by ten votes to four, with no abstentions. The Working Group was to address the appropriate cases for and methods of tax incentives in view of governments' financial needs and investors' need for tax relief; the appropriate methods for solving double taxation, especially considering the different interests of capital-importing and capital-exporting countries, and the availability of unilateral legislation and DTAs; and the uses of DTAs.

The Working Group's report to the Commission contained the following propositions that had been accepted by the majority (i.e. Poland excepted):[44]

was not a sufficient incentive per se to offset other unfavourable investment conditions in capital-seeking countries.

40 E/CN.8/SR.14 (18 May 1951) 10.

41 Ibid 11.

42 Ibid.

43 Ibid 11–12.

44 Fiscal Commission, 'Report of the Working Party on International Tax Problems', 3rd sess, Agenda item 3, Conference Room Paper No 8 (14 May 1951), NARAII:RG56-199-6; E/1993, annex 1, 26–7. The Working Group's deliberations are not known as no summary reports were found for it.

(i) there is normally no need or justification for countries seeking to attract capital and enterprise from abroad to offer as an incentive specially favourable tax treatment, as against the treatment accorded to their own national enterprises.
(ii) that international double taxation normally operates as one of the impediments to the free flow of trade and investment.
(iii) that the country in which income arises has an undoubted right in principle to tax that income.
(iv) that therefore the main burden of relief of double taxation must fall on the country where the income is also taxable as part of the income of a resident or national person or corporation.
(v) that, on the method of relief, the choice between exempting income from abroad or giving credit on account of the tax paid in the country in which the income arises is not one for which clearcut arguments are available pointing firmly one way or the other.
(vi) that while the relief of double taxation in a country charging income from abroad may be provided by unilateral legislation, which to a substantial extent can relieve the burden, the conclusion of bi-lateral agreements has the advantages of offering scope for the more effective provision of complete relief, of making possible the resolution of different approaches in the national laws of the contracting parties and also of providing the assured stability of an international treaty to enterprises of either country considering ventures in the other.
(vii) that such bilateral agreements can be concluded on the basis of the foregoing proposals between a so-called under-developed country and one in a more advanced state of development, with little sacrifice of national revenue on the part of the former, and that bilateral agreements on this footing can make their contribution to the general objectives of the United Nations for the encouragement of economic development in under-developed countries.
(viii) that therefore the conclusion of bilateral agreements for the relief of double taxation should find a place in the fiscal policy of member governments.

Plenary discussions resumed with Canada, France and the United States supporting the report, the United States claiming that the conclusions 'constituted the best possible solution at the present time'.[45] However, Poland and the USSR opposed the report, the latter observing, inter alia, that the conclusions merely 'coincided in the main with the views

[45] E/CN.8/SR.19 (5 June 1951) 3.

expressed by the United States and United Kingdom representatives during the general debate' and represented 'an attempt on the part of the monopolistic interests in the United States and United Kingdom to use the United Nations to bring underdeveloped countries under their control'.[46] Carroll, upon invitation by Cuba (as Chairman) to address the Commission, stated that while the conclusions could form a useful basis for double taxation relief, he disagreed with Paragraph 1 and proposed that the Commission discard the paragraph as countries were entitled to adopt special tax treatment for foreign investors for the following two reasons: (1) countries only sought to attract foreign capital 'when conditions were abnormal' (e.g. in wartime or in underdeveloped countries where 'the situation was chronically abnormal'), and (2) some countries had 'frequently complicated tax systems' that were 'difficult and inexpedient' to apply to foreign enterprise and which constituted 'a serious deterrent' to potential investors (e.g. extraterritorial taxation imposed by underdeveloped countries on dividend distributions by foreign enterprises operating within their borders).[47] At Belgium's request, voting on the report was postponed to await the French translation of the report.

Britain subsequently submitted a draft resolution[48] that incorporated most of the Working Group's propositions except for:

- paragraph (v) (regarding the imperceptible difference between the exemption and tax credit system as the preferable method of relief);
- the phrase in paragraph (vi) that set forth that unilateral relief measures relieved a substantial extent of double taxation; and
- the phrase in paragraph (vii) that referred to the general UN objectives of encouraging economic development in underdeveloped countries.

The preamble of the resolution declared the propositions to apply between underdeveloped countries and those in a more advanced state of development, and called for the Secretariat to continue its studies and analysis of double taxation relief methods, DTAs, national legislation and the effects of taxation on foreign trade and investment.

Discussions resumed with France (as the Working Group's Chairman) declaring that the UK draft resolution accurately reflected the

[46] Ibid 4.
[47] Ibid 2–3.
[48] Fiscal Commission, 'United Kingdom: Draft Resolution', 3rd sess, Agenda item 3, Conference Room Paper No 16 (15 May 1951), NARAII:RG56–199–6.

conclusions of the majority of the Working Group. Venezuela queried why the references in paragraphs (v) and (vi) had been omitted and reserved the right to propose their later insertion as it considered them extremely important. Britain (as Rapporteur) responded that those paragraphs had been omitted for 'technical reasons connected with method and not with the substance of the question' and that 'the fundamental ideas underlying those [paragraphs]' were still sufficiently reflected in the resolution.[49] France endorsed Britain's remarks. Meanwhile China considered that the preamble of the resolution was too limiting in scope in its specific application to relations between underdeveloped and developed countries. France agreed with this interpretation; however, Belgium unreservedly supported the UK resolution. Venezuela requested for Britain to re-insert the paragraph (vii) reference, which the latter accepted. The UK resolution, as amended, was adopted by twelve votes to three.

9.2.3 *Taxation of Foreign Nationals, Assets and Transactions*

Discussions began with Bloch explaining that while the Division had received more government replies to its questionnaire, they were still insufficient to produce a general survey. Some disagreement arose in the Commission as to whether the item was related to methods to solve double taxation or discriminatory taxation, the latter interpretation being espoused by the United Kingdom. The item was turned over to the Working Group, a move which was opposed by the Soviets, but the Working Group made no decision on the matter and simply recommended urging governments to reply to the questionnaire and the Secretariat to make studies without waiting for all replies to be received.

9.2.4 *The Commission's Report*

The Commission made only a few changes to Morton's reporting of the above items in his draft report for the session.[50] The major amendments consisted of, firstly, the appending of both working groups' reports to the Commission's report. This had been suggested by Pakistan but opposed by Britain and Belgium. Pakistan's proposal was adopted by five votes to

49 E/CN.8/SR.20 (29 May 1951) 5.

50 Fiscal Commission, *Draft Report to the Economic and Social Council on the Third Session of the Commission, Held at Lake Success, New York, from 7 to 17 May 1951*, UN Docs E/CN.8/L.1 and Corr.1–Corr.2 (16 May 1951).

two, with five abstentions. The second amendment was the inclusion of a brief account of the Soviet opposition to the position taken by the Commission regarding double taxation relief of foreign enterprise profits. This had been requested by the Soviets and was adopted by fourteen votes to one (China). The UK resolution reflecting the Working Group's conclusions was finalised as Draft Resolution B-II on 'International Tax Problems' among the draft resolutions recommended for adoption by ECOSOC.[51]

The Secretariat's future work programme was now organised according to continuing and ad hoc projects. The former was composed of technical assistance; the fiscal information service (which included the World Tax Service); periodic review of fiscal developments; and the collection of and comparative studies on the taxation of foreign nationals, assets and transactions. The latter included the continuation of studies on the effects of taxation on foreign trade and investment; the taxation of corporate profits and dividends; problems of fiscal administration and management; fiscal problems of agriculture; problems of municipal finance; and further refinement and broadening of fiscal classification and presentation systems. No mention was made concerning the consideration of the Mexico and London Models.

9.3 Deliberations in ECOSOC (July–August 1951)

At ECOSOC's Thirteenth Session,[52] the Commission's report was first considered by the Economic Committee, which completed its general discussion of the report and dealt with all the resolutions (except that relating to the taxation of international air transport[53]) at its 116th meeting on 31 July.[54] Belgium commented that Draft Resolution B-II appeared 'wholly acceptable' and that 'double taxation could easily be made the subject of general rules based on certain principles; but in practice it should be resolved primarily through bilateral agreements'.[55] However, the USSR and Poland proposed to abolish the Commission on the grounds, inter alia,

[51] E/1993, 14–15. Draft Resolution B-II (entitled 'International Tax Problems') is reproduced in Appendix E.

[52] ECOSOC membership in 1951 comprised Belgium, Canada, Chile, China, Czechoslovakia, France, India, Iran, Mexico, Pakistan, Peru, the Philippines, Poland, Sweden, the United Kingdom, the United States, Uruguay and the USSR.

[53] See Chapter 11, Section 11.8.

[54] Economic Committee, *Summary Record of the 116th Meeting*, UN ESC, 13th sess, 116th mtg, Agenda item 10, UN Doc E/AC.6/SR.116 (6 September 1951).

[55] Ibid 4.

that the majority of the Commission was attempting to exploit ECOSOC's authority by pushing through conclusions that were contrary to the principle of non-interference in states' domestic affairs, and which essentially promoted conditions favourable to the activities of British and American monopolies to the detriment of underdeveloped countries' interests and contrary to UN Charter aims. Britain supported the Soviet proposals to wind up the Commission's activities, albeit for a different reason, specifically that the preparatory work for ECOSOC in the fiscal field could be more effectively carried out by small groups of experts with the Secretariat's assistance rather than by a permanent functional commission. Only the United States defended the Commission's work for facilitating cooperation and closer relations between governments, and a greater flow of trade which ultimately helped to increase general living standards. The Chairman then closed the debate and the majority of the Committee went on to vote in favour of all the draft resolutions that the Commission had recommended for ECOSOC's adoption.

Draft Resolution B-II was adopted by thirteen votes to three, with two abstentions. France declared its full support of the resolution but remarked that as DTA negotiations were a long-term affair, it was desirable, wherever possible, for states 'to grant unilaterally exemption from taxation on income earned in other countries'.[56] Uruguay stated that it had voted affirmatively because sub-paragraph (ii) of the resolution (which stated 'the country in which income arises has an undoubted right in principle to tax that income') 'recognized the principle of taxation at source, which was traditional in [Uruguay]'.[57] The Philippines also expressed its approval of sub-paragraph (ii) but stated 'that it would have been preferable to have omitted the phrase "little sacrifice of national revenue" from sub-paragraph (v), since . . . no sacrifice at all should be called for from under-developed countries'.[58] The Philippines also considered that the word 'normally' in the recommendation against the offer by capital-seeking countries of special tax treatment 'detracted from the general tone of the resolution'.[59] The USSR, which voted against the resolution, observed, inter alia, 'that draft resolution B-II admitted only "in principle" the right to tax income in the country in which it arose. Such a limitation was unacceptable'.[60]

[56] Ibid 8.
[57] Ibid 8.
[58] Ibid 8–9.
[59] Ibid 9.
[60] Ibid 8.

At ECOSOC's 496th meeting on 10 August, debate on Draft Resolution B-II arose over sub-paragraph (ii).[61] Uruguay, supported by Chile and Pakistan, contended that the words 'in principle' were ambiguous, weakened the principle expressed in the statement and should be eliminated. However, Belgium stated that the words simply served to remind that a general rule was involved, allowing thus for 'flexibility in application' so that states were 'not invariably bound to tax' income arising within their territories and could also negotiate DTA provisions that diverged from that principle.[62] India urged the retention of those words to leave 'room for a certain amount of variation' for countries such as India where the word 'resident' encompassed a person whose 'income arising in India in a particular year exceeded his income arising from outside the country'.[63] Upon a vote, a joint Chilean-Uruguayan proposal to delete the words was rejected by nine votes to five, with three abstentions. A Philippines proposal to reconcile the Uruguayan and Belgian views by deleting those words and inserting the phrase 'as a general principle' after the words 'in which income arises has' was instead adopted by seven votes to three, with eight abstentions.[64] The resolution, as amended, was adopted as ECOSOC Resolution 378B (XIII) by fourteen votes to three, with one abstention.[65]

9.4 Commentary

By the time of the Third Session, the Division's reported output was largely focused on developing country-related issues – an inevitable outcome of the Expanded Programme of Technical Assistance, the Financing Economic Development agenda, the OEEC's monopolisation of Western Europe's economic concerns[66] and the intense Cold War

[61] UN ESCOR, UN Doc E/SR.496 (10 August 1951) 146–51.

[62] Ibid 146.

[63] Ibid 147. Discussions at this point were interrupted by Czechoslovakia, which argued for the Commission's discontinuance on the grounds that it had only mainly focused on double taxation, its goal of standardising fiscal legislation interfered in states' internal affairs and its work had been directed by capitalist states along 'lines favourable to their foreign investments and against the economic interests of under-developed countries'.

[64] Ibid.

[65] *International Tax Problems*, ESC Res 378B (XIII), UN ESCOR, UN Doc 2152 (10 October 1951, adopted 10 August 1951). This resolution is reproduced in Appendix F. ECOSOC adopted the other resolutions approved by the Committee without amendment.

[66] See Chapter 4, Section 4.1.3.

which made concentration on economic development issues the path of least resistance. The Division's studies and recommendations, however, were constrained in any overt mention of value judgements held by the Division regarding DTAs that might antagonise states, such as its policy against reciprocal exemption provisions,[67] the possible sufficiency of unilateral relief provisions by capital-exporting countries, the unequal revenue sacrifice underdeveloped countries stood to incur under DTAs or the potential means of DTAs to address tax bargaining arrangements. Rather, the Division focused on emphasising the potential advantages of DTAs in enabling developing countries to increase their tax rates, in facilitating mutual administrative assistance and in assuring capital-exporting countries' relief of double taxation – none of which, incidentally, reflected the US or UK objectives for DTA negotiations.

While some of the Division's policies may be traceable to Bloch's own long-held views,[68] it is queried whether its relatively recent shift in couching DTAs in a positive light for application to developing countries, in direct contrast with the positions taken in Sundelson's Report, may have been due to political pressures to ingratiate itself with the United States by showing general support of DTAs between developed and underdeveloped countries. After all, the Division, along with the Commission, had just narrowly escaped being terminated,[69] and Secretary-General Trygve Lie had fallen out with the USSR in supporting the US-led UN intervention in the North Korean invasion of South Korea.[70] McCarthyism hysteria, moreover, had infiltrated the UN with Lie sending the State Department, from 1948 and under confidential arrangements, lists of UN staff members who were US nationals for anti-communist investigation and security clearance.[71] The State Department was closely monitoring the UN: Bartelt was required to report on, inter alia, 'foreign participants ... attitudes toward the United States and its

[67] See also Chapter 11, Sections 11.2–11.7, regarding the Division's behind-the-scenes fight against ICAO's promulgation of this principle for the taxation of international air transport.

[68] See Chapter 7, Section 7.5. Such policies must have frustrated the NGOs, especially the ICC, in their active campaign for the very opposite positions.

[69] While debate on the Commission's continuance was public knowledge, it is unknown whether the Division was aware that it had earned the State Department's displeasure.

[70] Thant Myint-U and Amy Scott, *The UN Secretariat: A Brief History (1945–2006)* (International Peace Academy, 2007) 20; Brian Urquhart, *Hammarskjold* (The Bodley Head, 1972) 10.

[71] Abdelaziz Megzari, *The Internal Justice of the United Nations: A Critical History 1945–2015* (Brill Nijhoff, 2015) 130–2.

positions',[72] 'outstandingly effective or ineffective members as to constructive, indifferent or destructive contributions or activities', and 'the performance of key United Nations secretariat staff'.[73] Bartelt in turn would advise the State Department that 'systematic effort should be made by the United States delegation to keep in touch with the Secretariat (the Fiscal Division), so as to guide and be conversant with the scope and nature of its work between sessions of the Commission'.[74] Literature on UN intellectual history indicates that McCarthyism's advent in this period crippled the Secretariat's 'self-confidence to raise issues and concerns about forces that might undermine the path toward [the UN's founding ideals of global] unity'.[75] Even State Department officials were said to have been 'in a state of alarm and defeatism over the inroads of McCarthyism into their department'.[76] With the Red Scare affecting politicians, journalists, courts and bureaucrats, and 'Conservatives ... finding [of] Communist fingerprints on any policy they disagreed with',[77] it is plausible that the Division felt compelled to some middle ground between the United States' strident defence of private foreign capital, extreme positions being asserted by the NGOs and the need to ensure that the Secretariat's own views were not construed as linked to general Soviet positions. The Division's positive spin on DTAs would nevertheless be short-lived (see Section 9.5).

Although the Commission's records show that the Division had a silent role in the discussions apart from its introductory presentation of each agenda item, it may have been privately influential as indicated by its

[72] Memorandum by State Department to Bartelt, undated (around May 1951), NARAII: RG56-199-6.

[73] State Department, 'Outline of Suggested Form of Report to Chief of the United States Mission to the United Nations for Use by US Representatives to Commissions, Sub-Commissions, etc., of ECOSOC at Conclusion of Sessions', 18 May 1951, NARAII: RG56-199-6.

[74] Bartelt letter, 19 June 1951, 6.

[75] John Toye and Richard Toye, *UN and Global Political Economy: Trade, Finance, and Development* (Indiana University Press, 2004) 111.

[76] Urquhart, *Hammarskjold*, 62.

[77] Ellen Schrecker, 'McCarthyism: Political Repression and the Fear of Communism' (2004) 71(4) *Social Research* 1041, 1053. See also Frank D McCann, *Brazil and the United States during World War II and Its Aftermath: Negotiating Alliance and Balancing Giants* (Palgrave Macmillan, 2018) (noting that '[o]pposition to American views was easily labeled as Communist' in 'a Washington infected with McCarthyism' (at 258)); Urquhart, *Hammarskjold* (noting that from the time of the Korean War in 1950, the Secretariat 'had become the arena for an anti-Communist witch-hunt by the US authorities' (at 50) and 'been violently attacked in the United States' for being 'a stooge' of the USSR (at 60)).

pro-developing country policies that were reflected in the Working Group's propositions,[78] which were most likely incorporated at Pakistan's insistence.[79] The Secretariat's recommendation against exemption systems, however, may have been overridden by France, Pakistan and the NGOs in the Working Group, although Britain was subsequently successful in deleting from the final resolution the statement regarding the inappreciable difference between the credit and exemption methods.

The Third Session followed the pattern of previous sessions in that the Commission failed to deliberate much of the content of the Secretariat's documents and took a passive attitude towards interest shown in double taxation matters outside the Commission.[80] An insightful explanation for this is found in Bartelt's report to the State Department in which he states that many of the Commission's experts were intensively preoccupied with national fiscal legislation during the first half of the year, which prevented them from undertaking adequate preparation for the session as well as placed them 'under pressure to shorten the session as much as possible, to the detriment of sound policy formulation'.[81] Those representing industry nevertheless appeared to have become bolder in advancing positions inimical to developing countries' interests. It is curious why Cuba did not participate in the Working Group despite its expressed interest in finding common ground between the Models, or why the Latin Americans did not assert, as they would just one month later in ECLA,[82] for exclusive source taxation rights over income originating within the country or, alternatively, the exemption by capital-exporting countries from taxing foreign income of their nationals.[83]

78 Specifically, the recommendation against underdeveloped countries' provision of special tax treatment, the near sufficiency of unilateral measures in relieving double taxation and the utility of DTAs as a means of fulfilling UN objectives of encouraging economic development in underdeveloped countries.

79 This attribution is indicated by Carroll (see Chapter 10, Section 10.1); Britain's efforts to remove these statements from the Commission's resolution; and Morton's reporting to Inland Revenue that 'Qadir [the Pakistan representative], by the way, makes Pahdi of India, look like the most flexible and adaptable of mortals': Letter from Morton to Verity, 16 May 1951, TNA: IR40/9959(1).

80 According to Chairman Perez, nevertheless, this session was regarded as the appropriate 'time . . . for the Commission to make concrete recommendations on fiscal policy', the previous sessions having 'been largely preparatory': E/CN.8/SR.11, 5.

81 Bartelt letter, 19 June 1951, 5. Bartelt suggested that the timing of the Commission's sessions be moved to the fall of the year. However, the State Department and Treasury later determined that this was not a convenient time for the United States: Note by Bartelt to Ecker-Racz, 17 July 1952, NARAII:RG56–199–6.

82 See Chapter 10, Section 10.2.

83 The United States had in fact expected that the underdeveloped countries, especially Latin America, would sponsor a resolution calling for either policy because of their 'growing

Perhaps Perez had prioritised Pakistan for participation in the Working Group in his efforts to be a fair Chairman[84] and the Latin Americans felt inhibited by their lack of numbers or the Division's backing of the credit system. Whatever the reasons, the lack of activism by the developing countries was regrettable as Britain's confining of the Working Group to a small composition and its opportunistic capitalisation on its position as Rapporteur to omit statements inconvenient to its interests[85] essentially produced a resolution which, as noted by the USSR, conceded little ground to developing countries.

Conversely, Resolution B-II largely delivered the results that the United States and the United Kingdom had set out to achieve, Bartelt reporting that, except for the outcome regarding the taxation of international air transport, '[t]he action taken by the Commission ... conforms closely to the [US] views' and that Resolution B-II successfully

concern' of '[t]he relationship between taxation and international investment' and their shared views that the US system of taxation was 'an important impediment to the flow of investment capital'. As the United States 'would not subscribe to this theory', it had been prepared to propose a substitute resolution urging capital-exporting countries to defer taxing foreign income until such income was repatriated. This view was considered, '[f]rom an equity viewpoint ... more tolerable' and had been adopted by the Truman Administration 'in the legislation it ha[d] recommended to Congress in connection with the Point IV program': UN Economic Subcommittee of the Executive Committee on Economic Foreign Policy, Position Paper on 'Taxation of Foreign Income' for the US Delegation to the Third Session of the Fiscal Commission, 3 May 1951, 2–3, NARAII: RG59–UD-07D_73B(Lot56D479)–4.

84 See Chapter 11, Section 11.7, n 245.

85 Such interests being those of a debt-ridden power in need of imports of foodstuffs and raw materials yet had few prospects for affording these essentials, let alone making rapid economic recovery: the nation had negligible export trade due to declining industrial competitiveness, it faced formidable American competition, the pound had suffered a precipitous drop in open trading and sterling convertibility had been suspended. From Britain's perspective, DTAs with underdeveloped countries were aimed at helping to re-establish British presence in its lost markets by minimising taxes levied on British corporations. Economic development was not a goal in such negotiations. In fact, British policy-makers held that 'taxation, as an influence on development, operates only as a marginal discouragement' and that '[w]hat is required is an assurance against discriminatory rates of tax and the adoption of a fair method of assessment', both of which 'commonly form part of bilateral agreements': CSCIO, *Draft Brief for United Kingdom Representative to the 3rd Session of the Fiscal Commission Economic and Social Council Prepared by Board of Inland Revenue*, IOC(51)52 (30 April 1951) 1–2, TNA:IR40/9959(1). Inland Revenue further acknowledged it 'false to infer that parity of sacrifice is required ... with the flow preponderatingly from the undeveloped country to the developed country' but considered that DTAs 'need not be costly to the underdeveloped country' (at 2). The emphasis on non-discrimination would appear hypocritical in view of Britain's discriminatory trade and payments system instituted in the sterling area to rectify imbalances between the sterling and dollar worlds (see further Chapter 10, Section 10.5).

contained 'an implicit recognition that the home country may properly tax income from foreign investment' given that the view had 'been challenged from time to time by some underdeveloped countries, particularly in Latin America'.[86] Inland Revenue similarly regarded that Resolution B-II 'clearly accepts the co-existence of domicile taxation and taxation in the country of origin of the income and places the burden of relief on the country of fiscal domicile', although the Commission's deliberations were 'to some extent inconclusive'.[87] According to Morton:

> The most important thing we have done is to record certain principles on which the relief of double taxation as between developed and under-developed countries, can be based. The propositions are, I think, all right and may help the Latin American countries to begin discussions. I have little doubt though that some of them will be used to our disadvantage from time to time but I don't see how that can be helped.[88]

He also stated:

> The policy outlined in this Resolution is an important one from the point of view of the United Kingdom which has been extending its network of double taxation agreements with a view to encouraging overseas trade but (like the United States whose policy is similar) has met with some reluctance on the part of under-developed countries to negotiate agreements. If it were more widely recognised that these agreements can be concluded with comparatively small cost by under-developed countries greater success in negotiating them would no doubt be achieved.[89]

Although Morton concluded that the session had been 'only modestly productive', he considered it had been 'probably worth holding', specifically because the relevant discussions 'provided valuable exchanges of view' and Resolution B-II 'should be of some continuing value'.[90]

86 Bartelt letter, 19 June 1951, 1–2.

87 Letter from Nicholas to Daniel, 19 June 1952, TNA:IR40/11173(2).

88 Morton letter, 16 May 1951.

89 CSCIO, IOC(51)110, 3.

90 CSCIO, *Fiscal Commission: Third Session (Lake Success, 7th to 17th May, 1951), Report by United Kingdom Representative*, IOC(51)105 (24 July 1951) 3, TNA:IR40/9959(1). Morton, however, felt 'less sanguine of the somewhat academic work on public finance, on which the Commission seems in real danger of embarking'. This may have been a reason, along with the Commission's slow progress, why the United Kingdom proposed in ECOSOC to replace the Commission with a small group of experts. The United States, nevertheless, was clearly satisfied with the purposes being served by the Commission as indicated by the US representative's defence of the Commission's work. The immediate shutting down of the debate regarding the Commission's termination just after the US advocacy illustrates the decisiveness of US support to any UN endeavour.

The session may have helped stimulate interest in DTAs: after the Commission's meetings, the Pakistan representative (Abdul Qadir) 'visited Washington and held discussions with Treasury officials on various technical matters, including a possible tax treaty'.[91] Qadir, as well as the South African representative (MJ Wells), also visited London but Morton predicted that 'neither, I believe, has any plan for substantive action'.[92]

9.5 Subsequent Secretariat Work

The Division's work generally progressed according to the work programme set by the Commission with much of its efforts consumed by technical assistance activities.[93] Work on international tax matters consisted of continuing the *ITA* series[94] and studies on the taxation of foreign nationals, assets and transactions (now retitled 'taxation of foreign taxpayers and foreign income'); taxation on foreign investment; and corporate tax problems. The Division also began a joint study with FAO on the taxation of agriculture. The public finance work encompassed quantitative data on government finance,[95] regional and country surveys and information papers, and problems of fiscal administration and management.[96] The Division continued to struggle to obtain replies from Latin America to its inquiries for information,[97] mainly due to the refusal by the Secretariat's translation division to provide Spanish editions of the Fiscal Division's documentation (including 'model replies' to guide governments in preparing their responses).[98] The Division also continued to report to US officials on its progress of

91 Bartelt letter, 19 June 1951, 6.

92 Morton letter, 16 May 1951.

93 Fiscal Commission, *Programme of Secretariat Work: Action Taken since Third Session of Fiscal Commission and Proposed List of Future Priorities*, Note by the Secretary-General, UN Doc E/CN.8/75 (3 December 1952).

94 This comprised collecting DTAs and publishing volume 3 in French and Spanish.

95 This work involved publications for the UN Statistical Yearbook and further collaboration with the IMF on a supplementary questionnaire on ownership of public debt.

96 This category broadly comprised the sub-projects of government accounting and budget execution (of which a volume entitled *Government Accounting and Budget Execution* was published in 1952), fiscal classification and presentation, and problems of provincial and local finance.

97 Letter from Bloch to Swenson, 27 March 1952, UNARMS:AG-025-002—S-0441-0464-23412.

98 Memorandums between Karakacheff and Le Bosquet, 8 and 15 February 1952, UNARMS: AG-025-002—S-0441-0464-23412.

work.[99] In July 1952, funding for the World Tax Service came through with the receipt by HLS of a $200,000 grant from the Ford Foundation.[100] The Division was relieved that the grant had come 'early enough' to be able to use some of the funds for the study of the taxation in capital-exporting and capital-importing countries of foreign private investment in Latin America ('FPILA Taxation') as 'only a limited amount could be allocated by the UN'.[101] This communication reveals how financial constraints were significantly impeding the Division's progress of its international tax work.

The UN at this stage appeared out of favour with the United States. ECOSOC and the Assembly were issuing resolutions calling for time and cost estimates on economic and social projects to avoid short-term activities from becoming permanent or long term, and to focus resources on the priority projects.[102] Although these resolutions only addressed considerations of budget in ECOSOC and the Assembly, the State Department would instruct the US Delegation to the Commission's Fourth Session to require the Secretariat to provide 'cost estimates for all projects' to the Commission as such programmes, once approved, were 'difficult to alter in the superior bodies'.[103] The Delegation was also instructed to employ 'appropriate tactics' at its discretion as the Secretariat would 'resist this interpretation', and to 'carefully screen the total program in an endeavor to reveal any possible economies, and . . . oppose any program proposals which would result in any additional request for funds in 1953'.[104] In September 1951, ECOSOC decided to convene the Fiscal Commission, along with five other commissions, once

[99] See, for example, Letter from Bloch to Bartelt, 5 September 1952, NARAII:RG56–199–2.

[100] Letter from Bloch to Surrey, 26 August 1952, 1, UNARMS:AG-025-002—S-0441–0468–23886(B). The grant also allowed HLS to establish a program of tax research and training that supported the UN technical assistance fellowship and scholarship program: see, for example, Memorandum by Daniel to Bloch, 14 November 1952, UNARMS:AG-025-002—S-0441–0468–23886(B).

[101] Bloch letter, 26 August 1952, 2.

[102] *Co-ordination between the United Nations and the Specialized Agencies: Concentration of Effort and Resources*, GA Res 533B (VI), UN Doc A/RES/533(VI) (4 February 1952); *Co-ordination among the United Nations and the Specialized Agencies*, ESC Res 402B (XIII), UN ESCOR, UN Doc E/2152 (10 October 1951, adopted 17 September 1951); *Co-ordination of the Work of the United Nations and the Specialized Agencies*, ESC Res 451 (XIV), UN ESCOR, UN Doc E/2332 (13 August 1952, adopted 28 July 1952).

[103] Position Paper on 'Concentration of Effort and Resources' for the US Delegation to the Fourth Session of the Fiscal Commission, 22 April 1953, 4, NARAII:RG56–199–6.

[104] Ibid 4, 2.

every two years, and not to convene the Fiscal Commission (and two other commissions) until 1953.[105] In addition, in early 1952, the Secretariat's independence began to be officially challenged with the unleashing of the McCarthy witch-hunts in the UN, which eventually led to Lie's resignation in November.[106] In January 1953, the US Federal Bureau of Investigation began operating in the UN Building to investigate and interrogate Americans employed by the UN.[107] The Secretariat is described as being then 'a complete mess, disorganized, and with poor staff morale'.[108] Dag Hammarskjöld would begin as the new Secretary-General in April 1953 and almost immediately began instituting management reforms in the Secretariat.[109] Although the impact of tensions during this Red Scare era on the Division is not known, in July 1952, American Roy Blough had been appointed as DEA's new Principal Director, and the Division soon began reporting to him.[110] Blough was formerly Director of Tax Research of the US Treasury, an economics professor, and had been an adviser on the US delegation to the Commission's Third Session, alternating for Bartelt in several of the meetings.

At end 1952, two of the Division's documents circulated to the Commission indicated that DTAs were neither being recommended by technical assistance experts nor embraced by developing countries, the latter situation likely a corollary of the former. The first document

105 *Organisation and Operation of the Council and Its Commissions*, ESC Res 414 (XIII), UN ESCOR, UN Doc E/2152 (10 October 1951, adopted 18–20 September 1951) para 18(g) and (h). ECOSOC also discontinued three other commissions/sub-commissions (para 18(b)–(d)). See also *France: Working Paper Concerning the Functional and Regional Commissions*, UN ESC, 13th sess, Agenda item 36, UN Docs E/AC.24/L.36 and Corr.1 and Corr.2 (7 September 1951).

106 Megzari, *Internal Justice*, ch 6.

107 Urquhart, *Hammarskjold*, 61–2.

108 Myint-U and Scott, *UN Secretariat*, 35.

109 Ibid 27; Urquhart, *Hammarskjold*, 67–83; *Organization of the Secretariat*, Report of the Secretary-General, UN GA, UN Doc A/2554 (12 November 1953).

110 See, for example, Memorandum by Bloch to Blough, 3 November 1952, UNARMS:AG-025-002—S-0441-0468-23889(B). This coincides with Owen ceasing to be DEA's head, becoming instead the Executive Chairman of the Technical Assistance Board on 1 August. Blough's new position had itself been vacant since 1950: see 'The Secretariat' [1950] *Yearbook of the United Nations* 125, 148; 'The Secretariat' [1951] *Yearbook of the United Nations* 107, 126. This position, as well as Blough's employment within the Secretariat, ceased to exist in 1955, which coincides with Hammarskjöld's reorganisation of the Secretariat: see 'Structure of the United Nations' [1954] *Yearbook of the United Nations* 554, 568; cf 'Structure of the United Nations' [1955] *Yearbook of the United Nations* 456, 473–4.

concerned the report of the Technical Assistance Conference on Comparative Fiscal Administration held in Geneva in July 1951 under the joint auspices of the Division and the TAA.[111] The report made almost no mention of DTAs in the evaluation of the role of fiscal policy in economic development.[112] In brief, the Conference had determined, inter alia, that many underdeveloped countries had yet to fully grasp the role taxation played in capital formation, economic stabilisation and the various types of investment required for economic development. Most had only rudimentary income tax systems, globally exposed economies and less capable tax administrations. Regarding fiscal incentives for attracting foreign capital, the Conference only endorsed two recommendations of the Fiscal Commission and ECOSOC (as contained in ECOSOC Resolution 378B (XIII) II) in setting forth that revenue sacrifices for the avoidance of double taxation should be made by capital-exporting countries, and that it was not 'technically wise for capital importing countries to make any concessions on any basis other than for a limited time period'.[113]

The second document concerned US taxation laws applying to private investment in Latin America ('US FPILA Taxation'), written by consultants Surrey and Dan Throop Smith[114] of HLS as part of the Division's FPILA Taxation study. In it, the authors noted that 'little progress' had been made on the treaties that had long been under consideration between the United States and several Latin American countries. The explanation provided was likely because these treaties were less important to the Latin American countries than to the United States since the former did not ordinarily tax foreign income of their residents or corporations and felt that US investors were sufficiently protected by the US FTC provisions.[115] A memorandum of the Division, nevertheless, reveals

[111] Fiscal Commission, *Report on the Technical Assistance Conference on Comparative Fiscal Administration (Geneva 16–25 July 1951)*, 4th sess, UN Doc E/CN.8/67 (also ST/TAA/M/3) (5 December 1952). This was a lengthy document comprising a main report and annexes of recommendations of various UN, World Bank and US technical missions. It would be published in 1955 as *Taxes and Fiscal Policy in Under-Developed Countries* with the TAA as the issuing division.

[112] The only mention of the potential use of DTAs was in relation to their mutual administrative assistance provisions. This had been suggested by the UN mission to Bolivia to help in the tax assessment of foreign corporations: E/CN.8/67, 70.

[113] Ibid 43–4.

[114] Fiscal Commission, *Taxation in Capital-Exporting and Capital-Importing Countries of Foreign Private Investment in Latin America*, 4th sess, UN Doc E/CN.8/69 (5 December 1952). Smith later joined the Treasury Department as Assistant to the Secretary of the Treasury.

[115] Ibid 78.

a further partial reason: the 'dichotomy' between the major capital-exporting countries' steadfast 'position of limiting tax relief to the granting of credit for foreign taxes' and the Latin Americans' own steadfast 'position that total exemption should be granted by the capital-exporting country'.[116]

The Commission's Fourth Session had originally been scheduled for January 1953 but was postponed to April at the United States' request to allow the new Eisenhower Administration to formulate its views on international tax problems.[117]

[116] KE Lachmann, Memorandum on 'Tax Incentives to Foreign Investment in Underdeveloped Countries', undated, 2, attached to Memorandum by Bloch to Owen, 18 June 1952, UNARMS:AG-025-002—S-0441–0468–23888.

[117] Note by Bartelt to Vakil, 30 December 1952, NARAII:RG56–199–6.

10

Related Intervening Developments (May 1951–April 1953)

10.1 Carroll's Pursuit of Double Taxation Issues in IFA

After the Third Session, Carroll would write one of the rare contemporaneous accounts of the Commission for the *Bulletin for International Fiscal Documentation*[1] that censured the developing countries' postures at, and double taxation resolutions which had emanated from, that session. He reported that 'the obstructive attitudes of the underdeveloped countries', aided by 'the general opposition of the Communist representatives', had led to resolutions on general double taxation relief principles and the tax treatment of air transport companies[2] that had worrying implications 'in the field of primary interest to American and European countries engaged in investing or carrying on business abroad'.[3] He stated that, while 'attention had been given to his arguments' concerning 'necessary or justifiable' instances for countries to provide tax incentives, the Commission did not 'modify' its recommendations so as 'not to discourage underdeveloped countries from entering into [DTAs]'.[4] Carroll also described various political aspects of the discussions: India had led the underdeveloped countries' opposition to 'any concessions to foreign airlines'; Pakistan had influenced the recommendation against underdeveloped countries' offer of special tax concessions; and '[t]alks with various representatives of countries which have in the past supplied

[1] Mitchell B Carroll, 'Report on the Meeting of the United Nations Fiscal Commission, Lake Success, May 7–17, 1951' (1951) 5(5) *Bulletin for International Fiscal Documentation* 309 ('3rd Sess Report'). The Bulletin at this time was in its early years of publication, had a practitioner rather than 'scientific' focus and catered predominantly to Western European subscribers as the official journal of IFA with its distribution linked to IFA membership subscriptions: see Willem Dirksen, *IFA: International Fiscal Association, 1938–1988* (Kluwer Law and Taxation, 1988) 43–4, 171–2, 245–6, 253–5.

[2] See Chapter 11, Section 11.7 regarding the latter resolution.

[3] Carroll, '3rd Sess Report', 309.

[4] Ibid 310.

capital indicated resignation to this attitude on the grounds that otherwise no agreements with underdeveloped countries are likely to be possible'.[5] In concluding, he stated that while 'most of the European countries' had 'made concessions to attract foreign capital and enterprise' in their DTAs with the United States, 'they recognized that similar concessions are not to be expected of the so-called underdeveloped countries'.[6] Carroll's account offers some insight that developed countries and private businesses had an unabashed lack of concern for developing countries' development, seeking DTAs thus for the sole purpose of reducing source taxation.[7]

At IFA's 1951 Zurich Congress, Carroll suggested a resolution recommending that the IFA Council appoint a committee to study whether concessions, including for sea and air transport enterprises, might necessarily or justifiably be made by capital-seeking countries.[8] This resolution was adopted, as was another proposal (also by Carroll) to appoint a committee to study DTAs in force between Western European countries with the possibility and desirability of formulating a multilateral convention for the avoidance of multiple, extraterritorial and discriminatory taxation in view of Europe's growing regional integration.

5 Ibid 312. Carroll also briefly mentioned a third line of conflict existing between, on the one hand, the western European countries and, on the other, the United States and British Commonwealth countries, in addition to the lines of conflict existing between the Soviets and Anglo-American group, and between the underdeveloped and capital-supplying countries (at 309). No elaboration of this conflict, however, was provided.

6 Ibid 312.

7 Despite the rarity of 'developing countries without an adequate infrastructure . . . represented within IFA' at this time (Dirksen, *IFA*, 253), such members nevertheless did exist and Carroll appears cognisant of them as he tempers his account by praising the Cuban representative (Perez) for having 'handled very adroitly the problems raised' in his role as Chairman (Carroll, '3rd Sess Report', 312). In Carroll's 1953 account of the Fourth Session, he would again compliment Perez for having 'urged eloquently' for the adoption of the principle of exclusive source country taxation of foreign investment income (a principle that business circles also espoused): Mitchell B Carroll, 'Action on Tax Treatment of Foreign Income at Session of United Nations Fiscal Commission, April 27 to May 8, 1953' (1953) 7(5) *Bulletin for International Fiscal Documentation* 183, 187. These kind references appear attributable to Perez's IFA connection: Perez had become an IFA member in 1947 and would play an important role in the Cuban IFA national branch set up in February 1954, which became the second IFA base in Latin America after Brazil: Dirksen, *IFA*, 105.

8 'Themes and Resolutions of the 1951 IFA Zurich Congress', undated, UNARMS:AG-025-002—S-0441-0054-0001.

At its 1952 Brussels Congress, IFA adopted a resolution that declared 'the special problem' that taxation posed to shipping and airline enterprises based on 'the almost insoluble difficulty of sub-dividing by countries the net profits resulting from their international transport business', and recommended that:

> The taxation of net profits resulting from international transport by sea or by air should be reserved exclusively for the country in which the enterprises is actually domiciled, and no other country should be entitled to participate in such taxation.[9]

10.2 Growing Pressures for Residence Country Exemption of Foreign Source Income

Between 1951 and 1952, there were at least five developments that showed a gathering momentum in the Americas as well as in the UN itself under the Financing Economic Development agenda for capital-exporting countries to exempt the taxation of foreign investment income.

Firstly, in March 1951, the US International Development Advisory Board (IDAB), which comprised a board of prominent private citizens established in September 1950 under Rockefeller's leadership to oversee implementation of Truman's Point Four Program, delivered its report *Partners in Progress* ('Rockefeller Report'). The Report recommended, inter alia, that '*income from foreign sources should be free of United States tax to the extent necessary to stimulate the flow of private capital to underdeveloped areas*', which could be achieved by '*adoption of the principle that business enterprises located abroad should be taxed only in the country where their incomes are earned*'.[10] It further recommended that the United States 'should continue to press for DTAs purposed at eliminating discriminatory taxes levied on United States corporations abroad', and '*that Congress authorize the inclusion in bilateral tax treaties of a provision that income of business establishments of one country located in the other shall be subject to taxation only in the*

[9] IFA, *International Fiscal Association Resolutions Book* (IBFD, 1988) 26.

[10] IDAB, *Partners in Progress: A Report to the President by the International Development Advisory Board* (USGPO, 1951) 79 (emphasis in original). The IDAB considered this necessary to (1) offset high risks of foreign investment; (2) remove competitive disadvantage faced by US foreign companies operating against other foreign companies that were exempt from home country taxation on foreign income; and (3) prevent nullification of the low tax attraction offered by underdeveloped countries.

country where earned'.[11] The IDAB, supported by other important American business interests, considered the development of underdeveloped areas as entirely purposed at keeping up the supply of raw materials for the US rearmament effort, and to this end foreign economic assistance was held to be 'justified only if the quid pro quo is a larger flow of raw materials and extended export markets for United States industry'.[12]

Secondly, in May 1951, a group of experts appointed by the Secretariat[13] delivered a report *Measures for the Economic Development of Under-Developed Countries* (E/1986)[14] which set forth, inter alia, that the flow of private investment to underdeveloped countries was neither sufficient nor were governments of such countries able to borrow much in private capital markets to meet the large-scale capital inflow necessary to accelerate their economic development. The

11 Ibid 81 (emphasis in original). The Report cited eighteen European countries, including Soviet countries, that had concluded DTAs 'for reciprocal exemption from income tax of income from the business establishments of their nationals located in the territory of the other nation'.

12 Herman Olden and Paul Phillips, 'The Point Four Program: Promise or Menace?' (1952) 16(3) *Science and Society* 222, 245. Olden and Phillips concluded that the absence of any mention by these actors of the industrialisation of underdeveloped areas indicates that such was 'not contemplated', and that the Point Four Program was simply 'an attempt to maintain and extend wherever possible the economic and military domination of the colonial areas' (at 245–6).

13 The appointment was made pursuant to *Full Employment*, ESC Res 290 (XI), UN ESCOR, UN Doc E/1849 (31 August 1950, adopted 15 August 1950) and *Mechanization and Unemployment in Under-Developed Countries*, GA Res 408 (V), UN Doc A/RES/408(V) (12 December 1950), which requested the study of national and international measures to reduce unemployment and underemployment in underdeveloped countries. The group met between February and May 1951 and comprised five experts (mostly professors of economics), namely: Nobel Prize winners Ted Schultz (United States) and Arthur Lewis (United Kingdom), with the remaining three from developing countries – Alberto Baltra Cortez (Chile), DR Gadgil (India) and George Hakim (Lebanon).

14 DEA, *Measures for the Economic Development of Under-Developed Countries: Report by a Group of Experts Appointed by the UN Secretary-General*, UN Doc ST/ECA/10 (also E/1986) (UN, 1951). This report contained sixteen major recommendations, many of which dealt with methods of financing economic development, including for the World Bank to begin lending $1 billion annually to underdeveloped nations, and for developed countries to provide sizeable and increasing grants-in-aid to underdeveloped countries and to take action to eliminate the volatile and cyclical fluctuations in primary commodities prices. The report is noted to have given rise to 'in-depth discussion in ECOSOC' and to have 'had a major impact on development thinking at that time': Richard Jolly, Louis Emmerij and Dharam Ghai, *UN Contributions to Development Thinking and Practice* (Indiana University Press, 2004) 60.

report observed that traditional forms of private investment (i.e. private buying of foreign government bonds) had virtually ceased and that almost all private foreign investment then taking place consisted of FDI in undertakings, especially subsidiaries or PEs, that were established and effectively controlled in capital-exporting countries.[15] Around 70 per cent of such FDI had gone into petroleum, with very little occurring outside the oil-bearing countries. The report concluded with regard to taxation that double taxation was one of three obstacles to FDI expansion to underdeveloped countries,[16] and that such countries would derive 'more taxes from foreign enterprises, if the governments of the capital exporting countries would universally adopt arrangements for exempting foreign earned income from double taxation' (Recommendation 11(c)).[17]

The report was considered at ECOSOC's Thirteenth Session (the same session that considered the Fiscal Commission's report of its Third Session).[18] In the Economic Committee, Chile, Pakistan and India were among several other countries which favoured all the recommendations of the report;[19] however, Recommendation 11(c), among others, did not make it into the Committee's draft resolution. Instead, the draft resolution reversed the onus as to which country-type bore responsibility for improving FDI flows by calling on capital-exporting countries to simply undertake measures such as negotiating DTAs and providing tax credits, while recommending that capital-importing countries '[u]ndertake through legislative or administrative measures and the negotiation of tax treaties, to eliminate discriminatory taxation of foreign enterprises and to resolve issues of taxability arising from various types of income taxes, varying concepts of taxable net income and overlapping concepts of source of income'.[20] Such drafting suggests US and/or UK authorship.

15 E/1986, 80–2.

16 The other two were restrictions placed by underdeveloped countries due to fear of foreign control and fear by investors of arbitrary acts by underdeveloped country governments.

17 E/1986, 38. The report also noted that there were foreign companies in underdeveloped countries that were making and exporting exorbitant profits, most frequently because the local government had, whether through ignorance, corruption or external political pressure, signed away some national resource or monopoly without demanding adequate royalty or rental in return. This remark corroborates the findings in Sundelson's Report.

18 'Economic Development of Under-Developed Countries' [1951] *Yearbook of the United Nations* 376, 381–2.

19 Ibid 382.

20 Economic Committee, *Economic Development of Under-Developed Countries: Report of the Economic Committee*, UN ESC, 13th sess, Agenda item 4, UN Doc E/2061 (28 July 1951) 3–4.

Upon further debate by ECOSOC in plenary, these paragraphs were truncated by Britain and France's joint amendments that removed the references to tax credits and their related definitional issues.[21] The relevant resolution was adopted as Resolution 368B (XIII).[22]

Thirdly, at ECLA's Fourth Session in June 1951,[23] ECLA adopted Resolution 3 (IV) on financing economic development,[24] which, inter alia, recognised that Latin American countries regarded 'the suppression of double taxation' through exclusive source taxation of income earned within the country as 'one of the most effective incentives' enabling 'adequate expansion' of FDI flows to the region, but that 'some other countries' considered a system of tax credits, combined with a DTA programme, 'to be a flexible and effective weapon' for eliminating double taxation and tax deterrents to free FDI flows, 'while preserving the equity of the separate tax systems'.[25] The resolution recommended that the UN Secretariat study the influence that capital-exporting countries' fiscal systems had on private investors in making foreign investment decisions. It also recommended that ECOSOC consider adopting resolutions that established certain formulae for eliminating double taxation which paid 'special attention to creating fiscal incentives' for FDI in underdeveloped countries. When Resolution 3 (IV) was distributed at the UN headquarters, the Fiscal Division was annoyed that the passages 'not only fail[ed]

[21] *France and United Kingdom: Amendments to Draft Resolution Contained in the Report of the Economic Committee (E/2061)*, UN ESC, 13th sess, Agenda item 4(a), UN Doc E/L.219 (21 August 1951). Pakistan unsuccessfully attempted to amend the paragraph applying to capital-importing countries to include a reference that the elimination of discriminatory taxation in DTAs be based on the Fiscal Commission's recommendations: *Pakistan: Amendments to the Draft Resolution Contained in the Report of the Economic Committee (E/2061) and the Uruguay and US Amendments (E/L.207) to that Draft Resolution*, UN ESC, 13th sess, Agenda item 4(a), UN Doc E/L.210 (17 August 1951).

[22] *With the Object of Achieving an Expansion and Steadier Flow of Private Foreign Capital*, ESC Res 368B (XIII), UN ESCOR, UN Doc 2152 (10 October 1951, adopted 22 August 1951). The relevant paragraphs of this resolution are reproduced in Appendix G.

[23] At this time, ECLA had just been confirmed as a permanent regional commission and was expanding and strengthening its Secretariat's scope beyond producing mere research reports into practical activities and concrete policy work: Edgar J Dosman, *The Life and Times of Raúl Prebisch, 1901–1986* (McGill-Queen's University Press, 2008) 271. Dosman notes that US sentiment against the UN and ECLA was now 'hardening' but that ECOSOC was 'a consistent source of support' to ECLA (at 289).

[24] *Financing of Economic Development*, Resolution approved 16 June 1951, UN ECLA, 4th sess, Agenda Item 5, UN Doc E/CN.12/272 (16 June 1951). This resolution was reproduced as Resolution 3 (IV) in Economic Commission for Latin America, *Annual Report*, 4th sess, UN Doc E/2021 (15 June 1951) 73–8.

[25] Ibid 74.

to refer to the action in this field taken by the Fiscal Commission, but also to the work of the Fiscal Division, on which such action was based'.[26]

Fourthly, at ECOSOC's Fourteenth Session (June–July 1952),[27] ECOSOC adopted Resolution 416D (XIV), which recognised that DTAs and unilateral relief measures had not positively encouraged FDI from highly developed countries to underdeveloped countries. The resolution requested the Fiscal Commission, in its consideration of taxation problems relating to foreign investments, to examine the principle of exclusive source-country taxation of income from foreign investments in underdeveloped countries, with corresponding residence-country exemption of taxation of foreign-source income by capital-exporting countries (hereinafter 'SoCtyTax/ResCtyExempt(FoInvInc)') for recognition in DTAs and unilateral measures.[28] This resolution had originated with Cuba's submission of a draft resolution (L.365) that more forcefully asserted for this principle to be adopted 'as one of the most effective means' of increasing FDI to underdeveloped countries, to be transformed 'rapidly into a practical reality' through 'necessary unilateral legislative action' and to be recognised in DTAs concluded by highly developed countries with underdeveloped countries.[29] Cuba supported L.365 with lengthy arguments, citing authorities such as the Rockefeller Report and ECLA Resolution 3 (IV). Its arguments included that the avoidance of double taxation merely created a condition of tax neutrality without providing positive incentives to financiers of foreign investments, who would naturally be discouraged by the risks involved with exporting capital. Also, while the SoCtyTax/ResCtyExempt(FoInvInc) principle may have been prejudicial to underdeveloped countries 'in earlier days' in enabling large companies to exert pressure to obtain preferential tax treatment, such fears were 'no longer valid' as capital-importing

[26] Memorandum by Lachmann to Caustin, 29 October 1951, UNARMS:AG-025-002—S-0441-0463-23403. See also Memorandum by Malinowski to Lachmann, 8 November 1951, UNARMS:AG-025-002—S-0441-0463-23403.

[27] The relevant debates took place in the 610th, 613th–615th and 626th–627th plenary meetings. Unless otherwise stated, the material regarding these discussions have been drawn from the following ECOSOC *Summary Records*: UN ESCOR, UN Docs E/SR.610 (18 June 1952), E/SR.613–615 (20–23 June 1952), E/SR.626–627 (1 July 1952).

[28] *Fiscal Incentives to Increase the International Flow of Private Capital for the Economic Development of Under-Developed Countries*, ESC Res 416D (XIV), UN ESCOR, UN Doc 2332 (13 August 1952, adopted 1 July 1952). This resolution is reproduced in Appendix H.

[29] *Cuba: Draft Resolution*, UN ESC, 14th sess, Agenda item 5(b), UN Docs E/L.365 and Rev.1 (16 June 1952).

countries had learnt 'hard lessons' that offering such treatment 'endangered' their economic development and sovereignty.[30]

L.365 was met with unanimous opposition from the developed countries (especially Belgium, France, the United Kingdom and the United States) as well as China.[31] Iran also observed that foreign capital 'made investments only in branches of industry that promised very rich profits' and was neither concerned about nor contributed to the balanced development of underdeveloped countries.[32] The United States, '[a]s a tactical measure', suggested referring the proposal to the Fiscal Commission and for its joint study by the Fiscal Division and ECLA Secretariat.[33] Cuba sought the advice of the Division, which pointed out that various ECOSOC resolutions had so far failed to adopt the position and that it would be difficult to persuade the major capital-exporting countries to relinquish their traditional claim to tax foreign income.[34] The Division also emphasised that the Secretariat's FPILA Taxation study would demonstrate how the tax systems of the capital-exporting and capital-importing countries could be 'more effectively adjusted towards each other' to reduce the effective tax burden on foreign investors, such 'development of intermediate solutions' having 'the greatest chance of [gaining acceptance by both groups of countries and] being implemented for the better promotion of foreign investment'.[35] Cuba resultingly formulated a substitute resolution.[36] Meanwhile, the United States had drafted alternations to L.365 that it thought would 'be acceptable to the Cubans and others'.[37] This new text would essentially form the substance of Resolution 416D (XIV).[38] Britain considered that the new resolution

[30] E/SR.626, 441. This acknowledgement would appear to be an about-face of Cuba's refutation during the Fiscal Commission's Second Session of the tax bargaining practices referenced in Sundelson's Report.

[31] Memorandum by Lachmann to Bloch, 31 October 1952, UNARMS:AG-025-002—S-0441-0468-23889(B).

[32] E/SR.615 (23 June 1952) 348.

[33] Memorandum by Gordon to Bartelt, 20 June 1952, NARAII:RG56-199-4.

[34] Memorandum by Bloch to Owen, 18 June 1952, and attached memorandum by KE Lachmann on 'Tax Incentives to Foreign Investment in Underdeveloped Countries', undated, 2–5, UNARMS:AG-025-002—S-0441-0468-23888; Lachmann memo, 31 October 1952.

[35] Lachmann, 'Tax Incentives', 3, 5.

[36] Memorandum by Bloch to Owen, 20 June 1952, UNARMS:AG-025-002—S-0441-0468-23888; Lachmann memo, 31 October 1952.

[37] Telegram No 403 from New York (UK Delegation to UN) to Foreign Office, 23 June 1952, TNA:IR40/11173(2).

[38] See Telegram No 404 from New York (UK Delegation to UN) to Foreign Office, 23 June 1952, TNA:IR40/11173(2).

would 'do no harm' as it did 'no more than instruct the Fiscal Commission to make certain enquiries without prejudging their outcome'.[39] This was preferable to 'a full debate on the substance of the question and possibly the passage of a hostile resolution'.[40] Also, an 'enquiry by the Fiscal Commission could have a certain educational value'.[41] Britain nevertheless insisted on a textual change to ensure that the statement regarding the insufficiency of DTAs and unilateral relief measures in encouraging FDI read as 'a mere statement of fact rather than an implication that more incentive should be given than the mere removal of deterrents through double taxation agreements'.[42] This new text was incorporated by Cuba in a compromise draft joint resolution (L.383), which it submitted jointly with Iran and the Philippines.[43]

Lengthy discussions followed in which Belgium, Canada, China, France, Iran, Sweden, the United Kingdom and the United States indicated their preparedness to support L.383. Notably, France stated that its own problems of reconstruction, investment and equipment, as well as its concern for capital flight and the consequent aggravation of inflationary trends meant that 'it could only associate itself very cautiously with measures . . . which tended to provide too great a facility for the investment of French capital in foreign countries'.[44] France considered that the Fiscal Commission's Resolution B-II (of its Third Session) accurately balanced 'the legitimate aspirations of underdeveloped countries and the assistance which France could reasonably contribute at the present time' while noting that the exemption proposal went too far.[45] Sweden considered it premature to take an immediate stance on the issue before the Commission, as the competent body, had studied the draft. Britain cautioned that a proposal requiring capital-exporting countries to relinquish all claims to foreign-sourced income would not necessarily increase outward FDI but would give old investments an arbitrary advantage, entailing a considerable loss of revenue to capital-exporting countries and a discriminatory tax system with rates varying from country to country. Belgium considered that the exemption proposal

39 UK Delegation, Telegram No 403.
40 Ibid.
41 Ibid.
42 Ibid.
43 *Cuba, Iran and the Philippines: Joint Draft Resolution*, UN ESC, 14th sess, Agenda item 5, UN Docs E/L.383 and Corr.1 (26 June 1952).
44 E/SR.626, 441.
45 Ibid.

effectively required capital-exporting countries to penalise capital invested in their own countries or in their overseas territories. France and Belgium also considered that the proposal would encourage the extension of a system of lower tax rates by underdeveloped countries to attract capital which would jeopardise the financial and social structure of those countries. After minor revision, L.383 was eventually adopted as Resolution 416D (XIV) by a vote of fifteen votes to none, with three abstentions by the Soviet members.

The Division's records indicate that it played a mediating role between the United States and Cuba, but the Division evidently also had its own agenda: Bloch reported to Owen that '[t]here is thus good reason to expect that this entire matter will result principally in a renewed endorsement of our current studies in the field'.[46] The raising of international tax relations under this agenda item in ECOSOC had nevertheless been unexpected by the Division, and Bloch remained concerned that it might 'again be raised formally' before 'the Commission has had a chance to discuss it on the basis of our studies'.[47] The developed countries themselves also appeared to have been taken by surprise: the British delegation would report to the Foreign Office that '[i]nvesting countries were . . . coming to understand that they could not exploit or put pressure on weaker countries'.[48]

Fifthly, in November 1952, the IACCP adopted a resolution at its meeting in Lima, Peru, recommending that governments of American nations negotiate treaties for the elimination of double, extraterritorial and discriminatory taxation, and accept the principle that business profits should be subject to taxation only in the countries where earned.[49]

10.3 US Foreign Development Policy

In 1952, as the Cold War deepened, the United States expanded its economic aid to Asia as part of its communist containment strategy; Latin America's share of development aid from Washington now fell to

46 Bloch memo, 20 June 1952.

47 Memorandum by Bloch to Blough, 3 November 1952, UNARMS:AG-025-002—S-0441-0468-23889(B).

48 Telegram No 180 from New York (UK Delegation to UN) to Foreign Office, 4 July 1952, TNA:IR40/11173(2).

49 *Memorandum by the Secretary-General on Action Taken to Stimulate the International Flow of Private Capital*, UN ESC, 17th sess, Agenda item 3(c), UN Doc E/2546 (19 February 1954).

1 per cent with the Truman Administration becoming increasingly uninterested in Latin America.[50] That being said, at least in late October 1951, the United States was still 'endeavor[ing] to encourage healthy bilateral economic relations with Argentina' to improve 'overall relations' and to 'maintain a practical friendly situation in the economic field which will serve to mitigate periods of strain in other fields for the sake of hemisphere security'.[51] Despite growing rapprochement between the two countries, the United States was 'holding up action on the double taxation treaty'.[52] Argentina incidentally had 'its heart set on' being elected as an ECOSOC member, and the United States was hopeful that this campaign would cause the former to 'deviate from its usual aloofness from multilateral economic cooperation'.[53]

In January 1953, Eisenhower became President, and his Administration would institute a more conservative ideology that supported increased military use, budgetary restraint and the phasing out of the development aid programme, thus leaving economic assistance to developing countries

[50] Dosman, *Prebisch*, 274. See also James M Hagen and Vernon W Ruttan, 'Development Policy under Eisenhower and Kennedy' (1988) 23(1) *The Journal of Developing Areas* 1, 3.

[51] 'Policy Statement Prepared in the Department of State', 26 October 1951, in State Department, *Foreign Relations of the United States, 1951* (USGPO, 1979) vol 2: The United Nations; The Western Hemisphere, Doc 680. The second goal was considered 'especially significant at this time' as 'solidarity among the world's anti-communist forces is sorely needed'. Part of the US 'tactics' to 'obtain Argentine economic collaboration in the present emergency' was 'making representations On [sic] behalf of US business', including by 'emphasizing the damage which Argentina does to its credit by pursuing nationalistic economic policies which discourage new capital from entering the country and cause foreign enterprise now in the country to operate on a frightened wait-and-see basis'.

[52] Ibid. See Chapter 11, Section 11.10, n 302 for further details regarding the extent of US–Argentina economic relations and cooperation at this time.

[53] State Department, 'Policy Statement', 26 October 1951. The State Department indicated that '[d]uring the period that we continue to employ correct tactics toward Argentina, we shall not urge it to cooperate with our objectives in international economic bodies'. These tactics included being 'friendly to the Argentines at international meetings, . . . and vot[ing] for their candidates when they are the obvious choice of those voting or of the Latin American caucus'. The United States was moreover so pleased with Argentina's support of the United States on questions concerning China's seat in the UN and specialised agencies, and its declaration of the PRC as 'an aggressor' that, in one instance, the State Department 'instructed our [its] Embassy in Buenos Aires formally to express our appreciation'.

Argentina would in fact be elected to ECOSOC beginning in January 1952 ('Functions and Membership of the Principal and Subsidiary Organs' [1952] *Yearbook of the United Nations* 29, 36) and would be a leading voice among the developing countries in asserting for radical source taxing rights in ECOSOC's deliberations over the Fiscal Commission's 1953 resolution concerning double taxation: see Chapter 12, Section 12.3.

to the sphere of private enterprise.[54] Eisenhower had also made election promises to improving US–Latin American relations under a 'Good Partner' approach.[55] In his State of the Union message in February 1953, Eisenhower stated that his foreign economic policy was '[d]oing whatever our government properly can do to encourage private American investment abroad', with 'a serious and explicit purpose' being to encourage 'a hospitable climate for such investment' in foreign nations.[56] The IDAB and State Department assumed that Eisenhower mainly envisioned those of 'the so-called underdeveloped nations of Asia, Africa and Latin America' which had the 'greatest' need of capital, 'richest' opportunities for new enterprise and 'most acute' problem of an 'unfriendly "climate"' then widespread in the developing world, which the United States attributed to 'unreasonable fears or to misunderstanding of our aims and methods'.[57] The IDAB and State Department proposed 'to try to put the thinking of those countries right' by sending special representatives to, inter alia, promote 'our conviction that American capital can make a material and constructive contribution . . . to economic progress in other countries'; 'explain how normal it is, under our system, for private enterprise to participate in the execution of public policy'; and 'emphasize our certainty that our self-interests and the self-interests of all nations in the free world are, in the long run, synonymous'.[58] In private communications with UK officials, the US officials 'hinted that the new administration might well be more liberal than the old towards investors in Latin America'.[59]

The power of the US private sector at this time cannot be overestimated. The spreading Cold War was providing a boon to the US economy with 'the country enjoy[ing] prosperity and international power on a scale not seen in recent memory, and arguably never before seen in human history'.[60] Following the Military Keynesianism of NSC-68,[61] tax

54 Hagen and Ruttan, 'Development Policy', 4.

55 Dosman, *Prebisch*, 285–6.

56 Eric Johnston, 'Proposal Regarding Investment Climate in Underdeveloped Countries', undated, 1, NARAII:RG56-199-6.

57 Ibid 1, 4.

58 Ibid 4, 3.

59 Letter from New York (UK Delegation to UN) to Foreign Office, 2 January 1953, TNA:IR40/11173(2).

60 Jeffrey A Engel, *Cold War at 30,000 Feet: The Anglo-American Fight for Aviation Supremacy* (Harvard University Press, 2007) 128.

61 The NSC-68 (US National Security Council paper 68) was a policy directive carried out beginning in July 1950 that engendered a massive rearmament programme to deal with the Soviet threat and the international balance of payments problem posed by the dollar gap: see Daniel R Fusfeld, 'Economics and the Cold War: An Inquiry into the Relationship

cuts, investment incentives and threefold increase in military spending at consistently high levels of $40–$50 billion annually were spawning 'an interlinked grouping of major businesses that catered extensively and for the most part profitably to the needs of the defense community, and so had vested interests in maintaining a massive military sector'.[62] The Third World represented an important cog in the wheel for its role in the stockpiling of strategic raw materials, in the resumption of triangular trade,[63] and as areas for private investment expansion and potential markets for Western manufactures.[64]

10.4 Soviet Aid and Trade Relations with the Third World

Stalin's death in March 1953 'prompted a fundamental reassessment of Soviet diplomacy and the place of the global South in it',[65] resulting in a breakaway from a European orientation towards friendlier and active

between Ideology and Theory' (1998) 32(2) *Journal of Economic Issues* 505, 505–7; Curt Cardwell, *NSC 68 and the Political Economy of the Early Cold War* (Cambridge University Press, 2011).

62 Priscilla May Roberts (ed), *The Cold War: Interpreting Conflict through Primary Documents* (ABC-CLIO, 2019) vol 1: 1917–1957, 332. The links between the military and business were so strong, and the interconnected network of business and government institutions so vast, as was the US economy's reliance on military expenditures, that Eisenhower, upon leaving office in 1961, would caution the nation against the influence of this interest group which he termed the 'military-industrial complex': see Cardwell, *NSC 68*, 21; 'President Dwight D Eisenhower's Farewell Address (1961)', *The National Archives* (Web Page, 26 September 2022) <www.archives.gov/milestone-documents/president-dwight-d-eisenhowers-farewell-address>.

63 Triangular trade was the pattern of trade used in the prewar period 'whereby Europe's colonies and protectorates sold raw materials to the United States and then spent the dollars they earned in Europe for manufactures, thus providing Europe dollars to spend in the United States': Cardwell, *NSC 68*, 119.

64 Ibid 114–20. US officials and other elites nevertheless noted that American corporations were disinclined to build factories in underdeveloped countries, except where related to the oil industry. Turning such countries into steady consumers of European products manufactured from commodities bought from those countries moreover required a long investment period and 'was dependent on "induc[ing] under-developed areas of the world to forego plans for industrialization and self-sufficiency and rather expand exports to Europe in two-way mutually advantageous trade"' (at 116, quoting a 19 May 1950 document from the Gordon Gray Papers at the Truman Library that commented on a memorandum of the US Economic Cooperation Administration entitled 'The Way Out for Europe: A Projection of World-Wide Trade and Payments Adjustments to Declining Marshall Plan Aid').

65 Mark Philip Bradley, 'Decolonization, the Global South, and the Cold War, 1919–1962' in Melvyn P Leffler and Odd Arne Westad (eds), *The Cambridge History of the Cold War* (Cambridge University Press, 2010) vol 1: Origins, 464, 475.

policy with the new Asian-Arab nations to foster 'closer cooperation against "imperialism and colonialism"' and prevent these nations from joining 'the comprehensive alliance systems the United States was in the process of building up'.[66] Moreover, the superpower was also now in a stronger material position to use economic assistance and trade as global policy instruments: it had completed its own reconstruction, strengthened its military power and was enjoying high production levels for 'almost all types of goods'.[67] The USSR would begin to contribute to UN technical assistance programmes, conclude trade treaties with under-developed countries and supply financial aid to Afghanistan, Egypt, India, Indonesia and Syria.[68]

10.5 Britain's External Economic Relations

By 1952, Britain's finances were in a very parlous state despite years of Marshall Plan aid. The dollar gap, foreign trade deficit and rationing of certain foodstuffs and industrial materials continued; housing costs were four times that in 1939; the country had yet to reach the economic equilibrium necessary to ease its dependence on American aid; and the extraordinary assistance received under the European Recovery Program was set to end in June 1952.[69] Britain moreover faced 'the skyrocketing cost of maintaining a top spot in Washington's hierarchy of allies' in view of its 'full-fledged commitment to the global anticommunist fight',[70] which 'divert[ed] resources from exports and investment, to the detriment of the balance of payments and the efficiency of the

66 Geir Lundestad, *East, West, North, South: International Relations since 1945* (Sage, 7th ed, 2014) 59.

67 Ibid.

68 Joan E Spero and Jeffrey A Hart, *The Politics of International Economic Relations* (Routledge, 5th ed, 1997) 169.

69 Engel, *Aviation Supremacy*, 113, 126.

70 Ibid 127. This included Britain's rearmament programme prompted by the Korean War and its 'far-flung burdens' of patrolling areas in Germany, Trieste, Hong Kong, the Middle East, Indian Ocean and Mediterranean, and just off China. Although these overseas commitments were 'fundamental elements' to preserving Britain's 'claim to great-power status', they 'were also assumed in no small part so as to remain in Washington's good graces as a peerless ally' which was 'vital to Britain's chance at eventual economic revitalization'. By 1951, Britain's military expenses had increased to 18 per cent of Gross National Product from 6.5 per cent in 1949, and total foreign debt was anticipated to exceed $2.1 billion by 1952 (at 125–7). Prime Minister Churchill, back in power after winning the election in October 1951, would travel to Washington in January 1952 to not only seek further aid but also to reduce Britain's 'global military presence' (at 128).

economy'.[71] In its relations with the Third World, mushrooming nationalisation and independence crises in vital British-controlled, commodity-producing regions which earned scarce dollars for the sterling area[72] further beckoned Britain's financial ruin, impaired its prestige and expended its resources.[73]

By late 1952, however, Britain's economic woes had eased due to the commodity boom induced by European reconstruction, Marshall Aid and the Korean War; increasing exports in a growing world economy;[74] and American private investment flows.[75] Multilateralists in the British government and Bank of England had moreover regained their influence following Churchill's election victory,[76] and the UK Treasury and the Bank set their sights on attaining full convertibility with the dollar and on liberalising trade with the aim of re-establishing London as a global financial centre.[77] These plans involved a reconsideration of the integrated sterling area economic development that had been instituted in the late 1940s when Britain sought 'a close association with the empire in

[71] GC Peden, 'Suez and Britain's Decline as a World Power' (2012) 55(4) *The Historical Journal* 1073, 1075.

[72] The sterling area, formed in 1939, was a currency bloc made up of countries of, or closely associated with, the Commonwealth which pegged their currencies to the sterling, thus requiring any country trading with Britain to only spend its sterling earnings in Britain or other countries within the bloc. After 1945, the area 'was more tightly controlled[,] ... discriminated against trade with "hard currency" areas, particularly the United States, and became largely a device for dollar earning': Nicholas J White, *Decolonisation: The British Experience since 1945* (Routledge, 2nd ed, 2014) 13.

[73] These confrontations included Iran's nationalisation of the British-owned Anglo-Iranian Oil Company; Egypt's denouncement of the 1936 Anglo-Egyptian Treaty that granted Britain a twenty-year lease on the Suez Canal, leading Britain to send its entire strategic reserve to the Canal zone; and colonial wars in Malaya and Kenya, where use of force was employed to retain British presence, particularly in mines and estates: see Anthony Adamthwaite, 'Overstretched and Overstrung: Eden, the Foreign Office and the Making of Policy, 1951–5' (1988) 64(2) *International Affairs* 241, 242–3; PJ Cain and AG Hopkins, *British Imperialism: 1688–2015* (Routledge, 3rd ed, 2016) 671; Nico Schrijver, *Sovereignty Over National Resources: Balancing Rights and Duties* (Cambridge University Press, 1997) 41–2; White, *Decolonisation*, 38–9.

[74] Britain had also just produced the world's first commercial jet airliner, which greatly promised to change Britain's fortunes in 'revolutioniz[ing] air travel and monopoliz[ing] aircraft markets for years to come': Engel, *Aviation Supremacy*, 125. See further Chapter 11, Section 11.1.2 (regarding the importance of the aviation industry to the British economy and great power status).

[75] Cain and Hopkins, *British Imperialism*, 668, 672.

[76] Gerold Krozewski, *Money and the End of Empire: British International Economic Policy and the Colonies, 1947–58* (Palgrave, 2001) 71.

[77] Cain and Hopkins, *British Imperialism*, 668–9; Peden, 'Suez', 1084.

discriminatory economic policies' designed to maintain the value of the pound and prevent leakages of the dollar.[78] Such policies had included import and exchange restrictions, higher taxation in the colonies, dollar-pooling arrangements, as well as colonial economic development funded by free capital flows from the metropole, loans raised on the London money market, British private investment, local revenues and the use of colonial currency reserves.[79]

The development of colonies in particular had not only been directed at boosting commodity production for dollar earning and dollar substitution, as well as providing secure markets for British manufactures,[80] but had enabled London to control expenditures from the colonies' sizeable sterling accounts to keep these balances at high levels to avert inflationary pressures.[81] By 1953, however, these initiatives were finding less support for not having delivered 'the much hoped for magical, "multiplier effect" for the metropolitan economy'.[82] The new Churchill Administration moreover believed that Britain's financial autonomy and future hinged on mastering high-technology exports and its ability to sell them.[83] As the thrust of British foreign policy turned towards trade with North America and Europe, Treasury and the Bank viewed accumulated colonial sterling holdings as deferred claims on British resources and sought to reduce them to increase confidence in sterling by promoting colonial self-financing.[84] The export of capital to the colonies was further considered to divert funds from domestic export industries, hence contributing to Britain's uncompetitiveness.[85] Consequently, development financing and private sector investment subsequently ceased and colonial loans floated on the London market were shunned.[86] In addition, restraints were imposed on the portion of currency reserves colonies could use for local investment, restrictions governing colonial

[78] Krozewski, *Money*, 61.

[79] Ibid 64–6, 70; Allister E Hinds, 'Imperial Policy and Colonial Sterling Balances, 1943–56' (1991) 19(1) *The Journal of Imperial and Commonwealth History* 24, 32.

[80] White, *Decolonisation*, 14–17 (noting that 'Treasury's penchant for maximum primary production for export to the dollar area and the Board of Trade's desire to uphold markets for metropolitan manufactures in the colonies ... meant a return to a reliance on the private sector and the chief engine of economic growth (albeit in partnership with the colonial state)' (at 16–17)).

[81] Krozewski, *Money*, 71; Cain and Hopkins, *British Imperialism*, 671.

[82] White, *Decolonisation*, 34. See also Krozewski, *Money*, 66.

[83] Engel, *Aviation Supremacy*, 130.

[84] Peden, 'Suez', 1084; Krozewski, *Money*, 71, 109.

[85] White, *Decolonisation*, 35.

[86] Ibid. See also Krozewski, *Money*, 117.

expenditure in the dollar area were not relaxed and deferring the independence of certain colonies was also contemplated to prevent the rapid withdrawal of sterling balances that could threaten the stability of the British economy.[87] These policies perpetuated the development struggles of colonies, many of which now faced inflationary conditions from the prolonged shortage of goods fostered under the sterling area system where they had not been permitted to liquidate their export earnings to purchase dollar imports,[88] nor had British manufacturing capacity been able to meet such requirements.[89] From 1953, the imperial economy would be progressively marginalised and the Empire dismantled with the shifting of Britain's strategic interests.[90]

[87] Hinds, 'Imperial Policy', 36–40.

[88] Hard currency earned from such colonial exports had in fact been bought by Britain, which would in turn credit the colonial sterling balances and issue the colonies with an allocation of sterling: White, *Decolonisation*, 13.

[89] Ibid 14.

[90] This shift correlates not only with Britain's conclusion of DTAs with North America and Europe from this time onwards in contrast to its preceding focus on negotiating such treaties with its Empire-Commonwealth since World War II (see DESA, *International Tax Agreements*, UN Doc ST/ECA/SER.C/8, Suppl 3 (1968) vol 8: World Guide to International Tax Agreements, Country Table: United Kingdom, 9–27), but also its removal of its limited unilateral foreign tax credit instituted in 1950 under which relief up to 50 per cent of the UK rate had been provided for foreign taxes paid, with a more generous allowance for 75 per cent in the case of taxes paid to Commonwealth countries (Peter Andrew Harris, *Corporate/Shareholder Income Taxation and Allocating Taxing Rights between Countries: A Comparison of Imputation Systems* (IBFD, 1996) 308).

11

The Taxation of International Air Transport and Contending with ICAO (1947–1951)

This chapter narrates the jurisdictional conflict that transpired between the UN and ICAO over the taxation of income of international air transport, and the former's vehement opposition to the latter's sponsorship of the reciprocal exemption principle.[1] Section 11.1 provides the background and context in outlining the League's development of this income item, the postwar global aviation landscape as dominated by the United States and ICAO's relevant institutional and decision-making framework. Sections 11.2–11.9 detail the events generated by the clash of competencies between the two organisations, their opposing policy positions, their supposed collaboration through a jointly funded study by an expert and the political machinations that eventually saw ICAO undermine the Fiscal Division and Fiscal Commission to advance an agenda inimical to developing countries. Section 11.10 concludes with a brief commentary.

11.1 Background and Context

11.1.1 The Development of the Tax Treatment of International Air Transport under the League

The history of the tax treatment of air navigation is inextricably linked to the taxation of shipping income and has been well addressed by the literature.[2] Briefly, while the taxation of profits of shipping companies

1 While ICAO addressed a range of direct and indirect taxes connected to international aviation during this period, this chapter focuses on double taxation of income of international airlines as this was the chief issue of concern for the Division and the issue that came before the Commission for final debate.

2 Guglielmo Maisto, 'The History of Article 8 of the OECD Model Treaty on Taxation of Shipping and Air Transport' (2003) 31(6/7) *Intertax* 232; Jacques Sasseville, 'Historical Background of Proposed Changes to Articles 8 and 15(3) OECD Model' in Guglielmo Maisto (ed), *Taxation of Shipping and Air Transport in Domestic Law, EU*

was studied and discussed under the auspices of the League from the time of the 1923 Economists' Report until the Sub-Committee's 1940 Hague draft convention, no special study had ever been undertaken on double taxation of air navigation. Rather, income from air navigation first received mention in the three 1928 draft bilateral conventions where it was categorised alongside maritime shipping income.[3] The view expressed in the 1928 drafts was for such income to be exclusively taxed by the state of real centre of management and the provision was couched as an exception to the general principle governing business profits. This exemption position, however, was by no means unanimous. While the League's studies on shipping income up until 1927 preferred the principle of exclusive domicile (or real centre of management) taxation on the grounds of expediency, no affirmative position was ever expressed due to the concern that countries without domestic shipping industries would not relinquish revenue sharing.[4] Furthermore, acknowledgement was made on the need for reciprocity as well as the need for valid application of the exemption principle through bilateral conventions in recognition of the right of source countries (i.e. countries of operation of the vessel) to tax companies that had significant presence in their territories. Disagreement on the conflict of interest between residence and source states was still rife in the meetings leading up to the 1928 outcome.[5] Similar tentativeness was also displayed in the views of industry: in 1923, the Taxation Committee of the International Shipping Conference endorsed the exclusive residence taxation principle, but in 1926, the Conference took the view that such taxation had to be dealt with within the context of a more comprehensive tax treaty to provide counter-benefits to the source country.[6] In practice, the reciprocal exemption principle had been adopted by the United States, the United Kingdom, Japan and many European countries in unilateral relief measures, a number of limited scope treaties and a handful of general bilateral

Law and Tax Treaties (IBFD, 2017) 73; Sunita Jogarajan, *Double Taxation and the League of Nations* (Cambridge University Press, 2018) 221–2.

[3] Maisto, 'History of Article 8', 238–9; General Meeting of Government Experts on Double Taxation and Tax Evasion, *Double Taxation and Tax Evasion: Report*, League Doc C.562. M.178.1928.II (October 1928) 8 (Draft 1a, Article 5), 12 (Draft 1b, Article 5), 16 (Draft 1c, Article 2). For the limited discussion regarding this income item that took place among only a handful of the participants at the 1928 meeting of technical experts with industry bodies having a major say, see Jogarajan, *Double Taxation*, 221–2.

[4] Maisto, 'History of Article 8', 235–8; Jogarajan, *Double Taxation*, 41–7, 82.

[5] Maisto, 'History of Article 8', 239; Jogarajan, *Double Taxation*, 144–7, 216–21.

[6] Maisto, 'History of Article 8', 236–7.

treaties, although apportionment was provided for in one treaty.[7] While the 1928 drafts were influential on treaties subsequently concluded and the exemption principle was applied in some commercial treaties, countries such as Australia and South Africa continued to assert source taxing powers, including through the use of apportionment.[8]

In his 1933 study on the *Methods of Allocating Taxable Income*, Carroll claimed that 'the problem of allocation has been almost completely eliminated in the case of sea transport companies because of the almost universal adoption of the [exemption] principle'.[9] In the 1935 draft convention that considered the allocation of profit of special classes of international enterprises, income from shipping and air transport was segregated from the business profits article and dealt with in a separate provision.[10] The Fiscal Committee (which included Carroll) explained the change as being primarily driven by the tendency of the principle of taxing maritime and air navigation enterprises at the place of real centre of management 'to become more and more general as a result of the bilateral treaties concluded'.[11] Wording changes were subsequently introduced in the Hague, Mexico and London drafts (in all of which Carroll played an influencing role); however, in essence, the residence principle (whether determined by place of incorporation, registration of the aircraft or real centre of management) still applied.[12]

In short, the treatment of air transportation profits had simply been decided in 1928 by appending the subject to the determination made for shipping profits. Despite the conflict between source and residence countries that still existed then over shipping income, the exemption principle was never seriously re-examined again by an international forum of experts akin to that of the 1926–7 meetings of technical experts. This is not surprising given the collapse of international diplomacy in the 1930s, the mostly European and developed-country/colonial-power composition of the Fiscal Committee and the relatively early stage of commercial air transport in developing countries. Moreover, Carroll's 1933 definitive statement of the exemption principle as a League

[7] Ibid 232–4.

[8] Ibid 239.

[9] Mitchell B Carroll, *Taxation of Foreign and National Enterprises* (League of Nations, 1933) vol 4: Methods of Allocating Taxable Income, 147 et seq.

[10] Maisto, 'History of Article 8', 241.

[11] Fiscal Committee, *Report to the Council on the Fifth Session of the Committee*, League Doc C.252.M.124.1935.II.A (17 June 1935) annex I, 3.

[12] Maisto, 'History of Article 8', 242–3.

Secretariat expert and his key involvement in the drafts produced between 1935 and 1946 likely played an influential role in overshadowing the consideration of alternative approaches as well as the views and practices of various source countries.[13] While the principle's solidification in the London Model was expected given the developed country composition of the 1946 London Meeting, its inclusion in the Mexico Model appears peculiar given that certain Latin American countries which had been part of the Mexico Conference, such as Colombia, were refusing to entertain the principle in national legislation or limited-purpose treaties in 1948 with regards to shipping.[14]

Latin America's 1943 acceptance of the exemption principle in relation to the airline industry appears all the more curious seeing that most Latin American countries were opposed to the premier US international air carrier that monopolised commercial aviation in the Western Hemisphere, Pan American Airways (Pan Am), which they perceived as 'an agent of Yankee imperialism, like other US corporations'.[15] From the late 1920s, Pan Am had, with the diplomatic and financial support of the US government, demanded air and landing rights,[16] rights to operate both foreign and domestic air transportation, exclusive rights to transport airmail, land expropriation rights, unfettered usage of government facilities and infrastructure, and tax, duties and customs exemptions from Bolivia, Chile, Colombia, Costa Rica, El Salvador, Guatemala, Peru and Venezuela, much to their resistance, leading to protracted negotiations.[17] By the mid-1930s, Pan Am had acquired many local airlines of Chile,

[13] For example, Australia applied a method of calculating shipping profits at 5 per cent of the gross freights: C John Taylor, '"I Suppose I Must Have More Discussion on this Dreary Subject": The Negotiation and Drafting of the UK–Australia Double Taxation Treaty of 1946' in John Tiley (ed), *Studies in the History of Tax Law* (Hart, 2010) vol 4, 213, 229. In Britain's negotiations with Australia in 1945 on the UK–Australia DTA (concluded in 1946), the former would refer to the League's Fiscal Committee acceptance of the residence basis for taxing shipping and air transport to support its proposal for Australia to surrender its source taxation of such revenue (at 231, 240).

[14] See Chapter 5, Section 5.6, n 94.

[15] Jenifer Van Vleck, *Empire of the Air: Aviation and the American Ascendency* (Harvard University Press, 2013) 69.

[16] Prior to December 1943, carriers negotiated directly with foreign governments for commercial aviation rights. After this time, in anticipation of the importance of postwar commercial aviation, the State Department assumed conducting such negotiations for new or additional landing rights: Richard Y Chuang, *The International Air Transport Association: A Case Study of a Quasi-Governmental Organization* (AW Sijthoff, 1972) 19.

[17] Van Vleck, *Empire of the Air*, 70–2. See also Erik Benson, 'The Chosen Instrument? Reconsidering the Early Relationship between Pan American Airways and the US Government' (2004) 22 *Essays in Economic and Business History* 97, 101–5.

Colombia, Cuba, Mexico and Peru, allowing it to 'enjoy economic privileges that it could not obtain by government contract', including tax exemptions.[18] By 1941, the privately owned company had such extensive operations that the Roosevelt Administration was able to commission it to maintain the Western Hemisphere aerial defence by building over fifty-five airbases, along with other facilities (including military installations), in fifteen Latin American countries.[19] Such construction was not only achieved with extensive local labour toiling under deplorable conditions but was also carried out under the cloak of Pan Am's own ongoing expansion; Latin American governments being kept in the dark about the military significance or the US government's role and funding lest the United States be seen to violate its war neutrality and good neighbourliness in infringing state sovereignty.[20] Such secrecy was also expedient for other purposes: knowledge of the US government's role could have provided Axis influence in Latin America with fodder to 'use the airfields as evidence of "the imperialistic ambitions of the United States"' and, furthermore, 'complicate negotiations for postwar rights to these airfields'.[21]

Given the region's subordinated aviation capacity and stature, history of signing away taxing rights, and airline industries heavily owned by foreign private investment, Latin America probably entered the 1943 negotiations with little to bargain against the residence exemption principle. Yet there are further political factors that likely had bearing on the negotiations. Since its inception in 1927, Pan Am had functioned as the US government's 'chosen instrument' in upholding US political, economic and military interests in the region by containing European (especially German) ventures in the lucrative air transport market, safeguarding US sovereignty over the Panama Canal, fostering US cultural diplomacy and goodwill, while facilitating commercial expansion, which included transporting the rich natural resources and commodities extracted by US firms.[22] In Latin America, Pan Am invested heavily in publicity strategies that promoted pan-Americanism and the Good Neighbor Policy with the

18 Van Vleck, *Empire of the Air*, 2. In the case of Colombia, Pan Am's acquisition of the local airline's stock from European owners was undertaken secretly to prevent inciting a national backlash: Erik Benson, 'Flying Down to Rio: American Commercial Aviation, the Good Neighbor Policy, and World War Two, 1939–45' (2001) 19(1) *Essays in Economic and Business History* 61, 64.

19 Van Vleck, *Empire of the Air*, 83–4; Benson, 'Flying Down', 66.

20 Van Vleck, *Empire of the Air*, 83–6. See also Benson, 'Flying Down', 66.

21 Van Vleck, *Empire of the Air*, 84.

22 Van Vleck, *Empire of the Air*, 64–9, 72–82; Benson, 'Chosen Instrument?', 99–107; Benson, 'Flying Down', 63.

airline portraying itself 'as a model for a newly respectful, and mutually profitable, relationship' as part of the effort to redeem the United States' past exploitation of Latin America.[23] From 1939, commercial aviation was a key military defence strategy of the Roosevelt Administration to secure the Americas against Axis attack and later to facilitate Lend-Lease supplies and war-related passengers to Allied positions in Europe, North Africa and Middle East.[24] Pan Am was accordingly encouraged to expand, including through the provision of technical assistance to and the acquisition of controlling share interests in Latin American airlines, while the government financed the development of airfields and navigational facilities throughout the continent.[25] These plans also served a dual purpose: they would secure the United States' long-term economic supremacy not only by assuring control over the good neighbourly skyways but also by laying the experiential groundwork for conquering commercial air routes across the Pacific and Atlantic after the war. Such expansionist ambitions had already been envisioned by 1938 by both Pan Am's founder and president Juan Trippe and Secretary of State Hull in anticipation of the vast role international air traffic would play in linking industrial powers and trade markets, and in their determination that the United States would not lose to the Europeans in dominating transatlantic aviation as it had in transatlantic shipping.[26] From early 1941, aviation discourse and imagery became deeply ingrained in American culture as US government and business elites worked to project the airplane, in its facilitation of the liberal movement of products and peoples, as heralding the dawn of the 'American Century' – the utopian vision of American internationalism wherein the United States had a duty and entitlement to global ascendency to universalise its culture, technology and values (including concepts of democracy, freedom and justice) in uniting the world in peace and prosperity.[27] As the war progressed, the State Department worked to

[23] Van Vleck, *Empire of the Air*, 72–8. In the United States conversely, advertising and media accounts presented a more patronising discourse, typically depicting the inter-American air travel as US benevolence to Latin American backwardness and the effective means of securing US business hegemony in the region (at 78–82).

[24] Ibid 87, 100, 135–40. See also Theodore Joseph Crackel, *A History of the Civil Reserve Air Fleet* (Air Force History & Museums Program, 1998) ch 2.

[25] Van Vleck, *Empire of the Air*, 82–3, 106.

[26] Ibid 98. See also Jeffrey A Engel, *Cold War at 30,000 Feet: The Anglo-American Fight for Aviation Supremacy* (Harvard University Press, 2007) 39–42.

[27] Van Vleck, *Empire of the Air*, 3–5, 10–13, 89–90, 92, 106–8, 173–4. This vision was articulated by powerful publishing magnate Henry Luce in his famous editorial 'The American Century' published in February 1941, republished in Michael J Hogan (ed),

close off Latin American aviation operations to any perceived British toehold in the region in anticipation of a future clash over international commercial aviation with European rivals.[28]

In April 1943, just before the 1943 Mexico Conference, American captivation with the fusion of aviation and globalism appeared to be at a high with the release of the enormously bestselling book *One World* by prominent Republican internationalist Wendell Wilkie.[29] Through this book, and buttressed by similar views from government leaders, the media, the academia and airline advertisements, Wilkie promoted aviation as the conduit for postwar international cooperation, global economic stability and an American extraterritorial 'empire' built not on the European and Axis imperialism of colonies and conquest, but on markets and commerce.[30] That same month, the Interdepartmental Committee on International Aviation formed by Hull at the start of 1943 released its preliminary report supporting the liberal internationalist view that an 'open sky' policy (i.e. minimum air rights restrictions and maximum access to foreign markets) would best serve US interests in ensuring national prosperity and the capitalist world order by dismantling the protectionism, including the imperial trade preference, that restricted US operations in foreign countries.[31]

Given the US national and strategic interests at stake, one imagines that whatever reservations the Latin Americans might have had at Mexico, the State Department's senior representation, Carroll's persuasiveness and US de facto control over international commercial aviation made for the residence exemption principle to be an immovable point.[32] Deperon at this time does not appear to have proffered any contrary view as he would

The Ambiguous Legacy: US Foreign Relations in the 'American Century' (Cambridge University Press, 1999) 11.

28 Benson, 'Flying Down', 67–70.

29 Van Vleck, *Empire of the Air*, 108–10.

30 Ibid 3–6, 109–29, 168–9. See also Engel, *Aviation Supremacy*, 39–40; James Gormly, 'The Counter Iron Curtain: Crafting an American-Soviet Bloc Civil Aviation Policy: 1942–1960' (2013) 37(2) *Diplomatic History* 248, 249, 251.

31 Van Vleck, *Empire of the Air*, 175–7.

32 It is possible that Argentina, which played a principal role in expressing the Latin American views in the lead up to the 1943 Mexico regional tax conference (see Chapter 2, Section 2.1.3), may have had a part in overlooking this provision, with reference to Gómez's observation in her report of her 1947–8 Latin American mission (see Chapter 5, Section 5.6) that the principle of reciprocity was 'more acceptable' in Argentina because of the size of its merchant marine: Memorandum by Gómez del Rey to Lachmann, 6 May 1948, UNARMS:AG-004-001—S-0979-0003-22. See also Pedro CM Teichert, 'The Development of Argentina's Four State Fleets' (1959) 82 *Weltwirtschaftliches Archiv* 313 (which provides a history of Argentina's merchant fleets and explains that many Latin American countries only began to look into the development of national shipping after World War II (at 314)).

five years later as a secretariat member of the ostensibly egalitarian and independently financed UN.[33] While this may have been attributable to the League's endorsement of the exemption principle since 1928, the Princeton Mission could not have been impervious to the sentiments and sensitivities regarding aviation resonating then in its host country, the world's most powerful nation. With the Mission reliant on private business circles and the US government to support its work, and given Pan Am's close connections in Washington, on Wall Street, and with US multinationals operating in Latin America,[34] there were impelling disincentives for the consideration of

In addition, practices then in force regarding the tax treatment of shipping income may have influenced Latin America's acceptance of the provision: many Latin American countries, including Argentina, Brazil, Chile, Nicaragua, Dominican Republic, Panama, Paraguay, Guatemala, Honduras, Uruguay and Venezuela, in fact, were noted to have 'satisfied the reciprocal exemption requirements of the Revenue Code' (Hermon Manning Wells, 'United States Policies in International Double Taxation of Income' (Thesis No 74, Graduate Institute of International Studies, University of Geneva, 1950) 83), either because they imposed no income tax on or because they exempted the shipping earnings of US residents and corporations, which enabled them to be deemed to grant equivalent reciprocal exemption within the meaning of s 29.212-2, reg 111 (see US Internal Revenue Bureau, *Regulations 111 Relating to the Income Tax under the Internal Revenue Code: With Amendments to July 31, 1951, including TD 5841* (Lawyers Co-operative, 1951) 323).

33 See Section 11.2. Presumably, Deperon then supported residence exemption given that he was well aware of Carroll's advocacy of the principle for aviation and shipping in the latter's wartime promotion of DTAs and the League's double taxation work in the United States: see, for example, Letter from Carroll to Deperon, 15 June 1944, with attached Mitchell B Carroll, 'Outline of Post-War Programs on Prevention of Double Taxation' (Speech, NAM, document dated 5 June 1944) UNOG:PO—C.1646/30/1 (in which Carroll asserts: 'One can imagine the obstacle to the development of air transport after the war if each country tries to tax the earnings of an international company on such basis as the miles flown over its territory, or the proportion of the earnings corresponding to receipts for passengers and freight loaded in its territory' (at 5–6)).

34 Van Vleck, *Empire of the Air*, 66–70, 83–5; Benson, 'Chosen Instrument?', 101–7. A Rockefeller family member was an original board member and financial backer of Pan Am, as were many other financial scions (Van Vleck, *Empire of the Air*, 66; Anthony J Mayo and Nitin Nohria, *In Their Time: The Greatest Business Leaders of the Twentieth Century* (Harvard Business School Press, 2005) 95). Pan Am had also since 1929 operated a joint venture, Pan American-Grace Airways, with shipping conglomerate WR Grace & Company which networked the United States with the west coast of South America spanning Panama and the Panama Canal Zone, Colombia, Ecuador, Peru, Bolivia, Chile and Argentina. WR Grace itself not only controlled shipping between North and South America but was also a giant in Latin America with interests in mining, other commodities, industrial production, trading, finance and infrastructure: see 'Amazing Grace: The Story of WR Grace and Co' (1976) 10(3) *NACLA's Latin America and Empire Report* 3, 6–8. These linkages suggest that shipping had parallel significance as aviation for US commercial dominance and that similar pressures would have applied at Mexico regarding US insistence on (and ability to insist upon) the residence exemption principle for shipping.

alternative solutions that could be perceived as restricting US commerce and foreign relations. The tax treatment of airlines was in all probability never up for negotiation at Mexico.

11.1.2 The Postwar Global Aviation Frontier and US Ascendency

In 1944, in pursuit of an open skies policy, the United States began negotiations with other governments for air rights.[35] These diplomatic efforts included an attempt at multilateral settlement at the International Civil Aviation Conference held in Chicago in November 1944 ('Chicago Conference'), attended by fifty-two major Allied states at the invitation of the US government, the USSR withdrawing abruptly just days before the meeting began.[36] The conference did not bring about US visions for unrestricted commercial skyways as many nations resisted what could only pave the way for Pax-Americana.[37] The United States was then unrivalled in its commercial aviation leadership: its myriad airlines flew the great proportion of transatlantic traffic and the world's total passenger miles; it had a legion of skilled pilots already accustomed to Lend-Lease routes; and its surplus of transport planes churned out from the Anglo-American division of wartime aircraft production (Britain focusing on fighters and bombers) stood poised for conversion into passenger planes.[38] Britain, France, Portugal and the Netherlands in particular refused to cede cabotage rights over their colonies, while Australia and New Zealand even proposed a radical plan of

[35] Van Vleck, *Empire of the Air*, 167–8, 179–83; Gormly, 'Counter Iron Curtain', 254–7. Outside the Western Hemisphere, the United States at this time only had limited landing rights in Britain, France and Portugal and no peacetime commercial entry rights to most of Europe, Africa and the Middle East, nor to the USSR, China, India and Australia. In June 1944, the US government had already determined the specific global areas for US exploitation, subsequently inviting US airlines to apply for the award of world routes: Crackel, *Civil Reserve Air Fleet*, 58.

[36] Van Vleck, *Empire of the Air*, 170, 184–5; Gormly, 'Counter Iron Curtain', 257–9.

[37] Van Vleck, *Empire of the Air*, 170, 185–92; Engel, *Aviation Supremacy*, 96.

[38] Van Vleck, *Empire of the Air*, 170, 179; Crackel, *Civil Reserve Air Fleet*, 43; Engel, *Aviation Supremacy*, 29–32, 53; ' The Ins and Outs of IATA: Improving the Role of the United States in the Regulation of International Air Fares' (1972) 81(6) *The Yale Law Journal* 1102, 1111; Alan Dobson, *A History of International Civil Aviation: From Its Origins through Transformative Evolution* (Routledge, 2017) 38, 40. Aviation industries of Western Europe, the British Commonwealth and underdeveloped nations were moreover often public corporations or mixed undertakings following widespread nationalisation in the years leading up to, and during and after the war, entailing that many such governments had, inter alia, direct economic interest in air transport enterprises (Chuang, *International Air Transport Association*, 18), hence good cause to maintain protectionist policies.

international ownership and operation of world trunk routes.[39] During 1945 and 1947, the State Department under the new Truman Administration would instead secure air rights for US airlines through more aggressive bilateral negotiations with numerous nations, leveraging on US military and economic might as a bargaining chip.[40] Such settlements were facilitated by the global political changes underway that enabled aviation to be indissolubly 'wedded to international affairs' rather than perceived 'solely as an instrument of trade'.[41] The war had ended, international commerce had resumed and nations already heavily indebted for US wartime loans were in need of ongoing economic lifelines.[42] Airpower was also no longer just the harbinger of fortune but of annihilation in the dawn of the atomic age and Cold War era.[43] As the Iron Curtain descended, closing off Eastern European skies, the United States would implement, on the tail of the Truman Doctrine and Marshall Plan, its own increasingly stringent exclusionary air policy towards the Soviet bloc beginning from January 1948.[44] US concerns about surviving the air age[45] would only continue to heighten when the USSR exploded its first nuclear bomb in 1949 and its jet fighters, first produced in late 1948, 'hopelessly outclassed' and 'rendered obsolete every American plane' brought to the Korean War in late 1950.[46]

[39] Van Vleck, *Empire of the Air*, 185, 186; Eugene Sochor, 'International Civil Aviation and the Third World: How Fair Is the System?' (1988) 10(3) *Third World Quarterly* 1300, 1305.

[40] Van Vleck, *Empire of the Air*, 193–4; Dobson, *History of International Civil Aviation*, 53–8; Baldev Raj Nayar, 'Regimes, Power, and International Aviation' (1995) 49(1) *International Organization* 139, 157–8; Melina Piglia, '"Carry Our Colours and Defend Our Interests under the Skies of Other Continents". Argentinian Commercial Aviation Policy in the *Peronista* Decade (1945–1955)' (2019) 40(1) *The Journal of Transport History* 44, 49–52.

[41] Gormly, 'Counter Iron Curtain', 250.

[42] See Van Vleck, *Empire of the Air*, 193–4.

[43] Engel, *Aviation Supremacy*, 8–10, 45–9.

[44] Gormly, 'Counter Iron Curtain', 259–70.

[45] Such appeared to be the overpowering outlook of the panel appointed by Truman to comprehensively review the state of US military and commercial aviation, as encapsulated in the title of the panel's report: President's Air Policy Commission, *Survival in the Air Age: A Report by the President's Air Policy Commission* (USGPO, 1948). For a brief background of the panel and its recommendations, see Van Vleck, *Empire of the Air*, 206–8; Karen Miller, '"Air Power Is Peace Power" The Aircraft Industry's Campaign for Public and Political Support, 1943–1949' (1996) 70(3) *Business History Review* 297, 307–9, 326.

[46] Robert Frank Futrell, *The United States Air Force in Korea, 1950–1953* (Office of Air Force History, United States Air Force, rev ed, 1983) 244. See also Van Vleck, *Empire of the Air*, 199; Miller, '"Air Power is Peace Power"', 326–7; Engel, *Aviation Supremacy*, 119–20.

There are several aspects to the above developments that are vital to understanding the complex underlying political and economic dynamics at play at the time the taxation of income of international air transport came before the international community for consideration. Firstly, the State Department, and to some extent US airlines, would continue to take a major role in civil aviation matters as American military and civil policy once again became integrated in the emerging national security state, this time in response to mounting US concerns about the Soviet threat. In early 1947, the Air Coordinating Committee, an interdepartmental body comprising representatives of the Departments of State, Treasury, Commerce, Post Office, Army, Navy and Air Force, as well as the Civil Aeronautics Board (CAB)[47] and Federal Communications Commission, began overseeing the organisation of the civil reserve air fleet for Cold War mobilisation.[48] From 1947, the US commercial aviation industry would benefit from federal defence spending as airlines committed aircraft and equipment to augment military airlifts, ferrying critical cargo during the Berlin Airlift between June 1948 and May 1949, and during the Korean War from 1950 to 1953.[49]

A flourishing civil aviation industry also served other strategic purposes for Washington policymakers. Keeping US flag carrier services in the lead on the world's skyways had Cold War propaganda value in projecting America's unparalleled technological supremacy through expanded international route systems that included round-the-world flights.[50] Tourism, moreover, was considered an immeasurably powerful tool in buttressing US foreign policy by exporting American dollars, culture and capitalism while solving the balance of payments crisis and strain on federal coffers caused by foreign aid programmes, even stirring

[47] The CAB was the federal agency formed in 1938 to regulate commercial aviation.

[48] Crackel, *Civil Reserve Air Fleet*, 59. For a history of this Committee, established in September 1946, see Walter H Wager, 'The Air Coordinating Committee' (1949) 2(4) *Air University Quarterly Review* 17. For insight into the role that US aircraft manufacturers (which by 1947 were facing potential bankruptcy due to the cessation of wartime government contracts, sagging postwar commercial markets, labour strikes and shortage of raw materials) played in creating a climate where airpower garnered political, industry, military and public support as a solution to national defence and budgetary problems, see Miller, '"Air Power is Peace Power"'.

[49] Van Vleck, *Empire of the Air*, 206–8; Crackel, *Civil Reserve Air Fleet*, 55, 59–62. Regarding the airlines' influencing say in negotiations with the government and military to birth the civil airlift reserve, see Crackel at 62–71. The airlines also provided services sustaining air force operations, Pan Am for example managing and maintaining missile testing stations from Florida through the Caribbean in 1953: Van Vleck at 208.

[50] Van Vleck, *Empire of the Air*, 209.

other governments towards enterprising activity to attract such tourist dollars.[51] From 1947, Washington and US airlines consequently began collaborating to promote travel to Western Europe to the American public as a patriotic duty that would revive fellow capitalist economies, export American political values, diminish the lure of communism, close the dollar gap and reduce federal government expenditures.[52] In 1949, to make travel more affordable for the average American, Pan Am sought to introduce reduced fares for tourists on transatlantic flights – a matter which was not only regulated by the global industry body of international airlines, the International Air Transport Association (IATA),[53] but also opposed by competing Western European and Canadian airlines in their concern over the increasing US conquest of the global air transport market through cut-throat fares that only US airlines could offer.[54] Pan Am would eventually obtain this approval at IATA's annual meeting in September 1951 after repeated threats to unilaterally implement the reductions.[55]

Secondly, Britain and other Western European nations were resistant to and suspicious of US aviation policy that not only advanced American monopolisation of the world aviation market but also restricted their own expansion plans.[56] The dependence of the Marshall Plan nations on their benefactor, including for aircraft procurement to replace their obsolete equipment, nevertheless elicited a measure of cooperation. At Chicago, the United States' repeated emphasis on the capacity of its colossal aviation industry to aid other nations in establishing their own airlines and air forces led to the reporting that 'Nobody votes against Santa Claus'.[57] From 1948, Washington worked to persuade other Western nations to block the sale and export of aviation technology and materials to Eastern Europe, and to embargo Soviet bloc flights to the Middle East, South Asia and Africa in the effort to quarantine the bloc and prevent British and Western European competition from gaining commercial aviation advantages denied to the United States.[58] In 1951, it was successful in persuading

51 Ibid 211–12.

52 Ibid 200–1, 209–17.

53 A brief background of IATA is provided in nn 99 and 100.

54 Van Vleck, *Empire of the Air*, 214.

55 Ibid 215.

56 See Gormly, 'Counter Iron Curtain', 265–72. See also Van Vleck, *Empire of the Air*, 187; Nayar, 'Regimes', 163; Engel, *Aviation Supremacy*, 102.

57 Van Vleck, *Empire of the Air*, 187 (quoting the statement given by an anonymous delegate to the Chicago Daily Tribune).

58 Gormly, 'Counter Iron Curtain', 264–72; Engel, *Aviation Supremacy*, 98–102, 183–4.

Britain, France, Belgium and the Netherlands to curtail Czech flights over West Germany or to their countries, although it never achieved full implementation of its extensive containment policy.[59]

US coercive economic diplomacy was intensely deployed in Anglo-American relations given Britain's position as the only other nation with the global influence as well as the manufacturing, technical and resource capability to challenge the United States for aircraft and airline dominance in the immediate war aftermath.[60] Strong-arm tactics, especially threats of aid withdrawal, were used not only to pry open the British Empire's skies and give US airlines extended use of British air bases but also to thwart British aircraft exports to anti-American or communist nations, including Argentina, the USSR and Yugoslavia.[61] London's capitulations were bitter blows to British policymakers who had perceived in aircraft sales and airline services the crown jewel revenue sources to restore the nation's financial independence, trade patterns, colonial ties and great power status through lucrative markets and routes for British economic exploitation and influence.[62]

Thirdly, developing countries had little say in crafting postwar aviation policy. In fact, in the aforementioned negotiations over air rights, the major powers had bargained on behalf of dependencies on the presumption that the prewar system of colonial possessions and spheres of influence would continue unchanged.[63] The United States even bartered for landing rights to British strongholds in the Mediterranean by offering Britain quid pro quo entry into Latin America without consulting the latter's nations.[64] At Chicago, Asian and African nationalist leaders were left out of aviation policy discussions, and the representation of key British colonies (including India, Egypt, Iraq and Lebanon) by delegates appointed by the Britain government ensured that the imperial line was toed regardless of the

[59] Gormly, 'Counter Iron Curtain', 272–3.

[60] Engel, *Aviation Supremacy*, 6–7, 33–40, 51–2, 59. Only these two nations 'could offer every type of plane a country or airline might need', while other European countries could only 'supply one model or choose to specialize in a particular type of plane' (at 6). See also Alan P Dobson, 'The Other Air Battle: The American Pursuit of Post-War Civil Aviation Rights' (1985) 28(2) *The Historical Journal* 429, 429–30.

[61] Engel, *Aviation Supremacy*, 61–89, 112–16, 147–58; Van Vleck, *Empire of the Air*, 194. London was also pressed to interfere with rule of law processes to prevent Mao's regime from taking possession of the former Nationalist's fleet of airliners and transports headquartered in Hong Kong: Engel at 104–17.

[62] See Engel, *Aviation Supremacy*, 7–8, 33–9, 49, 51, 53–76, 85, 87, 97–102, 130–58.

[63] Sochor, 'International Civil Aviation', 1305; Van Vleck, *Empire of the Air*, 187–8.

[64] Benson, 'Flying Down', 70.

indignation this roused in the colonies themselves.[65] Meanwhile, nineteen Latin American nations united as a bloc to oppose US proposals for an international aviation organisation governed by the Big Five.[66]

For the developing world, especially for new nations established at war's end, airpower's significance was no less than it was for developed world. Aircraft ownership not only offered prestige, autonomy and the opportunity to industrialise, but was even considered one of the three prerequisites legitimising a nation's claim to true sovereignty (the other two being an army and a flag).[67] Enormous impediments nevertheless stood in the way of launching and growing a national airline let alone competing with established operators, and most developing countries were then 'for the most part destination points rather than sources of traffic[,] . . . compet[ing] with one another to attract foreign carriers and establish themselves as importing air junctions'.[68] From 1946, both the US government and US airlines began supplying civil aviation technical assistance, however, only to developing countries of diplomatic and strategic interest (e.g. Saudi Arabia, Turkey and Pakistan) for purposes that ranged from accessing rich oil fields and creating local air services that fed into US airlines' trunk routes to shoring up pro-American goodwill and allegiance, and counteracting Soviet propaganda and influence.[69]

[65] Van Vleck, *Empire of the Air*, 185.

[66] Ibid 186.

[67] Engel, *Aviation Supremacy*, 6; Sochor, 'International Civil Aviation', 1313; Chuang, *International Air Transport Association*, 15.

[68] Sochor, 'International Civil Aviation', 1304–5.

[69] Van Vleck, *Empire of the Air*, 230–2. This early technical assistance consisted of training pilots and ground crew, overseeing airport construction and guiding airline management. In 1952, the augmentation of such programmes was proposed in view of the purposes they served in: (1) increasing the recipient nation's defence potential; (2) improving facilities for the United States and its allies for emergency use; (3) promoting the sale of, and hence long-term markets for, US aeronautical equipment and material; (4) promoting US techniques; and (5) providing the US government with intelligence opportunities: 'Memorandum by Robert A Thayer of the Office of Near Eastern Affairs to the Acting Deputy Director of the Office of Transport and Communications Policy (Klemmer)', 6 March 1952, in State Department, *Foreign Relations of the United States, 1952–1954* (USGPO, 1983) vol 1, pt 1: General: Economic and Political Matters, Doc 123 ('*FRUS, 1952–1954*, vol 1, pt 1'). See also, 'Memorandum by Conversation, by Robert A Thayer of the Bureau of Neat Eastern, South Asian, and African Affairs', 11 September 1952, in State Department, *Foreign Relations of the United States, 1952–1954* (USGPO, 1983) vol 11, pt 1: Africa and South Asia, Doc 221 (regarding keeping a Liberian airfield open for civil aviation and standby military use despite the expenditure involved).

The upshot of the aforementioned dynamics on the international civil aviation landscape of the first postwar decade was a United States that reigned as the preeminent aerial power with not only the ability to direct international policy and to function as gatekeeper to other nations' aviation development, but with also the only population prosperous enough to make tourism an export commodity. While the rest of the First World countries were cynical about America's open skies deregulation and liberalism, they faced considerable pressure to concede. Developing countries themselves were largely bystanders, many lacking established, even fully locally owned or operated, aviation industries, and were perceived by the major powers as territorial extensions.

Given the urgency and centrality of the US commercial aviation enterprise to American ascendency and security, not to mention the nation's position to immediately capitalise on the growth of the industry, there were compelling reasons for the global superpower to promptly seek widespread international agreement to reduce or eliminate foreign aviation taxation. It stands to reason that a multilateral forum governed by beholden nations with common interests and unencumbered by Soviet presence and developing country numbers would have appeared the most expedient channel to pursue this agenda, which marks the entry of ICAO into double taxation matters.

11.1.3 ICAO Institutional and Decision-Making Framework

ICAO came into being in April 1947 upon the entry into force of the *Convention on International Civil Aviation*[70] which had been drafted at Chicago Conference.[71] The organisation was set up in Montréal,[72]

[70] Opened for signature 7 December 1944, 15 UNTS 295 (entered into force 4 April 1947) ('*ICAO Convention*').

[71] A provisional ICAO (PICAO) operated from July 1945 to April 1947 and '[b]y the end of its existence . . . was a virile, going concern with a great number of successes to its credit' that the transition to the permanent organisation was little more than a formality: Jacob Schenkman, *International Civil Aviation Organization* (Librairie E Droz, 1955) 118. In contrast, the UN 'had not managed to pass the stage of preliminary groping' (quoting A Verdurand of the ICAO French delegation).

[72] David MacKenzie, *ICAO: A History of the International Civil Aviation Organization* (University of Toronto Press, 2010) 48, 78. The decision was a compromise: the United States, Latin America and Australia wanted the organisation in the Western Hemisphere, the Europeans and India desired it in Paris and the British ultimately agreed on neutral Canada to prevent the 'tend[ency] to increase still further the preponderating influence which America already yields' (at 78). Canada itself had an elevated status in civil aviation due to 'the great circle routes that traversed its territory': Van Vleck, *Empire of the Air*, 185–6.

replacing the largely European-membered and Paris-based International Commission for Air Navigation (ICAN) created in 1919 as well as the rival inter-American initiative, the 1928 Pan American Convention on Commercial Aviation.[73] ICAN had been linked with the League, the latter concerning itself with particular aspects of international civil aviation, for example, the economic and legal aspects of commercial air transport.[74]

ICAO was purposed 'to develop the principles and techniques of international air navigation and to foster the planning and development of international air transport' for a number of enumerated purposes.[75] It had no regulatory authority, and accordingly could only recommend, advise and urge its members to accept and implement decisions.[76] Taxation issues were not specifically addressed in the Convention and, moreover, negotiations over economic questions reached an impasse at Chicago and were left for later discussions.[77]

ICAO discharged its functions through its Assembly, Council and Secretariat. All member states were represented in the Assembly where each had one vote. ICAO membership was open to the wartime Allies, their associates and neutrals.[78] Between 1947 and 1953, the new states of Burma, Ceylon, Indonesia, Israel, Libya and Pakistan became members, bringing ICAO's membership up to fifty-eight members.[79] Eight states that were UN members but not ICAO members during the Fiscal Commission years were the USSR, Byelorussian SSR, Ukraine SSR, Yugoslavia, Costa Rica,

[73] MacKenzie, *ICAO*, 15–16, 22–3.

[74] Although ICAN was placed under the direction of the League pursuant to its founding convention, the relationship in practice became one of 'friendly cooperation' between the two bodies. ICAN's fate was similar to that of the League: its headquarters were closed when Paris was invaded in 1940: Schenkman, *International Civil Aviation Organization*, 44; MacKenzie, *ICAO*, 22–3.

[75] *ICAO Convention* art 44. The purposes that arguably gave ICAO competence over tax matters include 'meet[ing] the needs of the peoples of the world for safe, regular, efficient and economical air transport' (art 44(d)) and 'promot[ing] generally the development of all aspects of international civil aeronautics' (art 44(i)). However, see n 77.

[76] MacKenzie, *ICAO*, 194.

[77] Ibid 34, 46. Many states preferred such questions to be left to the individual states and airlines. By 1950, in fact, the United States so opposed commercial regulation by ICAO over matters regarding rate, frequency or capacity controls that ICAO thereon 'would develop primarily as a technical organization . . . overseeing all the non-economic aspects of international commercial aviation' (at 127).

[78] Ibid 75. Conditions applied to the admission of ex-enemy states, and former colonial territories of a member state or newly partitioned states did not automatically acquire membership upon gaining independence: Thomas Buergenthal, *Law-Making in the International Civil Aviation Organization* (Syracuse University Press, 1969) 30.

[79] Schenkman, *International Civil Aviation Organization*, 128.

Panama, Saudi Arabia and Yemen.[80] Voting rights (in the Assembly or Council) could be suspended where a member was unable to meet its financial obligations to the organisation.[81] In the first postwar decade, the economic difficulties of many, especially smaller, members caused them to lag in their payments, and in 1948 and 1949, Bolivia, El Salvador, Jordan, Nicaragua, Paraguay and Poland had their voting rights suspended.[82] The full Assembly met in 1947 and 1948 but the expense, extensive preparations required and the lack of necessity for frequent full-scale meetings led to a limited assembly in 1949.[83] In 1950, the full Assembly agreed to limit full sessions to once every three years to coincide with electing the new Council.[84]

The Council consequently evolved as the central and executive institution in ICAO's framework, becoming a permanent body in virtually continuous session at the headquarters[85] and the legislative organ in adopting and amending international standards and recommending practices.[86] It comprised twenty-one member states elected for a three-year term. Council members were to reflect adequate representation of the following three categories, in order of importance and election: the chief air operators, the largest contributors of air facilities and the major geographic areas of the world.[87] Decisions were made by a majority[88] and, as members were to function as government representatives, the

[80] Ibid 129.

[81] *ICAO Convention* art 62.

[82] MacKenzie, *ICAO*, 164–5; Schenkman, *International Civil Aviation Organization*, 196. In 1951, Bolivia, Czechoslovakia, El Salvador, Guatemala, Jordan and Poland were in arrears and were suspended the following year.

[83] MacKenzie, *ICAO*, 147.

[84] Ibid; Schenkman, *International Civil Aviation Organization*, 147. In the intervening years, the Assembly would hold 'limited' sessions to deal with budgetary and administrative matters or such other matters that the Council considered to be of urgent importance.

[85] Schenkman, *International Civil Aviation Organization*, 164. In 1950, the Assembly passed a resolution requiring Council member states to appoint and support full-time representatives at the ICAO headquarters. By the end of 1952, all Council member states were maintaining offices with permanent representatives in the headquarters building.

[86] It had 'a multitude of functions, both mandatory and permissive, of a legislative, judicial and administrative character': Buergenthal, *Law-Making*, 8. This assumption of both 'routine and extraordinary functions' of ICAO entailed that the Council '[stood] somewhat above corresponding bodies in other international organizations': Christopher T Tourtellot, 'Membership Criteria for the ICAO Council: A Proposal for Reform' (1981) 11(1) *Denver Journal of International Law and Policy* 51, 52.

[87] *ICAO Convention* art 50.

[88] Ibid art 52.

Council was essentially a political body[89] with national interests and political motives the driving force in its discussions and operations.[90] The criteria for Council membership ensued in relatively little change in Council membership among the Category 1 and 2 states: the United States, the United Kingdom, Belgium, France, Ireland, the Netherlands, Portugal, Australia, Canada, Argentina, Brazil, Mexico, India, Iraq and Egypt were members throughout the Commission period.[91] The President (Edward Warner) was an American, and officers of the Council came from First World countries.[92] The Council's Air Transport Committee (ATC) was the relevant subordinate special advisory body in charge of handling economic questions, including taxation.[93] This Committee comprised twelve members selected for a term of three years from the Council representatives.[94]

The first Secretary-General of ICAO was Albert Roper (France), who had also been the Secretary-General of ICAN throughout its existence.[95] The Secretariat was mainly staffed by aviation professionals from developed nations, especially Canada, France, the United Kingdom and the United States.[96] Deep frustrations over language emerged in ICAO: although English, French and Spanish were the official languages, English was the common language of the Secretariat and staff, and it was common practice for all working papers and documents to be printed only in English.[97]

ICAO is reported as having 'worked to achieve standardization in civil aviation through a systematic policy of coordination with other international organizations'.[98] Its closest relationship was with IATA,[99] which was also based in Montréal and whose representatives were present for

[89] MacKenzie, *ICAO*, 54; Schenkman, *International Civil Aviation Organization*, 158.

[90] MacKenzie, *ICAO*, 153; Schenkman, *International Civil Aviation Organization*, 158.

[91] 'Election of Contracting States to the Represented on the Council', ICAO Assembly, 14th sess, Agenda item 9, ICAO Doc A14-WP/2 (15 January 1962) 2–3. In the 1950 elections, Denmark, Italy, the Philippines, South Africa and Venezuela replaced the Category 3 countries of Chile, China, Czechoslovakia, Peru, Sweden and Turkey (Spain later elected in 1951 to fill the one remaining Council seat).

[92] Schenkman, *International Civil Aviation Organization*, 166–9.

[93] Ibid 175; MacKenzie, *ICAO*, 55.

[94] Schenkman, *International Civil Aviation Organization*, 176.

[95] MacKenzie, *ICAO*, 66.

[96] Ibid 132; Schenkman, *International Civil Aviation Organization*, 218–19.

[97] MacKenzie, *ICAO*, 155–7. Translations in the other official languages either were not made or contained errors, and the cost of translation into a non-official language had to be borne by the country seeking such translation.

[98] Ibid 180.

[99] The new IATA was established in 1945, succeeding its Hague-based predecessor that had been formed in 1919. The old IATA had in fact played a role in encouraging the extension

most meetings of the ATC. Importantly, IATA was responsible for establishing the economic rules for international air transport and governments rarely interfered in its recommendations.[100] ICAO was a specialised agency of the UN, and pursuant to the agreement between them, both organisations were to cooperate to the fullest extent possible to secure maximum coordination and uniformity as well as efficiency and economy in their administrative operations.[101] Although ICAO would work with the UN in providing technical assistance to the developing world from the 1950s and had some relations with the Transport and Communications Division (similar to that between ICAN and the League counterpart),[102] the UN archival records indicate that its relations with the Fiscal Division during the Commission years were neither cordial nor genuinely cooperative in trying to find common ground over tax policy.

In summary, at the time of ICAO's study on double taxation of air transport income, the organisation was largely controlled by an élite group of powerful or richer states which were not only solely concerned with their own national interests, but also had essentially permanent positions and people in the Council and the even smaller ATC. Most of these states had long-established aviation industries and were in comparable stages of development. Several were also colonial powers that were seeking to re-establish their empires and hold on to their territories, including by reserving colonial services for the metropole.[103] The ICAO Secretariat had

of the exemption rule for shipping companies to the airline industry: Jogarajan, *Double Taxation*, 221–2.

100 IATA was created at Havana by thirty-four airlines to resolve the economic issues left unaddressed at the Chicago conference. It would provide the machinery for setting fares and rates on international routes, and its position of input to ICAO is reflected in the annexes of the ICAO Convention. Much of IATA's early work was technical and mostly performed by a dozen of the larger carriers. The Association was closely linked to governments as the majority of IATA airlines (US carriers excepted) were government-owned or controlled and most governments intended that, at its formation, it would be the counterpart of ICAO in the economic sphere: John C Leslie, 'International Air Transport Association: Some Historical Notes' (1971) 13(3/4) *Journal of Interamerican Studies and World Affairs* 319, 320, 322, 326–7; Ludwig Weber, *International Civil Aviation Organization (ICAO)* (Kluwer Law International, 2015) [6]–[7]; Sochor, 'International Civil Aviation', 1307; Chuang, *International Air Transport Association*, 26–7, 29–30.

101 *Agreement between the United Nations and the International Civil Aviation Organization*, signed 13 May 1947, 8 UNTS 315 (entered into force 3 October 1947). See also Schenkman, *International Civil Aviation Organization*, 193.

102 MacKenzie, *ICAO*, 183–9; Schenkman, *International Civil Aviation Organization*, 194.

103 MacKenzie, *ICAO*, 33 (noting that the French government believed strongly in regarding colonial services as internal services).

the benefit of a smaller bureaucracy than its UN counterpart and continuity from its provisional operations from 1945 as well as from the ICAN Secretariat. The organisation accordingly enjoyed considerable cohesive leadership and operational advantage in contrast to the UN, which was still carrying out its work in various locations, whose Fiscal Commission was only meeting biennially with more variable (especially developing country) composition, and whose Fiscal Division was struggling to recruit staff while undergoing a change of leadership and facing intense political pressures. ICAO had no developing country personnel in relevant senior positions, nor any taxation experts. Its limited working language effectively discriminated against states less versed in English, and its primary working relationship with IATA gave precedence to the concerns of industry on economic matters. There was accordingly little representation of the interests of developing countries. Only in September 1952 (i.e. after the events of interest concerning the Fiscal Commission story) did the ICAO Council come to agree that as the ATC dealt with problems that affected states individually, it was necessary for it to 'take a cross-section of the opinion of contracting states' in seeking solutions to these problems.[104] It would further take until the end of the decade before the ranks of the ICAO Secretariat began to be 'increasingly . . . filled by civil servants and government officials rather than aviation professionals of the early years'.[105]

11.2 ICAO's Excursion into Tax Matters (May 1947–December 1948)

At ICAO's First Assembly in May 1947, it was stated that 'onerous economic burdens on the development of international air transport could result from (i) double taxation; . . . '.[106] The Assembly resolved

[104] Schenkman, *International Civil Aviation Organization*, 178.

[105] MacKenzie, *ICAO*, 132.

[106] The other 'burden' related to 'the taxation of fuel and equipment not consumed within the jurisdiction of the country imposing such tax': see *Proceedings of the First Session of the Assembly, 6–27 May 1947*, ICAO Assembly, 1st sess, ICAO Doc 7325-C/852 (December 1952) Resolution A1-42, 269. This statement likely originated with the United States in view of US policies concerning the open skies, promotion of American travel abroad, aviation mobilisation planning as well as the cultivation of foreign markets for aircraft and aeronautical equipment given the financial straits of US aircraft manufacturers. Negotiations in IATA to fix prices for international air travel had commenced at this stage, raising the possibility that Pan Am had some input in this proposition to ICAO given its experience in securing tax exemptions from Latin American governments during the interwar years. See further 'Current Economic Developments: Review Completed of US Aviation Policy', 11 May 1954, in State

that the Council should study the matter, and the latter subsequently requested member governments to provide, by 1 November 1947, information concerning their national taxation practices that affected international air transport. IATA's views were also invited.[107]

In April 1948, the Fiscal Division had prepared a brief for ICAO's Second Assembly, which summarised the relief provisions in existing treaties that dealt with the various types of air navigation taxation, including of airlines, salaries of airline employees, fuel and lubricants, and equipment.[108] This brief stated, inter alia, that although the general reciprocal exemption treatment could be applied between creditor countries or countries in a similar stage of development, it was 'doubtful' that debtor countries and those behind in aircraft development would be prepared to enter into treaties based on the concept since most of the traffic in persons and goods would originate from their own countries, while the residence of such aircraft operators would likely be in other countries. Giving up their right to 'tax on the traffic would seem to be sacrificing a rich field for revenues without any compensation in other directions'.[109] To make DTAs attractive to such countries, the brief suggested provisions based on 'the test of registration or nationality of the aircraft' to make profits from such undertakings 'locally taxable'.[110] Where an aircraft was registered in more than one country, apportionment could be applied based on the volume of business and amount of profits earned.[111]

At this time, ICAO had not received sufficient government replies to prepare a study.[112] Instead, the subject was broadly discussed by the ATC's Division of Facilitation of International Air Transport, which

Department, *FRUS, 1952–1954*, vol 1, pt 1, Doc 135 (regarding US national interest considerations to facilitate sales of aircraft and related equipment 'to friendly nations').

107 See *Report of the Council to the Assembly on the Activities of the Organization June 1, 1947–March 1, 1948*, ICAO Assembly, 2nd sess, ICAO Doc 5221, A2/B-5 (19 March 1948) 52.

108 Fiscal Division, 'Brief on Double Taxation of International Air Transport', 16 April 1948, UNARMS:AG-025-002—S-0441-0469-23893(A).

109 Ibid 3–4.

110 Ibid 3.

111 Ibid 4. A further draft indicated that 'it may be possible to foresee methods by which new criteria for the taxation of such profits could be adopted which would rely more on the economic contribution of each country than on the former criteria of residence and registration': Fiscal Division, Draft on 'Double Taxation of International Air Transport Enterprises', 21 May 1948, UNARMS:AG-004-001—S-0979-0004-11.

112 Fiscal Commission, *References of Interest to the Fiscal Commission Contained in the Proceedings of the Second Assembly of the International Civil Aviation Organization, Geneva, 1–21 June 1948*, UN Doc E/CN.8/40 (20 December 1948) 1.

recommended that states 'adopt all practicable measures . . . to eliminate multiple, unfairly burdensome, or discriminatory taxation of airlines and their employees'.[113] At ICAO's Second Assembly in June, the UN was represented by Louis Delanney from the Transport and Communications Division ('Transport Division')[114] who explained 'the complexities of this entire subject', that the Fiscal Commission 'had it generally under consideration' and that ICAO should concentrate 'on the purely aviational aspects'.[115] Deperon also submitted a memorandum that indicated 'that a comprehensive study of the tax problems of international air transport was included in the over-all research program of the Division'.[116] The Assembly took no action on the subject and adopted a resolution directing the Council 'to continue to maintain close and co-operative relationship with the United Nations'.[117]

Back at the UN, Deperon assured the Secretariat's Co-ordination Division that the Fiscal Division had already embarked on work 'of direct concern to those engaged in international air transport' through its *ITA series* and questionnaires to governments to obtain comprehensive tax information.[118] He suggested that these 'comprehensive studies . . . be adapted toward satisfying . . . [ICAO's] needs for information, and for action on the basis of such information' as the tax problems of air transport were 'best . . . studied and dealt with as part of the over-all tax treatment of persons and enterprises engaged in international business transactions'.[119]

In December 1948, at ICAO, the ATC Chairman (PT David (United States)) submitted a resolution (AT-WP/30) that called for the total or partial reciprocal exemption of six major tax categories[120] affecting aviation on the basis that such 'multiple, unfairly burdensome and discriminatory

[113] Ibid 2. It is no small coincidence that the US Congress had on 4 May 1948 approved the amendment of relevant sections of its *Internal Revenue Code* relating to the reciprocal exemption of shipping profits to also apply to the earnings of air transport enterprises: Wells, 'United States Policies', 84; US National Archives and Records Administration, 'Proposed Rule Making: Department of Treasury' (1948) 13(162) *Federal Register* 4793, 4795.

[114] Memorandum by Lukae to Owen, 7 June 1948, 1, UNARMS:AG-025-002—S-0441-0469-23893(A).

[115] E/CN.8/40, 2.

[116] Ibid.

[117] Ibid 3.

[118] Memorandum by Deperon to Yates, 4 June 1948, 1, UNARMS:AG-025-002—S-0441-0469-23893(A).

[119] Ibid 2.

[120] These categories covered income and property taxes, fuel taxes, customs duties and excise taxes and personal income taxes of airline employees.

taxation' impeded 'the development of international air transport'.[121] David supported the resolution by referring to discussions with the 'experts on tax treaties of the US Treasury Department',[122] and also stressed the interest of IATA in this subject.[123] AT-WP/30 had been 'cleared in principle' by the US government prior to submission[124] and the United States would consistently advocate 'the broadest possible area of reciprocal tax exemption' throughout the ICAO discussions regarding taxation during this period.[125] AT-WP/30 would not be communicated to the UN until September 1949.[126] Ignorant of this development, the Fiscal Division communicated to the Fiscal Commission a brief document that simply set out the excerpts of the various ICAO bodies up until June 1948.[127]

11.3 Deliberations at the Fiscal Commission's Second Session (January 1949)

At the Commission's Second Session, New Zealand suggested that studies on the double taxation problems mentioned by ICAO should be given priority.[128] The subject was assigned for deliberation by the Working Party[129] but was only briefly discussed at its first and third meetings. At the first meeting, Britain stated that the question of the taxation of fuel and

121 ATC, *Proposed ICAO Council Resolution on Taxation*, ICAO Doc AT-WP/30 (14 December 1948), UNARMS:AG-025-002—S-0441-0469-23893(A). This resolution is reproduced in Appendix I.

122 Letter from Bloch to King, 4 October 1949, UNARMS:AG-025-002—S-0441-0469-23893(A) (citing ICAO Doc 6564-AT/687(Pt 17) (18 May 1949)).

123 See Fiscal Division, 'Memorandum on ICAO Preliminary Report on Multiple, Discriminatory and Unfairly Burdensome Taxation (AT-WP/85; 14 September 1949)', 31 October 1949, 2, UNARMS:AG-025-002—S-0441-0469-23893(A) ('Aide-mémoire'). This memorandum was primarily prepared by Lachmann.

124 State Department, 'Fiscal Commission - Second Session: Annotated Agenda', 6 January 1949, 2, NARAII:RG84-A1_1030E-8.

125 These policy recommendations had in fact been part of the US position from the time of the 1944 Chicago Conference: UNEC, Position Paper on 'Multiple Taxation of Aviation Operations' for the US Delegation to the Third Session of the Fiscal Commission, 3 May 1951, 1-2, NARAII:RG59-UD-07D_73B(Lot56D479)-4 ('US Position (Aviation Taxation)').

126 Letter from Moulton to Kremery, 19 September 1949, UNARMS:AG-025-002—S-0441-0469-23893(A).

127 E/CN.8/40.

128 Unless otherwise stated, the material regarding these discussions has been drawn from the following *Summary Records* of the Commission's Second Session (UN Doc E/CN.8/SR.9 (20 January 1949)) and its Working Party on International Tax Problems (UN Docs E/CN.8/AC.1/SR.1 (19 January 1949) and E/CN.8/AC.1/SR.3 (24 January 1949)).

129 See Chapter 7, Section 7.2 for details of the Working Party.

equipment might be of interest to another specialised agency and that the Division should be instructed to ensure no duplication of work. The United States reserved its position. After Ukraine SSR expressed the general Soviet positions, South Africa suggested that these views be reflected in the Commission's report and that any action to be taken would be made clear in the Commission's resolution. At the third meeting, Lachmann raised the subject, highlighting that ICAO was leaving it to the Commission to undertake the background studies. However, Cuba, with whom Belgium (as Chairman) agreed, stated that the question had already been settled in the earlier meeting. That concluded the Working Party's discussion, and no further deliberation took place in the plenary Commission. The Commission's report merely stated that the Commission, in its consideration of the Division's future work programme, 'took note' of the Division's document concerning ICAO's proceedings.[130]

The Working Party's dismissive treatment of the subject (and of Lachmann) was possibly attributable to the strained relations between the Division and Commission due to the former's overall disorganised preparatory work and its representation by new faces,[131] and perhaps also because the short-staffed Division had not provided any background explanation or the issues of concern for developing countries. The apparent British and American disinterest may also have discouraged closer examination of the problem, particularly without the presence of New Zealand to advocate its prioritisation.

It is worth noting that the introduction of AT-WP/30 followed on the heels of Latin America's pursuit of source taxation rights at the Havana and Bogotá Conferences, trends which were anticipated to take place in the UN in view of the Division's efforts at these conferences to safeguard its double taxation jurisdiction.[132] Moreover, in its brief to ICAO, the Division had indicated its approach to prevent developing countries' revenue sacrifice. The US pursuit of the residence exemption principle in ICAO, as well as its silence concerning AT-WP/30 in the Commission,[133] suggests that it may have been seeking to hasten an

[130] Fiscal Commission, *Report of the Second Session of the Fiscal Commission, Held at Lake Success, New York, 10 to 25 January 1949*, 2nd sess, UN Docs E/1104 and Corr.1 (also E/CN.8/49/Rev.2) (3 February 1949) 9–10 [22(ii)].

[131] See Chapter 7, Sections 7.1 and 7.2.

[132] See Chapter 6, Section 6.1.

[133] Interestingly, the State Department had initially anticipated that AP-WP/30 would be notified to the Division and had instructed Bartelt to propose, when the subject was before the Commission, that the Division keep itself and the Commission informed of the ICAO developments and to cooperate with ICAO to the extent appropriate: State

ICAO decision to pre-empt UN study and debate that could result in undesirable recommendations.

11.4 The Clash of Competencies and the Uneasy Alliance (1949)

From mid-January to mid-March 1949, the UN and ICAO Secretariats engaged in correspondence in which each attempted to form some baseline of cooperation while maintaining primary competence over tax matters concerning aviation. Each communication appeared to lead to further misinterpretation, culminating in an understanding that both organisations would not make studies on the subject without consulting the other. This began with a letter from ER Marlin (ICAO External Relations Officer) stating that ICAO would not duplicate the Fiscal Division's data collection activity but that the latter's research would not affect ICAO's prerogative to draw up draft conventions or recommendations for tax exemption where it considered that the special characteristics of air transport called for such separate treatment.[134] Lachmann replied, stating that the Fiscal Commission's and Division's comprehensive mandate encompassed international transactions and enterprises concerning air transportation and that it would make the results of its studies available when ICAO found it desirable to initiate and negotiate agreements to eliminate special tax burdens on air transport.[135] Marlin responded that the Division's studies 'goes beyond what I thought we had agreed' and that duplication was 'inevitable' if the Division 'intends to conduct studies of a purely aeronautical character'.[136] Marlin suggested that the two Secretariats 'keep each other informed of their activities in this field in order that their endeavours may be kept separate and distinct'.[137] Lachmann replied that 'there is full agreement that such special studies would not be undertaken, either by your Organization or by this Division, without previous consultation' and affirmed Marlin's suggestion 'to postpone final decision as

Department, 'Fiscal Commission – Second Session', 2. ICAO's failure to notify the Division and Bartelt's corresponding silence suggests that a new strategy had been devised.

134 Letter from Marlin to Lachmann, undated (received 26 January 1949 in the UN), UNARMS:AG-025-002—S-0441-0469-23893(A).

135 Letter from Lachmann to Marlin, 7 February 1949, UNARMS:AG-025-002—S-0441-0469-23893(A).

136 Letter from Marlin to Lachmann, undated (received 2 March 1949 in the UN), UNARMS:AG-025-002—S-0441-0469-23893(A).

137 Ibid.

to where the studies are carried out, until each occasion may arise'.[138] Marlin appeared satisfied with the answer.[139]

At the end of March, AT-WP/30 was considered by the ATC; however, at that meeting 'great stress was placed on the work already undertaken in this field by the Fiscal Commission . . . and on the necessity of using the material and information collected by the UN Secretariat on the subject'.[140] Some delegates 'expressed doubts as to the immediate usefulness of such a study' pending the completion of the UN's more comprehensive study, and highlighted 'the notorious difficulty of obtaining general acceptance for the proposed tax exemption measures'.[141] The ATC and Council decided that a preliminary review was necessary 'to determine aspects of the problem that called for a more thorough study' and that the ATC's budget should be increased to allow additional staff for the work.[142] ICAO's Third Assembly, however, rejected all proposed staff increases for 1950.[143] The ATC and Council, with the knowledge that 'no staff was available to do the work in the existing Secretariat', nevertheless instructed the ICAO Secretariat 'to consider how staff might be provided to undertake this work in the near future'.[144] In July, American Edward Weld (Director, Air Transport Bureau, ICAO Secretariat)[145] visited the UN to study the Division's materials on documents published by the League and UN on double taxation.[146] In September, Weld published the preliminary study (AT-WP/85)[147] and submitted draft resolution AT-WP/30 to the ATC, which decided to wait for IATA's input before submitting the documents to the ICAO

138 Letter from Lachmann to Marlin, 7 March 1949, 2, UNARMS:AG-025-002—S-0441-0469-23893(A).

139 Letter from Marlin to Lachmann, undated (received 18 March 1949 in the UN), UNARMS:AG-025-002—S-0441-0469-23893(A).

140 Fiscal Division, 'Aide-mémoire', 2. This statement was likely made by a representative from the UN Transport Division.

141 Ibid.

142 Ibid.

143 Ibid.

144 Letter from Lester to Kremery, 12 July 1949, UNARMS:AG-025-002—S-0441-0469-23893(A).

145 The Director also served as Assistant Secretary-General of Air Transport and as permanent secretary to the ATC: Schenkman, *International Civil Aviation Organization*, 212.

146 Letter from Weld to Muller, 28 June 1949, UNARMS:AG-025-002—S-0441-0469-23893 (A). The Division later mailed its materials to ICAO: Letter from Kremery to Lester, 29 July 1949, UNARMS:AG-025-002—S-0441-0469-23893(A).

147 *Multiple, Discriminatory and Unfairly Burdensome Taxation*, Preliminary Report by the ICAO Secretariat, ATC, 8th sess, ICAO Doc AT-WP/85 (14 September 1949).

Council.[148] RJ Moulton (Chief, Facilitation Section) sent the Fiscal Division copies of AT-WP/85 and AT-WP/30, stating that the ICAO Secretariat 'has encountered in its study many problems which, if more time had been available, could have been explored more thoroughly and perhaps given rise to proposals of a more concrete nature' but that AT-WP/85 nevertheless 'represents a reasonably comprehensive examination of the matter and provides a substantial basis for further study of the problem'.[149]

The Division was incensed: firstly, by ICAO's lack of consultation concerning AT-WP/85; secondly, because the ICAO Secretariat 'recommends special tax privileges for international airlines, especially at the expense of underdeveloped countries, and disguises this recommendation under the cloak of a fight against tax discrimination'; thirdly, because ICAO had not shown that the taxes under study uniquely affected international aviation, or were quantitatively or qualitatively more burdensome than those incurred by other international enterprises; and fourthly, which the Division considered '[t]he most annoying fact', because 'the Report misquotes the UN Fiscal Commission on important points of fact and policy'.[150] The Division's analysis found AT-WP/85 biased and riddled with contradictions and errors, and its conclusions presumptuous and unsubstantiated.

In general, the Division held that AT-WP/85 had taken the statements in AT-WP/30 as foregone conclusions by working to buttress, rather than test, those assumptions, and had gone further than a preliminary review to advance 'far-reaching recommendations without adequate study' and with evidence that 'fails almost without exception'.[151] AT-WP/85 also did not establish the necessary conditions for tax privileges to 'be defended, if at all' in proving that the taxes constituted 'a heavy burden whose removal would supply an incentive to the international aviation industry' or that 'the industry economically needs and politically justifies such special privileges as against domestic aviation on the one hand, and other international transport and general enterprises on the other'.[152]

148 Fiscal Division, 'Aide-mémoire', 2.

149 Moulton letter, 19 September 1949.

150 Memorandum by Bloch to Owen, 25 October 1949, UNARMS:AG-025-002—S-0441–0469–23893(A).

151 Fiscal Division, 'Aide-mémoire', 3.

152 Ibid 4. AT-WP/85 in fact gave contradictory statistics, namely: that 'very little factual data has as yet been found bearing on the magnitude of aviation's tax problem' (at 7 [10]); that industry data showed that for 1947, all taxes (except income taxes) on international air transport amounted to '2% of the total operating costs', while income

Regarding the subject of multiple taxation, the Division considered that AT-WP/85 made 'sweeping denunciation' of 'the taxation by several countries of the same item' without any 'thorough fiscal and economic analysis' before proceeding to limit the discussion to 'ways and means of eliminating it'.[153] AT-WP/85 misrepresented international opinion and practice by claiming that the universal adoption of the exemption rule had 'already substantially been realized' not only in national tax legislations and DTAs,[154] but also in the League's 'endorsement' of it and the UN's acceptance of it 'in its studies thus far', including the *Mexico/*

taxes were 'a negative quantity' since 'most operators lost money' (at 8 [11]); and that the burden of double taxation was 'slight', estimated at 1 per cent of total costs, with an 'absence of complaint [found] against such taxation' (at 8 [11]). Notwithstanding these figures, AT-WP/85 concluded that 'the problem is important enough at the international level to warrant making use of precedents and instruments at hand in order to prevent double taxation from becoming prevalent' (at 9 [13]), citing as support a CAB expert study on internal taxation of domestic US airlines (*Multiple Taxation of Air Commerce*, 79th US Congress, 1st session, House Document No 141, 12 April 1945 ('*CAB Study*')). The Division criticised the reference as inapplicable as it was not only a domestic study but was also outdated and 'unsuited for comparison with the over-all international picture, where the tax burden amounts to only one-tenth of this figure': Fiscal Division, 'Aide-mémoire', 4–5 (citing that the *CAB Study* had indicated that the tax burden on domestic air transport in the United States in 1943 amounted to 19.5 per cent with approximately 10.5 per cent of this comprising income taxes (*CAB Study*, 83)). The Division considered that the 'small amounts involved [in the international burden] . . . would in effect amount to a demand for absolute justice in taxation': Fiscal Division, 'Aide-mémoire', 5.

153 Fiscal Division, 'Aide-mémoire', 6. Conversely, the Division thought it 'doubtful whether super-imposition of taxes by several governmental authorities should be considered obnoxious per se' and 'even more doubtful whether it is always restrictive of international trade'. The Division also criticised AT-WP/85's recommendation that the exemption rule in the Model drafts be extended to the personal income tax of employees and to Social Security taxes, noting that no country, in the interests of preventing tax avoidance, applied such a rule (at 9).

154 Although AT-WP/85 listed eight ICAO member states (Australia, Belgium, China, Egypt, Greece, Iraq, Philippines and Siam) as favouring the allocation theory, it asserted that the application of the reciprocal exemption theory to the taxation of shipping and airline income by sixteen other member states (Canada, Denmark, Finland, France, Iceland, India, Ireland, Italy, the Netherlands, New Zealand, Norway, Sweden, Switzerland, South Africa, the United Kingdom and the United States) had led to the principle's extensive implementation via reciprocal exemption agreements: AT-WP/85, 11–12 [18]–[20]. AT-WP/85 also gave emphasis to the US practice as well as Britain's and France's recent reaffirmations of 'their strong adherence to the principle', citing as support the Division's study concerning member governments' tax laws and regulations governing foreign nationals, resources and transactions (at 12 [20], referring to Fiscal Commission, *Tax Treatment of Foreign Nationals, Resources and Transactions*, Note by the Secretariat, UN Docs E/CN.8/45 and Add.1 (31 December 1948); *Tax Treatment of Foreign Nationals, Assets and Transactions: Replies of Member Governments to*

London Models Commentary 'prepared by the UN Secretariat'.[155] AT-WP/85 also took no account of authorities that endorsed apportionment over the exemption rule,[156] asserting instead that 'water and air carriers … [,] in the absence of special tax treatment, would be handicapped by problems of income allocation between countries and the needs to comply with the requirements of numerous tax jurisdictions'.[157]

Questionnaire of 5 August 1948 (E/CN.8/W.19), UN Docs E/CN.8/46 and Add.1–2 (6 January 1949)).

The Division considered these statements overgeneralisations, particularly as E/CN.8/45 and 46 had indicated that Britain and France, along with Czechoslovakia, Denmark, Ecuador and Turkey, not only applied the allocation principle in their national legislation, but also in the absence of special agreements, taxed the profits of non-resident air transport enterprises on an allocation basis: Fiscal Division, 'Aide-mémoire', 8. Furthermore, even where these countries or any other country mentioned in AT-WP/85 (including the United States) applied the exemption rule in their DTAs, 'it was frequently hedged in by important reservations (designed to prevent tax evasion) which still leave room for taxation by allocation among the several countries where the air transport enterprise operates' (at 8–9). Some countries (e.g. Australia), moreover, had only agreed to the exemption rule in certain DTAs because of substantial concessions being granted in exchange rather than a regard for the principle's soundness, while the 'unfairness' of the rule largely accounted for 'the total absence of such tax agreements with underdeveloped countries having no national airlines of their own' (at 9). In addition, regarding US practice concerning international shipping, where no agreement for reciprocal exemption was in place, the United States 'recognized the existence of juridical limits to its taxing powers' in its income tax regulations (s 29.119–13, reg 111) which provided a formula restricting 'American tax on a foreign shipping enterprise to income measured primarily by the distance run and the time spent within the [US] territorial waters': Memorandum by Kremery to Lachmann, 20 December 1949, UNARMS:AG-025-002—S-0441-0469-23893(A).

155 AT-WP/85, 12 [20]–[21]. In the Division's view, it had been made explicitly clear in the relevant League publications that the Fiscal Committee had not proposed the Mexico and London drafts as final solutions but as requiring further expert and balanced examination, and that the *Mexico/London Models Commentary* had been the work of the League Secretariat and was not to be taken as representing the views of the Fiscal Committee: Fiscal Division, 'Aide-mémoire', 7–9. The UN itself had yet to produce any study on the principle as the Fiscal Commission had not 'at any time discussed the question, much less taken a stand on it' (at 8).

156 These included (1) the *CAB Study*, which concluded that US interstate reciprocal exemption rules had 'led to much litigation, tax avoidance and no little confusion, particularly in the field of property taxation', while 'a far more wholesome relationship between Government and the taxpayer is attained through the use of allocation methods' (*CAB Study*, 44–5); (2) the Model Bill adopted by the US Council of State Governments on 18 January 1947; and (3) published scholars in the field (i.e. Richard W Lindholm, *Public Finance of Air Transportation: A Study of Taxation and Public Expenditures in Relation to a Developing Industry* (Ohio State University, 1948) 90; James J Arditto, 'State and Local Taxation of Scheduled Local Airlines' (1949) 16(2) *Journal of Air Law and Commerce* 162, 167).

157 AT-WP/85, 12 [21].

In the Division's view, the exemption rule favoured airlines which stood to make tax savings and the more highly developed countries in which they were located, while 'deny[ing] all tax revenue to countries which have no airlines of their own, yet make an important contribution in passengers and freight to the operations of international aviation'.[158] As AT-WP/85 had not shown that preferential relief techniques were justified or that the PE allocation technique was any more complex for international aviation as compared to other multinational trading enterprises,[159] the Division concluded that 'the question is far from foreclosed by precedent, and that a thorough study of actual conditions should precede any general recommendation to apply specially favourable rules'.[160]

Regarding the subject of discriminatory and unfairly burdensome taxes, the Division held that AT-WP/85 had incorrectly defined discriminatory taxes as taxes 'imposed on aviation but not on other activities, provided there is no acceptable reason for such differentiation'.[161] The report did not refer to any existing instances of such discrimination. While unfairly burdensome taxes were not defined, they were said to include multiple and discriminatory taxes as well as all indirect taxes (including customs duties or import and excise taxes on fuel, lubricants, equipment, supplies and sales of international air transportation).[162] The

158 Fiscal Division, 'Aide-mémoire', 7. AT-WP/85 itself acknowledged that 'countries not operating air transport services find it difficult to surrender a possible lucrative tangible source of taxation in return for the less tangible advantages pertaining to the receipt of air service', although it surmised that this was '[t]he only weakness in the application of this principle': AT-WP/85, 12 [22].

159 On the contrary, AT-WP/85 indicated that the problem of double taxation faced by airline enterprises had fundamentally similar features to that faced by other international enterprises, before asserting that as air and shipping enterprises kept their property mostly at the home port or 'en route on the high seas . . . outside any tax jurisdiction', it was 'not unnatural for foreign jurisdictions to cede all taxing authority to the home state of the vessel': AT-WP/85, 10–11 [16]. The Division considered this argument 'remains doubtful' in the case of shipping lines, and 'wholly inapplicable' to aviation enterprises as 'flights over the high seas consume but a small percentage of their total mileage': Fiscal Division, 'Aide-mémoire', 7.

160 Fiscal Division, 'Aide-mémoire', 9.

161 AT-WP/85, 6 [6]. This was despite AT-WP/30 having defined it correctly as taxes levied differently on nationals and foreigners: Fiscal Division, 'Aide-mémoire', 10 (citing AT-WP/30, 4, annex I, para 1).

162 AT-WP/85, 6 [7]–[8]. In the case of fuel taxes, AT-WP/85 had further argued, in the interest of convenience, not only for their exemption and reduction because of the 'negligible' income to be derived from them 'as far as most states are concerned', but also for their 'uniformity at the level of zero . . . [as] by far the easiest uniformity to attain' (at 21 [48]). The Division contended that decisions of revenue sacrifice were the

Division considered that an analysis of fact was required in each case of alleged differentiation or unfairly burdensome taxation before they could be declared to exist, particularly as AT-WP/85's characterisations were 'contradicted by accepted tax practice'.[163]

In view of the aforementioned criticisms, the UN Secretariat officials felt that 'a strong stand should be taken in the matter' and that ICAO should be prevailed upon to withdraw AT-WP/85,[164] given 'the important precedent it might establish'.[165] Although detailed and strongly worded drafts were initially written, the final letter sent by Owen to Roper was brief and courteous, explaining that the subject of AT-WP/85 came within the UN's competence and work, the report contained errors of fact on the UN's position and there was 'considerable measure of doubt' as to its recommendations and conclusions.[166] Owen ended by requesting joint consideration of 'practical steps [that] might be taken to improve the arrangements [between the two organisations] in the future' and that their 'responsible officials ... consult together' before AT-WP/85 was finalised.[167] In early November, an ICAO Secretariat member (AM Lester) calling on the Division encountered a stern Lachmann. During their exchange, Lester 'explained that consultation had probably not taken place because AT-WP/85 had to be prepared in a great hurry', 'Weld himself had been under pressure of time' and there 'were no tax experts at all' under the ICAO 'set-up' who might 'have usefully discussed it with

prerogative of governments, to be determined on a case-by-case basis by examining 'that industry's intrinsic usefulness' and 'its comparative value as against other industries which would have to carry a heavier tax burden to make up for the loss of revenue': Fiscal Division, 'Aide-mémoire', 11.

163 Fiscal Division, 'Aide-mémoire', 10. According to the Division, the levying of excises was 'a legitimate revenue technique' imposed on all transport, not just aviation, and on domestic transport generally, not just international transport. Nothing in the nature of excises thus made them 'necessarily unfairly burdensome by definition', although they could constitute a burden on the activity and possibly be excessive or discriminatory. The Division also refuted AT-WP/85's argument for the exemption of international shipping activities from certain excises and duties to be analogously applied to international airlines (AT-WP/85, 18 [37]), noting that such exemption 'was limited to fuel and stores kept under bond in territorial waters and used only on the high seas outside of the limits of all taxing authorities', whereas airlines had 'scant opportunity to use stores and fuel outside the limit of national boundaries': Fiscal Division, 'Aide-mémoire', 10.

164 Bloch memo, 25 October 1949.

165 KE Lachmann, 'Notes for a Letter to Dr Roper', 21 October 1949, UNARMS:AG-025-002—S-0441-0469-23893(A).

166 Letter from Owen to Roper, 4 November 1949, UNARMS:AG-025-002—S-0441-0469-23893(A). Earlier drafts were dated 24 and 26 October 1949 (same folder).

167 Ibid.

[the Division]'.[168] Lester nevertheless 'stressed that no harm would come from the Report since no final action had yet been taken on its proposals' and that '[i]t was indeed the desire of ICAO always to proceed in full accord with [the Division]'.[169]

By mid-November, the UN Secretariat had looked into sharing the costs of engaging a consultant to work for four weeks to provide additional study.[170] It contacted tax economist George Mitchell (Director of the Department of Finance, State of Illinois)[171] to discuss the planning of the study and to advise on a suitably qualified expert, specifically a person 'outside the aviation industry' with 'knowledge of the economic issues involved, some actual experience in tax administration and a sufficient founding in legal aspects'.[172] Weld expressed surprise at the speed at which the UN was moving.[173]

Meanwhile, at ICAO, AT-WP/85 had not been withdrawn and was being used as the basis for debate by the ATC. While both France and Mexico found the evidence in AT/WP-85 'insufficient to form the basis for specific recommendations in most of the fields of taxation studied',[174] the Canadian Chairman (CS Booth) nevertheless submitted a draft report (AT-WP/120) containing draft resolutions on double taxation of income and property, customs duties and excise taxes on fuels and lubricants, and taxes on the sale or use of international air transport to be circulated to member states.[175] The draft resolution concerning double taxation called upon member states to adopt the reciprocal exemption rule in their bilateral agreements and national legislation on the basis that the rule had 'been widely accepted'; was 'favoured in the drafting of international tax conventions'; and could

168 Memorandum by Lachmann to Bloch, 7 November 1949, UNARMS:AG-025-002—S-0441-0469-23893(A).

169 Ibid.

170 Letter from Bloch to Weld, 18 November 1949, UNARMS:AG-025-002—S-0441-0469-23893(A).

171 Letter from Shere to Mitchell, 12 January 1950, UNARMS:AG-025-002—S-0441-0469-23893(B). Mitchell had been consultant for CAB and the director of the *CAB Study* and was also head of research of the Federal Reserve Bank of Chicago and consultant to the Internal Revenue Bureau.

172 Letter from Mitchell to Bloch, 14 December 1949, UNARMS:AG-025-002—S-0441-0469-23893(A).

173 Letter from Weld to Bloch, 25 November 1949, UNARMS:AG-025-002—S-0441-0469-23893(A).

174 UNEC, 'US Position (Aviation Taxation)', 1–2.

175 ATC, *Draft Report to Council by the Chairman of the Air Transport Committee*, 8th sess, ICAO Doc AT-WP/120 (18 November 1949), UNARMS:AG-025-002—S-0441-0469-23893(A).

effectively prevent double taxation, although some states 'would find it more practicable to deal with the problem . . . as part of the problem of relief from double taxation of trade and industry in general'.[176]

On 23 November, before the ATC could take action on AT-WP/120, the ICAO Secretariat informed it of the UN Secretariat's reservations on AT-WP/85[177] and that Roper, Booth and Weld, in consultation, had instructed the ICAO Secretariat to prepare a paper for the ATC detailing the communications between the two secretariats and the UN Secretariat's misgivings.[178] This paper (AT-WP/122) concluded that the UN Secretariat felt that ICAO 'had absorbed too much of an industry . . . viewpoint', was 'giving international bilateral agreements too much prominence at the expense of national legislation' and 'had tended to regard aviation taxation too much as being a separate subject'.[179] AT-WP/122 was submitted to the ATC on 28 November without consulting the UN Secretariat and contained errors in its details of the latter's views.[180] The State Department informed Lachmann by telephone of AT/WP/122's issuance before Weld, also by telephone, apprised the Division of the existence of AT-WP/120 and AT-WP/122.[181]

Bloch and Delanney travelled to Montréal to attend the ATC meeting of 5 December to emphasise the unfairness of ICAO's recommendation of reciprocal exemption to underdeveloped countries, clarify ICAO's misrepresentations in AT-WP/85 and AT-WP/122 of the UN Secretariat's position and obtain ICAO's agreement for a cooperative study by the two secretariats.[182] At the meeting, Weld made a public apology and the ATC decided not to submit AT-WP/120 to the ICAO Council, although it considered circulating it to member states to obtain their views. Bloch and Delanney thought this 'an entirely unnecessary and even harmful procedure' but 'were in no position to interfere'.[183] They reported that '[t]he discussion showed clearly that the members who suggested the circulation of documents did so in order to have

[176] Ibid app I.

[177] UNEC, 'US Position (Aviation Taxation)', 2.

[178] Weld letter, 25 November 1949.

[179] ATC, *Relations with United Nations*, 8th sess, ICAO Doc AT-WP/122 (28 November 1949) 3, UNARMS:AG-025-002—S-0441-0469-23893(A).

[180] Memorandum by Bloch and Delanney to Goldet, 8 December 1949, UNARMS:AG-025-002—S-0441-0469-23893(A).

[181] Memorandum by Goldet to Owen, 1 December 1949, UNARMS:AG-025-002—S-0441-0469-23893(A).

[182] Bloch and Delanney memo, 8 December 1949.

[183] Ibid 2.

something to show to the Council for their labors', that these members were 'also unwilling to reverse themselves completely on matters which had already received prior Committee approval' and that if 'the entire program completed so far would be scrapped and a new study begun, it would be considered a failure for the [ATC]'.[184] Once back at the UN, Bloch informed Marlin that the UN was issuing a report based on the proceedings of the Committee of Experts on Financing Economic Development,[185] which 'contain[ed] a definite endorsement of general preference for tax credits as against exemptions in the field of income and profits taxation'.[186] He asked Marlin to bring this to ATC's attention.

Meanwhile, the ATC issued its report to the Council (*20th Report*), in which it recommended transmitting its draft resolutions to member states, indicating that it would review the matter '[i]n light of the replies received' before submitting 'its final recommendations to Council'.[187] The *20th Report* made no mention of the misrepresentations of the UN Secretariat's position or the latter's problems with its views, but instead stated that '[i]n the final stages of its discussion, the Committee had the benefit of [the UN Secretariat's] advice', and proposed collaboration with the UN Secretariat in 'supplementing' AT-WP/85 for 'the main purposes of (1) expanding the factual and legal background material, and (2) analyzing and interpreting the material and the problems presented from the point of view of international taxation theory and practice'.[188] The Council approved the ATC's *20th Report* on 13 December.[189] The draft resolution concerning double taxation contained therein was virtually identical to the version in AT-WP/120.[190]

184 Ibid.

185 *Methods of Increasing Domestic Savings and of Ensuring Their Most Advantageous Use for the Purpose of Economic Development*, Study by the Secretary-General, UN ESC, 10th sess, Agenda item 9(c), UN Doc E/1562 (16 December 1949). See Chapter 9, Section 9.2, n 22 for a background of this report.

186 Letter from Bloch to Marlin, 8 December 1949, UNARMS:AG-025-002—S-0441-0469-23893(A). The Division itself considered that 'a credit rule can better combine the conflicting requirements of revenue and incentive needs': Note (untitled) on work plan of the Fiscal Division, 20 December 1949, 5, UNOG:UNOGRFP—G.X.25/1.

187 ATC, *20th Report to Council by the Chairman of the Air Transport Committee*, ICAO Council, 8th sess, ICAO Doc C-WP/509 (9 December 1949) 2, UNARMS:AG-025-002—S-0441-0469-23893(A).

188 Ibid 3.

189 Letter from Weld to Bloch, 13 December 1949, UNARMS:AG-025-002—S-0441-0469-23893(A).

190 'Draft Resolution on Taxation of Income and Property of Airlines' in ATC, *20th Report*, app III. This draft resolution is reproduced in Appendix J.

11.5 The Jointly Funded Expert Study by Shere (January–May 1950)

Throughout December, the Division vetted potential candidates to undertake the study,[191] ultimately deciding on a consultant from Weld's list,[192] Loius Shere (Director of Tax Research and Professor of Economics at the University of Indiana, and former Associate Director of the US Treasury's Tax Research Division).[193] The UN and ICAO each committed $1,000 for the research project ($1,500 to pay Shere, and $500 for his travelling expenses).[194] At ICAO's insistence, Shere was placed on its payroll;[195] Bloch consented, remarking to DEA that he was 'in favor of making all concessions in matters of form but to resist all concessions in matters of principle'.[196] Shere set to work almost immediately despite not yet receiving the official appointment by ICAO,[197] nor formal objectives.[198] Lachmann advised him of the delicate UN–ICAO relations, stating that

> it would perhaps be preferable to postpone establishing a precise list of the issues to be studied until our joint meeting with ICAO in Montréal. If

191 See, for example, Mitchell letter, 14 December 1949.

192 The ICAO Secretariat had considered this list of candidates in 1948 to carry out 'the original basic work on multiple taxation' before it undertook the study in-house: Letter from Weld to Bloch, 9 December 1949, UNARMS:AG-025-002—S-0441-0469-23893(A).

193 Letter from Bloch to Mitchell, 3 January 1950, UNARMS:AG-025-002—S-0441-0469-23893(A). Bloch regarded Shere 'a very good man' for the role and knew him 'from long association in the Treasury Department': Letter from Bloch to Weld, 13 December 1949, UNARMS:AG-025-002—S-0441-0469-23893(A). Shere had 'written extensively in the field of taxation and ... [had] made considerable contributions to the field of international tax relations': Memorandum by Bloch to Green, 22 December 1949, 2, UNARMS:AG-025-002—S-0441-0469-23893(A). He had also initially declined to do the research project for ICAO in 1948 and ICAO was reportedly 'very pleased that he has now consented to do this work': Ibid. Mitchell felt confident that Shere would do a competent job: Letter from Mitchell to Bloch, 6 January 1950, UNARMS:AG-025-002—S-0441-0469-23893(B).

194 Bloch memo, 22 December 1949.

195 Letter from Lachmann to Shere, 5 January 1950, UNARMS:AG-025-002—S-0441-0469-23893(A).

196 Bloch memo, 22 December 1949, 2.

197 Despite several reminders and assurances that it would be sent, Shere only received this letter in mid-March when he wanted to incorporate it in the front of his report to give the latter a proper reference: Letter from Shere to Weld, 13 March 1950, UNARMS:AG-025-002—S-0441-0469-23893(B).

198 These were only confirmed much later and mirrored the purposes set out in the ATC's *20th Report*: Letter from ICAO Secretary-General to Shere, 13 March 1950, UNARMS:AG-025-002—S-0441-0469-23893(B).

> I attempted now to prejudge that decision, no matter how tentatively, there is under the circumstances a danger than such procedure may be taken amiss by ICAO.[199]

This meeting took place between 26 and 27 January, with Shere in attendance.[200] The study was to deal primarily with income and property taxes, fuel taxes, taxes on the sale and use of international air transport, and certain customs duties on equipment and parts. Emphasis was to be made on differences between the taxation of international and national air transport, and between international transport and general international business enterprises. Regarding the taxation of income and property, the advisability of reciprocal exemption and the practicability of allocation was to be examined. The study was to be completed by 1 April with both secretariats to meet before 15 April to arrive at a joint report for submission to the ATC and Fiscal Commission.

Shere consulted an extensive range of source material provided by the UN, ICAO and Mitchell.[201] He found ICAO's data, inter alia, incomplete and inconsistent, frequently requesting Moulton to furnish further material.[202] Moulton was evidently annoyed at one point, stating:

> There is no inconsistency in the material furnished on 'reciprocal exemption' versus 'allocation' techniques, for the reasons you mentioned. Re the facts, I simply feel you will have to do what you can with such evidence as is available. ... To me the evidence available is clear on the basis of international action, i.e., bilateral agreements between countries wherein aviation and shipping are handled; and the internal or domestic policy of individual countries or even the views offered on any given occasion by them . . . have relatively little significance. In other words, it is my personal view that you will have to treat the subject on the basis of international evidence, small though it might be, forgetting for the moment the views

[199] Letter from Lachmann to Shere, 11 January 1950, UNARMS:AG-025-002—S-0441-0469-23893(B).

[200] Memorandum by Lachmann to Bloch, 7 February 1950, UNARMS:AG-025-002—S-0441-0469-23893(B). Lachmann was the only UN representative, whereas ICAO was represented by Warner, Roper, Weld and Moulton. Separate meetings were also held with the American (David) and French (M Bouché) representatives on the ICAO Council because of their particular interest in the project. Although Mitchell, at the Division's request, was supposed to join the meeting, the Montréal venue precluded his attendance: Letters between Mitchell to Bloch, 6 and 11 January 1950, UNARMS:AG-025-002—S-0441-0469-23893(B).

[201] This source material is indicated among the various correspondence in UNARMS:AG-025-002—S-0441-0469-23893(B).

[202] See, for example, Letters from Shere to Moulton, 23, 24, 25 and 26 February 1950, UNARMS:AG-025-002—S-0441-0469-23893(B).

> expressed by either fiscal or aviation experts as to what they think the practice ought to be.[203]

The study proved formidable: Shere wrote to Lachmann saying, it 'has been a much bigger job than either of us contemplated' and 'has become a labor of love long ago, about 1/3 the way through to be exact, but I don't mind'.[204] The former hoped that the report would 'be of service and of some permanent value . . . for development of international tax principles and practice generally'.[205] On 28 March, Shere sent his report to both Secretariats.[206] In brief, and according to Delanney, the report approached

> the problem mostly from the point of view of the impact of taxation on the international airlines, of the justification of the various taxes in force, of the possible alternatives which might be advocated and of their respective merits. In other words, emphasis is clearly placed on the airlines as taxpayers and the main question is whether they are right when complaining of 'multiple, discriminatory and unfairly burdensome taxation'.[207]

The report concluded that there was a lack of evidence showing why international aviation should benefit from a special tax regime and that airlines should be subjected to the generally accepted allocation method under which each country was entitled to tax the domestic profits of a foreign enterprise.[208]

[203] Letter from Moulton to Shere, 21 February 1950, 2, UNARMS:AG-025-002—S-0441-0469-23893(B) (emphasis in original).

[204] Letters by Shere to Lachmann, 11 and 18 March 1950, UNARMS:AG-025-002—S-0441-0469-23893(B).

[205] Ibid.

[206] Letter from Shere to Bloch, 28 March 1950, UNARMS:AG-025-002—S-0441-0469-23893(B).

[207] Memorandum by Delanney to Bloch, 24 April 1950, 1, UNARMS:AG-025-002—S-0441-0469-23893(B). Delanney considered '[t]his point of view is undoubtedly accurate, all the more so as ICAO has placed the problem on this ground, which is more particularly its own'. However, Delanney believed there was a second important aspect to be considered that was 'also essential in order to obtain a complete picture of the situation', but which Shere 'only touches upon and from a different angle'. This aspect concerned the question of fair allocation between States interested in international air transport of the revenues deriving from this transport to balance the differing interests of, on the one hand, 'countries running international airlines, i.e., are at the same time carriers and users', and, on the other, 'countries which are only used by international air transport' (emphasis in original).

[208] Memorandum by Lachmann to Bloch, 17 April 1950, UNARMS:AG-025-002—S-0441-0469-23893(B). Shere's report pointed out that the evidence showed that the United States, Canada and some European countries which were important in international air transportation favoured reciprocal exemption while less-industrialised countries preferred allocation.

On 7 April, Bloch, Lachmann, Delanney, Weld, Moulton and Shere met at the UN to discuss the report.[209] The ICAO members strongly objected to, while Bloch and Lachmann agreed with, the conclusions. Regarding double taxation, the ICAO members felt that reciprocal exemption was 'the only proper solution' because it was 'the effective system for 95% of international air transport . . . therefore any change in the rule would have to be justified on very strong grounds'; and allocation presented 'enormous difficulties' in determining a uniform detailed formula for each country's share that would be universally accepted.[210] Conversely, Bloch, Lachmann and Shere argued that reciprocal exemption, though simpler in administration, could not 'be defended on any rational ground' and that their position 'was not purely a narrow tax administrator's view of the problem' on the grounds, inter alia, that:[211]

- allocation was an important tax policy that entitled countries in which enterprises carried on profitable operations to their corresponding share of revenue, this tradition alone having precedence over 'the unexplained exception made for air transport and shipping in the past';
- allocation presented no heavier calculation burden for aviation enterprises than other multinationals enterprises operating in several countries, airlines themselves using bookkeeping revenue allocation to calculate the profit/loss of different routes of their operations; and
- reciprocal exemption left underdeveloped countries as 'the losers taxwise' and was 'in fundamental conflict' with capital exporting countries' undertaking to shoulder the financial burden resulting from eliminating double taxation rather than impose it on underdeveloped and economically weaker countries.

The meeting failed to lead to any agreement on the main points of contention. The ICAO members indicated that the ATC and Council would likely 'overlook' Shere's report and 'act in conformity with the policy advocated in the draft resolutions' on the basis that governmental replies to their draft resolutions indicated that governments were 'favourable to the point of view expressed by the ICAO Secretariat'.[212] The

209 Ibid.

210 Ibid 5.

211 Ibid 6–8.

212 Memorandum by Delanney to Lukac and Higgins, 13 April 1950, 3, UNARMS:AG-025-002—S-0441-0469-23893(B). Interestingly, ICAO had not received any such replies by 10 March and had extended the deadline to 15 April: Letter from Moulton to Shere,

meeting made 'clear' that if the Fiscal Commission endorsed the UN Secretariat's views, 'there would be a conflict between the two Organizations and therefore a need for arbitration'.[213] The parties decided that comments, including observations by Mitchell and other experts, would be sent to Shere for drafting changes by 30 April, and Shere was to send the revised text to ICAO before the ATC meeting around 15 May.[214] The ICAO Secretariat would prepare a brief introductory note agreed upon by the two Secretariats, but they were neither to give endorsement nor circulate comments that would reveal their disagreement. The ICAO officials indicated that Shere's report would only likely be examined in September as ICAO would be occupied with its Assembly until then. The report, along with an account of the action taken by the ATC and Council, would be submitted to the Fiscal Commission in 1951.

In May, Bloch wrote to Weld, objecting that ICAO Council's report to its Assembly (A4-P/1) did not correctly present the joint study in 'fail[ing] to indicate the reasons and the nature of the [UN's] participation ... in the study'.[215] Bloch suggested that A4-P/1 clarify that the joint study had been made, firstly, 'to avoid overlapping activities and conflicts in policy recommendations' because international aviation taxation was 'part and parcel' of the UN's 'over-all field of fiscal policy and of the taxation of international trade and investment' studies, 'especially in its role in the economic development of underdeveloped countries', and secondly, because further study by an outside expert had been necessary to expand 'the limited material' in AT-WP/85 and provide an analysis and interpretation 'from the point of view of international tax

10 March 1950, UNARMS:AG-025-002—S-0441-0469-23893(B). No replies were forwarded to Shere as he revised his report. Only in July did ICAO print the twelve replies in ICAO Doc AT-WP/153, which it forwarded to the Division: Letter from Weld to Bloch, 6 July 1950, UNARMS:AG-025-002—S-0441-0469-23893(B). By April 1951, ICAO had received replies from twenty-four states and nine dependent territories, which indicated conflicting positions between developed and underdeveloped countries: Memorandum by Delanney and Lachmann to Owen, 4 April 1951, UNARMS:AG-025-002—S-0441-0469-23893(B). Of these replies, all independent underdeveloped countries (except Indonesia) opposed the resolution, 'chiefly on the ground that reciprocal exemption was appropriate only where there was actual reciprocity among the countries in the volume of air traffic exchanged': Letter from Bloch to Saksena, 11 April 1951, 1, UNARMS:AG-025-002—S-0441-0469-23893(B).

213 Delanney memo, 13 April 1950, 3.

214 Memorandum by Bloch to Owen, 13 April 1950, UNARMS:AG-025-002—S-0441-0469-23893(B).

215 Letter from Bloch to Weld, 10 May 1950, UNARMS:AG-025-002—S-0441-0469-23893 (B) (citing *Report of the Council to the Assembly on the Activities of the Organization in 1949*, ICAO Assembly, 4th sess, ICAO Doc 6968, A4-P/1 (March 1950)).

theory and practice'.[216] Bloch also suggested that A4-P/1 clarify that the draft resolutions circulated to member states had been done to elicit their comments 'but without prejudice to its [the ICAO Council's] ultimate view as to the character of the taxes in question and the measures to be recommended in order to solve such tax problems as might be found by the joint enquiry to exist'.[217] Weld, however, declined Bloch's suggestions on the grounds of policies applicable to its governing structure, including that A4-P/1 was of the Council and not the Secretariat, and that in the Council's view, the study of the problem was 'still in the early stage of reference to the [ATC]'.[218] It further indicated that its supplementary report would not discuss the work done by Shere in the first five months of 1950. In July, Shere's report was reproduced by ICAO as AT-WP/154.[219]

11.6 ICAO's Rejection of Shere's Report (March–April 1951)

In February 1951, the ATC began its review by establishing a Working Group comprising its Brazilian, Danish, UK and US members.[220] In six meetings, the Working Group examined ICAO's draft resolutions

216 Ibid 1–2.

217 Ibid 2.

218 Letter from Lester to Bloch, 10 May 1950, UNARMS:AG-025-002—S-0441-0469-23893(B). Lester further stated that '[t]he existence of our permanent governing bodies makes the relationship between our own Secretariat and the Assembly very different from that between your Secretariat and your Assembly'.

219 Letters by Weld to Bloch, 6 and 20 July 1950, UNARMS:AG-025-002—S-0441-0469-23893(B). See n 296 for details regarding the number of copies printed and made available to the Division.

220 ATC, *39th Report to Council by the Chairman of the Air Transport Committee*, ICAO Council, 12th sess, ICAO Doc 7145, C/824 (18 April 1951) 4–5, UNARMS: AG-025-002—S-0441-0469-23893(B) ('*39th Report*'). Although a developing country, Brazil would likely not have been disadvantaged by the exemption method as one of the eight ICAO Category A states (i.e. states of chief importance in air transport): State Department, *International Civil Aviation, 1945–1948* (USGPO, 1948) 8. As for political reasons to align with the United States and the United Kingdom, these two were Brazil's largest investors and main suppliers of aircraft, and Brazil had closer relations with the United States than any other South American country and was then still expecting US economic assistance without resorting, as other nations had, to blackmailing Washington by threatening to turn to the Soviets for help: Louis J Rodriguez, 'A Comparison: United States Economic Relations with Argentina and Brazil, 1947–1960' (LSU Historical Dissertations and Theses No 854, Louisiana State University and Agricultural & Mechanical College, 1963) 65–70, 73; Frank D McCann, 'Brazil, the United States, and World War II: A Commentary' (1979) 3(1) *Diplomatic History* 59, 73. The United States had also 'never challenged Brazilian ownership of the facilities [air bases]' that the former spent millions in building during World War II: Frank

in view of the replies received from member states, Shere's report and IATA's comments. In its draft report (AT-WP/208), the Working Group concluded that 'the original Resolutions had been framed on a sound basis' and that the 'evidence in general confirmed the earlier views of the Committee and Council that adoption of the resolutions in substantially the form originally conceived ... [would] obtain a favourable response from a large majority of Contracting States and would assist in the healthy development of international civil aviation.[221] AT-WP/208 maintained that reciprocal exemption was the exclusive solution to eliminating double taxation given its almost universal acceptance in practice as reflected in its incorporation in all existing bilateral agreements.[222] AT-WP/208 also cited ECOSOC Resolution 226D (IX)[223] as authority for states to negotiate DTAs wherever possible.[224] The UN Secretariat considered that AT-WP/208 misinterpreted international practice as agreements concluded up to that point only comprised those 'of developed countries and their dependencies', and also represented Resolution 226D (IX) in a 'misleading' manner that 'could convey the idea that ... [ECOSOC] favoured the principle of reciprocal exemption'.[225] The UN Secretariat approached the ICAO Secretariat to correct these factual errors; however, the latter refused.

In March 1951, at the ATC meeting discussing AT-WP/208, Lachmann and Delanney explained their issues with the report, highlighting that while ICAO focused on 'the purely aviation aspect of taxation', the UN had to 'reconcile the aviation aspect with the broader aspects' of 'taxation problems concerning the entire economic field', including important questions of general policy and effects on the revenue of underdeveloped countries.[226] The UN officials advocated allocation as 'the most satisfactory way of avoiding double taxation' and stressed that ICAO 'would be contributing to a rupture in the

D McCann, *Brazil and the United States during World War II and Its Aftermath: Negotiating Alliance and Balancing Giants* (Palgrave Macmillan, 2018) 250.

221 ATC, *39th Report*, 2.

222 Delanney and Lachmann memo, 4 April 1951, 2.

223 See Chapter 7, Sections 7.2.6–7.3 regarding the resolution and its background. See also Section 7.4 regarding the resolution's importance to the State Department, which further suggests, inter alia, US authorship of AT-WP/208.

224 Delanney and Lachmann memo, 4 April 1951, 2.

225 Ibid.

226 Ibid 3.

coordinating process' if it did not allow the Fiscal Commission and ECOSOC the opportunity to form a position before final action.[227]

In the subsequent discussion, representatives of underdeveloped countries (e.g. Argentina, India, Iraq and Mexico), supported by Australia and France, expressed their opposition to AT-WP/208's prejudice and, regarding the resolution on taxation of income and property,[228] proposed that action be deferred, while the Netherlands, the United Kingdom and the United States favoured AT-WP/208's conclusions.[229] The resolution was adopted by a split vote of six to five, with one abstention,[230] and the ATC adopted AT-WP/208 in its report ('*39th Report*') with the recommendation that the Council withhold final endorsement of that resolution until the UN bodies had decided on the question.[231] On 13 April, the Council approved the report, withheld its formal approval of the resolution and referred the resolution to the Fiscal Commission and ECOSOC.[232] Bloch was nevertheless informed that the resolution already had the Council's 'informal support' but that it would not be circulated to ICAO member states until ICAO took action on it. Bloch reported to Owen, saying '[t]his is precisely the outcome we had wanted'.[233]

11.7 Deliberations at the Fiscal Commission's Third Session (May 1951)

Just prior to the start of the session, the Division distributed to the Commission Shere's report and the ATC's *39th Report*, accompanied by the letter from Roper to Lie,[234] which stated that the ICAO Council had found its resolution acceptable but was transmitting it to the Fiscal Commission and ECOSOC to ensure that its substance was 'not inconsistent

227 UNEC, 'US Position (Aviation Taxation)', 5.

228 'Council Resolution on Taxation of the Income and Flight Equipment of International Air Transport Enterprises' in ATC, *39th Report*, app III. This resolution is reproduced in Appendix K.

229 Delanney and Lachmann memo, 4 April 1951, 3. See also Bloch letter, 11 April 1951.

230 Letter from UK ICAO Council Representative (Pugh) to Ministry of Civil Aviation, 5 April 1951, TNA:IR40/9959(1).

231 ATC, *39th Report*, 5–6. Conversely, the other three resolutions calling for reciprocal exemption of taxes on fuel, lubricants and other consumable technical supplies, and the elimination or reduction 'to the fullest possible extent' of taxes on the sale or use of international air transport, received formal endorsement.

232 Letter from Roper to Lie, 1 May 1951, UNARMS:AG-025-002—S-0441-0469-23893(B).

233 Memorandum by Bloch to Owen, 18 April 1951, UNARMS:AG-025-002—S-0441-0469-23893(B).

234 Roper letter, 1 May 1951.

with any action taken or policy adopted by them up to and including these meetings'.[235] In its draft note on the agenda item, the Division briefly stated that Shere's report had concluded that while 'reciprocal exemption among countries on a similar level of economic development is adequate', underdeveloped countries with 'no airlines of their own . . . should not be asked to renounce all tax revenue from operations of foreign airlines in their territories'.[236] However, at ICAO's insistence,[237] the phrase 'should not be asked' was changed to read 'would not be likely'.[238] The Division issued no other official communication detailing the background of its dealings with ICAO. Bloch does appear to have written to at least one Commission member, India, outlining the thrust of Shere's report and underdeveloped countries' opposition to the resolution in the ATC.[239] Meanwhile, ICAO sent communications to nine of its Council member countries which were represented on the Commission, presumably to influence their views, advising them that the Council 'was in substantial approval of the [39th] Report as indicating the views of this organization on the subject'.[240] The State Department advised the US delegation to the Commission that 'no attempt [had been made] to evaluate the arguments used' in Shere's report, although acknowledging that the report 'was largely concerned with taxation theories on which Treasury experts are most competent'.[241] The British delegation itself was instructed by Inland Revenue to 'follow the line developed by the UK representative to ICAO that the correct solution lies in the provision of reciprocal exemption under bilateral agreements'.[242]

235 Fiscal Commission, *Taxation of International Air Transport*, Note by the Secretariat, 3rd sess, Agenda item 3(b), UN Doc E/CN.8/57 (3 May 1951) 2.

236 Fiscal Commission, *Note on the Agenda of the Third Session*, Note by the Secretariat, 3rd sess, UN Doc E/CN.8/52 (21 February 1951) 2.

237 Letter from Weld to Lachmann, 13 April 1951, UNARMS:AG-025-002—S-0441-0469-23893(B).

238 Fiscal Commission, *Note on the Agenda of the Third Session: Corrigendum*, Note by the Secretariat, 3rd sess, UN Doc E/CN.8/52/Corr.2 (16 April 1951).

239 Bloch letter, 11 April 1951.

240 Memorandum by Warner to Council Representatives of Australia (on behalf of New Zealand), Belgium, Canada, France, India, South Africa, the United Kingdom, the United States and Venezuela, 18 April 1951, contained in UNEC, 'US Position (Aviation Taxation)', 8–9.

241 Ibid 5.

242 CSCIO, *Draft Brief for United Kingdom Representative to the 3rd Session of the Fiscal Commission Economic and Social Council Prepared by Board of Inland Revenue*, IOC(51) 52 (30 April 1951) 2, TNA:IR40/9959(1). The UK ICAO representative had, inter alia, advised that the allocation system would 'resolve itself into hard bargaining' and lead to 'the development of a large number of bilateral allocation systems based on widely varying

The subject was the most contentious topic of the Third Session and was discussed over the course of eight of the Commission's thirteen plenary meetings.[243] The deliberations were chaotic, repetitious, frequently interrupted or diverted, and never allowed to acquire any technical depth. ICAO's representatives, Weld and Moulton, spoke at length, often at the invitation of the United States, and their positions were virtually identical to those expressed by the United States. Apart from the US delegation, which had been thoroughly briefed by the State Department,[244] no other Commission delegation appeared knowledgeable about the background events leading up to the matter's presentation before the Commission. At no point did the Division speak, nor was it invited to speak. It appeared unable to present data or arguments refuting ICAO's resolution, clarify misinformation in claims made by proponents of reciprocal exemption (particularly by ICAO and the United States), or even affirm the UN's competence in the matter. Shere's report, although stressed by Pakistan as representing the only reliable conclusions on which the Commission could reach in absence of additional proof, was never discussed as Weld stated that it had been rejected by ICAO. Above all, confusion abounded in the Commission as to the issue for decision due to the continual insistence by ICAO and the United States that ICAO's resolution had been referred simply as a matter of courtesy and required no positive action or even expression in favour of any solution. This was compounded by the United States' almost-immediate introduction of a resolution approving the ICAO text at the start of the discussions. Thereafter, a further four conflicting resolutions would be submitted (and a fifth drafted but not formally presented) by other countries at various points in the discussions, even when agreement by vote had already been reached on earlier proposals. In addition, procedural debates arose regarding whether the Commission could vote on ICAO's resolution, the order in which the competing resolutions/amendments should be voted on, and the USSR's and China's frequent assertions that the Commission could not deal with the technicalities of a matter that fell within ICAO's exclusive competence.[245]

principles and factors [which] would be a formidable barrier in the way of an ultimate multilateral approach': Pugh letter, 5 April 1951.

243 Unless otherwise stated, the material regarding these discussions has been drawn from the following *Summary Records* of the Commission's Third Session: UN Docs E/CN.8/SR.13–16 and SR.20–23 (17 May–14 June 1951).

244 See UNEC, 'US Position (Aviation Taxation)'.

245 When the USSR made this assertion, along with the argument that specialised agencies could not submit proposals, Cuba, India and the United States objected on the grounds that ICAO had clearly asked for the Commission's view and that the Commission should

The contending arguments between developed and developing countries, the latter group somewhat supported by the Soviet members,[246] may be summed up as follows. ICAO and the United States argued that reciprocal exemption was the most workable and equitable solution to deal with double taxation and administrative and accounting difficulties in view of the unique nature of the aviation industry, and that it was preferred by most experts, having been successfully applied in shipping, recommended in the League's model conventions and implemented in practically all existing bilateral agreements on air transport. They stated that ICAO was the competent organisation equipped to decide on the question, that there was no inconsistency between ICAO's resolution and the Commission's general policies, and that while it had been suggested that underdeveloped countries with no airlines of their own might be reluctant to adopt the method, air transport could nevertheless render important services to such countries which would far outweigh any revenue loss. The United States also indicated that ICAO's resolution had resulted after frequent exchanges of views between the UN and ICAO Secretariats, that ICAO anticipated a positive confirmation to its inquiry, and that while Shere had proposed two relief systems (i.e. apportionment or exclusive state-of-origin taxation with reciprocal exemption in other countries), no allocation formula had been recommended by Shere or any other authority that would be supported by enough States to be generally acceptable.[247]

encourage the various bodies which applied to it for advice. The United States also stated that the topic was among those which the Commission could have dealt with on its own initiative and that ICAO had acted correctly in submitting a question that came within the Commission's competence.

Morton reported the Chairman as having facilitated the lengthy procedural debates: 'We have a Cuban in the chair and now and again he demonstrates his Latin American temperament, getting us all into a procedural tangle which may take an hour or more to resolve': Letter from Morton to Verity, 16 May 1951, TNA:IR40/9959(1). Bartelt, also reported that the Chairman had 'worked diligently' but 'was not always successful' due to 'language difficulties and his zealousness to be courteous to all the members of the Commission': Letter from Bartelt to Secretary of State, 19 June 1951, 2, NARAII:RG56-199-2.

246 Morton and Bartelt reported to their respective governments that the developing countries' resistance to the Western bloc attracted the support of the Soviet group: CSCIO, *Fiscal Commission: Third Session (Lake Success, 7th to 17th May, 1951), Report by United Kingdom Representative*, IOC(51)105 (24 July 1951) 2, TNA:IR40/9959(1); UNEC, Position Paper on 'Report of the Third Session of the Fiscal Commission (Item 10)' for the US Delegation to ECOSOC 13th Session, SD/E/557, 3 July 1951, 3–4, NARAII:RG59-UD-07D_73B(Lot56D479)-4 ('US Position (ECOSOC)').

247 Bartelt also claimed that attempts to apply allocation in federal US States had resulted in injustices instead of eliminating double taxation (E/CN/8/SR.15 (24 May 1951) 5). This assertion, however, seemingly contradicted the findings of the *CAB Study*: see n 156.

Canada, ICAO, the ICC and Carroll agreed that a generally acceptable system of allocation was too complex to establish, especially for larger airlines that operated in many territories. Britain and Canada also remarked that ICAO's resolution offered governments the freedom to decide the method most appropriate to their situation if they found reciprocal exemption unacceptable.

Conversely, India and Pakistan, supported by Venezuela, argued that the ICAO text advanced a preconceived, exclusive method that was not reliable, reasonable or fair; assumed that difficulties incurred by any other double taxation relief method would be very considerable; and overlooked the situation where the air transport resources between the two negotiating countries differed greatly. Pakistan disagreed with the claim of insuperable accounting difficulties based on the successful application of the allocation system in the Pakistan–Indian air relations. India stated that it was necessary to determine whether countries' individual application of fiscal rules gave rise to practical difficulties, and whether countries willing to grant exemption could rely upon receiving benefits equal to the sacrifices it was prepared to make. India also argued that the endeavour to allocate profits should not be abandoned until genuine effort had been made to formulate such a system. The USSR argued that the ICAO resolution was purposed at obtaining fiscal advantages for some countries at the expense of others and that the League's models not only sought to compel countries to adopt a standard formula, irrespective of their individual circumstances, but had also not been approved by ECOSOC or the General Assembly. The USSR and India also stated that DTAs should not adhere to a preconceived plan, and that countries were entitled to frame them according to their circumstances.

Regarding the six resolutions proposed, the US resolution declared that ICAO's resolution reflected the policies in the London and Mexico Models, as well as many bilateral agreements, and was not inconsistent with any action taken by ECOSOC.[248] France and China in essence supported the US resolution, but it was opposed by India, the USSR and Venezuela. Venezuela also sought the deletion of the reference to the League's models and existing agreements on the basis that these were mere points of fact that neither constituted supporting arguments for reciprocal exemption nor made it acceptable for other countries in other

[248] Fiscal Commission, 'United States of America: Draft Resolution', 3rd sess, Agenda item 3(b), Conference Room Paper No 3 (10 May 1951), NARAII:RG56-199-6, reproduced in Appendix L, Section L.1.

circumstances. The United States was prepared to accept this deletion as it, along with France and the United Kingdom, sought to hurry a vote on the resolution.

Pakistan drafted a resolution that recommended that countries only apply reciprocal exemption of airlines in the context of comprehensive DTAs in view that Shere had found no evidence to recommend the principle and that ICAO's resolution presumed that negotiating parties to a bilateral agreement each had airlines operating in the other country.[249] However, Pakistan appeared to have withdrawn this resolution upon its proposal, supported by India and Venezuela, to wait for the Commission's Working Group to issue its conclusions regarding principles to apply in tax relations between developed and developing countries given that the taxation of airlines was only one aspect of this broader question. Pakistan's proposal was adopted by three votes to none, with seven abstentions.

After the Working Group had issued its propositions (which eventuated as Resolution B-II),[250] India, Pakistan and Venezuela submitted a joint amendment to the US resolution that mentioned Shere's report, declared ICAO's resolution as inconsistent with the principle of equality of sacrifice as far as underdeveloped countries were concerned and recommended that double taxation relief for international airlines be obtained through bilateral agreements based on the Working Group's recommended principles.[251] Britain, however, urged a compromise and proposed that the Commission not express any preference for a particular solution as 'that text would enable the Commission to reach greater unanimity while acting in a manner completely in accordance with its previous debates'.[252] Britain's proposal was supported by the United States, Canada, France and ICAO, whose various arguments included that the joint amendment went too far (France and Canada), that there was no direct contradiction between ICAO's recommendation and

249 Fiscal Commission, 'Pakistan: Draft Resolution', 3rd sess, Agenda item 3(b), Conference Room Paper No 4 (11 May 1951), NARAII:RG56–199–6, reproduced in Appendix L, Section L.2. No discussion of this draft resolution is found among the summary records. A handwritten note among the US records states that it was not distributed to the Commission although the US delegation received a copy.

250 See Chapter 9, Sections 9.2.2 and 9.2.4.

251 Fiscal Commission, 'India, Pakistan and Venezuela: Joint Amendments to the Draft Resolution of the United States of America (Conference Room Paper 3)', 3rd sess, Agenda item 3(b), Conference Room Paper No 10 (15 May 1951), NARAII: RG56–199–6, reproduced in Appendix L, Section L.3.

252 E/CN.8/SR.20 (29 May 1951) 10.

Resolution B-II as the latter only laid down general trends rather than strict relief methods for any type of enterprise (France and ICAO), and that compensation could be ensured by other means in DTAs (Britain, France and ICAO). Moulton also insisted that ICAO could not accept the joint amendment as the ICAO Council considered its own resolution 'a good one', that the joint amendment 'would jeopardise the freedom of negotiation of countries and place the Commission in an embarrassing position', and that the Commission should take a decisive stand on ICAO's Resolution as 'it was now for the first time being contended' that apportionment should be applied to civil air and sea transport.[253] The joint amendment was, nevertheless, adopted by seven votes to six, with two abstentions.

Britain, however, subsequently submitted an amendment which declared the ICAO resolution as 'not inconsistent' with the Commission's policies and that 'the whole result' of any bilateral agreement between an underdeveloped and a developed country should conform with the principles in Resolution B-II.[254] Pakistan and Venezuela in turn jointly submitted an amendment that stated that ICAO's resolution was only consistent with Resolution B-II to the extent it was part of a broader agreement offering compensatory concessions pursuant to the principle of equality of sacrifice.[255] The USSR opposed Britain's amendment as out of order and being part of the British and American manoeuvre to reverse the majority's decision and to force through ICAO's resolution which was inimical to underdeveloped countries' interest. Although the Chairman (Cuba) ruled in favour of the USSR, Britain challenged the decision and the Chairman was overruled by eight votes to seven, with no abstentions.

After deadlock ensued over the United Kingdom and the Pakistan–Venezuela amendments, India submitted an alternative amendment, based on a proposal by China to break the stalemate,[256] that simply requested the UN Secretary-General to forward a copy of Resolution

[253] Ibid 18, 13, 15.

[254] Fiscal Commission, 'United Kingdom: Amendment to United States Draft Resolution as Amended (Conference Room Paper No 3)', 3rd sess, Agenda item 3(b), Conference Room Paper No 17 (16 May 1951), NARAII:RG56–199–6, reproduced in Appendix L, Section L.4.

[255] Fiscal Commission, 'Pakistan and Venezuela: Amendment to United States Draft Resolution as Amended (Conference Room Paper No 3)', 3rd sess, Agenda item 3(b), Conference Room Paper No 18/Rev.1 (16 May 1951), NARAII:RG56–199–6, reproduced in Appendix L, Section L.5.

[256] Bartelt letter, 19 June 1951, 3. See also E/CN.8/SR.20, 14.

B-II and the Commission's summary records of its meetings to ICAO.[257] India explained that the solution would avoid controversy while acquainting ICAO with the Commission's views so that it could reconsider its resolution. The Chairman observed that the amendment was furthest removed from the original text but that it would settle the question if adopted. India's proposal was adopted by eight votes (Cuba, India, Pakistan, Venezuela, the USSR, Czechoslovakia, Poland and China) to seven (Belgium, Canada, France, New Zealand, South Africa, the United Kingdom and the United States). The final resolution (Resolution D) was accordingly composed of, in the following order, one paragraph of the US resolution, three paragraphs of the India–Pakistan–Venezuela joint amendment, and the text of India's amendment.[258]

At the final meeting of the session, the Commission debated the four-sentence paragraph in the Rapporteur's draft report that summarised the discussion.[259] Pakistan, supported by Venezuela, objected that the account was not a sufficiently full representation of the debate and requested that the various amendments be cited in the paragraph and included in an annex. However, Britain (as Rapporteur) objected on the basis that it might mislead ECOSOC if the report reproduced draft resolutions that had not been adopted. The paragraph was retained without change by five votes to two, with five abstentions. As the Commission finalised other sections of its report, the USSR's successful request to incorporate general Soviet positions in the report enabled India (supported by Pakistan, Venezuela and the USSR, but opposed by Britain and China) to reopen the discussion by submitting an amendment that provided a more detailed account of the debate.[260] This amendment was adopted by seven votes to none, with eight abstentions. The final text comprised the first three sentences of the Rapporteur's original paragraph and an additional five paragraphs that, inter alia,

[257] Fiscal Commission, 'India: Amendment to United States Draft Resolution as Amended (Conference Room Paper No 3)', 3rd sess, Agenda item 3(b), Conference Room Paper No 21 (16 May 1951), NARAII:RG56–199–6, reproduced in Appendix L, Section L.6.

[258] The text of Resolution D (entitled *International Air Transport*), in the manner it was contained in the Commission's final report, is reproduced in Appendix M.

[259] Fiscal Commission, *Draft Report to the Economic and Social Council on the Third Session of the Commission, Held at Lake Success, New York, from 7 to 17 May 1951*, 3rd sess, UN Docs E/CN.8/L.1 and Corr.2 (16 May 1951).

[260] Fiscal Commission, 'India: Proposed Amendment Paragraph 16 (E/CN.8/L.1)', 3rd sess, Agenda item 3(b), Conference Room Paper No 22 (17 May 1951), NARAII: RG56–199–6.

referred to the principle of equality of sacrifice, the situation of underdeveloped countries and Resolution B-II.[261]

Venezuela then highlighted that Resolution D was not in conformity with the style of the Commission's other draft resolutions in that it began with the words 'The Fiscal Commission' instead of 'The Economic and Social Council'. Britain (as Rapporteur) stated it was a purely procedural matter which could be left to the Secretariat. Bloch replied that the paragraph could begin either way. Venezuela accordingly decided to leave Resolution D unaltered. The Commission adopted its draft report before closing its session (17 May); however, the final version of the report issued by the Rapporteur and the Secretariat on 31 May separated Resolution D into a section entitled 'Resolution adopted by the Commission' (hereinafter referred to as 'Resolution X'), while listing the Commission's other resolutions under a different section on draft resolutions for adoption by ECOSOC.[262] Furthermore, the Division modified, at ICAO's instruction, its summary records concerning the statements of the ICAO representatives had made during the discussions.[263] Owen subsequently forwarded the relevant sections and resolutions in the report, the summary records of the meetings and the Working Group's report to ICAO[264] and the President of ECOSOC.[265]

In their respective reports to their governments, Morton described the compromise as 'a non-committal amendment' which allowed an interpretation that the Commission 'reached no conclusion on the matter',[266] while Bartelt similarly reported that 'the Commission took no position on the issue'.[267] Bartelt further advised that as this outcome 'was not in accord with the US position', the United States could either 'reopen . . . the question' in ECOSOC or take 'a noncommittal attitude on the Commission's action' to allow ICAO 'to debate the issue' as the 'better forum'.[268]

261 Fiscal Commission, *Report to the Economic and Social Council on the Third Session of the Commission, Held at Lake Success, New York, 7–17 May 1951*, UN Doc E/1993 (also E/CN.8/62) (31 May 1951) 9–10 [20]. This text is reproduced in Appendix N.

262 See Appendix M.

263 Letter from Lachmann to Weld, 29 June 1951, UNARMS:AG-025-002—S-0441-0469-23893(C).

264 Letter from Owen to Roper, 14 June 1951, UNARMS:AG-025-002—S-0441-0469-23893(C).

265 *Letter Dated 14 June 1951 from the Secretary-General to the President of the Council*, UN ESC, 13th sess, Agenda item 10, UN Doc E/2015 (14 June 1951).

266 CSCIO, IOC(51)105, 2.

267 Bartelt letter, 19 June 1951, 3. Bartelt also reported that the Pakistan, India and Venezuela representatives were 'able and tenacious exponents of their country's views' (at 6).

268 Ibid 3.

11.8 Deliberations in ECOSOC (July–August 1951)

The UK delegation entered ECOSOC's Thirteenth Session having been briefed that:

> It is virtually certain that a reopening of the subject in . . . [ECOSOC] will throw up a similar sharp division of view, which is unlikely to be capable of resolution in the way in which we should wish. Fortunately, perhaps, the Resolution passed by the Fiscal Commission is not a draft Resolution for the approval of . . . [ECOSOC] and strictly, therefore, there is no need for the matter to be referred to in the Council. It can go through under the general formula of 'taking note of the Report'. The best course seems to be to let this happen.[269]

The US delegation had initially been similarly instructed to 'avoid raising the issue', but that if such occurred, to state, inter alia, 'that ICAO is the proper organisation to handle this matter and that ECOSOC should not consider it until ICAO has taken final action'.[270] However, it was later advised that as the State Department had approved its position paper on ICAO's annual report to ECOSOC and as Owen had forwarded relevant communications to the President of ECOSOC, the US delegation was to now '[p]oint out that the Commission should not have referred its action on the matter directly back to ICAO, but that, as a question of procedure, . . . should have transmitted its view to ICAO through the Council [ECOSOC]'; and to maintain the US 'position on the substance of the issue',[271] being 'mindful . . . that their government is fully committed to the doctrine of reciprocal exemption'.[272]

When Resolution X was before the Economic Committee at its 116th and 117th meetings (31 July–1 August),[273] Belgium expressed its full agreement with all the conclusions of the Commission, whereas Pakistan proposed that the principles in Resolution B-II be applied to the earnings

[269] CSCIO, *Draft Brief for United Kingdom Delegation to the 13th Session of the Economic and Social Council: Report on the Third Session of the Fiscal Commission*, IOC(51)110 (25 July 1951) 5, TNA:IR40/9959(1) (emphasis in original).

[270] UNEC, 'US Position (ECOSOC)', 1. If the matter were raised, nevertheless, the delegation was 'to abstain from any vote' as such 'would do the least harm to support of the Fiscal Commission' (referring to the US desire to maintain the Commission's ongoing viability) (at 4).

[271] Ibid corrigendum (25 July 1951).

[272] Ibid 4.

[273] The material in these discussions has been drawn from the following *Summary Records* of ECOSOC, 13th sess (UN ESCOR, UN Doc E/SR.496 (10 August 1951)) and its Economic Committee (UN Docs E/AC.6/SR.116–117 (6 September 1951)).

of aviation enterprises.[274] The Chairman (Belgium) asked the Committee to decide whether Resolution B-II, which it had just adopted, conflicted with ICAO's resolution. Britain proposed that no further action be taken, stating that those resolutions 'could not be regarded as necessarily incompatible' and that ICAO's resolution seemingly accommodated Resolution X in providing that agreement could be reached through comprehensive DTAs.[275] France, however, acknowledged the considerable differences in both resolutions, stating that if the topic were regarded as part of the general double taxation problem, then Resolution B-II would suffice. Conversely, if it were regarded a separate problem requiring special solutions, then the question required careful study of data which was not in the Committee's possession. The United States supported Britain's proposal on the grounds that it saw no inconsistencies between the two resolutions that 'some delegations professed to find', that the Committee would be rectifying 'a procedural error without drawing attention to it', and that the Committee anyhow was unlikely to reach a considered decision since it had fewer fiscal experts than the Commission and given that this 'highly complex' matter had already been studied by various expert committees within ICAO for three years.[276] Britain's proposal was adopted by thirteen votes to none, with three abstentions. The Committee's report to ECOSOC, which incorporated the Commission's report, omitted the inclusion of Resolution X but included a paragraph that stated that as the Committee had taken note of the Commission's report and requested the Secretary-General to forward Resolution B-II to ICAO, the necessary action had been taken and no further steps were called for ('Paragraph 4').[277]

When Paragraph 4 was discussed by ECOSOC in plenary at its 496th meeting, Marlin (ICAO), on invitation to speak, stated that the Fiscal Commission and the Economic Committee had concluded that the transmission of their respective records and decisions to ICAO were adequate

[274] See Chapter 9, Section 9.3 for ECOSOC's composition and a background of its discussion of the Commission's report and other resolutions. This composition entailed that India and Pakistan were the only developing countries in ECOSOC which had also been represented on the Commission, while the other developing countries of Chile, Iran, Mexico, Peru, the Philippines and Uruguay were encountering the subject for the first time. On the other hand, five Western countries (Belgium, Canada, France, the United Kingdom and the United States) and China had been represented on the Commission.

[275] E/AC.6/SR.117, 3.

[276] Ibid 5–6.

[277] Economic Committee, *Report of the Economic Committee*, UN ESC, 13th sess, Agenda item 10, UN Doc E/2063 (3 August 1951) 9 [4].

steps in providing policy guidance to ICAO. The matter was now within ICAO's competence to decide whether this answer sufficed. In the ensuing debate, Belgium, China, Poland, the United Kingdom, the United States and the USSR took the position that no decision was called for as neither the Fiscal Commission had submitted a proposal nor had the Economic Committee submitted a recommendation to ECOSOC. Britain added that ICAO 'had adopted a somewhat doubtful procedure' in transmitting its request to the Commission, and that the Commission had not attempted to decide the question but had merely been prepared to give ICAO its general views on double taxation.[278]

India objected, stating that ECOSOC would not be answering ICAO's inquiry by merely noting the Commission's report and that if it subscribed to Paragraph 4, it would commit itself to approving ICAO's interpretation of the policy guidance provided by the UN bodies. India insisted that ECOSOC could not be a party to any such interpretation, especially when certain delegations had the impression that ICAO intended to indirectly impose a certain course of action on ECOSOC. However, Chile and Pakistan appeared to think that the Committee's lack of action indicated that ECOSOC was not being swayed in any direction and that Paragraph 4 indicated that the Committee had concurred with the Commission's solution. At Belgium's persuasion that there were no grounds to continue the discussion and that considerable preparatory work was required if ECOSOC wished to examine the substance of the problem, the President of ECOSOC closed the examination of the Committee's report.

11.9 ICAO Resolution (October 1951)

The ICAO Secretariat reported the actions of the Commission and ECOSOC to the ICAO Council on 28 September.[279] On 4 October, the ICAO Council adopted its resolution without change, except for an amendment of dates mentioned within it.[280] It then circulated a State Letter on 18 October containing the resolution to member states with the request that they notify ICAO by 1 March 1952 of the extent to which

[278] E/SR.496, 150.

[279] See Letter from Lachmann to Moulton, 23 October 1951, UNARMS:AG-025-002—S-0441-0469-23893(C).

[280] Letter from Moulton to Lachmann, 17 October 1951, UNARMS:AG-025-002—S-0441-0469-23893(C).

they were prepared to take action in accordance with the principles therein.[281]

Lachmann enquired with Moulton regarding 'further steps' which could be expected, for example, whether the matter would come before the ICAO Assembly, or further discussions in the ATC or ICAO Council based on the replies from member governments.[282] Moulton replied that no further steps were contemplated as the ICAO Council's 'action is final'.[283] In November, ICAO issued a news release entitled 'Burdensome Taxation to Be Reduced'.[284] In March 1953, in its report to the Seventh Assembly, the Council stated that twenty states had responded, indicating they were, or would shortly be, largely applying these principles.[285] The Council also indicated its intention of publishing a circular reporting the extent to which these principles were being applied worldwide.

11.10 Commentary

The UN–ICAO saga over the taxation of aviation income is a remarkable chronicle in the context of its place in the dawning commercial aviation frontier that was the making of empires. The matter was not, as the vague official narratives portrayed, simply an episode of contending views between developed and developing countries and of intersecting compasses between international institutions. Rather, it is a story of how the UN Secretariat and a handful of developing countries, in persisting to broker equitable global tax rules, unknowingly defied and disrupted US designs for an American ascendency that had not only been long in planning but also involved coordinated interdepartmental strategising and effort at the highest levels. With the nation's economic and political influence, federal budget and military security at stake, it was likely that no other tax outcome but residence exemption would have been acceptable to both US policymakers and US airlines, as appears confirmed by the State Department's close monitoring of the relevant developments in both

281 See Lachmann letter, 23 October 1951.

282 Ibid.

283 Letter from Moulton to Lachmann, 26 October 1951, UNARMS:AG-025-002—S-0441-0469-23893(C).

284 Letter from Dolbeare to Boussard, 21 November 1951, UNARMS:AG-025-002—S-0441-0469-23893(C).

285 *Report of the Council to the Assembly on the Activities of the Organization in 1952*, ICAO Assembly, 7th sess, ICAO Doc 7367, A7-P/1 (31 March 1953) 50.

international organisations and its detailed briefings for US delegations to the UN bodies.

It is difficult to gauge the extent to which (if at all) DEA, even former Treasury official Bloch, were aware of the importance of aviation to US policy and of the malleability of the postwar economic order by US dominance.[286] There is no overt indication that the UN officials, and perhaps many of the developing country membership of the Fiscal Commission and ECOSOC, perceived the United States as driving the residence exemption principle or that its controlling influence in and throughout the ICAO structure and operations enabled the advancement of its policies with minimal obstruction or challenge.[287] The power imbalances between the ICAO and UN Secretariats were stark – the former acted as one with its ATC/Council, often displayed condescension towards the UN Secretariat, and refused to rectify errors in its documents flagged by the UN Secretariat, although could conversely insist on the latter's amendments of its own documents to reflect what the former preferred. Such conduct was strongly reflective of having been emboldened by US support, even imperialist attitudes, as indicated by the coordinated actions of the various ICAO bodies to make the US-introduced resolution a certainty. On ICAO's part, Shere's engagement appeared merely lip service: it imposed a significant time constraint for Shere to complete what would prove to be monumental work, even though the ATC would not consider it for months; it dragged its feet in sending Shere his appointment letter and formal objectives; it was immediately dismissive of Shere's conclusions; and Moulton became irritated with Shere's inquires, even instructing the latter how he should conduct this work. ICAO's insistence on placing Shere on its payroll gave it control over the distribution of Shere's report, which appears not to have been disseminated beyond the ATC and Fiscal Commission. Had Shere been engaged as a UN expert, it is possible the report may have seen a wider

[286] As these events took place prior to the apex of the Korean War and McCarthy eras, the heady idealism of the organisation's mandate, the belief that the UN was the centre of the interlocking network of postwar international organisations, and possibly the careful exercise of US diplomacy up to this point likely spurred the UN Secretariat's thinking and efforts in this field.

[287] Presumably, those member countries of the Commission or ECOSOC which were member countries of ICAO were aware of these influences. Even so, no such country which opposed residence exemption raised this contention, possibly for diplomatic reasons, although the situation of being insufficiently informed might have been a factor.

distribution, including its translation for broader readership, especially in Latin America.[288]

In view of the odds stacked against it, including the institutional hurdles of a resource-strapped Division that had poor collaborative relations with an intermittently-meeting Commission, the UN Secretariat's persistence in its efforts to protect underdeveloped countries' revenue interests were fair, even creditable. It is nevertheless evident that it was inhibited from acting with boldness and bluntness, and its apparent voicelessness in presenting its own views and research may be said to have hindered the development of apportionment methods for aviation (and perhaps even shipping) profits. While there are indications that the Division may have been influential in its private communications with some developing country members in the Commission,[289] its silent public role was arguably the ultimate disservice to genuine and reasonable negotiations in leaving many arguments and misleading statements advanced by ICAO, the United States and other developed countries unchallenged and uncorrected.

Despite their broadly disadvantaged position from an informational perspective, developing countries appear to have circumnavigated some of the tactics employed against them, particularly in their use of the Working Group's decision to challenge ICAO's resolution. If not for Britain's intervention, supported by the developed countries, the initially approved India–Pakistan–Venezuela amendment might have become an official proclamation by the UN preventing the adoption of reciprocal tax exemption for aviation profits where developing countries were concerned. The final compromise, however, only contained subtle reservations rather than an unequivocal refutation of ICAO's endorsed policy, and the subsequent ECOSOC outcome further served to remove this decision from the record of published ECOSOC resolutions which could have potentially enabled the matter to be pursued in the Assembly.

The West's supply, control and predominant use of aviation technology, as well as the promise of vast worldwide profit for an industry that was often government subsidised or owned, gave powerful motivation

[288] The fact that Shere was still engaged in August 1952 as a consultant on UN fiscal projects indicates that his expert opinion was highly valued by the Division: see Letter from Bloch to Surrey, 26 August 1952, UNARMS:AG-025-002—S-0441-0468-23886. It is nevertheless doubtful that Shere's report, or part of it, would have been made into a UN sales publication as this may have required budgetary approval by the Fifth Committee.

[289] Apart from Bloch's written communications to India, Venezuela's request to remove references to the League's models and existing treaty practice suggest a Division origin.

for nations with more highly developed aviation industries to support policies that protected their interests and ambitions in the long-term against a rising Third World. Yet imperialist economic considerations alone do not explain the unity of the First World members in the Commission.[290] This is most evident in the case of France, which had just the month prior objected to the residence exemption principle's bias in the ATC's discussions.[291] New Zealand's position also appears surprising in view of its desire for supranational ownership and operation of international airlines at Chicago, as well as Australia's opposition to the ICAO text in the ATC. It is similarly questionable why South Africa was prepared to surrender source taxing rights when its flag carrier was focused on the domestic market.[292] While it is possible that the positions of these countries may have been swayed by their international routes to Third World countries,[293] there are strong indications that the political

[290] With the Cold War upon them, it is possible that most Western governments by then were primed for their airlines to provide, inter alia, logistical support in transporting war personnel and material as had occurred during World War II, particularly in view of the North Atlantic Treaty Organization (NATO) that had been formed in April 1949 between the United States and eleven other Western nations as a collective security system against the USSR. Van Vleck, moreover, notes that 'US airlines' ongoing international expansion created tensions with NATO allies' (Van Vleck, *Empire of the Air*, 201), which suggests that many First World countries were resentful of the profits that were mostly accruing to the United States.

[291] See Section 11.6. France's initial position in ICAO may have been attributable to its inability to seriously compete in international aviation markets due to its humbled postwar circumstances: see Engel, *Aviation Supremacy*, 40. Assuming that this position was based on its revenue interests, its complete shift in the UN suggests that there was some pressure to show coalition solidarity with other Western industrialised countries, especially the United States, which was then not only stepping up enormous aid to help France's military effort in the Vietnam War but was, through NATO, also building defences in Western Europe (with military headquarters set up in early 1951 near Paris) and supplying nearly $6 billion in arms and military equipment to European allies to prevent Soviet conquest of the region: see Julius W Pratt, *A History of the United States Foreign Policy* (Prentice-Hall, 3rd ed, 1972) 445–6, 492.

[292] See Oswald Mhlanga and JN Steyn, 'The Aviation Industry in South Africa: A Historical Overview' (2016) 5(4) *African Journal of Hospitality, Tourism and Leisure* 1, 2–3.

[293] In particular, the New Zealand and South African national airlines were leading carriers for their respective regional networks given the largely underdeveloped or non-existent aviation industries of nearby nations. Until the 1960s, the international routes of New Zealand's Tasman Empire Airways (which it jointly owned with Australian and British interests) were focused on Fiji, Samoa, the Cook Islands and Tahiti, apart from trans-Tasman services: see Air New Zealand, 'History' (February 2006), available at <https://web.archive.org/web/20070621151238/http://www.airnz.co.nz/resources/company_history_feb_06.pdf>. Meanwhile, South African Airways' international routes mainly serviced flights to Kenya, Sudan, Egypt, Libya and Britain: 'Brief History', *South African Airways* (Web Page, 2022) <www.flysaa.com/about-us/leading-carrier/about-saa/brief-history>.

dynamics in the UN did appreciably affect voting behaviour. Scholars have in fact observed that France and New Zealand at this time overwhelmingly voted with the Western bloc, and South Africa with the Imperial bloc, in all UN matters.[294] The presence of such strong political alignments in the deadlocked Commission raises questions about the role of Nationalist China in its swing vote and persuasiveness in bringing about the watered-down compromise by developing countries. Given that the nation not only had no airlines of its own,[295] but was also completely dependent on US support and economic aid for its existence, its compromised position and proposed solution in the negotiations could be said to have been ultimately directed at serving US interests, even if it was not the unambiguous pronouncement that the latter sought.

By the time the debate reached ECOSOC, there appears to have been some degree of coordination among the Western countries as indicated by the way in which the proceedings transpired. The United States, France and Belgium stressed that the Council was not equipped to deliberate the topic when no precedent existed for preparatory information to be supplied at the ECOSOC level.[296] Britain cast doubt on the propriety of ICAO's referral, while the United States remained silent despite having contested such a view when it was put by the USSR in the Commission. The United Kingdom and the United States claimed a lack of inconsistency between Resolution B-II and ICAO's Resolution and capitalised on the

[294] Randall G Holcombe and Russell S Sobel, 'The Stability of International Coalitions in United Nations Voting from 1946 to 1973' (1996) 86(1/2) *Public Choice* 17, 27. Political motivations can even almost entirely explain South Africa's acceptance of the residence exemption rule. The new apartheid regime faced isolation in a postwar political climate that was moving away from racial discrimination and the government was striving to carve its place within the Western power bloc in its need for certain goods and export markets and its search for military and foreign security: NM Van der Waag-Cowling, 'South Africa and the Korean War, the Politics of Involvement' (2016) 44(1) *Scientia Militaria* 224, 228–9; 'South Africa's Foreign Relations during Apartheid, 1948', *South Africa's History Online* (Web Page, 2019) <www.sahistory.org.za/article/south-africas-foreign-relations-during-apartheid-1948>. Between 1950 and 1958, it would sign thirteen limited DTAs on the taxation of income from maritime and air transport enterprises with predominantly European and Scandinavian states (DESA, *International Tax Agreements*, UN Doc ST/ECA/SER.C/8, Suppl 3 (UN, 1968) vol 8: World Guide to International Tax Agreements, xx–xxi) despite none of its airlines flying routes to these nations: see Mhlanga and Steyn, 'Aviation Industry', 2–3; South African Airways, 'Brief History'.

[295] See Engel, *Aviation Supremacy*, 105–6.

[296] This is evident in Bloch's request for only 25 copies of Shere's report in addition to the two that were initially sent by Weld to the Division out of ICAO's printing (of which 125 copies were stated as being 'available immediately'): Letters between Weld and Bloch, 6 and 14 July 1950, UNARMS:AG-025-002—S-0441-0469-23893(B).

'procedural error' of Resolution X.[297] Conversely, the lack of resistance by developing countries generally suggests their unpreparedness for the discussion, their unsuspectingness of the tactical non-action being urged by the developed countries, as well as an inability to seek immediate directions from their own governments,[298] especially amid the rushed deliberations. While India appeared to have become informed in time to mount a challenge in plenary discussions, its opposition necessarily failed without the backing of other developing countries.

In summary, the taxation of international aviation enterprises has never been the subject of technical study or negotiation by international tax experts. The incorporation of reciprocal exemption in the Mexico and London Models came to be used by aviation professionals, heavily influenced by the United States,[299] to justify the method's international acceptance and universal application despite the weight of contrary opinion expressed by tax experts in academia, US government service and the UN, as well as the use of allocation in practice by several countries around the world. The United States and the United Kingdom, the two major international civil aviation powers, played leading roles in manoeuvring the negotiations in the UN to ensure that the residence exemption provision was not upended. A Western-dominated ICAO, which was primarily created as a technical body to facilitate matters such as safety and standardisation regarding air navigation, came to promulgate the recommended rule to be applied to the taxation of international air transport.

It is possible to infer ICAO's influence in setting tax treaty precedent and consensus regarding the double taxation of air transport enterprises by reference to the number of limited DTAs concluded regarding the subject after October 1951 up until 1968 when the UN Group of Experts

[297] This is somewhat ironic considering that the drafting of Resolution X had resulted from a combination of the original US resolution and the British Rapporteur's and Bloch's misdirection to the Commission. Bloch's own error in this regard may have stemmed from his newness to his role.

[298] Communication via telephone in this era is noted to have 'necessitated multiple operators' and been 'extraordinarily inaccessible', thus 'plac[ing] major constraints on non-elites' ability to mobilize': John W McArthur and Eric Werker, 'Developing Countries and International Organizations: Introduction to the Special Issue' (2016) 11(2) *Review of International Organizations* 155, 156. ECOSOC's Thirteenth Session furthermore was held in Geneva, placing the developing country representatives away from their permanent delegations in New York.

[299] Also note the compelling indication that US private aviation enterprises had a significant role in shaping US policy regarding airline taxation.

was formed.[300] After World War II, but prior to October 1951, a total of three agreements on the taxation of income from air transport enterprises and twenty-four agreements on the taxation of income from maritime and air transport enterprises were concluded.[301] All but two of these limited agreements were negotiated by Argentina, Greece or South Africa, their circumstances of the time indicative that political and geostrategic factors were overriding impetuses in their forming of these treaties.[302] From October 1951, thirty-three agreements on the taxation

300 IFA itself may have also been influential in this regard in view of its 1952 resolution that vigorously defended the residence exemption principle: see Chapter 10, Section 10.1.

301 DESA, *International Tax Agreements*, vol 8, xvi, xx. Before World War II, only four agreements on the taxation of income from air transport enterprises had been concluded among Britain and other Western European states.

302 Ibid xx. Eighteen of the DTAs on shipping and airline income were concluded by Argentina between October 1948 and August 1950 with European and Scandinavian states, other Latin American nations, Britain and Canada. Argentina was then in a precarious economic state following prolonged US economic boycott, which had extended to obstructing British and European procurement of Argentinian goods, Argentina's imports from other Latin American countries and the expansion of Argentina's merchant navy: Carlos Escudé, 'The US Destabilization and Economic Boycott of Argentina of the 1940s, Revisited' (Serie de Documentos de Trabjo No 323, Área de Ciencia Polílitica, Universidad del CEMA, July 2006) 8–9; Gabriel Porcile, 'The Challenge of Cooperation: Argentina and Brazil, 1939–1955' (1995) 27(1) *Journal of Latin American Studies* 129, 137–8. This conflict with the United States, disruption to essential imports and the dollar shortage would accordingly dictate postwar Argentine foreign policies, leading it to 'deploy … intense diplomacy activity aimed at reaching bilateral trade and payments agreements with European and Latin America countries' (Porcile, 'Challenge of Cooperation', 138). The eighteen Argentine limited DTAs thus appear to fall squarely within Argentina's efforts to improve its position in the new world order, particularly as its international airline, first created in 1946, did not generate direct economic benefit nor fly to most of these treaty partners: see Piglia, '"Carry Our Colours"', 55 (indicating further at 48–59 that Argentina's commercial aviation policy was more directed at affirming its sovereignty, strengthening its national defence, investing in its geopolitical and symbolic prestige, creating conditions for industrial export expansion and limiting US expansion in the Southern Cone). In July 1950, Argentina signed a limited DTA on shipping and airline income with the United States, which marks the time when the latter sought to improve relations with the former, including through a supplement Friendship, Commerce and Navigation Treaty, a comprehensive DTA, a bilateral air transport agreement and encouragement of tourism: see 'Policy Statement Prepared in the Department of State: Argentina', 26 October 1951, in State Department, *Foreign Relations of the United States, 1951* (USGPO, 1979) vol 2: The United Nations; The Western Hemisphere, Doc 680. A key US objective in these efforts was 'to defend the legitimate rights of US firms doing business in or with that country', particularly concerning the aviation, transport, petroleum, film, shipping and meat industries. The United States also considered it 'in the US interest to have Argentina on our side in case of an outside attack on the other American republics or on ourselves' as Argentina was not only 'politically, economically and

militarily one of the most powerful of the American Republics' but also 'strategically situated with respect to South Atlantic shipping routes and the Straits of Magellan and would be in wartime a much needed supplier of food and raw materials to the US and its allies'.

South Africa's first three limited DTAs covering shipping and airline income during this time frame were concluded with Scandinavian countries (see n 294 for its likely motives). Meanwhile, Greece's early limited DTAs involving air transport income with Switzerland, Britain, France and the Netherlands were concluded from 1950, just after the end of its civil war in which the United States supplied massive military and financial aid through the Marshall Plan to prevent the Soviet spread in the Eastern Mediterranean and to protect Middle East oil supplies as well as important sea trade routes: see Lawrence S Wittner, *American Intervention in Greece, 1943–1949* (Columbia University Press, 1982) 53–4, 76. Not only was Greece then one of the poorest European economies (Ibid 190), but Greek airlines, which were for the most part unsuccessful and then in financial straits, would barely fly to these Western destinations until the late 1950s (see Graham M Simons, *Olympic Airways: A History* (Air World, 2019) ch 2, 72, 76). The Greek air force, nevertheless, had been a decisive factor in the civil war (Amikam Nachmani, 'Civil War and Foreign Intervention in Greece: 1946–49' (1990) 25(4) *Journal of Contemporary History* 489, 509) and US aid would continue to flow to the nation as a Western bloc member most exposed to Soviet bloc aggression: see 'The Chief of the Joint United States Military Aid Group to Greece (Jenkins) to the Joint Chiefs of Staff', 26 July 1950, and 'Memorandum by the Acting Secretary of State to the Executive Secretary of the National Security Council (Lay)', 19 September 1950, in State Department, *Foreign Relations of the United States, 1950* (USGPO, 1978) vol 5: The Near East, South Asia and Africa, Docs 166 and 181. It appears more than coincidental that the three latter Western European treaty partners were NATO members with valuable Cold War air bases and air defence operations (see Donald Mitchell, 'Strategy of the Mediterranean' (1955) 29(168) *Current History* 65, 68–70; Shannon W Caudill (ed), *Defending Air Bases in an Age of Insurgency* (Air University Press, 2015) 82) and that these treaties were signed during the Korean War, in which the four contracting parties supplied infantry (as well as transport aircraft on the part of Greece) for UN forces (see James F Schnabel and Robert J Watson, *The Joint Chiefs of Staff and National Policy* (Office of Joint History/Office of the Chairman of the Joint Chiefs of Staff, 1998) vol 3:1950–1951, The Korean War: pt 1, 68–9, 178). Greece's treaty with neutral Switzerland was plausibly motivated by the latter's role as protecting power, the extension of credits by the Swiss government and banks to Marshall Plan countries, and the humanitarian services provided the Geneva-based International Committee of the Red Cross: see 'Policy Statement Prepared in the Department of State', 17 August 1950, in State Department, *Foreign Relations of the United States, 1950* (USGPO, 1977) vol 3: Western Europe, Doc 694.

The remaining two limited DTAs, both signed in 1951, comprised a treaty between Brazil and France, and one between Israel and Switzerland. Brazil's civil aviation was controlled by its air force for decades after World War II (McCann, *Balancing Giants*, 250), suggesting that military considerations were a factor in its treaties. Nevertheless, the fact that the largest and only one of Brazil's multitude airlines that had international routes outside the Western Hemisphere was a subsidiary of Pan Am also suggests an influencing role by the parent company: see 'Panair do Brasil', *Aviaçãocomercial.net* (Web Page, 2012) <www.aviacaocomercial.net/english/panair.htm> (as contrasted with the routes of other airlines operating at that time, e.g. Cruzeiro do Sul, REAL, VASP and

of income from air transport enterprises, as well as fifty-seven agreements on the taxation of income from maritime and air transport enterprises, were concluded, mostly among First World nations.[303] The majority of the few treaties that involved a Third World nation were concluded by Iran, Egypt and Lebanon with European and Scandinavian nations, while in the remaining treaties, neutral Switzerland was often the First World contracting party. This trend corresponds with the turning of Western focus to the Middle East from the mid-1950s following the rise of nationalism and the expansion of Soviet power in the strategic and oil-rich region, suggesting that these agreements were largely influenced by politics rather than any strong conviction in the residence exemption principle.[304]

The widespread acceptance of the reciprocal residence exemption principle through limited and comprehensive DTAs among the First World nations likely did advance the tourism promotion element of the US foreign economic programme: by 1954, more Americans were travelling abroad by air, surpassing steamship travel, and the travel boom as well as US airlines' international expansion would continue into the 1960s.[305] While few developing countries concluded tax treaties with the

Varig). In the case of the Israel–Switzerland treaty, while Switzerland's protecting power status and its Red Cross were likely supporting factors in view of the young state's recent emergence from its War of Independence and ongoing conflict with its Arab neighbours, other political and economic motivations appear to have been equally paramount. Civil aviation was especially critical in flying in essential supplies and equipment and providing a link to the outside world with Israel blockaded on all its land frontiers and its ships, or ships with Israeli cargo, denied access through the Suez Canal by Egypt. While Israel's national airline, incorporated in late 1948, did fly to key European cities, it mostly served as an immigrant carrier for mass Jewish immigration from the Middle East, Europe and other areas; outbound travel then limited by the austerity system: see Marvin G Goldman, *El Al: Israel's Flying Star* (rev ed, 2020) chs 2 and 3, available at *Israel Airline Museum* (Web Page) <www.israelairlinemuseum.org/el-al-israels-flying-star>; Moshe Naor, 'Israel's 1948 War of Independence as a Total War' (2008) 43(2) *Journal of Contemporary History* 241, 252; Pratt, *United States Foreign Policy*, 514.

303 DESA, *International Tax Agreements*, vol 8, xvi–xvii, xx–xxii.

304 Apart from an earlier treaty with Switzerland, Egypt (under President Gamal Abdel Nasser) began concluding these limited DTAs with Benelux and Scandinavian countries from the time of the Suez Canal Crisis from which Britain and France would lose their prestige and influence in the region. As Nasser's leadership, supported by the USSR, began to rouse Arab unity and collaboration leading to the toppling of Western-oriented governments in several of the region's nations, Western intervention enabled other nations, including Iran and Lebanon, to be distanced from the Arab resistance: see Pratt, *United States Foreign Policy*, 516–22; Paul Salem, 'The Middle East: Evolution of a Broken Regional Order' (Carnegie Paper No 9, Carnegie Middle East Centre, June 2008) 4–5.

305 See Van Vleck, *Empire of the Air*, 215–25.

developed world, there were other means by which the United States or US airlines may have spread this principle among developing countries. Specifically, as the Cold War shifted to the Third World in the mid-1950s following the spread of communist influence, which included the USSR's resolute and robust entry into global civil air routes, the United States responded by underwriting the development of national airlines in Asian, African and Latin American countries of strategic interest.[306] US airlines were again contracted into these projects that not only established new tourist destinations and supplied domestic feeder lines, but also propagated capitalist business practices and American customs and values. Such aviation development assistance possibly facilitated preferential tax treatment by developing country governments to US aviation enterprises, much in the way as Pan Am had obtained from Latin American countries in the interwar years. Certainly the fact that no alternative tax rule had ever been put forward by an international organisation would have impaired the position of weaker nations to assert for source taxing rights. ICAO, moreover, would continue to reaffirm its 1951 resolutions and recommendation in subsequent policy documents and resolutions issued in 1966, 1986 and 2000.[307]

The residence exemption principle appears to have been so fairly entrenched by the time of the work of the 1968 Group of Experts that the Group chose to retain the method despite several developing country members highlighting that source-country taxation of profits from where passengers or freight were booked (i.e. one of Shere's proposals) was a more reasonable approach in view of the 'very substantial expenditure that developing countries incurred in the construction of airports'.[308] For the briefest moment in time, the activism of the UN Secretariat and developing countries in the Fiscal Commission, backed by the Soviet

306 Ibid 200–1, 228–37. Such grants 'enabled recipient governments to finance aircraft purchases, to employ US technical advisers, and to construct or improve airports and communications facilities' (at 230).

307 These documents are available at 'Doc Series 8632: ICAO's Policies on Taxation in the Field of International Air Transport', *ICAO* (Web Page) <www.icao.int/publications/pages/publication.aspx?docnum=8632>. In 2000, all four of the 1951 resolutions were consolidated into a single resolution. IATA has also upheld and promoted ICAO's taxation policies: see, for example, 'Guidelines for Taxation of International Air Transport Profits', *IATA* (Web Page, May 2015) <www.iata.org/contentassets/a72d8d3cfaf84529bcdef6b2dc59f224/taxation_intl_air_transport20profits_final.pdf>.

308 DIESA, *United Nations Model Double Taxation Convention between Developed and Developing Countries*, UN Doc ST/ESA/102 (UN, 1980) 101–2 (commentary to Article 8B [1]).

countries, might have changed the course of history for reciprocal exemption in aviation taxation. As it turned out, their many labours were in vain and not only had the Division vexed the State Department for intervening in US proposals in ICAO,[309] but Britain also appeared to have earmarked the Commission for dissolution.[310]

309 See Chapter 8, Section 8.1.

310 See Chapter 9, Section 9.3.

12

Fourth Session of the Fiscal Commission and Aftermath (1953)

12.1 Preparatory Documents of the Fiscal Division

Beginning in late November 1952, the Division circulated seven documents to the Commission: three papers related to international taxation, two regarding technical assistance,[1] one review of fiscal developments[2] and one summary report of its work and activities.[3] The three papers concerning international taxation comprised the Division's work-in-progress on corporate tax problems,[4] the

[1] Fiscal Commission, *Report on the Technical Assistance Conference on Comparative Fiscal Administration (Geneva 16–25 July 1951)*, 4th sess, UN Doc E/CN.8/67 (5 December 1952); E/CN.8/72 (20 November 1952).

[2] Fiscal Commission, *Review of Fiscal Developments, 1951–52*, 4th sess, UN Doc E/CN.8/74 (16 December 1952).

[3] Fiscal Commission, *Programme of Secretariat Work: Action Taken since Third Session of Fiscal Commission and Proposed List of Future Priorities*, Note by the Secretary-General, 4th sess, UN Doc E/CN.8/75 (3 December 1952).

[4] Fiscal Commission, *Corporate Tax Problems*, 4th sess, UN Docs E/CN.8/66 and addenda (25 November 1952). This study, which totalled over 140 pages, was described as 'in the nature of a progress report' with '[i]ts limits . . . set by the still rudimentary stage of practical tax research, especially with regard to underdeveloped countries' (at 4). It addressed theoretical problems from the perspective of lawmakers, economists and the Secretariat, and had an annex which provided a review of various DTA provisions (divided according to continental European agreements and Anglo-American agreements) that resolved conflicts in the domestic law of contracting parties which affected the same profits or dividends. Addenda to the study comprised country studies of Argentina, Britain, Belgium, Canada, France, the Netherlands and New Zealand. The Division was planning further studies on Egypt, India and the United States and capsule studies of thirty more countries, including all the Latin American countries (Fiscal Commission, *Summary Record of the 27th Meeting*, 4th sess, 27th mtg, UN Doc E/CN.8/SR.27 (14 May 1953) 3).

taxation of foreign taxpayers and foreign income,[5] and FPILA Taxation.[6]

Although the Division set out, in its summary report, the operative parts of ECOSOC Resolution 416D (XIV) and ECLA Resolution 3(IV) (described as interest expressed in the study on taxation of foreign investment), its FPILA Taxation paper contained no recommendations concerning the proposal for SoCtyTax/ResCtyExempt(FoInvInc), as had been requested by these resolutions.[7] The Division also failed to mention the conclusions of the group of experts' E/1986 report.[8] These limited references, especially in view of the thorough information on fiscal-related discussions by other UN bodies that had typically been reported in previous sessions by the Division to the Commission, suggest an attempt by the Division to avoid discussion of the SoCtyTax/ResCtyExempt(FoInvInc) proposal. The Division's work in fact now appeared to largely comply with the US agenda for its activities: apart from being pleased with the Division's presentation of its work programme,[9] the State Department briefed Bartelt to commend the Secretariat for the lack of duplication of effort with other regional economic commissions and specialised agencies, and that if he were to become aware of any such duplication, to 'feel free to call attention to it, and recommend its termination'.[10]

5 Fiscal Commission, *Taxation of Foreign Taxpayers and Foreign Income*, Note by the Secretary-General, 4th sess, UN Docs E/CN.8/68 and addenda (22 December 1952). This document was composed of only a short note on the structure and concepts of key income items, and four country studies of Argentina, Canada, Israel and New Zealand. Further country studies on Chile, Britain, Belgium and India were being prepared. The Division also reported it had detailed information transmitted by thirty-five governments on the relevant provisions of their national tax systems as modified by international tax agreements to which they were parties.

6 Fiscal Commission, *Taxation in Capital-Exporting and Capital-Importing Countries of Foreign Private Investment in Latin America*, 4th sess, UN Doc E/CN.8/69 (5 December 1952). This document was composed of the US FPILA Taxation report later published in January 1953 as DEA, *Taxation in Capital-Exporting and Capital-Importing Countries of Foreign Private Investment in Latin America: United States Income Taxation of Private United States Investment in Latin America*, UN Doc ST/ECA/18 (1953), as well as a country report for Mexico. See Chapter 9, Section 9.5 for a background of the FPILA Taxation study and US FPILA Taxation report.

7 See Chapter 10, Section 10.2 for the background of these resolutions.

8 See ibid for details of this report.

9 Position Paper on 'Concentration of Effort and Resources' for the US Delegation to the Fourth Session of the Fiscal Commission, 22 April 1953, 3, NARAII:RG56–199–6.

10 Ibid 2.

12.2 Deliberations in the Fiscal Commission (27 April–8 May 1953)

The Commission members of the Fourth Session comprised Belgium, Canada, Chile, China, Colombia, Cuba, Czechoslovakia, France, India, Pakistan, South Africa, Sweden, the United Kingdom, the United States and the USSR (Chile, Colombia and Sweden having replaced New Zealand, Poland and Venezuela).[11] This made for a membership composed of seven First World countries, five developing countries (the largest in any session so far), two Soviet countries and China. Certeux was appointed Chairman, Jaroslav Rybar (Czechoslovakia) and Qadir as Vice-Chairmen, and Albert Eaton (Canada) as Rapporteur. Bloch served as Secretary to the Commission, with Lachmann and Rossen as Assistant Secretaries.[12] This session saw, for the first time, attendance by observer countries comprising Argentina, Australia and Yugoslavia. Other observers included FAO, the ILO, the IMF, the ICC, IFA and NAM (Carroll).

The Commission held ten plenary meetings over nine days, with eight of the meetings spent in substantive discussions.[13] Two-thirds of these substantive discussions were taken up with technical assistance, the fiscal information service, public finance and the taxation of agriculture.[14] The

[11] Fiscal Commission, *Provisional List of Participants*, 4th sess, UN Doc E/CN.8/INF.2/Rev.1 (30 April 1953). Of the individual delegates, nine had represented (including as alternate) their country at the Third Session: Callebaut (Belgium), Eaton (Canada), Kan Lee (China), Perez (Cuba), Certeux (France), Qadir (Pakistan), Wells (South Africa), Bartelt (United States) and Chechetkin (USSR): see Appendix B, Table B.1.

[12] Blough also attended half of the plenary meetings.

[13] Unless otherwise stated, the material regarding the Commission's discussions has been drawn from the *Summary Records* of the Commission's Fourth Session (UN Docs E/CN.8/SR.24–33 (14–22 May 1955)); and the Commission's report of its session (Fiscal Commission, *Report to the Economic and Social Council on the Fourth Session of the Fiscal Commission, Held at Headquarters, New York, from 27 April to 8 May 1953*, UN Doc E/2429 (also E/CN.8/78) (8 May 1953)).

[14] The Secretariat's work on these matters was simply noted and approved. The United States dominated these discussions with long speeches by the various advisers on its delegation while the developing countries expressed their support for any work that purportedly fostered their economic development. Conversely, the European countries, Britain, Canada and South Africa made little contribution. The UK representative (Nicholas) reported to his government that these delegations had 'not had the time (or possibly the inclination) to master the material', especially regarding government accounting and budgetary problems which the United States pressed the Secretariat to further develop: CSCIO, *Fiscal Commission, Fourth Session, 27th April to 8th May 1953: Report by United Kingdom Representative*, IOC(53)128 (22 July 1953) 3, TNA:IR40/11173(2).

remaining third was spent on international tax matters, which was largely consumed with the taxation of foreign investment.[15] The topic was 'the most heated subject' of the session,[16] attracting broad participation among participants and showcasing the South's heightening frustration with the North of the little that was being done to aid their development. During these deliberations, the USSR and Czechoslovakia reprised the general Soviet positions expressed at previous sessions.[17] They also unsuccessfully moved to exclude the Chinese member (Lee) and to have him replaced with a PRC representative.[18] The Soviet oppositions were generally regarded by America and Britain to be more customary than hostile: Bartelt reported to his government that the Soviet 'attempts at political coloration of the proceedings did not appear to have any influence on the other delegations';[19] British records indicated that 'it is really very easy to dispose of [the Chinese representation question] as it has become such a routine question, and in any case the Russians are not being difficult just now'.[20]

The Commission established a Working Group on International Tax Problems ('Working Group') at the end of the second meeting, which met three times around the plenary sessions.[21] The Working Group was entirely occupied with deliberations concerning the taxation of foreign investment and was attended by eleven members: Belgium, Canada, Chile, China, Cuba, India, Pakistan, South Africa, Sweden, the United Kingdom and the United States. Eight of these members came on board by an initial show of interest, and Erik Lindahl (Sweden) was appointed as Chairman of the Working Group. Eaton was appointed to the group in his capacity as Rapporteur, with Lachmann as Secretary. China and Cuba

[15] The Commission's discussions on corporate tax problems and the taxation of foreign taxpayers and foreign income were brief and uneventful with only the United States and Chile making specific suggestions on how the corporate tax study could be enhanced and expanded. In particular, Chile, with whom the United States and France agreed, considered that the study needed to encompass the structure of corporations, not just their fiscal aspects, as underdeveloped countries needed economic information on the types and nature of corporations most suitable for their requirements and for stimulating entrepreneurship.

[16] Letter from Bartelt to Secretary of State, 29 June 1953, 2, NARAII:RG56–199–6.

[17] See Chapter 7, Section 7.2, Chapter 9, Section 9.2 and Chapter 11, Sections 11.3 and 11.7.

[18] Fiscal Commission, *Union of Soviet Socialist Republics: Draft Resolution on Question of the Representation of China*, 4th sess, UN Doc E/CN.8/L.2 (27 April 1953). This proposal was overruled by a vote of nine to four, with one abstention.

[19] Bartelt letter, 29 June 1953, 1.

[20] Letter from Meade to Nicholas, 14 April 1953, TNA:IR40/11173(1).

[21] This was the only working group established at this session.

joined the Working Group later: Cuba made its request in plenary session while China made its request privately to France (as Chairman), presumably to avoid Soviet objection. When the Commission later sat to discuss the Working Group's conclusions, the Soviet members expressed their outrage to learn of China's inclusion.

In briefing the US delegation to the session, the State Department anticipated that the discussion on the taxation of foreign investment would culminate in a proposed resolution for SoCtyTax/ResCtyExempt(FoInvInc) by a Latin American delegation, which would draw the support of Pakistan, India, South Africa, other Latin American countries and possibly the Soviet bloc, making for a majority vote.[22] The US strategy was to explain that it could take no position on the question as the new administration was reviewing the tax system as it affected foreign income and had yet to draw any conclusions.[23] The delegation was to stress that the United States considered a conducive local climate for investment, and not the US tax system, as the critical factor in determining FDI flows abroad; that the tax credit device was giving an impetus to underdeveloped countries to adopt high income taxes unjustified by their social and economic development; and that the United States was considering revisions to its FTC to credit other types of taxation that underdeveloped countries found more desirable as sources of revenue. The delegation was to also emphasise 'the detrimental effect of the so-called "Nationalization Resolution"' and to place the onus on underdeveloped countries to develop an investment climate that attracted FDI from capital-exporting countries.[24] The

[22] Position Paper on 'Taxation of Foreign Investment' for the US Delegation to the Fourth Session of the Fiscal Commission, 20 April 1953, 3, NARAII:RG56–199–6 ('US Position (FoInv Taxation)').

[23] Ibid 1, 4.

[24] Ibid 4. This 'Nationalization Resolution' referred to GA Res 626 (VII) (entitled *Right to Exploit Freely Natural Wealth and Resources*), UN Doc A/RES/626(VII) (21 December 1952) was adopted after heated debates and declared the right of states to permanent sovereignty over their national resources. This principle had been advanced by the Latin American countries as part of their growing 'uneasiness about their relationship with the United States, which they perceived as very unequal': Nico Schrijver, *Sovereignty Over National Resources: Balancing Rights and Duties* (Cambridge University Press, 1997) 36. The resolution originated from a Uruguayan draft resolution calling for the recognition of underdeveloped countries' right to nationalise and freely exploit their own natural resources, which included selling products to buyers of their own choice, and for this right to not be confused with the 'manifestations of an aggressive and destructive ideology' (at 42–3). This proposal was received negatively by Western delegations, media and business organisations (including the ICC) (at 43–8). Years later, the US delegate to these debates would write that the resolution 'may have had some

delegation was to ideally defer action on a substantive resolution 'by having the Commission request for further studies'; however, 'a realistic assessment of the situation suggest[ed] that such a resolution' had to come from the floor.[25] If a substantive resolution endorsing SoCtyTax-ResCtyExempt(FoInvInc) was put to a vote, the delegation was to abstain or to vote in the negative. At best, it was hoped a resolution would be introduced calling for an adjustment by capital-exporting countries of their foreign tax credit provisions to give effect to tax incentive schemes that were being increasingly adopted in underdeveloped countries.[26]

Meanwhile, the British government considered the taxation of investment 'without doubt, the most important item on the Commission's agenda'[27] and 'fear[ed]' that underdeveloped countries would approach the agenda item 'not so much from the purely fiscal angle . . . but from the political angle' with Cuba attempting to garner

> support for some objectionable recommendation . . . that capital-exporting countries should exercise self-denial over the taxation of their foreign investments specifically as a means towards the financing of economic development, and regardless of technical arguments.[28]

The UK delegation was briefed to employ 'tactics', including 'prior consultation with the representatives of other capital-exporting countries',[29] and to hold the attitude that any SoCtyTax/ResCtyExempt(FoInvInc) proposal was 'too sweeping' and 'unacceptable' on the grounds of the technical difficulties of administration and inequalities resulting from the tax discrimination of income received from different sources.[30] It was also to indicate that if capital-exporting countries were 'to feel compelled by a resolution of an international body to make taxation concessions',

beneficial effects as a safety valve for letting off steam, and as a timely reminder to the United States that many of the other free countries do not share our views' (at 48–9, quoting Edmund Halsey Kellogg, *The 7th General Assembly 'Nationalization' Resolution: A Case Study in United Nations Economic Affairs* (Woodrow Wilson Foundation, 1955) 15).

25 'US Position (FoInv Taxation)', 5.

26 The US expected that Britain would sponsor such a resolution as the Royal Commission on the Taxation of Profits and Income had recently suggested a similar proposal: Ibid 5.

27 CSCIO, *Draft Brief for United Kingdom Representative to the Fourth Session of the Fiscal Commission of the Economic and Social Council, Prepared by the Board of Inland Revenue*, IOC(53)46 (15 April 1953) 1, TNA:IR40/11173(2).

28 Letter from Bartlett to Green, 9 April 1953, 1, TNA:IR40/11173(1).

29 Ibid 2.

30 CSCIO, IOC(53)46, 2.

budgetary concerns might necessitate such countries imposing a limitation on the flow of investment abroad.[31]

12.2.1 Taxation of Foreign Private Investment

Discussions began with Bloch outlining the Division's FPILA Taxation work, stating that no conclusions had yet been reached at this stage of the inquiry, which so far consisted of factual studies and theoretical analysis. The United States then presented a lengthy speech that, inter alia, covered the substance of the delegation's prepared representations with a focus on promoting the merits of the tax credit mechanism and discrediting tax exemption.[32] These representations included that the Eisenhower Administration disagreed with the encouragement the Truman Administration had given to other countries to adopt income taxation at comparable rates to US taxation as 'a desirable, incidental result of the tax-credit provision'; yet in spite of this, the US FTC was still 'an effective device to minimize international double taxation of income, especially when used in conjunction with tax treaties to help define income and establish rules for its allocation', and hence should not be 'hastily rejected or superseded by any other procedure'.[33] The United States argued that its deferral system enabled foreign countries to use low tax rates to attract US FDI to establish foreign subsidiaries and foster expansion through accumulated profits (even though small).[34] It stated that the exemption system to capital-exporting countries resulted in lower aggregate taxes on foreign corporate income that was 'inequitable and discriminatory against domestic investment'; raised 'difficult administrative problems in the determination of foreign income'; and could be costly, including to the United States, which 'was in a tight budget position' even though its net receipts from its taxation of foreign income after allowance for FTCs were generally relatively low at $150 million in comparison to the total US budget that exceeded $70 billion.[35] It also argued that while economists considered that tax exemption 'might attract attention to foreign investment and make it interesting, even fashionable', such hopes were 'largely illusory' as the 'principal barriers to capital export do not arise from tax factors', but rather from financial

[31] Ibid.

[32] The US was mostly represented by Dan Throop Smith in these discussions.

[33] E/CN.8/SR.25 (14 May 1953) 5–6.

[34] Ibid 7.

[35] Ibid 7–9.

and political risks from expropriation and restrictions on money, trade and operations of foreign firms.[36]

Britain itself stated that it was 'opposed to the suggestion that other incentives should be granted to investment abroad' other than the avoidance of double taxation by a credit system, and had reservations on 'allowing the direction of capital investment to be guided by the taxation systems of the capital-importing countries'.[37] It nevertheless stated that it, like the United States, was reviewing its taxation system through its Royal Commission on the Taxation of Profits and Income ('Royal Commission'), which had in consideration the 'desirability of capital investment in the under-developed areas', and that until the Royal Commission's report was considered by the British government, Britain could not reach any conclusions beyond those adopted at the Third Session.[38]

The US views were heatedly contested by Belgium, Chile, China, Cuba, India and Pakistan, whose arguments centred along the following lines: firstly, that while fiscal incentives might be insufficient in themselves to induce large-scale investment, the initiative in such matters still lay with capital-exporting countries rather than capital-importing countries, particularly as flows of capital abroad were necessary to address the financial and political risks faced by underdeveloped countries (Chile, China, Cuba, India and Pakistan). India indicated that prospective US foreign investors had stated their willingness to invest abroad if their capital investment could be repatriated in a shorter time and that such statements should be kept in view as it was for the Commission, not the United States, to 'consider how the best methods of ensuring a flow of capital investment could be linked with the fiscal systems of the recipient countries'.[39] Chile also indicated that double standards were being imposed as the European countries had faced such instability themselves stemming from the two world wars, and the Middle East, Africa and Latin America were in a similar state with respect to currency control and political stability, yet US aid still flowed to such selected countries. Pakistan censured the United States for 'considering the situation in terms of dollars rather than of pressing needs' when 'poverty, disease and hunger predominated in many areas' and that peace would be elusive unless the means to combat these problems were found.[40] China

[36] Ibid 8–9.
[37] Ibid 11.
[38] Ibid.
[39] Ibid 12.
[40] Ibid 10.

expressed the hope that capital-exporting countries, in determining their economic policies, 'would not fail to come to grips with the seriousness and reality of the situation' faced by underdeveloped countries 'in view of the abnormal times', which could not be solved by private investment alone.[41]

Secondly, the US justifications for maintaining its credit system and for underdeveloped countries to keep their tax rates low were self-serving, presumptuous and hypocritical (Belgium, China, India and Pakistan). Pakistan highlighted that such positions were inconsistent with the recent declaration by President Eisenhower, supported by the British Prime Minister, 'that all possible help would be given for the development of the under-developed countries'.[42] China stated that any reduction of taxation by underdeveloped countries as an incentive to FDI flows would be undermined under the credit system. India clarified that it had determined its income tax system based on its own requirements and not by US tax levels, and that this 'should to be made clear, since India needed foreign capital investment and it was likely that the United States would be the main source'.[43] Belgium pointed out that the US credit system contradicted ECOSOC Resolution 416D (XIV), which requested the Commission to explore the exclusive source-based jurisdiction of underdeveloped countries to tax foreign investment, and that Belgium's unilateral deduction mechanism proved that such a request was feasible as this system not only did not require DTAs to provide full double taxation relief but was also the reverse of the credit system in that any tax reduction accorded by the capital-importing country did not result in an increase of the tax due in Belgium.

In setting out their general Soviet positions, the USSR, supported by Czechoslovakia, cautioned that US corporations were deriving great profits from overseas investments through their predatory exploitation of natural resources and cheap labour, and urged that economic and trade relations with underdeveloped countries be conducted in a manner which promoted their national industries, agriculture and transport.[44] This was exemplified by the USSR, which supplied capital and durable goods and equipment in exchange for those countries' traditional exports

[41] E/CN.8/SR.26 (14 May 1953) 12.
[42] E/CN.8/SR.25, 10.
[43] Ibid 11.
[44] The USSR also accused the US technical assistance and economic development programmes as being conditioned on economic or political demands, including for territorial use for military purposes.

without intervening in their domestic affairs.[45] Czechoslovakia added that tax policy was a most important means for underdeveloped countries to prevent exploitation by foreign capital, to reduce the profits extracted from them by foreign companies and to strengthen domestic capital resources. It warned that foreign investment in some areas caused unbalanced production and dependence on a single export commodity, which led to the lowering of living standards and general reduction in tax revenue. It considered that the SoCtyTax/ResCtyExempt(FoInvInc) principle would only lead to an increase in profits, benefitting the capitalist monopolies.

At Pakistan's suggestion, the Working Group was established to invite an exchange of views on double taxation relief solutions and the extent to which ECOSOC Resolution 416D (XIV) could be implemented. Cuba subsequently submitted a resolution (L.3) which essentially declared that the incentive to FDI offered by the lower tax rates of underdeveloped countries was nullified by capital-exporting countries' taxation of income earned from investments in such countries.[46] L.3 recommended that the SoCtyTax/ResCtyExempt(FoInvInc) principle be adopted as 'one of the most effective means of increasing the flow of private capital to the under-developed countries', and 'transform[ed] ... rapidly into a practical reality' through unilateral legislative action and DTAs between highly developed countries and underdeveloped countries.[47] Canada commented that Cuba's resolution would cause a 'minor revolution in the fiscal practices of a number of States if the policies were adopted'.[48]

In the Working Group, L.3 was defeated by vote of four to three.[49] Subsequent discussions led to a compromise solution, greatly facilitated

[45] China observed in response that barter trading 'offered greater opportunities for exploitation than normal investment practices if equal value was not obtained in the exchange'; that '[m]any countries were being bled white, not by investors, but by "barterers"'; and that '[f]ew economic systems were good or bad in themselves; everything depended upon the way they were used and by whom': E/CN.8/SR.26, 12.

[46] Fiscal Commission, *Cuba: Draft Resolution on Fiscal Incentives to Increase the International Flow of Private Capital for the Economic Development of Under-Developed Countries*, 4th sess, Agenda item 3(a), UN Doc E/CN.8/L.3 (29 April 1953). This draft resolution is reproduced in Appendix O.

[47] Ibid.

[48] E/CN.8/SR.27, 13.

[49] CSCIO, *Draft Brief for United Kingdom Delegation to the Sixteenth Session of the Economic and Social Council: Report on the Fourth Session of the Fiscal Commission*, IOC(53)78 (12 June 1953) 3, TNA:IR40/11173(2). The other Working Group attendees presumably abstained. Cuba and Pakistan, supported by Chile, were reported as driving the SoCtyTax/ResCtyExempt(FoInvInc) proposal as they wished to offer foreign

by India,[50] that was consolidated into a resolution drafted by Pakistan (L.6) and adopted by all the Working Group members with one abstention.[51] The operative part of L.6 contained two paragraphs: the first generally affirmed the source taxation rights of countries ('Paragraph 1'), while the second recommended that highly developed countries, in unilateral legislation or DTAs, 'give sympathetic consideration to the feasibility of taxing such income [income arising from investments in underdeveloped countries] only or primarily in [those countries]' ('Paragraph 2').[52]

When the plenary meetings resumed, Cuba resubmitted L.3, explaining that it had no alternative but to maintain its resolution as the UN had not been created to merely discuss abstract principles but to achieve practical results, foremost among which was the development of underdeveloped countries. L.3 was rejected by a vote of seven to four, with four abstentions. The Commission then considered the Working Group's resolution, to which Cuba and Czechoslovakia expressed their dissatisfaction with the text. Cuba stated that the solution fell short of meeting its needs and appealed to the more developed countries to 'reflect on the fact that international solidarity was essential in the present world situation' and that it was in their own interest to increase FDI flows for the development of underdeveloped countries before they found themselves deprived of foreign markets at some stage.[53] Czechoslovakia considered that the resolution only served the interests of the more highly developed countries to the detriment of the underdeveloped countries. The United States and Chile, however, expressed full support for the resolution, although the latter also expressed reservations on the provision of favourable tax treatment to foreign capitalists exploiting a country's natural resources given that the profits of such enterprises were essentially derived from the exhaustion of such resources, which were a danger to the country's future revenue source. The Working Group's resolution was adopted upon a vote of thirteen to none, with two abstentions by the Soviets.

investors lower tax rates, with Pakistan also offering tax holidays for new industries. Chile nevertheless remarked that tax incentives would still not induce sufficient FDI 'to make more than a small contribution to the needs of the underdeveloped countries' (at 2). The ICC was also in favour of tax exemption but agreed with the United States and the United Kingdom that non-tax factors had more influence on FDI flows.

50 E/CN.8/SR.30 (20 May 1953) 6.

51 Fiscal Commission, *Pakistan: Draft Resolution on Fiscal Incentives to Increase the International Flow of Private Capital for the Economic Development of Under-Developed Countries*, Working Group, 4th sess, Agenda item 3(a), UN Doc E/CN.8/L.8 (4 May 1953).

52 See Appendix P for the text of this resolution in its adopted form.

53 E/CN.8/SR.30, 6.

When the Commission came to discuss the future work programme of the Secretariat, Pakistan, supported by Cuba and India, submitted that the Secretariat's study regarding the effects of taxation on foreign investment be focused on the effect of the outcome of the Working Group's resolution on countries' taxation policies. Pakistan accordingly proposed that the project be renamed 'Effect of taxation on foreign investment in under-developed countries as a result of resolution ___ [Resolution number to be inserted]'.[54] This was generally opposed by China, the United States and Canada: China, with which the United States agreed, considered that the underdeveloped countries should not monopolise the Secretariat's work; the United States claimed that the directive would unduly limit the Secretariat's work (to which Bloch indicated that such would not necessarily result); and Canada argued that it was impracticable for the Secretariat to assess the effect of the operative part of the resolution (to which Pakistan indicated that the Secretariat's survey could be carried out by annually transmitting a letter to governments inquiring of their actions in response to the resolution).[55] Ensuing debate eventually led to an amended proposal that more tenuously addressed such a focus, which was adopted by ten votes to none, with three abstentions.

The Commission's report was discussed in the last two meetings of the session, in which Cuba was not present. The draft report that was circulated by Canada (as Rapporteur) prior to these meetings proffered, within the account of the debate concerning the taxation of foreign investment, a summary of the arguments of 'capital-exporting countries' and 'capital-importing countries'.[56] This summary went into some detail of the technical arguments of the former group but more briefly described the latter group's contentions, with some implication that they were unsupported by technical grounds. When the Commission sat to discuss the draft report, however, the Rapporteur submitted changes that deleted this summary.[57] At the same time, the USSR and Czechoslovakia also submitted amendments to incorporate into the

[54] E/CN.8/SR.31 (21 May 1953) 4.

[55] Bloch here cautioned that government replies to questionnaires were not always forthcoming and that it could take several years before there were enough replies for a proper analysis.

[56] Fiscal Commission, *Draft Report to the Economic and Social Council on the Fourth Session of the Fiscal Commission, Held at New York, from 27 April to 8 May 1953*, 4th sess, UN Doc E/CN.8/L.9 (7 May 1953) 8–9 [13]–[14]. This text is reproduced in Appendix Q.

[57] Fiscal Commission, *Draft Report to the Economic and Social Council on the Fourth Session of the Fiscal Commission, Held at New York: Changes Submitted by Rapporteur, from 27 April to 8 May 1953*, 4th sess, UN Doc E/CN.8/L.9/Add.1 (8 May 1953).

report Soviet positions on the various agenda items as well as their views on China's illegal representation.[58] Chile, supported by Belgium, objected to all the proposed changes as they would not only extensively revise the original draft but also reduce it to a 'unilateral document' that represented the views of one delegation at length.[59] At Chile's suggestion that all delegations should be allowed to submit changes they wished to have incorporated, a lengthy procedural debate arose as to whether the report should represent a consensus document or whether individual delegations were entitled to have their views recorded. Chile, Czechoslovakia, India and the USSR supported the inclusion of minority views, while the United States, Belgium and China advocated that the report should focus on the majority viewpoint. Although the Commission adjourned the meeting at the suggestion of France (as Chairman) to enable delegations to submit further desired amendments to the report, none did so.

Discussions resumed with the Commission proceeding to vote on each paragraph of the draft report and the amendments that had been submitted. The Rapporteur's amendments were adopted without argument and no indication was given among the records of the votes that carried these changes through. On the other hand, the votes regarding the Soviet amendments were recorded, with the changes generally adopted by a vote carried by the USSR, Czechoslovakia and India, while the rest of the Commission abstained. A Chilean proposal for the report to include a statement that the Chinese representative had considered the Soviet motion to exclude him illegal was adopted by four votes to two, with eight abstentions.[60]

12.2.2 The Commission's Report

The Working Group's resolution was finalised as Draft Resolution B in the Commission's report of its Fourth Session.[61] The Secretariat's future work programme was almost identical to that which had been adopted at

[58] Fiscal Commission, *Czechoslovakia and Union of Soviet Socialist Republics: Amendments to Draft Report to the Economic and Social Council on the Fourth Session of the Fiscal Commission, Held at New York, from 27 April to 8 May 1953 (E/CN.8/L.9)*, 4th sess, UN Doc E/CN.8/L.12 (8 May 1953).

[59] E/CN.8/SR.32 (21 May 1953) 4.

[60] India explained that it had abstained but that this should not be interpreted as a variation to India's constant effort to invite PRC representatives to all UN bodies. See Chapter 4, Section 4.1.1, n 28 (regarding India's early support of China's representation in the UN by PRC representatives after the PRC's establishment).

[61] E/2429, 6 [50]. This resolution (entitled *International Tax Problems*) is reproduced in Appendix P.

the Third Session. The continuing projects comprised technical assistance, the fiscal information service, the World Tax Service (now listed separately), the review of fiscal developments and the taxation of foreign taxpayers and foreign income.[62] The ad hoc projects included 'Continuation of studies on the effects of taxation on foreign investment, especially in under-developed countries, in the light of draft resolution B' as well as corporate tax problems, fiscal administration and management, fiscal problems of agriculture and problems of municipal finance.[63]

The report's account of the debate concerning the taxation of foreign investment income merely stated that the Commission had been 'divided' on the question presented by ECOSOC Resolution 416D (XIV) as to the role that tax exemption of income from foreign investment by capital-exporting countries played in facilitating FDI flows to underdeveloped countries, before outlining the respective resolutions of Cuba and the Working Group and the outcome of the Commission's vote on each resolution.[64]

12.3 Deliberations in ECOSOC (July 1953)

At ECOSOC's Sixteenth Session,[65] the Commission's report was considered at the 710th, 711th, 712th and 719th meetings on 3, 4 and 9 July and at the Economic Committee's 131st and 132nd meetings on 6 and 7 July.[66] The United Kingdom and the United States praised the Secretariat's work, and Argentina, France, India, the United Kingdom and the United States generally commended the Commission's work and report, although India considered the report was too brief in its summary of some of the discussions that had taken place. While ECOSOC adopted all the Commission's resolutions other than Draft Resolution B without

62 Ibid 5–6 [48].

63 Ibid 6 [48].

64 These sentences are reproduced in Appendix Q.

65 ECOSOC membership in 1953 comprised Argentina, Australia, Belgium, China, Cuba, Egypt, France, India, the Philippines, Poland, Sweden, Venezuela, Turkey, the United Kingdom, the United States, Uruguay, the USSR and Yugoslavia.

66 Unless otherwise stated, the material regarding these discussions have been drawn from the following *Summary Records* of ECOSOC, 16th sess (UN ESCOR, UN Docs E/SR.710–712 (3–4 July 1953); E/SR.719 (9 July 1953)) and its Economic Committee (UN Docs E/AC.6/SR.131–132 (12–13 August 1953)); and the Economic Committee's report (Economic Committee, *Report of the Economic Committee*, UN ESC, 16th sess, Agenda item 9, UN Doc E/2478 (7 July 1953)).

issue, Draft Resolution B was the subject of acrimonious and protracted debate, drawing broad participation and seven resolutions from among the First World and developing country delegations. Except for Yugoslavia, the Communist delegations largely did not participate in the discussions and refrained from voting on the matter.[67]

The discussions were preceded by resolutions submitted by Cuba and Argentina separately. Cuba's resolution (L.510) was submitted as a replacement for Draft Resolution B and basically replicated L.3 that had been rejected in the Commission.[68] Argentina's resolution (L.515) amended L.510 to incorporate bolder assertions,[69] including that 'the taxation facilities of all kinds granted by developing countries' to stimulate FDI might 'be ineffective' if the SoCtyTax/ResCtyExempt(FoInvInc) principle was 'not universally accepted', and for the principle to be incorporated into governments' fiscal legislation 'with the least possible delay' and in all DTAs concluded thereon with no distinction as to the stage of development of the contracting parties.[70]

In the deliberations, L.510 was outrightly opposed by Australia, Belgium, China, France, Sweden, the United Kingdom and the United States for reasons that included:[71] the Fiscal Commission was the competent expert body to decide on the subject and its carefully considered decision should be respected, especially as the credit system was an equitable approach (the United Kingdom and the United States); developed nations still required capital for reconstruction and modernisation,

67 Yugoslavia observed that the subject should more appropriately be discussed under the agenda item on 'Economic development of under-developed countries' and that such discussions were 'useless' on the basis that fiscal policy was unlikely 'to have important repercussions on the economic picture as a whole'.

68 *Cuba: Draft Resolution*, UN ESC, 16th sess, Agenda item 9, UN Doc E/L.510 (1 July 1953), reproduced in Appendix R, Section R.1.

69 *Argentina: Amendment to the Cuban Draft Resolution (E/L.510)*, UN ESC, 16th sess, Agenda item 9, UN Doc E/L.515 (2 July 1953), reproduced in Appendix R, Section R.2.

70 L.515 also requested that the Secretariat bring this issue to the attention of the group of experts to be set up pursuant to GA Resolution 623 (VII) to be considered among the practical measures the group was to recommend on financing the economic development of underdeveloped countries. GA Resolution 623 (VII) was concerned with the prices of primary commodities and undue fluctuations in the terms of trade. When L.515 was discussed by the Economic Committee, the question of taxation was generally considered to be quite irrelevant to the subject matter of this resolution. The British delegation nevertheless reported to the Foreign Office that Cuba still assumed that the substance of the SoCtyTax/ResCtyExempt(FoInvInc) proposal would be referred to the group; however, the Secretariat had assured the British delegation that it would not take any such action: Letter from Anderson to Cooks, 13 July 1953, 2, TNA:IR40/11173(1).

71 The summary records do not indicate that these countries addressed L.515.

and had to prevent capital flight to countries with lower tax rates or weaker administrative capacity in tax collection (Belgium, France and Sweden);[72] and more study was required to demonstrate the benefits of such a resolution on developing economies and the consequences it would have on industrialised economies (China, France and Sweden).[73] L.510 was also criticised for serving 'no useful purpose' as taxation did not significantly influence FDI (Australia); being too prescriptive and interfering with countries' tax sovereignty (Australia, China, France, Sweden, the United Kingdom and the United States); encouraging tax evasion in capital-exporting countries (France and Sweden) and tax competition among capital-importing countries (Sweden); discouraging DTAs, thereby frustrating the elimination of existing double taxation (Sweden); and conferring legal validity on a principle that would embarrass the treasury departments of various countries (France and Sweden) and compel capital-exporting countries to exempt taxing income from all foreign sources (Sweden).

On the other hand, Egypt, Venezuela, Uruguay and the Philippines backed L.510 (the former three also backing L.515), while India supported the underlying principle of L.510 but considered the resolution too far-reaching.[74] In explaining its resolution, Cuba stated that L.510 fulfilled a duty to all the underdeveloped countries of the world in advancing 'precise and realistic ideas' that had not only been approved by the twenty Latin American UN members in ECLA but which had also found approval in General Assembly Resolution 520 (VI) in directing ECOSOC to continue studying the problem of financing the economic development of under-developed countries.[75] Cuba further stated that the Commission had been inhibited in its technical consideration of the former's proposals as the latter had been dominated by political considerations. Argentina agreed, asserting that the Commission should not

[72] Sweden and France also indicated that revenue loss resulting from the application of L.510 would force highly developed countries to impose capital export restrictions and curtail their contributions to underdeveloped countries' economic development, such as technical assistance.

[73] France also pointed out that technical difficulties arose in determining the definition of developed and underdeveloped countries.

[74] India generally insisted that the Commission had done excellent work in reaching a compromise in Draft Resolution B (likely because of the conciliator role played by India in the Commission).

[75] E/SR.710 (3 July 1953) 43–4 (referring generally to *Financing of Economic Development of Under-Developed Countries*, GA Res 520 (VI), UN Doc A/RES/520(VI) (12 January 1952)).

have discarded proposals simply because they were contrary to the established practices of certain governments, nor should it have issued such a 'weak and somewhat ambiguous'[76] and 'unworthy'[77] solution as Draft Resolution B. Argentina argued that the Commission's basic function was to devise the best solutions to problems based on their intrinsic merit, establish principles that were capable of commanding universal recognition and make definite recommendations for adoption by governments. As Cuba's proposals were 'logical and in accordance with the highest principles of justice' in meeting both the objectives of eliminating double taxation and taking 'every possible step . . . to improve conditions in the countries suffering from a low standard of living',[78] Argentina explained it had accordingly submitted amendments to broaden the application of L.510.

Cuba and Egypt, supported by Argentina and Venezuela, also extensively rebutted arguments that had been advanced by the opposing countries; their reasons referenced to the insufficiency of public funds and technical assistance flowing to underdeveloped countries, their difficulties in securing foreign capital[79] and developed countries' own declaration in resolutions of ECOSOC and the Assembly that the economic development of underdeveloped countries was 'a matter of urgency'.[80] These counterarguments included that UN resolutions had no binding force to infringe on nations' sovereignty;[81] that Draft Resolution B itself recognised the value of favourable tax treatment in incentivising FDI but that underdeveloped countries' willingness to supply low taxation was rendered ineffective without corresponding

[76] E/SR.711 (3 July 1953) 46.

[77] E/SR.712 (4 July 1953) 55. Argentina and the Philippines also considered the reaffirmation of 'a generally accepted principle' in Paragraph 1 of Draft Resolution B 'useless, and possibly dangerous'.

[78] E/SR.711, 45–6.

[79] This situation had been published in the Secretariat's *World Economic Report 1951–52* (UN, 1953) and adopted at ECOSOC's Fifteenth Session in 1952.

[80] E/SR.711, 50. Egypt highlighted that the World Bank had prioritised Europe's reconstruction over economic development, while Cuba criticised France's threat to reduce technical assistance funding as a 'somewhat paradoxical' and 'greatly deplor[able]' development.

[81] Egypt further pointed out that France itself, in a preceding discussion, had clarified that governments retained the freedom to determine how to give recommendations suitable legal expression in national provisions, the former adding that while it was understandable if underdeveloped countries considered particular measures recommended in UN resolutions to infringe upon their sovereignty 'in view of the feeling of inferiority under which some of them at times laboured', it was 'very surprising to hear developed countries advance such an argument': Ibid.

tax exemption by capital-exporting countries; that the revenue sacrifice incurred by developed countries' treasuries was unlikely to be substantial; and that the Commission's findings had simply reflected the one-sided views of the developed countries represented in the majority on the Commission and now here in ECOSOC, just as the views of the developing countries aligned with those expressed in L.510.

The developed countries' refusal to accept L.510 led to a further four resolutions to amend Draft Resolution B submitted by Argentina (L.517),[82] Australia (L.518)[83] and the United States (L.520),[84] and jointly by Argentina, Cuba, Uruguay and Venezuela (L.61),[85] as well as to the referring of the debate to the Economic Committee. In general, the amendments by the developing countries sought to strengthen the recommendation for the implementation of the SoCtyTax/ResCtyExempt(FoInvInc) proposal and to keep the examination of the proposal on the Fiscal Commission's priority agenda, especially with the aim of producing practical solutions to the problem. Conversely, the amendments suggested by Australia and the United States effectively weakened the proposals of the developing countries. The discussions eventuated in a joint resolution submitted by Argentina, Cuba, Egypt, the Philippines, Uruguay and Venezuela (L.62) that attempted to consolidate the various views that had been put forward.[86] Ensuing debate on verbal alterations proposed by the United States resulted in further dilution of the thrust of the statements as drafted in L.62. In particular, the directives to the Commission to produce practical recommendations and further analysis regarding the SoCtyTax/ResCtyExempt(FoInvInc) principle were removed, leaving just an acknowledgment that the Commission would be continuing its studies on the subject. Also, the word 'favourable' in the recommendation for highly developed countries to 'give favourable consideration to the feasibility of taking action to ensure that' income from foreign

[82] *Argentina: Amendment to Draft Resolution B (E/2429)*, UN ESC, 16th sess, Agenda item 9, UN Docs E/L.517 and Corr.1 (3 July 1953), reproduced in Appendix R, Section R.3.

[83] *Australia: Amendment to Draft Resolution B in the Report of the Commission (E/2429–paragraph 50)*, UN ESC, 16th sess, Agenda Item 9, UN Doc E/L.518 (3 July 1953), reproduced in Appendix R, Section R.4.

[84] *United States of America: Amendment to Draft Resolution B of the Report of the Fiscal Commission (E/2429)*, UN ESC, 16th sess, Agenda item 9, UN Doc E/L.520 (4 July 1953), reproduced in Appendix R, Section R.5.

[85] Economic Committee, *Argentina, Cuba, Uruguay and Venezuela: Amendments to the Draft Resolution B (E/2429)*, UN ESC, 16th sess, Agenda item 9, UN Doc E/AC.6/L.61 (6 July 1953), reproduced in Appendix R, Section R.6.

[86] Economic Committee, *Argentina, Cuba, Egypt, Philippines, Uruguay and Venezuela: Joint Amendments to Draft Resolution B (E/2429)*, UN ESC, 16th sess, Agenda item 9, UN Doc E/AC.6/L.62 (6 July 1953), reproduced in Appendix R, Section R.7.

investment was taxable 'only or primarily' in source countries was changed to 'special' (hereinafter referred to as the 'Operative Paragraph') to prevent any prejudgement of the direction in which governments' decisions should take.[87] This final solution was adopted by a vote of fifteen to none, with three abstentions by the Soviet members. When Poland inquired about L.510, Cuba indicated that it would introduce its draft resolution 'again at a suitable time in the appropriate body'.[88]

In plenary session, ECOSOC adopted, by the same majority, the resolution approved by the Economic Committee as ECOSOC Resolution 486B (XVI) of 9 July 1953.[89] Cuba was again questioned about the status of L.510, this time by the United States, to which Cuba affirmed that its resolution was no longer before the Council but that it intended to reintroduce it 'at the appropriate time and place'.[90]

12.4 Deliberations in the General Assembly (September–December 1953)

At the Assembly's Eighth Session, during discussions on the Financing of Economic Development agenda, Cuba, Iraq and Saudi Arabia introduced a resolution to the Second Committee which, although primarily directed at calling for immediate steps towards the establishment of the International Finance Corporation (IFC), also incorporated a modified version of the Operative Paragraph in ECOSOC Resolution 486B (XVI) that omitted the words 'or primarily'.[91] In reporting to the Foreign Office, the UK delegation described the resolution as one 'in horrifying terms . . . conceived by . . . Saudi Arabia' which also dealt with 'the old Cuban taxation gambit'.[92] The UK delegation was instructed to move to restore the words 'or primarily' into the paragraph, and failing that, to vote against

[87] The word 'favourable' had previously replaced the word 'sympathetic' as found in the Commission's Draft Resolution B as Argentina had considered that the latter epithet presented the problem 'in rather too sentimental terms' (E/AC.6/SR.131 (13 August 1953) 5) given its 'emotional connotation' in the Spanish version (at 7). India conversely thought the adjective had 'a practical rather than an emotional connotation' (at 6).

[88] E/AC.6/SR.132 (12 August 1953) 11.

[89] *International Tax Problems*, ESC Res 486B (XVI), UN ESCOR, UN Doc 2508 (15 August 1953, adopted 9 July 1953). This resolution is reproduced in Appendix S.

[90] E/SR.719, 101.

[91] Telegrams No 232, 25 October 1953, and No 242 and No 243, 3 November 1953, from New York (UK Delegation to UN) to Foreign Office, TNA:IR40/11173(1).

[92] UK Delegation, Telegram No 232.

the paragraph.[93] While the final resolution hammered out by the Committee 'left out all references to taxation',[94] the Cuba–Iraq–Saudi Arabia resolution had provoked concerns in Inland Revenue as it 'affect-[ed] the whole structure of our double taxation agreements' and the Royal Commission, which was 'approaching the final stages of their deliberations', had been closely following the discussion of the problem in the Assembly.[95]

12.5 Commentary

The Commission's Fourth Session showed a seemingly acquiescent Fiscal Division focused on relatively uncontentious work, reluctant even to report on UN reports (i.e. the E/1986 report) that supported views contrary to US positions. While this may have been partly attributable to the conclusions of E/1986 having been overridden in ECOSOC as well as the Division's own disapproval of the exemption system, the impact of 'the height of the McCarthy era in 1953'[96] itself could not have been lost on the Secretariat's keeping of a low profile.[97] US dominance appeared to be in its element: Bartelt made changes to the Division's summary records of the session,[98] and the UK representative (RO Nicholas) reported to his government that he, along with the Belgian, Canadian and French representatives, had been so annoyed by

> [the United States'] long prepared speeches on all subjects, . . . apparent desire to advertise that the new administration was going to introduce new policies (not clearly specified) and . . . passion for collecting more studies and more statistics[,]

as well as by underdeveloped countries' 'loosely co-ordinated plan of campaign and a tendency to support the US in the hope of favours to

93 Telegram No 919 from Foreign Office to New York (UK Delegation to UN), 7 November 1953, TNA:IR40/11173(1).

94 Note of Telephone Conversation, 31 December 1953, TNA:IR40/11173(1). See *Financing of Economic Development of Under-Developed Countries*, GA Res 622 (VII), UN Doc A/RES/622(VII) (21 December 1953).

95 Letter from Thorpe to Goodman, 29 December 1953, TNA:IR40/11173(1).

96 Abdelaziz Megzari, *The Internal Justice of the United Nations: A Critical History 1945–2015* (Brill Nijhoff, 2015) 182.

97 See Edgar J Dosman, *The Life and Times of Raúl Prebisch, 1901–1986* (McGill-Queen's University Press, 2008) 287 (indicating that close US scrutiny of the UN only eased in mid-1954).

98 Letter from Bloch to Bartelt, 25 May 1953, NARAII:RG56–199–6.

come'[99] that the four had contemplated that the Commission might have 'come to the end of its useful life'.[100]

Indeed, there seemed little the Commission could accomplish but rubber stamp the US-approved work of the Division. While the taxation of foreign investment was the '[o]nly question of substance'[101] that engaged broad interest and participation, the discussions were not underpinned by technical studies but were suffused with underlying political tensions and alliances. In particular, the United States took pains to belabour the economic nationalism spreading through Latin America; the need for such emphasis indicative of the pressure large US corporations (especially those exploiting land, minerals and petroleum, or providing utilities) were exerting in lobbying Washington for support.[102] Meanwhile, the developing countries, overlooked by US aid and resentful of Western imperialism, barely contained their frustrations. In their reports to their respective governments, Nicholas noted that Cuba spoke 'with great eloquence and feeling' and Pakistan 'with some

[99] R Nicholas, 'Note for Next Session of the Fiscal Commission', undated (around July 1953), TNA:IR40/11173(1). Certeux even proposed that the four (whom Nicholas referred as the 'more dispassionate and reasonable group') 'meet together a few days in advance' for future sessions to agree on 'the line they were going to take during the discussions' to be more 'effective' given that 'it was undesirable that the initiative should always be left to the US and the under-developed countries'. This irritation with the United States appears to reflect the latter's deteriorating standing even among the Western nations it economically supported, John Colville, Churchill's Private Secretary, having noted in June 1952 that '[b]ut now England, and Europe, distrust, dislike and despise the United States': Anthony Adamthwaite, 'Overstretched and Overstrung: Eden, the Foreign Office and the Making of Policy, 1951–5' (1988) 64(2) *International Affairs* 241, 243. See also Chapter 14, n 15.

[100] CSCIO, IOC(53)128, 3.

[101] CSCIO, IOC(53)78, 1.

[102] Rory M Miller, 'Economic Nationalism and British Investments in Post-War Latin America, 1945–1970' in Thomas C Mills and Rory M Miller (eds), *Britain and the Growth of US Hegemony in Twentieth-Century Latin America: Competition, Cooperation and Coexistence* (Palgrave Macmillan, 2020) 151, 152, 154. In contrast, the British government and British firms were able to adapt to the new climate with greater success. At the time of the session, the United States was intervening in the Bolivian nationalisation of tin companies (Noel Maurer, *The Empire Trap: The Rise and Fall of US Intervention to Protect American Property Overseas, 1893–2013* (Princeton University Press, 2013) 298–9) and its relations with Guatemala were fast deteriorating with the launch of a Communist smear campaign by the powerful American-owned United Fruit Company and the Central Intelligence Agency (CIA) against Guatemala's 1952 land reforms that threatened the company's extensive landholdings (Sharon I Meers, 'The British Connection: How the United States Covered Its Tracks in the 1954 Coup in Guatemala' (1992) 16(3) *Diplomatic History* 409, 413).

bitterness',[103] while Bartelt recorded that Pakistan became 'somewhat irritated' with the US refusal to support it and had challenged the United States to prove its desire to encourage private foreign investment 'with action rather than words'.[104]

Moreover, despite the European countries' own exemption or deduction systems for foreign-source income and the South African territorial tax system, political ties evidently bound the First World countries to vote as a unit.[105] Similarly, India's support of Soviet submissions reflected the improved Indo-Soviet relations following the Kremlin's 1952 assurances of assistance for Indian development projects and expressed interest in closer trade relations.[106] The United States thus need not have been concerned – India's conciliatory role[107] at this session and the Soviets' aversion to US capitalist business benefiting from the exemption principle left the Latin Americans and Pakistan far in the minority. Draft Resolution B accordingly gave little ground to the developing countries. In fact, Paragraph 1, in its reaffirmation of source-country taxation rights, possibly implied a concession being granted by the developed countries to developing countries, as suspected by Argentina and the Philippines.[108] Paragraph 2 was a fairly weak compromise, Nicholas reporting that '[i]t really carries things no further' although it could be adversely used by countries with which Britain was trying to negotiate DTAs.[109] The developing countries' attempt to overcome the benign resolution by demanding accountability over Paragraph 2's implementation would seem to evidence their growing fatigue with solutions that had futile impact on actual practice.

Canada's last-minute deletions to its draft report suggest that they were prompted, presumably by the United States, to preclude any public record of fundamental discord in the Commission, especially one

[103] 'Note Given to Anderson of United Kingdom Permanent Delegation to United Nations', undated (around June 1953), 2, TNA:IR40/11173(1).

[104] Bartelt letter, 29 June 1953, 2.

[105] CSCIO, IOC(53)78, 3 (regarding America and Britain being supported by Belgium, Canada, France, South Africa).

[106] Vijay Sen Budhraj, 'Major Dimensions of Indo-Soviet Relations' (1975) 31(1) *India Quarterly* 11, 12.

[107] See Stanley A Kochanek, 'India's Changing Role in the United Nations' (1980) 53(1) *Pacific Affairs* 48, 49 (regarding India's general policy as mediator between power blocs during this period).

[108] See n 77. Britain itself regarded Paragraph 1 'a gratuitous reaffirmation': Anderson letter, 13 July 1953, 1.

[109] CSCIO, IOC(53)78, 3.

between developed and developing countries.[110] Why developing countries neither contested the deletions nor made submissions of their own despite indication by Chile that it wished to do so suggests that the United States might also have been persuasive behind the scenes in preventing further amendments. The brevity of the Commission's report and the lack of impartial reporting or study by the Division had the most disadvantage for developing countries unfamiliar with double taxation, as indicated by Turkey during the ECOSOC discussions where it stated that it was unable to form an opinion on the Cuban resolution as it had little understanding of its import.[111]

The discussions in ECOSOC reveal heightened degrees of antagonism between the two groups of countries in their fortified numbers: the developed group not shy in resorting to duplicitous, condescending and even bullying arguments, and the developing group similarly uninhibited in their exasperation with indeterminate resolutions, hollow promises and double standards, as well as in their determination to keep the SoCtyTax/ResCtyExempt(FoInvInc) proposal on the table and to compel responding action by the former group. Although the entry of the then powerful developing countries Argentina and Egypt into the debate greatly strengthened the 'hard bargaining'[112] between the two groups, the stark power and economic imbalances allowed developed countries to remain intransigent. The diplomatic accommodation of various countries' proposals possibly even weakened Draft Resolution B further. In addition, developing countries' hope that further study of the problem might yield outcomes in their favour appeared misplaced as the Division showed no inclination for pursuing examination of the proposal.

Developing countries' prospects of carving out a place on the world stage appeared to be becoming bleaker. By this time, the reconstruction of Western Europe and Japan was virtually complete and these areas, along with other industrialised countries and centrally planned economies, had entered into the postwar economic boom later identified as the 'Golden Age' of economic growth.[113] Western Europe was progressing in its

[110] This is analogous to the US efforts at the First Session to exclude the 'counter-balance' views presented by the USSR regarding the safeguarding of underdeveloped countries' interests against developed country positions (see Chapter 5, Section 5.2).

[111] E/SR.711, 49–50 [45]–[46]. Turkey nevertheless indicated that its position at that point did not pre-judge its future attitude on any discussion of the question at the next General Assembly session.

[112] Note from Cooks to Nicholas, 8 July 1953, TNA:IR40/11173(1).

[113] DESA, *World Economic and Social Survey 2017: Reflecting on Seventy Years of Development Policy Analysis*, UN Doc E/2017/50/Rev/1 (also ST/ESA/365) (UN, 2017)

economic integration and looked upon the UN 'as only another international organization, one not even as important to them as the European common market'.[114] The Commonwealth economic network was still functioning, and Canada, Australia and New Zealand had already turned to relationships with the United States, the IMF and the World Bank for capital supplies.[115] The developed nations had a choice of forums with the global marketplace largely controlled by GATT, the IMF and the World Bank.

Meanwhile, the UN's analysis of development advanced that technical progress in underdeveloped countries as primary producers, in contrast to technical progress in manufacturing industries, led to declining terms of trade in the long term, which was exacerbated by short-term volatility of commodity prices (the 'Prebisch-Singer thesis').[116] This revolutionary thinking not only challenged the main tenet of free trade, which promoted exports as the driver of growth, but also held that domestic industrialisation through import substitution and protection of local industries from foreign competition was the decisive factor in the economic development of underdeveloped countries. Igniting such industrialisation, however, required a large injection of financing, and developing countries' campaign to establish 'fair' international prices for primary commodities,[117] SUNFED or the IFC[118] in the UN, as urged by the Secretariat's and other expert reports,[119] were being hamstrung by the First World countries. Their acts of economic nationalisation to advance national autonomy

ch 2; Tamás Vonyó, 'Post-War Reconstruction and the Golden Age of Economic Growth' (2008) 12(2) *European Review of Economic History* 221.

114 E Appathurai, 'Permanent Missions to the United Nations' (1970) 25(2) *International Journal* 287, 299.

115 See Paul L Robertson and John Singleton, 'The Commonwealth as an Economic Network' (2001) 41(3) *Australian Economic History Review* 241.

116 John Toye and Richard Toye, *UN and Global Political Economy: Trade, Finance, and Development* (Indiana University Press, 2004) ch 5; Richard Jolly, Louis Emmerij and Dharam Ghai, *UN Contributions to Development Thinking and Practice* (Indiana University Press, 2004) 55–64 (quoting Singer's conclusion that 'the industrialised countries have had the best of both worlds, as consumers of primary commodities and as producers of manufactured articles; the underdeveloped countries have had the worst of both worlds, as consumers of manufactures and as producers of raw materials' (at 58)).

117 'Paper Prepared by the United Nations Planning Staff, Bureau of United Nations Affairs', undated (around July 1953), in State Department, *Foreign Relations of the United States, 1952–1954* (USGPO, 1979) vol 3: United Nations Affairs, Doc 31.

118 Eric Toussaint, *The World Bank: A Critical Primer*, tr Elizabeth Anne et al, ed Sylvain Dropsy (Pluto Press, 2008) 32–3. See also Telegram No 212 from New York (UK Delegation to UN) to Foreign Office, 3 November 1953, TNA:IR40/11173(1).

119 Jolly, Emmerij and Ghai, *UN Contributions*, ch 3.

and limit foreign control of domestic resources were moreover condemned by the United States as 'misguided', even amounting to communist subversion.[120] The Eisenhower Administration, in its preoccupation with the Cold War, intended to extend little foreign aid to non-European areas unthreatened by communism and was endeavouring to induce 'private enterprise to take up the slack' to venture more capital abroad,[121] even though private enterprise was then only interested in accessing strategic raw materials in such regions.

Moreover, developing countries themselves were being pressured to bear the onus of responsibility in attracting private capital as their economic panacea, and this extended even to the role tax measures were to play, resulting in incongruent advice. Just two years prior, developing countries were counselled (by the Secretariat and the compromise reached at the Third Session) against offering preferential tax treatment to attract FDI and that capital-exporting countries would absorb, through their provision of double taxation relief, the former's increases of income taxes as a means of fostering their development. Now the United States claimed that it could not spare any revenue sacrifices, however low, and that developing countries' low tax rates were a necessary incentive to FDI, while contradictorily acknowledging that such benefit was effectively nullified under a credit system and that tax incentives had little influence on fostering actual investment. In their desperation to obtain capital, many developing countries appeared to be caving into the demands of the United States and private businesses: Cuba and Pakistan in the Commission indicated their preparedness to offer lower taxes, and India, Pakistan, Ceylon and other British colonies had begun offering 'pioneer industries' reliefs.[122] On the other hand, other developing countries, such as Brazil, would be spurred towards further nationalism in their desire to retain sovereignty over their economic development and their aversion towards accepting US private investment.[123]

120 Stephen G Rabe, 'Eisenhower and Latin America' in Chester J Pach (ed), *A Companion to Dwight D Eisenhower* (Wiley-Blackwell, 2017) 435, 443.

121 'Mr Humphrey's Dinner', *New York Times*, 22 June 1953, 20. See also Kevin E Grimm, 'Eisenhower and the Third World' in Chester J Pach (ed), *A Companion to Dwight D Eisenhower* (Wiley-Blackwell, 2017) 473, 481; Dosman, *Prebisch*, 291.

122 Letter from Green to Smith, 28 August 1953, TNA:IR40/11173(1).

123 In October 1953, the Brazilian Congress approved its Petrobras law that placed petroleum development under a state-owned monopoly, thus putting an end to US efforts from the mid-1940s under the Truman Administration to prevent Brazil from passing laws shutting out foreign participation in the industry: Frank D McCann, *Brazil and the United States during World War II and Its Aftermath: Negotiating Alliance and Balancing*

Although developing countries had not been overly successful at this stage in getting the United States or the United Kingdom to relinquish taxation of income earned from foreign investments, there were nevertheless developments that indicated that the resolutions they had managed to wring out, however weak, were having some impact at least on Britain, in view of pressures being applied by industry and international experts. In August 1953, the British delegation to the Third Session of ECAFE's working party of experts on financing of economic development (September 1953), which had under consideration the Commission's views as part of the agenda item on taxation as an instrument of development policy, was briefed to defend the position that the country of origin only had a 'primary right' to tax business and trading profits and did 'not necessarily [have] the superior right' to tax other income.[124] The British government was also then being lobbied to provide matching relief for the 'pioneer industries' incentives being granted by overseas countries based on the recommendation of the Royal Commission's interim report[125] issued earlier in February.[126] The Commission's views would later that year be used by British overseas mining interests to argue that Britain's taxation of foreign income at 'onerous taxation rates' was hampering 'the opening-up of under-developed territories' and 'provoking growing irritation abroad, particularly within the Commonwealth', in deterring developing countries from offering incentives to encourage new mining in their territories 'if the gainer was to be the UK Treasury'.[127]

Giants (Palgrave Macmillan, 2018) 258, 252. The United States 'responded by reducing drastically the amount of an already agreed upon loan from the Export-Import Bank', which in turn provoked Brazil to issue 'a decree limiting the repatriation of profits of American firms operating in Brazil' (at 258–9).

The mounting concern of private business over nationalism is reflected in IFA's resolution on 'Tax measures to facilitate international movements of capital' adopted at its 1954 Cologne Congress, which stated that the organisation:

> Condemns any legal or administrative measures discriminating against capital and enterprises from abroad as compared with national capital and enterprises especially with regard to the calculation of taxable profits, and
> Recommends, on the contrary, all and every means to bring tax systems close together and to prevent double taxation.

(IFA, *International Fiscal Association Resolutions Book* (IBFD, 1988) 36).

124 Green letter, 28 August 1953.

125 Royal Commission on the Taxation of Profits and Income, *Interim Report* (Her Majesty's Stationery Office, 1953).

126 Green letter, 28 August 1953.

127 'British Overseas Mining Association', *Financial Times* (London), 21 December 1953, 4. These pressures by the mining industry must have been significant: at this stage, despite

12.6 Subsequent Secretariat Work

From July 1953, at the request of the UN Educational, Scientific and Cultural Organization, the Division began looking into the double taxation of authors and artists on copyright royalties.[128] By mid-1954, the Division's research work on agricultural taxation, land taxation, taxation and capital formation, taxation of international investment and tax administration was largely being carried out in cooperation with the HLS International Tax Program.[129] The Secretariat and HLS would also complete arrangements for the latter to take over the preparation and publication of the World Tax Service.[130] Not surprisingly, the Division appeared not to have progressed any examination of the SoCtyTax/ResCtyExempt(FoInvInc) proposal, as indicated in its communications with the Chilean Embassy in June 1954. The latter had written to Bloch, asking for his 'personal opinion' on 'the practical measures that could be adopted' at the Conference of Ministers of the Treasury of the Inter-American System (the first of its kind) to be held in Rio de Janeiro as Argentina had requested for double taxation to be included in the discussion on financing economic development.[131] Bloch replied vaguely that it was 'rather difficult' for him to provide such and that 'the best solution would be a strong support for bilateral agreements'.[132] By the year's end, the Division had published volumes 4 and 5 of the *ITA* series.[133] The Division reported considerably more progress and achievement concerning its work on technical assistance, public finance information service, and budget classification and management.[134]

over £260 million having been raised between 1946 and 1952 in the London market for overseas mines, only £15 million had been invested as additional capital in existing overseas mines directed from Britain, while no new mines had been registered since 1939. Moreover, over a quarter of the latter figure had been raised by companies that had since migrated to where their mines were located.

128 Letter from Evans to Hammarskjöld, 20 July 1953, UNARMS:AG-025-002—S-0441-0470-23900.

129 Memorandum by Surrey to Cavers, 26 May 1954, UNARMS:AG-025-002—S-0441-0468-23886(B).

130 'Fiscal Questions' [1954] *Yearbook of the United Nations* 179, 181.

131 Letter from Valenzuela to Bloch, 21 June 1954, UNARMS:AG-025-002—S-0441-0463-23403.

132 Letter from Bloch to Valenzuela, 25 June 1954, UNARMS:AG-025-002—S-0441-0463-23403.

133 DEA, Fiscal Division, *International Tax Agreements*, UN Doc ST/ECA/SER.C/4 (UN, 1954) vol 4; DEA, Fiscal Division, *International Tax Agreements*, UN Doc ST/ECA/SER.C/5 (UN, 1954) vol 5: World Guide to International Tax Agreements.

134 UN Yearbook, 'Fiscal Questions', 179–81.

Two reports issued by the Secretariat in early 1954, both in response to requests by the Assembly under the Financing Economic Development agenda,[135] are worthy of some note for their rather dissuasive effect on DTAs between developed and developing countries. The first was a publication entitled *The International Flow of Private Capital, 1946–1952*,[136] which analysed the volume, direction, types and fields of application of postwar FDI flows, and set forth the main reasons for the continued inadequacy of such flows in underdeveloped countries as well as certain conclusions concerning policy formulation for promoting economic development with the aid of FDI. The report did not mention double taxation as a deterrent to investment nor any unilateral or bilateral relief solutions in its policy recommendations. The second report was the Secretariat's memorandum on 'Action Taken to Stimulate the International Flow of Private Capital',[137] which summarised the studies conducted and action taken by the UN, specialised agencies, NGOs and governments to stimulate FDI for economic development. Regarding national action on fiscal measures, the report indicated, inter alia, that the introduction of tax concessions and incentives[138] by several underdeveloped countries had little significance to foreign investors whose home country applied the tax credit mechanism.[139] Most independent underdeveloped countries had accordingly remained outside the bilateral treaty network as DTAs proposed or concluded by capital-exporting countries maintained the obligation of the parent enterprise to national tax laws. Increasing attention was hence being placed on 'action by capital-exporting countries to modify their taxation of foreign investment income' to allow parent enterprises to take advantage of lower foreign tax liabilities that would effectively reduce the total amount of tax due.[140] However, while such recommendations, as well as 'more far-reaching proposals' such as complete tax exemption of foreign-sourced income, had been advanced in the United Kingdom

135 GA Res 622C (VII).

136 DEA, *International Flow of Private Capital, 1946–1952*, UN Doc E/2531 (also ST/ECA/22) (UN, 1954).

137 *Memorandum by the Secretary-General on Action Taken to Stimulate the International Flow of Private Capital*, UN ESC, 17th sess, Agenda item 3(c), UN Doc E/2546 (19 February 1954).

138 For example, tax holidays, lower tax rates, allowance of accelerated depreciation and depletion in the early years of investment, and reduced rate of tax on earnings reinvested.

139 E/2546, 61.

140 Ibid 62.

and the United States, they had not matured into legislative proposals in either country.[141] The principle of exclusive source-country taxation referred to in ECOSOC Resolution 486B (XVI) 'thus had not been adopted as the basis of tax policy by governments of major capital-exporting countries'.[142]

[141] Ibid 69–70.
[142] Ibid 70.

13

Dissolution of the Fiscal Commission and Birth of the OEEC Fiscal Committee

13.1 Abolition of the Fiscal Commission (August 1954)

The dissolution of the Fiscal Commission in August 1954 appeared sudden, at least publicly. Even in May, the Commission's Fifth Session had been tentatively scheduled for 17 January 1955,[1] and in June, seven countries (Colombia, Denmark, Indonesia, Pakistan, Panama, Syria and the United States) had indicated their interest in being elected or re-elected to the Commission to replace the four that were due to retire (Colombia, Pakistan, Sweden and the United States).[2]

However, as early as February 1954, as Britain made plans for ECOSOC's discussion on the reorganisation of ECOSOC and its commissions,[3] Inland Revenue considered that the Fiscal Commission 'might have come to the end of its useful life' on the grounds that

> the United Kingdom is in danger of finding itself in an isolated position [on the question of the taxation of income arising from investments in underdeveloped countries]. We are one of the few countries in the world charging tax in full on business profits arising abroad, and we have been under some pressure, which has been reflected in views expressed in the Fiscal Commission by Latin America and other underdeveloped countries, to give up or at least modify this charge. ... At the last Session, we were forced into the position of accepting an ambiguous compromise resolution on this question which may be embarrassing to us in future negotiations for double taxation agreements. We feel that at future Sessions, we may be placed in an even more difficult position; particularly if the United

[1] Note by McKenna, 18 May 1954, NARAII:RG56–199–7.

[2] *Election of One-Third of the Membership of the ECOSOC Functional Commissions*, UN ESC, 18th sess, Agenda item 31(a), UN Doc E/2630 (3 July 1954).

[3] CSCIO, *Economic and Social Council: Seventeenth Session, Organisation and Operation of Economic and Social Council and Its Commissions (Memorandum by the Foreign Office)*, IOC(54)11 (9 February 1954) TNA:IR40/11173(1).

> States of America changes its attitude. ... For this reason, we should be quite happy to see the Fiscal Commission wound up.[4]

Nevertheless, as '[t]his reason of expediency ... could obviously not be put forward in ECOSOC', Inland Revenue suggested to offer the 'fair' and 'perfectly true' reason that the Commission had 'reached the end of its useful life and that the research work ... being carried out by the Secretariat in the fiscal field could well be continued without the supervision of the Commission'.[5]

Britain's fears had more cause to grow in the coming months. In June, the Commission's views, along with the ICC's, would be cited in the Royal Commission as evidence that 'the trend of international thought ... is steadily moving towards the view that the country of origin has not only the first claim but the only claim to tax profits arising within its jurisdiction'.[6] On the UN front itself just a couple of months prior, the United States had called a private meeting with the delegations from Australia, Belgium, Britain, France, Pakistan, Turkey and Venezuela[7] at ECOSOC's Seventeenth Session (March–April) to discuss a resolution it intended to submit which contained recommendations on efforts to be continued by both 'countries seeking to attract private foreign capital' and 'countries able to export capital'.[8] The paragraph regarding taxation recommended that

[4] Letter by MHC (for JMG) to Bartlett, 15 February 1954, TNA:IR40/11173(1).

[5] Ibid.

[6] Royal Commission on the Taxation of Profits and Income, *Minutes of Evidence*, 2 June 1954 [4777], available at *Internet Archive* (Web Page) <https://archive.org/stream/op1265422-1001/op1265422-1001_djvu.txt>.

[7] The three underdeveloped countries were here invited as their 'policies on this subject seem particularly satisfactory to the United States': Telegram No 222 from New York (UK Delegation to UN) to Foreign Office, 2 April 1954, TNA:IR40/11173(1).

[8] Telegram No 223 from New York (UK Delegation to UN) to Foreign Office, 2 April 1954, TNA:IR40/11173(1). This resolution reflected Eisenhower's foreign economic policy, which proposed to give no more grants-in-aid (except to support military forces or operations connected with US security) but to instead provide incentives to induce private investors to fill this role: see Commission on Foreign Economic Policy, *Report to the President and the Congress* (USGPO, 1954) ('*Randall Report*'). To this end, proposed tax incentives included a reduced tax rate on income from foreign PEs, the treatment of US foreign branches as subsidiaries to access the benefits of deferral, and the extension of the scope of the FTC. The *Randall Report* ignored earlier official reports that stated uncompromisingly that private investment alone could not be expected to solve the problem of financing development (Gordon Gray, *Report to the President on Foreign Economic Policies* (USGPO, 1950); IDAB, *Partners in Progress: A Report to the President by the International Development Advisory Board* (USGPO, 1951)) and paid lip service to the importance of technical assistance in improving living standards and countering Communist influence in underdeveloped countries, when total US appropriations for such programmes barely

capital-exporting countries 'continue studies on the desirability and feasibility of changes in their taxation systems which might encourage the international flow of private capital' ('Paragraph 3').[9] Britain generally 'deprecated'[10] discussion on private investment capital at this session as being neither 'necessary' nor 'advisable', 'premature', 'bound to lead to a lengthy scrimmage over ground already well trampled' and providing 'the Soviet delegation numerous opportunities to harangue us on east–west trade'.[11] However, as there was 'no chance of riding the Americans off',[12] Britain proposed, inter alia, modifying Paragraph 3 'to apply to "countries whose economies are able to support a substantial increase in the flow of private capital investment"' as it considered the paragraph 'difficult for us' given that Britain's existing tax structure only allowed as much capital to flow overseas in 'those channels . . . the economy can afford without the danger of either hampering international investment or of inflation'.[13] Meanwhile, the United States had decided to substitute Paragraph 3 with a sub-paragraph which recommended that capital-exporting countries 'adopt within the framework of their institutions, measures on taxation that will reduce progressively international double taxation with a view to its final elimination' ('Sub-paragraph 2(e)').[14] On 27 April, the draft resolution, jointly sponsored by Belgium, China, Pakistan, Turkey, the United States and Venezuela, was tabled in the Economic Committee.[15] Sub-paragraph 2(e) was adopted by a vote of thirteen to two, with three abstentions.[16] On

exceeded $100 million (see Richard N Gardner, 'Review: Report to the President and the Congress (Randall Report) by The Commission on Foreign Economic Policy' (1954) 63 (5) *The Yale Law Journal* 751, 755). The *Randall Report* also stated boldly that America 'recognize[d] no . . . right' to the claim by underdeveloped areas to economic aid from the United States (Commission on Foreign Economic Policy, *Randall Report*, 9).

9 UK Delegation, Telegram No 223, 2–3.

10 Telegram No 247 from New York (UK Delegation to UN) to Foreign Office, 7 April 1954, 1, TNA:IR40/11173(1).

11 UK Delegation, Telegram No 222, 1. In private, the British delegation also asked the US delegation whether the latter 'seriously thought they would get the draft through without it being so mangled in the process as to become unacceptable to themselves'.

12 Ibid 2.

13 Telegram No 396 from Foreign Office to New York (UK Delegation to UN), 6 April 1954, 2, TNA:IR40/11173(1).

14 UK Delegation, Telegram No 247. The word 'final' was later inserted after 'many lengthy private discussions' by the US with Egypt and India.

15 Economic Committee, *Belgium, China, Pakistan, Turkey, US and Venezuela: Revised Joint Draft Resolution*, UN ESC, 17th sess, Agenda item 3, UN Doc E/AC.6/L.79/Rev.3 (27 April 1954).

16 Economic Committee, *Report of the Economic Committee*, UN ESC, 17th sess, Agenda item 3, UN Doc E/2588 (29 April 1954). Although Britain had 'misgivings' on parts of the

30 April, the Council adopted, without discussion, the resolution as ECOSOC Resolution 512B (XVII) by a vote of fifteen to two, with one abstention.[17]

At ECOSOC's Eighteenth Session (June–August),[18] when the Co-ordination Committee sat to consider the reorganisation of ECOSOC and its commissions, the US private position at the start of the discussion was that the Commission

> should be continued if there is strong feeling especially among smaller nations that Commission has further useful purpose to serve. Hence USDEL should support such a move but should neither take initiative to keep Commission alive nor urge its continuance if apparent consensus is opposed. ... Particularly, USDEL should avoid lining up with few large countries either to keep Commission or abolish it in opposition to small nations.[19]

resolution that called for the negotiation of treaties (including DTAs) and the consideration of establishing investment corporations to stimulate FDI to underdeveloped countries, it voted for the resolution to avoid having to explain an abstaining vote, which 'would be so embarrassing to the United States': Telegram No 353 from New York (UK Delegation to UN) to Foreign Office, 27 April 1954, TNA:IR40/11173(1).

17 Telegram No 102 from New York (UK Delegation to UN) to Foreign Office, 4 May 1954, TNA:IR40/11173(1); *International Flow of Private Capital for the Economic Development of Under-Developed Countries*, ESC Res 512B (XVII), UN ESCOR, UN Doc E/2596 (May 1954, adopted 30 April 1954).

18 ECOSOC membership in 1954 comprised Argentina, Australia, Belgium, China, Cuba, Czechoslovakia, Ecuador, Egypt, France, India, Turkey, Norway, Pakistan, the United Kingdom, the United States, the USSR, Venezuela and Yugoslavia.

19 Telegram message by Fields to Hotckiss and Kotsching, 9 July 1954, NARAII:RG56-199-2. This tokenistic reason for the Commission's existence strongly points to the delicate tightrope in international relations the United States was walking over the public backlash to the CIA-led coup of Guatemalan President Arbenz for suspected communism (see Michelle Denise Getchell, 'Revisiting the 1954 Coup in Guatemala' (2015) 17(2) *Journal of Cold War Studies* 73, 99–100). There is further strong implication that the United States saw the need to ultimately side, albeit not publicly, with the preferences of the 'large countries' – a strategy that contrasts starkly with its attitude just a year prior when it boldly asserted its own agenda without regard for other Western nations' interests: see Chapter 12, Section 12.5 (regarding US domination of the Commission's Fourth Session). Broader political developments again offer an explanation: American's need for Western solidarity was then at a high. In August 1953, the USSR had detonated its first thermonuclear bomb, and in May 1954, a squadron of mammoth Soviet long-range jet bombers had been sighted, stoking American fear that their country was now 'a reachable target': Jeffrey A Engel, *Cold War at 30,000 Feet: The Anglo-American Fight for Aviation Supremacy* (Harvard University Press, 2007) 174. That same month, Ho Chi Minh's Viet Minh forces decisively defeated the US-backed French forces at Dien Bien Phu, and since January 1954, the United States had been pressuring Britain to block arms shipments by other Western nations to Guatemala, so much so that the Foreign Office considered that 'Washington put critical European relationships at risk to advance its Guatemala campaign': Sharon I Meers, 'The British Connection: How the United States

On July 13, well into the Committee's discussions, Czechoslovakia submitted a 'comprehensive' draft resolution that ostensibly incorporated various countries' proposals and views on a range of matters.[20] This resolution proposed the discontinuance of the Fiscal and Population Commissions broadly on the grounds of concentrating ECOSOC's activities 'on the most important and pressing problems'.[21] Czechoslovakia subsequently submitted a replacement resolution which contained a new paragraph that hinted heavily at British origins, namely: that the activity of both Commissions were 'no longer useful'.[22] In the ensuing debate, Czechoslovakia amended this resolution only to apply to the Fiscal Commission.[23] This amended resolution was adopted by a vote of ten to six, with two abstentions[24] – an outcome that strongly reflected a vote largely carried by the developed and Soviet members.[25] Before ECOSOC in plenary, Cuba submitted amendments that sought less derogatory reasons for the Commission's termination.

Covered Its Tracks in the 1954 Coup in Guatemala' (1992) 16(3) *Diplomatic History* 409, 414 (noting further that London relented to US demands for fear that 'American hysteria on this whole subject will be sharpened and they may do something silly').

20 See *Organization and Operation of the Council and Its Commissions: Report of the Co-ordination Committee*, UN ESC, 18th sess, Agenda item 29, UN Doc E/2649 (4 August 1954) 4, 7, 11–12.

21 Co-ordination Committee, *Czechoslovakia: Draft Resolution*, UN ESC, 18th sess, Agenda item 29, UN Doc E/AC.24/L.98 (13 July 1954).

22 Co-ordination Committee, *Czechoslovakia: Draft Resolution*, UN ESC, 18th sess, Agenda item 29, UN Doc E/AC.24/L.104 (29 July 1954).

23 E/2649, 16.

24 Ibid 17.

25 ECOSOC's composition (n 18) made for six First World countries, three Communist countries, China and eight developing countries. A similar voting pattern is observed in Argentina and Pakistan's unsuccessful joint attempt to revive the Economic, Employment and Development Commission during these debates, which was defeated by nine to eight, with one abstention (E/2649, 14–16). It is speculated that Czechoslovakia's long-standing gripe concerning the Commission's superfluousness was an ideal and convenient hook for Britain to hang the Commission on without leaving any official trace to itself. Moreover, US concurrence with the Commission's abolition, in view of the opposition by developing countries and the Population Commission's salvaging, highly suggests the Fiscal Commission may have been part of the 'diplomatic trading arrangement' then being worked out with Britain under which the latter considered the United States indebted to it for supporting US positions in the UN on the Guatemalan crisis and China's representation (see Meers, 'British Connection', 424). Scholars note the mutually dependent Anglo-American relationship at this time with Britain having particular influence over the United States due to the former's importance to NATO and US security in providing Cold War military support throughout its informal and formal empire, as well as broad political support, including a Security Council veto: see Engel, *Aviation Supremacy*, 129; Helen Leigh-Phippard, *Congress and US Military Aid to Britain: Interdependence and Dependence, 1949–56* (St Martin's Press in association with Palgrave Macmillan, 1995) 113–14.

The amendments replaced the word 'useful' with 'necessary' and inserted a paragraph that acknowledged the importance of fiscal aspects of economic problems, the established nature of the UN's fiscal work, and that the Secretariat had been 'adequately' guided by the Commission and ECOSOC.[26] Cuba's amendment was accepted, and the final resolution was adopted on 5 August as ECOSOC Resolution 557C II (XVIII) by thirteen votes to one, with four abstentions.[27]

The Commission's dissolution appeared to raise concerns among developing countries, almost certainly led by Cuba, that the SoCtyTax/ResCtyExempt(FoInvInc) proposal would cease to have an avenue on the UN agenda. During the discussions on the Financing Economic Development agenda at the Assembly's Ninth Session (September–December), Chile, Colombia, Cuba, Iraq, Mexico, the Philippines and Venezuela submitted a joint draft resolution (L.241) which called upon the Secretariat, in view of the Fiscal Commission's discontinuance, to continue its studies concerning action taken by capital-exporting countries on the taxation of foreign investment income earned in underdeveloped countries pursuant to ECOSOC Resolution 486B (XVI).[28] At the Second Committee's 329th Meeting (2 December), both formal[29] and verbal amendments were proposed by Cuba, Egypt, Peru, South Africa and Australia.[30] These amendments mainly concerned broadening the resolution to apply generally to capital-importing countries, and also to encompass the Division's other ongoing studies. Regarding the former issue, Australia, Norway, South Africa and Venezuela insisted that the reference to underdeveloped countries be replaced with capital-importing countries as those studies affected

[26] *Cuba: Proposed Amendments to Draft Resolution B II Contained in the Report of the Co-ordination Committee E/2649*, UN ESC, 18th sess, Agenda item 29, UN Doc E/L.643 (4 August 1954).

[27] 'Fiscal Questions' [1954] *Yearbook of the United Nations* 179, 179; *Fiscal Commission*, ESC Res 557C II (XVIII), UN ESCOR, UN Doc E/2654 (15 August 1954, adopted 5 August 1954). This resolution is reproduced in Appendix T.

[28] Second Committee, *Chile, Colombia, Cuba, Iraq, Mexico, Philippines and Venezuela: Joint Draft Resolutions*, UN GA, 9th sess, Agenda item 25(c), UN Doc A/C.2/L.241 (30 November 1954).

[29] Second Committee, *Chile, Colombia, Cuba, Iraq, Mexico, Philippines and Venezuela: Revised Joint Draft Resolution*, UN GA, 9th sess, Agenda item 25(c), UN Doc A/C.2/L.241/Rev.1 (2 December 1954); Second Committee, *Egypt: Amendments to Joint Draft Resolution A/C.2/L.241*, UN GA, 9th sess, Agenda item 25(c), UN Doc A/C.2/L.245 (2 December 1954); Second Committee, *Text Proposed by the Chairman for the Operative Paragraph 1(a) of A/C.2/L.241/Rev.1*, UN GA, 9th sess, Agenda item 25(c), UN Doc A/C.2/L.246 (2 December 1954).

[30] Second Committee, *Summary Record of the 329th Meeting*, UN GAOR, UN Doc A/C.2/SR.329 (2 December 1954) 196–7.

them (i.e. countries that were considered to be economically developed but were nevertheless capital importers) as much as they did underdeveloped countries. Cuba, Egypt and Iraq opposed this as they considered that resolutions under this agenda item should solely relate to the economic development of underdeveloped countries. Meanwhile, Britain, Canada and Blough (representing the Secretariat) questioned the resolution's necessity given that the Secretariat was already authorised to carry out fiscal studies of the nature being discussed. The compromise resolution, adopted by thirty votes to none, with five abstentions, called upon the Secretariat to 'continue . . . studies of the taxation by capital-exporting and capital-importing countries on the income from foreign investments, particularly those made in the under-developed countries' with 'a view to accelerating the rate of economic development of under-developed countries'.[31] On 11 December, the Assembly adopted this resolution as Resolution 825 (IX) by fifty-one votes to none, with five abstentions.[32] The Foreign Office reported to Inland Revenue that the resolution 'aroused little interest',[33] presumably because of its generality and in view of the other items being debated, which included SUNFED, the IFC and underdeveloped countries' frustration with the insufficiency of FDI flows to meet their economic needs and with the 'disappointing results' of measures that had already been taken in various countries to encourage such flows.[34]

13.2 The UN's Role in the OEEC's Entry into Double Taxation Matters (July 1954–May 1956)

The ICC's urging of the OEEC to take up the mantle of double taxation work and the OEEC's subsequent assumption of the function have been

[31] This resolution (entitled *International Tax Problems*), as adopted by the Assembly, is reproduced in Appendix U.

[32] *Verbatim Records of the 510th Plenary Meeting*, UN GAOR, UN Doc A/PV.510 (11 December 1954). Note that GA Resolution 824 (IX) (entitled *International Flow of Private Capital for the Economic Development of Underdeveloped Countries*), which was adopted that same day and contained recommendations addressed to both capital-exporting and capital-importing countries, simply advised the negotiation of DTAs to stimulate capital flows to underdeveloped countries without specifying any applicable principles.

[33] Memorandum by Brinson to Wainwright, 25 March 1955, TNA:IR40/11173(1).

[34] 'Economic Development of Under-Developed Areas' [1954] *Yearbook of the United Nations* 119, 133–6. See also Telegram from New York (UK Delegation to UN) to Foreign Office, 8 December 1954, TNA:IR40/11173(1).

well documented in the literature.[35] The following brings to light the UN's role in these developments.

When the ICC called upon the OEEC in early July 1954 to recommend that its member countries conclude DTAs based on the London Draft as rapidly as possible among themselves, adopt unilateral measures such as those recommended by the ICC in its resolutions and reports and investigate the possibility of concluding a multilateral tax convention,[36] the OEEC responded by requesting the ICC's assistance in compiling DTAs in force between OEEC member and associated countries.[37] The ICC in turn sought this information from the Fiscal Division which collated and supplied the requested data.[38] Between November and December 1954, the OEEC circulated the ICC resolution and the compilation of DTAs to its member countries,[39] and in February 1955, the OEEC Council adopted a recommendation calling upon member governments to conclude DTAs with one another and to review existing agreements which might no longer be adequate to deal with double taxation.[40] The recommendation also requested the OEEC Secretariat to collect information on European agreements, contemplated double taxation studies regarding indirect taxation and referred to the possibility of establishing a committee on taxation.

UN officials discussed the resolution, querying whether the ICC had 'drafted the resolution' as it had 'aroused OEEC's interest in the matter', and considered 'pointing out to the ICC that they could have known that

[35] See, for example, AJ Van den Tempel, *Relief from Double Taxation* (IBFD, 1967) 10; Frank Pötgens, *Income from International Private Employment* (IBFD, 2006) 41–2. The texts of relevant OEEC documents may be found at *History of Tax Treaties* (Web Page) <https://taxtreatieshistory.org>.

[36] Executive Committee of the ICC, *Double Taxation in Europe*, Resolution adopted by the Executive Committee at its 51st session on 2 July 1954, Doc No 510/36Rev (30 July 1954) UNARMS:AG-025-002—S-0441-0468-23410.

[37] Letter from Barton and Vassuer to Lusardi, 23 July 1954, UNARMS:AG-025-002—S-0441-0468-23410. This appeal, made while the Commission was still in existence and on substantially the same propositions the ICC had submitted to the Commission in 1947, suggests that the ICC had deserted the Commission as a forum to advance its views.

[38] See correspondence between Lusardi and Lachmann, July–September 1954 in UNARMS: AG-025-002—S-0441-0468-23410.

[39] OEEC Council, *Double Taxation in Europe: Resolution Adopted by the Executive Committee of the International Chamber of Commerce*, Note by the Secretary-General, C(54)294 and addendum (12 November and 8 December 1954).

[40] OEEC Council, *Recommendation of the Council Concerning Double Taxation*, Adopted by the Council at its 274th meeting on 25 February 1955, C(55)37(Final) (28 February 1955).

overlapping would result from this resolution'.[41] In July 1955, the Division (now called the Fiscal and Financial Branch ('Fiscal Branch')) contacted the OEEC to initiate direct relations to avoid duplication in the collection and status update of tax treaties and because of the seeming complementarity of their work programmes.[42] In private discussions with the OEEC Secretary-General (René Sergent) and Deputy Secretary-General (HJB Lintott) in September, Bloch indicated that the UN was responsible for continuing the League's work in collecting tax agreements but that there would be no duplication in the fields of intra-European indirect taxes or double taxation as the UN would have difficulty conducting 'this kind of work outside of a regional pattern, because conclusions applicable for relations between European countries would not be applicable for relations between developed and under-developed countries'.[43] Moreover, the Fiscal Branch no longer had contacts with European Treasuries nor dealt with the matter on a technical level since the Commission's abolition. Bloch nevertheless highlighted that the work was highly specialised and the UN staff suitably skilled. When Lintott explained that the OEEC had no experts in the field, Bloch flagged the possibility of seconding an International Tax Section official for a few months to furnish the OEEC Secretariat with technical support while gaining European government contacts for the UN from which country information could be gathered. Lintott and Sergent indicated that they had 'no real interest' in the subject and suggested that it be discussed at the technical level between the Secretariats' officials.[44]

In January 1956, the OEEC Council appointed an ad hoc group which met in February in Paris.[45] Lintott requested that Fiscal Branch be represented to describe the scope of its work.[46] Bloch sent Certeux (former French member of the Commission and occasional consultant to the

[41] Memorandum by Heide to Bloch, 16 June 1955, UNARMS:AG-025-002—S-0441-0468-23410.

[42] Memorandum by Lachmann to Bloch, 20 October 1955, UNARMS:AG-025-002—S-0441-0468-23410.

[43] Memorandum by Bloch to Carlson, 20 October 1955, 1, UNARMS:AG-025-002—S-0441-0468-23410. These discussions took place at the Annual Meetings of the World Bank and IMF in Istanbul.

[44] Ibid 2.

[45] OEEC Council, *Council Resolution on the Study of Fiscal Questions*, Adopted by the Council at its 307th meeting on 13 January 1956 after consideration of C(55)307, C(56)1 (19 January 1956).

[46] Cable by Lintott to Bloch, 30 January 1956, UNARMS:AG-025-002—S-0441-0468-23410.

Fiscal Branch) as UN observer to the meeting, urging that the latter stress that while the Fiscal Commission had been on hiatus for three years, the Secretariat was continuing the work programme pursuant to the ECOSOC and Assembly resolutions, which included income tax treaties and international tax relations, as demonstrated by the Fiscal Branch's various publications and manuscripts that Certeux was to supply to the ad hoc group.[47] Bloch indicated that if the OEEC undertook tax studies of relevance to European integration, coordination of work between the two Secretariats could be easily organised, especially since more OEEC members had recently become UN members and even Western Germany and Switzerland, which were not UN members, regularly sent information upon request to the UN for publication in official documents.

Certeux reported to Bloch and Philippe de Seynes (head of the Department of Economic and Social Affairs, which had succeeded DEA) that the study programme envisaged by the OEEC was extensive and overlapped to a large extent with the UN's work programme.[48] Certeux advised the UN Secretariat to consider whether it wished to have unofficial or official cooperation and that the OEEC Secretariat had informally indicated that official liaison would undoubtedly be justified if it was confirmed that the Commission had not been definitively dissolved. Certeux personally considered that relations should be formalised for genuine bilateral and fully effective collaboration to prevent the risk of one-sided exchanges of information and to enable the Fiscal Branch's workload to benefit from an appreciable supplement. He suggested that the UN Secretariat announce its views before the OEEC Council decided on the ad hoc group's proposals in March.[49] Folke Hilgerdt (Deputy Director of the Bureau of Economic Affairs (UN Secretariat)), however, interpreted this as 'an attempt to get the Secretary-General to pronounce himself before the end of this month in favour of a revival of the Fiscal Commission', and reminded de Seynes that the Commission had been

[47] Letter from Bloch to Certeux, 3 February 1956, UNARMS:AG-025-002—S-0441-0468-23410.

[48] Letter from Certeux to Bloch, 16 February 1956; Letter from Certeux to Seynes, 17 February 1956, UNARMS:AG-025-002—S-0441-0468-23410.

[49] Certeux's suggestion appears to have been the result of a misunderstanding stemming from his inquiry to Bloch whether the Commission might be reconvened to consider the progress of the Secretariat's work (Letter from Certeux to Bloch, 13 January 1956, UNARMS:AG-025-002—S-0441-0468-23410), which Bloch never addressed in his reply (see Bloch letter, 3 February 1956). It could be said that Bloch even encouraged the view that the Commission had not been permanently terminated with reference to the representations that were made to the OEEC.

abolished because it was 'no longer necessary'.[50] In this deliberation, the Fiscal Branch appears to have emphatically stressed that

> the double taxation study of the United Nations, which is concerned with the encouragement of the flow of capital from developed countries to under-developed countries, can not [sic] be accomplished within the framework of the OEEC and . . . must be continued independently. It must also be understood that the reporting on tax agreements can never be done on a purely regional basis, but that OEEC must draw on United Nations publications, which are the only available series in this field covering the entire world.[51]

Certeux's discussions at the ad hoc group's meeting prompted the OEEC Secretariat to inquire whether the Commission 'had been actually dissolved or whether its meetings had temporarily been suspended',[52] to which Bloch replied that the UN's international tax work was 'not affected by its [the Commission's] status' but that ECOSOC had 'been dealing with these questions' since the Commission's discontinuance and the subject 'International Tax Problems' was on the agendas of the forthcoming ECOSOC and Assembly sessions.[53] On 24 February, the ad hoc group proposed the creation of a permanent committee, and on 16 March, the OEEC Council established the Fiscal Committee.[54] Informal relations and liaison were subsequently established with the UN Secretariat, with UN observers invited to the Fiscal Committee's first meeting in May 1956.[55]

From his strong representations to the OEEC through efforts reminiscent of Division's turf battles with the ITO, the PAU/OAS and ICAO, Bloch evidently envisaged at this stage that the UN would be progressing double taxation questions between developed and developing countries. No such official studies, however, would be produced until the work of the 1968 Group of Experts. The general silence in the literature concerning the UN–OECD relationship in the OEEC's work also suggests that the UN's contribution was negligible, at least from an OEEC perspective.

50 Memorandum by Hilgerdt to Seynes, 21 February 1956, UNARMS:AG-025-002—S-0441-0468-23410.

51 Fiscal Branch, Memorandum on 'Permanent Fiscal Experts Committee to be Established by OEEC', 16 February 1956, 2, UNARMS:AG-025-002—S-0441-0468-23410.

52 Letter from Erichsen to Bloch, 22 February 1956, UNARMS:AG-025-002—S-0441-0468-23410.

53 Letter from Bloch to Erichsen, 8 March 1956, UNARMS:AG-025-002—S-0441-0468-23410.

54 OEEC Council, *Resolution of the Council Creating a Fiscal Committee*, Adopted by the Council at its 321st meeting on 16 March 1956, C(56)49(Final) (19 March 1956).

55 Letter from Lintott to Bloch, received 26 April 1956, UNARMS:AG-025-002—S-0441-0468-23410.

14

Conclusion

This archival and contextual story of the Fiscal Commission, including its origins in the Princeton Mission's wartime efforts in the Americas, presents a compelling case for revising prevailing understandings in tax history concerning developing countries engagement with, and the role of international institutions in, early international tax coordination, as well as the progress of double taxation in the first post–World War II decade. This new historical interpretation and perspective, as revealed through the surviving evidence and deeper consideration of the relevant surrounding influences, may be summarised as follows.

Firstly, the narratives supplied in the literature concerning the League Fiscal Committee after 1939 and the UN Fiscal Commission are fragmentary or skewed towards private business and developed country interests in advancing the elimination of double taxation and DTAs. In the case of the League, the writings of Carroll and Deperon were geared towards promoting and lending credibility to the work of the Mission, particularly that which was accomplished through the regional tax conferences. These texts have tended to exaggerate Latin America's interest as well as concealed the involvement of the US government and the connection with the Rockefeller Foundation. In the case of the UN, the various literature that have been based on the Commission's reports do not provide an accurate picture of the UN's progress on double taxation due to the following combination of factors: the brevity and bias of the reports, the imprecision of the Commission's resolutions, efforts by the United States to preclude mention of positions contrary to its own, and Soviet insistence on the separate representation of their views, not to mention the assumption by respective authors that the UN institutional structure facilitating fiscal activities operated similarly to the League's. The consequence has been an extremely sketchy UN history overlaid with perceptions of overriding East–West tensions and moderate North–South division, little recognition of US domination and misinterpretation of the import of the Commission's resolutions. There is, moreover, almost a complete lack of awareness of ECOSOC's modifications of the Commission's decisions as well as of the pursuit of double taxation in other forums which impacted on the Commission's work and the development of double taxation principles. Anecdotal accounts of the Commission, which were authored by private business or US officials, have bolstered some of these misconstructions as well as been dismissive of the Commission's work, likely discouraging research into the Commission period.

Secondly, the induction of developing countries into double taxation concerns during World War II was conducted under dubious objectives and circumstances, forcing a reconsideration of the long-held presumption that the Mexico Model formed part of the Fiscal Committee's work and was negotiated among willing and informed participants. DTAs were marketed to Latin America as a key form of development assistance and component of interdependent world economic relations which the region greatly aspired to. This was conducted during a time when the Fiscal Committee was no longer functioning, the Mission had only cursory knowledge of developing country economies and almost non-existent ideas on development, the Latin American economy was virtually subjugated to that of the United States and when the region's governments not only had little revenue from their rudimentary income tax systems but had also undiversified economies dependent on a few basic commodities. The Mission utilised the dialogue on double taxation to further its own quasi-political agenda in the region as well as the interests of the United States and private business. Once the threat of an Axis-dominated world ceased, attention was drawn away from the region.

Thirdly, the continuation of the League's Fiscal Committee in the UN was largely fictional. The Fiscal Commission did not 'inherit' a double taxation mandate to reconcile the Mexico and London Models. Rather, such aims, along with other designs for the work of the Commission, had been formulated by Deperon, supported by the remnant League, Carroll and US officials. These plans found underwhelming support and were never carefully examined in the fledging UN, and the Commission was ultimately an afterthought establishment born of the League's networks. The plans would, moreover, prove overly ambitious in view of the global political-economic climate of the post–World War II world and the changed institutional framework and membership of the UN from that of the League. The Commission would not function as a technical body and would be attended by participants of varying competence and expertise. Its wide-ranging work had little broad applicability to the diverse tax systems and economies of the UN membership. Importantly, the two most powerful capitalist actors, the United States and the United Kingdom, considered that little remained to be progressed in the double taxation field except to promote (particularly to developing countries) DTAs that were essentially based on the provisions of the London Model and on the tax credit system. Given this lack of influential support for the making of a new model convention, work on improving the Models not surprisingly came to an end with Deperon's departure.

Fourthly, although the Mexico and London Models had negligible impact in fostering the conclusion of DTAs among the international community,[1] they appeared to have had more impact on international tax practice than has been generally appreciated. The existence of both Models would be used by developed countries during the Commission period to cement the principle of reciprocal exemption of income of international airline enterprises and to support the presumption of the suitability and benefit of DTAs between developed and developing countries despite contrary research and expert recommendations. Also, the Mission's wartime efforts in Latin America that led to the negotiation of the Mexico Model effectively turned the region's attention to viewing double taxation relief measures as a means for promoting its economic development through attracting private capital. This would rally Latin American countries to form strong views concerning source-country taxing rights with respect to income earned from inbound investment, including the tax exemption by the United States of income derived by its nationals/residents from such outbound investment. These countries were never sufficiently persuaded of whether the Mexico Model represented a fair bargain, and during the Commission years, they would lead the contention for the SoCtyTax/ResCtyExempt(FoInvInc) principle, attracting other Third World countries to their cause as well as triggering the collapse of DTA negotiations with the United States. Meanwhile, the London Model intrinsically affirmed the positions of the developed countries and the ICC, which not only precluded any role for the UN on the subject in relation to their interests (and perhaps any serious effort by the developed countries to renegotiate international tax principles that might find widespread acceptance among the new global balance of power), but also empowered the ICC to successfully press the OEEC to begin investigations into the uniform development of DTAs premised on

[1] John F Avery Jones, 'The UK's Early Tax Treaties with European Countries' in Peter Harris and Dominic de Cogan (eds), *Studies in the History of Tax Law* (Hart, 2017) vol 8, 295, 298.

this Model. It may thus be said that the collective labours of the League Secretariat, developed countries and the ICC enabled the international tax regime to develop on a basis that saw the 'remarkably intact' survival of the fundamental principles laid down by the League in the 1920s.[2]

Fifthly, private business interests, especially through industry bodies, American private foundations and key individuals, have had a vital role in generating and directing international tax action than has previously been explored. Tax history knowledge regarding such influences has tended to be limited to the Rockefeller grants that enabled the League Fiscal Committee's 1930s work, and the ICC's involvement in the League's peacetime work and OEEC's entry into double taxation matters. Less known are the wartime funding by private foundations and the activities of industry bodies (in which Carroll was prominent) that furthered the movement for the elimination of double taxation in the Americas to the detriment of Latin America, even if inadvertent. Even lesser known are the private business pressures and multinational corporations which shaped international tax policies that facilitated the exploitation of the Third World. The influence of private business should not be underestimated in view of the growth of the military-industrial complex and the centrality of private enterprise to international capital flows, especially where other financing avenues were lacking. The Mission itself recognised that initiative from the private sphere was necessary to propel governmental interest in double taxation; relatively recent scholarship explains how the private foundations propelled the ideas and basis behind the postwar international economic order;[3] and the British government faced considerable pressures by industry bodies to change its tax practices concerning foreign-source income. US firms moreover were able to elicit the assistance of the State Department to make representations on their behalf and to defend their interests, at least in Latin America and particularly where US economic and security interests were concerned. Segments of American business community were so influential that they were even responsible for the State

[2] Michael J Graetz and Michael M O'Hear, 'The "Original Intent" of US International Taxation' (1997) 46(5) *Duke Law Journal* 1021, 1023–4.

[3] See, for example Inderjeet Parmar, *Foundations of the American Century: The Ford, Carnegie, & Rockefeller Foundations in the Rise of American Power* (Columbia University Press, 2012); Ludovic Tournès, 'The Rockefeller Foundation and the Transition from the League of Nations to the UN (1939–1946)' (2014) 12(3) *Journal of Modern European History* 323; Patricia Clavin, *Securing the World Economy: The Reinvention of the League of Nations, 1920–1946* (Oxford University Press, 2013).

Department's 1949 shelving of the economic charter being negotiated with Latin America.[4]

In addition, the recommendations of the UN Secretariat and resolutions of the Fiscal Commission against developing countries' grant of preferential tax incentives to attract FDI went unheeded, suggesting that the demands and advocacy by private business had more compelling force. The continual advocacy by such business or business-related interests for the SoCtyTax/ResCtyExempt(FoInvInc) principle also likely fuelled Latin America's resolve to see this measure enforced, even in the face of Secretariat studies that indicated taxation not being a major deterrent to FDI flows and despite the region's own ambivalent feelings towards Western corporations.

Sixthly, the League and UN secretariats have played greater roles in the development of international tax rules and policy than have ever been recognised.[5] The League Secretariat was mainly responsible for bringing about the output of the 'Fiscal Committee' produced after the outbreak of the war, namely: the 1940 Mexico Draft, the Mexico and London Models and even the less-known *PFI Conditions* report, which on the whole favoured developed countries' interests. Its methods and motives, however, were far from impartial, even if justified by the belief that DTAs underpinned global economic welfare. The League sprung the 1940 Mexico Draft on an unprepared Latin America, worked persistently to promote DTAs to the suspicious and lukewarm continent (including helping to mobilise a movement for such treaties from American and inter-American private business circles) and determined the composition of the country participants to the various wartime conferences that produced the fiscal (or fiscal-related) work. It successfully worked to secure its institutional survival by producing results that generally aligned with the goals of its sponsor, the Rockefeller Foundation, and its host government and then most powerful country in the world, the United States, as well as by exceeding its boundaries in engaging with non-League members and political aspects of international relations.

On the other hand, the UN Secretariat's own endeavours to become the foremost global fiscal authority and independent actor in the fiscal field, and to mediate between developed and developing country interests, would, for the most part, fail, with deleterious consequences for itself

[4] Stephen G Rabe, 'The Elusive Conference: United States Economic Relations with Latin America, 1945–1952' (1978) 2(3) *Diplomatic History* 279, 290.

[5] The same may also be said of the ICAO Secretariat in supplying the supporting study enabling the ATP and Council to endorse the reciprocal exemption principle.

and the latter country group. The Fiscal Division's pioneering of relevant and equitable development of international tax rules and policies – noticeably through its interference in ICAO's actions to promulgate the residence exemption principle for the taxation of international air transport, its research into tax bargaining contracts between developing country governments and foreign firms, its appointment of expert consultants Sundelson and Shere, and perhaps even its technical assistance policies that were at variance with the IMF – was not only suppressed but also led the United States to rein in the UN's fiscal sphere. Although the Division had more success in securing its jurisdiction and in upholding its own views against the exemption system in the ITO talks as well as in PAU/OAS and ECLA, this came at the expense of frustrating developing countries' pursuit of the SoCtyTax/ResCtyExempt(FoInvInc) principle, arguably further impairing their already disadvantaged bargaining position. This somewhat dismal record of the UN's achievement in charting fair global tax principles or even a level playing field nevertheless may have been mitigated by its technical assistance activities, which perhaps explain why few DTAs between developing and developed countries were concluded in the subsequent decades despite ongoing efforts on the part of the latter group.

Lastly, and most importantly, politics is an unignorable, even inseparable, factor not only in the tax and trade relations between developed and developing countries but also in the operations of international governing organisations, at least during the historical period addressed in this research.[6] The League was astutely aware of this in engineering its extension in the Americas and its rebirth in the UN by discreetly cultivating the necessary constructive public opinion and relations with key governments, especially the United States, while overtly appearing as a disinterested global organisation. The Mexico Model, and the concessions to source countries therein, was only afforded by the United States when it was preoccupied with hemispheric defence and when Latin Americanists in the State Department had preponderant influence. Latin America itself was

[6] Such considerations likely extend to any international economic efforts at any time. Even the United States and the USSR appeared to have acknowledged this as early as October 1945 in the context of the transfer of the League's technical functions to the UN: the USSR noting that 'there was no exact dividing line between economic and political activities', and the United States admitting that 'in theory this may be true': 'Telegram by Stevenson to Secretary of State', 10 November 1945, in State Department, *Foreign Relations of the United States: Diplomatic Papers, 1945* (USGPO, 1967) vol 1: General: The United Nations, Doc 342.

only open to considering DTAs, and even so reluctantly, in view of the Good Neighbor relations that had been fostered for nearly a decade and its expectation of long-term US commitment to inter-American economic relations. Once the United States was no longer dependent on its southern neighbours, it would, along with the other Western industrialised countries (especially the colonial powers), seek to remake a world that reinforced their dominance (or former dominance) and capitalist expansionism, heedless of any Allied solidarity with and contribution by the developing nations. Interestingly, as Latin America's treasure trove of raw materials beckoned once again with the Cold War heating up towards 1950,[7] the State Department appeared to be willing to sign DTAs with Latin America that caved into the latter's pursuit of greater source taxing rights over business profits earned by US firms in their countries; the US Treasury, however, put an end to such developments.

In the first postwar decade, US ascendency, and to a lesser extent fading but still potent British power, assured that the international tax order progressed along the lines which the two powers were prepared to accept. Like the League Secretariat, the UN Fiscal Division was cognisant that its survival and success depended on being backed by powerful sponsors, hence its adoption of a work programme largely approved by the United States and its subtle entreaties to developing countries to abandon tax positions that were unacceptable to developed countries.[8] While it did attempt to carve out an independent role in living up to the UN Charter ideals, it would effectively be prevented from producing, at least officially, any novel work and be relegated to the role of a mostly public finance information service. Developing countries could neither advance nor defend their source taxing rights in view of their development needs, the United States backpedalled on earlier agreed-upon tax policies and priorities, and the developed countries used their superior bargaining power and alliances to prevent the Third World's attempts to rise to economic equality. The industrialised countries, in particular the United States and the United Kingdom, in fact showed clear imperialistic intentions in desiring to spread their DTA networks to developing countries to assure privileged access to Southern markets, with no consideration for reciprocal

7 See Gabriel Kolko, *Confronting the Third World: United States Foreign Policy, 1945–1980* (Pantheon Books, 1988) 38 (noting that '[i]t was [US] official policy … that in case of a world war that the region's main function would be to supply raw materials').

8 Even despite its reservations concerning DTAs, the Division never overtly contradicted the US policy of promoting DTAs to developing countries, choosing instead to improvise different purposes for such DTAs.

trade relations in seeking to preserve their residence taxation rules, even to reverse developing countries' trend towards economic nationalism, by using DTAs to reduce source taxation and discourage discriminatory and extraterritorial taxation.

Such Western postures strongly indicate that the eventual immobilisation of the Fiscal Commission and Fiscal Division was inevitable even without the Cold War, particularly in view of developed countries' usage of 'Western' institutions of GATT, the IMF, the World Bank and ICAO to serve the First World's interests, and that only the less contentious of ECOSOC's functional commissions in the economic sphere remained by 1955.[9] In this light, the Cold War's role in the Commission story was largely tangential, although still significant. The Soviet presence to some extent helped to rebalance the power and information asymmetries by providing counterweight arguments to US positions and, at least at the Third Session, voting support to the outnumbered developing countries. Overall, however, the complete suffusion of the international diplomatic climate by Cold War attitudes appeared more harmful to the South's struggles against the North during the Commission years, seeing that the Western nations held the purse strings as the USSR was not a contender as a source of capital flows. Soviet denunciations of American capitalist policies and predatory expansionism in the Commission marred the United States' public image, contributing grounds to the latter's contemplation of abolishing the Commission;[10] Latin America's acts of economic nationalism heightened US hysteria over Communist subversion;[11] and US economic favour would only flow to areas it considered essential to the East–West confrontation.[12]

[9] These consisted of the Statistical and the Transport and Communications Commissions. The Economic, Employment and Development Commission, which had been charged with considering the economic development of underdeveloped areas, had been discontinued in September 1951 and its two sub-commissions (the Sub-Commission on Employment and Economic Stability and the Sub-Commission on Economic Development) abolished in August 1950: see 'The Economic and Social Council' [1947–8] *Yearbook of the United Nations* 500, 502; 'Functions and Organization of the United Nations' [1950] *Yearbook of the United Nations* 12, 59, 79–81; 'Functions and Organization of the United Nations' [1951] *Yearbook of the United Nations* 49, 60–67; 'Structure of the United Nations' [1955] *Yearbook of the United Nations* 456, 465.

[10] Such representations would have not been insignificant given the integrated role of propaganda in the foreign policies of the major Cold War actors: see generally Gary D Rawnsley, *Cold-War Propaganda in the 1950s* (MacMillan Press, 1999).

[11] See Noel Maurer, *The Empire Trap: The Rise and Fall of US Intervention to Protect American Property Overseas, 1893–2013* (Princeton University Press, 2013) 314.

[12] Even in the largely overlooked Latin America, the Eisenhower Administration is said to have spent most of the 1950s 'busy hugging and bestowing medals on dictators who professed to be anticommunists': Stephen G Rabe, 'Eisenhower and Latin America' in

The USSR also added to stifling the Secretariat's attempts to guide the fiscal work programme, and Soviet contempt for the Commission became a useful rhetorical cudgel for the Western nations to bring about the Commission's dissolution.

The political dimension of international tax coordination becomes even more intriguing when considered from the perspective of how the fluidity of the political context at the time and after the closure of the Commission could have turned the tide against the privileged nations and towards a Third World that had not even existed as a 'self-aware, self-defining group of countries'[13] when the UN was being designed, not to mention when racial discrimination (including segregation in the United States) was pervasive across the globe.[14] By 1954, the contours of world power were once again shifting with US global prestige waning,[15] the colonial powers unable to sustain the costs of holding on to their empires[16] and multinational corporations rising as the principal actors in the global political economy.[17] Double taxation discussions were beginning to attract vociferous participation by formidable Third World countries governed by charismatic, anti-imperialist leaders and which were fostering burgeoning South–South connections and solidarities.[18] Even the United States and the United Kingdom each suspected that the other might yield to allowing more source taxation demands, and strategic Third World countries were indicating their interest in membership in the Commission. In April 1955, the heads of states and governments of twenty-nine Asian and African countries or colonies would meet in Bandung for a conference that would be the precursor to the Non-Aligned Movement and which would rouse the United States and the USSR to accelerate their strategies to win over and

Chester J Pach (ed), *A Companion to Dwight D Eisenhower* (Wiley-Blackwell, 2017) 435, 436.

13 John Toye and Richard Toye, *UN and Global Political Economy: Trade, Finance, and Development* (Indiana University Press, 2004) 26.

14 See generally Azza Salama Layton, 'International Pressures and the US Government's Response to Little Rock' (1997) 56(3) *The Arkansas Historical Quarterly* 257.

15 See 'Special Report Prepared by the Psychological Strategy Board', 11 September 1953, in State Department, *Foreign Relations of the United States, 1952–1954* (USGPO, 1983) vol 1, pt 2: General: Economic and Political Matters, Doc 223.

16 Heather Streets-Salter and Trevor R Getz, *Empires and Colonies in the Modern World: A Global Perspective* (Oxford University Press, 2016) 441–2, 466–9.

17 See generally Kema Irogbe, 'Global Political Economy and the Power of Multinational Corporations' (2013) 30(2) *Journal of Third World Studies* 223.

18 See Lily Pearl Balloffet, 'Argentine and Egyptian History Entangled From Perón to Nasser' (2018) 50(3) *Journal of Latin American Studies* 549.

influence post-colonial countries.[19] By the end of the year, a large en bloc admission of sixteen new members to the UN[20] had ensued and a subsequent influx of new members from the Afro-Arab-Asian bloc set off a steady decline in the US power base in the organisation.[21] The UN hence 'began to show new vigor'[22] and to develop from a Western-dominated agency into a more genuine world forum.[23] By 1958, developing countries had the numbers to vote SUNFED into being.[24] Latin America had, moreover, 'become of real importance both politically and economically' to the United States and the United Kingdom for its 'relatively secure sources of supply and expanding markets' following the invasion of Egypt by Britain (in alliance with France and Israel) that culminated in the Suez Crisis.[25] In 1961, the Non-Aligned Movement emerged, and in 1965, ECOSOC's membership was increased to

[19] Jürgen Dinkel, *The Non-Aligned Movement: Genesis, Organization and Politics (1927–1992)*, tr Alex Skinner (Brill, 2018) 42–83. On the USSR's part, this included donating 'billions of rubles in military and economic aid to states such as India, Indonesia, and Egypt, which would become leaders of the Non-Aligned Movement, in an effort to draw them into the Soviet orbit' (Mark Philip Bradley, 'Decolonization, the Global South, and the Cold War, 1919–1962' in Melvyn P Leffler and Odd Arne Westad (eds), *The Cambridge History of the Cold War* (Cambridge University Press, 2010) vol 1: Origins, 464, 475), leading the United States to expand its foreign aid programme in the 'fear that the desperate masses of many developing countries would turn to the Soviet camp for relief from their poverty' (James M Hagen and Vernon W Ruttan, 'Development Policy under Eisenhower and Kennedy' (1988) 23(1) *The Journal of Developing Areas* 1, 2).

[20] SC Res 109, UN SCOR, UN Doc S/3509 (14 December 1955).

[21] David Armstrong, *The Rise of the International Organisation: A Short History* (Macmillan, 1982) 60; Toye and Toye, *UN*, 2. For the impact of the Bandung Conference on the process of decolonisation, see Dinkel, *Non-Aligned Movement*, 78–9.

[22] Julius W Pratt, *A History of the United States Foreign Policy* (Prentice-Hall, 3rd ed, 1972) 422.

[23] Toye and Toye, *UN*, 2.

[24] This, however, was not the fund of capital financing that developing countries had wanted but a compromise of augmented technical assistance with long-term low-interest loans for building infrastructure: see Ronald A Manzer, 'The United Nations Special Fund' (1964) 18(4) *International Organization* 766; D John Shaw, 'Turning Point in the Evolution of Soft Financing: The United Nations and the World Bank' (2005) 26(1) *Canadian Journal of Development Studies* 43.

[25] Rory M Miller, 'Economic Nationalism and British Investments in Post-War Latin America, 1945–1970' in Thomas C Mills and Rory M Miller (eds), *Britain and the Growth of US Hegemony in Twentieth-Century Latin America: Competition, Cooperation and Coexistence* (Palgrave Macmillan, 2020) 151, 161 (quoting the Foreign Office's communication of a minute by the US Secretary of State). See also 'Progress Report by the Operations Coordinating Board to the National Security Council', 19 January 1955, in State Department, *Foreign Relations of the United States, 1952–1954* (USGPO, 1983) vol 4: The American Republics, Doc 13 (regarding renewed US efforts towards Latin America's economic development to counteract communist penetration into the region).

twenty-seven,[26] thereby altering the regional balance in the Council's composition, which resulted in an increasing shift in emphasis to development concerns. Importantly, under activist Secretary-General Hammarskjöld, who had particular expertise in economic and social affairs, a complete reorganisation of the Secretariat was initiated in 1955 which led to major changes in management practices, policies, structure and composition of the senior echelon that revived the independence, efficiency and morale of the Secretariat.[27] Britain's eagerness to dispose of the Commission in 1954 could therefore have pre-empted a very real threat of the international tax regime developing more favourably towards source taxation interests in view of the changing UN membership, the growing influence and coalition of the Third World, and the Secretariat reforms.

On the other hand, there are strong indications that the UN would never have, in any event, become a force as an overarching international tax authority. Even when developing countries were able to convert their increasing numbers into resolutions, they still could not compel implementation by reluctant developed states.[28] The Secretariat's studies and surveys, while being 'factually complete and comprehensive', remained necessarily restrained in analysis and conclusions to avoid stirring up political controversy.[29] The UN generally would not have much effectiveness in economic activities given the ideological conflict and power games in North–South relations and its inefficient and costly bureaucracy.[30] It would instead be described as operating in a 'climate of unreality' where resolutions proliferated, in which 'the most forceful conclusions . . . consist in calling for yet a further report from the Secretary-General'; where principles were approved 'which no one intends to respect'; and where interim plans adopted were 'so vaguely formulated as to render verification of their implementation impossible'.[31] Given the longevity of such

[26] *Question of Equitable Representation on the Security Council and the Economic and Social Council*, GA Res 1991B (XVIII), UN Doc A/RES/1991(XVIII) (17 December 1963, entry into force 31 August 1965).

[27] Bob Reinalda, 'Institutional Development of the United Nations Secretariat' (2020) 26(2) *Global Governance* 325, 331. See also Pratt, *United States Foreign Policy*, 422.

[28] For example, SUNFED was stillborn as it failed to obtain financial resources from Western donors: Thomas G Weiss et al, *The United Nations and Changing World Politics* (Routledge, 8th ed, 2017) 251.

[29] Leland M Goodrich, *The United Nations* (Thomas Y Cromwell, 1959) 280.

[30] See Maurice Bertrand, *The United Nations: Past, Present and Future* (Kluwer Law International, 1997) 94.

[31] Ibid 66.

characteristics that had materialised during the Commission years,[32] it might have been inevitable that another institution, particularly one controlled by the Western nations, would have eventually stepped in to assume the functions that could not be progressed by the UN.

It is difficult to sum up the Commission's double taxation story when many pieces of international tax history have yet to be filled, such as archival narratives from other informational sources and those regarding the work and impact of the UN Secretariat through technical assistance activities and fellowship and scholarship programmes to train officials and lawyers from developing countries in tax law and administration. Nevertheless, there is sufficient evidence to conclude that the Commission was the creation and casualty of empire-building by various stakeholders, particularly an idealistic Secretariat, imperialistic developed countries, aspirational developing countries and self-interested private business. The Commission existed at an exceptional juncture when the position of incoming hegemon America 'was truly unique in history',[33] while that of outgoing hegemon Britain, along with other European powers, was so battered and dwindling that great power engagement to construct a new future or reclaim a glorious past was vigorous, even hawkish. In addition, a Cold War of indeterminate scope and duration loomed over their existence, a Third World was birthed that began to claim sovereignty over natural resources and foreign investments, corporate–government cooperation was in keeping with the business of government[34] and the internationalism of the 1940s withered as rapidly as it had sprung. For a brief epoch, the activism of the Secretariat

[32] The UN's institutional and bureaucratic incapacities have continued into present times and are well recognised by the tax literature as precluding it from developing and implementing tax policy standards: H David Rosenbloom, Noam Noked and Mohamed S Helal, 'The Unruly World of Tax: A Proposal for an International Tax Cooperation Forum' (2014) 15(2) *Florida Tax Review* 57, 69. The UN also remains a resource-strapped organisation in perpetual financial crisis: UN Secretary-General António Guterres, 'Improving the Financial Situation of the Organization' (Speech, Fifth Committee, General Assembly, 4 June 2019) <www.un.org/sg/en/content/sg/statement/2019-06-04/secretary-generals-remarks-the-fifth-committee-improving-the-financial-situation-of-the-organization-delivered>.

[33] Lundestad describes the United States as then 'in a league of its own', 'by far the strongest power the world had ever seen' and incomparable to 'earlier Great Powers ... [i]n the overwhelming size of its economy, in its superior military strength, and in its popular message to the world, its soft power': Geir Lundestad, '"Empire by Invitation" in the American Century' in Michael J Hogan (ed), *The Ambiguous Legacy: US Foreign Relations in the 'American Century'* (Cambridge University Press, 1999) 52, 59–60.

[34] See John Lewis Gaddis, 'The Corporatist Synthesis: A Skeptical View' (1986) 10(4) *Diplomatic History* 357, 359.

and the Third World in charting new global tax principles redefining tax relations between developed and developing countries so vexed the dominant powers that they consigned the Division to relatively uncontentious endeavours and the Commission to the forgotten annals of history. With this the death knell sounded for the UN's original presiding role in formulating and influencing tax policy and for developing countries' voice and seat at the double taxation negotiating table in a forum that recognised the formal equality of states. A very different history of postwar international tax developments would thus emerge.

The Commission story (and prehistory) perhaps finds greatest historical import in the insights offered regarding the facilitators and complications behind international tax coordination between developed and developing countries. These may be said to consist, in particular, of the following: firstly, there is direct correlation between the success of overtures by developed countries to negotiate DTAs with developing countries and broader interest being shown by the former in the latter's economic concerns. Secondly, there is clear value (and even need), in the interest of fairness, for an autonomous body to safeguard the revenue interests of weaker nations. Thirdly, 'outside–insiders' – that is, 'closely associated' yet independent actors such as NGOs, experts and consultants – play an integral role, for better or worse, in the work and impact of world organisations.[35] Fourthly, it is critical that negotiations over international tax norms be conducted allowing not just broad and informed participation but also transparency and acknowledgement of the political dimensions involved in the process. Remarkably, these themes have come full circle, but with an ostensibly more positive trajectory, in the revival of global multilateral cooperation kindled by the BEPS projects since 2013.

These relatively recent efforts have of course stemmed from the pressures of the 2008 financial crisis that left governments scrambling to claw back revenue losses and the breaking point reached in the international tax regime over the untenability of the long-standing and fundamental norms to handle the digital economy, tax competition and tax avoidance.[36] Such

[35] Weiss, Carayannis and Jolly coin this the 'Third UN', defining it as 'comprising NGOs, academics, consultants, experts, independent commissions, and other groups of individuals who routinely engage with the First UN [the UN of governments] and the Second UN [the UN of the Secretariat] and thereby influence UN thinking, policies, priorities, and actions': Thomas G Weiss, Tatiana Carayannis and Richard Jolly, 'The Third United Nations' (2009) 15(1) *Global Governance* 123, 127.

[36] Mindy Herzfeld, 'The Case against BEPS: Lessons for Tax Coordination' (2017) 21(1) *Florida Tax Review* 1, 4–5.

drivers are perhaps not dissimilar to the economic devastation, nationalistic tendencies, unilateralism and lack of global tax coherence faced by countries in the postwar world of the mid-twentieth century, especially in view of the hard times, trade collapse and protectionist responses brought about by the novel coronavirus (COVID-19) pandemic since 2020. However, the major differences now include, importantly, the shifts in the global balance of power and international capital movements with the rise of emerging economies as twenty-first-century economic powerhouses[37] and the recognition by the original OECD member countries that they can no longer drive international standards-setting by themselves without true global consensus.[38] In addition, individuals, NGOs and private businesses have once again been roused to international action, albeit this time respectively through tax data leaks, tax justice journalism and advocacy, and multinational tax avoidance.[39] Politics and technocracy are working in an ordered and concerted manner.[40] Inclusivity and pluralism are now characteristic of international tax policymaking through the OECD/G20 Inclusive Framework on BEPS (IF), which to date has brought together over 140 countries, the 3 leading international organisations (i.e. the UN, the IMF and the World Bank) as well as regional tax organisations to collaborate on the implementation of the BEPS Package stemming from the work accomplished between 2012 and 2015 (BEPS 1.0).[41] Moreover, regionally based networks of tax policy and administration officials operate to engage a broader group of smaller

37 Richard Vann, 'Current Trends in Balancing Residence and Source Taxation' in Yariv Brauner and Pasquale Pistone (eds), *BRICS and the Emergence of International Tax Coordination* (IBFD, 2015) 367, 386–7.

38 Ruth Mason, 'The Transformation of International Tax' (2020) 114(3) *The American Journal of International Law* 353, 398.

39 Shu-Yi Oei and Diane Ring, 'Leak-Driven Law' (2018) 65(3) *UCLA Law Review* 532, 545–68, 582–9; Allison Christians, 'BEPS and the New International Tax Order' [2016] (6) *Brigham Young University Law Review* 1603, 1627, 1646–7.

40 See OECD, *OECD Secretary-General Tax Report to G20 Finance Ministers and Central Bank Governors – February 2021* (2021) pt 1, ch 1 ('*2021 Tax Report*').

41 'What is BEPS', *OECD* (Web Page) <www.oecd.org/tax/beps/about/>. The inclusivity in the work of the OECD's Committee of Fiscal Affairs and its subsidiary bodies began with the addition of eight G20/non-OECD members and the three countries then applying for OECD membership to the thirty-four OECD countries at the start of BEPS. In 2015, sixty-two countries were involved, and plans were underway for the broadening participation to be formalised in 2016 under the IF: OECD, *OECD/G20 Base Erosion and Profit Shifting Project: Explanatory Statement* (2015) 4, 11, 19 n 2. Despite not having direct participation in the discussions, dozens of other low-income countries were consulted for their input even within the first year of the project: OECD, *Two-Part Report to G20 Developing Working Group on the Impact of BEPS in Low Income Countries* (2014).

and poorer developing countries which are unable to participate in the Paris-based BEPS consultations.[42] The OECD, the UN, the IMF and the World Bank have converged to strengthen capacity building in developing countries through the PCT as well as the OECD's Global Relations Programme and Tax and Development Programme.[43]

These developments appear seismic when contrasted with the problems that plagued the Commission years in relation to the fragmentation of institutional authority, clandestine motives and procedures, muddled political and technical thinking at the working and decision-making levels and above all, marginalisation and general lack of support faced by developing countries. So, while many scholars note that BEPS 1.0 did not deliver the necessary reforms in rewriting the international tax framework,[44] as other commentators have stressed, BEPS has effected significant (though undervalued) change to international tax by addressing and bringing together many of its interlocking elements, including participants, institutions, process, politics, policy and practice.[45] The transformation is far from utopian: critics, for example, observe that weaker and poorer developing nations have had limited influence on agenda-setting or policy decision,[46] and perceive that the IF is simply a conduit for the OECD to impose its agenda on the rest of the world and to solidify its legitimacy as an inclusive supranational body against the UN.[47] However, as the hindsight of history suggests, a change in the stakeholders tends to set into motion changes to the scope of coordination and the norms to be developed, meaning that the current trajectory holds some promise for a more equitable international tax order. As

[42] OECD, 'The BEPS Project and Developing Countries: From Consultation to Participation' (November 2014) 2–3 <www.oecd.org/ctp/strategy-deepening-developing-country-engagement.pdf>. Current information on the work of these regional meetings may be found at 'Regional Meetings of the Inclusive Framework on BEPS', *OECD* (Web Page) <www.oecd.org/tax/beps/beps-regional-meetings.htm>.

[43] 'Global Relations and Development', *OECD* (Web page) <www.oecd.org/ctp/tax-global/>. See also Richard Vann, 'International Tax Policy and International Tax Institutions: Never the Twain?' in Guglielmo Maisto (ed), *Current Tax Treaty Issues: 50th Anniversary of the International Tax Group* (IBFD, 2020) 41, 72 (noting that both the UN and IMF have chosen to cooperate and complement, rather than compete with, the OECD work by focusing on an agenda concerning developing countries' issues not covered by BEPS).

[44] See Mason, 'Transformation', 353 n 1 for a listing of such scholarly literature.

[45] Vann, 'Never the Twain', 74; Mason, 'Transformation', 354, 401.

[46] Reuven S Avi-Yonah and Haiyan Xu, 'Evaluating BEPS: A Reconsideration of the Benefits Principle and Proposal for UN Oversight' (2016) 6(2) *Harvard Business Law Review* 185, 211.

[47] Christians, 'BEPS', 1604, 1646.

transpired under the BEPS 2.0 work, emerging economies led an aggressive push for more source taxing rights[48] and the OECD Two Pillar blueprints accommodated developing countries' concerns and priorities to an extent.[49] The UN itself began to reposition itself in the global tax order by providing contending source tax solutions.[50] That being said, the historical multilateral agreement achieved in October 2021 regarding the OECD's overhaul plan on how to divide the global revenue pie[51] fell short in benefitting all countries equally, even being criticised for giving priority to residence countries to the detriment of developing countries' interests.[52] This pessimistic start appears emblematic of an international tax system refractory to change and hence set to perpetuate its historical legacies.

But the story is not over yet and in a more positive light, it is possible to say that the restoration of developing countries to the main negotiating table, their unprecedented involvement to date and their growing economic weight[53] foreshadow that their perspectives and presence will no longer be as easily displaced as it was for the first ninety years of international tax coordination. At the very least, the present situation is

48 Vann, 'Current Trends', 387–91.

49 OECD, *Tax Challenges Arising from Digitalisation – Report on Pillar One Blueprint* (2020) 9, 15; OECD, *Tax Challenges Arising from Digitalisation – Report on Pillar Two Blueprint* (2020) 12; OECD, *Tax Challenges Arising from Digitalisation – Economic Impact Assessment* (2020) 169–73.

50 For discussion concerning this work in April 2022, see Committee of Experts on International Cooperation in Tax Matters, *Report on the Twenty-Fourth Session (Virtual Session, 4–7 and 11–12 April 2021)*, UN ESCOR, Supplement No 25A, UN Doc E/2022/45/Add.1 (also E/C.18/2022/2) (2022).

51 As at 4 November 2021, 137 IF countries have agreed to the OECD's Two-Pillar Solution of October 2021: 'Statement on a Two-Pillar Solution to Address the Tax Challenges Arising from the Digitalisation of the Economy – 8 October 2021', *OECD* (Web Page) <www.oecd.org/tax/beps/statement-on-a-two-pillar-solution-to-address-the-tax-challenges-arising-from-the-digitalisation-of-the-economy-october-2021.htm>.

52 See, for example, Sarah Paez, 'OECD Global Tax Agreement Draws Mixed Reactions' (18 October 2021) 104 *Tax Notes International* 342; Sol Picciotto, The BEPS Monitoring Group, 'Comments of the G24 on the Statement on a Two-Pillar Solution to Address the Tax Challenges Arising from the Digitalisation of the Economy' (5 October 2021), available at <www.bepsmonitoringgroup.org/news/2021/10/5/comments-of-the-g24-on-the-proposed-two-pillar-solution>. Argentina even voiced that developing country policymakers had been 'forced to choose between something bad and something worse': Stephanie Soong Johnston, 'Argentina Says Global Tax Deal Is Bad for Developing Nations' (11 October 2021) 104 *Tax Notes International* 13.

53 'Economy: Developing Countries Set to Account for Nearly 60% of World GDP by 2030, According to New Estimates', *OECD* (Web Page, 16 June 2010) <www.oecd.org/development/economydevelopingcountriessettoaccountfornearly60ofworldgdpby2030accordingtonewestimates.htm>.

a vast improvement from the Commission period regarding the transparency of proceedings, availability of independent critique and support, absence of hegemonic dominance and a better understanding of sustainable politico-socio-economic development. Novel alternatives to multilateral cooperation approaches have been advanced in recent years,[54] the Group of 77 in 2021 demanded the establishment of a full intergovernmental tax body under UN auspices to rival the OECD as the main multilateral institution of the international tax regime,[55] and the Second Committee of the General Assembly in November 2022 adopted by consensus a resolution paving the way for intergovernmental discussions to begin at the UN 'on ways to strengthen the inclusiveness and effectiveness of international tax cooperation'.[56] Moreover, the overt recognition of the role of politics and coordination in governance in international tax, in contrast to the prevailing preference for a technocratic approach,[57] is a welcome development to international

[54] See, for example, Rosenbloom, Noked and Helal, 'Unruly World of Tax'; Tsilly Dagan, *International Tax Policy: Between Competition and Cooperation* (Cambridge University Press, 2018).

[55] See Financial Accountability Transparency and Integrity (FACTI) Panel, *Financial Integrity for Sustainable Development: Report of the High Level Panel on International Financial Accountability, Transparency and Integrity for Achieving the 2030 Agenda* (UN, 2021) (especially Recommendations 2, 4, 11A, 14B); José Antonio Ocampo and Heidemarie Wieczorek-Zeul, 'An Intergovernmental Tax Body at the United Nations', Implementation Note on FACTI Panel on Recommendation 14B (July 2021).

[56] *Nigeria: Draft Resolution: Promotion of Inclusive and Effective International Tax Cooperation at the United Nations*, UN GA, 2nd Comm, 77th sess, Agenda Item 16, UN Doc A/C.2/77/L.11/Rev.1 (16 November 2022), adopted at 25th mtg on 23 November 2022. Ironically, it was the group of developing countries absent from participation during the Fiscal Commission years – the Group of African States – that spearheaded this resolution. The United States attempted to delete from the relevant operating paragraph mention of 'the possibility of developing an international tax cooperation framework or instrument that is developed and agreed upon through a United Nations intergovernmental process' but was unsuccessful: *United States: Amendment to Draft Resolution A/C.2/77/L.11/Rev.1*, UN GA, 2nd comm, 77th sess, Agenda item 16, UN Doc A/C.2/77/CRP.2 (22 November 2022); *Recorded Vote: A/C.2/77/CRP.2 – Amendment to A/C.2/77/L.11/Rev.1*, UN GA, 2nd comm, 77th sess, 25th mtg, Agenda Item 16 (23 November 2022) <https://www.un.org/en/ga/second/77/docs/voting/CRP.2.pdf>. At the time of this writing, this recommended resolution has yet to be confirmed by the plenary Assembly; its budgetary implications (*Program Budget Implications of Draft Resolution A/C.2/77/L.11/Rev.1*, Statement submitted by the Secretary-General in accordance with rule 153 of the rules of procedure of the General Assembly, 2nd Comm, 77th sess, 2nd Comm, Agenda Items 16 and 138, UN Doc A/C.2/77/L.75 (21 November 2022)) requiring it to be first considered by the Fifth Committee before it can be adopted in plenary.

[57] Mason, 'Transformation', 393.

tax knowledge. This may well prove significant as the world faces escalating trade tensions and global economic upheaval from the continuing COVID-19 pandemic,[58] but also economic war, rearmament and greater military spending increases as a result of the resurgence of (and threats of future) geopolitical conflicts.

As a final note, the insights from the Commission narrative have shown the tremendous value of historical and international relations perspectives in understanding and framing the deep-seated problems that have troubled international tax coordination and global tax governance. Global political economy and governance would appear to be indivisible attributes of international tax relations between developed and developing countries, and as the international relations discipline itself affirms: 'History matters for international politics'.[59] It is hoped that such intermingling of perspectives will invite future interdisciplinary scholarship to expand the areas of international tax history involving developing countries that remain uncharted to bring us closer to determining how international taxation may best be reformed to equitably reconcile the interests of developed and developing countries.

[58] It is worth noting that even with the COVID-19 global economic scarring, the G20 indicated that the OECD's efforts 'to build effective tax systems and fortify domestic resource mobilisation' in developing countries 'remain a priority during the recovery phase' (OECD, *2021 Tax Report*, 28) and that such was being dealt with comprehensively with other infrastructure and financing challenges faced by vulnerable countries, including through enhanced global liquidity under the IMF, promoting sustainable capital flows and strengthening local capital markets (see G20 Finance Ministers and Central Bank Governors, *Italian G20 Presidency: Second G20 Finance Ministers and Central Bank Governors Meeting – Communiqué* (G20 Italia 2021, 7 April 2021)). In October 2021, the OECD provided a follow-up reporting on the progress of these commitments and recommended further assessments on a regular basis (see OECD, *Developing Countries and the OECD/G20 Inclusive Framework on BEPS: OECD Report for the G20 Finance Ministers and Central Bank Governors, October 2021, Italy* (2021)). The United States' overhauling of its international tax policies to end its participation in tax competition, increase taxes on corporations and incentivise domestic investment (see US Senate Finance Committee, *Overhauling International Taxation: A Framework to Invest in the American People by Ensuing Multinational Corporations Pay Their Fair Share* (Report, April 2021); US Department of the Treasury, *Made in America Tax Plan* (Report, April 2021)) may well herald in a new era towards truly global tax cooperation.

[59] Robert O Keohane, 'Observations on the Promise and Pitfalls of Historical Institutionalism in International Relations' in Orfeo Fioretos (ed), *International Politics and Institutions in Time* (Oxford University Press, 2017) 321, 321. See also Thomas Rixen, 'Historical Institutionalism and International Relations' in Thomas Rixen, Lora Anne Viola and Michael Zürn (eds), *Historical Institutionalism and International Relations: Explaining Institutional Development in World Politics* (Oxford University Press, 2016) ch 1.

APPENDIX A

Cast of Key Characters

The following provides a non-exhaustive list of key characters referred to in this book.

A.1 Key Characters in the Double Taxation Work of the League's Princeton Mission Years (1940–1946)

Carroll, Mitchell B	Acted as consultant to the Princeton Mission albeit without official status;[1] served as Member of the 1940 and 1943 Mexico Regional Meetings and the 1946 Tenth Session of the Fiscal Committee; Fiscal Committee member of the 1945 Special Joint Committee on Private Foreign investment
Deperon, Paul	League Secretariat member of the Princeton Mission responsible for fiscal work;[2] acted as Secretary to the 1943 Mexico Regional Meeting and the 1946 Tenth Session of the Fiscal Committee; primarily responsible for the investigations and preparatory work on the report of the 1945 Special Joint Committee on Private Foreign Investment
Elliott, C Fraser	Commissioner of Income Tax, Department of National Revenue (Canada) at the time of the 1943 Mexico

[1] Prior to 1940, Carroll attended the 1927 and 1928 Meetings of the Technical Experts and the Fiscal Committee's Second Session (1930) as assistant to Professor TS Adams; was a consultant expert for the League Secretariat for its *Taxation of Foreign and National Enterprises* study; and was the US member of the Fiscal Committee's Fifth to Ninth Sessions (1935–1939), serving as Chairman at the Eighth and Ninth Sessions.

[2] Deperon joined the League Secretariat in 1931: Percy G Watterson, 'Note on P Deperon', 30 September 1941, UNOG:PO—C.1626/523/10/1. During the Princeton Mission years, apart from his work on fiscal matters, Deperon, inter alia, prepared public finance sections of the League's *World Economic Survey* publication; conducted the investigations and preparatory work on the League's study on private foreign investment; was responsible for most of the liaison work with Latin America (including for the League's Washington Office for the Permanent Central Opium Board); and acted as legal adviser to the Mission, especially in connection with taxation questions: Alexander Loveday, 'Annual Report: Mr P Deperon – January 1st, 1943–January 1st, 1944', 1 January 1944; 'Annual Report: Mr P Deperon – January 1st–December 31st, 1944)', 1 January 1945; 'Annual Report: Mr P Deperon – January 1st–December 31st, 1945', 4 January 1946; Note (untitled) on Deperon's work for 1941, 9 January 1942, UNOG:PO—C.1626/523/10/1.

	conference; later Deputy Minister of National Revenue for Taxation (Canada)
Goytia, Medardo	Director of Internal Taxes, Ministry of Finance (Chile)
King, Eldon P	Special Deputy Commissioner, Bureau of Internal Revenue, Treasury Department (US)
Loveday, Alexander	Director of the Economic, Financial and Transit Department of the League's Princeton Mission

A.2 Key Characters in the Double Taxation Work of the UN Fiscal Commission Years (1946–1954)

A.2.1 The UN Secretariat

Bloch, Henry S	Director of the Fiscal Division (1949–1954+)
Blough, Roy	Principal Director of the Department of Economic Affairs (1952–1954)
Delanney, Louis	Member of the Transport and Communications Division (at least from 1948–1951+)
Deperon, Paul	Director of the Fiscal Division (1946–1948)
Kremery, Karol	Member of the Fiscal Division (1948–unknown)
Lachmann, Karl E	Chief of the International Tax Section of the Fiscal Division (1948–1954+)
Owen, A David K	Assistant Secretary-General for the Department of Economic Affairs (1946–1952)

A.2.2 The UN Fiscal Commission[3]

Bartelt, Edward F	US member of the Fiscal Commission (1947–1954); Fiscal Assistant Secretary, Treasury Department (US)
Certeux, Jacques	French member of the Fiscal Commission (1947–1954); Inspector of Finance, and Chief of the Service of Co-ordination of Financial Administrations, Ministry of Finance (France)
Morton, WW	British representative on the Fiscal Commission (1949–1951); Assistant Secretary, Board of Inland Revenue (UK)

[3] The details of the select members of the Commission who began serving in 1947 are those that stood as at July 1947: *Biographical Data on the Members of the Fiscal Commission*, UN ESC, UN Doc E/453 (8 July 1947). The details of the British members are those as found in the British Archives records in TNA:IR40/9959(1) and IR40/11173(1).

Nicholas, RO	British representative on the Fiscal Commission (1953); Assistant Secretary, Board of Inland Revenue (UK)
Perez Cubillas, José M	Cuban member of the Fiscal Commission (1947–1954); Technical Adviser, Ministry of Finance (Cuba)
Chernyshev, PM	Soviet member of the Fiscal Commission (1947–1951); Economic Adviser, USSR delegation to the UN

A.2.3 ICAO

Moulton, RJ	Chief of the Facilitation Section (ICAO Secretariat)
Weld, Edward M (US)	Director of the Air Transport Bureau; Assistant Secretary-General of Air Transport (ICAO Secretariat); Secretary to the Air Transport Committee of the ICAO Council
David, PT (US)	Chairman of the Air Transport Committee of the ICAO Council
Warner, Edward (US)	Permanent President of the ICAO Council
Marlin, ER	External Relations Officer (ICAO Secretariat)

A.2.4 NGO Representatives

Bower, Frank	British member of the ICC's Committee of Taxation
Carroll, Mitchell B	Official representative of the National Association of Manufacturers (US); President of IFA (1939–1971)

APPENDIX B

Members and Participants of the Fiscal Commission's Sessions

The following tables list the delegations of the member countries and other participants (i.e. observer countries, specialised agencies and NGOs) to the Fiscal Commission's sessions.[1]

[1] This information has been drawn from the following Fiscal Commission documents: *Provisional List of Participants*, 1st sess, UN Doc E/CN.8/19/Rev.2 (21 May 1947); *Report to the Economic and Social Council on the Work of the First Session of the Commission by Dr ARF Mackay, Representative for New Zealand, General Rapporteur*, 1st sess, UN Doc E/440 (29 May 1947); *Provisional List of Participants*, 2nd sess, UN Doc E/CN.8/W.29/Rev.3 (10 January 1949); *Report of the Second Session of the Fiscal Commission, Held at Lake Success, New York, 10 to 25 January 1949*, UN Doc E/1104 (also E/CN.8/49/Rev.2) (3 February 1949); *Provisional List of Participants*, 3rd sess, UN Doc E/CN.8/INF.1/Rev.1 (4 May 1951); *Report to the Economic and Social Council on the Third Session of the Commission, Held at Lake Success, New York, 7–17 May 1951*, UN Doc E/1993 (also E/CN.8/62) (31 May 1951); *Provisional List of Participants*, 4th sess, UN Doc E/CN.8/INF.2/Rev.1 (30 April 1953); *Report to the Economic and Social Council on the Fourth Session of the Fiscal Commission, Held at Headquarters, New York, 27 April to 8 May 1953*, 4th sess, UN Doc E/2429 (also E/CN.8/78) (8 May 1953).

Table B.1 *Member countries' delegations to the sessions of the Fiscal Commission*

Member Countries	Delegation Members			
	First Session	Second Session	Third Session	Fourth Session
De facto Permanent Members (Big Five)				
China	TY Wu (Observer)	Hsiu Cha (Alternate)	Kan Lee (Representative)	Kan Lee (Representative)
France	Jacques Certeux (Representative) A Boissard (Adviser)	Jacques Certeux (Representative) Jacques Devinat (Alternate)	Jacques Certeux (Representative)	Jacques Certeux (Representative)
UK	RG Hawtrey (Representative) JACC Alexander (Adviser)	WW Morton (Alternate) JT Fearnley (Adviser)	WW Morton (Representative)	RO Nicholas (Alternate)
US	Edward F Bartelt (Representative) Laszlo Ecker-Racz (Adviser) Cyril E Heileman (Adviser) LH Hyde (Adviser)	Edward F Bartelt (Representative) Eldon P King (Adviser) Frederick P Livesey (Adviser) Boyd Evans (Observer)	Edward F Bartelt (Representative) Roy Blough (Adviser) Nathan N Gordon (Adviser) Eldon P King (Adviser)	Edward F Bartelt (Representative) Dan Throop Smith (Principal Adviser) Eldon P King (Adviser) Frederick P Livesey (Adviser)

	Eldon P King (Adviser) Frederick P Livesey (Adviser) Austin Nisonger (Adviser) IC Olsen (Adviser)	Nathan N Gordon (Observer) IC Olsen (Observer) R Sherfy (Observer) Max J Wasserman (Observer)	Frederick P Livesey (Adviser)	Ray Sherfy (Adviser)
USSR	Pavel M Chernyshev (Representative)	Pavel M Chernyshev (Representative)	Pavel M Chernyshev (Representative) IV Chechetkin (Alternate)	IV Chechetkin (Representative) VA Krivitsky (Adviser)
<u>Elective members</u>				
Belgium	Rodolphe Putnam (Representative) Jules Woulbroun (Adviser)	Jules Woulbroun (Alternate)	Paul Callebaut (Alternate) D Driz (Adviser) Jules Woulbroun (Adviser)	Paul Callebaut (Representative) Edgard Schreuder (Alternate) Marcel D'Haeze (Alternate)
Canada			Albert K Eaton (Representative)	Albert K Eaton (Representative)
Chile				Carlos Valenzuela (Representative) Sergio Molina (Alternate)

Table B.1 (*cont.*)

Member Countries	Delegation Members			
	First Session	Second Session	Third Session	Fourth Session
Colombia	Jorge Ortiz Rodriguez (Alternate) Diego Mejia (Adviser) Hernan Samper Gomez (Adviser)	Jorge Ortiz Rodriguez (Alternate) Eduardo Carrizosa (Adviser)		Eduardo Carrizosa (Representative) Edmundo Castollo Jr (Alternate)
Cuba	José M Perez Cubillas (Representative)	José M Perez Cubillas (Representative)	José M Perez Cubillas (Representative)	José M Perez Cubillas (Representative)
Czechoslovakia	Karel Czesany (Representative)	Karel Czesany (Representative)	J Nosek (Alternate) M Glozar (Adviser)	Joseph Vins (Representative) Jaroslav Rybar (Alternate) Frantisek Lukes (Alternate)
India	N Sundaresan (Representative)		Shri Ramji Ram Saksena (Representative) AN Sattanathan (Alternate)	Arthur S Lall (Representative) PK Banerjee (Alternate)
Lebanon	Edward Ghorra (Alternate)	George Hakim (Representative) Edward Ghorra (Alternate)		

New Zealand	ARF Mackay (Representative) Helen M Hampton (Adviser)	DWA Barker (Representative) WB Sutch (Alternate)	JH Weir (Representative)	
Pakistan		MAK Nawab Gurmani (Alternate) M Shaffi (Adviser)	Abdul Qadir (Alternate)	Abdul Qadir (Representative)
Poland	Jan Drewnowski (Alternate)	RM Tychanowicz (Alternate)	S Boratynski (Alternate) S Matusisk (Adviser)	
South Africa	*Unrepresented*	JL Barrie (Alternate)	MJ Wells (Representative)	MJ Wells (Representative)
Sweden				Erik Lindahl (Representative)
Ukraine SSR	I Tolkhunov (Representative)	AI Galagan (Alternate)		
Venezuela			A Nass (Alternate)	

Notes:
'Representative' refers to the Official Representative whose appointment was confirmed by ECOSOC.
Empty cells represent periods during which the country was not a member of the Fiscal Commission.

Table B.2 *Other participants and observers to the sessions of the Fiscal Commission*

Other Participants and Observers	Delegation Members			
	First Session	Second Session	Third Session	Fourth Session
Observer Countries				
Argentina	-	-	-	Agustin M Bartol
Australia	-	-	-	PS McGovern
Yugoslavia	-	-	-	Janez Stanovnik
Specialised Agencies				
Food and Agriculture Organization	David W Lusher	M Ezekiel FL McDougall	M Ezekiel	Alicia Banos
International Bank for Reconstruction and Development	Georges de Fleurieu	-	John E Adler	-
International Civil Aviation Organization	EW Deutschler	R Weld	Edward M Weld RJ Moulton	-
International Labour Office	-	EJ Riches	RA Metall AAP Dawson	AAP Dawson
International Monetary Fund	Gyan-Chaned Gordon Williams	JJ Polak	Earl Hicks E Birnbaum	HL Dey Richard Goode Earl Hicks Paul Brand

Non-governmental Organisations				
American Federation of Labour	Toni Sender William Withers Peter Garvan	Toni Sender Alfred Brauthal	-	-
International Air Transport Association	-	-	John A Lundmark	-
International Chamber of Commerce	Ellsworth C Alvord Victor Schoepperle Edith Sansom	Frank Bower Henry B Fernald Ellsworth C Alvord Edith Sansom	Frank Bower Ellsworth C Alvord Henry B Fernald Maurice J Smits Edith Sansom	Ellsworth C Alvord Thomas J Green Roberta M Lusardi
International Confederation of Free Trade Unions	-	-	Arthur Edler J Brophy	Arthur Elder
International Conference of Catholic Charities	-	-	-	L Longarzo
International Federation of Women Lawyers	-	-	-	AV Smith
International Fiscal Association	-	-	Felix Dayton	George F James Gerard Ph Helders Robert C Plumb Felix Dayton

Table B.2 (*cont.*)

Other Participants and Observers	Delegation Members			
	First Session	Second Session	Third Session	Fourth Session
				Raymond L Brittenham
International Institute of Public Finance	-	-	Carl Shoup	Carl Shoup
International Union of Local Authorities	-	-	Charles S Asher	Charles S Ascher
Inter-American Council of Commerce and Production	-	-	Noel Sargent	E Cruickshank
National Association of Manufacturers (US)	-	Mitchell B Carroll	Mitchell B Carroll	Mitchell B Carroll

APPENDIX C

Deperon's Illustrative Lists of Fiscal Problems for the Tasks of the Fiscal Commission (1947)[1]

Annex A Illustrative List of Basic Problems in the Field of Public Finance

I. Standards of public finance organization, administration and audit

1. Fiscal powers and responsibilities of the national government;

2. Co-ordination of national, state and local fiscal systems; fiscal functions of state and local authorities; means of financing state and local expenditure; supervision;

3. Preparation and implementation of a budget (or budgets) or similar financial plans;

4. Contents and classification of the various budgetary estimates and accounts including those of government enterprises, monopolies and corporations;

5. Contents, comprehensiveness, form, periodicity and publicity of the various documents relating to the expenditure, receipts, debt, financial position as well as assets and liabilities of the government and its institutions;

6. Management, accounting and audit of funds and property of the government and its institutions;

7. Transactions, transfers, credits among government departments and institutions.

II. Relations between public spending and financing

1. Influence of local conditions, particularly the economic, financial and social structure, of a country on the distribution and forms of its public expenditure and receipts;

[1] Contained in Fiscal Commission, *Remarks Concerning the Tasks of the Fiscal Commission*, Note by the Secretariat, 1st sess, Provisional Agenda items 6 and 9, UN Doc E/CN.8/6 (10 April 1947) annexes A and B, 11–15.

2. Specific sensitiveness (timing and magnitude) of the various classes of public expenditure and receipts to structural changes, business fluctuations and relating factors, according to the different types of countries;

3. Economic and other effects of the various classes of public spending and public financing, according to the different types of countries;

4. Selection of form of financing for the various classes of public spending, according to economic, financial and social structure and policies;

5. Fiscal organization and temporary or permanent measures to promote economic stability and development as well as advancement, according to types of countries.

III. Structure and administration of tax systems

1. Principles of tax organization and management in the light of fiscal, economic and social objectives, local conditions and overall costs;

2. Definition of tax bases, determination and selection of tax rates, criteria and methods of assessment, collection procedures, prevention of fraud and evasion, protection of taxpayers;

3. Classification and treatment of individual and corporate taxpayers, internal double taxation, economic and social exemptions;

4. Methods of compilation and presentation, and uses, of tax statistics;

5. Collection and codification of tax laws, regulations and decisions, publicity of tax measures, techniques of guidance to taxpayers;

6. Techniques for the improvement and complication of obsolete or inadequate tax institutions and procedures.

IV. International tax problems

1. Effects of tax barriers on world trade and on the economic stability and development of various types of countries;

2. International double taxation of income, property, capital, estates and successions, transactions, legal and commercial instruments;

3. Taxation of foreigners and non-residents, particularly extra-territorial taxation and discriminatory taxation;

4. Taxation of international enterprises, transactions and transfers;

5. Taxation of international travel, transport and communications including tax treatment of tourists, business visitors, border commuters, migratory workers, of telecommunications and of means of land, sea and air transportation;

6. Mutual assistance between national tax administrations regarding the assessment and collection of taxes, especially exchange of information and prevention of international tax evasion;

7. Standards for domestic legislation, and treaty negotiation, on international tax matters; model bilateral and multilateral tax treaties; draft tax provisions for insertion in other treaties; application of most-favoured-nation clause in tax matters; development of an international tax law.

Annex B Illustrative List of General Fiscal Problems of Immediate Interest

I. Fiscal administration in general

1. Nomenclature and classification of government budgets and accounts;
2. Financing and accounting of government current expenditure and capital outlay;
3. Transactions, transfers and credits among government departments and institutions;
4. Relations between national, state and local fiscal systems;
5. Cost of fiscal administration;
6. Recruitment and training of fiscal personnel;
7. Adaptation of fiscal systems to national economic and social structures.

II. Current economic and social aspects of fiscal systems and techniques

1. Fiscal measures for the control of inflation;
2. Fiscal measures for the promotion of economic stability, particularly in economically advanced countries;
3. Fiscal measures for the promotion of economic development and diversification and of investment, particularly in economically less advanced countries;
4. Financing of social expenditures and public works;
5. Fiscal measures in the field of housing and urban planning;
6. Tax status of the family.

III. Basic problems of internal taxation

1. Analysis of theories on the effects of taxation;
2. Sensitiveness of tax yields to economic fluctuations and structural changes;
3. Recent developments in the techniques and theory of taxation;

4. Methods of tax reform;
5. Devices for preventing tax fraud and evasion.

IV. International tax relations
1. Effects of tax obstacles to international economic relations;
2. Trends in international tax treaties;
3. Operation and results of existing tax treaties;
4. International tax evasion.

APPENDIX D

ECOSOC Resolution 226D (IX) (22 July 1949)[1]

226 (IX). REPORT OF THE SECOND SESSION OF THE FISCAL COMMISSION

. . .

D

Promotion and Adoption of Bilateral Agreements for the Avoidance of Double Taxation

The Economic and Social Council,

Having in mind the importance of utilizing all appropriate means to promote the expansion of trade and investment among nations,

Having in mind the obstructions to the flow of trade and investment which may result from the unco-ordinated action of Governments in the field of taxation,

Having in mind the studies made in this field by the Fiscal Committee of the League of Nations and by private international and national organizations in numerous conferences, and the continuing work of the Fiscal Commission of the Council in this field, and

Having in mind the important progress in this field already achieved through bilateral agreements for the avoidance of double taxation, and the special suitability of such bilateral action to the task of assuring concrete co-ordination among the diverse national regime of taxation expressed in the complex and detailed tax legislation and regulations of the various countries of the world,

Recommends to Governments Members of the United Nations that they actively pursue a policy of negotiating bilateral agreements, wherever appropriate, for the avoidance of double taxation.

[1] Contained in UN ESCOR, UN Doc E/1553 (15 August 1949) 22–3.

APPENDIX E

Draft Resolution B-II (Fiscal Commission, Third Session)[1]

VII. Draft Resolution Recommended for Adoption by the Economic and Social Council

B

International Tax Problems

. . .

II

The Economic and Social Council,

Recognizing that, in the relations between under-developed countries and countries in a more advanced state of development,

(i) international double taxation normally operates as one of the impediments to the free flow of trade and investment;

(ii) the country in which income arises has an undoubted right in principle to tax that income;

(iii) therefore the main burden of relief of double taxation must fall on the country where the income is also taxable as part of the income of a resident or national person or corporation;

(iv) the conclusion of bilateral agreements has the advantage of offering scope for the more effective provision of complete relief, of making possible the resolution of different approaches in the national laws of the contracting parties, and also of providing the assured stability of an international treaty to enterprises of either country considering ventures in the other;

(v) such bilateral agreements can be concluded on the basis of the foregoing propositions between an under-developed country and one in a more advanced state of development with little sacrifice of national revenue on the

[1] Contained in Fiscal Commission, *Report to the Economic and Social Council on the Third Session of the Commission, Held at Lake Success, New York, 7–17 May 1951*, UN Doc E/1993 (also E/CN.8/62) (31 May 1951) 14–15 [34].

part of the former, and bilateral agreements on this footing can make their contribution to the general objectives of the United Nations for the encouragement of economic development in under-developed countries.

Recommends that,

there is normally no need or justification for countries seeking to attract capital and enterprise from abroad to offer as an incentive specially favourable tax treatment, as against the treatment accorded to their own national enterprises;

Recommends again,

that the conclusion of bilateral agreements for the relief of double taxation should find a place in the fiscal policy of Member governments.

Requests the Secretary-General:

to continue his study and analysis of the methods for relief from double taxation through bilateral tax agreements and national legislation.

APPENDIX F

ECOSOC Resolution 378B (XIII) (10 August 1951)[1]

378 (XIII). REPORT OF THE FISCAL COMMISSION (THIRD SESSION)

...

B

International Tax Problems

...

II

The Economic and Social Council,

Recognizing that in the relations between under-developed countries and countries in a more advanced state of development:

(a) International double taxation normally operates as one of the impediments to the free flow of trade and investment;

(b) The country in which income arises, as a general principle, has an undoubted right to tax that income;

(c) Therefore, the main burden of relief of double taxation must fall on the country where the income is also taxable as part of the income of a resident or national person or corporation;

(d) The conclusion of bilateral agreements has the advantage of offering scope for the more effective provision of complete relief, of making possible the resolution of different approaches in the national laws of the contracting parties, and also of providing the assured stability of an international treaty to enterprises of either country considering ventures in the other;

(e) Such bilateral agreements can be concluded on the basis of the foregoing propositions between an under-developed country and one in a more advanced state of development with little sacrifice of national revenue on the

[1] Contained in UN ESCOR, UN Doc 2152 (10 October 1951) 23–4.

part of the former, and bilateral agreements on this footing can make their contribution to the general objectives of the United Nations for the encouragement of economic development in under-developed countries;

1. *Recommends that* there is normally no need or justification for countries seeking to attract capital and enterprise from abroad to offer as an incentive specially favourable tax treatment as against the treatment accorded to their own national enterprises;

2. *Recommends again*, that the conclusion of bilateral agreements for the relief of double taxation should find a place in the fiscal policy of Members States; and

3. *Requests* the Secretary-General to continue his study and analysis of the methods for relief from double taxation through bilateral agreements and national legislation.

APPENDIX G

ECOSOC Resolution 368B (XIII) (22 August 1951)[1]

368 (XIII). METHODS OF FINANCING ECONOMIC DEVELOPMENT OF UNDER-DEVELOPED COUNTRIES

The Economic and Social Council,

. . .

3. *Is convinced* that, in order to promote a larger and steadier flow of public and private capital from the more developed to the under-developed countries, various measures need to be taken at this time; and to this end submits the following recommendations for action by the governments of the Member States, the Secretary-General and the specialized agencies concerned:

. . .

B

With the Object of Achieving an Expansion and Steadier Flow of Private Foreign Capital

5. *Recommends* that countries able to export capital:

. . .

(b) Undertake measures for the avoidance of double taxation, such as the negotiation of appropriate tax treaties;

. . .

6. *Recommends* that countries seeking to attract private foreign capital:

. . .

(c) Undertake, through legislative or administrative measures and the negotiation of tax treaties, to safeguard foreign investors against discriminatory taxation and to resolve other taxation issues, including the issue of double taxation,

[1] Contained in UN ESCOR, UN Doc 2152 (10 October 1951) 3–7.

Provided that the provisions of sub-paragraphs (b) and (c) will be without prejudice to the right to the government of a Member State to take any appropriate safeguards necessary to ensure that foreign investment is not used as a basis for interference in its internal affairs or national policies;

. . .

APPENDIX H

ECOSOC Resolution 416D (XIV) (1 July 1952)[1]

416 (XIV). ECONOMIC DEVELOPMENT OF UNDER-DEVELOPED COUNTRIES

D

Fiscal Incentives to Increase the International Flow of Private Capital for the Economic Development of Under-Developed Countries

The Economic and Social Council,

Recognizing:

(a) The great importance for the acceleration of economic development of finding means of stimulating the flow of private investment capital from the highly developed to the under-developed countries,

(b) That the present international flow of private investment capital is insufficient for development needs,

(c) That in so far as international double taxation constitutes a deterrent to foreign investment this deterrent has been greatly reduced through international tax agreements and unilateral measures for the avoidance of such double taxation,

(d) That the measures heretofore adopted for the avoidance of double taxation do not, however, appear to afford a positive incentive to foreign private investment,

(e) That further examination is needed of: (i) the extent to which fiscal measures may afford an incentive to the flow of foreign investment from the highly developed to the under-developed countries; and (ii) the feasibility and desirability of such measures,

1. *Notes* that in the field of international tax problems:

(a) In accordance with Council resolution 378 B (XIII), the Secretary-General is continuing to study 'the effects of taxation on foreign trade and investment'; and

[1] Contained in UN ESCOR, UN Doc 2332 (13 August 1952) 3–4.

(b) In accordance with resolution 3 (IV) of 16 June 1951 of the Economic Commission for Latin America, a study is being undertaken jointly by the Headquarters Secretariat and the secretariat of the Economic Commission for Latin America of 'the influence that the fiscal systems of capital-exporting countries may have on the decisions of private investors in those countries to make foreign investments';

2. *Requests* that, in the light of the results of the further studies being made by the Secretary-General and of the study which is being undertaken jointly by the Headquarters Secretariat and the secretariat of the Economic Commission for Latin America, the Fiscal Commission give further consideration to the problems of taxation in relation to foreign investments;

3. *Further requests* the Fiscal Commission, in the consideration of such problems:

(a) To examine further the proposal that, through bilateral agreements or unilateral measures, income from foreign investments in under-developed countries should be taxed only in these countries, with such income being exempted from taxes by countries other than those in which the foreign investments are made; and

(b) To submit the results of such examination to the Council in a special section of its next report.

APPENDIX I

Proposed ICAO Council Resolution on Taxation (December 1948)[1]

Draft of Proposed ICAO Council Resolution on Taxation (In substitution for Chapter 16 and para. 11.1. of FAL Standards as proposed by FAL Division, Second Session)

WHEREAS it appears that the development of international air transport is impeded by multiple, unfairly burdensome, and discriminatory taxation of airlines, their employees, and their customers

THE COUNCIL RESOLVES

1. That Contracting States should notify the Council by (date) of any difficulties they foresee in implementing the provisions of Annex '1' to this Resolution, together with their suggested amendments to the said provisions;

2. That Contracting States should endeavour, as far and as soon as may be practicable, to put the said provisions into effect.

Annex I

1. Each Contracting States should adopt all practicable measures, in cooperation with other States concerned, to eliminate multiple and unfairly burdensome, or discriminatory taxation of airlines and employees, and customers of airlines of other Contracting States.

2. For the purpose of accomplishing the objectives contemplated by paragraph 1, Contracting States should, wherever possible,

(a) extend to airlines of other Contracting States reciprocal exemption from income and gross receipts taxes;

(b) extend to airlines of other Contracting States reciprocal exemption from property taxes on aircraft;

[1] ATC, *Proposed ICAO Council Resolution on Taxation*, ICAO Doc AT-WP/30 (14 December 1948) 3–4.

(c) extend to airline employees of other Contracting States reciprocal exemption from personal income taxes to the extent necessary to prevent multiple taxation of their incomes;

(d) admit free of customs duty or excise tax any air navigational ground equipment imported from a Contracting State by an airline of a Contracting State for the purpose of providing services to international air navigation;

(e) exempt reciprocally from customs duty or excise tax any other aviation ground equipment imported from a Contracting State by an airline of a Contracting State for direct use in the servicing of the internationally operated aircraft of such airline;

(f) exempt reciprocally from excise taxes all aircraft stores, parts, supplies, and equipment used in international air navigation by airlines of any other Contracting State;

(g) agree reciprocally to the elimination, or reduction of taxes on fuels and lubricants used in international air navigation by airlines of any Contracting State;

(h) reduce or eliminate excise taxes on the sale of international transportation by air.

APPENDIX J

ICAO Council Draft Resolution on Taxation of Income and Property of Airlines (9 December 1949)[1]

Draft Resolution on Taxation of Income and Property of Airlines

WHEREAS the principle of reciprocal exemption from taxation of the earnings of international water and air transportation enterprises has been widely accepted; and

WHEREAS the application of the same principle to the property taxation of vessels and aircraft operated in international transportation has been favoured in the drafting of model international tax conventions; and

WHEREAS double taxation of the above mentioned earnings and property of international air transportation enterprises can be effectively prevented by the application of the rule of reciprocal exemption; and

WHEREAS it is the understanding of Council that some States would find it more practicable to deal with the problem of relief from taxation of air transport enterprises as part of the problem of relief from double taxation of trade and industry in general;

THE COUNCIL RESOLVES THAT:

(1) Each Contracting State should, to the fullest possible extent, grant reciprocally to air transport enterprises of other Contracting States

(a) exemption from taxation on the income and gross receipts derived in that State from the operation of aircraft in international air transportation; and

(b) exemption from property taxes, capital levies, increment of wealth or other similar taxes on aircraft engaged in international air transportation.

(2) Each Contracting State should endeavour to give effect to paragraph (1) above, in bilateral agreements relating to double taxation generally, or by such other methods as the inclusion of appropriate provisions in bilateral agreements for the exchange of commercial air transport rights, or by legislation granting such exemption on a reciprocal basis;

[1] Contained in ATC, *20th Report to Council by the Chairman of the Air Transport Committee*, ICAO Doc C-WP/509 (9 December 1949) app III.

(3) Each Contracting State should notify the Council on or before Sept 1950 of the extent to which it is prepared to apply the provisions of this Resolution as from 1 January 1951;

(4) Any Contracting State which has not made notification pursuant to Para (3) above may notify the Council at any time of the extent to which it is prepared to apply the provisions of this Resolution, and of the date that such application will become effective;

(5) All Contracting States be advised of the notifications so received.

APPENDIX K

ICAO Council Resolution on Taxation of the Income and Flight Equipment of International Air Transport Enterprises (18 April 1951)[1]

Council Resolution of Taxation of the Income and Flight Equipment of International Air Transport Enterprises

WHEREAS the Economic and Social Council of the United Nations has recommended to governments that they actively pursue a policy of negotiating bilateral agreements, wherever appropriate, for the avoidance of double taxation; and

WHEREAS in such bilateral agreements completed to date the principle of reciprocal exemption from taxation of the earnings of international water and air transport enterprises has been widely accepted; and

WHEREAS the application of the same principle to the property taxation of vessels and aircraft operated in international transport has been favoured in the drafting of model international tax conventions; and

WHEREAS double taxation of the above mentioned earnings and property of international air transport enterprises can be effectively prevented by the application of the rule of reciprocal exemption; and

WHEREAS for international air transport enterprises the absence of reciprocal exemption involves either double taxation or considerable difficulties of income allocation in a very large number of taxing jurisdictions; and

WHEREAS it is the understanding of Council that some States would find it more practicable to deal with the problem of relief from double taxation of air transport enterprises as part of the problem of relief from double taxation of trade and industry in general;

[1] Contained in ATC, *39th Report to Council by the Chairman of the Air Transport Committee*, ICAO Council, 12th sess, ICAO Doc 7145, C/824 (18 April 1951) app III.

THE COUNCIL RESOLVES THAT

(1) Each Contracting State should, to the fullest possible extent, grant reciprocally to air transport enterprises of other Contracting States

(a) exemption from taxation on the income and gross receipts derived in that State from the operation of aircraft in international air transport; and

(b) exemption from property taxes, capital levies, increment of wealth or other similar taxes on aircraft engaged in international air transport;

(2) Each Contracting State should endeavour to give effect to paragraph (1) above, by the bilateral negotiation of agreements relating to double taxation generally, or by such other methods as the inclusion of appropriate provisions in bilateral agreements for the exchange of commercial air transport rights, or by legislation granting such exemption on a reciprocal basis;

(3) Each Contracting State should notify the Council, on 1 January 1952 or as soon thereafter as possible, of the extent to which it is prepared to take action in accordance with the principles of this Resolution;

(4) All Contracting States be advised of the notifications so received.

APPENDIX L

Proposed Resolutions on the Taxation of International Air Transport (Fiscal Commission, Third Session)[1]

L.1 United States: Draft Resolution[2]

The Fiscal Commission,

Considering that the Council of the International Civil Aviation Organization has been considering a resolution on the taxation of the income and flight equipment of international air transport enterprises (as recorded in document E/CN.8/57, Appendix III), and

Considering that the policy established in this resolution reflects the policies contained in both the London and Mexican drafts of model bilateral tax conventions, as well as in many bilateral tax agreements negotiated by member countries, and

Recognizing that the policy recommended in such resolution is designed to promote the growth of international civil aviation and is not inconsistent with any action taken by this body in the past,

Recommends that the Economic and Social Council convey its appreciation to the International Civil Aviation Organization for the close working relationship which has been maintained with the United Nations, and inform ICAO that its resolution on the taxation of income and flight equipment is not inconsistent with any action taken by the Economic and Social Council.

L.2 Pakistan: Draft Resolution[3]

The Fiscal Commission,

Considering that Professor Shere who was appointed as a consultant by the United Nations and ICAO could not find evidence to recommend exemption of airlines from international taxation, and

[1] The following conference room papers containing the proposed resolutions may be found in NARAII:RG56-199-6.

[2] Fiscal Commission, 'United States of America: Draft Resolution', 3rd sess, Agenda item 3(b), Conference Room Paper No 3 (10 May 1951).

[3] Fiscal Commission, 'Pakistan: Draft Resolution', 3rd sess, Agenda item 3(b), Conference Room Paper No 4 (11 May 1951).

Recognizing that reciprocal exemption recommended by ICAO in their resolution (E/CN.57) presumes that both countries entering into a bilateral agreement have airlines operating in the other country,

Recommends that the principle of reciprocal exemption of airlines from taxation suggested by ICAO should be applied by contracting parties after concluding bilateral agreements in respect of taxation.

L.3 India, Pakistan and Venezuela: Joint Amendments to the US Draft Resolution[4]

Replace paragraphs 2, 3 and 4 by the following:

Having considered the report submitted by Professor Louis Shere, a joint consultant to the ICAO and the United Nations, on taxation of International Air Transport,

Appreciates the courtesy extended to it by the ICAO Council in referring its draft resolution for an expression of its views,

Recognizes the importance of International Air Transport as a means for the development of international trade and understanding, and of the part which relief from double taxation can play in its development,

Considers that the grant of reciprocal exemption from taxation by Contracting States to the fullest possible extent, as recommended in the resolution of the ICAO Council is not consistent in so far as under-developed countries are concerned with the principle of equality of sacrifice,

Recommends that relief from double taxation for International Air Transport enterprises should be obtained through bilateral agreements based on the principles formulated by the Working Group of the Fiscal Commission in respect of avoidance of double taxation.

L.4 United Kingdom: Amendment to the Joint Amendments[5]

Delete the last two paragraphs and substitute:

Acknowledges that the draft resolution of ICAO on the Taxation of Income and Flying Equipment is not inconsistent with the policies of the Fiscal Commission, it being understood that in any bi-lateral [sic] agreement between an under-developed country and a country in a more advantageous

[4] Fiscal Commission, 'India, Pakistan and Venezuela: Joint Amendments to the Draft Resolution of the United States of America (Conference Room Paper 3)', 3rd sess, Agenda item 3(b), Conference Room Paper No 10 (15 May 1951).

[5] Fiscal Commission, 'United Kingdom: Amendment to United States Draft Resolution as Amended (Conference Room Paper No 3)', 3rd sess, Agenda item 3(b), Conference Room Paper No 17 (16 May 1951).

state of development the whole result should conform with the principles adopted in the Commission's resolution on this subject.

L.5 Pakistan and Venezuela: Amendment to the Joint Amendments[6]

Delete the last two paragraphs and substitute:

4. Considers that insofar as under-developed countries are concerned the grant of reciprocal exemption from taxation by Contracting States, as recommended in Appendix III of the Report of the ICAO Council, is consistent with the principles formulated by the Fiscal Commission in its Resolution on International Tax Problems, of 15 May 1951, only if such grant is part of a broader agreement offering compensatory concessions in accordance with the principle of equality of sacrifice.

L.6 India: Amendment to the Joint Amendments[7]

Delete last two paragraphs and substitute:

Requests the Secretary-General to forward a copy of the resolution of the Fiscal Commission on the subject of Avoiding Double Taxation, (dated 15 May 1951), and also the summary records of these meetings.

[6] Fiscal Commission, 'Pakistan and Venezuela: Amendment to United States Draft Resolution as Amended (Conference Room Paper No 3)', 3rd sess, Agenda item 3(b), Conference Room Paper No 18/Rev.1 (16 May 1951).

[7] Fiscal Commission, 'India: Amendment to United States Draft Resolution as Amended (Conference Room Paper No 3)', 3rd sess, Agenda item 3(b), Conference Room Paper No 21 (16 May 1951).

APPENDIX M

Resolution on International Air Transport (Fiscal Commission, Third Session)[1]

VI Resolution Adopted by the Commission

International Air Transport

The Fiscal Commission,

Considering that the Council of the International Civil Aviation Organization has been considering a resolution on the taxation of the income and flight equipment of international air transport enterprises (as recorded in document E/CN.8/57, Appendix III), and

Having considered the report submitted by Professor Louis Shere, a joint consultant to the ICAO and the United Nations, on taxation of International Air Transport,

Appreciates the courtesy extended to it by the ICAO Council in referring its draft resolution for an expression of its views,

Recognizes the importance of International Air Transport as a means for the development of international trade and understanding, and of the part which relief from double taxation can play in its development,

Requests the Secretary-General to forward to the President of the Economic and Social Council and to the Secretary-General of the ICAO copies of Draft Resolution B, II on International Tax Problems, and also the summary records of these meetings.

[1] Contained in Fiscal Commission, *Report to the Economic and Social Council on the Third Session of the Commission, Held at Lake Success, New York, 7–17 May 1951*, UN Doc E/1993 (also E/CN.8/62) (31 May 1951) 13 [31].

APPENDIX N

Account of the Debate on the Taxation of International Air Transport, Report of the Fiscal Commission (Third Session)[1]

20. On the taxation of income and flight equipment of international air transport enterprises (items 3 (b) (2) and 3 (b) (3) of the agenda, which had been referred to the Fiscal Commission and the Economic and Social Commission by the Council of the International Civil Aviation Organization), the Commission found itself more evenly divided than on any other item. On the one hand, there were those members who acknowledged that international air transport, like international shipping, presented a special problem in relieving double or multiple taxation, and believed that the most practicable method was to concede on the basis of bilateral agreements or otherwise that exemption from tax should be accorded in the countries in which air enterprises operate, there being reserved to the country in which the enterprise was located the exclusive right to tax. On the other hand, there were others who regarded a system which required the exemption from tax of air transport profits in countries in which operations are carried on by foreign air enterprises as involving an absence of true reciprocity, particularly in the case of under-developed countries.

The United States representative proposed a resolution endorsing the draft resolution of the ICAO. An amendment to this, proposed by the Indian, Pakistani, and Venezuelan representatives stating that the draft resolution of the ICAO was not consistent with the principle of equality of sacrifice as far as under-developed countries are concerned and recommending appropriate relief by bilateral agreements was passed in the first instance.

Before the original United States draft resolution, as thus amended, was put to the vote, a further amendment by way of compromise was proposed by the United Kingdom representative to the effect that the ICAO draft resolution was not inconsistent with the principles formulated by the Fiscal Commission, it being understood that in a bilateral agreement between an under-developed country and a country in a more advanced state of development, the overall result should conform with the principles laid down in Draft Resolution B, II.

[1] Contained in Fiscal Commission, *Report to the Economic and Social Council on the Third Session of the Commission, Held at Lake Success, New York, 7–17 May 1951*, UN Doc E/1993 (also E/CN.8/62) (31 May 1951) 9–10 [20].

As a matter of compromise, another amendment was proposed by the Pakistani and Venezuelan representative [sic], stating that the draft resolution of the ICAO was consistent with the principles formulated in Draft Resolution B, II only if the grant of reciprocal exemption from taxation by the contracting parties was part of a broader agreement offering compensatory concessions in accordance with the principles of equality of sacrifice.

The Indian representative in an attempt to avoid controversy, proposed an amendment suggesting that the Secretary-General should be requested to forward a copy of Draft Resolution B, II and of the summary records of these meetings to the President of the Economic and Social Council and to the Secretary-General of the International Civil Aviation Organization.

The Indian amendment, being farthest removed from the original resolution, was put to the vote and adopted resulting in the Resolution shown in Section VI below. [See Appendix M]

APPENDIX O

Proposed Cuban Resolution on the Taxation of Foreign Investment (Fiscal Commission, Fourth Session)[1]

Fiscal Incentives to Increase the International Flow of Private Capital for the Economic Development of Under-developed Countries (Cuba: Draft Resolution)

The Economic and Social Council,

Recognizing:

(a) The great importance of finding means to stimulate the flow of private investment from the highly developed to the under-developed countries, in order to accelerate the economic development of the latter,

(b) That the present flow of capital exported to the under-developed countries is insufficient for their development needs,

(c) That low taxation relatively to the rates in force in the more developed countries is one of the attractions which the under-developed countries can offer to foreign capital as an incentive to investment, provided that the highly developed countries accept the principle of non-taxation of the income from national capital earned in under-developed countries,

(d) That this incentive becomes ineffective – although international double taxation is avoided – if the capital-exporting countries apply to the income from investments in under-developed countries any further taxation beyond that already paid in the latter,

(e) That income should be taxed solely in that under-developed country in which the capital is invested,

1. Declares that income from foreign investments in under-developed countries should be taxed only in those countries, and should be exempted from taxation in all other countries;

2. Recommends the adoption of this principle as one of the most effective means of increasing the flow of private capital to the under-developed countries;

3. Recommends also that the necessary unilateral legislative action be taken to transform this principle rapidly into a practical reality;

[1] Fiscal Commission, *Cuba: Draft Resolution on Fiscal Incentives to Increase the International Flow of Private Capital for the Economic Development of Under-Developed Countries*, 4th sess, Agenda item 3(a), UN Doc E/CN.8/L.3 (29 April 1953).

4. Recommends likewise that the highly developed countries should, when concluding bilateral tax agreements with under-developed countries stipulate that income earned by their residents from investments in the other country should be taxed only in the country in which the income was produced.

APPENDIX P

Draft Resolution B (Fiscal Commission, Fourth Session)[1]

VIII. Draft Resolutions Recommended for Adoption by the Economic and Social Council

. . . .

B

International Tax Problems

Fiscal Incentives to Increase the International Flow of Private Capital for the Economic Development of Under-developed Countries

The Economic and Social Council,

Recognizing:

(a) The great importance of finding means to stimulate the flow of private investment from the highly developed to the under-developed countries, in order to accelerate the economic development of the latter,

(b) That the present flow of capital exported to the under-developed countries is insufficient for their development needs,

(c) That relatively low taxation in force in the under-developed countries is one of the attractions which such countries can offer to foreign capital as an incentive to investment,

(d) That this incentive becomes ineffective – although international double taxation is avoided – if the capital-exporting countries apply to the income

[1] Contained in Fiscal Commission, *Report to the Economic and Social Council on the Fourth Session of the Fiscal Commission, Held at Headquarters, New York, from 27 April to 8 May 1953*, UN Doc E/2429 (also E/CN.8/78) (8 May 1953) 6 [50].

from investments in under-developed countries any further taxation beyond that already paid in the latter,

(e) That favourable tax treatment is one of the many factors affecting the flow of foreign capital,

1. *Reaffirms* that the country in which income arises has as a general principle an undoubted right to tax that income;

2. *Recommends* that the highly developed countries acting unilaterally or when concluding tax agreements should give sympathetic consideration to the feasibility of taxing such income only or primarily in the country in which the income was produced.

APPENDIX Q

Account of the Debate on the Taxation of Foreign Investment, Report of the Fiscal Commission (Fourth Session)[1]

[The underlined text in the following extract represents the text in the original draft report[2] that was deleted from the final report.]

16. The discussion centred around the question of tax exemption as raised in this resolution of the Council [ECOSOC Resolution 416D (XIV)]. Most of the Representatives were agreed that it was highly desirable and indeed necessary to facilitate the flow of private investment from capital-exporting to under-developed countries. They were, however, divided as to the question of the role to be played by tax exemption of such income in capital-exporting countries. The Representatives of the latter countries pointed to the revenue loss and the administrative difficulties which would result from tax exemption, as well as to its discriminatory features. They also felt doubts as to the comparative importance of the tax factor in influencing the flow of private capital to under-developed countries. On the other hand, they did state that the credit system, while substantially eliminating double taxation, did not offer positive tax advantages to foreign investment as such; that such advantages might in certain cases be desirable and were in fact granted in the tax legislation of some of the capital-exporting countries represented on the Commission. Several of the Representatives point to the fact that their Governments were currently engaged in a re-examination of their tax systems, including the provisions affecting the taxation of income from foreign investment. A further view which was put forward in opposition to the introduction of outright tax exemption in all capital-exporting countries was that a single standard could not appropriately be applied to all the varied tax systems prevailing in capital-exporting countries.

Representatives of capital-importing countries emphasized their belief in the effectiveness of tax exemption, even in the face of non-tax factors; they considered that the revenue loss which it would cause to the capital-exporting

1 Contained in Fiscal Commission, *Report to the Economic and Social Council on the Fourth Session of the Fiscal Commission, Held at Headquarters, New York, from 27 April to 8 May 1953*, UN Doc E/2429 (also E/CN.8/78) (8 May 1953) 2–3 [15]–[20].

2 Fiscal Commission, *Draft Report to the Economic and Social Council on the Fourth Session of the Fiscal Commission, Held at New York, from 27 April to 8 May 1953*, 4th sess, UN Doc E/CN.8/L.9 (7 May 1953) 8–9 [13]–[14].

countries would not be significant. They saw in the adoption of the exemption device an outstanding contribution on the part of capital-exporting countries to the expansion of the flow of private foreign investment for economic development.

17. The representative of Cuba introduced a draft resolution recommending tax exemption in the highly developed countries of income earned by their residents from investments in under-developed countries.

18. The Commission established a Working Group on International Tax Problems to seek a reconciliation of these viewpoints so as to arrive at a draft resolution on this question which could be submitted to the Economic and Social Council in the requested special section of the Commission's report. This special section is contained in section VI below.

19. The Working Group submitted a draft resolution proposed by the representative of Pakistan, to the Commission, recommending that the highly developed countries give sympathetic consideration to the feasibility of taxing income earned in under-developed countries only or primarily in such countries.

20. After receiving the report of the Working Group (which is published as an annex), the Commission rejected the draft resolution proposed by the representative of Cuba by a vote of 4 in favour, 7 against, with 4 abstentions. The Commission adopted by 13 votes in favour, none against, with 2 abstentions draft resolution B proposed by the Working Group.

APPENDIX R

Proposed Resolutions on the Taxation of Foreign Investment (ECOSOC, Sixteenth Session)

R.1 Cuba: Draft Resolution (L.510)[1]

The Economic and Social Council,

Recognizing:

(a) The great importance of finding means to stimulate the flow of private investment from the highly developed to the under-developed countries, in order to accelerate the economic development of the latter;

(b) That the present flow of capital exported to the under-developed countries is insufficient for their development needs;

(c) That lower taxation relatively to the rates in force in the more developed countries is one of the attractions which the under-developed countries can offer to foreign capital as an incentive to investment, always provided that the highly developed countries accept the principle of non-taxation of the income from national capital earned in under-developed countries;

(d) That this incentive is removed – although international double taxation is avoided – if the capital-exporting countries apply to the income from investments in under-developed countries any further taxation beyond that already paid in the latter;

(e) That income should be taxed solely in that under-developed country in which the capital is invested;

1. Declares that income from foreign investments in under-developed countries should be taxed only in those countries, being exempt from taxation in any other country;

2. Recognizing that the adoption of this principle is one of the most effective means of increasing the flow of private capital to the under-developed countries;

3. Recognizing, further, that the necessary unilateral legislative action should be taken to put this principle rapidly into effect;

4. Recommends, accordingly, to the highly developed countries that in carrying out their policy of concluding bilateral fiscal agreements with under-developed countries, they stipulate that the income of their residents from investments in the other country shall be taxed only in the country where such income was produced.

[1] *Cuba: Draft Resolution*, UN ESC, 16th sess, Agenda item 9, UN Doc E/L.510 (1 July 1953).

R.2 Argentina: Amendment to the Cuban Draft Resolution (L.515)[2]

1. Paragraph (c)
Substitute the following text:

> (c) that the taxation facilities of all kinds granted by developing countries in order to stimulate the flow and investment of foreign capital may be ineffective if the principle of non-taxation of the income earned by nationals in developing countries is not universally accepted;

2. Paragraph 3
Substitute the following text:

> 3. Recommends governments which have not incorporated this principle in their fiscal legislation to undertake the reforms required to ensure that it will be effectively applied throughout the world with the least possible delay;

3. Paragraph 4
Substitute the following paragraph:

> 4. Recommends, accordingly, that bilateral fiscal agreements concluded hereafter shall stipulate that the income of residents of one country from investments in the other country shall be taxed only in the country where such income was produced.

4. Add the following new paragraph:

> 5. Requests the Secretary-General to bring this important problem to the notice of the group of experts to be set up in accordance with resolution 623 (VII) of the General Assembly, so that it may be duly taken into account in connexion with the practical measures which the group is to recommend for the financing of the economic development of developing countries.

R.3 Argentina: Amendment to Draft Resolution B of the Fiscal Commission (L.517)[3]

1. Paragraph (c)
Substitute the following text:

> (c) That the taxation facilities of all kinds granted by countries in process of development in order to stimulate the flow and investment

[2] *Argentina: Amendment to the Cuban Draft Resolution (E/L.510)*, UN ESC, 16th sess, Agenda item 9, UN Doc E/L.515 (2 July 1953).

[3] *Argentina: Amendment to Draft Resolution B of the Fiscal Commission (E/2429)*, UN ESC, 16th sess, Agenda item 9, UN Docs E/L.517 and Corr.1 (3 and 4 July 1953).

of capital from foreign countries may be ineffective unless the principle is universally accepted that the income shall be taxable only in the country where it is earned;

2. Add a further paragraph (f) to the preamble, to read as follows:

(f) That notwithstanding the above, the criteria for deciding this important matter are not yet sufficient;

3. Replace the operative part by the following:

1. Requests the Fiscal Commission to continue its study of the problem of international double taxation and to report on the matter to the Economic and Social Council after its next meeting.

R.4 Australia: Amendment to Draft Resolution B of the Fiscal Commission (L.518)[4]

Replace paragraph 2 by the following:

Recommends that the highly developed countries acting unilaterally or when concluding tax agreements should give sympathetic consideration to the feasibility of taking action to ensure that such income is taxable only or primarily in the country in which the income was produced.

R.5 United States: Amendment to Draft Resolution B of the Fiscal Commission (L.520)[5]

1. Add a further paragraph (f) to the preamble to read as follows:

(f) that further study and analysis of the problem referred to in paragraph (d) above is needed before governments can be prepared to take a definitive position on this matter.

2. Add a paragraph 3 to the operative part as follows:

3. Notes that the Fiscal Commission plans to continue its study of the problem referred to in paragraph (d) above and anticipates a report on the results of its further studies to the Economic and Social Council after the next meeting of the Fiscal Commission.

[4] *Australia: Amendment to Draft Resolution B in the Report of the Commission (E/2429–Paragraph 50)*, UN ESC, 16th sess, Agenda Item 9, UN Doc E/L.518 (3 July 1953).

[5] *United States of America: Amendment to Draft Resolution B of the Report of the Fiscal Commission (E/2429)*, UN ESC, 16th sess, Agenda item 9, UN Doc E/L.520 (4 July 1953).

R.6 Argentina, Cuba, Uruguay and Venezuela: Joint Amendments to Draft Resolution B (L.61)[6]

1. Add further paragraphs (f) and (g) to the preamble to read as follows:

(f) that further study and analysis of the problem referred to in paragraph (d) above is needed before governments can be prepared to take a definitive position on this matter.
(g) the desirability that all countries should continue to lend special interest and consideration to the feasibility of taking action to ensure that such income is taxable only or primarily in the country in which the income was produced.

2. Replace the operative part by the following:

Notes that the Fiscal Commission plans to continue its study of the problem referred to in paragraph (d) above and anticipates a report on the results of its further studies to the Economic and Social Council after the next meeting of the Fiscal Commission.

R.7 Argentina, Cuba, Egypt, Philippines, Uruguay and Venezuela: Joint Amendments to Draft Resolution B (L.62)[7]

1. Replace paragraph (c) by the following:

That the fact that the taxation levels in force in the under-developed countries are lower than those in capital exporting countries constitutes one of the attractions which under-developed countries offer to foreign capital as an incentive to investment.

2. Add further paragraph (f) to the preamble to read as follows:

(f) that further analysis and factual study of the problem referred to in paragraph (d) above is needed, together with recommendations for practical measures to solve the problem.

3. Replace paragraph 1 by the following:

Notes that the Fiscal Commission plans to continue its study of the problem referred to in paragraph (d) above and anticipates a report on

6 Economic Committee, *Argentina, Cuba, Uruguay and Venezuela: Amendments to the Draft Resolution B (E/2429)*, UN ESC, 16th sess, Agenda item 9, UN Doc E/AC.6/L.61 (6 July 1953).

7 Economic Committee, *Argentina, Cuba, Egypt, Philippines, Uruguay and Venezuela: Joint Amendments to Draft Resolution B (E/2429)*, UN ESC, 16th sess, Agenda item 9, UN Doc E/AC.6/L.62 (6 July 1953).

the results of its further studies to the Economic and Social Council after the next meeting of the Fiscal Commission.

4. Replace paragraph 2 by the following:

Recommends meanwhile, pending the further analysis and factual study of the problem referred to in paragraph (d) above, that the highly developed countries acting unilaterally or when concluding tax agreements should give favourable consideration to the feasibility of taking action to ensure that such income is taxable only or primarily in the country in which the income was produced.

APPENDIX S

ECOSOC Resolution 486B (XVI) (9 July 1953)[1]

486 (XVI). REPORT OF THE FISCAL COMMISSION (FOURTH SESSION)

...

B

International Tax Problems

The Economic and Social Council,

Recognizing:

(a) The great importance of finding means to stimulate the flow of private investment from the highly developed to under-developed countries, in order to accelerate the economic development of the latter,

(b) That the present flow of capital exported to the under-developed countries is insufficient for their development needs,

(c) That relatively lower taxation in force in the under-developed countries, as compared with capital exporting countries, is one of the attractions that under-developed countries may be in a position to offer to foreign capital as an incentive to investment,

(d) That this incentive becomes less effective – although international double taxation is avoided – if the capital-exporting countries apply to the income from investments in under-developed countries any further taxation beyond that already paid in the latter,

(e) That favourable tax treatment is one of the many factors affecting the flow of foreign capital,

(f) That further analysis and factual study of the problem referred to in paragraph (d) above is needed, together with such practical recommendations as may emerge from this further study and analysis,

1. *Notes* that the Fiscal Commission plans to continue its study of the problem referred to in paragraph (d) above and anticipates a report on the

[1] Contained in UN ESCOR, UN Doc 2508 (15 August 1953) 3.

results of its further studies to the Council after the next meeting of the Commission;

2. *Recommends*, meanwhile, that the highly developed countries, acting unilaterally or when concluding tax agreements, should give special consideration to the feasibility of taking action to ensure that such income is taxable only or primarily in the country in which the income was produced.

APPENDIX T

ECOSOC Resolution 557C II (XVIII) (5 August 1954)[1]

557 (XIII). ORGANIZATION AND OPERATION OF THE COUNCIL AND ITS COMMISSIONS

...

C

Functional Commissions

...

II

Fiscal Commission

The Economic and Social Council,

Bearing in mind the major economic and social problems on which the Council should concentrate its attention and efforts in the immediate future,

Recognizing that the fiscal aspects of economic problems are important; that the fiscal work of the United Nations is well established; and that the Secretariat has received adequate guidance from the Fiscal Commission and the Council.

1. *Considers* that the activity of the Fiscal Commission is no longer necessary;
2. *Decides* to discontinue the activity of this Commission.

[1] Contained in UN ESCOR, UN Doc E/2654 (15 August 1954) 24–5.

APPENDIX U

General Assembly Resolution 825 (IX) (11 December 1954)[1]

825 (IX). INTERNATIONAL TAX PROBLEMS

The General Assembly,

Noting that in resolution 486 (XVI) the Economic and Social Council, in addition to establishing the future lines of work of the Secretariat in the fiscal field, stated that it expected a report by the Fiscal Commission on the results of its future studies on the problem of the imposition by capital-exporting countries of any further taxes on the income from investments in under-developed countries beyond those applied by these latter countries,

Considering that, as one of the results of its review of the organization and operation of its commissions, the Economic and Social Council, by resolution 557 C (XVIII), section II, decided to discontinue the activity of the Fiscal Commission before it could complete the studies envisaged under resolution 486 (XVI) mentioned above,

Noting with satisfaction that the Secretary-General intends to continue his studies on the fiscal aspects of economic problems referred to in Economic and Social Council resolutions 486 (XVI) and 557 C (XVIII), section II,

1. *Requests* the Secretary-General:

(a) With a view to accelerating the rate of economic development of under-developed countries, to continue his studies of the taxation by capital-exporting and capital-importing countries on the income from foreign investments, particularly those made in the under-developed countries, making use in such studies of an analysis of replies of Governments to his questionnaire[*] concerning the taxation of foreign nationals, assets and transactions;

(b) To submit his studies to the Economic and Social Council;

[1] Contained in UN Doc A/RES/825(IX) (11 December 1954).

2. *Requests* the Economic and Social Council to consider the reports of the Secretary-General mentioned in paragraph 1 above and to transmit the results of its deliberations to the General Assembly.

---

* See document E/CN.8/W.19.

SELECT BIBLIOGRAPHY

League of Nations Publications

Bruins, GWJ et al, *Report on Double Taxation Submitted to the Financial Committee*, League Doc E.F.S.73.F.19 (League of Nations, 1923)

Carroll, Mitchell B, *Prevention of International Double and Fiscal Evasion: Two Decades of Progress under the League of Nations* (League of Nations, 1939)

Carroll, Mitchell B, *Taxation of Foreign and National Enterprises* (League of Nations, 1933) vol 4: Methods of Allocating Taxable Income

Committee of Technical Experts on Double Taxation and Tax Evasion, *Double Taxation and Tax Evasion: Report*, League Doc C.216.M.85.1927.II (April 1927)

Economic and Financial Committees, *Report to the Council on the Work of the 1943 Joint Session, Princeton, December 1943*, League Doc C.I.M.I.1944.II.A (February 1944)

Economic and Financial Organization, *Conditions of Private Foreign Investment: Report by the Special Joint Committee*, League Doc C.14.M.14.1946.II.A (1946)

Fiscal Committee, *London and Mexico Model Tax Conventions: Commentary and Text*, League Doc C.88.M.88.1946.II.A (November 1946)

Fiscal Committee, *Report on the Work of the Tenth Session*, League Doc C.37.M.37.1946.II.A (25 April 1946)

Fiscal Committee, *Report to the Council on the Fifth Session of the Committee*, League Doc C.252.M.124.1935.II.A (17 June 1935)

Fiscal Committee, *Report to the Council on the Fourth Session of the Committee*, League Doc C.399.M.209.1933.II.A (26 June 1933)

Fiscal Committee, *Report to the Council on the Seventh Session of the Committee*, League Doc C.490.M.331.1937.II.A (16 October 1937)

Fiscal Committee, *Report to the Council on the Work of the Eighth Session of the Committee*, League Doc C.384.M.229.1938.II.A (25 October 1938)

Fiscal Committee, *Report to the Council on the Work of the Ninth Session of the Committee*, League Doc C.181.M.110.1939.II.A (21 June 1939)

Fiscal Committee, *Report to the Council on the Work of the Second Session of the Committee*, League Doc C.340.M.140.1930.II (31 May 1930)

Fiscal Committee, *Report to the Council on the Work of the Third Session of the Committee*, League Doc C.415.M.171.1931.II.A (6 June 1931)

General Meeting of Government Experts on Double Taxation and Tax Evasion, *Double Taxation and Tax Evasion: Report*, League Doc C.562.M.178.1928.II (October 1928)

League of Nations, *Brief Statement on the Activities of the League of Nations and Its Organs in 1940 and 1941, Submitted by the Acting Secretary-General*, League Doc C.41.M.38.1941 (June 1941)

League of Nations, *The League Hands Over* (1946)

League of Nations, *Taxation of Foreign and National Enterprises* (1933) vols 1–3

League of Nations, *Ten Years of World Co-Operation* (1930)

Technical Experts to the Financial Committee of the League of Nations, *Double Taxation and Tax Evasion, Report and Resolutions*, League Doc F.212 (7 February 1925)

United Nations Publications

Alonso, José Antonio, Ana Luiza Cortez and Stephan Klasen, 'LDC and Other Country Groupings: How Useful Are Current Approaches to Classify Countries in a More Heterogeneous Developing World?', UN Doc ST/ESA/2014/CDP/21 (Committee for Development Policy Background Paper No 21, United Nations, September 2014)

Department of Economic Affairs, *Domestic Financing of Economic Development: Methods of Increasing Domestic Savings and of Ensuring Their Most Advantageous Use for the Purpose of Economic Development*, UN Publication Sales No 1951.II.B.1 (United Nations, 1950)

Department of Economic Affairs, *The Effects of Taxation on Foreign Trade and Investment*, UN Doc ST/ECA/1 (United Nations, 1950)

Department of Economic Affairs, *International Flow of Private Capital, 1946–1952*, UN Doc E/2531 (also ST/ECA/22) (United Nations, 1954)

Department of Economic Affairs, *International Tax Agreements*, UN Doc ST/ECA/SER.C/8, Suppl 3 (United Nations, 1968) vol 8: World Guide to International Tax Agreements

Department of Economic Affairs, *Measures for the Economic Development of Under-Developed Countries: Report by a Group of Experts Appointed by the UN Secretary-General*, UN Doc ST/ECA/10 (also E/1986) (United Nations, 1951)

Department of Economic Affairs, *Taxation in Capital-Exporting and Capital-Importing Countries of Foreign Private Investment in Latin America: United States Income Taxation of Private United States Investment in Latin America*, UN Doc ST/ECA/18 (United Nations, 1953)

Department of Economic Affairs, *World Economic Report 1951–52*, UN Doc ST/ECA/19 (United Nations, 1953)

Department of Economic Affairs, Division of Economic Stability and Development, *Methods of Financing Economic Development in Under-Developed Countries*, UN Doc E/1562 (United Nations, 1949)

Department of Economic Affairs, Fiscal Division, *Budgetary Structure and Classification of Government Accounts*, UN Doc ST/ECA/8 (United Nations, 1951)

Department of Economic Affairs, Fiscal Division, *Government Accounting and Budget Execution*, UN Doc ST/ECA/16 (United Nations, 1952)

Department of Economic Affairs, Fiscal Division, *International Tax Agreements*, UN Doc E/CN.8/30 (United Nations, 1948)

Department of Economic Affairs, Fiscal Division, *International Tax Agreements*, UN Doc ST/ECA/SER.C/3 (United Nations, 1951) vol 3: World Guide to International Tax Agreements 1843–1951

Department of Economic Affairs, Fiscal Division, *International Tax Agreements*, UN Doc ST/ECA/SER.C/4 (United Nations, 1954) vol 4

Department of Economic Affairs, Fiscal Division, *International Tax Agreements*, UN Doc ST/ECA/SER.C/5 (United Nations, 1954) vol 5: World Guide to International Tax Agreements

Department of Economic Affairs, Fiscal Division, *Public Debt, 1914–1946*, UN Publication Sales No 1948.XVI.1 (United Nations, 1948)

Department of Economic Affairs, Secretariat of the Economic Commission for Latin America, *Economic Survey of Latin America 1948* (United Nations, 1949)

Department of Economic and Social Affairs, *Guidelines for Tax Treaties between Developed and Developing Countries*, UN Doc ST/ECA/14 (United Nations, 1974)

Department of Economic and Social Affairs, *Manual for the Negotiation of Bilateral Tax Treaties between Developed and Developing Countries*, UN Doc ST/ESA/PAD/SER.E/37 (United Nations, 2003)

Department of Economic and Social Affairs, *Manual for the Negotiation of Bilateral Tax Treaties between Developed and Developing Countries 2019*, UN Doc ST/ESA/PAD/SER.E/M319 (United Nations, 2019)

Department of Economic and Social Affairs, *United Nations Model Double Taxation Convention between Developed and Developing Countries*, UN Doc ST/ESA/PAD/SER.E/21 (United Nations, 2001)

Department of Economic and Social Affairs, *United Nations Model Double Taxation Convention between Developed and Developing Countries*, UN Doc ST/ESA/340 (United Nations, 2011)

Department of Economic and Social Affairs, *United Nations Model Double Taxation Convention between Developed and Developing Countries: 2017 Update*, UN Doc ST/ESA/PAD/SER.E/213 (United Nations, 2017)

Department of Economic and Social Affairs, *World Economic and Social Survey 2017: Reflecting on Seventy Years of Development Policy Analysis*, UN Doc E/2017/50/Rev/1 (also ST/ESA/365) (United Nations, 2017)

Department of International Economic and Social Affairs, *Manual for the Negotiation of Bilateral Tax Treaties between Developed and Developing Countries*, UN Doc ST/ESA/94 (United Nations, 1979)

Department of International Economic and Social Affairs, *United Nations Model Double Taxation Convention between Developed and Developing Countries*, UN Doc ST/ESA/102 (United Nations, 1980)

Department of Public Information, *Yearbook of the United Nations* [1947–1948]

Department of Public Information, *Yearbook of the United Nations* [1948–1949]

Department of Public Information, *Yearbook of the United Nations* [1950]

Department of Public Information, *Yearbook of the United Nations* [1951]

Department of Public Information, *Yearbook of the United Nations* [1952]

Department of Public Information, *Yearbook of the United Nations* [1954]

Department of Public Information, *Yearbook of the United Nations* [1955]

Financial Accountability Transparency & Integrity (FACTI) Panel, *Financial Integrity for Sustainable Development: Report of the High Level Panel on International Financial Accountability, Transparency and Integrity for Achieving the 2030 Agenda* (United Nations, 2021)

Technical Assistance Administration, *Taxes and Fiscal Policy in Under-Developed Countries: A Report Based on Technical Assistance Experience, with Special Reference to Field Missions and to the Technical Assistance Conference on Comparative Fiscal Administration, Geneva, 16–25 July 1951*, UN Doc ST/TAA/M/8 (United Nations, 1955)

Secondary Sources

Aaronson, Susan, 'How Cordell Hull and the Postwar Planners Designed a New Trade Policy' (1991) 20 *Business and Economic History* 171

Adamthwaite, Anthony, 'Overstretched and Overstrung: Eden, the Foreign Office and the Making of Policy, 1951–5' (1988) 64(2) *International Affairs* 241

'Amazing Grace: The Story of WR Grace and Co' (1976) 10(3) *NACLA's Latin America and Empire Report* 3

Andrés Aucejo, Eva, 'The Primary Legal Role of the United Nations on International Tax Cooperation and Global Tax Governance: Going on a New International Organization on Global Tax Cooperation and Governance under the UN "Family"' (2020) 21 *Revista de Educación y Derecho* 31297: 1–34

Appathurai, E, 'Permanent Missions to the United Nations' (1970) 25(2) *International Journal* 287

Arditto, James J, 'State and Local Taxation of Scheduled Local Airlines' (1949) 16(2) *Journal of Air Law and Commerce* 162

Armstrong, David, *The Rise of the International Organisation: A Short History* (Macmillan, 1982)

Avery Jones, John F, 'The UK's Early Tax Treaties with European Countries' in Peter Harris and Dominic de Cogan (eds), *Studies in the History of Tax Law* (Hart, 2017) vol 8, 295

Avi-Yonah, Reuven S, *Advanced Introduction to International Tax Law* (Edward Elgar, 2015)

Avi-Yonah, Reuven S and Haiyan Xu, 'Evaluating BEPS: A Reconsideration of the Benefits Principle and Proposal for UN Oversight' (2016) 6(2) *Harvard Business Law Review* 185

Baker, Philip, *Double Taxation Conventions and International Tax Law: A Manual on the OECD Model Tax Convention on Income and on Capital of 1992* (Sweet & Maxwell, 2nd ed, 1994)

Balloffet, Lily Pearl, 'Argentine and Egyptian History Entangled: From Perón to Nasser' (2018) 50(3) *Journal of Latin American Studies* 549

Benson, Erik, 'The Chosen Instrument? Reconsidering the Early Relationship between Pan American Airways and the US Government' (2004) 22 *Essays in Economic and Business History* 97

Benson, Erik, 'Flying Down to Rio: American Commercial Aviation, the Good Neighbor Policy, and World War Two, 1939–45' (2001) 19(1) *Essays in Economic and Business History* 61

Bertrand, Maurice, *The United Nations: Past, Present and Future* (Kluwer Law International, 1997)

Bird, Richard M, 'Taxing Electronic Commerce: The End of the Beginning?' (2005) 59(4) *Bulletin for International Taxation* 130

Bird, Richard M and Oliver Oldman, *Taxation in Developing Countries* (John Hopkins University Press, 4th ed, 1990)

Blair, Alasdair, *Britain and the World since 1945* (Routledge, 2015)

Blank, Stephen, 'Britain: The Politics of Foreign Economic Policy, the Domestic Economy, and the Problem of Pluralistic Stagnation' (1977) 31(4) *International Organization* 673

Bloch, Henry S and Cyril E Heilemann, 'International Tax Relations' (1946) 55(5) *Yale Law Journal* 1158

Boianovsky, Mauro, 'Beyond Capital Fundamentalism: Harrod, Domar and the History of Development Economics' (2017) 42(2) *Cambridge Journal of Economics* 477

Bowett, DW, *The Law of International Institutions* (Steven, 4th ed, 1982)

Bradley, Mark Philip, 'Decolonization, the Global South, and the Cold War, 1919–1962' in Melvyn P Leffler and Odd Arne Westad (eds), *The Cambridge History of the Cold War* (Cambridge University Press, 2010) vol 1: Origins, 464

Brauner, Yariv, 'An International Tax Regime in Crystallization' (2003) 56(2) *Tax Law Review* 259

Breda dos Santos, Norma, 'Latin American Countries and the Establishment of the Multilateral Trading System: The Havana Conference' (2016) 36(2) *Brazilian Journal of Political Economy* 309

Budhraj, Vijay Sen, 'Major Dimensions of Indo-Soviet Relations' (1975) 31(1) *India Quarterly* 11

Buergenthal, Thomas, *Law-Making in the International Civil Aviation Organization* (Syracuse University Press, 1969)

Bulkeley, J Russell, 'Depoliticizing United Nations Recruitment: Establishing a Genuinely International Civil Service' in Paul Taylor, Sam Daws and Ute Adamczick-Gerteis (eds), *Documents on Reform of the United Nations* (Dartmouth, 1997) 267

Bulmer-Thomas, Victor, *The Economic History of Latin America since Independence* (Cambridge University Press, 2014)

Cain, PJ and AG Hopkins, *British Imperialism: 1688–2015* (Routledge, 2016)

Cárdenas, Emilio J, R Carlos Sersale di Cerisano and Oscar A Avalle, 'Financing the United Nations' Operations: A Frustrating Nightmare' in Harlan Cleveland, Hazel Henderson and Inge Kaul (eds), *The United Nations: Policy and Financing Alternatives: Innovative Proposals by Visionary Leaders* (Elsevier Science, 1995) 145

Cardwell, Curt, *NSC 68 and the Political Economy of the Early Cold War* (Cambridge University Press, 2011)

Carnegie Endowment for International Peace, 'The United States and World Organization during 1939' (1940) 20(June) *International Conciliation* 209

Carroll, Mitchell B et al, 'Report of the Committee on International Double Taxation' [1946] *Proceedings of the Section of International and Comparative Law (American Bar Association)* 40

Carroll, Mitchell B, 'Action on Tax Treatment of Foreign Income at Session of United Nations Fiscal Commission, April 27 to May 8, 1953' (1953) 7(5) *Bulletin for International Fiscal Documentation* 183

Carroll, Mitchell B, 'The Development of International Tax Law: Franco-American Treaty on Double Taxation – Draft Convention on Allocation of Business Income' (1935) 29(4) *The American Journal of International Law* 586

Carroll, Mitchell B, 'Development of International Tax Law in the Americas' (1941) 8(4) *Law and Contemporary Problems* 793

Carroll, Mitchell B, 'Developments in International Tax Law in 1937 – and Suggestions to Protect American Foreign Trade' (1938) 16(2) *The Tax Magazine* 75

Carroll, Mitchell B, 'Germany, Japan and Sweden Show the United States How to Reach Tax Treaties with South American Countries' (1969) 38(2) *George Washington Law Review* 199

Carroll, Mitchell B, *Global Perspectives of an International Tax Lawyer* (Exposition Press, 1978)

Carroll, Mitchell B, 'The Historical Development of Tax Treaties' in Jon E Bischel (ed), *Income Tax Treaties* (Practising Law Institute, 1978) 51

Carroll, Mitchell B, 'IFA's Growth with International Tax Law' (1971) 5(3) *The International Lawyer* 558

Carroll, Mitchell B, 'Income Tax Conventions as an Aid to International Trade and Investment' (1962) 6(3) *Section of International & Comparative Law Bulletin* 16

Carroll, Mitchell B, 'International Double Taxation' (1938) 16(10) *The Tax Magazine* 588

Carroll, Mitchell B, 'International Double Taxation' in Harriet Eager Davies (ed), *Pioneers in World Order: An American Appraisal of the League of Nations* (Columbia University Press, 1944) 171

Carroll, Mitchell B, 'International Tax Law: Benefits for American Investors and Enterprises Abroad: Part I' (1968) 2(4) *The International Lawyer* 692

Carroll, Mitchell B, 'Postwar International Organization and the Work of the Section of International and Comparative Law of the American Bar Association' (1945) 39(1) *The American Journal of International Law* 20

Carroll, Mitchell B, 'Removal of Tax Barriers to American Foreign Trade' (1940) 18(10) *Taxes – The Tax Magazine* 616

Carroll, Mitchell B, 'Report on the Meeting of the United Nations Fiscal Commission, Lake Success, May 7–17, 1951' (1951) 5(5) *Bulletin for International Fiscal Documentation* 309

Carroll, Mitchell B, 'Tax Inducements to Foreign Trade' (1946) 11(4) *Law and Contemporary Problems* 760

Carroll, Mitchell B, 'Tax Trends and Relief for US Companies Trading Abroad' (6 December 1943) *Export Trade and Shipper* 5

Caudill, Shannon W (ed), *Defending Air Bases in an Age of Insurgency* (Air University Press, 2015)

Chase, Eugene Parker, *The United Nations in Action* (McGraw-Hill, 1950)

Chiang, Pei-heng, *Non-Governmental Organizations at the United Nations: Identity, Role, and Function* (Praeger, 1981)

Chrétien, Maxime, 'Contribution a l'Étude du Droit International Fiscal Actuel: Le Rôle des Organizations International dans le Règlement des Questions d'Impôts entre les Divers États' (1954 II) 86 *Recueil des Cours* 5 (Translation: Contribution to the Study of Current International Tax Law: The Role of International Organizations in the Settlement of Tax Matters among Various States)

Christians, Allison, 'BEPS and the New International Tax Order' [2016] (6) *Brigham Young University Law Review* 1603

Christians, Allison, 'Hard Law, Soft Law, and International Taxation' (2007) 25(2) *Wisconsin International Law Journal* 325

Chuang, Richard Y, *The International Air Transport Association: A Case Study of a Quasi-Governmental Organization* (AW Sijthoff, 1972)

Claude Jr, Inis L, *The Changing United Nations* (Random House, 1967)

Claude Jr, Inis L, *Swords into Plowshares: The Problems and Progress of International Organization* (Random House, 4th ed, 1971)

Clavin, Patricia, *Securing the World Economy: The Reinvention of the League of Nations, 1920–1946* (Oxford University Press, 2013)

Cobbs, Elizabeth A, 'Entrepreneurship as Diplomacy: Nelson Rockefeller and the Development of the Brazilian Capital Market' (1989) 63(1) *Business History Review* 88

Cockfield, Arthur J, 'The Rise of the OECD as Informal "World Tax Organization" through National Responses to E-commerce Tax Challenges' (2006) 8 *Yale Journal Law and Technology* 136

Commission on Foreign Economic Policy (United States), *Report to the President and the Congress* (United States Government Printing Office, 1954)

Costanza, Robert et al, 'Beyond GDP: The Need for New Measures of Progress' (The Pardee Papers No 4, The Frederick S Pardee Center for the Study of the Longer-Range Future, Boston University, January 2009)

Court, JF, 'Some Reflections on the Experience of the UN Model in Tax Treaties between Developed and Developing Countries' in International Fiscal Association, *Double Taxation Treaties between Industrialised and Developing Countries: OECD and UN Models, a Comparison* (Kluwer, 1990) 15

Crache, Daniel, 'The Short but Significant Life of the International Trade Organization: Lessons for Our Time' (Working Paper No 62/00, Centre for the Study of Globalisation and Regionalisation, University of Warwick, November 2000)

Crackel, Theodore Joseph, *A History of the Civil Reserve Air Fleet* (Air Force History & Museums Program, 1998)

Cracolici, Maria Francesca, Miranda Cuffaro and Peter Nijkamp, 'The Measurement of Economic, Social and Environmental Performance of Countries: A Novel Approach' (2010) 95(2) *Social Indicators Research* 339

Craig, Campbell, 'The Resurgent Idea of World Government' in Paul F Diehl and Brian Frederking (eds), *The Politics of Global Governance: International Organizations in an Interdependent World* (Lynne Rienner, 4th ed, 2010) 397

Cramer, Gisela and Ursula Prutsch, 'Nelson A. Rockefeller's Office of Inter-American Affairs (1940–1946) and Record Group 229' (2006) 86(4) *Hispanic American Historical Review* 785

Dagan, Tsilly, *International Tax Policy: Between Competition and Cooperation* (Cambridge University Press, 2018)

Dang, Giang and Low Sui Pheng, *Infrastructure Investments in Developing Economies: The Case of Vietnam* (Springer, 2015)

Davies, David R, *Principles of International Double Taxation Relief* (Sweet & Maxwell, 1985)

de Goede, Jan and Fraser Dickinson, 'The UN Model (2001) Special Issue – The Context and Contents' (2012) 66(11) *Bulletin for International Taxation* 587

Deperon, Paul, *International Double Taxation* (Committee on International Economic Policy in cooperation with Carnegie Endowment for International Peace, 1945)

Díaz-Bonilla, Eugenio and María Victoria del Campo, *A Long and Winding Road: The Creation of the Inter-American Development Bank* (Lulu, 2010)

Diehl, Paul F and Brian Frederking, 'Introduction' in Paul F Diehl and Brian Frederking (eds), *The Politics of Global Governance: International Organizations in an Interdependent World* (Lynne Rienner, 4th ed, 2010) 1

Dinkel, Jürgen, *The Non-Aligned Movement: Genesis, Organization and Politics (1927–1992)*, tr Alex Skinner (Brill, 2018)

Dirksen, Willem, *IFA: International Fiscal Association, 1938–1988* (Kluwer Law and Taxation, 1988)

Dobson, Alan, *A History of International Civil Aviation: From Its Origins through Transformative Evolution* (Routledge, 2017)

Dobson, Alan P, 'The Other Air Battle: The American Pursuit of Post-War Civil Aviation Rights' (1985) 28(2) *The Historical Journal* 429

Domhoff, G William, 'The Council on Foreign Relations and the Grand Area: Case Studies on the Origins of the IMF and the Vietnam War' (2014) 2(1) *Class, Race and Corporate Power* 1: 1–41

Dosman, Edgar J, *The Life and Times of Raúl Prebisch, 1901–1986* (McGill-Queen's University Press, 2008)

Dubin, Martin D, 'Towards the Bruce Report' in UN Library/Graduate Institute of International Studies, *The League of Nations in Retrospect: Proceedings of the Symposium* (Walter de Gruyter, 1983) 59

Engel, Jeffrey A, *Cold War at 30,000 Feet: The Anglo-American Fight for Aviation Supremacy* (Harvard University Press, 2007)

Escudé, Carlos, 'The US Destabilization and Economic Boycott of Argentina of the 1940s, Revisited' (Serie de Documentos de Trabjo No 323, Área de Ciencia Polílitica, Universidad del CEMA, July 2006)

Falk, Richard, 'Explaining the UN's Unhappy 50th Anniversary: Toward Reclaiming the Next Half-Century' in Dimitris Bourantonis and Marios Evriviades (eds), *A United Nations for the Twenty-First Century: Peace, Security and Development* (Kluwer Law International, 1996) 89

Farrell, Jennifer E, *The Interface of International Trade Law and Taxation* (International Bureau for Fiscal Documentation, 2013)

Figueroa, AH, 'Comprehensive Tax Treaties' in International Fiscal Association, *Double Taxation Treaties between Industrialised and Developing Countries: OECD and UN Models, a Comparison* (Kluwer, 1990) 9

FitzGerald, EVK, 'ECLA and the Formation of Latin American Economic Doctrine' in David Rock (ed), *Latin America in the 1940s: War and Postwar Transitions* (University of California Press, 1994) 89

Ford, Alan, 'The Secretariat' in BA Wortley (ed), *The United Nations: The First Ten Years* (Oceana, 1957) 81

Friedlander, Lara and Scott Wilkie, 'Policy Forum: The History of Tax Treaty Provisions – and Why It Is Important to Know About It' (2006) 54(4) *Canadian Tax Journal* 907

Fusfeld, Daniel R, 'Economics and the Cold War: An Inquiry into the Relationship between Ideology and Theory' (1998) 32(2) *Journal of Economic Issues* 505

Futrell, Robert Frank, *The United States Air Force in Korea, 1950–1953* (Office of Air Force History, United States Air Force, rev ed, 1983)

Gaddis, John Lewis, 'The Corporatist Synthesis: A Skeptical View' (1986) 10(4) *Diplomatic History* 357

Gardner, Richard N, 'Review: Report to the President and the Congress (Randall Report) by The Commission on Foreign Economic Policy' (1954) 63(5) *The Yale Law Journal* 751

Getchell, Michelle Denise, 'Revisiting the 1954 Coup in Guatemala' (2015) 17(2) *Journal of Cold War Studies* 73

Gilderhus, Mark T, 'An Emerging Synthesis? US–Latin American Relations since the Second World War' in Michael J Hogan (ed), *America in the World: The Historiography of American Foreign Relations since 1941* (Cambridge University Press, 1995) 424

Gilpin, Robert, *US Power and the Multinational Corporation: The Political Economy of Foreign Direct Investment* (Macmillan Press, 1975)

Glazebrook, G deT, 'The Middle Powers in the United Nations System' (1947) 1(2) *International Organization* 307

Goldman, Marvin G, *El Al: Israel's Flying Star* (rev ed, 2020), available at *Israel Airline Museum* (Web Page) <www.israelairlinemuseum.org/el-al-israels-flying-star>

Goodrich, Leland M, *The United Nations* (Thomas Y Cromwell, 1959)

Goodspeed, Stephen S, *The Nature and Function of International Organization* (Oxford University Press, 2nd ed, 1967)

Gordon, Nathan N, 'The Role of Tax Treaties' (1965) 46(7) *Taxes – The Tax Magazine* 463

Gordon, Nathan N, 'The Second Session of the United Nations Fiscal Commission' (1949) 2(2) *National Tax Journal* 166

Gormly, James, 'The Counter Iron Curtain: Crafting an American-Soviet Bloc Civil Aviation Policy: 1942–1960' (2013) 37(2) *Diplomatic History* 248

Grady, Henry F, 'World Economics' in Harriet Eager Davis (ed), *Pioneers in World Order: An American Appraisal of the League of Nations* (Columbia University Press, 1944) 156

Graetz, Michael J and Michael M O'Hear, 'The "Original Intent" of US International Taxation' (1997) 46(5) *Duke Law Journal* 1021

Graff, Michael, AG Kenwood and AL Lougheed, *Growth of the International Economy, 1820–2015* (Routledge, 5th ed, 2014)

Gray, Gordon, *Report to the President on Foreign Economic Policies* (United States Government Printing Office, 1950)

Gregg, Robert W, 'UN Economic, Social, and Technical Activities' in James Barros (ed), *The United Nations: Past, Present and Future* (The Free Press, 1972) 218

Gregg, Robert W, 'The UN Regional Economic Commissions and Integration in the Underdeveloped Regions' (1966) 20(2) *International Organization* 208

Grimm, Kevin E, 'Eisenhower and the Third World' in Chester J Pach (ed), *A Companion to Dwight D Eisenhower* (Wiley-Blackwell, 2017) 473

Group of Twenty Finance Ministers and Central Bank Governors, *Italian G20 Presidency: Second G20 Finance Ministers and Central Bank Governors Meeting – Communiqué* (G20 Italia 2021, 7 April 2021)

Hagen, James M and Vernon W Ruttan, 'Development Policy under Eisenhower and Kennedy' (1988) 23(1) *The Journal of Developing Areas* 1

Hammarskjöld, Dag, 'The International Civil Servant in Law and Fact' in Robert W Gregg and Michael Barkun (eds), *The United Nations System and Its Functions: Selected Readings* (D Van Nostrand, 1968) 215

Hanhimäki, Jussi M, *The United Nations: A Very Short Introduction* (Oxford University Press, 2008)

Harris, Peter and David Oliver, *International Commercial Tax* (Cambridge University Press, 2010)

Harris, Peter Andrew, *Corporate/Shareholder Income Taxation and Allocating Taxing Rights between Countries: A Comparison of Imputation Systems* (International Bureau for Fiscal Documentation, 1996)

Haynes, Jeff, *Politics in the Developing World: A Concise Introduction* (Blackwell, 2002)

Haynes, Jeff, *Third World Politics: A Concise Introduction* (Blackwell, 1996)

Hearson, Martin, *Imposing Standards: The North–South Dimension to Global Tax Politics* (Cornell University Press, 2021)

Henrikson, Alan K, 'Great Powers, Superpowers, and Global Powers: Managerial Succession for a New World Order' in Dimitris Bourantonis and Marios Evriviades (eds), *A United Nations for the Twenty-First Century: Peace, Security and Development* (Kluwer Law International, 1996) 65

Herring Jr, George C, 'The United States and British Bankruptcy, 1944–1945: Responsibilities Deferred' (1971) 86(2) *Political Science Quarterly* 260

Herzfeld, Mindy, 'The Case against BEPS: Lessons for Tax Coordination' (2017) 21(1) *Florida Tax Review* 1

Hettne, Björn, 'The Development of Development Theory' (1983) 26(3/4) *Acta Sociologica* 247

Hinds, Allister E, 'Imperial Policy and Colonial Sterling Balances, 1943–56' (1991) 19(1) *The Journal of Imperial and Commonwealth History* 24

Hofman, André A, *The Economic Development of Latin America in the Twentieth Century* (Edward Elgar, 2000)

Hogan, Michael J (ed), *The Ambiguous Legacy: US Foreign Relations in the 'American Century'* (Cambridge University Press, 1999)

Hogg, Roy D, 'Canada–US Tax Relations' (1995) 43(5) *Canadian Tax Journal* 1547

Holcombe, Randall G and Russell S Sobel, 'The Stability of International Coalitions in United Nations Voting from 1946 to 1973' (1996) 86(1/2) *Public Choice* 17

Houston, John A, *Latin America in the United Nations* (Carnegie Endowment for International Peace, 1956)

Hovet Jr, Thomas, *Bloc Politics in the United Nations* (Harvard University Press, 1960)

Hubbard, Ursula Phalla, 'The Cooperation of the United States with the League of Nations, 1931–1936' (1937) 18(April) *International Conciliation* 295

Humphreys, RA, *Latin America and the Second World War* (Athlone Press, 1982) vol 2: 1942–1945

Hune, Shirley and Jayantha Dhanapala, 'Non-Aligned Movement' in Joel Krieger (ed), *The Oxford Companion to International Relations* (Oxford University Press, 2014) [e-Resource]

'The Ins and Outs of IATA: Improving the Role of the United States in the Regulation of International Air Fares' (1972) 81(6) *The Yale Law Journal* 1102

'The Inter-American Bar Association: Resolutions of the XXX Conference' (1993) 25(1) *The University of Miami Inter-American Law Review* 161

'Inter-American Council of Commerce and Production' in Union of International Associations, *Yearbook of International Organizations* (Brill, 2007) [e-Resource]

'The Inter-American Economic and Social Council' (1946) 80(1) *Bulletin of the Pan American Union* 12

Interim Committee to Consultative Non-Governmental Organizations, *Consultation between the United Nations and Non-Governmental Organizations*, United Nations Studies 3 (Carnegie Endowment for International Peace, December 1949)

International Chamber of Commerce, *Settlement of Difficulties and Disputes Arising Out of Double Taxation Agreements: Statement Adopted by the Executive Committee of the ICC (February 1959) and Report of Its Commission on Taxation* (1959)

International Development Advisory Board (United States), *Partners in Progress: A Report to the President by the International Development Advisory Board* (United States Government Printing Office, 1951)

International Fiscal Association, *International Fiscal Association Resolutions Book* (International Bureau for Fiscal Documentation, 1988)

Irogbe, Kema, 'Global Political Economy and the Power of Multinational Corporations' (2013) 30(2) *Journal of Third World Studies* 223

Isenbergh, Joseph, *International Taxation* (Foundation Press, 3rd ed, 2000)

Jogarajan, Sunita, *Double Taxation and the League of Nations in the 1920s* (Cambridge University Press, 2018)

Johnston, Stephanie Soong, 'Argentina Says Global Tax Deal is Bad for Developing Nations' (11 October 2021) 104 *Tax Notes International* 224

Jolly, Richard, Louis Emmerij and Dharam Ghai, *UN Contributions to Development Thinking and Practice* (Indiana University Press, 2004)

Kedar, Claudia, *The International Monetary Fund and Latin America: The Argentine Puzzle in Context* (Temple University Press, 2013)

Kennedy, Dane, *Decolonization: A Very Short Introduction* (Oxford University Press, 2016)

Keohane, Robert O, 'Observations on the Promise and Pitfalls of Historical Institutionalism in International Relations' in Orfeo Fioretos (ed), *International Politics and Institutions in Time* (Oxford University Press, 2017) 321

Kimball, Warren F, 'Lend-Lease and the Open Door: The Temptation of British Opulence, 1937–1942' (1971) 86(2) *Political Science Quarterly* 232

Kochanek, Stanley A, 'India's Changing Role in the United Nations' (1980) 53(1) *Pacific Affairs* 48

Kolko, Gabriel, *Confronting the Third World: United States Foreign Policy, 1945–1980* (Pantheon Books, 1988)

Krozewski, Gerold, *Money and the End of Empire: British International Economic Policy and the Colonies, 1947–58* (Palgrave, 2001)

Kust, Matthew J, 'Tax Treaties with the Underindustrialized Countries' (1961) 13(3) *Tax Executive* 175

Layton, Azza Salama, 'International Pressures and the US Government's Response to Little Rock' (1997) 56(3) *The Arkansas Historical Quarterly* 257

Leigh-Phippard, Helen, *Congress and US Military Aid to Britain: Interdependence and Dependence, 1949–56* (St Martin's Press in association with Palgrave Macmillan, 1995)

Lennard, Michael, 'The Purpose and Current Status of the United Nations Tax Work' (2008) 14(1) *Asia-Pacific Tax Bulletin* 23

Leslie, John C, 'International Air Transport Association: Some Historical Notes' (1971) 13(3/4) *Journal of Interamerican Studies and World Affairs* 319

Lewis, W Arthur, 'The Economic and Security Council' in BA Wortley (ed), *The United Nations: The First Ten Years* (Oceana, 1957) 34

Lie, Trygve, 'Summary of Work of the United Nations' (1946) 32(9) *American Bar Association Journal* 553

Lindholm, Richard W, *Public Finance of Air Transportation: A Study of Taxation and Public Expenditures in Relation to a Developing Industry* (Ohio State University, 1948)

Little, IMD and JM Clifford, *International Aid: The Flow of Public Resources from Rich to Poor Countries* (Routledge, 2017)

Loveday, Alexander, 'An Unfortunate Decision' (1947) 1(2) *International Organization* 279

Luard, Evan, *A History of the United Nations* (Macmillan Press, 1982) vol 1: The Years of Western Domination, 1945–1955

Luard, Evan, *The Management of the World Economy* (Macmillan Press, 1983)

Luard, Evan, *The United Nations: How It Works and What It Does* (Palgrave Macmillan, 1979)

Luck, Edward C, 'Reforming the United Nations: Lessons from a History of Progress' in Paul F Diehl and Brian Frederking (eds), *The Politics of Global Governance: International Organizations in an Interdependent World* (Lynne Rienner, 4th ed, 2010) 366

Lundestad, Geir, *East, West, North, South: International Relations since 1945* (Sage, 7th ed, 2014)

Lundestad, Geir, '"Empire by Invitation" in the American Century' in Michael J Hogan (ed), *The Ambiguous Legacy: US Foreign Relations in the 'American Century'* (Cambridge University Press, 1999) 52

Macekura, Stephen, 'The Point Four Program and US International Development Policy' (2013) 128(1) *Political Science Quarterly* 127

Machlup, Fritz, *A History of Thought on Economic Integration* (Macmillan Press, 1977)

MacKenzie, David, *ICAO: A History of the International Civil Aviation Organization* (University of Toronto Press, 2010)

Maisto, Guglielmo, 'The History of Article 8 of the OECD Model Treaty on Taxation of Shipping and Air Transport' (2003) 31(6/7) *Intertax* 232

Malinowski, WR, 'Centralization and Decentralization in the United Nations Economic and Social Activities' (1962) 16(3) *International Organization* 521

Manzer, Ronald A, 'The United Nations Special Fund' (1964) 18(4) *International Organization* 766

Margold, Stella K, 'The National Foreign Trade Council Convention, 1939' (1939) 102(4) *World Affairs* 208

Mason, Ruth, 'The Transformation of International Tax' (2020) 114(3) *The American Journal of International Law* 353

Maurer, Noel, *The Empire Trap: The Rise and Fall of US Intervention to Protect American Property Overseas, 1893–2013* (Princeton University Press, 2013)

Mayo, Anthony J and Nitin Nohria, *In Their Time: The Greatest Business Leaders of the Twentieth Century* (Harvard Business School Press, 2005)

McArthur, John W and Eric Werker, 'Developing Countries and International Organizations: Introduction to the Special Issue' (2016) 11(2) *Review of International Organisations* 155

McCann, Frank D, 'Brazil, the United States, and World War II: A Commentary' (1979) 3(1) *Diplomatic History* 59

McCann, Frank D, *Brazil and the United States during World War II and Its Aftermath: Negotiating Alliance and Balancing Giants* (Palgrave Macmillan, 2018)

McIntyre, Michael J, 'Developing Countries and International Cooperation on Income Tax Matters: An Historical Review' (Unpublished manuscript, 2005)

McKenzie, Francine, 'Imperial Solutions to International Crises: Alliances, Trade and the Ottawa Imperial Economic Conference of 1932' in John Fisher, Effie GH Pedaliu and Richard Smith (eds), *The Foreign Office, Commerce and British Foreign Policy in the Twentieth Century* (Palgrave Macmillan, 2016) 165

McQuaid, Kim, 'Corporate Liberalism in the American Business Community, 1920–1940' (1978) 52(3) *Business History Review* 342

Meers, Sharon I, 'The British Connection: How the United States Covered Its Tracks in the 1954 Coup in Guatemala' (1992) 16(3) *Diplomatic History* 409

Megzari, Abdelaziz, *The Internal Justice of the United Nations: A Critical History 1945–2015* (Brill Nijhoff, 2015)

Menzies, A Alexander, 'Technical Assistance and the League of Nations' in UN Library/Graduate Institute of International Studies, *The League of Nations in Retrospect: Proceedings of the Symposium* (Walter de Gruyter, 1983) 295

Messere, Ken, 'The 1992 OECD Model Treaty: The Precursors and Successors of the New OECD Model Taxation Convention on Income and Capital' (1993) 33(8) *European Taxation* 246

Mhlanga, Oswald and JN Steyn, 'The Aviation Industry in South Africa: A Historical Overview' (2016) 5(4) *African Journal of Hospitality, Tourism and Leisure* 1

Miller, Karen, '"Air Power is Peace Power" The Aircraft Industry's Campaign for Public and Political Support, 1943–1949' (1996) 70(3) *Business History Review* 297

Miller, Rory M, 'Economic Nationalism and British Investments in Post-War Latin America, 1945–1970' in Thomas C Mills and Rory M Miller (eds), *Britain and the Growth of US Hegemony in Twentieth-Century Latin America: Competition, Cooperation and Coexistence* (Palgrave Macmillan, 2020) 151

Mills, Thomas C, 'British Industry and US–UK Economic Diplomacy during the Second World War' in John Fisher, Effie GH Pedaliu and Richard Smith (eds), *The Foreign Office, Commerce and British Foreign Policy in the Twentieth Century* (Palgrave Macmillan, 2016) 233

Mitchell, Donald, 'Strategy of the Mediterranean' (1955) 29(168) *Current History* 65

Mutén, Leif, 'Double Taxation Conventions between Industrialised and Developing Countries' in International Fiscal Association, *Double Taxation Treaties between Industrialised and Developing Countries: OECD and UN Models, a Comparison* (Kluwer, 1990) 3

Myint-U, Thant and Amy Scott, *The UN Secretariat: A Brief History (1945–2006)* (International Peace Academy, 2007)

Nachmani, Amikam, 'Civil War and Foreign Intervention in Greece: 1946–49' (1990) 25(4) *Journal of Contemporary History* 489

Naor, Moshe, 'Israel's 1948 War of Independence as a Total War' (2008) 43(2) *Journal of Contemporary History* 241

Nayar, Baldev Raj, 'Regimes, Power, and International Aviation' (1995) 49(1) *International Organization* 139

Oei, Shu-Yi and Diane Ring, 'Leak-Driven Law' (2018) 65(3) *UCLA Law Review* 532

Olden, Herman and Paul Phillips, 'The Point Four Program: Promise or Menace?' (1952) 16(3) *Science and Society* 222

Organisation for Economic Co-operation and Development, *Fiscal Incentives for Private Investment in Developing Countries: Report of the Fiscal Committee* (1965)

Organisation for Economic Co-operation and Development, *Model Tax Convention on Income and on Capital 2017 (Full Version)* (2019)

Organisation for Economic Co-operation and Development, *OECD Secretary-General Tax Report to G20 Finance Ministers and Central Bank Governors – April 2021* (2021)

Organisation for Economic Co-operation and Development, *OECD/G20 Base Erosion and Profit Shifting Project: Explanatory Statement* (2015)

Organisation for Economic Co-operation and Development, *Tax Challenges Arising from Digitalisation – Economic Impact Assessment* (2020)

Organisation for Economic Co-operation and Development, *Tax Challenges Arising from Digitalisation – Report on Pillar One Blueprint* (2020)

Organisation for Economic Co-operation and Development, *Tax Challenges Arising from Digitalisation – Report on Pillar Two Blueprint* (2020)

Organisation for Economic Co-operation and Development, *Two-Part Report to G20 Developing Working Group on the Impact of BEPS in Low Income Countries* (2014)

Paez, Sarah, 'OECD Global Tax Agreement Draws Mixed Reactions' (18 October 2021) 104 *Tax Notes International* 342

Parmar, Inderjeet, *Foundations of the American Century: The Ford, Carnegie, & Rockefeller Foundations in the Rise of American Power* (Colombia University Press, 2012)

Paterson, Thomas G, *Soviet-American Confrontation: Postwar Reconstruction and the Origins of the Cold War* (Johns Hopkins University Press, 1973)

Perez Cubillas, José, 'New Decisions of Fiscal Commission: Review of Third Session' (1951) 10(12) *United Nations Bulletin* 598

Picciotto, Sol, *International Business Taxation* (Quorum Books, 1992)

Piglia, Melina, '"Carry Our Colours and Defend Our Interests under the Skies of Other Continents". Argentinian Commercial Aviation Policy in the *Peronista* Decade (1945–1955)' (2019) 40(1) *The Journal of Transport History* 44

Pires, Manuel, *International Juridical Double Taxation of Income* (Kluwer Law and Taxation, 1989)

Porcile, Gabriel, 'The Challenge of Cooperation: Argentina and Brazil, 1939–1955' (1995) 27(1) *Journal of Latin American Studies* 129

Pötgens, Frank, *Income from International Private Employment* (International Bureau for Fiscal Documentation, 2006)

Pratt, Julius W, *A History of the United States Foreign Policy* (Prentice-Hall, 3rd ed, 1972)

President's Air Policy Commission, *Survival in the Air Age: A Report by the President's Air Policy Commission* (United States Government Printing Office, 1948)

Qureshi, NM, 'Tax Treaty Needs of Developing Countries' in International Fiscal Association, *UN Draft Model Taxation Convention* (Kluwer, 1979) 31

Rabe, Stephen G, 'Eisenhower and Latin America' in Chester J Pach (ed), *A Companion to Dwight D Eisenhower* (Wiley-Blackwell, 2017) 435

Rabe, Stephen G, 'The Elusive Conference: United States Economic Relations with Latin America, 1945–1952' (1978) 2(3) *Diplomatic History* 279

Rappard, William E, 'Small States in the League of Nations' (1934) 49(4) *Political Science Quarterly* 544

Rawnsley, Gary D, *Cold-War Propaganda in the 1950s* (MacMillan Press, 1999)

Reimer, Ekkehart and Alexander Rust (eds), *Klaus Vogel on Double Taxation Conventions* (Kluwer Law International, 4th ed, 2015) vol 1

Reinalda, Bob, 'Institutional Development of the United Nations Secretariat' (2020) 26(2) *Global Governance* 325

Reinalda, Bob, *Routledge History of International Organizations: From 1815 to the Present Day* (Routledge, 2009)

Ridgeway, George L, *Merchants of Peace: Twenty Years of Business Diplomacy through the International Chamber of Commerce, 1919–1938* (Columbia University Press, 1938)

Ring, Diane M, 'Who is Making International Tax Policy? International Organizations as Power Players in a High Stakes World' (2010) 33(3) *Fordham International Law Journal* 649

Rivas, Darlene, *Missionary Capitalist: Nelson Rockefeller in Venezuela* (University of North Carolina Press, 2002)

Rivas, Darlene, 'United States–Latin American Relations, 1942–1960' in Robert D Schulzinger (ed), *A Companion to American Foreign Relations* (Blackwell, 2006) 230

Rixen, Thomas, 'Historical Institutionalism and International Relations' in Thomas Rixen, Lora Anne Viola and Michael Zürn (eds), *Historical Institutionalism and International Relations: Explaining Institutional Development in World Politics* (Oxford University Press, 2016) 3

Roberts, Priscilla May (ed), *The Cold War: Interpreting Conflict through Primary Documents* (ABC-CLIO, 2019) vol 1: 1917–1957

Robertson, Paul L and John Singleton, 'The Commonwealth as an Economic Network' (2001) 41(3) *Australian Economic History Review* 241

Rock, David, 'War and Postwar Intersections: Latin America and the United States' in David Rock (ed), *Latin America in the 1940s* (University of California Press, 1994) 15

Rodriguez, Louis J, 'A Comparison: United States Economic Relations with Argentina and Brazil, 1947–1960' (LSU Historical Dissertations and Theses No 854, Louisiana State University and Agricultural & Mechanical College, 1963)

Rohatgi, Roy, *Basic International Taxation* (BNA International, 2nd ed, 2005)

Rosenbloom, H David, Noam Noked and Mohamed S Helal, 'The Unruly World of Tax: A Proposal for an International Tax Cooperation Forum' (2014) 15(2) *Florida Tax Review* 57

Rostow, WW, *The Stages of Economic Growth: A Non-Communist Manifesto* (Cambridge University Press, 1960)

Salem, Paul, 'The Middle East: Evolution of a Broken Regional Order' (Carnegie Paper No 9, Carnegie Middle East Centre, June 2008)

Sasseville, Jacques, 'Historical Background of Proposed Changes to Articles 8 and 15(3) OECD Model' in Guglielmo Maisto (ed), *Taxation of Shipping and Air Transport in Domestic Law, EU Law and Tax Treaties* (International Bureau for Fiscal Documentation, 2017) 73

Scammell, WM, *The International Economy since 1945* (Macmillan, 2nd ed, 1983)

Schenkman, Jacob, *International Civil Aviation Organization* (Librairie E Droz, 1955)

Schnabel, James F and Robert J Watson, *The Joint Chiefs of Staff and National Policy* (Office of Joint History, Office of the Chairman of the Joint Chiefs of Staff, 1998) vol 3: 1950–1951

Schrecker, Ellen, 'McCarthyism: Political Repression and the Fear of Communism' (2004) 71(4) *Social Research* 1041

Schrijver, Nico, *Sovereignty over National Resources: Balancing Rights and Duties* (Cambridge University Press, 1997)

Shaw, D John, 'Turning Point in the Evolution of Soft Financing: The United Nations and the World Bank' (2005) 26(1) *Canadian Journal of Development Studies* 43

Simons, Graham M, *Olympic Airways: A History* (Air World, 2019)

Simontacchi, Stefano, *Taxation of Capital Gains under the OECD Model Convention: With Special Regard to Immovable Property* (Kluwer, 2007)

Singer, Hans W and Javed A Ansari, *Rich and Poor Countries* (Allen & Unwin, 2nd ed, 1978)

Smith, Joseph, *The United States and Latin America: A History of American Diplomacy, 1776–2000* (Routledge, 2005)

Sochor, Eugene, 'International Civil Aviation and the Third World: How Fair is the System?' (1988) 10(3) *Third World Quarterly* 1300

Solarz, Marcin Wojciech, '"Third World": The 60th Anniversary of a Concept that Changed History' (2012) 33(9) *Third World Quarterly* 1561

Spellacy, Amy, 'Mapping the Metaphor of the Good Neighbor: Geography, Globalism, and Pan-Americanism during the 1940s' (2006) 47(2) *American Studies* 39

Spero, Joan E and Jeffrey A Hart, *The Politics of International Economic Relations* (Routledge, 5th ed, 1997)

Steiner, Zara, 'Introductory Essay' in United Nations Library/Graduate Institute of International Studies, *The League of Nations in Retrospect: Proceedings of the Symposium* (Walter de Gruyter, 1983) 1

Stinsky, Daniel, 'Western European vs All-European Cooperation? The OEEC, the European Recovery Program, and the United Nations Economic Commission for Europe (ECE), 1947–1952' in Matthieu Leimgruber and Matthias Schmelzer (eds), *The OECD and the International Political Economy since 1948* (Palgrave Macmillan, 2017) 65

Streets-Salter, Heather and Trevor R Getz, *Empires and Colonies in the Modern World: A Global Perspective* (Oxford University Press, 2016)

Sweetster, Arthur, 'The Non-Political Achievements of the League' (1940) 19(1) *Foreign Affairs* 179

Szirmai, Adam, *The Dynamics of Socio-Economic Development: An Introduction* (Cambridge University Press, 2005)

Taylor, C John, '"I Suppose I Must Have More Discussion on This Dreary Subject": The Negotiation and Drafting of the UK–Australia Double Taxation Treaty of 1946' in John Tiley (ed), *Studies in the History of Tax Law* (Hart, 2010) vol 4, 213

Teichert, Pedro CM, 'The Development of Argentina's Four State Fleets' (1959) 82 *Weltwirtschaftliches Archiv* 313

Thorp, Rosemary, 'The Latin American Economies in the 1940s' in David Rock (ed), *Latin America in the 1940s* (University of California Press, 1994) 41

Thuronyi, Victor, *Comparative Tax Law* (Kluwer Law International, 2003)

Titlow, Richard E, 'International Double Taxation and the United States' (1968) 46(3) *Taxes – The Tax Magazine* 135

Todaro, Michael P and Stephen C Smith, *Economic Development* (Pearson, 12th ed, 2015)

Tournès, Ludovic, 'The Rockefeller Foundation and the Transition from the League of Nations to the UN (1939–1946)' (2014) 12(3) *Journal of Modern European History* 323

Tourtellot, Christopher T, 'Membership Criteria for the ICAO Council: A Proposal for Reform' (1981) 11(1) *Denver Journal of International Law and Policy* 51

Toussaint, Eric, *The World Bank: A Critical Primer*, tr Elizabeth Anne et al, ed Sylvain Dropsy (Pluto Press, 2008)

Toye, John and Richard Toye, *UN and Global Political Economy: Trade, Finance, and Development* (Indiana University Press, 2004)

Trask, Roger R, 'Spruille Braden versus George Messersmith: World War II, the Cold War, and Argentine Policy, 1945–1947' (1984) 26(1) *Journal of Interamerican Studies and World Affairs* 69

Tsakaloyannis, Panos, 'International Society at a Crossroads: The Problem of Conceptualization' in Dimitris Bourantonis and Marios Evriviades (eds), *A United Nations for the Twenty-First Century: Peace, Security and Development* (Kluwer Law International, 1996) 19

United States Department of State, *Foreign Relations of the United States: Diplomatic Papers, 1945* (United States Government Printing Office, 1967) vol 1: General: The United Nations

United States Department of State, *Foreign Relations of the United States, 1946* (United States Government Printing Office, 1972) vol 1: General: The United Nations

United States Department of State, *Foreign Relations of the United States, 1948* (United States Government Printing Office, 1976) vol 1, pt 2: General: The United Nations

United States Department of State, *Foreign Relations of the United States, 1950* (United States Government Printing Office, 1977) vol 1: National Security Affairs; Foreign Economic Policy

United States Department of State, *Foreign Relations of the United States, 1950* (United States Government Printing Office, 1976) vol 2: The United Nations; The Western Hemisphere

United States Department of State, *Foreign Relations of the United Sates, 1950* (United States Government Printing Office, 1977) vol 3: Western Europe

United States Department of State, *Foreign Relations of the United States, 1950* (United States Government Printing Office, 1978) vol 5: The Near East, South Asia, and Africa

United States Department of State, *Foreign Relations of the United States, 1951* (United States Government Printing Office, 1979) vol 2: The United Nations; The Western Hemisphere

United States Department of State, *Foreign Relations of the United States, 1952–1954* (United States Government Printing Office, 1983) vol 1, pt 1: General: Economic and Political Matters

United States Department of State, *Foreign Relations of the United States, 1952–1954* (United States Government Printing Office, 1983) vol 1, pt 2: General: Economic and Political Matters

United States Department of State, *Foreign Relations of the United States, 1952–1954* (United States Government Printing Office, 1979) vol 3: United Nations Affairs

United States Department of State, *Foreign Relations of the United States, 1952–1954* (United States Government Printing Office, 1983) vol 4: The American Republics

United States Department of State, *Foreign Relations of the United States, 1952–1954* (United States Government Printing Office, 1983) vol 11, pt 1: Africa and South Asia

United States Department of State, *International Civil Aviation, 1945–1948* (United States Government Printing Office, 1948)

United States Department of State, *Postwar Foreign Policy Preparation 1939–1945* (United States Government Printing Office, 1949)

United States Department of the Treasury, *Made in America Tax Plan* (Report, April 2021)

United States Senate Finance Committee, *Overhauling International Taxation: A Framework to Invest in the American People by Ensuing Multinational Corporations Pay Their Fair Share* (Report, April 2021)

Urquhart, Brian, *Hammarskjold* (The Bodley Head, 1972)

Van den Tempel, AJ, *Relief from Double Taxation* (International Bureau for Fiscal Documentation, 1967)

Van der Waag-Cowling, NM, 'South Africa and the Korean War, the Politics of Involvement' (2016) 44(1) *Scientia Militaria* 224

Van Vleck, Jenifer, *Empire of the Air: Aviation and the American Ascendency* (Harvard University Press, 2013)

Vann, Richard, 'Current Trends in Balancing Residence and Source Taxation' in Yariv Brauner and Pasquale Pistone (eds), *BRICS and the Emergence of International Tax Coordination* (International Bureau for Fiscal Documentation, 2015) 367

Vann, Richard, 'International Tax Policy and International Tax Institutions: Never the Twain?' in Guglielmo Maisto (ed), *Current Tax Treaty Issues: 50th Anniversary of the International Tax Group* (International Bureau for Fiscal Documentation, 2020) 41

Vann, Richard, 'Travellers, Tax Policy and Agency Permanent Establishments' [2010] (6) *British Tax Review* 538

Vann, Richard J, 'A Model Tax Treaty for the Asian-Pacific Region?' (1991) 45(3) *Bulletin for International Fiscal Documentation* 99

Vital, David, *The Inequality of States: A Study of the Small Power in International Relations* (Clarendon Press, 1967)

Vonyó, Tamás, 'Post-War Reconstruction and the Golden Age of Economic Growth' (2008) 12(2) *European Review of Economic History* 221

Wager, Walter H, 'The Air Coordinating Committee' (1949) 2(4) *Air University Quarterly Review* 17

Wang, Ke Chin, 'International Double Taxation of Income: Relief through International Agreement 1921–1945' (1945) 59(1) *Harvard Law Review* 73

Weber, Ludwig, *International Civil Aviation Organization (ICAO)* (Kluwer Law International, 2015)

Weiss, Thomas G et al, *The United Nations and Changing World Politics* (Routledge, 8th ed, 2017)

Weiss, Thomas G, Ramesh Thakur and John Gerard Ruggie, *Global Governance and the UN: An Unfinished Journey* (Indiana University Press, 2010)

Weiss, Thomas G, Tatiana Carayannis and Richard Jolly, 'The Third United Nations' (2009) 15(1) *Global Governance* 123

Wells, Bret and Cym Lowell, 'Tax Base Erosion and Homeless Income: Collection at Source Is the Linchpin' (2012) 65(3) *Tax Law Review* 535

Wells, Hermon Manning, 'United States Policies in International Double Taxation of Income' (Thesis No 74, Graduate Institute of International Studies, University of Geneva, 1950)

Wells, Sidney, 'The Developing Countries GATT and UNCTAD' (1969) 45(1) *International Affairs* 64

White, Christopher M, *A Global History of the Developing World* (Routledge, 2014)

White, Nicholas J, *Decolonisation: The British Experience since 1945* (Routledge, 2nd ed, 2014)

Wilkins, Mira and Frank Ernest Hill, *American Business Abroad: Ford on Six Continents* (Wayne State University Press, 1964)

Wittner, Lawrence S, *American Intervention in Greece, 1943–1949* (Columbia University Press, 1982)

Wolf-Phillips, Leslie, 'Why Third World?' (1979) 1(1) *Third World Quarterly* 105

Wood, Bernard, 'Towards North-South Middle Power Coalitions' in Cranford Pratt (ed), *Middle Power Internationalism: The North-South Dimension* (McGill-Queen's University Press, 1990) 69

Woods, Randall B, 'Conflict or Community? The United States and Argentina's Admission to the United Nations' (1977) 46(3) *Pacific Historical Review* 361

INDEX

For EU product safety concerns, contact us at Calle de José Abascal, 56–1°, 28003 Madrid, Spain or eugpsr@cambridge.org.

www.ingramcontent.com/pod-product-compliance
Lightning Source LLC
LaVergne TN
LVHW011656200926
848484LV00004B/963

* 9 7 8 1 0 0 9 1 8 0 4 6 7 *